THE GREAT
GANGSTER PICTURES
II

by
James Robert Parish
and
Michael R. Pitts

The Scarecrow Press, Inc.
Metuchen, N.J., & London
1987

Library of Congress Cataloging-in-Publication Data

Parish, James Robert.
  The great gangster pictures II.

    1. Gangster films--Catalogs. I. Pitts, Michael R.
II. Title. III. Title: Great gangster pictures 2.
IV. Title: Great gangster pictures two.
PN1995.9.G3P364 1987   016.79143'09'09   86-28002
ISBN 0-8108-1961-9

For

REGIS TOOMEY

ACKNOWLEDGMENTS

Academy of Motion Picture Arts & Sciences'
   Film Information Service

Richard Bojarski

John Cocchi

Film Favorites (Bob & Charles Smith)

Pierre Guinle

Kent State University Library (Alex Gildzen)

Gary Kramer

The Library of Congress--Motion Picture, Broadcasting
   & Recorded Sound Division (Katharine Loughney)

Alvin H. Marill

Doug McClelland

Jim Meyer

Mrs. Peter Smith

T. Allan Taylor

Vincent Terrace

Dr. Ray White

CONTENTS

INTRODUCTION

Since its publication in 1976, <u>The Great Gangster Pictures</u> has probably been the best received of our four-volume <u>The Great ... Pic-
tures</u> series for Scarecrow Press. Therefore, it is with great pleasure that we have compiled a companion volume which looks at still
more gangster movies. Like the other volumes, the word "Great"
in the book's title does not necessarily refer to the individual titles
included but to the gangster film genre itself.

Next to the Western, there have probably been more gangster
motion pictures produced than in any other genre, although the science fiction film seems to be quickly catching up in the 1980s. Because of the number of gangster movies which have been released,
we were able to pick and choose from a large quantity of titles for
inclusion in this book. We limited our selection to feature films,
serials, and telefilms of four reels or more. The main criterion was
to include titles readily available to the reader. When our initial volume was published more than a decade ago, there were hundreds of
gangster movies available, but most viewers were able to see only
whatever local television stations or theaters played. With the advent of cable television and video home recorders in recent years,
this limitation no longer applies, and the viewer now has access to
literally thousands of movies. For example, thanks to cable companies
like the Satellite Program Network (SPN), even the most obscure
poverty row gangster movies of the 1930s have surfaced.

In preparing this volume, therefore, we have tried to include
a wide variety of titles for the reader's consumption. Naturally, we
have chosen scores of movies issued since our base volume (B/V),
and we have also gone back and included titles from previous decades, back into the silent era. Also included are serials, TV movies,
and genre titles from abroad.

Defining the gangster movie can be a difficult task, something
that can be said for most types of films. Basically, our criteria for
including a title was to insure that it has thematic ties in some ways
with the underworld or organized crime. Generally, we have omitted
titles which deal with a loner, or loners, out to take revenge on society. Since the problem of the international drug trade has worsened
in recent years, we have chosen to include several titles which deal

with this situation, especially since such trade could not exist without the underworld's network.

While various film genres come and go in popularity, the gangster movie seems to continue in a steady stream of popularity, as it has since the early silent film days. Although there have been no major gangster movie blockbusters in recent years, there have been scores of genre films released, and gangster movies still continue to be a commercial success both on the big and small screens around the world. Since underworld activities exist globally, it is only natural that movies depicting gangsters should have continuing worldwide appeal.

Like the spy movie, gangster films continue to grab headlines in the media, reminding the public of the lawlessness which is rampant around them. The gangster movie, therefore, gives the viewer a vicarious look at the denizens of the underworld whose appeal has, and will, remain constant.

As with the other volumes in our series, we have presented the American release title as the main entry title, with cross references to appropriate native and multi co-production titles. The abbreviation, B/V, refers to our base volume.

Since there are so many gangster movies to look at and evaluate, we hope to be back with you in the not too distant future with still a third volume on one of the movies' most enduring genres.

James Robert Parish   Michael R. Pitts
Los Angeles, California   Chesterfield, Indiana

July 4, 1986

THE GREAT GANGSTER PICTURES

ABSENCE OF MALICE (Columbia, 1981) C 116 mins.

Executive producer, Ronald L. Schwarz; producer-director, Sydney Pollack; screenplay, Kurt Luedtke; music, Dave Grusin; costumes, Bernie Pollack; art director, Terence Marsh; assistant directors, David McGiffert, Rafael Elortegui; camera, Owen Roziman; editor, Sheldon Kahn.

Paul Newman (Michael Gallagher); Sally Field (Megan Carter); Bob Balaban (Elliot Rosen); Melinda Dillon (Teresa Perrone); Luther Adler (Malderone); Barry Primus (Waddell); Josef Sommer (McAdam); John Harkins (Davidek); Don Hood (Quinn); Wilford Brimley (Wells); Arnie Ross (Eddie Frost); Anna Marie Napoles (Nicke); Shelley Spurlock (Sarah Wylie); Shawn McAllister, Joe Petrullo (Hoods); Rooney Kerwin (Walker); Oswaldo Calvo (John); Clardy Malugen (Donna); Sharon Anderson (Secretary); Jody Wilson (Raggedy Lady); Ilse Earl (Nun); Alfred Alvarez Colderon (Rodriguez); Pat Sullivan (Meersman); Bill Hindman (Priest); John Archie, Timothy Hawkins, Ricardo Marquez (FBI Agents); Diane Zolten, Kathy Suergui, Jeff Gillen (Reporters); Ted Bartsch (Beverage Manager); Sugar Ray Mann (Copy Boy); Richard O'Feldman (Driver); Chuck Lupo (Dock Boy); John DiSanti (Longshoreman); Laurie V. Logan (McAdam's Assistant); Patricia Matzdorff (Susan); Gary Van Auiken (Marshall); Jack McDermott, Mark Harris, Bobbie-Ellyne Kosstrin, Lynn Parraga, Lee Sandman, Barry Hober (News Staff).

In today's film climate, especially with the continued lionization of the news media (mostly by itself despite continued polls which show great public distrust in the "media"), it is surprising that a film like this, which takes a hard look at journalist responsibilities, would be made by mainstream Hollywood, especially since the star is Paul Newman, an actor renowned for his liberal politics. (The role had originally been planned for Al Pacino.) Still, the movie (which cost $13,000,000+) is an honest presentation of the need for journalistic responsibility, especially since harmful, sloppy reporting can tremendously affect the lives of many innocent people.

Set in Miami, the story tells of a newspaper reporter, Megan Carter (Sally Field), who is looking into the disappearance of a local longshoreman labor leader. Elliot Rosen, the chief (Bob Balaban) of a government agency investigating the matter, persuades Field to write a story implicating Michael Gallagher (Paul Newman) as a prime

suspect in the case. Newman, though an honest businessman, is the
son of a deceased gangster and his mobster ties include his corrupt
uncle (Luther Adler). It is hoped the expose will force Newman into
aiding the government to solve the case. However, he has an alibi
since he was in Atlanta with a friend (Melinda Dillon) at the time of
the longshoreman's disappearance. Because Dillon was arranging an
abortion for herself resulting from an affair with another man, she
begs Field not to use her name in print, but in the name of "truth"
Field publishes the story, which destroys Dillon's life and Dillon commits suicide. Eventually, another government agent (Wilford Brimley)
solves the case and the newspaper must print a retraction. The cal-
lous editor of the paper (Josef Sommer), who initially had urged
Field to write the story, fires her.

Although the gangster theme takes a second seat to yellow
journalism in this "splendidly disturbing look at the power of sloppy
reporting to inflict harm on the innocent" (Variety), the gangland
activities are the unsavory crux upon which this stout drama is constructed.

ACROSS 110TH STREET (United Artists, 1972) C 102 mins.

Executive producers, Anthony Quinn, Barry Shear; producer, Ralph
Serpe; director, Shear; based on the novel by Wally Ferris; screen-
play, Luther Davis; music, J. J. Johnson; songs, Johnson and Bobby
Womack; art director, Perry Watkins; assistant director, John E.
Quill; camera, Jack Priestley; editor, Byron Brandt.

Anthony Quinn (Captain Frank Mattelli); Yaphet Kotto (Detective
Lieutenant Pope); Anthony Franciosa (Nick D'Salvio); Paul Benjamin
(Jim Harris); Ed Bernard (Joe Logart); Richard Ward (Doc Johnson);
Norma Donaldson (Gloria Roberts); Antonio Fargas (Henry J. Jack-
son); Gilbert Lewis (Shevvy); Marlene Warfield (Mrs. Jackson); Nat
Polen (Lieutenant Reilly); Tim O'Connor (Lieutenant Hartnett); Frank
Mascetta (Don Gennaro); Charles McGregor (Chink); Joe Attles (Mr.
Jessup); Betty Haynes (Mrs. Jessup); and: Frank Adu, Frank Arno,
Gerry Black, Alex Brown, Anthony Cannon, Joe Canutt, Keith Davis,
George Garro, Joseph George, Hilda Haynes, Gloria Hendry, Pete
Hock, Nick La Padula, Norma Matlock, Robert Sacchi, Eddie Smith,
Adam Wade, Marvin Walter, Mel Winkler, Burt Young.

In Harlem, three black punks (Paul Benjamin, Ed Bernard, Antonio Fargas) attempt to cut into the Mafia's take by stealing $300,000
the "family" has gathered from various illegal street activities. Mafia
don Nick D'Salvio (Anthony Franciosa) provides quick justice by murdering one of the gang and beating another and then dropping him
out of a twenty-story window. He and his thugs then go after the
last member of the trio, who takes refuge in a condemned tenement.
In the meantime, corrupt police captain Frank Mattelli (Anthony Quinn)
and his new but honest partner, Detective Lieutenant Pope (Yaphet

Anthony Quinn in ACROSS 110th STREET (1972).

Kotto), are assigned to find the man before the gangsters reach him. When the hunted man's girlfriend (Norma Donaldson) brings him epilepsy medicine, the hoodlums corner their victim in the building and a gunfight ensues, but the police arrive on the scene. Mortally wounded, the man throws the loot into a schoolyard below and the children playing there retrieve it, while Quinn is killed by a sniper.

As Video Movies magazine assessed in retrospect, "ACROSS 110TH STREET is sort of like an R-rated KOJAK.... Produced in the era of blaxploitation films, ACROSS 110th STREET is surprisingly sensitive in its portrayal of ghetto blacks who have to make their own opportunities outside the dominant white culture. And the character played by Quinn is far more complex and interesting than might otherwise be expected." On the other hand, Jerry Renninger, writing in the Palm Beach Post at the time of the film's release, noted, ACROSS 110TH STREET could have been an intriguing look at organized crime in the ghetto. Instead, it's a shallow though extremely brutal shoot-'em-up.... The film's biggest fault is its failure to take a point of view or settle on just whose film it's supposed to be. It

jumps back and forth between what the mob, black and white, is
doing, what the police are doing and what the robbers are trying
to do to avoid the other two groups.... If all the bloodletting
served any purpose besides taking up space on film and keeping
the makeup men busy, it's well hidden."

While Anthony Franciosa is top notch as the colorful Mafia
man, Anthony Quinn is miscast as the crooked policeman with a
sense of duty, and the totally uncorrupt character played by Kotto
is hard to accept, especially when all the other members of the police force are depicted as being on the take. Roger Greenspun
(New York Times) carped: "... it manages at once to be unfair to
blacks, vicious towards whites, and insulting to anyone who feels
that race relations might consist of something better than impro-
vised genocide."

AD OGNI COSTO see: GRAND SLAM

AGAINST ALL ODDS (Columbia, 1984) C 128 mins.

Executive producer, Jerry Bick; producers, Taylor Hackford, Wil-
liam S. Gilmore; associate producer, William R. Borden; director,
Hackford; based on the screenplay Out of the Past by Daniel Main-
waring; assistant directors, Tom Mack, Bill Elvin; costumes, Michael
Kaplan; music, Michel Colombier, Larry Carlton; art director,
Richard James Lawrence; camera, Donald Thorin; editors, Fredric
Steinkamp, William Steinkamp.

Rachel Ward (Jessie Wyler); Jeff Bridges (Terry Brogan); James
Woods (Jake Wise); Alex Karras (Hank Sully); Jane Greer (Mrs.
Wyler); Richard Widmark (Ben Caxton); Dorian Harewood (Tommy);
Swoosie Kurtz (Edie); Saul Rubinek (Steve Kirsch); Pat Corley (Ed
Phillips); Bill McKinney (Head Coach); Allen Williams (Bob Soames);
Sam Scarber (Assistant Coach); Jon St. Elwood (Ahmad Cooper);
Tamara Stafford (Kirsch's Girlfriend); Jonathan Terry (Ryskind);
Paul Valentine (Councilman Weinberg); Ted White (Guard with Dog);
Stone Bower (Security Guard); Mel Scott-Thomas (Quarterback);
Barnetta McCarthy, Ginger LaBrie (Receptionists); David Dayan
(Car Valet); Tom Kelly (Football Announcer); August Darnell (Kid
Creole); Gary Davis, Carey Loftin, Carl Ciarfalio (Stunts).

Producers Taylor Hackford (who also directed) and William B.
Gilmore made a valiant attempt to recreate the film noir vogue of the
1940s with this lavish remake of the 1947 classic, OUT OF THE PAST
(see: B/V). The overall result was a "sexy remake [that] just
misses." (Variety) Among the new version's liabilities are a strung-
out scenario, a non-definite finale, and a well stated but out of context auto chase along Sunset Boulevard. On the plus side is the
sterling ambiance of mystery and the filmmakers' attempt to combine
the new and old Hollywoods with a superb cast: the latter represented

Jeff Bridges and Rachel Ward in AGAINST ALL ODDS (1984).

by Richard Widmark and Jane Greer, with Ms. Greer portraying the mother of the femme fatale she created originally in OUT OF THE PAST.

The narrative tells of Terry (Jeff Bridges), a fast fading football star who has crooked connections with low-life Los Angeles bookie-gangster Jake (James Woods), the lover of Jessie (Rachel Ward). She is the woman the footballer craves and the daughter of the lady (Greer) who owns the team for which he plays. When Bridges is cut from the squad and needs money, he accepts Woods' offer to find Ward, who has left their love nest and headed to Mexico. Eventually, a confrontation develops between the two men over the woman they both desire.

In addition to its main themes of love and lust, AGAINST ALL ODDS was saddled with all variations of offshoot happenings, such as the team owner's alliance with a handsome lawyer (Widmark) in a real estate scheme, Greer forcing her daughter into housekeeping with the sleazy Woods, and the actions of Bridges' best pal (Alex Karras), a teammate.

Boasting excellent scenery and striking photography, the main draw of this production is the steamy sensuality of Ward as the amoral vixen.

AGENCY (Jensen Farley, 1981) C 94 mins.

Producers, Robert Lantos, Stephen J. Roth; associate producer, Robert Baylis; director, George Kaczender; based on the novel by Paul Gottlieb; screenplay, Noel Hynd; music, Lewis Furey; production designer, Bill Brodie; art director, Alica Gurnsky; assistant directors, Charles Braive, Dani Hausmann; costumes, Olga Dimitrov; camera, Milkos Lente; editor, Kirk Jones.

Robert Mitchum (Ted); Lee Majors (Philip); Valerie Perrine (Brenda); Saul Rubinek (Sam); Alexandra Stewart (Mimi); Hayward Morse (Tony); Anthony Parr (Charlie); Michael Kirby (Peters); Gary Reineke (Jones); Goerge Touliatos (Sergeant Eckersly); Jonathan Welsh (Detective Ross); Hugh Webster (Inamte); Franz Russell (George); Malcolm Nelthorpe (Cy); Marlin Gardner (Jill); Eric Donkin (Henry); Donald Davis (Alexander); and: Pierre Sevigny, Anthony Sherwood, Patti Oatman, Don Arioli, Henry Gasner, Militia Battlefield, Camille Belanger, Rollie Nincheri, Barry Simpson, Jande W. Woods, John Lefebvre, Jim Walton, Wally Martin, Celina Bacon, Catherine Vaneri, Martin Kevin, Robert Bolduc, Shawna Sexsmith, Wally Boland, Eric Cord, Francois Pratt.

The stereotype of the gangster, and gangster film, revolves around slick hoodlums, gangs, tommy guns, 1920s Chicago and New York, and the like. Of course, there are all kinds of gangsters and hoodlums, and this Canadian-produced feature focuses on one of the most insidious kinds of underworld figures, the respectable businessman fronting an organization which in reality is being used for nefarious purposes to defraud and mislead the public. This brand of hoodlum is probably the most despicable of all. Nevertheless, AGENCY failed to generate much excitement in its presentation of the subject.

Mysterious businessman Ted Quinn (Robert Mitchum) becomes the head of an established advertising firm and begins a series of changes which include a new campaign for a mainstream product. Unaffected by the new set-up is the firm's chief designer (Lee Majors), but copywriter Sam Goldstein (Saul Rubinck) becomes concerned and voices his opinion to Majors. He later turns up dead, officially a suicide. The man's demise, however, causes Majors to investigate, and he uncovers a clue which he shares with his girlfriend (Valerine Perrine). The police, in league with Mitchum and his henchmen, find the evidence and set about engineering the man's "suicide." However, Majors emerges victorious in the showdown with Mitchum and his minions.

ALCATRAZ: THE WHOLE SHOCKING STORY (NBC-TV, 11/5-6/80) C 200 mins.

Executive producer, Pierre Cossette; producers, Ernest Tidyman, James H. Brown; director, Paul Krasny; story, Clarence Carnes,

Don DeVevi; teleplay, Tidyman; music, Jerrold Immel; production designer, William L. Campbell; camera, Robert B. Hauser; editors, Donald R. Rode, Lee Green.

Michael Beck (Clarence Carnes); Art Carney (Robert Stroud); Alex Karras (Jughead Miller); Telly Savalas (Cretzer); Will Sampson (Clarence's Father); Ronny Cox (Bernard Coy); Richard Lynch (Sam Shockley); Robert Davi (Hubbard); John Amos (Bumpy Johnson); James MacArthur (Walt Stomer); Ed Lauter (Frank Morris); Joe Pantoliano (Ray Neal); Louis Giambalvo (Clarence Anglin); Jeffrey Tambor (Dankworth); Paul Mantee (Ordway); Charles Aidman (Warden Johnson); Jack Rader (Weinhold); Walter Mathews (Corwin); Spencer Milligan (Fred Haskell); Sidney Clute (Miller); Redmond Gleeson (Jackson); Brad English (Thompkins); Antony Ponzini (John Anglin); Paul Picerni (Lieutenant Lagason); Burt Marshall (Guard); Lois Red-Elk (Clarence's Mother); David Boyle (Guard); Sandy Ward (McIntire); Tom Lupo (Dunslay); Ken Lettner (Armory Lieutenant); Al Gingolani (Carroll); Peter Coyote (Courtney Taylor); Peter Jason (Lieutenant Micklin); James Harrison (Dumpy); James Jeter (Guard Fairgate); Angelo Crisante (Convict); Nick Eldredge (Larwin); Johnny Weissmuller, Jr. (Felish); Jim Haunie (Salkin).

This well-executed telefeature recounts the stark life of Alcatraz prisoner Clarence Carnes (Michael Beck), an Oklahoma Indian, who is sent to the "Rock" on a 99-year murder conviction after escaping from several other penal institutions. There he joins forces with a cellblock leader (Telly Savalas) in plotting another escape. In 1946 the attempt is made, with three prisoners and two guards being killed before the convicts are captured. Beck is given another life sentence for his part in the escape attempt. During the 1940s Beck is asked to try yet another escape, but his fellow isolation area inmate Robert "Birdman of Alcatraz" Stroud (Art Carney) dissuades him. In 1960 a trio makes a successful break from Alcatraz and in 1963 the maximum security prison is closed. Beck is transferred to Leavenworth and is paroled a decade later.

The New York Times decided this telefilm was "dedicated more to simplicity and economy than drama," although few could argue with Beck's performance as Clarence Carnes or Carney's underplayed interpretation of Robert Stroud (an interesting contrast to Burt Lancaster's characterization in 1962's BIRDMAN OF ALCATRAZ --see: B/V). Although overlapping the scope of ESCAPE FROM ALCATRAZ (1979, q.v.), this film offers a dramatic presentation of the grotesque world of prisons, the stopping off point for gangsters and criminals of all variations.

ALIAS THE CHAMP (Republic, 1949) 60 mins.

Producer, Stephen Auer; director, George Blair; screenplay, Albert DeMond; song, Ned Washington, Al Newman, and Richard Cherwin; camera, John MacBurnie; editor, Harold Minter.

Gorgeous George (Himself); Robert Rockwell (Lieutenant Ron Peter-
son); Barbra Fuller (Colette); Audrey Long (Lorraine); Jim Nolan
(Al Merlo); John Harmon (Chuck Lyons); Sammy Menacker (Sam);
Joseph Crehan (Tim Murphy); John Hamilton (Police Commissioner
Bronson); Stephen Chase (District Attorney Gould); Frank Scan-
nelli (Bert Tracy); Frank Yaconelli (Head Waiter); Emmett Vogan
(Doc Morgan); John Wald (Telecaster); Bomber Kulkovich [Henry
Kulky], Mike Ruby, Jim Lennon, Billy Varga, Bobby Mangoff,
George Temple, Super Swedish Angel [Tor Johnson], Jack Sockeye
McDonald (Themselves).

In the late 1940s and early 1950s millions of television sets
were sold so people could view Milton Berle and Gorgeous George,
the latter TV personality responsible for the revival in popularity
of professional wrestling. Under his real name, George Wagner,
"The Toast of the Coast," he had been a champion amateur grap-
pler and his talent in drawing a crowd through showmanship was
emulated by many, including Muhammad Ali. At the peak of his
professional popularity, Gorgeous George starred in this Republic
programmer, and while his histrionics were thin, his ring flair made
this feature an enjoyable event.
    East coast mobster Al Merlo (Jim Nolan) and his henchman
Chuck (John Harmon) figure to muscle in on the popularity and
profit of wrestling on the West Coast and they want the sport's
premiere star, Gorgeous George (himself) to join with them. When
he refuses, the gangsters poison his ring opponent (Sammy Menacker) and implicate George in the crime. Homicide police lieutenant
Ron Peterson (Robert Rockwell), who is also a wrestling code ad-
ministrator, believes George is innocent and sets out to establish
that. Along the way, he romances pretty Lorraine (Audrey Long).
By re-screening a TV film of the wrestling match in which Menacker
died, Rockwell proves George's innocence and later corners the
mobsters, who die in a shootout.

AMBUSH (Paramount, 1939) 60 mins.

Director, Kurt Neumann; story, Robert Ray; screenplay, Laura and
S. J. Perelman; camera, William Meller; editor, Stuart Gilmore.

Gladys Swarthout (Jane Hartman); Lloyd Nolan (Tony Andrews);
William Henry (Charlie Hartman); William Frawley (Inspector Weber);
Ernest Truex (Mr. Gibbs); Broderick Crawford (Randall); Rufe
Davis (Sheriff); Raymond Hatton (Hardward Store Keeper); Hartley
Tufts (Sidney); Antonio Moreno (Captain Gonzales); Harry Fleisch-
mann (Captain Rosen); Clem Bevans (Pop Stebbins); Billy Lee
(Boy in Restaurant); Polly Moran (Cora); Wade Boteler (Bank Guard).

In the mid-1930s, when pretty opera singers were the vogue of
Hollywood films, Paramount imported Gladys Swarthout from the Met-
ropolitan Opera to star in a series of big-budget motion pictures like

GIVE US THIS NIGHT and ROSE OF THE RANCHO (both 1936). By
the end of the decade the operatic fad was over, and the lovely
soprano completed her studio contract with this "B" gangster item;
in the proceedings she sings not one note. Also of interest is that
the film was scripted by S. J. and Laura Perelman, mainly known
for comedy. The New York Times endorsed, "As an unblushing
excursion in the cops-and-robbers vein, with just enough comic by-
play to keep it unmistakenly within the bounds of purest fiction, it
is lively, amusing stuff."
    Gangsters led by the brainy Mr. Gibbs (Ernest Treux) pull
off a job, only to have their escape muffed by the secretary sister
(Swarthout) of a cowardly gang member (William Henry). Hoping to
get her brother away from the mob, she asks truck driver Tony
Andrews (Lloyd Nolan) to help her in following the gang, but the
two are captured by Treux, who must figure out what to do with
them as the police, led by Inspector Weber (William Frawley), close
in.

THE AMSTERDAM KILL (Columbia, 1977) C 93 mins.

Executive producer, Raymond Chow; producer, Andrew Morgan;
director, Robert Clouse; story, Gregory Teifer; screenplay, Clouse,
Teifer; music, Hal Schaefer; assistant directors, Louis Shektin,
Chaplin Chang; art directors, John Blezard, K. S. Chen; sound,
Peter Davies, Charles McFadden; special effects, Gene Grigg;
camera, Alan Hume; editors, Allan Holzman, Gina Brown.

Keye Luke and Robert Mitchum in THE AMSTERDAM KILL (1977).

Robert Mitchum (Quinlan); Bradford Dillman (Odums); Richard Egan (Ridgeway); Leslie Nielsen (Knight); Keye Luke (Chung Wei); George Cheung (Jimmy Wong); Chan Sing (Assassin).

The aging chief (Keye Luke) of a worldwide Oriental-based drug syndicate enlists the aid of Quinlan (Robert Mitchum), a former agent of the U.S. Drug Enforcement Agency who has been forced to resign, as a go-between with the agency and to bargain for his safe trip to America in return for information on the international drug trade. Mitchum goes to Hong Kong to meet the chief, but once there all his plans go awry and he finds that he is detested by both the agency head (Bradford Dillman) and the local police. Eventually being kidnapped and beaten and with only a clue to the case, he goes to Amsterdam and finally discovers the city is the European base for the drug traffic from the Orient, the dope then being smuggled out of Europe and into the western nations. Locating the headquarters of the drug smugglers, Mitchum demolishes it with a caterpillar truck and also reveals who is involved in the murderous operation. As a result the international drug traffic syndicate is destroyed--at least for now.

Although filled with interesting scenic shots of Hong Kong and Amsterdam, and greatly benefitting from Mitchum's strong performance as the world-weary Quinlan, the movie's chief fault is its predictability.

THE AMSTERDAM KILL was the initial international production from Golden Harvest Productions, a feature film company which previously had been releasing kung fu movies, particularly those with Bruce Lee. It proved to be one of the first features to explore the actual drug connections between Hong Kong, Amsterdam, and the United States.

AND HOPE TO DIE (Twentieth Century-Fox, 1982) C 140 mins.

Producer, Serge Siberman; director, Rene Clement; based on the novel Black Friday by David Goodis; screenplay, Sebastien Japrisot; music, Francis Lai; camera, Edmond Richard; editor, Roger Dwyre.

Robert Ryan (Charley); Aldo Ray (Mattone); Tisa Farrow (Pepper); Jean-Louis Trintignant (Tony); Lee Massari (Sugar); Jean Gaven (Rizzio); Nadine Nabokov (Majorette); Andrew Lawrence (Gypsy); Daniel Breton (Paul).

This French-Italian co-production, filmed in English in Canada, apparently was an attempt by French director Rene Clement and that country's major star, Jean-Louis Trintignant, to become international box-office properties. If so, the effort was not successful, as the resulting feature was a drawn out and violent gangster entry which received neither critical nor audience endorsement. For the director of such highly regarded Continental features as PLEIN SOLEIL [Purple Noon] (1959) and LE PASSAGER DE LA PLUIE [Rider on the Rain] (1968), this attempt was a dismal creative affair indeed.

The muddled story tells of a Frenchman (Trintignant) who is on the run from gypsies after he crash lands his plane on a beach, killing one of their children. In Montreal he is thrown together with Charley (Robert Ryan), the head of a small-time gang which is planning a robbery. He joins the group, which contains two mental defectives, and they are hired by an Italian gangster (Jean Gaven) to kidnap a mentally retarded girl the police are guarding in a skyscraper. The clique find the girl has committed suicide, but plan to carry out the kidnapping anyway, substituting another girl, so they can collect their million dollar fee.

Only the strong work of Robert Ryan as the gang leader and nice support from Aldo Ray and Tisa Farrow, plus the Montreal locales, hold any viewer interest.

French title: LE COURSE DU LIEVRE A TRAVERS LES CHAMPS [Cross Your Heart and Hope to Die].

ANGELS' ALLEY (Monogram, 1948) 64 mins.

Producer, Jan Grippo; director, William Beaudine; screenplay, Edmond Seward, Tim Ryan, Gerald Schnitzer; art director, Dave Milton; set decorator, Ray Bottz; music, Edward Kay; assistant director, Wesley Barry; sound, Franklin Hansen; camera, Marcel LePicard; editor, William Austin.

Leo Gorcey (Slip Mahoney); Huntz Hall (Sach); Billy Benedict (Whitey); David Gorcey (Chuck); Gabriel Dell (Ricky); Frankie Darro (Jimmie); Nestor Paiva (Tony Lucarno); Nelson Leigh (Father O'Hanlon); Geneva Gray (Josie O'Neill); Rosemary La Planche (Daisy Harris); John Eldredge (District Attorney); Mary Gordon (Mrs. Mahoney); Richard Paxton (Jockey Burns); Buddy Gorman (Andy Miller); Tommie Menzies (Boomer); Benny Bartlett (Jag Harmon); Dewey Robinson (Moose); John H. Elliott (Magistrate); Robert Emmett Keane (Felix Crowe); William Ruhl (Brian Watson); Wade Crosby (Mike); Meyer Grace (Welder).

Recently released convict Jimmy Mahoney (Frankie Darro) moves in with his cousin Slip (Leo Gorcey) and the latter's mother (Mary Gordon). Unable to find a job, Darro goes to work for Tony Lucarno (Nestor Paiva), a businessman who runs a car theft operation. When Gorcey finds out, he goes to a warehouse to prevent Darro from committing a theft and is himself caught by the police. To protect his mother's feelings for Darro, Gorcey claims to have committed the crime. He is sentenced to jail but a priest (Nelson Leigh) takes responsibility for him and this allows Gorcey et al. to obtain the needed information to smash Paiva's gang.

A typical entry in the long running "Bowery Boys" series, ANGELS' ALLEY looks more like one of the group's earlier "East Side Kids" outings in that the character of Slip Mahoney is allowed to be humanized, while the movie also brings back Mary Gordon as his mother, a part she played repeatedly in the earlier entries.

Douglas Fairbanks, Jr. and Rita Hayworth in ANGELS OVER BROAD-
WAY (1940).

ANGELS OVER BROADWAY (Columbia, 1940) 78 mins.

Producer, Ben Hecht; associate producer, Douglas Fairbanks, Jr.;
directors, Hecht, Lee Garmes; screenplay, Hecht; assistant director,
Clifton Broughton; art director, Lionel Banks; camera, Garmes; editor, Gene Havlick.

Douglas Fairbanks, Jr. (Bill O'Brien); Rita Hayworth (Nina Barona);
Thomas Mitchell (Gene Gibbons); John Qualen (Charles Engel);
George Watts (Hopper); Ralph Theodore (Dutch Enright); Eddie
Foster (Louie Artino); Jack Roper (Eddie Burns); Constance Worth
(Sylvia Marbe); Richard Bon (Sylvia's Escort); Frank Conlan (Joe);
Walter Baldwin (Rennick); Jack Carr (Tony); Al Seymour (Jack);
Jimmy Conlin (Proprietor); Ethelreda Leopold (Cigarette Girl);
Catherine Courtney (Miss Karpin); Al Rhein, Jerry Jerome, Roger
Gray, Harry Strang (Gamblers); Carmen D'Antonio (Specialty Danc-
er); Carleton Griffin (Waiter); Stanley Brown (Master of Ceremon-
ies); Blanche Payson (Large Woman); Walter Sande (Lunch Wagon
Waiter); Art Howard (Night Court Judge); Billy Wayne (Taxi Driver);

Lee Phelps (Police Lieutenant); Harry Antrim (Court Clerk); Ben Hecht (Bit); Tommy Dixon (Checkroom Boy); Bill Lally (Doorman); Edward Earle (Headwaiter).

On a rainy night at a New York City cafe, a poor clerk (John Qualen) admits he has stolen $3,000 while on the job to appease his extravagant wife and that he will kill himself if he cannot repay the money. Overhearing the confession is a drunken but once famous Pulitzer Prize winning playwright (Thomas Mitchell), and he develops a scheme to help the man. His plan involves a con artist (Douglas Fairbanks, Jr.) and a down-on-her-luck young girl (Rita Hayworth). The playwright has the cardshark start a poker game with gangsters, with the clerk as a participant, and let him win the money he needs, leaving the hoodlums as the losers.

Screenwriter Ben Hecht, who co-directed this affair with Lee Garmes, used ANGELS OVER BROADWAY as a comeback vehicle, but the results were downbeat. Although well executed, and some say well ahead of its time, the drama was too much a fantasy which had little appeal to pre-World War II audiences. Co-star Rita Hayworth had not yet attained the box-office pull requisite to make the feature a success.

As noted by the Hollywood Reporter, the film as "a strangely compelling drama of shadowy seams in the background of Broadway's nocturnal glitter, marked for its brilliant interpretation of a brilliant script, ANGELS OVER BROADWAY is so far off the beaten track that it fits into none of Hollywood's formulized categories." Perhaps the movie's emphasis on its fragile head characters rather than the underworld background predetermined its financial failings. In his book, The Films of Rita Hayworth (1974), Gene Ringgold analyzed, "ANGELS OVER BROADWAY, however, is still the film that marked Hollywood's prewar 'coming of age' so to speak, and deserves recognition for everything it attempted and succeeded in saying and doing and not disparagement for its minor flaws or being a financial failure."

ARCTIC MANHUNT (Universal, 1949) 69 mins.

Producer, Leonard Goldstein; associate producer, Billy Grady, Jr.; director, Ewing Scott; based on the story "Narana of the North" by Scott; screenplay, Oscar Brodney, Joel Malone; art directors, Bernard Herzbrun, Robert Boyle; set decorators, Russell Gauzman, Al Fields; music, Milton Schwarzwald; makeup, Bud Westmore; sound, Leslie I. Carey, Joe Lapis; exterior camera, Kay Norton; camera, Irving Glassberg; editor, Otto Ludwing.

Mikel Conrad (Mike Jarvis); Carol Thurston (Narana); Wally Cassell (Tooyuk); Helen Brown (Lois Jarvis); Harry Harvey (Carter); Russ Conway (Landers); Paul E. Burns (Hotel Clerk); Quianna (Eskimo Girl); Chet Huntley (Narrator).

Narrated by newsman Chet Huntley, this anemic gangster movie takes place in the unlikely setting of Alaska. Variety termed it "a slow moving drama of the frozen north that has little to recommend it" and added that "the natural background isn't sufficient to offset a lustreless plot." Scott and star Mikel Conrad later collaborated on the spy melodrama THE FLYING SAUCER (1950) which utilized footage shot for this production.

Gangster Mike Jarvis (Conrad) is released from prison, having served time for armored car robbery. He heads to Alaska but is followed by the authorities, who seek the location of the hidden loot from the heist. In Alaska Conrad pretends to be a missionary and romances pretty Eskimo girl Narana (Carol Thurston), but eventually dies in the wilderness trying to elude the law. The obvious morale is: "Crime does not pay."

ARSON FOR HIRE (Allied Artists, 1959) 67 mins.

Producer, William F. Broidy; director, Thor Brooks; screenplay, Tom Hubbard; camera, William Margulies; editor, Herbert R. Hoffman.

Steve Brodie (John); Lyn Thomas (Keely); Frank Scannell (Pop); Antony Carbone (Foxy); John Merrick (Clete); Jason Johnson (Yarbo); Robert Riordan (Boswell); Wendy Wilde (Marily); Walter Reed (Hollister); Lori Laine (Cindy); Reed Howes (Barney); Lyn Osborn (Jim); Frank Richards (Dink); Ben Frommer (Hot Dog Vender); Lester Dorr (Dispatcher); Florence Useem (Nurse); Tom Hubbard (Ben).

This is the type of old-fashioned feature the studios churned out in the 1930s-40s as a double-bill item. Coming at the end of the 1950s, the film is definitely out of place. The only saving grace is that screenwriter Tom Hubbard played the villain and is top notch in his characterization.

Gangsters are on a rampage, setting fire to large buildings and then shaking down the owners for the insurance money they collect. Arson squad head John (Steve Brodie) is baffled because the gang seems to have an inside track involving his investigations into their activities. With the aid of one of the victims (Lyn Thomas), he is finally able to track down the leader, who turns out to be his second-in-command on the arson squad.

ARSON, INC. (Screen Guild, 1949) 64 mins.

Producer, William Stephens; director, William Berke; screenplay, Arthur Caesar, Maurice Tombragel; art director, Martin Objina; set decorator, Joseph Kish; music director, Raoul Kraushaar; sound, William Randall, Lyle Cain; camera, Carl Berger; editor, Edward Mann.

Robert Lowery (Joe Martin); Anne Gwynne (Jane); Marcia Mae Jones
(Bella); Douglas Fowley (Fender); Edward Brophy (Pete); Byron
Foulger (Peyson); Gaylord Pendleton (Murph); Maude Eburne (Grand-
ma); Lelah Tyler (Mrs. Peyson); William Forrest (Firechief); John
Maxwell (Detective); Richard David (Junior Peyson); Emmett Vogan
(Night Watchman).

An arson gang is using the blind of setting fires to carry out
their heists with firebug Pete (Edward Brophy) as their chief torch.
Fire department arson investigator Joe Martin (Robert Lowery) is
assigned to the case while romancing pretty school teacher Jane
(Anne Gwynne). To expose the gang, Lowery infiltrates their operations and eventually brings the arsonists to justice.

Done in a semi-documentary fashion, this low budget programmer cost only $60,000 to make, taking intelligent advantage of stock
footage. The result was a superior little picture, reflecting the full
ambiance of the arson-bent gangsters.

ARSON RACKET SQUAD (Republic, 1938) 54 mins.

Associate producer, Herman Schlom; director, Joseph Kane; screenplay, Alex Gottlieb, Norman Burstine; additional dialogue, Joseph
Hoffman; music director, Alberto Colombo; camera, Ernest Miller;
editor, Edward Mann.

Bob Livingston (Bill O'Connell); Rosalind Keith (Joan); Jackie Moran
(Jimmy); Warren Hymer (Tom); Jack LaRue (Morgan); Clay Clement
(Hamilton); Selmer Jackson (Commissioner Benton); Emory Parnell
(Riley); Walter Sande (Oscar); Dick Wessel (Slugs); Jack Rice
(Bradbury); Lloyd Whitlock (Martin).

Handsome Robert Livingston finally found stardom at Republic
Pictures in the mid-1930s after kicking around Hollywood since the
beginning of the sound era. At Republic he became a utility star of
"B" films, working in all kinds of genres including gangster movies
such as FEDERAL MANHUNT (q.v.) and this one before settling
down as the efficient star of series Westerns.

ARSON RACKET SQUAD deals with an arson gang which has
been causing havoc in New York City with the metropolis' Fire Department officials at a loss to stop them. Finally, a young fire captain, arson investigator Bill O'Connell (Livingston), must gain the
evidence necessary to bring the gang to justice. To accomplish his
mission, the department permits him to set a series of fires, which
causes pretty newspaperwoman Joan (Rosalind Keith) to turn onto
the story. Eventually, she and Livingston fall in love.

While the hard-to-please New York Times complained that the
film "is worse 'n arson; it's murder," the programmer is a pleasing
interlude, aided by Warren Hymer's comedy relief.

A.k.a.: ARSON GANG BUSTERS.

THE ASPHALT JUNGLE see: CAIRO

ASSIGNMENT REDHEAD see: MILLION DOLLAR MANHUNT

AT ANY COST see: GRAND SLAM

BABY FACE KILLERS see: PRIVATE HELL 36

BACK DOOR TO HEAVEN (Paramount, 1939) 81 mins.

Producer, William K. Howard; associate producer, Johnnie Walker; director-story, Howard; screenplay, John Bright, Robert Tasker; assistant director, Harold Godsoe; music supervisor, Erno Rapee; camera, Hal Mohr; editor, Jack Murray.

Aline McMahon (Miss Williams); Jimmy Lydon (Frankie the Youth); Anita Magee (Carol); William Harrigan (Mr. Rogers); Jane Seymour (Mrs. Rogers); Robert Wildhack (Rudolph Herzing); Billy Redfield (Charley Smith); Kenneth LeRoy (Bob Hale); Raymond Roe (John Sheilley); Al Webster (Sheriff Kramer); Joe Garry (Reform School Superintendent); Wallace Ford (Frankie As An Adult); Stuart Erwin (Jud); Bert Frohman (The Mouse); Kent Smith (John Shelley); Bruce Evans (Charley Smith); George Lewis (Bob Hale); Doug McMullen (Wallace Kishler); Helen Christian (Mrs. Smith); Robert Vivian (George Spelvin); Hugh Cameron (Penitentiary Warden); Iris Adrian (Sugar); Georgette Harvey (Mrs. Hamilton).

BACK DOOR TO HEAVEN is one of the most sadly neglected gangster films of the 1930s. Filmed at Paramount's Astoria Studios in New York City, the movie was given some screenings late in 1938 but did not go into general release until early in 1939. The last major United States production directed by William K. Howard, the film seems much more vintage than it is, due primarily to the anti-quated equipment used on the Astoria lot. Add to this a dated storyline and melodramatic plot developments, and this feature seems hopeless, but it has so many good points that it becomes rewarding viewing to the discerning.

The picture is divided into two sections: The Prologue and The Play. The former takes place in the pre-Roaring Twenties era in a small town where a young boy, Frankie (Jimmy Lydon), is about to graduate from grammar school. He is poor, living on the wrong side of the tracks with his drunken father and slatternly mother. The only person who really takes an interest in him is Miss Williams (Aline McMahon), his teacher, and since all the other children are going to do something for graduation, Lydon steals a harmonica to play for the event. As a result he is sent to reform school and later to jail and then to the state penitentiary. The Play then takes over

with Frankie (Wallace Ford) now an adult and being paroled from
prison after five years. He and his two pals (Stuart Erwin and
Bert Frohman) go back to his hometown. He visits the now elderly
teacher and finds out she has been forcibly retired from her job by
the head (Bruce Evans) of the school board, one of Ford's ex-
classmates. Ford then goes to the big city where he finds Carol
(Patricia Ellis), his childhood sweetheart, who is now an unsuccess-
ful showgirl. The two fall in love but Ford is forced to flee when
his pals rob a diner and he gets the blame for killing a clerk. He
is sentenced to die for the crime, after having been defended unsuccessfully by another ex-classmate, broke lawyer John Shelley
(Van Heflin). Ellis returns for her class reunion hoping that
Evans will help Ford. Ford escapes from prison, returns to the
nostalgic gathering, and minutes after bidding them farewell, he is
cornered and killed by the law.

The film's social implications are complex. Actually, the production contains neither hero nor villains. Written by Robert Tasker
and John Bright (the latter also collaborated on THE PUBLIC ENEMY
--see: B/V), who were known as social reformers, the picture is a
brutal attack on the capitalistic system and the way it delivers "justice." The central character of Frankie is depicted as nothing more
than a pawn, a predestined victim because he was born poor. On
the other hand, the banker character is shown to have been born
assured of success by society.

Unlike many gangster epics of its period, BACK DOOR TO
HEAVEN is surprisingly light on violence. Almost all of the action,
such as the robbery and shooting in the diner and the final gunning
down of Ford, occur out of camera range. The rather abrupt editing
gives the film good pacing, and the musical supervision of Erno
Rapee is to be commended. He was a Hungarian conductor popular
in the 1930s for his radio work, but best known for co-writing such
popular 1920s tunes as "Charmaine," "Diane," and "Angela Mia."

BADGE 373 (Paramount, 1973) C 116 mins.

Producer-director, Howard W. Koch; screenplay, Pete Hamill; music,
J. J. Jackson; art director, Philip Rosenberg; assistant director,
Michael P. Petrone; sound, Dennis Maitland; camera, Arthur J.
Ornitz; editor, John Woodcock.

Robert Duvall (Eddie Ryan); Verna Bloom (Maureen); Henry Darrow
(Sweet William); Eddie Egan (Scanlon); Felipe Luciano (Ruben); Tina
Cristiani (Mrs. Caputo); Manna Durell (Rita Garcia); Chico Martinez
(Frankie Diaz); Jose Duval (Ferrer); Louis Cosentino (Gigi Caputo);
Peter Hamill (Reporter).

The exploits of real-life New York City vice cop Eddie Egan
was the colorful basis for THE FRENCH CONNECTION (1971) (see:
B/V) and its sequel THE FRENCH CONNECTION II (q.v.), four
years later. Sandwiched in between was BADGE 373, which not only

Eddie Egan in BADGE 373 (1973).

continued Egan's (called Eddie Ryan here) exploits, but also featured brash Egan as his actual department boss. In addition he served as the film's technical advisor. Sadly, all these hats worn by Egan did little for the film, which was dreary.

New York City policeman Eddie Ryan (Duvall) is determined to halt vicious crime boss Sweet William (Henry Darrow), who controls the Puerto Rican section of town. Never holding to the letter of the law, the iconoclastic Duvall conducts unauthorized drug raids, torments a gangster into falling off a building, endangers the lives of several bus passengers while giving chase to a hoodlum, and causes the death of his girl friend (Verna Bloom) when he forces her to help him follow a suspect. He does have his reward, for eventually he corners and kills the crime boss.

Cut from the "Dirty Harry" school of crime elimination, the protagonist here seems to break more laws than he enforces. Obviously, this cop feels that the end justifies the means, although in reality his character may be just plain mean and one who could have easily ended up on the other side of justice. For screen historians, this movie features Felipe Luciano, a leader in the Puerto Rican rights movement, in a screen counterpart role, and scripter-newspaper columnist Peter Hamill appears as a reporter.

BANK ALARM (Grand National, 1937) 64 mins.

Producer, George A. Hirliman; associate producer, Charles Hunt; supervisor, Sam Diege; director, Louis Gasnier; screenplay, David N. Levy, J. Griffin Jay; assistant director, Milton Brown; music supervisor, Abe Meyer; camera, Mack Stengler; editor, Dan Milner.

Conrad Nagel (Alan O'Connor); Eleanor Hunt (Bobbie Reynolds); Vince Barnett (Bulb); Frank Milan (Turner); Wilma Francis (Kay); William Thorne (Inspector Macy); Wheeler Oakman (Karbotti); Charles Delaney (Duke); Phil Dunham (Curtis); Sid D'Albrook (Grimes); Pat Gleason (Barney); Wilson Benge (Overman); Henry Roquemore (Sheriff).

G-man Alan O'Connor (Conrad Nagel) and his confederate, pretty Bobbie Reynolds (Eleanor Hunt), are after a bank robbery gang which also deals in counterfeiting and murder. As a ruse, Hunt permits herself to be taken hostage, only to be sprung by Nagel who rounds up the hoodlums.
One of three gangster programmers (the others are YELLOW CARGO and THE GOLD RACKET, qq.v.) built around the romantic tandem of the two government agents played by Nagel and Hunt, BANK ALARM is definitely the weakest. A fourth entry, NAVY SPY (1937), was in the spy motif.

BEHIND PRISON GATES (Columbia, 1939) 63 mins.

Director, Charles Barton; screenplay, Arthur T. Horman, Leslie T. White; camera, Allen G. Siegler; editor, Richard Fantl.

Brian Donlevy (Red Murray); Jacqueline Wells (Sheila Murray); Joseph Crehan (Warden O'Neil); Paul Fix (Petey Ryan); George Lloyd (Marty Conroy); Dick Curtis (Captain Simmons); Richard Fiske (Lyman).

The state's attorney intends to find out the location of hidden money taken in a robbery and assigns policeman Red Murray (Brian Donlevy) to the case. Donlevy becomes pals with the two crooks, but in order to find the money's whereabouts, he is forced to stage a prison break to get the duo on the outside so they will lead him to the cache. He accomplishes the escape, but his identity is uncovered and he nearly dies before being rescued by a fellow operative (Richard Fiske). Donlevy then unearths the cash and returns to work and a life of happiness with his girl (Jacqueline Wells).
Brian Donlevy gives credibility to this standard tale of life behind bars and the mentality of men serving time for their anti-social activities.

Jacqueline Wells [Julie Bishop] and Brian Donlevy in BEHIND PRISON GATES (1939).

BEHIND PRISON WALLS (Producers Releasing Corp., 1943) 64 mins.

Producer, Andre Dumonceau; director, Steve Sekely; story. W. A. Ulman, Jr.; screenplay, Van Norcross; dialogue director, Kurt Steinbait; assistant director, Chris Beute; sound, Ben Winkler; camera, Marcel Le Picard; editor, Holbrook N. Todd.

Alan Baxter (Jonathan MacGlennon); Gertrude Michael (Elinor Cantwell); Tully Marshall (James J. MacGlennon); Edwin Maxwell (Percy Webb); Jacqueline Dalya (Mimi); Matt Willis (Frank Lucacelli); Richard Kipling (Frederick Driscoll); Olga Sabin (Yettie Kropatchek); Isabelle Withers (Whitney O'Neil); Lane Chandler (Reagan); Paul Everton (Warden); George Guhl (Doc); Regina Wallace (Mrs. Cantwell).

Despite its title and prison setting, this PRC affair was not hardened-criminals-behind-bars melodrama but an intelligent and pleasant drama of corrupt businessmen. The movie was well acted and produced. As Don Miller judged in B Movies (1973): "It was a gentle, witty, somewhat intellectualized [entry].... An oddity from any company and a downright treasure coming from PRC, its soft-sell approach probably was the cause of its bypassing by most audiences.... For those who saw it, it was a pleasant surprise.

Alan Baxter and Gertrude Michael in BEHIND PRISON WALLS (1943).

It was also the last film for the elderly Tully Marshall, best remembered from the silent THE COVERED WAGON."
        Corrupt business tycoon James J. MacGlennon (Marshall) and
his social-welfare-minded son (Alan Baxter) are both sent to prison
for business fraud. The father, however, has little use for his
son's ideologies and attempts to conduct business as usual behind
bars. Baxter, though, receives a pardon and returns home to take
over family affairs from the crook who sent him to jail in the first
place. In revamping the business into a more humanitarian operation, he succeeds in revitalizing the company. It proves the theory
that honesty does pay.

BEHIND STONE WALLS (Action Pictures, 1932) 58 mins.

Supervisor, Cliff Broughton; director, Frank Strayer; screenplay,
George H. Seitz; camera, Jules Cronjager; editor, Byron Robinson.

Eddie Nugent (Robert Clay); Priscilla Dean (Esther Clay); Robert
Elliott (District Attorney John Clay); Ann Christy (Peg Harper);
Robert Ellis (Jack Keene); George Chesebro (Leo Drugget).

        The wife (Priscilla Dean) of a district attorney (Robert
Elliott) who is romancing a racketeer, kills him in a jealous pique.

Her stepson (Eddie Nugent), believing she is his real mother, takes the blame for the homicide and is prosecuted by his father and sentenced to prison for life. When a friend of the murdered gangster blackmails Dean, she tries to kill him, but her spouse, called to the scene by his son's ex-fiancee (Ann Christy), arrives and in the struggle shoots his erring wife. Nugent is released from prison and returns home to defend his father at the murder trial and wins an acquittal.

Released by Action Pictures, this poverty row outing is low grade technically and is hampered by an outrageous potboiler plot.

Popular silent screen star Priscilla Dean, who had appeared in pictures between 1918 and 1926 and is best remembered as Cigarette in UNDER TWO FLAGS (1922), attempted a screen comeback here, but overplayed the role of the murderous woman.

BEHIND THE HIGH WALL (Universal, 1956) 85 mins.

Producer, Stanley Rubin; director, Abner Biberman; story, Wallace Sullivan, Richard K. Polimen; screenplay, Harold Jack Bloom; music, Joseph Gershenson; camera, Maury Gertsman; editor, Ted J. Kent.

Tom Tully (Warden Frank Carmichael); Sylvia Sidney (Hilda Carmichael); Betty Lynn (Anne MacGregor); John Gavin (Johnny Hutchins); Don Beddoe (Todd MacGregor); John Larch (William Kiley); Barney Phillips (Tom Reynolds); Ed Kemmer (Charlie Rains); John Beradino (Carl Burkhardt); Rayford Barnes (George Miller); Nicky Blair (Roy Burkhardt); David Garcia (Morgan); Peter Leeds, Jim Hyland (Detectives).

Prison warden Frank Carmichael (Tom Tully) is kidnapped by escaping convicts; the gang forces fellow inmate Johnny Hutchins (John Gavin) to drive the getaway truck. When the vehicle crashes in the process, only the warden and Gavin survive. The former hides the $100,000 the escaping convicts had with them and returns to his job. Since a policeman died in the melee, Gavin is sentenced to be executed and Tully, despite appeals from his crippled wife (Sylvia Sidney) and the prisoner's fiancee (Betty Lynn), takes no steps to thwart the verdict. Finally, his conscience gets the best of him and he confesses. Gavin is set free.

Overreaching itself to be a major production, BEHIND THE HIGH WALL emerged routine and overlong. Besides offering veteran star Sylvia Sidney a cameo as the ailing wife of the warden, it presented the sophisticated situation of criminals being on both sides of the law.

BEHIND THE MASK (Columbia, 1932) 68 mins.

Director, John Francis Dillon; story-dialog, Jo Swerling; continuity, Dorothy Howell; camera, Teddy Tetzlaff; sound, Glenn Rominger; editor, Otis Garrett.

Jack Holt (Jack Hart); Constance Cummings (Julie Arnold); Boris Karloff (Jim Henderson); Claude King (Arnold); Bertha Mann (Edwards); Edward Van Sloan (Dr. Steiner); Willard Robertson (Hawkes).

Following his tremendous success as the monster in Universal's FRANKENSTEIN (1931), Boris Karloff was co-starred with Jack Holt in the latter's Columbia Pictures action series, resulting in the gangster melodrama BEHIND THE MASK. To milk the most of Karloff's new-found horrific popularity, the producers injected into the script a mad doctor majoring in vivisections, graveyards on stormy nights, exhuming of bodies, and exotic laboratory equipment. Audiences, no doubt, were disappointed since they were expecting a horror film. Secret Service agent Jack Hart (Holt) takes on the guise of prisoner to ingratiate himself with Jim Henderson (Karloff), a key man in a drug-running gang controlled by the mysterious Mr. X. Another cohort of Mr. X is Arnold (Claude King), and the agent falls in love with his daughter Julie (Constance Cummings). Mr. X, however, becomes suspicious and kills King, claiming he died after surgery. Holt proves this wrong. Mr. X then captures the law enforcer and plans to kill him via vivisection, but Cummings arrives for the rescue. Mr. X is unmasked as the seemingly kindly doctor (Edward Van Sloan).

Using sets from THE CRIMINAL CODE (1932) (see: B/V) plus stock footage from that production, which also featured Constance Cummings and Boris Karloff, this programmer boasted superior photography by Ted Tetzlaff.

BEVERLY HILLS COP (Paramount, 1984) C 105 mins.

Executive producer, Mike Moder; producers, Don Simpson, Jerry Bruckheimer; associate producer, Linda Horner; director, Martin Brest; story, Danilo Bach, Daniel Petrie, Jr.; screenplay, Petrie; production designer, Angelo Graham; art director, James T. Murakami; set decorators, Jeff Haley, John M. Dwyer; costume designer, Tom Bronson; music, Harold Faltermeyer; songs: Faltermeyer and Keith Forsey; Allee Willis and Danny Sembello; Sharon Robinson, John Giultin and Bunny Hull; Junior and Glenn Nightingale; Vanity; stunt coordinator, Gary McLarty; second unit director, Tom Wright; assistant directors, Peter Bogart, Richard Graves; makeup, Ben Nye, Jr., Leonard Engelman; technical consultant, Chuck Adamson; special effects, Kenneth D. Pepiot; camera, Bruce Surtees; editors, Billy Weber, Arthur Coburn.

Eddie Murphy (Axel Foley); Judge Reinhold (Detective Billy Rosewood); John Ashton (Sergeant Taggart); Lisa Eilbacher (Jenny Summers); Ronny Cox (Lieutenant Bogomill); Steven Berkoff (Victor Maitland); James Russo (Mikey Tandino); Jonathan Banks (Zack); Stephen Elliott (Chief Hubbard); Gilbert R. Hill (Inspector Todd); Art Kimbro (Detective Foster); Joel Bailey (Detective McCabe); Bronson Pinchot (Serge); Paul Reiser (Jeffrey); Michael Champion (Casey); Frank Pesce (Cigarette Buyer); Gene Borkan (Truck Driver); Michael

Gregory (Hotel Manager); Alice Cadogan (Hotel Clerk); Gerald Berns, William Wallace (Beverly Hills Cops); Israel Juarbe (Room Service Waiter); Chuck Adamson, Chip Heller (Crate Operators); Paul Drake, Tom Everett (Holdup Men); Jack Heller (Harrow Club Maitre D'); David Wells (Dispatcher); Dennis Madden, John Achorn, John Pettis (Detroit Police); Darwyn Carson (Barmaid); Mark E. Corry (Pool Player).

"BEVERLY HILLS COP is the sort of slick and sleek, unabashed high-style Hollywood entertainment that seduces you in spite of yourself. The plot may be formula, the intent may be narrow, but still the movie sparkles with intelligence. Crackling with energy, it races, skitters and leaps along, dragging you unresisting in its wake." (Michael Wilmington, Los Angeles Times) The feature has grossed nearly $200,000,000 to date!

In his third starring feature, Eddie Murphy created a box-office mega sensation in BEVERLY HILLS COP, a project which had been floating around Hollywood for years and was once considered as a vehicle for Sylvester Stallone.

Murphy is Detroit police detective Axel Foley, arresting contraband cigarette dealers. He bungles the assignment and returns home to find an old friend and ex-convict, Mikey Tandino (James Russo), at his apartment and carrying German bearer bonders. Thereafter Russo is murdered by mobsters. Although his police superior (Gilbert R. Hill) orders Murphy to stay clear of the matter, he takes a leave of absence and goes to Beverly Hills where his dead pal had worked at an art gallery. There he meets Jenny Summers (Lisa Eilbacher), a co-worker of Russo's, and art dealer Victor Maitland (Steven Berkoff) whom Murphy soon suspects is behind the murder. With the willing help of Eilbacher, Murphy pursues his theory, all the time being under the surveillance of the local police. The Detroit cop learns that Berkoff is smuggling bonds and dope into the United States. Gratefully, the two police (John Aston, Judge Reinhold) tailing Murphy come to his rescue, and as a team the three storm the gangster's villa, saving Eilbacher and killing the mobster. Justice and friendship triumph.

Relying heavily on Murphy's ability as a free-flowing standup comic, this smooth running comic cop-versus-gangster thriller seems all the more lighthearted for being set in a plush Beverly Hills locale. Like DOWN AND OUT IN BEVERLY HILLS (1985), which for different storyline purposes trades on the lushness of the famed movietown bedroom community, BEVERLY HILLS COP digs beneath the surface to re-emphasize that appearances are almost always deceiving. Herein, the revelation is that contrary to popular belief, the underworld does not always operate in covert manners and that the lifestyle of organized crime can be quite sophisticated and upscale.

In mid-1986 it was announced that Eddie Murphy would star in BEVERLY HILLS COP II.

THE BIG BOODLE (United Artists, 1957) 84 mins.

Producer, Lewis Blumberg; director, Richard Wilson; based on the
novel by Robert Sylvester; screenplay, Jo Eisenger; music, Paul
Lavista; camera, Lee Garmes; editor, Charles Kimball.

Errol Flynn (Ned Sherwood); Pedro Armendariz (Colonel Mastegul);
Rosanna Rory (Fina): Gia Scala (Anita); Sandro Giglio (Senor
Ferrer); Jacques Aubuchon (Collada); Carlos Rivas (Rubi); Charles
Todd (Griswold); Guillerme Alvaraz Guedes (Casino Manager);
Carlos Mas (Churchu); Rogelio Hernandez (Saicito); Vella Martinez
(Secretary); Aurora Pita (Sales Girl).

Havana gambling den croupier Ned Sherwood (Errol Flynn)
finds himself in the midst of a counterfeiting operation when a customer (Rosanna Rory) gives him a bill worth 500 pesos which turns
out to be phoney. As a result both the police chief (Pedro Armendariz) and the gangsters who are after the bogus plates think that
Flynn knows their whereabouts, and he is hunted by both sides.
With the aid of a pretty confederate (Gia Scala), he uncovers the
counterfeit ring.
Filmed in Havana, Cuba, prior to Fidel Castro's takeover,
THE BIG BOODLE provides an interesting look at the city in pre-
revolution days. (The climactic gun battle was lensed at the Morro
Castle.) Also of interest is Flynn's performance as the world-weary
croupier innocently involved with gangsters.

THE BIG CHASE (Sono Art-World Wide Pictures, 1930) 5,850'

Supervisor, James Cruze; director, Walter Lang; based on the play
by Milton Herbert Gropper, Max Marcin; adaptors-continuity-
screenplay, Walter Woods; songs, Lynn Cowan and Paul Titsworth;
sound, Fred J. Lau, W. C. Smith; camera, Jackson Rose.

Lola Lane (Shirley); Ralph Ince (Chuck); Guinn Williams (Tiger);
Stepin Fetchit (Spot); Wheeler Oakman (Steve); James Eagle (Les-
ter); Robert E. O'Connor (Detective); Edna Bennett (Winnie); Tony
Stabeneau (Battler); Larry McGrath (Pinkie); Frank Jonasson (Berrili).

A manicurist (Lola Lane) loves boxer Tiger (Guinn Williams)
but learns that her brother (James Eagle) has lost a big bet to a
gangster (Ralph Ince) and will be killed unless he pays off the
money quickly. Williams offers her the funds but she refuses and
later finds that Eagle has been accused of murdering the gangster's
bodyguard. Ince, working with Williams' crooked manager (Wheeler
Oakman), tells Lane they will cancel the debt if she slips Williams a
drug before his next bout. When she fails to do so, the manager
does. While the boxing match is taking place, Ince and his gang
have a shootout with the police and the hoodlum is killed. Williams
wins the bout since the waterboy (Stepin Fetchit) had substituted
real water for the drugged concoction.

Photoplay magazine found this drama "amusing enough" and added, "Stepin Fetchit almost shuffles off with the show." The real interest in this early talkie was its interpolation of the gangster theme with the world of prizefighting, making it a forerunner of such genre classics as KID GALAHAD (1939) and BODY AND SOUL (see both: B/V).

THE BIG CHASE (Lippert, 1954) 60 mins.

Producer, Robert L. Lippert, Jr.; director, Arthur Hilton; screenplay, Fred Freeberger; sound, Ben Winler; camera, John Martin; editor, Carl L. Pierson.

Glenn Langan (Pete Grayson); Adele Jergens (Doris Grayson); Lon Chaney (Kip); Jim Davis (Brad Miggs); Douglas Kennedy (Ned Daggart); Jay Lawrence (Jim Bellows); and: Phil Arnold, Jack Daly, Gil Perkins, Tom Walker, Jack Breed, Wheaton Chambers, Irish Menshell.

Working on the juvenile squad, a rookie policeman (Glenn Langan) passes up an assignment at the urging of his pregnant wife (Adele Jergens), who fears for his life. When gangsters rob a payroll train, the young cop gets into a shootout with the gang leader (Lon Chaney) and once he is authorized, he travels to Mexico in pursuit of the rest (Jim Davis, Douglas Kennedy) of the gang. Upon the completion of the mission, Langan returns home to find he is the father of a daughter.
The British Monthly Film Bulletin described this low budget production as: "A harsh, lucid and semi-documentary method, combined with rapidly paced cutting, gives this thriller more than the usual tension."
Some viewers, however, were disappointed at the film's brief one-hour running time and the fact that several of the players (i.e. Lon Chaney) had abbreviated roles. Actually, some of the film's footage, plus other shots not in the feature, were released the year before in the 25-minute color short, BANDIT ISLAND, which exploited the novelty of stereo vision 3-D. That outing was a condensation of THE BIG CHASE's plot with the police on the trail of a robbery gang.

BIG MONEY (Pathe, 1930) 80 mins.

Producer, E. B. Derr; director, Russell Mack; story-screenplay, Walter De Leon, Mack; art director, Carroll Clark; music director, Josiah Zuro; assistant director, Robert Fellows; costumes, Gwen Wakeling; sound, Charles O'Loughlin, Tom Carman; camera, John Mescall; editor, Joseph Kane.

Eddie Quillan (Eddie); Robert Armstrong (Ace); James Gleason (Tom);

Margaret Livingston (Mae); Miriam Seegar (Joan McCall); Robert
Edeson (Mr. McCall); Dorothy Christy (Leila); G. Pat Collins
(Smiley); Morgan Wallace (Durkin); Myrtis Crinley (Flora); Robert
Gleckler (Monk); Charles Sellon (Bradley); Kit Guard (Lefty);
Johnny Morris (Weejee); Frank Sabini, Harry Semels (Waiters);
Clara Palmer (Society Woman); Ed Deering (Detective); Spec
O'Donnell (Elevator Boy); Mona Rico (Maid); Murray Smith (Izzy);
Harry Tyler (Wendell); Jack McDonald (Butler); Zita Moulton
(Michael); Jack Hanlon (Office Boy); Richard Cramer (Detroit
Dan); Lewis Wilder (Maurice Black).

This early talkie allows viewers to see veteran character actor
Eddie Quillan in a starring role and one he handles convincingly.
Lasting stardom eluded this talented performer, whose career has
spanned from 1920s silents to nifty television performances in the
1970s and 1980s. BIG MONEY provides Quillan with the type of
screen role in which he excelled; that of the devil-may-care young
man caught up as a victim of circumstances, this time with murderous gangsters.

Here he is Eddie, a messenger boy for a brokerage firm who
is assigned to deliver $5,000 to the bank but who gets mixed up in
a crap game and arrives too late. He is forced to take the money
home with him. When the boss' (Robert Edeson) daughter (Miriam
Seegar) accepts his jokingly made dinner invitation, he is forced to
take her to a restaurant beyond his means and uses some of the company funds to pay the check. Later, two crooks (Robert Gleckler,
Kit Guard) attempt to mug him and in escaping ends up in a hotel
room pitted against a notorious gambler (Robert Armstrong), from
whom he wins a great deal of money. Quillan then proposes to his
girl but she refuses when she realizes he gambles. At a later poker
session Armstrong murders another player and Quillan is arraigned
as a witness to the murder. Eventually, the gambler confesses,
Quillan reforms, and he and his girlfriend are reunited.

As this complex plotline seeks to prove, the good of heart can
be tempted but cannot be corrupted by evil.

THE BIG OPERATOR (Metro-Goldwyn-Mayer, 1959) 90 mins.

Executive producer, Albert Zugsmith; producer, Red Doff; director,
Charles Haas; based on the story by Paul Gallico; screenplay, Rob-
ert Smith, Allen Rivkin; music, Van Alexander; camera, Walter H.
Castle; editor, Ben Lewis.

Mickey Rooney (Little Joe Braun); Steve Cochran (Bill Gibson);
Mamie Van Doren (Mary Gibson); Mel Torme (Fred McAfee); Ray
Danton (Oscar Wetzel); Jim Backus (Cliff Heldon); Ray Anthony
(Slim Cayhurn); Jackie Coogan (Ed Brannell); Charles Chaplin, Jr.
(Bill Tragg); Vampira (Gina); Billy Daniels (Tony Webson); Ben
Gage (Bert Carr); Jay North (Tommy Gibson); Lawrence Dobkin
(Emil Cernak); Lee Gordon (Danny Sacanzi); Donald Barry

Mel Torme, Jim Backus, Mamie Van Doren, and Steve Cochran in
THE BIG OPERATOR (1959).

(Detective Sergeant); Ziva Rodann (Alice); Joey Forman (Raymond
Bailey); Grabowski (Lou Green); Vido Musso (Picket Captain).

Prior to teaming up for the inane comedy THE PRIVATE LIVES
OF ADAM AND EVE (1960), producer Albert Zugsmith and star Mickey
Rooney made this "walloping labor rackets melo(drama)" (Variety)
which benefitted from a strong script, swift direction, and solid
performances. For Mickey Rooney, the production proved to be a
good continuation for the ruthless gangster characters he had offered in BABY FACE NELSON (1957) and THE LAST MILE (1959)
(see both: B/V), in deference to his more innocent-type role in
QUICKSAND (q.v.). The star's fine work is complemented by Steve
Cochran as his adversary, and Mamie Van Doren is seen to good advantage as the latter's wife.

Under investigation by a government rackets committee, evil
union leader Little Joe Braun (Rooney) lies about knowing thug
Oscar Wetzel (Ray Danton) who has done strong-arm work for him.
Two union members, Bill Gibson (Cochran) and Fred McAfee (Mel
Torme), however, agree to testify that they saw Rooney with Danton. In retaliation, Rooney threatens Cochran's wife (Van Doren)
and kidnaps their son (Jay North), while having his thugs beat up
Cochran and set Torme on fire. Cochran, nevertheless, fights back
with the aid of his friends and the law and brings about Rooney's
conviction.

Astute moviegoers noted this was a remake of JOE SMITH, AMERICAN (1941) with Steve Cochran assuming Robert Young's role.

THE BIG SCORE (Almi, 1983) C 85 mins.

Executive producers, Harry Hurwitz, David Forbes; producers, Michael S. Landes, Albert Schwartz; associate producer, Irving Schwartz; director, Fred Williamson; screenplay, Gail Morgan Hickman; camera, Joao Fernandes; editor, Dan Lowenthal.

Fred Williamson (Frank Hooks); Nancy Wilson (Angi); John Saxon (Davis); Richard Roundtree (Gordon); Ed Lauter (Parks); D'Urville Martin (Easy); Michael Dante (Goldy); Bruce Glover (Koslo); Joe Spinell (Mayfield); Frank Pesce (J.C); Tony King (Jumbo); James Spinks (Cheech); Chelcie Ross (Hoffa); Stack Pierce (New); Jerome Landfield (Chief Detective); Frank Rice (Pete); Karl Theodore (Huge); Ron Dean (Kowalski); Katherine Wallach (Prostitute); Ernest Perry, Jr. (Allen); Greg Noonan (Martin); and: The Ramsey Lewis Trio, Grand Slam (Themselves).

Police detective Frank Hooks (Fred Williamson) is accused of stealing money taken in a big drug raid and is fired from the force. He decides to round up the gangsters responsible for framing him.
Allegedly based on several screen projects by Gail Morgan Hickman for the "Dirty Harry" film series and purchased by star-director Fred Williamson from Clint Eastwood in the 1970s, this motion picture simply moved the locale from the West Coast to Chicago and made the chief protagonist black instead of white. Otherwise the Frank Hooks of THE BIG SCORE and Dirty Harry Callahan are pretty much from the same violent cloth.
Full of gratuitous thrills and some gripping Chicago background, this entry is more intriguing for its cast than its plot. Williamson is appropriately stalwart as the honest loner cop, while John Saxon and Richard Roundtree add flavor as his police force cohorts; Ed Lauter is particularly strong as his by-the-book police superior; and singer Nancy Wilson makes her film debut as Williamson's on-again-off-again girlfriend.

THE BIG SHAKEDOWN (First National, 1934) 64 mins.

Producer, Samuel Bischoff; director, John Francis Dillon; based on the story "Cut Rate" by Sam Engels; screenplay, Niven Busch, Rian James; camera, Sid Hickox; editor, James Gibbon.

Charles Farrell (Jimmy Morrell); Bette Davis (Norma Frank); Ricardo Cortez (Rick Barnes); Glenda Farrell (Lil); Allen Jenkins (Lefty); Henry O'Neill (Sheffner); G. Pat Collins (Gyp); Adrian Morris (Trigger); Dewey Robinson (Slim); John Wray (Gardinella); Philip

Faversham (John); Earle Foxe (Carey); Samuel S. Hinds (Kohlsadt);
Sidney Miller (Jewis Boy); Elinor Jackson (Woman); Charles B. Wil-
liams (Timid Man); Robert Emmett O'Connor (Regan the Bartender);
Ben Taggert (Cop); Oscar Apfel (Doctor); John Hyams (Smith);
Edward LeSaint (Fillmore); Frank Layton (Dr. Boutellier).

Leading men Charles Farrell and Ricardo Cortez were on the
descent from their career peaks as silent screen stars, while Bette
Davis, appearing surprisingly comely in this outing, was on the rise
when the trio was teamed for this gangster melodrama directed by
John Francis Dielon, who two years earlier had helmed another genre
opus, BEHIND THE MASK (q.v.) at Columbia.
Prohibition has just been repealed and mobster Nick Barnes
(Cortez) is without a racket since the bootlegging business is
over. To retain his lifestyle, he talks local druggist-chemist Jimmy
Morrell (Farrell) into brewing counterfeit patent medicines which
Cortez will sell at half the price of prescription drugs. Cortez convinces Farrell the business will save poor people money, and what
finally persuades him is his need for funds to marry Norma (Davis),
a pharmacy clerk. After their marriage, Davis wants her husband
out of the racket, but Cortez beats him up and threatens Davis, so
the chemist remains and is later forced to dilute his formulas which
make the medicines useless. Thereafter, Davis is given some of the
useless medicine at the hospital where she is undergoing a premature
delivery. The baby dies and she nearly does too. In anger, Farrell shoots Cortez, with the gangster falling into a vat of acid. At
the grand jury hearing, Farrell is found innocent of any crime because he was forced to work for the gangster. He and Davis are
able to reopen their drugstore.
This was another example of a Warner Bros. proletarian drama,
in which poor innocent dupes are at the mercy of a corrupt segment
of society but in a very timely fashion (since this was a programmer)
manage to emerge victorious.

THE BIG SLEEP (Warner Bros., 1946) 114 mins.

Producer-director, Howard Hawks; based on the novel by Raymond
Chandler; screenplay, William Faulkner, Leigh Brackett, Jules
Furthman; music, Max Steiner; orchestrator, Simon Bucharoff; as-
sistant director, Robert Freeland; art director, Carl Jules Weyl; set
decorator, Fred M. MacLean; gowns, Leah Rhodes; sound, Robert B.
Lee; special effects, E. Roy Davidson, Warren E. Lynch, William
McGann, Robert Burks, Willard Van Enger; camera, Sid Hickox;
editor, Christian Nyby.

Humphrey Bogart (Philip Marlowe); Lauren Bacall (Vivian Rutledge);
John Ridgely (Eddie Mars); Martha Vickers (Carmen Sternwood);
Dorothy Malone (Bookshop Proprietress); Peggy Knudsen (Mrs. Ed-
die Mars); Regis Toomey (Bernie Ohls); Charles Waldron (General
Sternwood); Charles D. Brown (Norris); Bob Steele (Canino);

Elisha Cook, Jr. (Harry Jones)1 Louis Jean Heydt (Joe Brody);
Sonia Darrin (Agnes); James Flavin (Captain Cronjager); Thomas
Jackson (District Attorney Wilde); Dan Wallace (Carol Lundgren);
Theodore Von Eltz (Arthur Gwynn Geiger); Joy Barlowe (Taxicab
Driver); Tom Fadden (Sidney); Ben Welden (Pete); Trevor Bardette
(Art Huck); Joseph Crehhan (Medical Examiner); Emmett Vogan (Ed).

THE BIG SLEEP (United Artists, 1978) C 99 mins.

Producers, Elliott Kastner, Michael Winner; director, Winner; based
on the novel by Raymond Chandler; adaptor, Winner; production
designer, Harry Pottle; music, Jerry Fielding; art director, John
Graysmark; costumes-wardrobe, Ron Beck; assistant director,
Michael Dryhurst; sound, Hugh Strain, Brian Marshall; camera,
Robert Paynter; editor, Freddie Wilson.

Robert Mitchum (Philip Marlowe); Sarah Miles (Charlotte Sternwood);
Richard Boone (Lash Canino); Candy Clark (Camilla Sternwood);
Joan Collins (Agnes Lozelle); Edward Fox (Joe Brody); John Mills
(Inspector Carson); James Stewart (General Sternwood); Oliver
Reed (Eddie Mars); Harry Andrews (Butler Norris); Colin Blakely
(Harry Jones); Richard Todd (Barker); Diana Quick (Mona Grant);
James Donald (Inspector Gregory); John Justin (Arthur Geiger);
Simon Turner (Karl Lundgren); Martin Potter (Owen Taylor); David
Savile (Rusty Regan); Dudley Sutton (Lanny); Don Henderson (Lou);
Nik Forster (Croupier); Joe Ritchie (Taxi Driver); Patrick Durkin
(Reg); Derek Deadman (Man in Bookstore).

Raymond Chandler's first novel The Big Sleep (1939) (the
title refers to death) is probably the most flagrant of his works with
its underlying theme of corruption. Here drugs, blackmail, illicit
sex, murder, and a host of other immoral activities are entwined
into a plot so complicated that even scripters William Faulkner, Leigh
Brackett, and Jules Furthman (for the 1946 version) had difficulty in
ferreting out all the characters and welding them into a cohesive unit.
One amusing story surrounding the filming of the 1940s version had
the filmmakers at a loss at one point as to who committed a certain
murder and a quick phone call to author Chandler resulted only in
the terse comment, "The butler did it!"
      The complex and often illogical plot has Los Angeles private
detective Philip Marlowe (Humphrey Bogart) hired by wealthy, but
dying General Sternwood (Charles Waldron) to look into a blackmailing attempt against his pretty younger daughter Carmen (Martha
Vickers) by bookstore owner Arthur Geiger (Theodore Von Eltz).
Wandron also advises Bogart that one of his employees, Shawn Regan,
has disappeared. The general's other daughter, Vivian (Lauren
Bacall) believes Bogart has been hired to find Regan. When Von
Eltz is murdered and a drugged Vickers is found at the scene,
Bogart takes her home. Later Von Eltz's clerk (Sonia Darrin) and
her associate Joe Brody (Louis Jean Heydt) attempt to take over the

dead man's blackmailing racket (here utilizing a set of nude photographs of Vickers), but Heydt is soon murdered by Von Eltz's friend.
In the meantime, Bogart falls into a net with gangster Eddie Mars
(John Ridgely) whose wife is believed to have run away with the elu-
sive Regan. At Ridgely's gambling casino Bogart encounters sultry
Bacall, who is a big winner there. Together they sort through the
clues leading to the missing Regan which point to Vickers apparently
having killed Regan. Still later, Ridgely shoots Vickers, Bogart
kills Ridgely. Bogart and Bacall then lie to the general about
Vickers' true nature to save his feelings, and are able to report
that Regan is really still alive.

Following their successful teaming in TO HAVE AND HAVE
NOT (1944), Humphrey Bogart and Lauren Bacall were assigned the
meaty roles of Philip Marlowe and Vivian Sternwood in this initial
screen adaptation of the Raymond Chandler work. The screen chemistry was still torrid between the two stars and their joint scenes
were a highlight of the motion picture. Outstanding among the superior supporting players was cowboy star Bob Steele as the cold
blooded killer Canino and Martha Vickers as the deadly nymphomaniac Carmen.

In 1978 the Chandler novel was reworked by director Michael
Winner, following the box-office success of the remake of FAREWELL,
MY LOVELY (q.v.) three years earlier. As in that feature, Robert
Mitchum played Philip Marlowe, and for the most part the movie was
an even more accurate adaptation of the novel than had been the
1946 edition. In fact, the film stayed so true to the novel that it
was sometimes necessary for Winner to utilize flashbacks within flashbacks to relate the narrative. The critics, however, lambasted this
remake, squashing any hope that Mitchum would continue in a series
of film adaptations of Chandler novels.

The plot of the remake was basically the same as its predecessor, but this time the sexual aspects of the plot were able to be
graphically shown, as was the work's excessive violence. What
galled the critics and Chandler purists alike was that the film was
updated in time and that its locale was changed to London (where
the movie was shot on location). Perhaps the weakest link in this
remake was Richard Boone's characterization of the hitman Canino.
He played the part as a hobbling, belicose, bellowing madman, lacking the cold, frightening aspects of the character so beautifully underplayed by Bob Steele in the Warner Bros. original.

THE BIG STEAL (RKO, 1949) 71 mins.

Executive producer, Sid Rogell; producer, Jack L. Gross; director,
Don Siegel; based on the story "The Road to Carmichael's" by
Richard Wormser; screenplay, Geoffrey Homes, Gerald Drayson Adams;
music, Leigh Harline; music director, C. Bakaleinikoff; art directors,
Albert D'Agostino, Ralph Berger; set decorators, Darrell Silvera;
Harley Miller; costumes, Edward Stevenson; makeup, Gordon Bau,
Robert Cowan; assistant director, Sam Ruman; camera, Harry J.
Wild; editor, Samuel E. Beetley.

Jane Greer and Robert Mitchum in THE BIG STEAL (1949).

Robert Mitchum (Duke); Jane Greer (Joan); William Bendix (Blake); Patrick Knowles (Fiske); Ramon Novarro (Colonel Ortega); Don Alvarado (Lieutenant Ruiz); John Qualen (Seton); Pasqual Garcia Pena (Manuel); Henry Carr, Jose Logan, Primo Lopez (Bellhops); Alfonso Dubois (Police Sergeant); Frank Hagney (Madden); Ted Jacques (Cole); Virginia Farmer, Carmen Morales, Lillian O'Malley (Women); Edward Colebrook (Mexican Tourist); Paul Castellanos, Dimas Sotello, Frank Leyva, Elios Gamboa, Juan Duval (Vendors); Rodolfo Hoyos (Custom Inspector); Salvador Baguez (Morale); Arturo Soto Rangel (Pedro); Beatriz Ramos (Carmencita); Tony Roux (Parrot Vendor); Felipe Turich (Guitar Vendor); Nacho Galindo (Pastry Vendor); Carl Sklover, Bing Conley (Dockhands); Gregorio Acosta (Chaney); Alfred Soto (Gonzales); Paul Guerrero (Pepe); Carlos Reyes (Taxi Driver); Alphonse Sanchez Tello (Basguez).

RKO mogul Howard Hughes pushed THE BIG STEAL into production in order to prove to the California courts that star Robert Mitchum was gainfully employed, hoping to reduce the actor's court sentence for being involved in a marijuana scandal. After fifty days behind bars, Mitchum was released to go to Mexico where he headlines in this actioner, much of the footage having been shot without him. With the publicity from Mitchum's ordeal, plus his reteaming with beautiful Jane Greer--his co-star of OUT OF THE PAST (1947) (see: B/V)--THE BIG STEAL proved to be a successful commercial entry despite the fact it was saddled with a mundane script.

Duke Haliday (Mitchum) gets off a steamer in Vera Cruz only to be arrested by policeman Blake (William Bendix) for the theft of $300,000 of Army payroll. Mitchum escapes with Bendix's papers and in tow has pretty passenger Chiquita (Greer) who has had $2,000 stolen from her by Jim Fiske (Patrick Knowles). Mitchum and Greer deduce that Knowles is also the culprit in the payroll theft and they trail him to Tehuacan where he is to meet his gangster boss (John Qualen), who also employs Bendix. Also involved in the case caper is Mexican police inspector Ortega (Ramon Navarro) and his lieutenant (Don Alvarado).

With its fast-paced action, ingratiating cast, tongue-in-cheek approach, and attractive Mexican locales, THE BIG STEAL is a modestly entertaining drama. Time magazine observed, "In fleeting moments the cockeyed speed of the chase recalls the wonderful jet-propelled jalopies of the old silent comedies."

BIG TOWN CZAR (Universal, 1939) 61 mins.

Associate producer, Ken Goldsmith; director, Arthur Lubin; story, Ed Sullivan; screenplay, Edmund L. Hartmann; assistant director, Vaughn Paul; camera, Ellwood Bredell; editor, Philip Cahn.

Barton MacLane (Phil Daley); Tom Brown (Danny Daley); Eve Arden (Susan Warren); Jack La Rue (Mike Luger); Frank Jenks (Sid Travis); Walter Woolf King (Paul Burgess); Oscar O'Shea (Pa Daley); Esther Daley (Ma Daley); Horance MacMahon (Puncky); Ed Sullivan (Himself).

The chief interest today in this dual bill item is that it is based on a story by newspaper columnist Ed Sullivan, who also served as the onscreen narrator. Of course, Sullivan later became world famous for his TV variety show, "The Toast of the Town," which aired for nearly a quarter of a century.

Barton MacLane headlines as Phil Daley, a big time gangster who has pulled himself up from the tenements. His controls a big Gotham racketeering operation and is chagrined when his younger brother Danny (Tom Brown) leaves college to join the operation. A rival gang, however, tries to use Brown against his brother, but MacLane comes to the rescue. He sets Brown on the right path, but ends up being arrested on a murder charge after escaping an ambush from his foes.

Keeping within the Production Code of the film industry, films such as this attempted to moralize by showing that even with gangsters, blood is thicker than water.

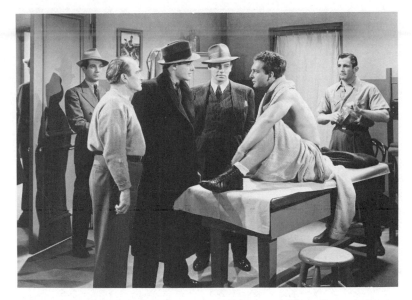

Cully Richards, John Sheehan, Jack LaRue, Carleton Young, Gordon Jones, and Billy McGowan in BIG TOWN CZAR (1939).

BLACK BELT JONES (Warner Bros., 1974) C 85 mins.

Producers, Fred Weintraub, Paul Heller; director, Robert Clouse; story, Alex Rose, Weintraub; screenplay, Oscar Williams; music, Luichi De Jesus, Dennis Coffy; set decorator, Charles Pierce; assistant director, Martin Hornstein; sound, Darin Knight; camera, Kent Wakeford; editor, Michael Kahn.

Jim Kelly (Black Belt Jones); Gloria Hendry (Sydney); Scatman Crothers (Pop); Alan Weeks (Dippy); Eric Laneuville (Quincy); Andre Phillipe (Don Steffano); Vincent Barbi (Big Tuna); Nate Esformes (Roberts); Malik Carter (Pinky); Mel Novak (Blue Eyes); Esther Sutherland (Lucy).

Producers Fred Weintraub and Paul Heller, director Robert Clouse, and star Jim Kelly, all involved with the previously successful ENTER THE DRAGON (q.v.), reteamed for this "minor exploitation programmer" (Variety).
Hoodlum Pinky (Malik Carter), the underling of mobster Don Steffano (Andre Phillips), is seeking land for a building project, but the owner (Scatman Crothers), who has a karate studio on the property, will not sell. The hoodlum then attempts to force a sale, but Pop's daughter's (Gloria Henry) boyfriend, Black Belt Jones

Jim Kelly (center) in BLACK BELT JONES (1974).

(Kelly) and his other blackmartial arts students come to his rescue by beating up the gangsters.

In actuality, BLACK BELT JONES is a hollow feature with the gimmick of martial arts special effects to hold up the plot ploy of good blacks versus bad whites. As a point of cinema history, the promotional trailer to BLACK BELT JONES was used as part of the contents of the sendup on bad cinema called IT CAME FROM HOLLY-WOOD (1982) and is one of the funniest segments in that compilation feature.

THE BLACK BIRD (Columbia, 1975) C 98 mins.

Executive producer, George Segal; producers, Michael Levee, Lou Lombardo; director, David Giler; based on a story by Don M. Mankiewicz, Gordon Cotler; screenplay, Giler; music, Jerry Fielding; production designer, Harry Horner; set decorator, Darrell Silvera; assistant director, Art Levinson; sound, Jack Solomon; camera, Phil Lathrop; editors, Margaret Booth, Walter Thompson.

George Segal and Elisha Cook, Jr. in THE BLACK BIRD (1975).

George Segal (Sam Spade, Jr.); Stephane Audran (Anna Kemidon);
Lionel Stander (Andrew Jackson Immelman); Lee Patrick (Effie
Perrine); Elisha Cook, Jr. (Wilmer); Felix Silla (Litvak); Signe Hasso
(Dr. Crippen); John Abbott (Du Quai); Connie Kreski (Decoy Gril);
Titus Napoleon, Harry Kenoi (Hawaiian Thugs); Howard Jerfrey
(Kerkurian); Richarrd B. Shull (Prizer); Ken Swafford (McGregor).

    Following the success of the 1941 version of THE MALTESE
FALCON (see: B/V), Warner Bros. announced a sequel to be called
THE FURTHER ADVENTURES OF THE MALTESE FALCON, planning
to reunite stars Humphrey Bogart, Mary Astor, and Sydney Green-
street. That exciting project never developed, although the trio
did redo the original on CBS radio in 1946 on "Academy Award
Theatre." For years, a sequel to the John Huston celluloid classic
was touted, and finally Columbia Pictures produced the much heralded THE BLACK BIRD in 1975, gearing it as a serio-comedy followup to Dashiell Hammett's work. The resulting production was
disappointing to purists while providing only occasional amusement
to the rest of its viewers.
    Like the original, the narrative is set in San Francisco, where
seedy Sam Spade, Jr. (George Segal) has inherited his father's detective business and his now bitter secretary Effie Perrine (Lee
Patrick). The part of town where his office is located is tawdry,
full of pimps and prostitutes. When the body of Kaspar Gutman

(who more than three decades before had involved his father in the search for the legendary Maltese Falcon) is found at the entrance to Segal's building, the latter finds himself solving the old caper. He locates what he thinks to be the bogus bird and pawns it, only to learn it is the genuine item. Several parties are after the treasure, including: mysterious Anna Kamidon (Stephane Audran); dwarf Litvak (Felix Silla); a neo-Nazi; and Wilmer (Elisha Cook, Jr.), Gutman's one-time gunsel. Aiding Spade in solving the case is his father's old pal Andrew Jackson Immelman (Lionel Stander). Eventually Segal finds himself caught between the machinations of Shanghai-born White Russian Audran and the Nazi dwarf, and his own greed.

This movie lacks the verve of a tongue-in-cheek joke and is not substantial enough to be a robust crime thriller. For nostalgia buffs, it was entertaining to have Patrick and Cook repeat their screen originals; especially Patrick, who stole the proceedings as the loud-mouth, blousy Effie.

THE BLACK COIN (Stage & Screen, 1936) fifteen chapters

Supervisor, Louis Weiss; director, Al Herman; story, George M. Merrick; screenplay, Eddy Graneman, Dallas M. Fitzgerald, Robert Lively, Albert Merman, music, Lee Zahler; sound, Corson Jowett; camera, James Diamond; editor, Earl Turner.

Ralph Graves (Prescott); Ruth Mix (Dorothy Dale); Dave O'Brien (Terry Navarro); Constance Bergan (Virginia Caswell); Mathew Betz (Jensen); Robert Frazer (Hackett); Snub Pollard (Vic Moran); Robert Walker (Shark Malone); Bryant Washburn (Caswell); Clara Kimball Young (Donna Luise); Josef Swickard (Don Pedro); Blackie Shiteford (McGuire); Yakima Canutt (Ed McMahan); Jackie Miller (Bobbie); Lane Chandler (Sir Philip); Richard Cramer (Hank); Roger Williams (Gleason); Walter Taylor (Herb); Pete de Grasse (Ali Ben Aba); William Desmond (Bartender); Joe Garcia (Ozzie); Juan Duval (Juan); Lew Meehan (Ortega); Carter Wayne (Anderson); Milburn Morante (Slim); Carl Matthews (Spotty).

Chapters: 1) Dangerous Men; 2) The Mystery Ship; 3) The Fatal Plunge; 4) Monsters of the Deep; 5) Wolves of the Night; 6) Shark's Fang; 7) Midnight Menace; 8) Flames of Death; 9) Smuggler's Lair; 10) Flaming Guns; 11) Wheels of Death; 12) The Crash; 13) Danger Ahead; 14) Hidden Peril; 15) The Phantom Treasure.

Two Federal agents (Ralph Graves, Ruth Mix) are on the trail of a gang of smugglers, whom they believe are headquartered at the Caswell Shipping Company. An employee of the operation, Terry Navarro (Dave O'Brien), also believes the smugglers are using the company as a front but he feels its president (Bryant Washburn) is innocent, especially since he loves the man's daughter (Constance Bergen). O'Brien is assigned by Washburn to take valuable papers to a deserted island, but ship captain Shark Malone (Robert Walker) thinks the documents contain part of the puzzle to a treasure map. A business associate (Robert Frazer) of Washburn and an Arab chieftain (Pete de Grasse) also want the papers, and the chase leads the participants from the Middle East to Africa and on to the United States before the smuggling operation is destroyed, Washburn is cleared, and O'Brien and Bergen can settle down to a life of contentment.

THE BLACK COIN was the finale in a trio of cliffhangers issued by Stage & Screen, a company attempting to win a piece of the 1930s independent market serial pie. This chapterplay was one of the few independent sound serials to utilize the gangster theme, here in the guise of a sea smuggling ring.

BLACK GUNN (Columbia, 1972) C 94 mins.

Producers, John Heyman, Norman Priggen; director, Robert Hartford-Davis; based on idea by Hartford-Davis and a screenplay by Robert Shearer; screenplay, Franklin Coen; art director, Jack DeShields; assistant director, Max Stein; music, Tony Osborne; camera, Richard H. Kline; editors, David De Wilde, Pat Somerset.

Jim Brown (Gunn); Martin Landau (Capelli); Brenda Sykes (Judith); Luciana Paluzzi (Toni); Vida Blue (Sam Green); Stephen McNally (Laurento); Keefe Brasselle (Winman); Timothy Brown (Larry); William Campbell (Rico); Bernie Casey (Seth); Gary Conway (Adama); Chuck Daniel (Mel); Tommy Davis (Webb); Rick Ferrell (Jimpy); Bruce Glover (Ray Kriley); Toni Holt (Betty); Herbert Jefferson, Jr. (Scott Gunn); Jay Montgomery (Junkie); Mark Tapscott (Cassidy); Gene Washington (Elmo); Jim Watkins (Lieutenant Hopper); Jonas Wolfe (Val); Tony Young (Dell); Sandra Giles (Prostitute); Kate Woodville (Louella); Gyl Roland (Celeste); Lavelle Roby (Jane); Jeanne Bell (Lisa); Tony Giorgio (Ben); Frank Bello (Robbo); Arell Blanton (Television Director); Manuel DePina (Bowling Alley Manager); Deacon Jones (Himself).

Another in the series of early 1970s cheaply made black exploitation features, BLACK GUNN was surprisingly produced by British craftsmen working in Hollywood. The results were passable entertainment, although the filmmakers suffered from naivete and a strong desire to preach.

Jim Brown, one-time football ace and often the lead in these violent screen epics, is cast as Gunn, the owner of a nightclub, whose young sibling (Herbert Jefferson, Jr.) is hooked up with a gang of militant black power guerillas. He makes the mistake of ripping off a Mafia-owned bookie operation and the "family" guns him down. Big brother swears revenge against the murderer, mob member Capelli (Martin Landau).

Regular filmgoers will notice a surprising number of familiar Hollywood faces (i.e. Luciana Paluzzi, Stephen McNally, Keefe

Brasselle, William Campbell, Gary Conway, et al) as well as such
personalities as Vida Blue and Deacon Jones. The film's title was
an ethnic exploitation of the Blake Edwards' created 1960s TV series "Peter Gunn" starring Craig Stevens which itself became a 1967
feature, GUNN.

BLACK MARKET BABIES (Monogram, 1946) 71 mins.

Producer, Jeffrey Bernard; director, William Beaudine; story, George
Morris; adaptor, George W. Sayre; camera, Harry Neumann; editor,
William Austin.

Ralph Morgan (Dr. Jordan); Kane Richmond (Eddie Condon); Teala
Loring (Evelyn Barret); Marjorie Hoshelle (Donna Corbett); George
Meeker (Anthony Marco); Jayne Hazard (Doris Condon); Dewey Rob-
inson (Barney); Alan Foster (Jake); Selmar Jackson (Mr. Andrews);
Nana Bryant (Mrs. Andrews); Maris Wrixon (Helen Roberts); Addi-
son Richards (Hamilton); Parker Gee (Paul Carroll); Terry Frost
(Sam).

A gangster, Eddie Condon (Kane Richmond), enlists the aid of
a physician (Ralph Morgan) and a crooked lawyer (George Meeker)
in running a hospital for wayward, pregnant girls. The young
ladies' unwanted offsprings are then put up for adoption with pro-
spective parents being bilked for lots of money, presumably to aid
the institution, but in reality most of the money going to the hoodlum. The operation is a financial success, but complaints bring the
authorities into the case. After a killing, the mobster tries to lay
the blame on the doctor, but the latter turns state's evidence and
brings Richmond to justice.
The black market baby racket has been a standard ploy in the
gangster film arena since the 1920s. This outing has a "timeliness
of theme and several good performances by the feature players"
(Variety) to make it a pleasing programmer.

BLACK MARKET BABY (Brut/ABC-TV, 10/7/77) C 100 mins.

Executive producer, James Green; producer, Milton Sperling; supervising producer, Allen S. Epstein; director, Robert Day; based on
the novel A Nice Italian Girl by Elizabeth Christman; teleplay, Andrew Peter Marin; music, George Wilkins, Richard Bellis; art director, Carl Anderson; camera, Richard C. Glouner; editor, George
Jay Nicholson.

Linda Purl (Anne Macarino); Desi Arnaz, Jr. (Steve Aletti); Jessica
Walter (Louise Carmino); David Doyle (Joseph Carmino); Tom Bosley
(Dr. Andrew Brantford); Bill Bixby (Herbert Freemont); Lucille
Benson (Mrs. Krieg); Annie Potts (Linda Cleary); Tracy Brooks
Swope (Babs); Allen Joseph (Albert Macarino); Mark Thomas (Mario

Macarino); Argentina Brunetti (Aunt Imelda); Tom Pedi (Uncle
Sanchi); Beulah Quo (Mrs. Yamato); Robert Resnick (Rick); Stuart
Nisbet (Professor Wellman); James Oliver (Waterman); James Fraracci
(Victorio); Shelly Hoffman (Sylvana); Ivana Moore (Gina); Andrew
Marin (Watcher).

Dr. Andrew Brantford (Bill Bixby) is the slick but corrupt
head of an adoption agency who uses pregnant, unwed girls in order to sell their babies to people desperately wanting children.
Since most of the girls who use the agency are college age and do
not have abortions, Bixby uses this information to blackmail them
into giving up their offsprings. A wealthy couple (Jessica Walter,
David Doyle) convince Bixby to get them a baby by hiring a young
man to impregnate a co-ed and then acquire her newborn infant.
The man chosen is Steve Aletti (Desi Arnaz, Jr.), a pre-med student,
and the girl is Anne Macarino (Linda Purl). The plan goes awry
when the couple plan to keep the child, only to find themselves
threatened by the black market adoption agency.
Made as DANGEROUS LOVE, this telefeature was based on
Elizabeth Christman's novel A Nice Italian Girl. It was shown
abroad as DON'T STEAL MY BABY. As social drama, the film was
exploitive; as entertainment it benefitted from the responsive acting
of Purl and Bixby.

THE BLACK RAVEN (Producers Releasing Corp., 1943) 62 mins.

Producer, Sigmund Neufeld; director, Sam Newfield; screenplay,
Fred Myton; assistant director, Melville De Lacy; music supervisor,
David Chudnow; sound, Hans Weeren; camera, Robert Cline; editor,
Holbrook N. Todd.

George Zucco (Amos Bradford); Wanda McKay (Lee Winfield); Noel
Madison (Mike Baroni); Bob Randall [Robert Livingston] (Allen
Bentley); Byron Foulger (Horace Weatherby); Charles Middleton
(Sheriff); Robert Middlemas (Tim Winfield); Glenn Strange (Sandy);
I. Stanford Jolley (Whitey Cole).

At a lonely roadside inn called "The Black Raven," near the
Canadian border, a motley group of people appear on a stormy night
and are provided sanctuary by the inn's owner, Amos Bradford
(George Zucco), a one-time criminal also known as "The Raven."
Among the guests are: an eloping couple (Wanda McKay, Robert
[Livingston] Randall); the girl's angry father (Robert Middlemas);
a runaway prisoner named Whitey Cole (I. Stanford Jolley) who is
on the run from the law and out to settle a score with Zucco; gang-
ster Mike Baroni (Noel Madison); and an embezzler (Byron Foulger).
As the evening progresses, several murders occur and the gangster
is finally brought to justice, but not before Zucco is fatally wounded.
THE BLACK RAVEN can best be described as PRC's GRAND
HOTEL. The movie, despite its poverty row origins, is well executed

Bob Randall [Livingston], George Zucco, and Wanda McKay in THE BLACK RAVEN (1943).

and filled with good atmosphere, some effective comedy dialogue, and fairly decent production values. Its mystery motif and a fine cast keep the movie entertaining, with Zucco especially good as the inn's none-too-honest proprietor, aided by Glenn Strange as his dimwit handyman and Charles Middleton as the local sheriff. The film's minor hero role was portrayed by Robert Randall, the real name of Robert Livingston, the Western star who had earlier head-lined several gangster exercises, including ARSON RACKET SQUAD and FEDERAL MANHUNT (qq.v.), both 1938 Republic releases.

BLONDE BAIT (Associated Film Distributing Corp, 1956) 70 mins.

Producer, Anthony Hinds; director, Elmo Williams; music, Leonard Salzedo; camera, Walter Harvey, William Whitley; editor, James Needs.

Beverly Michaels (Angela Booth); Jim Davis (Nick Randall); Joan Rice (Cleo); Richard Travis (Kent Foster); Paul Cavanagh (Inspector Hedges); Thora Hird (Granny); Avril Angers (Bessie); Gordon Jackson (Percy); Valeria White (Prison Governor); April Olrich (Marguerte); Ralph Michael (Julian Lord).

BLONDE BAIT is actually two movies for the price of one.

Originally made in Great Britain and issued there in 1956 by
Exclusive/Hammer Films as WOMEN WITHOUT MEN, this movie deleted some of its original footage and had new scenes shot with
American actors for its United States release the same year. In
the British edition, the character of gangster Nick Randall was
played by Paul Carpenter, but he was deleted entirely for the
American version with Jim Davis now playing the hoodlum. For
the U.S. outing, not only was Nick a murderous underworld figure,
but also a traitor, an enemy collaborator who had been a paid
courier for a foreign spy ring.

State Department agent Kent Foster (Richard Travis) relates
a case to his boss (Harry Lauter) and the film flashes back six
months to London where American singer Angela Booth (Beverly
Michaels) has become a major star. She is in love with Nick Randall (Davis) and promises to meet him in three months so they can
wed; she is unaware that he is a wanted gangster who plans to use
her in his latest underworld scheme. When Michaels goes to her
manager Julian Lord (Ralph Michael) for a release from her contract,
there is a struggle and she hits him with a mirror. Michael brings
charges against her and the actress is sentenced to six months in a
women's prison. Since the State Department had been secretly using
Michaels to get at Davis, Travis flies to London and asks Scotland
Yard Inspector Hedges (Paul Cavanagh) for help. The latter agrees
to allow Michaels to escape and to meet Davis. An old-time inmate
(Hird) is used to break Michaels out and she helps her keep her
New Year's Eve appointment with Davis. The police surround them
and in a shootout the gangster is killed. Because she was responsible for Davis' capture, Michael's sentence is commuted and she
resumes her career successfully.

THE BLONDE BANDIT (Republic, 1950) 60 mins.

Producer, Sidney Picker; director, Harry Keller; screenplay, John
K. Butler; assistant director, Nate Barranger; art director, Frank
Hotaling; set decorators, John McCarthy, Jr., James Reed; music,
Stanley Wilson; sound, Earl Crain, Sr.; camera, Ellis W. Carter;
editor, Arthur Hilton.

Dorothy Patrick (Gloria Dell); Gerald Mohr (Joe Sapelli); Robert
Rockwell (James Deveron); Larry J. Blake (Captain E. V. Roberts);
Charles Cane (Lieutenant Metzger); Richard Irving (Benny); Ar-
gentina Brunetti (Mama Sapelli); Alex Frazer (Winters); Nana Bryant
(Mrs. Henley); David Clarke (Lieutenant O'Connor); Jody Gilbert
(Bertha Fannon); Monte Blue (Chief Ramsay); Eve Shitney (Mara-
belle); Norman Budd (Gus); Bobby Scott (Mechanic); Bob Wilke
(Walker); Philip Van Zandt (Arthur Jerome); Ted Jacques (Bartend-
er); Walter Clinton (Waiter); Eva Novak (Jail Matron); Keith Richards
(Detective); Lester Dorr (Ticket Taker); Roy Gordon (Thorndyke).

Pretty Gloria Dell (Dorothy Patrick) comes to California with the promise of getting married, but once there she learns her intended has been arrested for bigamy. She is befriended by Joe Sapelli (Gerald Mohr), who turns out to be a racketeer bookie, and he talks her into taking part in a jewelry heist. Captured by the law, a district attorney (Robert Rockwell) convinces the once naive girl to get evidence to convict the hoodlum, but she falls in love with Mohr and after his arrest she agrees to wait for him to finish his prison term.

The major interest of this unassuming feature is its study of the distaff side of the gangster theme, or at least how a young woman can be lured into a life of crime by a slick hoodlum.

BLONDIE JOHNSON (First National, 1933) 67 mins.

Director, Ray Enright; story-screenplay, Earl Baldwin; dialogue director, Stanley Logan; camera, Tony Gaudio; editor, George Marks.

Joan Blondell (Blondie Johnson); Chester Morris (Curley Jones); Allen Jenkins (Louie); Claire Dodd (Gladys La Mann); Earle Foxe (Scannell); Mae Busch (Mae); Joseph Cawthorn (Jewelry Store Manager); Sterling Holloway (Red Charley); Olin Howland (Eddie); Arthur Vinton (Max Wagner); Donald Kirke (Joe); Tom Kennedy (Hype); Sam Godfrey (Freddie); Toshia Mori (Lulu).

After the death of her mother and the seduction and desertion of her young sister, pretty Blondie (Joan Blondell) takes to the street for a living when she cannot find a legitimate job. She becomes involved in the rackets and encounters petty gangster Curley Jones (Chester Morris) and they fall in love. She talks Morris into quitting his job with a big-time mobster and setting up his own racket. Eventually she is the cause of several shootings and is arrested and sent to prison for six years, finally realizing that crime does not pay.

Outside of solid emoting by Joan Blondell in the title role, Chester Morris as her hoodlum boyfriend, and Allen Jenkins as a wisecracking thug, BLONDIE JOHNSON is a rather complicated but not very realistic programmer. About the only credibility here is the fact that the Depression forced essentially moral girls into prostitution, but this portion of the plotline is subordinated to the gangster tale, which is not a strong one as presented here.

BODY AND SOUL (Cannon Group, 1981) C 115 mins.

Producers, Menahem Golan, Yoram Globus; director, George Bowers; screenplay, Leon Isaac Kennedy; art director, Bob Ziembicki; fight choreographer, Bob Minor; dance choreographers, Hope Clarke, Valentino; costumes, Celia; music, Webster Lewis; camera, James Forrest; editors, Sam Pollard, Skip Schoolnik.

Leon Isaac Kennedy (Leon); Jayne Kennedy (Julie); Peter Lawford
(Big Man); Perry Lang (Charles); Nikki Swassy (Kelly); Mike Gazzo
(Frankie); Kim Hamilton (Mrs. Johnson); Muhammad Ali (Himself);
Chris Wallace (Dr. Bachman); Robbie Epps (Iceman); J. B. William-
son (Assassin); Al Denavo (Mad Man Santiago); Mel Welles (Joe);
Danny Wells, Johnny Brown (Sports Announcers); DeForest Cowan
(Cut Man); Azizi Johnson (Pussy); Roseann Katon (Melody); Al
Garcia (Mad Man's Manager); Jimmy Lennon (Ring Announcer); Mike
Garfield (Official); Hazel Girtman (Nurse).

Leon Isaac Kennedy wrote and starred in this updated version
of the 1947 boxing classic (see: B/V) and co-featured his wife
Jayne. Unfortunately the result is a moribund affair which fails to
work energy into its dramatic/action sequences, and the comparisons
between Kennedy and John Garfield in the 1940s original is unfavor-
able to the newcomer. Most of the problem lies with Kennedy's lack-
lustre reworking of Abraham Polonsky's original screenplay, which
had provided a piercing study of the boxing world and the people
who control the so-called sport. Kennedy tries to emulate this theme
but fails due to an overemphasis on the gangster element as well as
lingering too long on the protagonist's private life.
Young medical student Leon (Kennedy) becomes a professional
boxer to earn money and becomes involved with a beautiful woman
(Kennedy). He is made the tool of a gangster (Peter Lawford) who
promises to take him to the top of the welterweight division. With
the help of his girlfriend and his faithful manager (Michael V. Gazzo), Kennedy ultimately double crosses the gang boss.

BOWERY AT MIDNIGHT (Monogram, 1942) 63 mins.

Producers, Sam Katzman, Jack Dietz; associate producer, Barney A.
Sarecky; director, Wallace Fox; story, Sam Robins; screenplay,
Gerald Schnitzer; art director, Dave Milton; music, Edward J. Kay;
camera, Mack Stengler; editor, Carl L. Pierson.

Bela Lugosi (Professor Brenner/Karl Wagner); Wanda McKay (Judy);
John Archer (Dennison); Tom Neal (Frankie Mills); Vince Barnett
(Charlie); J. Farrell MacDonald (Captain Mitchell); Dave O'Brien
(Sergeant); John Berkes (Fingers Dolan); Ray Miller (Big Tramp);
J. Farrell MacDonald (Captain Mitchell); Lew Kelly (Doc Brooks);
Lucille Vance (Mrs. Malvern); Anna Hope (Mrs. Brenner); George
Eldredge (Plainclothes Policeman); and: Wheeler Oakman.

In 1941 Bela Lugosi signed with producers Sam Katzman and
Jack Dietz for a series of low budget horror thrillers, beginning
with THE INVISIBLE GHOST that year and culminating with RETURN
OF THE APE MAN in 1944. At the time of their release, the movies
were considered grindhouse fodder, aimed chiefly at quick playoffs
to the juvenile trade. In recent years, however, the movies have
taken on a camp status and BOWERY AT MIDNIGHT is often considered

Wanda McKay and John Archer in BOWERY AT MIDNIGHT (1942).

the "best" of the lot. This production is really more of a gangster film, with science fiction tinges, and has only minimal horror elements. It has more than a passing resemblance to an earlier Lugosi starrer made in England, DARK EYES OF LONDON (q.v.).

Here Lugosi assumes dual roles, by day highly regarded college psychology professor Brenner and at night the kindly Kurt Wagner, the owner of a Bowery soup kitchen for the indigent. The professor, however, employs the latter guise as a front for committing robberies, using the skid row bums to carry out the tasks and then murdering them. Unknown to him, however, his deranged doctor-assistant (Lew Kelly) is reviving the victims and keeping them in a sub-basement of the professor's underground hideout. Working at the mission is a pretty girl (Wanda McKay) whose boyfriend (John Archer) is doing a sociological study and comes to the Bowery to research, only to end up a victim, as does a notorious hoodlum (Tom Neal) who tries to revolt against the professor. Eventually the girl brings in a police officer (Dave O'Brien) who unravels the case and as the professor seeks to escape via his sub-basement, he is murdered by the men he thought he had killed.

BOWERY AT MIDNIGHT is a somber affair, nicely capturing the atmosphere of skid row in the settlement house sequences. Lugosi properly handles his double assignment, although he is florid at times. His character may have been an intellectual gangster, but in the end, he met the same fate as the Tom Powers and Rico Bandello's of lesser education.

BOYS' REFORMATORY (Monogram, 1939) 62 mins.

Associate producer, Lindsley Parsons; director, Howard Bretherton; story; Ray Trampe, Norma S. Hall; screenplay, Trampe, Wellyn Totman; camera, Harry Newman.

Frankie Darro (Tommy); Grant Withers (Dr. Owens); David Durand (Knickles); Warren McCallum (Spike); Albert Hill, Jr. (Pete); Bob McClung (Blubber); George Offerman, Jr. (Joie); Frank Coghlan, Jr. (Eddie); Ben Welden (Mike Hearn); Lillian Elliot (Mrs. O'Mara).

Like most series films the Monogram entries starring Frankie Darro, issued in the late 1930s and early 1940s, had their ups and downs, but this outing is one of the poorest of the lot. Variety analyzed, "Has a memograph story without climactic punch or love interest, doesn't develop character or atmosphere, and it's shy on name value." In addition the film lacked proper character delineation and completely ignored its opportunity to take a poke at juvenile reformatory reform.

A gang of hoodlums led by Mike Hearn (Ben Weldon) frame a weak-willed kid (Frank Coghlan, Jr.) on a robbery charge. To save his mother's (Lillian Elliot) feelings, the boy's foster-brother Tommy (Darro) says he committed the heist and is sent to a boy's reformatory where the conditions are grim. Eventually he breaks out of the institution and aids the police in bringing the gangsters to justice.

THE BRAIN (Paramount, 1969) C 115 mins.

Producer, Alain Poire; director, Gerard Oury; screenplay, Oury, Marcel Jillian, Daniele Thompson; assistant director, Gerard Guerin; technical advisor for camera, Armand Thirard; second unit director, Claude Clement; art director, Jean Andre; music, Georges Delerue; song, Eddie Snyder and Larry Kulck; costumes, Tanine Autre; sound, Jean Rieul, Louis Hochet; camera, Vladimir Ivanov; editor, Albert Jurgenson.

David Niven (The Brain); Jean-Paul Belmondo (Arthur); Bourvil (Anatole); Eli Wallach (Scannapieco); Silvia Monti (Sofia); Fernand Valois (Bruno); Raymond Gerome (Commissioner); Jacques Balutin (Pochet); Jacques Ciron (Duboeuf); Fernand Guiot (Mazurel); Henri Genes (Chief Warder); Tommy Duggan (Superintendent).

Wanted by Scotland Yard for the robbery of a Glasgow-London train, an international criminal known as "The Brain" (David Niven) plans to rob $14,000,000 from a French train going to NATO headquarters in Brussels. He has himself assigned as security guard on the train and hires Scannapieco (Eli Wallach), a Mafia chief, to assist him. On the train, however, he finds that escaped prisoner Arthur (Jean-Paul Belmondo) and his pal (Bourvil) have already grabbed the money. Yet when they throw it off the train and over a bridge, Niven gets the money bags. Wallach then attempts to

8-40-11

Jean-Paul Belmondo in THE BRAIN (1969).

doublecross his employer because the latter has bedded his sister
(Silvia Monti). In Le Havre the police arrest Wallach thinking he is
really The Brain. Belmondo then discovers that the Mafia man has
hidden the money in a replica of the Statue of Liberty, but when it
is opened the wind blows the bills far away. Niven then teams with
Belmondo and Bourvil and the trio come to New York City, intent on
robbing a $50,000,000 gold shipment bound for Fort Knox.

The Monthly Film Bulletin called this British-Italian co-
production, "... another of those multi-nation comedies in which
national characteristics are presumed to be screamingly funny and
where the ill-assorted cast is therefore encouraged to overplay ad
lib." Despite its cosmopolitan cast and somewhat wry humor, THE
BRAIN is a disappointing gangster feature. In France, it was called
LE CERVEAU and in Italy, IL CERVELLO. Both titles translate as
THE BRAIN, but the outing was hardly cerebral.

BRANNIGAN (United Artists, 1975) C 111 mins.

Executive producer, Michael Wayne; producer, Jules Levy; director,
Douglas Hickox; story, Christopher Trumbo, Michael Butler; screen-
play, Trumbo, Butler, William P. McGivern, William Nortan; music,
Dominic Frontiere; art director, Ted Marshall; set decorator, Josie

John Wayne as BRANNIGAN (1975).

MacAvin; assistant director, Ted Sturgis; sound, Simon Kaye; camera, Gerry Fisher; editor, Malcolm Cooke.

John Wayne (Detective Jim Brannigan); Richard Attenborough (Commander Sir Charles Swann); Judy Geeson (Jennifer Thatcher); Mel Ferrer (Mel Fields); John Vernon (Larkin); Daniel Pilon (Gorman); John Stride (Traven); James Booth (Charlie); Del Henney (Drexel); Anthony Booth (Freddy); Brian Glover (Jimmy the Bet); Ralph Meeker (Captain Moretti); Arthur Batandides (Angell).

In the mid-1970s superstar John Wayne took a brief sabbatical from Westerns to make two popular police action thrillers, first McQ (see: B/V) and the British-lensed BRANNIGAN. While the former did big United States box-office business, it was less popular abroad while the opposite was true of BRANNIGAN. Both films are solid entertainment, embodying John Wayne's stalwart hero image set against a background of mobster corruption. While neither film was psychologically deep, both contain heavy doses of old-fashioned entertainment values, plus a view of modern day gangsters and their nefarious activities.

BRANNIGAN especially delivered solid dialogue dealing with American cop John Wayne fighting hoods on alien turf with methods somewhat foreign to the staid British law enforcers. His interrogation, for example, of a British thug included the line, "How would you like to apply for England's free dental treatment or will you answer my question?" The best line, however, in this vein is given to co-star Judy Geeson who informs Wayne of her late father's opinion of Yanks, "They're overfed, oversexed, and over here."

The complex tale has American police detective Jim Brannigan (Wayne) being dispatched to London to bring back racketeer Larkin (John Vernon) to stand trial. Scotland Yard has the man under surveillance, but before Wayne can corner him, the hoodlum is kidnapped and a ransom demanded. Scotland Yard Commander Sir Charles Swann (Richard Attenborough) joins forces with Wayne to locate Vernon, and pretty, petite Jennifer Thatcher (Geeson), a detective-sergeant, is assigned as Wayne's driver. Working through Vernon's slick but corrupt lawyer, Mel Fields (Mel Ferrer), negotiations take place for the racketeer's release, but in the meantime a hit man (Daniel Pilon) hired by Vernon tries to eliminate Wayne but succeeds only in shooting Geeson. Eventually Wayne realizes that the kidnap/ransom plots are merely a hoax planned by Vernon and Ferrer and he routs the underworld figure.

Filmed in London, BRANNIGAN includes scenic British landmarks such as Piccadilly Circus (during an especially suspenseful sequence involving the initial ransom pickup); Heathrow Airport, Tower Bridge, the dockland area with its shadowy wharves and piers; the deserted Beckton Gasworks on the Thames River and the Garrick Club, where a well-staged fist fight occurs. All in all, BRANNIGAN is one of the more entertaining gangster productions of the 1970s. Worth noting is that it was not overly violent and contained no overt sex scenes or strong language, elements which seemed necessary to filmmakers in the genre since the late 1960s.

THE BREAKING POINT (Warner Bros., 1950) 97 mins.

Producer, Jerry Wald; director, Michael Curtiz; based on the novel To Have and Have Not by Ernest Hemingway; screenplay, Ranald MacDougall; dialogue director, Norman Stuart; music director, Ray Heindorf; costumes, Phillips Leak Rhodes; art director, Edward Carrere; set decorator, George James Hopkins; assistant director, Sherry Shouds; sound, Lewslie G. Hewitt; camera, Ted McCord; editor, Alan Crosland, Jr.

John Garfield (Harry Morgan); Patricia Neal (Leona Charles); Phyllis Thaxter (Lucy Morgan); Juano Hernandez (Wesley Park); Wally Ford (Duncan); Edmon Ryan (Rogers); Ralph Dumke (Hannagan); Guy Thomajan (Danny); William Campbell (Concho); Sherry Jackson (Amalia); Donna Jo Royce (Connie); Victor Sen Yung (Mr. Sing); Peter Brocco (Macho).

World War II PT boat captain Harry Morgan (John Garfield) operates a boat service along the Southern California coast (which is the film's new setting), renting his in-debt power cruiser to private fishing parties. Needing money, he takes a client to Mexico but the client leaves without paying him, while also deserting alluring Leona Charles (Patricia Neal), who sets her sights on Garfield although he has a wife (Phyllis Thaxter) and children. In order to pay off the boat debts, Garfield becomes involved with the smuggling of Chinese laborers into the country as well as with mobsters. At the finale he turns on the criminals and brings about their destruction and returns to his family.

This John Garfield vehicle for Warner Bros. is only a quasi satisfactory remake of the 1944 TO HAVE AND HAVE NOT (see: B/V). "It strays even further than its predecessor from the Hemingway story line, but is apparently no more effective entertainment," deemed Variety. The New York Times on the other hand, called the feature an "excellent screen derivation" of Hemingway's work which was "adapted with lean crispness by Ranald MacDougall, commandingly directed by Michael Curtiz and solidly played, especially by John Garfield, as the dispirited operator of a sports fishing cruiser whose shady dabblings lead to his ruin ... a word should be said for Juano Hernandez, Garfield's Negro sidekick, whose death is one of the most moving things in the picture."

In 1958 Don Siegel would direct yet another remake of the Hemingway tale, this time entitled THE GUN RUNNERS and starring frequent Western star Audie Murphy as well as Eddie Albert and Patricia Owens.

THE BRIBE (Metro-Goldwyn-Mayer, 1949) 98 mins.

Producer, Pandro S. Berman; director, Robert Z. Leonard; story, Frederick Nebel; screenplay, Marguerite Roberts; music, Miklos Rozsa; song, Nacio Herb Brown and William Katz; art directors, Cedric Gibbons, Malcolm Brown; set decorators, Edward B. Willis,

Advertisement for THE BRIBE (1949).

Hugh Hunt; makeup, Jack Dawn; assistant director, Bert Glazer; sound, Douglas Shearer, Fred MacAlperin; special effects, Warren Newcombe, A. Arnold Gillespie; camera, Joseph Ruttenberg; editor, Gene Ruggiero.

Robert Taylor (Rigby); Ava Gardner (Elizabeth Hintian); Charles Laughton (J. J. Bealer); Vincent Price (Carwood); John Hodiak (Tug Hintian); Samuel S. Hinds (Dr. Warren); John Hoyt (Gibbs); Tito Renaldo (Emlio Gomez); Martin Garralaga (Pablo Gomez).

The United States Justice Department orders agents Rigby (Robert Taylor) to a small Caribbean seaport to investigate a war-surplus material operation run by cold-blooded gangster Carwood (Vincent Price) and his overweight beachcomber cohort Bealer (Charles Laughton). While investigating the case, Taylor meets and falls in love with cafe singer Elizabeth Hintian (Ava Gardner), who is married to a drunken former Air Force captain (John Hodiak). In order to half the investigation, Price orders Gardner to detain the agent romantically and at the same time has Laughton offer the law enforcer a $10,000 bribe to drop the case. Eventually Taylor succeeds in bringing about Price's downfall (in a rather spectacular climax intermingled with a firewords display) and wins the love of Gardner, whose spouse is now dead.

Despite its top-notch cast and the usual MGM posh production values, this turgid backlot melodrama is cheap stuff. Most of the film's publicity advertised the romantic pairing of Robert Taylor and Ava Gardner (in her first star billing), but the result was hardly one of the screen's memorable tandems--their love scenes lacked the necessary spark. On the plus side, the angle of smashing a war surplus racket was a legitimate plot ploy. It is a shame that this gangster story aspect wasn't expanded further.

BRIDGE OF SIGHS (Invincible, 1936) 65 mins.

Producer, Maury M. Cohen; director, Phil Rosen; story-adaptor, Arthur T. Horman; camera, M. A. Anderson; editor, Ernest J. Nims.

Onslow Stevens (Jeffrey Powell); Dorothy Tree (Marion Courtney); Jack LaRue (Packy Lacy); Mary Doran (Evelyn "Duchess" Thane); Walter Byron (Arny Norman); and: Oscar Apfel, Paul Fix, George "Gabby" Hayes.

When her brother (Paul Fix) is tried for a crime he didn't commit and is sentenced to die in the electric chair, a young woman (Dorothy Tree) sets out to prove his innocence. She tries to get the prosecuting attorney (Onslow Stevens) to help her and eventually she has herself put in jail in order to obtain the needed information to vindicate her sibling, proving a gangster (Jack LaRue) actually committed the murder.

BRIDGE OF SIGHS is a pleasant little "B" melodrama expertly helmed by Phil Rosen, an old hand at this type of entertainment. With its many scenes in various prisons and courtrooms, the film is quite flavorful and is basically a nonviolent genre outing, relying more on dialogue than machine guns. Onslow Stevens is convincing as the prosecuting attorney, but the drama is focused primarily on Dorothy Tree, who performs admirably. In his typecasting as a slick gangster, Jack LaRue provides another deft performance.

Originally released by Invincible Pictures, BRIDGE OF SIGHS received most of its theatrical plays from Grand National, a new studio which acquired several independent features to complete its release program.

THE BRINK'S JOB (Universal, 1978) C 103 mins.

Executive producer, Dino De Laurentiis; producer, Ralph Serpe; director, William Friedkin; based on the book by Noel Behn; screenplay, Walon Green; production designer, Dean Tavoularis; art director, Angelo Graham; assistant director, Terence A. Donnelly; music, Richard Rodney Bennett; sound, Jeff Wexler; camera, A. Norman Leigh; editors, Bud Smith, Robert K. Lambert.

Peter Falk (Tony Pino); Peter Boyle (Joe McGinnis); Allen Goorwitz (Vinnie Costa); Warren Oates (Specs O'Keefe); Gena Rowlands (Mary Pino); Paul Sorvino (Jazz Maffie); Sheldon Leonard (J. Edgar Hoover); Gerald Murphy (Sandy Richardson); Kevin O'Connor (Gus Gusciora); Claudia Peluso (Gladys).

Seven men (Peter Falk, Peter Boyle, Allen Goorwitz, Warren Oates, Paul Sorvino, Gerald Murphy, Kevin O'Connor) conceive the idea to rob the Brink's office in Boston when they learn it is poorly guarded. They formulate the plan for the heist, successfully carry it out, and then wait for the statute of limitations to expire before spending the $2,000,000+ they stole. However, one of them, Specs (Oates), is imprisoned for another robbery and by pressuring him via his ailing sister, the police make him tell the truth. Two days before the statute expires, the other gang members are arrested and soon sentenced to prison.

The details of the notorious "crime of the century" were previously described much better in the telefeature BRINKS; THE GREAT ROBBERY (q.v.) and the entertaining fictional SIX BRIDGES TO CROSS (1955) (see: B/V) starring Tony Curtis. Having accomplished the classic THE FRENCH CONNECTION (see: B/V) in 1971, director William Freidkin returned to the gangster mold for this heist tale, but he and scriptor Walon Green created a film with little general audience interest. One tremendous handicap was Falk's overacting in the pivotal role of Tony Pino, the gang leader.

BRINK'S: THE GREAT ROBBERY (Quinn Martin/Warner Bros. TV/ CBS-TV, 3/26/76) C 100 mins.

Executive producer, Quinn Martin; producer, Philip Saltzman; supervising producer, Russell Stoneham; director, Marvin J. Chomsky; teleplay, Robert W. Lenski; music, Richard Markowitz; art director, Richard Y. Maman; camera, Jacques R. Marquette; editor, Jerry Young.

Carl Betz (Paul Jackson); Stephen Collins (Agent Donald Nash); Burr DeBenning (Ernie Heideman); Michael V. Gazzo (Mario Russo); Cliff Gorman (Danny Conforti); Darren McGavin (James McNally); Art Metrano (Julius Mareno); Leslie Nielsen (Agent Norman Houston); Jenny O'Hara (Maggie Hefner); Bert Remsen (Ted Flynn); Jerry Douglas (Dennis Fisher); Laurence Haddon (Detective Russ Shannon); Philip Kenneally (Les Hayes); Byron Mabe (Jerry Carter); Barney Phillips (Thomas Preston); Amie Strickland (Neighbor Lady); Frank Borone (Bill Shadix); David Brandon (Robert Bloch); Hank Brandt (Lieutenant Lorin Pope); Dort Clark (Stoughton Cop); Nick Ferris (Doctor); Mary LaRoche (Betty Houston); Terry Lumley (Sherry); Stuart Nisbet (Pennsylvania Police Chief); John Perak (Dave Stanley); Artie Spain (Donald O'Leary); Marvin Miller (Narrator).

On January 17, 1950 over $2,750,000 was stolen from Brink's, Inc. in Boston in a daring robbery. For years the theft was thought to be the perfect crime until it was finally solved by the Federal Bureau of Investigation. This telefeature was a study of the famous event and was shown on CBS-TV as one of a series of films commemorating the nation's Bicentennial and the FBI's most famous cases. The result was average. As MOVIES ON TV (1985) analyzed, "The drama of law versus crooks feuding among themselves sounds more exciting than it really is."

A small gang has lock expert James McNally (Darren McGavin)

BRINK'S: THE GREAT ROBBERY (1976).

as its leader. The men feud among themselves about the best way
to execute the Brink's robbery and finally armed and wearing masks
they hold up the Brink's office on Boston's Prince Street and take
the loot and make good their getaway. The FBI then sets out to
solve what was the largest heist in history to that time. For the
next six years the law enforcers piece together various clues which
take them to some of the gang members and eventually to the arrest
of all those who participated in the crime.

BROADWAY AFTER MIDNIGHT (Krelbar Pictures, 1927) 6,199'

Presenter, Sherman S. Krellberg; director, Fred Windermere; story,
Frederic Bartel; screenplay, Adele Buffington; camera, Charles
Davis.

Matthew Betz (Quill Burke); Priscilla Bonner (Queenie Morgan/
Gloria Livingston); Cullen Landis (Jimmy Crestmore); Gareth
Hughes (Billy Morgan); Ernest Hilliard (Bodo Lambert); and:
Barbara Tennant, William Turner, Hank Mann, Paul Weigel.

To protect her brother (Gareth Hughes) nightclub entertainer
Queenie Morgan (Priscilla Bonner) is forced into marriage with

gangster Quill Burke (Matthew Betz). At the same time, her looka-like, society girl Gloria Livingston (Bonner), is forced to kill the man (Ernest Hilliard) who seduced her and she is blackmailed by the mob. Later they accidentally murder her when they try to ex-tort money from her wealthy parents. Her gangster husband then forces Queenie to impersonate Gloria and eventually the police trace the girl's homicide to her and she is tried for muder. She is exon-erated by the testimony of her maid and is reunited with her loyal boyfriend (Cullen Landis).

Adele Buffington, who worked mainly as a scriptor for "B" Westerns in both the silent and sound eras, kept this melodrama moving at a fast clip, but overall it was just another stale girl-caught-in-the-web-of gangsters affair somewhat benefitted by Priscilla Bonner's solid acting job in dual roles.

BROADWAY BIG SHOT (Producers Releasing Corp., 1942) 63 mins.

Producer, Jed Buell; director, William Beaudine; screenplay, Martin Mooney; camera, Jack Greenhalgh; editors, Robert Crandall, Guy Thayer.

Ralph Byrd (Jimmy O'Brien); Virginia Vale (Betty Collins); William Halligan (Warden Collins); Dick Rush (Tom Barnes); Herbert Raw-linson (District Attorney); Cecile Weston (Mrs. Briggs); Tom Her-bert (Carnation Charlie); Stubby Kruger (Dynamite); Frank Hagney (Butch); Jack Buckley (Windy); Harry Depp (Ben Narlo); Jack Roper (Nipper); Al Goldsmith (Coffee Cake George); Joe Oakie (Sneaky); John Ince (Judge Scott); Alfred Hall (Dr. Williams); Jimmy Aubrey (Orderly); Dick Cramer (Reilly); Jack Cheatham (Tim); Jack Perrin (Ed).

Ralph Byrd was a useful utility player in his more than fifteen Hollywood years, usually nothing better than a supporting or even bit player in big budget outings, but he headlined many a "B" adventure in various genres. He is best remembered for his con-vincing portrayal of the title character "Dick Tracy" in a quartet of serials for Republic and later replacing Morgan Conway in the part for two RKO programmers in the late 1940s before bringing the Chester Gould character to TV in the early 1950s. BROADWAY BIG SHOT was one of his several starrers in the "B" gangster field, but it was a poor offering seesawing between melodramatics and comedy "... all done by the cast with apparently no conception of what comedy is, or how to play it." (Don Miller, B Movies, 1973)

The story found Byrd as a newspaper reporter after a notori-ous gangster. In order to obtain the big scoop, he takes the rap for a crime and is sent to the "big house" to get evidence on an-other resident there, a hoodlum he believes is in the pay of "Mister Big." While there he becomes the coach of the prison football team and helps them win the championship, but the man he is tailing is murdered and he must start anew to acquire the needed evidence.

BRONK (Metro-Goldwyn-Mayer/CBS-TV, 4/17/75) C 74 mins.

Executive producers, Carroll O'Connor, Terry Becker; associate producer, Alan Godfrey; producer, Becker; director, Richard Donner; creators/story, O'Connor, Ed Waters; teleplay, Al Martinez, Waters; music, Lalo Schifrin; music supervisor, Harry Lojewski; art director, Jack Senter; set decorator, Don Sullivan; makeup, Bob Dawn; camera, Matthew F. Leonetti; editor, Jerry Taylor.

Jack Palance (Lieutenant Alex Bronkov); Tony King (Sergeant John Webster); Henry Beckman (Harry Mark); David Birney (Willie); Joseph Mascolo (Pete Santori); Joanna Moore (Shirley); George Brenlin (Sullivan); Dina Ousley (Ellen Bronkov); Chelsa Brown (Celeste); Ivor Francis (Eicher); Phil Bruns (Gunther); Conlan Carter (Meeker); Bart Burns (Ferris); Thom Christopher (Sergeant Nelson); Barbara Baldavin (Joan); Tony Georgio (Killer); Marcy Lafferty (Mayor's Secretary).

After the murder of a fellow officer and his own suspension from the police force, homicide Detective Alex Bronkov (Jack Palance) swears to get revenge on the mobsters responsible for these two events. Since the episodes were related to a narcotics investigation he was undertaking, Palance goes after the criminals running the operation and finds they are tied to corrupt law officials. Eventually he ferrets out the hoodlums and their governmental cohorts.

The strong suit of this small screen outing is Palance's performance. He handles the part with leathery efficiency and a minimum of emotions, although the later TV series had his daughter crippled and his wife murdered by mobsters. It is interesting to note that no longer are just the street hoodlums the villains of anti-law movies, but more and more films like this one are casting their lances at the powers within the law enforcement agencies, showing them to be frequently more evil than the hoodlums they are supposed to corral.

The CBS-TV hour-long series ran 24 episodes, starting September 21, 1975.

THE BURNING QUESTION see: REEFER MADNESS

C-MAN (Film Classics, 1949) 76 mins.

Producer, Rex Carlton; director, Joseph Lerner; screenplay, Berne Giler; music, Gail Kubik; camera, Gerald Hirschfield; editor, Geraldine Lerner.

Dean Jagger (Cliff Holden); John Carradine (Doc Spencer); Lottie Elwen (Kathe); Harry Landers (Owney); Rene Paul (Matty Royal); Walter Vaughan (Inspector Brandon); Adelaide Klein (Mrs. Hoffman); Edith Atwater (Lydia Brundage); Jean Ellyn (Birdie); Walter Brooke (Joe).

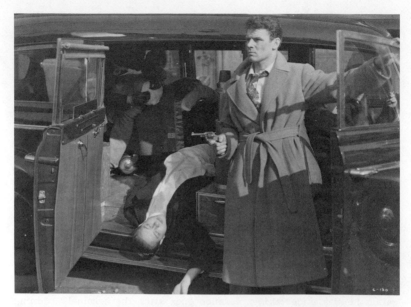

Harry Landers in C-MAN (1949).

  Cliff Holden (Dean Jagger), a United States Customs Service agent, must locate a smuggling operation in New York City. After tracing the gang through a series of beatings, kidnappings, and murders, he discovers the underworld activity is fronted by a supposedly respectable doctor (John Carradine) who hides stolen jewelry in the head bandages of a girl he has slugged. The customs agent halts the gang's activities.

  Having previously been teamed in the spy melodrama I ESCAPED FROM THE GESTAPO (1943), stars Dean Jagger and John Carradine did their best to hold this New York City-lensed feature together. While the script was limp and the acting mediocre, the movie captured the flavor of the big city plus the day-to-day workings of the Customs Service, the latter aspect in the usual solemn semi-documentary manner.

CAGE WITHOUT A KEY (Columbia Pictures Televison/CBS-TV, 3/14/75) C 100 mins.

Executive producer, Douglas S. Cramer; associate producer, Robert Mintz; producer-director, Buzz Kulik; teleplay, Joanna Lee; music, Jerry Fielding; art director, Ross Bellah; camera, Charles F. Wheeler; editor, Roland Gross.

Susan Dey (Valerie Smith); Jonelle Allen (Tommy); Sam Bottoms
(Buddy Goleta); Michael Brandon (Ben Holian); Anne Bloom (Joleen);
Karen Carlson (Betty Holian); Edith Diaz (Angel Perez), Susie Elene
(Suzy Kurosawa); Dawn Frame (Sarah); Katherine Helmond (Mrs.
Little); Vicky Huxstable (Jamie); Karen Morrow (Mrs. Turner);
Lani O'Grady (Noreen); Margaret Willock (Wanda Polsky); Marc
Alaimo (Workman); Lewis Charies (Liquor Customer); Jerry Crews
(Supervisor); Edward Cross (Social Worker); Ann D'Andrea (Mrs.
Smith); Joella Deffenbaugh (Girl in Corridor); Al Dunlap (Liquor
Counterman); Annette Ensdley (Rosie).

   Teenager Valerie (Susan Dey) accepts a ride with a stranger
and is soon involved in robbery and murder. She is mistakenly convicted of the latter crime and sentenced to a women's penal institution. Once there she not only must endure the hardships of incarceration, but she also learns the place is riddled with administrative
corruption. To survive, the naive girl turns into a tough criminal.
   Another indictment of the prison system, this time set against
the tribulations of an innocent teenager caught in its nasty web,
this telefilm is a "tedious run-of-the-cell-tale [which] resembles [a]
1940s B movie" (TV Movies, 1985). It should be noted that director
Buzz Kulik kept the project from becoming maudlin with his strong
direction and Susan Dey, formerly the sweet daughter on TV's "The
Partridge Family," demonstrated she was developing as an actress by
her deft handling of the role of Valerie.

CAGED WOMEN (MPM, 1984) C 96 mins.

Director, Vincent Dawn [Bruno Mattei]; screenplay, P. Molteni,
Oliver LeMat; music, Luigi Ceccarelli; art director, Maurizio Mammi;
assistant director, Claudio Fragasso; camera, Luigi Ciccarese; editor, Mattei.

Laura Gemser (Laura/Emanuelle); Gabriele Tinti (Dr. Moran);
Lorraine de Selle (Warden); and: Maria Romano, Ursula Flores, Raul
Cabrera.

   CAGED WOMEN is one of those foreign (Italian-French in this
instance) productions which uses the gangster theme as a spring-
board for assorted titillating activities for the grind house trade,
including sadistic treatment of female prisoners and lesbian sex.
Scores of such pictures have been released since the 1960s. CAGED
WOMEN is typical of this genre subtype.
   The story tells of world-traveled newswoman Emanuelle (Laura
Gemser) who takes on the guise of a hooker and is admitted to Santa
Catarina women's prison to do an expose on the harsh treatment of
the inmates as well as obtain evidence against the corrupt officials
who run the state institution. There she has a cellmate who keeps
a cockroach for a pet; is attacked by marauding rats; and is forced

to submit to gay sex. With the aid of a sympathetic doctor (Gabriele Tinti), she obtains the data she seeks.

No CAGED (see: B/V), is this women's prison melodrama which exploits its slim plot as an excuse for beatings, nudity, and soft-core sex. Filmed in Rome in 1982 as EMANUELLE REPORTS FROM A WOMAN'S PRISON, this is one of more than a dozen features made in the "Emanuelle" series since the mid-1970s, all starring Laura Gemser in the title role, with her husband Gabriele Tinti co-starring.

CAIRO (Metro-Golwyn-Mayer, 1963) 92 mins.

Producer, Ronald Kinnoch; director; Wolf Rilla; based on the novel by W. R. Burnett; screenplay, Joanne Court; music, Kenneth V. Jones; assistant director, George Pollark; art directors, Ivan King, Maher Abdel Nour; sound, J. B. Smith; camera, Desmond Dickinson; ecitor, Bernard Gribble.

George Sanders (Major); Richard Johnson (Ali); Faten Hamama (Amina); Eric Pohlmann (Nicodemos); Ahmed Mazhar (Kerim); Walter Rilla (Kuchuk); John Neillon (Willy); Kamal El Shennawy (Ghattas); Chewikar (Marie); Salah Nazmi (Commandant); Mona (Mamba); Said Abu Bakr (Osman); Salah Mansour (Doctor); Abdel Khalek Saleh (Assistant Minister); Youssef Shaaban, Captain Mohamed Abdel Rahman (Officers).

Producer Ronald Kinnoch, director Wolf Rilla, and star George Sanders, who had cinema success with the atmospheric science fiction thriller VILLAGE OF THE DAMNED (1960), reteamed for this limpid remake of THE ASPHALT JUNGLE (see: B/V) with the locale changed from big city America to Egypt. The result was a film "laden with cliches and riddled with holes" (Variety).

While serving a prison term, erudite Major Pickering (Sanders) devises a foolproof plan for stealing the Tut-ankh-Amen jewels from the Cairo museum. Once freed, he puts together a band of international criminals to aid him in his meticulous plans. However, the innate character weakness of his cohorts and Sanders' own lechery for belly dancers ironically bring about their downfall.

In comparison to the hard effectiveness of THE ASPHALT JUNGLE, this anemic remake is a sad mishmash indeed. What is especially distracting to the film's premise is how easily the thieves gain access to the museum containing the art treasures and how poorly guarded the facility is.

CALL A MESSENGER (Universal, 1939) 65 mins.

Producer, Ken Goldsmith; director, Arthur Lubin; story, Sally Sandlin, Michael Kraike; screenplay, Arthur T. Horman; music director, Hans J. Salter; art director, Jack Otterson; assistant director, Henry Spitz; sound, Bernard B. Brown; camera, Elwood Bredell; editor, Charles Maynard.

Sensuous and sinister...the dens of Cairo beckon...and if you come out broke–or manacled you're lucky... because there are those who never come out at all!

Metro · Goldwyn · Mayer
presents

GEORGE SANDERS · RICHARD JOHNSON

Actually filmed-in-the-flesh
...amid the terrors and
temptations of the sin city!

with
FATEN HAMAMA · Screenplay by JOANNE COURT · Directed by WOLF RILLA · Produced by RONALD KINNOCH

T H E A T R E

Advertisement for CAIRO (1963).

Billy Halop (Jimmy Hogan); Huntz Hall (Pig); David Gorcey (Yap); William Benedict (Trouble); Robert Armstrong (Kirk Graham); Mary Carlisle (Marge Hogan); Anne Nagel (Frances O'Neill); Victor Jory (Ed Hogan); Larry "Buster" Crabbe (Chuck Walsh); El Brendel (Baldy); Jimmy Butler (Bob Pritchard); George Offerman, Jr. (Big Lip); Jimmy O'Gatty (Al); Joe Gray (Nail); Cliff Clark (Sergeant Harrison); John Hamilton (Lieutenant Nelson); Anthony Hughes (Gardner); Kay Sutton (Virginia); James C. Morton, Frank O'Connors (Policemen); Sherwood Bailey (Sweeney); Joey Ray, Lyle Moraine (Clerks); Ruth Rickaby (Miss Clarington); Frank Mitchell (Barber); James Farley (Desk Sergeant); Payne Johnson (Kid); Jack Gardner (Paymaster); Kernan Cripps (Police Officer); Russ Powell (Watchman); Wilson Benge (Butler); Louise Franklin (Maid); Harris Berger, Hally Chester (Messengers).

"Dead End Kids" Billy Halop and Huntz Hall abandoned their screen teammates temporarily to headline this Universal programmer, "a rowdy, gripping production" (Variety), highlighted by fine performances from the two juvenile stars who were ably supported by a solid cast.

Halop is Jimmy Hogan, who with his pal Pig (Huntz Hall) is recruited by Kirk Graham (Robert Armstrong) to be messengers for his citywide service. Armstrong is actually working with law enforcement agencies in the hope that gainful employment will keep the boys from straying to the wrong side of the law. Halop, however, has problems on the homefront since a notorious gangster (Larry "Buster" Crabbe) has eyes for his pretty sister (Mary Carlisle), and his older brother (Victor Jory) has gotten out of prison and Halop is trying to keep him away from the criminal element.

CALL TO DANGER (Paramount Television/CBS-TV, 2/27/73) C
    78 mins.

Producer, Laurence Heath; director, Tom Gries; teleplay, Heath; music, Laurence Rosenthal; art director, William L. Campbell; camera, Ronald W. Browne; editors, Charles Freeman, John Loeffler.

Peter Graves (Doug Warfield); Diana Muldaur (Carrie Donovan); John Anderson (Edward McClure); Clu Gulager (Emmet Jergens); Tina Louise (April Tierney); Stephen McNally (Joe Barker); Ian Balin (Marla Hayes); Michael Ansara (Frank Mulvey); Roy Jenson (Dave Falk); William Jordan (Tony Boyd); Edward Bell (Reed); Paul Mantee (Adams); Wesley Lau (Police Sergeant); Victor Campos (Danny); Lesley Woods (Rosalind); Bart Barnes (Chairman); Dan Frazer (Reynolds).

During federal investigations by a committee studying organized crime, a gangster giving evidence against the mob is kidnapped and taken to the West Coast, where he is kept prisoner in a heavily fortified area. Wanting the man back, the Justice Department assigns

undercover agents the job and they hire, via a computer, Doug Warfield (Peter Graves), a one-time agent, to carry out the operation.
Producer-writer Laurence Heath, who conceived the highly
successful "Mission: Impossible" TV series that starred Graves,
persuaded the actor to headline this pale thriller.

CALLING HOMICIDE (Allied Artists, 1956) 60 mins.

Producer, Ben Schwab; director-screenplay, Edward Bernds; music,
Marlin Skiles; camera, Harry Neumann; editor, William Austin.

Bill Elliott (Lieutenant Doyle); Don Haggerty (Sergeant Duncan);
Kathleen Case (Donna); Myron Healey (Haddix); Jeanne Cooper
(Darlene); Thomas B. Henry (Gilmore); Lyle Talbot (Tony Fuller);
Almira Sessions (Mrs. Dunstetter); Herb Vigran (Ray Engel); James
Best (Arnholf); John Dennis (Benny).

After a series of "B" westerns for Allied Artists between
1952-54, William Elliott (a.k.a. Gordon Elliott, Bill Elliott, and Wild
Bill Elliott) remained with that studio to finish his over three decades in film with five detective dramas. Although each was produced on a limited budget, the series proved to be a good one.
Nicely paced-directed-acted, the movies have a subdued film noir
quality and they certainly provided Elliott with a suitable finale to
his many years in pictures.
Lieutenant Doyle (Elliott) is researching the death of a young
policeman blown up by a bomb planted in a car. At the same time
he also looks into the strangulation of a woman who owned a modeling school and he comes to believe the two deaths are related. Questioning those involved with the school, he learns the enterprise is
actually a blackmail operation centering around a black market baby
racket. One of the suspects in the woman's death is Haddox (Myron
Healey), a construction firm owner, who had been in love with the
woman when they were both in films. All of the evidence surrounding the extortion racket, however, is destroyed in an explosion and
a school employee is killed. Elliott and his crew suspect school janitor Benny (John Dennis) of the crimes and they wound him as he attempts to escape. Before he dies he admits to having killed his employer, and that she had hired him to kill the policeman who was
getting too close to the operation. He also explains the reason he
murdered her was because she had cruelly taunted him.

CANILOUE see: DOG DAY

CAUGHT IN THE ACT (Producers Releasing Corp., 1941) 60 mins.

Producer, T. H. Richmond; director, Jean Yarborough; story,
Robert Cosgriff; screenplay, Al Martin; camera, Mack Stengler.

Henry Armetta (Mike); Iris Meredith (Lucy); Robert Baldwin (Jim); Charles Miller (Brandon); Inez Palange (Mary); Dick Terry (Henderson); Joey Ray (Davis); Maxine Leslie (Fay); William Newell (Sergeant Reilly).

Mike (Henry Armetta), a construction company foreman, is promoted to salesman but becomes involved with gangsters working a construction company protection racket. As a result he has problems at home, gets mixed up with a gangster's moll, and even draws his boss in the situation until he aids the law in bringing about the downfall of the racket.

Chiefly a gangster-comedy vehicle for Italian character Henry Armetta, this feature is too slight in plot and action to sustain interest even for its brief one-hour running time.

CAXAMBU (W. Lee Wilder/Paramount TV Sales, 1968) C 85 mins.

Producer-director, W. Lee Wilder; screenplay, Weldon Wheeland; music, Albert Elms; camera, Hubert V. Theis; editor, Ronald Pole.

John Ireland (Vince); Carol Ohmart (Peggy Garrett); Keith Larsen (Garrett); Gordon Blackmon (Simon); and: Lucien Pan.

Four hoodlums steal two thousand carats of raw diamonds and take a diamond cutter (Keith Larsen) and his wife (Carol Ohmart) prisoners, planning to force the former to cut the diamonds so they can be sold on the black market. The group boards a plane, which crashes during a flight over the Amazon Basin. As the survivors work their way back to civilization, trouble develops between the gang and their hostages as well as the ever present danger threat from local headhunters. Ironically, in the midst of this crisis, the thieves learn that the gems are worthless.

The title of this melodrama comes from the Caxambu tribe of headhunters who dwell in the Amazon. Wilder, the producer-director brother of Billy Wilder, had made an auspicious directing debut with THE GLASS ALIBI (q.v.) but he did not live up to its promise with such later films as PHANTOM FROM SPACE (1953), THE SNOW CREATURE (1954), MANFISH (1956), and SPY IN THE SKY (1958).

LE CERCLE DES PASSIONS [Circle of Passion] (Ginis Films, 1983) C 110 mins.

Executive producer, Jean-Marie Bertrand; producer, Henry Lange; director, Claude d'Anna; screenplay, Laure Bonin, d'Anna; music, Egisto Macchi; assistant director, Olivier Coussemacq; art director, Jerome Allamand; sound, Michel Fano; camera, Patrick de Coninck; editors, D'Anna, Patrick de Coninck.

Giuliano Gemma (Anthony Tursi); Max Von Sydow (Carlo Di Villa-
fratti); Assumpta Serna (Elisa Di Vittafratti); Marcel Bozzuffi
(Turiddu Zangara); Francoise Fabian (Renata Strauss), Ofelia An-
gelica (Rosaria Croce); Jose Manuel Cervno (Le Meneur); Federico
Pacif (Silvio Croce); Dora Calindri (Lucia); Raoul Freire (D'Amico).

While the Mafia has often been the topic of American gangster
films, there have been few motion pictures which examine the organization in its native soil of Sicily and try to determine why the
Mafia exists there and how it became so powerful. While the French-
Spanish co-production LE CERCLE DES PASSIONS is not a gangster
movie in the strict sense, it does delve into the Mafia mystique as it
existed in turbulent 1950s Sicily.

American Anthony Tursi (Giuliano Gemma) returns his father's
body for burial in his native Sicily and there he is befriended by an
aristocratic family whose nymphomaniac daughter Elisa (Assumpta
Serna) tries to seduce him despite the fact that she is also involved
incestuously with her father, a count (Max Von Sydow), whose wife
committed suicide when she learned of the situation. The count is
also having trouble with his farm workers, who are striking and being agitated by Communists, while the Mafia is forcing their protection upon him and his neighbors, eventually leading to a bloody confrontation with the strikers.

In its florid manner, this feature captures the fabric of changing Italian aristocratic society of the Fifties. While the tale is out-
landish, it is well executed, especially by Giuliano Gemma as the
young man caught in the midst of social upheaval, and by Assumpta
Serna as the beautiful but half-witted daughter. The casting of
Swedish actor Max Von Sydow as a decadent Italian count leaves a
great deal to be desired.

LE CERVEAU see: THE BRAIN

IL CERVELLO see: THE BRAIN

CHAINED HEAT (Jensen Farley, 1982) C 95 mins.

Executive producers, Ernst Von Theumer, Lou Paciocco; producer,
Billy Fine; associate producer, Gerhard Scheurich; director, Paul
Nicolas; screenplay, Vincent Mongol, Nicolas; camera, Mac Ahlberg;
editor, Nino di Marco.

Linda Blair (Carol); John Vernon (Warden Blackman); Sybil Danning
(Ericka); Tamara Dobson (Dutchess); Stella Stevens (Captain Tay-
lor); Sharon Hughes (Val); Henry Silva (Lester); Michael Callan
(Martin); Nita Talbot (Kaufman); Louise Mortiz (Bubbles); and:
Edy Williams, Susan Meschner, Greta Blackburn, Robert Miano,
Jennifer Ashley, Kendall Kaldwell, Dee Biederbeck, Leila Chrystie.

Locked in a women's prison on drug charges, young Carol (Linda Blair) finds the institution is controlled by a lecherous, corrupt warden (John Vernon) and his disreputable captain (Stella Stevens). The latter has drug and prostitution rackets in the clinker with outside assistance from her boyfriend (Henry Silva). In jail Stevens works with two prisoners (Sybil Danning, Tamara Dobson) who keep control of the white and black populations, though one of them is in cahoots with Silva in a plot against Stevens. Subjected to the horrors of jail, Blair eventually convinces the two prisoner-leaders to stop fighting each other and to unite with her during a prison break to defeat the people in charge.

Made by producer Billy Fine as a followup to his earlier and popular THE CONCRETE JUNGLE (q.v.), the film stretches credibility with its exploitive elements (violence, nudity, dope, corruption, etc.) in deference for a needed picture of prison reform.

CHARLIE CHAN AND THE CURSE OF THE DRAGON QUEEN (American Cinema, 1981) C 97 mins.

Executive producers, Michael Leone, Alan Belkin; producer, Jerry Sherlock; director, Clive Donner; story, Sherlock; screenplay, Stan Burns, David Axelrod; costumes, Jocelyn Rickards; music, Patrick Williams; assistant directors, Richard Luke Rothschild, Rafael Elortegui, Pamela Eilerson; production designer, Joel Schiller; camera, Paul Lohmann; editors, Walt Hannemann, Phil Tucker.

Peter Ustinov (Charlie Chan); Lee Grant (Mrs. Lupowitz); Angie Dickinson (Dragon Queen); Richard Hatch (Lee Chan, Jr.); Brian Keith (Police Chief); Roddy McDowall (Gillespie); Rachel Roberts (Mrs. Dangers); Michelle Pfeiffer (Cordelia Farrington, III); Paul Ryan (Masten); Johnny Sekka (Stefan); Bennett Ohta (Hawaiian Chief of Police); David Hirokane (Lee Chan, Sr.); Karlene Crockett (Brenda Lupowitz); Michael Fairman (Bernard Lupowitz); James Ray (Haynes); Momo Yashima (Dr. Yu Sing); Alison Hong (Maysie Ling); and: Kael Blackwood, James Bacon, David Chow, Duane Tucker, Gerald Okamura, Peter Michas, Jim Winburn, Pavlo Ustinov, Trevor Hook, Paul Sanderson.

"Charlie Chan's" heralded return to the big screen after an absence of more than three decades met with all kinds of adverse publicity when Chinese-American actors picketed the film because British actor Peter Ustinov was chosen to play the part instead of someone of their own race. The eighth actor to portray the screen role, Ustinov took the brunt of the commotion although it should be noted that despite Earl Derr Biggers having created Chan as a Chinaman, not one Chinese actor has ever portrayed the Occidental detective in an American feature film. (Keye Luke, famous as Number One Son Lee Chan in the old [Twentieth Century-] Fox series, did supply the voice for the character in a 1970s children's TV cartoon series.) The hubbub was hardly worth it, as the resultant

Peter Ustinov, Richard Hatch, Michelle Pfeiffer, Lee Grant, Paul Ryan, Rachel Roberts, and Brian Keith in CHARLIE CHAN AND THE CURSE OF THE DRAGON QUEEN (1981).

feature was a weak tongue-in-cheek escapade vastly disappointing to Chan purists.

Chinese-American detective Charlie Chan (Ustinov), with the dubious aid of his clumsy Chinese-Jewish grandson Lee Chan Jr. (Richard Hatch), combats the evil Dragon Queen (Angie Dickinson) and her gangster minions, since their nefarious activities have resulted in several murders.

Variety observed, "... Ustinov adds absolutely nothing original to the role.... Worse still, when stumped for more stupid talk, [Director Clive] Donner falls back on every cliche stunt ever made."

CHICAGO AFTER MIDNIGHT (FBO Pictures, 1928) 66 mins.

Director, Ralph Ince; story, Charles K. Harris; continuity, Enid Hibbard; titles, George M. Arthur; camera, J. O. Taylor; editor, Arthur.

Ralph Ince (Jim Boyd); Jola Mendez (Betty Boyd/Mona Gale); Lorraine Rivero (Betty Boyd As a Baby); James Mason (Hardy); Carl Axzelle (Ike the Rat); Helen Jerome Eddy (Mrs. Boyd); Ole M. Ness (Tanner); Robert Seiter (Jack Waring); Frank Mills (Frank); Christian J. Frank (Casey).

The brother of Thomas H. Ince, Ralph Ince became a top actor and director in films through his association with Vitagraph,
where he began as a prop boy in 1907. Noted for his screen performances as Abraham Lincoln, Ince had a diverse career as an
actor-director and between 1912 and 1916 he directed all of Anita
Stewart's (his sister-in-law) features. He later became an independent producer and CHICAGO AFTER MIDNIGHT was a "vigorous
melodrama" (Photoplay magazine) he directed and starred in for
Joseph Kennedy's FBO Pictures.

After fifteen years, gangster Jim Boyd (Ince) is released from
prison, having been framed by rival Hardy (James Mason). Ince
goes to Chicago where Mason runs a speakeasy and there meets
pretty dancer, Mona (Jola Mendez), who is actually his daughter.
She is engaged to orchestra leader Jack Waring (Robert Seiter),
who is blamed when Ince kills Mason in a fight. In order to save
her lover, Mendez joins Ince's gang, but they learn she is a police
informant and torture her. When her father discovers her identity
and her whereabouts, he saves the girl but is mortally wounded by
one of his gang in the effort. He lives long enough to confess to
Mason's murder, thus setting Seiter free.

As in many silent films, this feature is crammed with plotline
and coincidence, but its raw reality provides interest.

CHICAGO STORY (Epipsychidion Inc/MGM Television/NBC-TV,
    3/15/81) C 100 mins.

Executive producer, Eric Bercovici; producer, John Cutts; director,
Jerry London; teleplay, Bercovici; music, Lalo Schifirn; art director, Ron Foremann; camera, Andrew Jackson; editor, John J. Dumas.

Vincent Baggetta (Lou Pellegrino); Dennis Franz (Officer Joe Gil-
land); Kene Holliday (Dr. Jeff House); Jack Hehoe (Officer Tony
Coswell); Craig T. Nelson (Kenneth A. Dutton); Kristoffer Tabori
(Dr. Max Carson); Gail Young (Elizabeth Bergstrom); Michael Hor-
ton (George Stepak); Charles Hallahan (John Ryan); Allan Rich
(G. W. Rosen); Richard Venture (Judge Harold Stankey); Brooke
Alderson (Margo Ryan); Luca Bercovici (Dukes); Kelly Hayden
(B. J. Ryan); Connie Foster (Ann Gilland); Lance Kinsey (Jerry
Stepak); Ralph Foody (Sergeant Hesper); Pauline Brailsford (Dr.
Dorothea Carroll); and: Fern Parsons, Judy Mockys, Bob Moomey,
Lara Staley, Al Nuti, Corney Morgan, Frank Rice, Tony Mockus, Jr.

A small girl is found shot on a playground with the chief
suspect being a retarded chestnut vendor (Michael Horton). The
assistant prosecutor (Craig T. Nelson) and public defender (Lou
Pellegrini), former law school roommates, prepare to battle the case
in court as the girl fights for her life and another case develops
which sheds light on this one.

Made as a pilot for a series dealing with law enforcement in
the city of Chicago, where it was filmed, this teleplay focused on

the individuals caught in the web of crime who are either basically victims or those chosen by the system to combat lawlessness. The substantial film has a distinct Windy City flavor.

CHICAGO SYNDICATE (Columbia, 1955) 84 mins.

Director, Fred F. Sears; story, William Sackheim; screenplay, Joseph Hoffman; music conductor, Ross D. Maggio; camera, Henry Freulich, Fred Jackman, Jr.; editor, Viola Lawrence.

Dennis O'Keefe (Barry Amsterdam); Abbe Lane (Connie Peters); Paul Stewart (Arnie Valent); Xavier Cugat (Benny Chico); Allison Hayes (Joyce Kern); Dick Cutting (David Healey); Chris Alcaide (Nate); William Challee (Dolan); John Zaremba (Robert Fenton); George Brand (Jack Roper); Mark Hanna (Brad Lacey); Carroll McComas (Mrs. Valent); Hugh Sanders (Pat Winters).

A citizen's group is determined to convict mobster Arnie Valent (Paul Stewart), who hides his racketeering behind legitimate business enterprises including a nightclub which offers entertainment by bandleader Benny Chico (Xavier Cugat) and thrush Connie Peters (Abbe Lane), the gangster's girl. Accountant Barry Amsterdam (Dennis O'Keefe), part of the citizens' committee, goes to work for Stewart, hoping to uncover needed evidence to send him to jail for income tax evasion. He is aided by Joyce Kern (Allison Hayes), who wants revenge on Stewart for the murder of her accountant father. Eventually, O'Keefe uncovers microfilm made by the murdered man and in a climactic shootout with the police, Stewart is killed.
CHICAGO SYNDICATE, with on-location shooting in the Windy City for added flavor, is a standard crime melodrama which moves quickly and spotlights a well shaded performance by Paul Stewart as the slippery mobster. The film's musical background is also satisfying, provided by the then husband-and-wife team of Xavier Cugat and Abbe Lane.

CHINATOWN AFTER DARK (Action Pictures, 1931) 50 mins.

Producer, Ralph M. Like; director, Stuart Paton; screenplay, Betty Burbridge; music, Lee Zahler; art director, Ben Dore; recording, James Stanley; assistant director, Wilfred Black; camera, Jules Cronjager; editor, Viola Roehl.

Rex Lease (Jim Bonner); Barbara Kent (Lotus); Edmund Dreese (Lee Fong); Carmel Myers (Madame Ying Su); Frank Mayo (Ralph Bonner); Billy Gilbert (Horatio Dooley); Lloyd Whitlock (Captain of Detectives); Laska Winter (Ming Fu); Michael Visaroff (Varanoff); Charles Murphy (Policeman); James B. Leong, Willie Fung (Servants).

Chinese Prince Lee Fong (Edmund Breese) is saved by an American during an uprising in his homeland, but the man dies as a result and Breese takes the man's daughter to America and cares for her. When the girl, Lotus (Barbara Kent) grows up, Breese needs money to get her accepted by her own people and he is promised his inheritance, an antique dagger, which is coveted by the underworld. The gangster asks the aid of Madame Ying Su (Carmel Myers) in obtaining the antique and when the go-between (Frank Mayo) attempts to deliver the dagger to Breese, Mayo is soon found dead and Breese's brother (Rex Lease) sets out to find his relative and the missing dagger. Meanwhile, a police detective (Billy Gilbert) believes Lease is in cahoots with the Chinese underworld but he traces the dagger to Myers' home, where he also locates the missing Chinese princess.

Films about the mysterious and exotic Chinese underworld in San Francisco had been popular since the silent era and this early talkie from poverty row was properly atmospheric in its presentation of the gangster motif, herein Chinese instead of American hoodlums. Silent screen star Carmel Myers is especially alluring as the dragon lady, while Barbara Kent is a fetching heroine in distress.

CIRCLE OF PASSION see: LE CERCLE DES PASSIONS

CITADEL OF CRIME (Republic, 1941) 56 mins.

Associate producer-director, George Sherman; screenplay, Don Ryan; music director, Cy Feuer; camera, Ernest Miller; editor, Les Orlebeck.

Robert Armstrong (Cal Fullerton); Frank Albertson (Jim Rogers); Linda Hayes (Ellie Jackson); Russell Simpson (Jess Meekins); Skeets Gallagher (Chet); William Haade (Turk); Jay Novello (Vince); Paul Fix (Gerro); Bob McKenzie (Martin Jackson); Wade Crosby (Rufe); William Benedict (Wes Rankins).

Big City mobsters devise a plan to get illegal alcohol by obtaining it through West Virginia moonshiners. They enlist the aid of Cal Fullerton (Robert Armstrong) and bring him to the big city where he joins the illegal operation. Framed on a subsequent murder charge, he returns home and persuades the head of the moonshiners (Russell Simpson) to supply corn liquor to the city mobsters. When the operation gets into full swing, the federal government has agent Jim Rogers (Frank Albertson) investigate and he goes to the mountains where he falls in love with the attractive daughter (Linda Hayes) of an innkeeper (Bob McKenzie) before battling the moonshiners and corraling the gangsters.

While its plot was farfetched, CITADEL OF CRIME emerged a "neat little package of gangster hokum" (Variety) which provided director George Sherman with his first non-Western feature assignment. As a result, Sherman fashioned a fast-paced, solid programmer which was greatly enhanced by the emoting of Robert Armstrong as the ex-mountaineer and Russell Simpson as the crusty head of the moonshiners. The movie's working title was TEN NIGHTS IN A BAR ROOM although this feature had nothing to do with the plot of that old theatrical chestnut.

CITTA VIOLENTA see: THE FAMILY

CITY HEAT (Warner Bros., 1983) C 97 mins.

Producer, Fritz Manes; director, Richard Benjamin; story, Sam O. Brown [Blake Edwards]; screenplay, Brown, Joseph C. Stinson; music, Lennie Niehaus; songs, Irene Cara, Bruce Roberts; Ted Koehler and Harold Arlen; George and Ira Gershwin; Cole Porter; Niehaus; production designer, Edward Carfagno; set decorator, George Gaines; costume designer, Norman Stalling; stung coordinator, Wayne Van Horn; assistant director, David Valdes; special effects, Joe Unsinn; sound, C. Darin Knight; camera, Nick McLean; editor, Jacqueline Cambas.

Clint Eastwood (Lieutenant Speer); Burt Reynolds (Mike Murphy); Jane Alexander (Addy); Madeline Kahn (Caroline Howley); Rip Torn (Primo Pitt); Irene Cara (Ginny Lee); Richard Roundtree (Dehl Swift); Tony Lo Bianco (Leon Coll); William Sanderson (Lonnie Ash); Nicholas Worth (Troy Roker); Robert Davi (Nino); Jude Farese (Dub Slack); John Hancock (Fat Freddie); Tab Thacker (Tuck); Gerald S. O'Loughlin (Counterman Louie); Jack Nance (Aram Strossell); Dallas Cole (Redhead Sherry); Lou Filippo (Referee); Michael Maurer (Vint Diestock); Preston Sparks (Keith Stoddard); Ernie Sabella (Ballistics Expert); Christopher Michael Moore (Roxy Cop); Carey Loftin (Roxy Driver); Harry Caesar (Locker Room Attendant); Hamilton Camp (Garage Attendant); Joan Shawlee (Peggy Barker); Minnie Lindsey (Bordello Maid); Darwyn Swalve (Bordello Bouncer); Bob Terhune (Billiard Soldier); Jim Lewis (Roxy Patron); Hanl Calia (Shorter Friend); Daphne Eckler (Agent); Bob Herron, Bill Hart (Garage Soldiers).

"Like many of the traditional film genres, ... the gangster film has gone through most of its possible permutations, and to be successful today, it must either elevate familiar material into a kind of epic dimension similar to THE GODFATHER (1972) [see: B/v] or find a new setting similar to that of WITNESS (1985) [q.v.], or regard the usual ingredients with some special angle of vision. In each of these cases, because the story focuses on a 'hero' of sorts, it is important to have a powerful personality or actor to center the story. Richard Benjamin's film CITY HEAT is not particularly original, but it combines some comfortably established conventions with a fairly bizarre, almost surrealistic style, and it has a cast of players of unusual interest, featuring most prominently Clint Eastwood, without whom, it might safely be assumed, the film would never have been made at all." (Leon Lewis, Magill's Cinema Annual, 1985)

Burt Reynolds' wavering screen popularity was positively jolted when he teamed with Clint Eastwood in this gangster entry which appears to be a straight drama once intended as tongue-in-cheek. Blake Edwards originally co-wrote and was to direct the project but was replaced by actor-director Richard Benjamin, who created a passable melodrama. As Richard Combs assessed in the British Monthly Film Bulletin, "Nothing that happens here ... does anything to compensate for the structural awkwardness. Reynolds is smugly confirmed in his Cary Grant irresponsibility-with-charm persona, and Eastwood plays a teeth-gritting parody of himself that is crude by comparison with the parodies of THE GAUNTLET or THE OUTLAW JOSEY WALES."

In 1933 Kansas City, police Lieutenant Speer (Eastwood) comes to the aid of his old comrade and now private detective Mike Murphy (Reynolds), who is about to have his auto repossessed by two thugs. Reynolds, however, soon comes into money when his partner (Richard Roundtree) shows up with loot he has acquired by a crooked scheme. He has taken ledgers from gangster Leon Coll (Tony Lo Bianco) and has offered to sell them to rival mobster Primo Pitt (Rip Torn) as well as extorting money from Lo Bianco for their return. Torn, however, murders Roundtree, but Eastwood saves the latter's girlfriend (Irene Cara) from the same fate. Reynolds is then abducted by Lo Bianco and he promises to return the missing ledgers for $50,000, but Torn kidnaps his girlfriend (Madeline Kahn) and holds her for the ledgers. Cara then tells Reynolds the location of the ledgers, but he is caught in a gun battle between the rival gangsters. Eastwood arrives and saves the day. At Torn's headquarter, Reynolds advises the mobster that the suitcase containing the ledgers is wired with dynamite. Eastwood shows up and in the ensuing battle Torn is killed. Lo Bianco then arrives to demand the suitcase which Reynolds gives him, but a few minutes later it explodes, killing the greedy mobster.

CITY OF SHADOWS (Republic, 1955) 70 mins.

Producer, William J. O'Sullivan; director, William Witney; screenplay, Houston Branch; music, R. Dale Butts; camera, Reggie Lanning; editor, Tony Martinelli.

Victor McLaglen (Big Tim Channing); John Baer (Dan Mason); Kathleen Crowley (Fern Fellows); Anthony Caruso (Toni Finetti); June Vincent (Linda Fairaday); Richard Reeves (Angelo Di Bruno); Paul Maxey (Davis); Frank Ferguson (District Attorney Hunt); Richard Travis (Phil Jergins); Kay Kuter (Kink); Nicolas Coster (Roy Fellows); Gloria Paul (Waitress); Fern Hall (Miss Hall).

Nearing the finale of his lengthy Hollywood career, Academy

Award winner Victor McLaglen headlined this "B" programmer and managed to breathe life into the proceedings with his typical characterization of a tough yet soft-hearted hoodlum. Greatly bolstered by a good supporting cast and by William Witney's careful direction, CITY OF SHADOWS is satisfying entertainment.

Big Tim Channing (McLaglen), a long-time minor league gangster befriends a young boy whom he puts through school and who becomes a lawyer and then is able to help McLaglen circumvent the law. The attorney (John Baer) also runs rackets for his mentor but in one of them is an employee (Richard Travis) who is secretly working for the local district attorney (Frank Ferguson); the latter is dedicated to putting McLaglen behind bars. This goal is accomplished not by the law but when Baer decides to go legitimate after falling in love with attractive Fern Fellows (Kathleen Crowley).

CITY OF SILENT MEN (Producers Releasing Corp., 1942) 64 mins.

Producer, Dixon R. Harwin; director, William Nigh; story, Robert E. Kent, Joseph Hoffman; screenplay, Hoffman; sound, Corson Jowett; camera, Gilbert Warrenton; editor, Carl Pierson.

Frank Albertson (Gil Davis); June Lang (Helen Hendricks); Jan Wiley (Jane Muller); Richard Clarke (Jerry Hendricks); William Gould (Mayor Hendricks); Emmett Lynn (Jeb Parker); Dick Curtis (Frank Muller); Barton Hepburn (Frank); Frank Jacquet (Judge); Frank Ferguson (Fred Bernard); Richard Bailey (Liptine); Jack Baxley (Police Chief); William Kellogg (Captain); Charles Jordon (Gordon); Pat Gleason (Manners).

The problem of ex-convicts trying to go straight and often being thwarted by society has occasionally been dealt with in feature films. One of the better examples is the PRC feature CITY OF SILENT MEN, which Variety classified a "sleeper." Realistic in detail, nicely controlled by William Nigh from a taut script by Joseph Hoffman and Robert E. Kent, this melodrama elicited a top-notch performance from Frank Albertson as a former prisoner out to become an honest citizen. Interwoven into the plotline is the theme of the lack of manpower due to the World War II effort and the possible utilization of rehabilitated ex-convicts to take up the slack.

Two ex-convicts (Albertson and Emmett Lynn) are released from jail and go from town to town, being rejected because of their past. Finally the mayor (William Gould) of one small community takes them under his "wing" and puts them to work running a canning factory which had to be closed due to the lack of manpower. The duo bring in other ex-cons to work at the factory, but the town's newspaper editor (Dick Curtis) seeks to disrupt the operation by planting fear in the townsfolk about having former convicts at large in their township. Eventually, though, he is thwarted and the factory, with the use of ex-convict labor, is a big success.

Linda Darnell and Michael Duane in CITY WITHOUT MEN (1943).

CITY WITHOUT MEN (Columbia, 1943) 75 mins.

Producer, B. P. Schulberg; director, Sidney Salkow; story, Budd
Schulberg, Martin Berkeley; screenplay, W. L. River, George Skier,
Donald Davis; additional dialogue, George Sklar, Donald Davis; art
directors, Lionel Banks, Cary Odell; set director, William Kiernan;
music director, Morris Stoloff; assistant director, Abby Berlin;
sound, Lambert Day; camera, Philip Tannura; editor, Al Clark.

Linda Darnell (Nancy Johnson); Edgar Buchanan (Judge Malloy);
Michael Duane (Tom Adams); Sara Allgood (Mrs. Barton); Glenda
Farrell (Billie LaRue); Leslie Brooks (Gwen); Doris Dudley (Winnie);
Margaret Hamilton (Dora); Constance Worth (Elsie); Rosemary De-
Camp (Gwen Salde); Sheldon Leonard (Monk LaRue); Joseph Crehan
(Father Burns); Don DeFore (Mr. Peters); Joseph Crehan (Prison
Chaplain); William B. Davidson (Warden); George Chandler (Chester
Salde).

  Unlike most prison pictures, CITY WITHOUT MEN does not
center around inmates but instead focuses on the women in their
lives and the long waits they have until their mates are freed. In
its offbeat way, this feature has merit.
  Pilot boat helmsman Tom Adams (Michael Duane) picks up two
Japanese spies who force him at gunpoint to outrun a Coast Guard

boat. When captured, the aliens claim Duane helped them and he is arrested and tried in U.S. District Court. He is sentenced to five years in prison. Believing in his innocence, his fiancee (Linda Darnell) takes up residence in the town where the federal prison is located, living in a boarding house for women whose men are behind bars. Darnell enlists the aid of once famous but now drunken lawyer Michael Malloy (Edgar Buchanan) to aid Duane and she takes a laundry job. When Duane tries to get himself and his fellow prisoners paroled to fight in the war effort, he's rejected and a riot ensues, with the men being placed in solitary confinement. Meanwhile, the wives at the house come up with a prison break plan in which Duane will be the leader. Darnell does not know about the break but proves Duane's innocence when she learns the Axis ship he saw drop off the spies has been sunk. Buchanan is now able to persuade the parole board to free Duane.

This film is best when focusing on the boarding house folk: a woman whose son is about to be executed; a young woman (Constance Worth) who has been there for seven years and who is now mentally unbalanced; the owner (Sara Allgood) whose husband is incarcerated for life; the hardened Billie LaRue (Glenda Farrell), loyal wife of gangster Monk (Sheldon Leonard); jovial Dora (Margaret Hamilton) whose spouse has been in seven prisons in eleven years; and seductive Gwen (Rosemary DeCamp) whose dimwit prisoner husband (George Chandler) remains unaware she is romancing the meter reader (Don DeFore).

THE COCAINE FIENDS (Willis Kent, 1935) 74 mins.

Producer, Willis Kent; director, William A. O'Connor; screenplay, no credit listed; camera, Jack Greenhalgh; editor, Holbrook N. Todd.

Lois January (Dorothy); Noel Madison (Nick); Sheila Mannors (Fanny); Dean Benton (Eddie Bradford); Lois Lindsay (Jane Bradford/Lil); Charles Delaney (Dan); Eddie Phillips (Escort); Frank Shannon (Farley); and: Gaby Fay, Maury Peck, Nona Lee, Gay Sheridan, Frank Collins.

On the lam from the law, gangster Nick (Noel Madison) takes refuge in a roadside restaurant run by comely Jane Bradford (Lois Lindsay) and he soon has her hooked on cocaine and takes her to the big city, turning her into a tough moll known as Lil. Her brother Eddie (Dean Benton) comes looking for her and gets a carhop job where he falls for pert Fanny (Sheila Mannors), one of Madison's customers. The two youths become dependent on cocaine while socialite Dorothy (Lois January) is infatuated with Madison. Benton and Mannors lose their jobs and move in together. To obtain dope for Benton, Mannors turns to prostitution and when she finds she is pregnant, she commits suicide. Lindsay discovers that her brother is a dope fiend and when Benton abducts January for the white slavery trade, Lindsay kills him and calls the police.

January's father (Frank Shannon) comes for her and is arrested by
her boyfriend (Charles Delaney), the head of the vice squad, since
the old man is actually the racketeer behind the city's drug trade.

A state's rights exploitation melodrama, also called THE PACE
THAT KILLS, this movie preaches against not only the use of drugs
but also against the racketeers who run the illegal trafficking, premarital sex, and the high life. Unlike REEFER MADNESS (q.v.),
which is a clean looking film despite its squalid theme and characters, THE COCAINE FIENDS is gritty, soiled, grainy photoplay
which appears as sordid as its plotline. Unlike most films of its
ilk, the movie is well acted, especially by Noel Madison as the slimy
gangster peddling dope to school children. Also very effective are
Sheila Mannors and Lois Lindsay as innocent young women lured into
the web of drugs.

CODE OF SILENCE (Orion, 1985) C 101 mins.

Producer, Raymond Wagner; director, Andrew Davis; story, Michael
Butler, Dennis Shryack; screenplay, Butler, Shryack, Mike Gray;
production designer, Maher Amed; set decorator, Karen O'Hara;
music, David Frank; costumes, Jay Hurley, Mickey Antonetti, Jennifer Jobst; makeup, Lillian Toth; stunt coordinator, Aaron Norris;
sound, Scott Smith; camera, Frank Tidy; editors, Peter Parsheles,
Christopher Holmes.

Chuck Norris (Detective Sergeant Eddie Cusack); Henry Silva (Luis
Comacho); Bert Remsen (Commander Kates); Mike Genovese (Tony
Luna); Nathan Davis (Felix Scalese); Ralph Foody (Crague); Allen
Hamilton (Pirelli); Ron Henriquez (Victor Comacho); Joseph Guzaldo
(Nick Kopalas); Molly Hagan (Diana Luna); Ron Dean (Brennan);
Wilbert Bradley (Spider); Dennis Farina (Dorato); Gene Barge
(Music); Mario Nieves (Pompas); Miquel Nino (Efren); Ronnie Bar-
ron (Doc); Joe Kosala (Kobas); Lou Damiani (Gamiani); Nydia Rod-
riquez Terracina (Partida); Andre Marquis (Sanches); John Mahoney
("Prowler" Representative); Dennis Cochrum, Zaid Farid (Hoods in
Tavern); Howard Jackson (Officer Johnson); Alex Stevens (Angel);
Don Pike (Hood on Yacht); Trish Schaefer (Molly Luna); Martha
Oton (Tony Luna's Mother); James Fierro (Vito); Tom Letuli (Sam);
Jeff Hoke (Gallery Artist); Gary T. Pike (Scalase's Driver); Frank
Storcchia (Police Gym Attendant); Jerry Tullos (Review Board
Clerk); Catalina Cacares (Grandmother at Hearing); Shirley Kelly
(Artist's Benefactor).

Chicago police attempt to crack open the cocaine dealing of
the sinister Comacho family, but everything goes afoul when competing gangsters led by Tony Luna (Mike Genovese) steal the dope
cache. In the aftermath, a police officer (Ralph Foody) shoots an
innocent youth and then claims self defense, but the truth is observed by his partner (Joseph Guzaldo), who for the time being
substantiates his co-worker's gross lie. Detective Sergeant Eddie

Cusack (Chuck Norris), in charge of the police operation, must now cope with gang retribution as Luis Comacho (Henry Silva) returns to town to seek revenge on the rival monsters. Silva's men massacre Genovese's family, but the latter's daughter, Diana (Moly Hagan), escapes and seeks safety at Norris' apartment, only to be later kidnapped by Silva's henchmen. All the while, Norris is losing the confidence of his fellow police officers because he insists that Foody, whom he has learned faked the self-defense situation, should no longer be allowed to continue active duty. After further mobster killings, macho Norris, using an armed police robot, storms Silva's stronghold (alone!!) and, in the final battle, kills his opponents. Finally, his co-workers on the force, having learned the truth about Foody, arrive to champion Norris' cause.

All in the name of justice triumphing over evil, this Chuck Norris action film sacrifices storyline credibility, characterization, and pacing to allow increasingly stoic hero Norris to be the champ at the finale. If any insight is shed into the workaday worlds of gangsters and law enforcers, it is how much at the mercy of the heads of the households are the families of both "sides." Never sure of their man's work schedule or loyalties or safety, it ultimately comes to roost that their only route to sanity is to ignore everything and live deliberately blinded to the man's activities. That their own lives are in constant danger goes with the territory.

COFFIN FROM HONG KONG see: EIN SARGAUS HONG KONG

COME OUT FIGHTING (Monogram, 1945) 62 mins.

Producers, Sam Katzman, Jack Dietz; director, William Beaudine; screenplay, Earl Snell; art director, David Milton; music director, Edward Kay; assistant director, Mel DeLay; sound, Tom Lambert; camera, Ira Morgan; editor, William Austin.

Leo Gorcey (Muggs McGinnis); Huntz Hall (Glimpy); Gabriel Dell (Talman); Billy Benedict (Skinny); Mende Koenig (Danny Moore); Bud Gorman (Sammy); Johnny Duncan (Gilbert Mitchell); Amelita Ward (Rita Joyce); June Carlson (Jane Riley); Addison Richards (Commissioner James Mitchell); George Meeker (Silk Henley); Pat Gleason (Pete Vargas); Robert Homans (Chief Tom Riley); Fred Kelsey (Mr. McGinnis); Patsy Moran (Mrs. McGinnis); Douglas Wood (Mayor); Alan Foster (Whitey); Davidson Clark (Officer McGowan); Meyer Grace (Jake); Betty Sinclair (Commissioner's Stenographer).

When the police commissioner (Addison Richards) rescues the East Side Kids by preventing the closing of their club house, the boys return the favor by teaching the man's sissy son (Johnny Duncan) how to be a boxer. Duncan, however, gets involved with gamblers who use him to ruin his father, and the boys must put a fast stop to the plan.

Using the gangster theme once more as a celluloid springboard for their special brand of shenanigans, the "East Side Kids" again demonstrate how much they were the kings of youthful proletarian slapstick comedy.

THE CONCRETE JUNGLE (Pentagon/Aquarius, 1982) C 99 mins.

Executive producers, Jay Schultz, Richard Feinberg; producer, Billy Fine; associate producer, Louis Paciocco; director, Tom DeSimone; screenplay, Alan J. Adler; music, Joe Conlon; camera, Andrew W. Friend; editor, Nine di Marco.

Jill St. John (Warden Fletcher); Tracy Bregman (Elizabeth Demming); Barbara Luna (Cat); June Barrett (Icy); Peter Brown (Danny); Aimee Eccles (Spider); Sondra Currie (Catherine); Susan Mechsner (Breaker); Nita Talbot (Shelly Meyers); Niki Dantine (Margo).

Elizabeth Demming (Tracy Bregman) is sent to a women's prison after being caught at an airport with a batch of cocaine, although she is really the dupe of her pusher boyfriend (Peter Brown). Behind bars, she finds the institution is run by a corrupt warden (Jill St. John) who is in cahoots with a drug dealing murderess (Barbara Luna) in control of a prison gang. When she refuses the sexual advances of the gang leader, Bregman is set up for rape by a prison guard, attacked by other inmates, and put into solitary confinement. Despite urging from a prison reformer (Nita Talbott), the girl will not snitch on her fellow prisoners, but after a time she realizes her no-good boyfriend won't help her, and she sets about to win her freedom as well as to revenge herself on those who have abused her.
Made for the exploitation trade, this R-rated, sleazy melodrama has little nudity, although a finale fight sequence between the female prisoners is a voyeurs' delight. Apparently THE CONCRETE JUNGLE calls for reform in women's prisons, but the overall plot is so tawdry that any hope of using this picture as a positive expose piece is lost in its brutal excesses.
The next year, a sensational semi-sequel, CHAINED HEAT (q.v.), would be released.

CONFIDENTIAL (Mascot, 1935) 68 mins.

Director, Edward L. Cahn; story, John Rathmell, Scott Darling; screenplay, Wellyn Totman, Olive Cooper; camera, Ernest Miller, Jack Marta; editor, Ray Curtiss.

Donald Cook (Dave Elliot); Evelyn Knapp (Maxine); Warren Hymer (Midget); J. Carrol Naish (Lefty); Herbert Rawlinson (J. W. Keaton); Theodore Von Eltz (Welsh); Morgan Wallace (Van Cleve); and: Kane Richmond, Clay Clements, Reed Howes, Edward Hearn, Alan Bridge,

Earl Eby, Lynton Brent, Monte Carter, George Chesebro, James
Burtis, Mary Guryane, Frank Marlowe, Lillian Castle, Donald Kerr,
Edwin Argus, Jack Gustin, David Worth, Allen Connor, Tom Brower.

To halt a numbers racket preying on the public, a G-Man
(Donald Cook) teams with the mob who murdered his pal. In the
meantime, he falls in love with the organization's attractive bookkeeper (Evelyn Knapp) who doesn't know of their activities since
she is employed by a supposedly honest businessman (Herbert Rawlinson). One of the gang members, a gunman (J. Carrol Naish),
believes he knows the new member from somewhere and eventually
recognizes Cook, all of which hastens the final showdown.
Obviously influenced by G-MAN (see: B/v), which Warner
Bros. issued six months earlier, this Mascot production was "one of
the best G-man dramas" (Film Daily). Directed with fine pacing by
Edward L. Cahn, the movie contained all the ingredients now associated with 1930s gangster melodramas, including Warren Hymer's
comedy relief as the gang's none-too-bright stooge. Donald Cook
was the typical stalwart hero, Evelyn Knapp the lovely heroine, and
Herbert Rawlinson the villainous head of the numbers racket.
In retrospect, Jon Tuska wrote of CONFIDENTIAL in his book
The Vanishing Legion: A History of Mascot Pictures 1927-35 (1982):
"Not merely did CONFIDENTIAL and so many like it indulge in self-
congratulatory fantasies about crime and law enforcement, ... but
they succeeded only in adding to the already distorted conception of
organized crime that had been put forth by the gangster film cycle
in the early thirties."

CONSPIRACY (RKO, 1930) 69 mins.

Producer, William Le Baron; associate producer, Bertram Millhauser;
director, Christy Cabanne; based on the novel by Robert Melville
Baker and John Emerson; screenplay-dialogue, Beulah Marie Dix;
art director, Max Ree; assistant director, Dewey Starkey; sound,
John Tribby; camera, Nich Musuraca; editor, Arthur Roberts.

Bessie Love (Margaret Holt); Ned Sparks (Winthrop Clavering);
Hugh Trevor (John Howell); Rita La Roy (Nita Strong); Ivan
Lebedeff (Butch Miller); Gertrude Howard (Martha); Otto Matieson
[James Morton] (Marco); Jane Keckley (Rose Towne); Donald
MacKenzie (Captain McLeod); George Irving (Mark Holt); Bert Moore-
house (Victor Holt); Walter Long (Weinberg).

When gangsters running a narcotics ring murder their father,
Margaret Holt (Bessie Love) and her brother Victor (Bert Moorehouse), vow revenge. Moorehouse becomes a district attorney and
obtains information on the gang, while Love becomes the secretary
to Marco (Otto Matieson), the head of the underworld activity.
When the gangster kingpin discovers her identity, he orders Moorehouse's death and Love stabs him, but is too late to save her brother.

Escaping, she meets reporter John Howell (Hugh Trevor) who persuades a mystery writer (Ned Sparks) to hire her as his secretary.
Trevor finds out Moorehouse is really still alive and a prisoner of
the hoodlums while Sparks deduces the identity of Love and invites
the gangsters to his apartment to get her. There, they are arrested while Trevor rescues Moorehouse.

Based on the 1913 novel by Robert Melville Baker and John
Emerson which was made into a silent feature, this Bessie Love
vehicle was so bad that hardly anyone had a kind word for it. Released only a short time before the ground breaking LITTLE CAESAR
and THE PUBLIC ENEMY (see both: B/V), this outdated melodrama
did little to enrich the popularity of the gangster film cycle.

CONTRACT ON CHERRY STREET (Columbia Pictures Television/
Artamis Productions/NBC-TV, 11/23/77) C 144 mins.

Executive producer, Renee Valente; producer, Hugh Benson; director, William A. Graham; based on the book by Phillip Rosenberg;
teleplay, Edward Anhalt; music, Jerry Goldsmith; art director, Robert Gundlach; camera, Jack Priestley; editor, Eric Albertson.

Frank Sinatra (Deputy Inspector Frank Hovannes); Jay Black (Tommy
Sinardos); Verna Bloom (Emily Hovannes); Martin Balsam (Captain
Ernie Weinberg); Joe DeSantis (Vincenzo Seruto); Martin Gabel
(Baruch Waldman); Harry Guardino (Ron Polito); James Luisi (Al
Palmini); Michael Nouri (Lou Savage); Marco St. John (Eddie Man-
zaro); Henry Silva (Roberto Obregon); Richard Ward (Jack Kittens);
Addison Powell (Bob Halloran); Steve Inwood (Frank Marks); Johnny
Barnes (Otis Washington); Lenny Montana (Phil Lombardi); Murray
Moston (Richie Saint); Robert Davi (Mickey Sinardos); Nicky Blair
(Jeff Diamond); Estelle Omens (Flo Weinberg); Ray Serra (Jimmy
Macks); Bill Jorgensen (Himself); Sol Weiner (Paul Gold); Jim Boyd
(Gallagher); Carmine Foresta (Saladino); Sonny Grosso (Rhodes);
Daniel Hannafin (Menneker); Randy Jurgensen (Al Jenner); Michael
Stroka (Mike Farren); Ruth Rivera (Cecelia Benitez); Keith Davis
(Jamie Leonx); Anna Berger (Mrs. Moore); Richard Corley (Desk
Clerk); Mitchell Jason (Leo Goffman); Johnny Smash (Bartender);
Louise Campbell (Admissions Nurse); Jilly Rizzo (Silvera); Gil
Frazier (Bodyguard); Neil Elliott (Medic); Tucker Smallwood (Bus
Driver); Phil Rubenstein (Deli Clerk); Robert Davis (Rabbi);
Michele Mais (Secretary).

"Aces to this fine thriller ... Above average," is how TV
Movies (1985) rated this telefeature starring Frank Sinatra in his
first made-for-TV movie and his return to filmmaking after a seven
year absence. Some years before, the crooner had purchased the
property, but not as a vehicle for himself; he was finally convinced
to take the starring role in the production by Columbia Pictures
Television. The telefeature was released abroad theatrically.

Filmed in New York City, the narrative tells of a 25-year

Frank Sinatra in CONTRACT ON CHERRY STREET (1977).

police force veteran, Deputy Inspector Frank Havannes (Sinatra), who is the chief of a special unit investigating and battling organized crime. When one of his men is murdered and his own actions are restrained by the courts and department superiors, Sinatra and three of his staff unite to wipe out the mob with an unorthodox, daring plan: they will ambush and murder an underworld kingpin, hoping the assassination will ignite a gang war between two rival mob factions.

Needless to say, more killings and violence ensues, all encased in a tale of morality.

CONVICTS AT LARGE (Principal, 1938) 57 mins.

Directors, Scott E. Beal, David A. Friedman; story, Ambrose Barker; screenplay, Walter James, Beal; camera, Marcel Le Picard.

Ralph Forbes (David); Paula Stone (Ruth); William Royle (Steve); John Kelly (Buggsie); George Travell (Gus); Charles Brokaw (Squire); Florence Lake (Hattie).

An architect (Ralph Forbes) has his clothes stolen by an escaped prisoner and he is forced to put on the man's prison duds. He ends up in the nightclub run by the gang to which the escaped convict belongs and there he tumbles for a pretty singer (Paula Stone) and soon becomes involved with the hoodlums while the police begin a crackdown on the town's bad element. Eventually Forbes helps the police capture the gangsters and also wins Stone's affection.

CONVICTS AT LARGE is a pointed illustration of the banal use of the gangster theme by poverty row companies in the 1930s. Since gangster movies were so popular, the small film outfits threw together threadbare (both in plot and budget) items like this for quick playoffs on the states' rights market, correctly assuming any movie dealing with gangsters and violence would bring a profit. Handsome British star Ralph Forbes had come down a long way to headline this trifle after appearing in such Hollywood classics as BEAU GESTE (1926).

COPACABANA (CBS-TV, 12/3/85) C 100 mins.

Executive producers, Dick Clark, Dan Paulson; producer, R. P. Goodwin; director, Waris Hussein; screenplay, James Lipton; music, Barry Manilow; songs, Manilow, Bruce Sussman, and Jack Feidman; choreography, Grover Dale; camera, Bobby Byrne; editor, Michael Jablow.

Barry Manilow (Tony Starr); Annette O'Toole (Lola Lamarr); Joseph Bologna (Rico Castelli); Ernie Sabella (Sam Gropper); Estelle Getty (Bella Stern); James T. Callahan (Dennis); Andra Akers (Pamela

Devereaux); Silvana Callardo (Rivera); Cliff Osmond (Angelo); Dwier Brown (Bibi).

Barry Manilow's Grammy winning 1978 record "Copacabana" was the inspiration for this glossy TV musical which highlighted the singer-songwriter in his first starring film. Glitsy at best, with rather wan production numbers and a silly storyline, COPACABANA is nonetheless better than average TV movie fare, due mainly to Annette O'Toole's ingratiating performance as Lola Lamarr with Manilow quite acceptable in the undemanding male lead. In TV Guide, Judith Crist called it a "delightfully deadpan pastiche of the old Hollywood musical" and added, "Manilow is disarmingly charming and O'Toole is a singing-dancing revelation."

Set in 1948, the story has aspiring entertainers Tony Starr (Manilow) and Lola Lamarr (O'Toole) as contestants on a radio singing quiz show, with Manilow winning a supposed engagement at the Copacabana nightclub which turns out to be a bartending job. O'Toole meanwhile ekes out a living as a dancehall hostess until the two meet and fall in love and audition for Copa club owner Sam Gropper (Ernie Sabella), who gives them jobs. O'Toole then draws the attention of gangster Rico Castelli (Joseph Bologna), who takes her to Havana to headline his Tropicana Club after she has a spat with Manilow. Manilow, however, learns of Bologna's underworld connections and heads to Cuba to rescue his girlfriend from Bologna's unwanted attentions and he is able to do so with the aid of a socialite (Andra Akers) who has a hankering for him. Manilow and O'Toole escape back to the United States in the socialite's plane and are married, but when they headline at the Copa, Bologna arrives on the scene and in a scuffle, Manilow is killed. At a modern-day disco, where the story began, the aged and half-crazy Lola remembers the happier times when she and Manilow were the club's headliners.

THE COTTON CLUB (Orion, 1984) C 128 mins.

Executive producer, Dyson Lovell; producer, Robert Evans; co-producers, Sylvio Tabet, Fred Roos; associate producer, Melissa Prophet; director, Francis Ford Coppola; story, William Kennedy, Coppola, Mario Puzo; screenplay, Kennedy, Coppola; production designer, Richard Sylbert; art directors, David Chapman, Gregory Bolton; set decorators, George Gaines, Lee Bloom; music, John Barry; music arranger, Sy Johnson; music recreations, Bob Wilbert; choreography, Michael Smith; tap choreography, Henry LeTang; montage-second unit director, Gian-Carlo Coppola; assistant directors, Robert V. Girolami, Henry Bronchtein, Louis D'Esposito; visual consultant, Antony Clavet; costume designer, Milena Canonero; makeup, Craig Lyman; special consultant, Ralph Cooper; stunt coordinators, Vic Magnotta, Bill Burton; sound, Jack Jacobsen; camera, Stephen Goldblatt; editors, Barry Malkin, Robert Q. Lovett.

Richard Gere (Dixie Dwyer); Gregory Hines (Delbert "Sandman"

Advertisement for THE COTTON CLUB (1984).

Williams); Diane Lane (Vera Cicero); Lonette McKee (Lila Rose Oliver); Bob Hoskins (Owney Madden); James Remar (Dutch Schultz); Nicolas Cage (Vincent Dwyer); Allen Garfield (Abbadabba Berman); Fred Gwynne (Frenchy Demange); Gwen Verdon (Tish Dwyer); Lisa Jane Persky (Frances Felgeheimer); Maurice Hines (Caly Williams); Julian Beck (Sol Weinstein); Novella Nelson (Madame St. Clair); Larry Fishburne (Bumpy Rhodes); John Ryan (Joe Flynn); Tom Waits (Irving Stark); Ron Karabarsos (Mike Best); Glenn Withrow (Ed Popke); Jennifer Grey (Patsy Dwyer); Wynonna Smith (Winnie Williams); Thelma Carpenter (Norma Williams); Charles "Honi" Coles (Sugar Coates); Larry Marshall (Cab Calloway); Joe Dallesandro (Charles "Lucky" Luciano); Ed O'Ross (Monk); Frederick Downs, Jr. (Sullen Man); Diane Venora (Gloria Swanson); Tucker Smallwood (Kid Griffin); Woody Strode (Holmes); Bill Graham (J.W.); Dayton Allen (Solly); Kim Chang (Ling); Ed Rown (Messiah); Leonard

Termo (Danny); Rony Clanton (Caspar Holstein); Damien Leake (Bub Jewett); Bill Cobbs (Big Joe Ison); Joe Lynn (Marcial Flores); Oscar Barnes (Spanish Henry); Sandra Beall (Myrtle Fay); Zane Mark (Duke Ellington); Tom Signorelli (Butch Murdock); Steve Vignari (Trigger Mike Coppla); Susan Meschner (Gypsie); Gregory Rozakis (Charlie Chaplin); Marc Coppola (Ted Husing); Norma Jean Darden (Elida Webb); Robert Earl Jones (Stage Door Joe); Vincent Jerosa (James Cagney); Rosalind Harris (Fanny Brice).

After reviving interest in the gangster film genre with two box-office blockbusters--THE GODFATHER in 1972 (see: B/V) and THE GODFATHER, PART II in 1974 (See: B/V)--both of which were consolidated into the TV film presentation THE GODFATHER SAGA (q.v.) in 1977, director Francis Ford Coppola returned to the genre in 1984 with THE COTTON CLUB. While not as long as its predecessors in running length (it was severely butchered for theatrical release), this movie is just as involved in its fictionaliza-tion of historical happenings and personages regarding the rivalry between white and black hoodlums in Prohibition-era Harlem.

Set in 1928 Harlem, the feature opens with musician Dixie Dwyer (Richard Gere) saving the life of gangster Dutch Schultz (James Remar), who has been ambushed by a rival (John Ryan) whom Remar later eliminates. Gere's brother Vince (Nicholas Cage) joins Remar's mob and at the same time gangster Owney Madden (Bob Hoskins) hires two black brother dancers, Sandman (Gregory Hines) and Clay (Maurice Hines) to work in his Cotton Club. Remar asks Gere to be a companion to his girlfriend, Vera Cicero (Diane Lane), whom Gere once knew. In the meantime, Gregory Hines is romanc-ing another black club entertainer (Lonette McKee).

While Remar plans to take over the Harlem numbers racket, Gere and Lane have an affair and Hoskins uses Gere as a front for his entering the movie business by making the handsome musician a screen star. Within two years the numbers racket war in Harlem is in full swing; Gere has made a name for himself in gangster mov-ies; and Lane owns a Broadway club where McKee (now passing for white and calling herself Angelina) sings. When Remar does not cut Cage into the numbers racket, he kidnaps rival gangster Frenchy Demange (Fred Gwynne). Later Remar has Cage murdered.

As time passes, black hoodlums try to take over the Cotton Club and Remar becomes mentally unstable. Gregory Hines saves Gere's life when Remar tries to kill him after learning about the latter's affair with Lane. Still later Remar is killed by a gangster alliance led by Hoskins and Lucky Luciano (Joe Dallesandro). As a result, Lane is free to stay with Gere, while Hines and McKee wed.

Long before the film reached completion, THE COTTON CLUB had become infamous for its runaway budget, in-staff fighting, and rampant rumors that it was a fiasco. Then, despite an enormously expensive publicity campaign, the elaborate movie--which insiders insisted had been cut to shreds in its release print--failed to arouse public response. It was quickly relegated to cable TV and video cassette versions, where it gained a better footing.

"Admitting, the story sets up one after another of the screen's oldest chestnuts (the 'I'm goin' solo now' scenes between partners; the death-in-a-machine-gun-riddled-phone-booth scene; the 'watch my girl, but don't lay a finger on her' admonition). They're saved by the lyrically laconic dialogue, and by Coppola's imagination and his cast's energy. (Watch the scene between warring gangsters, or the love-hate dance of Lane and Gere, staged with throwaway delight.) ... The spine of the film is its outrageous, joyous musical numbers by the singers, tap dancers, barbecue shouters and showgirls of the Cotton Club.... A sense of amplitude that's close to profligacy marks the staging of the songs and dances. These numbers are integral to the action and each one of them may be show stoppers, but this show never stops" (Sheila Benson, Los Angeles Times).

When viewers with a knowledge of history were not comparing THE COTTON CLUB's storyline with the real life biographies of Mae West, George Raft, and gangster Owney Madden, there was much else to hold the attention. Since the film's thrust was a dramatic panorama of a gangster era and its chief players, it is unfortunate that so much of the screen time was given to set pieces for musical interludes and that the mobsters--with the strong exception of Bob Hoskins' solid performance--are caricatures in search of a dimensional role to play. Moreover, as the British Monthly Film Bulletin reviewer observed, "... this treatment of the gangster narrative, involving history but paying it little regard, is matched by an opposite tendency: adorning with 'social significance' the musical romance between Delbert Williams and Lila Rose, the two main characters most clearly on the fringes of the white mobster world. Their relationship is traced in terms of race: skin color as an obstacle to desire, as an ambiguous 'grey area' for Lila Rose. It is exactly here, however, that one's doubts about THE COTTON CLUB start to firm up.... Coppola signally fails to establish any real link between the race question, as embodied in the couple, and its large manifestation in the Cotton Club itself." (It should be noted that in the actual Cotton Club, all the performers were black, but the patrons and owners were white.)

COUNTERFEIT PLAN (Warner Bros., 1957) 79 mins.

Producer, Alec C. Snowden; director, Montgomery Tully; screenplay, James Eastwood; music, Richard Taylor; camera, Philip Grinrod; editor, Geoffrey Meller.

Zachary Scott (Max); Peggie Castle (Carol); Mervyn Johns (Louie); Sydney Tafler (Flint); Lee Patterson (Duke); David Lodge (Watson); Mark Bellamy (Vik); Chili Bochier (Housekeeper); Robert Arden (Bob); Eric Pohlmann (Wandelman); Aubrey Dexter (Lepton); John Welsh (Police Inspector).

Beating a murder rap in France, gangster Max (Zachary Scott) comes to England where he blackmails an ex-forger (Mervyn Johns) into going into business with him in making counterfeit five pound notes at Johns' country home. With the aid of a fence (Lee Patterson), the men make a fortune in their operation, but things go bad when Johns' attractive daughter (Peggie Castle) arrives and Scott begins to court her. Seeing the illegal goings on, Castle persuades her father to go to the police, but he is later murdered by Scott. Thereafter, Scott and Patterson die when their jeep crashes in a police chase.

Made in Great Britain with American stars Zachary Scott and Peggie Castle, this entry was merely another of the several quickie movies Scott churned out in 1950s England.

THE COUNTERFEITERS (Twentieth Century-Fox, 1948) 73 mins.

Executive producer, Bert M. Stearn; producer, Maurice H. Conn; director, Peter Stewart [Sam Newfield]; story, Conn; screenplay, Fred Myton, Barbara Worth; assistant director, Stanley Newfield; music director, Irving Gertz; art director, Frank Dexter; set decorator, Elias H. Reif; sound, John H. Carter; camera, James S. Brown, Jr.; editor, Martin Conn.

John Sutton (Jeff MacAllister); Doris Merrick (Margo); Hugh Beaumont (Philip Drake); Lon Chaney (Louie); George O'Hanlon (Frankie);

George O'Hanlon, Lon Chaney, and John Sutton in THE COUNTERFEITERS (1948).

Douglas Blackley (Tony); Herbert Rawlinson (Norman Talbot); Pierre Watkins (Carter); Don Harvey (Dan Taggart); Fred Coby (Piper); Joi Lansing (Art Model); Gerald Gilbert (Jerry McGee).

Long-time denizens of Hollywood's poverty row, producer Maurice Conn, director Peter Stewart [Sam Newfield], and scripter Fred Myton joined for the B+ programmer. With its semi-documentary look--a popular device in gangster and espionage films of the day-- it proved a "good entry for the secondary market" (Variety).
Philip Drake (Hugh Beaumont) runs a counterfeiting ring and works with pal Frankie (George O'Hanlon) and dumb thug Louie (Lon Chaney). They are in cahoots with platemaker Carter (Pierre Watkins) with Beaumont romancing the latter's daughter (Doris Merrick). The government, however, is trailing his gang and a FBI man (Blackley) is teamed with his Scotland Yard counterpart (John Sutton) in catching the forgers. It develops that Merrick is only playing up to Beaumont to help her father go straight, and she is soon in league with the government men in stopping the illegal operation.

LA COURSE DU LIEVRE A TRAVERS LES CHAMPS see: AND HOPE
    TO DIE

CRASHOUT (Filmakers, 1955) 88 mins.

Producer, Hal E. Chester; director, Lewis E. Foster; screenplay, Chester, Foster; music, Leith Stevens; art director, Wiard Ihnen; camera, Russell Metty; editor, Robert Swink.

William Bendix (Van Duff); Arthur Kennedy (Joe Quinn); Luther Adler (Pete Mendoza); William Talman (Swanee Remsen); Gene Evans (Monk Collins); Marshall Thompson (Billy Lang); Beverly Michaels (Alice Mosher); Gloria Talbot (Girl on Train); Adam Williams (Fred); Percy Helton (Dr. Barnes); Melinda Markey (Girl in Bar); Chris Olsen (Timmy); Adele St. Maur (Mrs. Mosher); Edward Clark (Conductor); Tom Duran (Bartender); Morris Ankrum (Head Guard).

CRASHOUT is one of the more sadly neglected gangster movies of the 1950s, and it is one of the better ones. The movie is a tough, no-holds-barred look at men escaping from prison, their motives, their psychological makeup, and their desperate attempts to be free. The movie does not take a particular stand on the prison system or reform but instead studies the people involved in a crashout, or prison escape, and those outside the prison walls affected by their actions. This Filmakers release is exciting from start to finish.
    Five prisoners (William Bendix, Arthur Kennedy, Gene Evans, Luther Adler, Marshall Thompson) carry out a daring prison breakout. They take refuge in an abandoned tunnel where they remain until the coast is clear. Later, while holding up a roadhouse, two

CRASHOUT (1955).

policemen arrive and in a shootout the men escape, but one of them is injured. They bring in a doctor (Percy Helton) to care for him and then kill the medical man when they no longer have use for him. Continuing their escape, the convicts find sanctuary in a remote farm home and one (Thompson) of them falls in love with a girl (Beverly Michaels) who lives there. When it comes time to leave, Michaels goes with Thompson, who now wants no part of his cohorts' murderous ways. Eventually all the prisoners except Thompson are killed by the law and the survivor returns to prison knowing his love will be waiting for him upon his release.

William Bendix (in a dramatic change from his stereotyped role as situation comedy lead Chester A. Riley) plays the cold, conniving killer to the hilt, ably supported by Luther Adler as a slick womanizer, with Gene Evans a dumb thug, Arthur Kennedy as the intellectual prisoner, and Marshall Thompson as the innocent.

CRAZY MAMA (New World, 1975) C 82 mins.

Producer, Julie Corman; director, Jonathan Demme; story, Francis Duel; screenplay, Robert Thom; second unit director, Evelyn Purcell; art director, Peter Jamison; set decorator, Linda Spheeris; music coordinator, Marshall Leib; stunt coordinator, Alan Gibbs; camera, Bruce Logan; editors, Allan Holzman, Lewis Teague.

Cloris Leachman (Melba); Stuart Whitman (Jim Bob); Ann Sothern (Sheba); Tisha Sterling (Sheba in 1932); Jim Backus (Mr. Albertson); Donny Most (Shawn); Linda Purl (Cheryl); Bryan England (Snake); Merle Earle (Bertha); Sally Kirkland (Ella Mae); Clint Kimbrough (Daniel); Vince Barnett (Homer).

In the late 1950s, widow Melba (Cloris Leachman) and her mother Sheba (Ann Sothern) are tossed out of their beauty parlor for failure to pay the rent. Since the girl's father (Clint Kimbrough) was murdered by the law a quarter of a century before, the revengeful duo, along with Leachman's pregnant daughter (Linda Purl) and her boyfriend (Donny Most) go on a robbery spree, stealing cars as they head east. They also pick up another young man (Bryan England) who becomes involved with Purl. While in Las Vegas, a small town sheriff (Stuart Whitman) joins the gang as does elderly Bertha (Merle Earle) who has run away from her uncaring relatives. The bizarre group then decides to pretend the lawman has been kidnapped and get a large ransom. Along the way, the already married Whitman takes Leachman for his bride. But some are gunned down by lawmen. Later the surviving members of the group open a lunch room in Miami Beach.

Obviously a tongue-in-cheek takeoff on BONNIE AND CLYDE (see: B/V), CRAZY MAMA is a fast paced feature which seesaws unbelievably between drama, comedy, and violence in constant doses. While the family detailed here are low life, a useless bunch of thieves and murderers, it is the law which is pictured as the villain of the piece, especially in the scene where elderly Earle is ambushed by them in a wooded area.

The film's performances also vary, most being overripe, although Ann Sothern is amusing as the blowsy mother and Merle Earle steals the show as the strong-willed Bertha. Tisha Sterling, Ann Sothern's daughter, portrays her mother in the 1932 prologue sequence.

THE CRIME PATROL (Empire, 1936) 58 mins.

Producer, Harry S. Knight; director, Eugene Cummings; story, Arthur T. Horman; adaptor, Betty Burbridge; camera, Bert Longenecker; editor, Earl Neville.

Ray Walker (Bob Neal); Geneva Mitchell (Mary Prentiss); Herbert Corthell (Commissioner Cullen); Hooper Atchley (Doctor Simmons); Wilbur Mack (Vic Santell); Russ Clark (Patrolman Davis); Max Wagner (Bennie); Virginia True Boardman (Mrs. Neal); Henry Roquemore (Fight Promoter); Snub Pollard (Gyp).

Brash boxer Bob Neal (Ray Walker) joins the police force as a rookie so he can use the department's gym and boxing instructor. He also falls in love with a pretty nurse (Geneva Mitchell) who realizes that under his smug exterior is the man she loves. When gangsters from his old neighborhood pull a holdup and take two of his fellow policemen as hostages, Walker proves himself by rescuing the men and bringing in the gang.

This vehicle was just another outing for fast-talking comedian Ray Walker, who was usually typecast a nosey, near-obnoxious reporter.

CRIME RING (RKO, 1938) 69 mins.

Producer, Cliff Reid; director, Leslie Goodwins; story, Reginald Taviner; screenplay, J. Robert Bren, Gladys Atwater; music director, Roy Webb; camera, Jack MacKenzie; editor, Desmond Masquette.

Allan Lane (Joe); Frances Mercer (Judy Allen); Clara Blandick (Phoebe Sawyer); Inez Courtney (Kitty); Bradley Page (Whitmore); Ben Welden (Nate); Walter Miller (Jenner); Frank M. Thomas (Redwins); Jack Arnold (Buzzell); Morgan Conway (Taylor); George Irving (Clifton); Leona Roberts (Mrs. Wahrton); Charles Trowbridge (Marvin); Tom Kennedy (Dummy); Paul Fix (Slim); Jack Mulhall (Brady).

The plot ploy of phony spiritualists, psychics, and fortune tellers preying on a gullible public has long been grist for moviemakers and for years has been an integral part of the gangster film genre, since these charlatans either tend to be hoodlums themselves or are financially supported by mobsters. Many films have delved into these bogus rackets, such as THE MYSTIC CIRCLE MYSTERY (aka RELIGIOUS RACKETEERS, 1939) and MURDER, MY SWEET (q.v.). CRIME RINGS also studies these nefarious practices, and Variety claimed, "As such it may squelch careless spending for phoney crystal gazers. But as entertainment, the film badly misses its mark."

Fake spiritualists are using their rackets for blackmail, kidnapping, a stock-selling scheme, forgery, and even murder. All their activities are backed by local gangsters. Newspaper reporter Joe (Allan Lane) sets out to expose the crooks and he is aided by attractive dancer Judy (Frances Mercer), who joins the fake clairvoyant racket as an informer for the district attorney. As a result the two not only bring the hoodlums to justice, but also fall in love.

CRIME TAKES A HOLIDAY (Columbia, 1938) 59 mins.

Director, Lewis D. Collins; screenplay, Jefferson Parker, Henry Altimus, Charles Logue; camera, James S. Brown, Jr.; editor, Dwight Caldwell.

Jack Holt (Walter Forbes); Marcia Ralston (Peggy Stone); Russell Hopton (Jerry Clayton); Douglass Dumbrille (J. J. Grant); Arthur

Jack Holt, Tom Jackson, and Russell Hopton in CRIME TAKES A HOLIDAY (1938).

Hohl (Joe); Thomas Jackson (Brennan); John Wray (Howell); William Pawley (Spike); Paul Fix (Louie); Harry Woods (Stoddard); Joe Crehan (Governor Allen).

     Crusading District Attorney Walter Forbes (Jack Holt) wants to clean up the city's gangster element so he can run for governor. He intends to put underworld kingpin Grant (Douglass Dumbrille) behind bars but cannot get the information needed for his conviction. He then comes up with a scheme to prosecute an innocent man, who is sentenced to die in the electric chair, so the real hoodlum will show his hand. The plan, known only to Holt, almost backfires, but eventually the real criminal is brought to justice.
     This entry in Jack Holt's long-running action series for Columbia Pictures seems to have some basis in the career of New York crimebuster Thomas E. Dewey, who became governor of the state due to his anti-crime activities and who was twice Republican candidate for United States president. Leading man Holt did not participate in the scenario's romancing, but instead left leading lady Marcia Ralston (as the daughter of the falsely convicted man) to be courted by his assistant (Russell Hopton).

THE CRIMES OF DR. MABUSE see: THE TESTAMENT OF DR.
   MABUSE

CROSS YOUR HEART AND HOPE TO DIE see: AND HOPE TO DIE

CUSTOMS AGENT (Columbia, 1950) 71 mins.

Producer, Rudolph C. Flothow; director, Seymour Friedman; story, Hal Smith; screenplay, Russell S. Hughes, Malcolm Stuart Boylan; assistant director, Gilbert Kay; makeup, Ray Sebastian; art director, Harold MacArthur; set decorator, Sidney Clifford; music director, Mischa Bakaleinikoff; camera, Philip Tannura; editor, Aaron Stell.

William Eythe (Bert Stewart); Marjorie Reynolds (Lucille Gerrard); Griff Barnett (McGraw); Howard St. John (Charles Johnson); Jim Backus (Thomas Jacoby); Robert Shayne (J. G. Goff); Denver Pyle (Al); John Doucette (Hank); Harlan Warde (Perry); James Fairfax (Pettygill); Clark Howat (Phillips); Marya Marco (Miss Kung); Guy Kingsford (Watkins); William Phillips (Barton).

The success of THE THIRD MAN (1949) (see: B/V) emphasized the existing problem of the illegal smuggling and dilution of medicines by the black market. A number of films thereafter got on the commercial bandwagon by presenting exposes of these black marketeers; one of them was CUSTOMS AGENT.
Unreeled in a pseudo-documentary style, William Eythe starred as Bert Stewart, an American customs agent working in China on the path of drug smugglers. In reality he is following gangsters who are stealing streptomycin and diluting it and then selling the worthless drug on the illegal market. He trails the gang to the West Coast and in a showdown rounds up the illicit medicine peddlers.
Marjorie Reynolds (who gained her greatest show business fame as the sweet wife of Chester A. Riley in the long running teleseries "The Life of Riley") appeared as the blonde gang moll used to seductively sideline the no-nonsense customs agent.

THE CZAR OF BROADWAY (Universal, 1930) 60 mins.

Presenter, Carl Laemmle; director, William James Craft; story-continuity-dialog, Gene Towne; music arranger, Lou Handman; sound, C. Roy Hunter; camera, Hal Mohr; editor, Harry Lieb.

John Wray (Morton Bradley); Betty Compson (Connie Colton); John Harron (Jay Grant); Claud Allister (Francis); Wilbur Mack (Harry Foster); King Baggot (Dane Harper); Edmund Breese (McNab).

The editor of a New York City newspaper is determined to expose the activites of criminal boss Mort Bradley (John Wray) who has most of the city's press in his pay. The editor hires San Francisco newsman Jay Grant (John Harron) to work undercover on the assignment. The latter goes to the underworld czar's nightclub

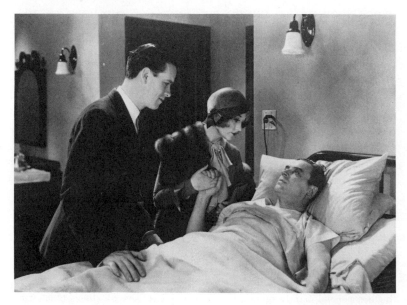

John Harron, Betty Compson, and John Wray in THE CZAR
OF BROADWAY (1930).

where he becomes friendly with Wray, who believes he is just a
country boy on the loose in the big city. When Harron falls for
Wray's ex-girlfriend (Betty Compson), the latter encourages the
romance. When Wray later finds that Harron is really a reporter,
he plans to have the reporter killed but rival mobsters shoot Wray
and his associate (Claud Allister). When Harron finds out that
Wray is dead, he destroys his expose story out of friendship for
the late crime lord. He and Compson leave the city.

Supposedly based on the life of mobster Arnold Rothstein,
Photoplay magazine labeled this film, "A not-so-good imitation of
that fine picture, STREET OF CHANCE" [q.v.]. THE CZAR OF
BROADWAY seemed more interested in its hokey subplot romance
theme than in a definitive character delineation of the big time
mobster. What might have been a top-notch gangster feature was
badly weakened by too many shrill dramatics.

DA NEW YORK: MAFIA UCCIDE see: HAIL! MAFIA

DANGER ZONE (Lippert, 1951) 55 mins.

Producer-director, William Berke; based on the radio series by

Louis Morheim, Herbert Margolis; screenplay, Julian Harmon; music, Bert Shefter; art director, F. Paul Sylos; set decorator, Harry Reif; makeup, Paul Stanhope; sound, Glen Glenn; special effects, Ray Mercer; camera, Jack Greenhalgh; editors, Carl Pierson, Harry Reynolds.

Hugh Beaumont (Dennis O'Brien); Edward Brophy (Professor Shicker); Richard Travis (Lieutenant Bruger); Tom Neal (Edgar Spadely); Pamela Blake (Vicki Jason); Virginia Dale (Claire Underwood); Ralph Sanford (Larry Dunlap); Paula Drew (Sheila Jason); Jack Reitzen (Cole); Edward Clark (Elderly Man); Richard Monahan (Henry the Bartender); Dan Garner (Bud Becker).

Private detective Dennis O'Brien (Hugh Beaumont) aids an attractive woman (Virginia Dale) to obtain a saxophone at an auction and is held up and knocked out for his trouble. Later he discovers that gangster Larry Dunlap (Ralph Sanford) took the instrument because it contains valuable jewels. Beaumont corners the gang at the local airport and brings them to justice for the murder of the instrument's real owner. Beaumont is then hired by a client (Pamela Blake) to be her escort on a yachting party and she is later blackmailed by another private eye (Tom Neal) since she is the wife of a wealthy man who turns up murdered. When the other detective is killed, Beaumont solves the caper by arresting Blake for both murders; she was after her husband's wealth.

DANGER ZONE has the honor of being the first telefeature in the United States. Originally conceived to be aired on TV, the movie was actually two segments of an unsold video series starring Hugh Beaumont as a detective and Edward Brophy as his sidekick. When the series failed to sell, the segments were slapped together and sold as a theatrical feature, the vanguard of a distribution operation still in practice today. As a theatrical release, Variety judged, "High voltage title but strictly low-juiced otherwise." Released simultaneously with DANGER ZONE were PIER 23 and ROARING CITY, each composed of two segments of the unsold series. Following their theatrical showings, the episodes were then aired on TV in their original form.

DANGEROUS BUSINESS see: PARTY GIRL (1930)

DANGEROUS MISSION (RKO, 1954) 75 mins.

Producer, Irwin Allen; director, Louis King; story, Horace McCoy, James Edmiston; screenplay, McCoy, W. R. Burnett, Charles Bennett; music, Roy Webb; camera, William Snyder; editor, Gene Palmer.

Victor Mature (Matt Hallett); Piper Laurie (Louise Graham); William Bendix (Joe Parker); Vincent Price (Paul Adams); Betta St. John (Mary Tiller); Steve Darrell (Katoonai); Marlo Dwyer (Mrs. Elster);

Walter Reed (Dobson); Dennis Weaver (Pruitt); Harry Cheshire (Elster); George Sherwood (Mr. Jones); Maureen Stephenson (Mrs. Jones); Fritz Apking (Hawthorne); Ken Dibbs (Johnny Yonkers); John Carlyle (Bellhop); Frank Griffin (Tedd); Trevor Bardette (Kicking Bear); Roy Engel (Hume); Grace Hayle (Mrs. Alvord); Jim Potter (Cobb); Sam Shack, Craig Moreland, Ralph Volkie, Mike Lally (Firefighters).

A young woman, Louise Graham (Piper Laurie) witnesses a mobster-staged murder in New York City and to save her own life flees west to a remote tourist hotel at Glacier National Park. Two men arrive on the scene, both of whom show a strong interest in her. One of them is Matt Hallett (Victor Mature), actually a New York undercover policeman sent to protect the girl, while the other is Paul Adams (Vincent Price), a syndicate gang member dispatched to silence her. In the meantime, Laurie is drawn into a local murder case after befriending Indian girl Mary Tiller (Betta St. John), whose father is a murder suspect hunted by Park Ranger Joe Parker (William Bendix) with St. John being romanced by Price.

Shot in 3-D and color on location at Glacier National Park, this potboiler had little to offer besides scenics and a good cast wasted in a mundane storyline. Although action was injected in the form of such tried-and-true methods as forest fires, chases through rough terrain, falling power lines, and an avalanche, the three-dimensional movie lacked juice.

DARK MOUNTAIN (Paramount, 1944) 56 mins.

Producers, William Pine-William Thomas; director, William Berke; story, Paul Franklin, Charles Royal; screenplay, Maxwell Shane; art director, F. Paul Sylos; assistant director, Nat Merman; sound, Ferol Redd; camera, Fred Jackman, Jr.; editor, Henry Adams.

Robert Lowery (Don Bradley); Ellen Drew (Kay Downey); Regis Toomey (Steve Downey); Eddie Quillan (Willie); Elisha Cook, Jr. (Whitey); Ralph Dunn (Sanford); Walter Baldwin (Uncle Sam); Rose Plummer (Aunt Pattie); Virginia Sale (Althea); Byron Foulger (Harvery Bales); John Fisher (Hunk); Alex Callan (Dave Lewis); Eddie Kane (Waiter); Angelos Desfia (Bookkeeper).

Produced by the Pine-Thomas economy unit at Paramount, DARK MOUNTAIN is a nifty thriller which demonstrates how good a low budget feature can be, even when modestly budgeted. Outside of its early nightclub sequence, the film has only a small, but highly competent cast and most of its footage is set in a forest locale, providing visual interest. Veteran actor Regis Toomey offers one of the best performances of his long career as the smooth, "honest" businessman who turns out to be a murderous criminal, while Ellen Drew is fetching as the heroine and Robert Lowery makes a reliable hero.

Regis Toomey, Ellen Drew, Robert Lowery, and Eddie Quillan in
DARK MOUNTAIN (1944).

Comely Kay Downey (Drew) drops her romance with a forest
ranger (Lowery) to marry a man (Toomey) in the shipping business.
Too late, she finds out her mate is actually a gangster involved in
the illegal shipment of stolen goods. After he commits a murder and
is hunted by the law, they take refuge in a remote mountain cabin
in an area patroled by the girl's ex-beau. Toomey threatens to kill
Drew if she does not help him make a getaway, but Lowery rescues
her. After a wild chase over curving and dangerous mountain
passes, Toomey dies when his speeding car is wrecked.
    To add authenticity to the film, the producers hired the super-
visor of the Tahoe National Forest, Guerdon Ellis, a U.S. Forest
Service employee, to instruct the lead players on the technical details of Forest Service activities.

DARK STREETS (First National, 1929) 55 mins.

Producer, Ned Marin; director, Frank Lloyd; story, Richard Connell; adaptor-dialogue, Bradley King; camera, Ernest Hallor; editor,
Edward Schroeder.

Jack Mulhall (Pat McGlone/Danny McGlone)l Lila Lee (Katie Dean);
Aggie Herring (Mrs. Dean); Earl Pingree (Cuneo); Will Walling

Jack Mulhall in a dual role in DARK STREETS (1929).

(Police Captain); E. H. Calvert (Police Lieutenant); Maurice Black (Beefy Barker); Lucien Littlefield (Census Taker); and: Pat Harmon.

Although extremely dated by today's standards, DARK STREETS was an important motion picture in its day since it was one of the first times an actor, in this case Jack Mulhall, performed dual roles in a talking picture. Further, it is the first gangster sound feature to attempt this feat, thus paving the way for such future portrayals. Thanks to Mulhall's smooth characterizations as the TWO brothers, DARK STREETS remains a special landmark in the gangster film genre.

Twin brothers Pat McGlone, a policeman, and Danny, a small-time hood (both played by Mulhall), love pretty Katie (Lila Lee), the daughter of their foster mother (Aggie Herring). Danny's gang pulls off a warehouse robbery and Pat is on the scene and shoots the getaway truck's driver and spots Danny in the vehicle. The gang plans to murder Pat and exchanges clothes with him. The gang shoots and kills Danny, believing they have eliminated his policeman brother.

THE DEAD EYES OF LONDON (Magna Pictures, 1965) 104 mins.

Executive producer, Horst Wendlandt; producer, Herbert Sennewald; director; Alfred Vohrer; based on the novel by Edgar Wallace; screenplay, Trygve Larsen; art director, Mathias Matthies; music, Heinz Funk; camera, Karl Lob; editor, Ina Orberg.

Joachim Fuchsberger (Inspector Larry Holt); Karin Baal (Nora Ward); Dieter Borsche (Reverend Dearborn); Wolfgang Lukschy (Steven Judd); Eddi Arent (Sergeant Harvey); Klaus Kinski (Jack); and: Harry Wustenhagen, Adi Berber, Bobby Todd, Rudolf Fenner, Ann Savo, Hans Paetsch, Ida Ehre, Fritz Schroder-Jahn, Walter Ladengast.

Several people are found dead in London and all of them are heavily insured. Scotland Yard assigns Inspector Larry Holt (Joachim Fuchsberger) to investigate the cases and he traces the killings to the Dead Eyes of London, an organization of blind peddlers. With the aid of a former nurse (Karin Baal) who has worked with the blind, Fuchsberger ferrets out that the leader (Dieter Borsche) of the peddlers who has been paying them to commit the killings since his insurance company has obtained huge premiums from the intended victims.

Based on Edgar Wallace's 1924 novel, The Dark Eyes of London, and a remake of the 1939 feature film (see THE HUMAN MONSTER q.v.) starring Bela Lugosi, this West German melodrama is a flavorful adaptation of the Wallace work. The motion picture was issued originally in West Germany in 1961 under the title DIE TOTEN AUGEN VON LONDON.

DEAD WRONG (Comworld International, 1983) C 93 mins.

Executive producer, Tony Parsons; producer-director, Len Kowalewich; screenplay, Ron Graham; music, Karl Kobylansky; art director, Ian Thomas; costumes, Trish Keating; sound, Larry Sutton; camera, Doug McKay; editor, Jana Fritsch.

Winton Rekert (Sean Phelan); Britt Eklund (Priscilla Lancaster/ Penny); Dale Wilson (Mike Brady); Jackson Davies (Inspector Fred Foster); Alex Daikun (The Stranger); Leon Bibb (Bahama Jones); Annie Kidder (Didi).

One of the few gangster movies to be produced in Canada, this $1,000,000 production (made with the aid of 50% salary deferrals from many of the production team) was the directorial debut of Canadian Broadcasting cameraman Len Kowalewich and proved to be an impressive cinema start. Add the fine cinematography by Doug McKay and a fairly gripping updating of themes from TREASURE OF THE SIERRA MADRE (1948) and the result is a compact, appealing thriller.

Fisherman Sean Phelan (Winston Rekert) is tied into smugglers due to an obligation to his friend (Dale Wilson). Rekert agrees to aid dope traffickers in bringing cocaine and marijuana from Colombia. The Canadian Mounties, however, are aware of this smuggling and set a trap for the mobsters, using agent Penny (Britt Eklund) to infiltrate the outlaw team; but she soon is romancing the duped skipper. There is a showdown between the mob and the country's armed forces.

DEADLINE--U.S.A. (Twentieth Century-Fox, 1952) 87 mins.

Producer, Sol C. Siegel; director-screenplay, Richard Brooks; music director, Lionel Newman; music, Cyril Mockridge; orchestrator, Edward Powell; special effects, Ray Kellogg; camera, Milton Krasner; editor, William B. Murphy.

Humphrey Bogart (Ed Hutcheson); Ethel Barrymore (Mrs. Garrison); Kim Hunter (Nora); Ed Begley (Frank Allen); Warren Stevens (Burrows); Paul Stewart (Thompson); Martin Gabel (Rienzi); Joseph De Santis (Schmidt); Joyce Mackenzie (Kitty Garrison Geary); Audrey Christie (Mrs. Willebrandt); Fay Baker (Alice Garrison Courtney); Jim Backus (Cleary); Carleton Young (Crane); Selmer Jackson (Williams); Fay Roope (Judge); Parley Baer (Headwaiter); Bette Francine (Telephone Operator); John Doucette (City News Editor); June Eisner (Bentley); Richard Monohan (Copy Boy); Harry Tyler (Headline Writer); Joe Sawyer (Whitey); Florence Shirley (Barndollar); Kasia Orzazewski (Mrs. Schmidt); Raymond Greenleaf (Mr. White); Alex Gerry (Attorney Prentiss); Irene Vernon (Mrs. Burrows); William Forrest (Mr. Greene); Edward Keane (Mr. Blake); Clancy Cooper (Captain Finlay); Tom Powers (Wharton); Thomas Browne Henry (Fenway); Ashley Cowan (Lefty); Howard Negley (Police Sergeant); Phil Terry (Lewis Schaefer); Joe Mell (Lugerman); Luther Corckett (National Editor); Joseph Crehan (City Editor); Larry Dobkin (Lawyer Hansen).

Director-scripter Richard Brooks and producer Sol C. Siegel were both former newspapermen and their expertise in the field breathed tremendous authenticity into this well executed melodrama, which deals with the daily activities of a big city newspaper, with one of its subplots having the journal's editor combatting a mobster. With much on-location footage shot in the newsrooms of the New York Daily News, the movie had a fine sense of the fourth estate. According to Variety, "It tells the story of the fundamental freedoms --press, integrity and incorruptibility--without preaching. Best of all it tells its story in action and purposeful cinematurgy without piling it on."

Ed Hucheson (Humphrey Bogart) is the editor of The Day, a 300,000 daily circulation newspaper which is in financial trouble. The widow (Ethel Barrymore) of the paper's founder is at odds with her socialite daughters (Joyce Mackenzie, Fay Baker) who want to sell the property and Bogart tries to convince her to thwart her offsprings' actions. Bogart is also romancing his ex-wife (Kim Hunter) who has become engaged to her advertising agency boss. When one of his crime reporters is badly beaton by syndicate goons working for crime boss Rienzi (Martin Gabel), Bogart uses the paper's power to expose and break up the mobster's operation, which includes controlling the local boxing racket. Gabel is finally brought to justice by the mother (Kasia Orzazewski) of a hooker he has used and murdered. The mobster's activities are detailed in the newspaper, which becomes popular again and is left unsold. Bogart is also able to convince his ex-wife to break her engagement.

Tightly edited and accomplished in a semi-documentary style, DEADLINE--U.S.A. is a hard hitting, realistic melodrama all too often overlooked today. Bogart has one of his more multidimensional roles as the newspaper chief and the supporting cast includes outstanding work by Martin Gabel as the mobster and Paul Stewart, Ed Begley, and Warren Stevens as his cohorts.

DEADLY CHINA DOLL (Metro-Goldwyn-Mayer/Panasia Films, 1973) C 90 mins.

Producer, Andrew G. Vajna; director, Huang Feng; screenplay, Ho Jen; music, Joseph Koo; assistant director, Chou Hsiao Pei; camera, Li Yiu Tang/ editor, Chiang Lung.

Angela Mao (center) in DEADLY CHINA DOLL (1973).

Angela Mao (Chin Su Hua); Carter Huang (Pai Chien); Yen I-Feng
(Han Fei); Nan Kung Hsun (Wu "Scareface" Szu); Ke Hsiang Ting
(Chin); Li Hung (Wang Tsai Sa); Yi Juan (Tsai Lao Ta); Lung Fei
(Hung Hsiao Pao); Travador Ramos (Fang Ping Yang).

An Agent (Carter Huang) for the Chinese government is combating drug smuggling along the border and is also out to revenge
himself on the gangster (Nan Kung Hsun) who killed his brother.
Huang is ambushed on two occasions by the hoodlum's men and the
second time he is aided by a restaurant proprietor (Ke Hsiang Ting)
and the man's lovely hapkido expert daughter (Angela Mao). In
reality, father and daughter are also secret agents and they aid the
government man in his quest. When the truck containing the opium
arrives in town, a battle breaks out between the drug smugglers
and hijackers; the gangster leader believes the agent is responsible
for the ambush and sets out to kill him, Huang, however, finds out
the consignment is nothing more than pebbles and he plans to upset
the smugglers' plans and bring them to justice.
    This Panasia Film Production is rather typical of the kung-fu
action thrillers made in the Far East; this one nicely combines the
gangster motif. The plot of government agents, smugglers, and hijackers all doing battle over an opium shipment is intriguing. As
expected from a kung fu film, the action is hot and heavy, with the
fight sequences well staged.
    With its exotic locales, fast moving plot, and major release in
this country from Metro-Goldwyn-Mayer, DEADLY CHINA DOLL
proved to be one of the more noticeable of the kung fu thrillers.
Not hindering the matter is comely Angela Mao in the title role of
Chin Su Hua.

DEATH RAGE (S. J. International Pictures, 1976) C 98 mins.

Producer, Raymond R. Homer [Alberto Giovine]; director, Anthony
M. Dawson [Antonio Margheretti]; screenplay, Guy Castaldo; music,
Guido de Angelis; special effects, Paolo Ricco; camera, Serge
D'Offizi.

Yul Brynner (Peter Marciani); Martin Balsam (The Inspector); Barbara Bouchet (Annie); Massimo Ranieri (Angelo).

    "The hunter is about to become the hunted.... A tale of be-
trayal and revenge" ran the blurbs for this Italian-made melodrama
which was originally called SHADOW OF A KILLER. A sluggish
thriller, it was hampered by grainy photography, a muddled plot,
overloud music, and only sporadic action. While Yul Brynner was
appropriately effective in the lead role as the mechanic (hit man),
he appeared old and tired and most of the action sequences were
left to Massimo Ranieri to carry off.
    Retired hit man Peter Marciani (Brynner) leaves New York
City for Naples to kill Mafia strongman Gallo, who was responsible

for Brynner's brother's murder. The mob wants Gallo rubbed out because he has been slicing into the stateside take from Italian horse racing. Once there, Brynner meets young race track habitue Angelo (Ranieri), who also wants Gallo dead because one of his victims had been a big winner and was killed before Ranieri got his cut. Through Ranieri, Brynner meets beautiful dancer Annie (Barbara Bouchet) and the two fall in love. Gallo learns of Brynner's mission and sends his goons to capture the hit man, but Brynner eliminates them and the locale police inspector (Martin Balsam) tries to get Brynner to help put Gallo in prison. Brynner finally succeeds in his murder task, but is mortally wounded doing so. At the funeral, Ranieri shoots the Mafia man who hired Brynner to kill Gallo since that man actually paid Gallo to kill Brynner's brother. In the end, Ranieri becomes Brynner's mob replacement.

THE DEATH SQUAD (ABC-TV, 1/8/74) C 78 mins.

Producers, Aaron Spelling, Leonard Goldberg; associate producer, Parke Perine; director, Harry Falk; teleplay, James D. Buchanan, Robert Austin; music, Dave Grusin; art director, Tracy Bousman; camera, Tim Southcott; editor, Stefan Arnsten.

Robert Forster (Eric Benoit); Michelle Phillips (Joyce Kreski); Claude Akins (Connie Brennan); Mark Goddard (Allen Duke); Melvyn Douglas (Captain Earl Kreski); Kenneth Tobey (Hartman); George Murdock (Vern Acker); Jesse Vint (Harmon); Stephen Young (Lieutenant Andrece); Julie Cobb (Sharon); Bert Remsen (The Chief); Dennis Patrick (The Commissioner); Janis Hansen (Dispatcher); Nate Esformes (Pela); Regis J. Cordic (Judge); Sidney Clute (Driver); Jeanne Byron (Commissioner's Wife); Claire Brennan (Waitress Max); Nick Dennis (Greek); Mel Scott (Officer); Ian Scott (Gunman); Trish Mahoney (Woman); Buddy Garion (Staley); Sally Frei (Girl).

"They were honest cops ... until they started their own war on crime and became judge and jury and executioner.... He was the one cop who stood in their way." Thus read the blurbs advertising this ABC-TV telefeature, which was very similar in theme to Clint Eastwood's theatrical feature, MAGNUM FORCE (q.v.). Critical reaction to the telefilm varied. TV Movies (1985) rated it "below average" while Movies on TV (1985) called it "a strong police yarn."

The film was the account of ex-cop Eric Benoit (Robert Forster) who has been dismissed from the force, later being called back to undercover duty by Captain Kreski (Melvyn Douglas) when the latter finds that a group of policemen in his precinct have banded together and are methodically killing alleged criminals who have been released by the court on technicalities. It is Forster's duty to infiltrate the "death squad" and bring them to justice.

Charles Bronson in DEATH WISH (1974).

DEATH WISH (Paramount, 1974) C 92 mins.

Executive producer, Dino De Laurentiis; producers, Hal Landers, Bobby Roberts; co-producer-director, Michael Winner; based on the novel by Brian Garfield; screenplay, Wendell Mayes; music, Herbie Hancock; production designer, Robert Gundlach; set decorator, George DeTitta; assistant director, Charles Okun; sound, Hugh Strain, James Sabat; camera, Arthur J. Ornitz; editor, Bernard Gribble.

Charles Bronson (Paul Kersey); Hope Lange (Joanna Kersey); Vincent Gardenia (Detective Ochoa); Steven Keats (Jack Toby); William Redfield (Sam Kreutzer); Stuart Margolin (Aimes Jianchill); Stephen Elliott (Police Commissioner); Kathleen Tolan (Carol Toby); Jack Wallace (Hank); Fred Scollay (District Attorney); Robert Kya-Hill (Officer Charles); Jeff Goldberg, Christopher Logan, Gregory Rozakis (Muggers).

DEATH WISH II (Filmways, 1982) C 93 mins.

Executive producers, Hal Landers, Bobby Roberts; producers, Manhem Golan, Yoram Globus; director, Michael Winner; based on characters created by Brian Garfield; screenplay, David Engelbach; production designer, William Hiney; assistant director, Russell

Vreeland; music, Jimmy Page; camera, Richard H. Kline, Tom Del
Ruth; editors, Arnold Crust, Julian Semilian.

Charles Bronson (Paul Kersey); Jill Ireland (Geri Nichols); Vincent
Gardenia (Frank Ochoa); J. D. Cannon (New York District Attorney);
Anthony Franciosa (L.A. Police Commissioner); Ben Frank (Lieutenant
Mankiewicz); Robin Sherwood (Carol Kersey); Silvano Gillardo (Ro-
sario); Robert F. Lyons (Fred McKenzie); Michael Prince (Elliott
Cass); Drew Synder (Deputy Commissioner Hawkins); Paul Lambert
(New York Police Commissioner); Thomas Duffy (Nirvana); Kevyn
Major Howard (Stomper); Stuart I. Robinson (Jiver); Laurence Fish-
burne III (Cutter); E. Lamont Johnson (Punkcut).

DEATH WISH III (Cannon, 1985) C 90 mins.

Producers, Menahem Golan, Yoram Globus; co-producer, Michael

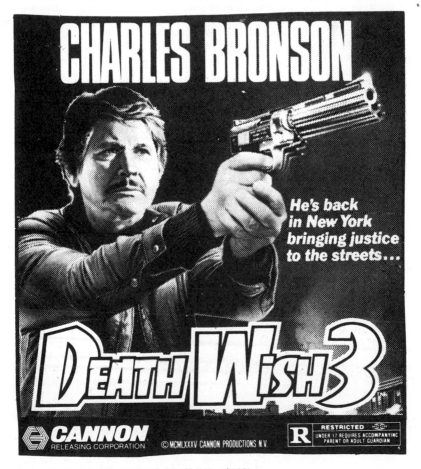

Advertisement for DEATH WISH III (1985).

Winner; associate producer, Michael Kagan; director, Winner; based
on characters created by Brian Garfield; screenplay, Michael Ed-
monds; production designer, Peter Mullins; art directors, David
Minty, James Taylor; set decorators, Robin Tarsnane, Gretchen Rau;
costumes, Peggy Farrell; makeup, Richard Mills, Carla White; stung
coordinators, Marc Boyle, Ernest Orsatti, Harry Hadsen; music,
Jimmy Page; sound, Derek Ball, William Daly; camera, John Stanier;
editor, Arnold Crust.

Charles Bronson (Paul Kersey); Deborah Raffin (Kathryn Davis);
Ed Lauter (Richard S. Shriker); Martin Balsam (Bennett); Gavan
O'Herlihy (Fraker); Kirk Taylor (Giggler); Alex Winter (Hermosa);
Tony Spiridakis (Angel); Ricco Ross (The Cuban); Tony Britts
(Tulio); Joseph Gonzalez (Rodriguez); Francis Drake (Charley);
Marina Sirtis (Maria); Nelson Fernandez (Chaco); Alan Cooke, Bob
Dysinger (Punks at Car); Barbie Wilde (Female Punk); Ron Hayes
(Lieutenant); Jery Phillips (Street Punk); Birdie M. Hale (Mugging
Victim); Dinah May, Steffanie Pitt (Nurses); Billy J. Mitchell (Frak-
er's Lawyer); Lee Patterson (TV Newscaster); Olivia Ward (Protest-
ing Lady); Mark Stewart, Nick D'Aviorro, Peter Banks, Tom Hun-
singer, Mac McDonald, Sam Douglas, William Roberts, Ralph Mopnaco,
Joe Cirillo (Policemen).

   The DEATH WISH series is among the most controversial in the
gangster film genre. The initial 1974 release of DEATH WISH proved
to be the vanguard of a host of action melodramas in which the hero
eliminates all types of vermin to protect himself, his family, and his
community. To the average grassroots American, and especially the
urban dweller besieged by street crime, Charles Bronson as Paul
Kersey in the DEATH WISH sagas became a knight in shining armor,
the vicarious character by whom each person could live out the
dream of fighting back and successfully destroying the type of scum
who make life unbearable. Filmgoers took these no-nonsense looks
at the individual combatting crime to their hearts, and the result
was big box office. Some critics and many vocal liberals denounced
the vividly violent films as anarchic in nature. But the best reply
to them came from star Charles Bronson himself when he stated, "We
don't make movies for critics, since they don't pay to see them any-
how."
   DEATH WISH is set in New York City of the 1970s and centers
around mild-mannered, politically liberal architect Paul Kersey (Bronson), an upper middleclass apartment dweller who is happy with his
job and only slightly concerned about the rampant street violence
around him. When brutal thugs (Jeff Goldberg, Christopher Logan)
break into his apartment and attack his wife (Hope Lange), who
dies as a result, and rape his married daughter (Kathleen Tolan),
leaving her permanently mentally scarred, Bronson is afraid yet revengeful. The police are impotent in finding the thugs and after
returning from a business trip to Arizona, Bronson finds he is the
owner of a handgun (an illegal act in New York City) given to him
by a client. Bronson begins to respond to the violence around him,

first by hitting a would-be mugger with a sock full of coins and
then by hunting and killing street thugs with his gun. His actions
make him known as "the vigilante" and the police fear he will ignite
a whole scale war on criminals which they will not be able to control.
Police Inspector Frank Ochoa (Vincent Gardenia) locates Bronson but
instead of arresting him, which would make his identity known and
cause him to be a greater hero, he is asked to leave town.

Critical reaction to the film was decidedly mixed, although its
box-office, both here and abroad, was potent. Writing in New York
magazine, Judith Crist termed the movie "a first-rate suspenser"
while in the New York Daily News Rex Reed wrote, "DEATH WISH
is a complex and startlingly original film that will anger and pro-
voke, but its most important questions are the ones it raises about
ourselves." On the other hand, Vincent Canby complained in The
New York Times, "The movie seems to have been made for no reason
except to exploit its audience's urban paranoia and vestigial fascina-
tion with violence for its own sake."

DEATH WISH was based on Brian Garfield's book. He did not
care for the movie version's open advocacy of vigilantism, and when
CBS-TV planned to air it in prime time he unsuccessfully asked the
network not to do so because he was afraid it might make the wrong
impression on those with immature minds. On the other hand it is
reported that when the movie first played in Manhattan, audiences
literally stood up and applauded when Bronson gunned down his
first street thug.

DEATH WISH II moved its locale to Los Angeles (the first
film ended with Bronson planning to start anew in Chicago) where
he now works for a large architectural concern and keeps company
with pretty TV news commentator Geri Nichols (Jill Ireland). One
day the two accompany Bronson's still mentally ill daughter (Robin
Sherwood) to an amusement park where they are harassed by a
group of young punks who steal Bronson's wallet. They find his
address and go there and rape and murder his housekeeper (Silvana
Gillardo). When Bronson and Sherwood arrive home they knock him
out and kidnap the girl, who they take to a deserted warehouse and
molest before she impales herself on a fence trying to escape. Again
the police are incompetent in trying to solve the crime and Bronson
takes up his gun and heads to the skid row section of Los Angeles
and systematically tracks down and kills the attackers one by one.
After several such homicides, in one of which he saves a couple
being tortured by thugs in a parking garage, the police commissioner (Anthony Franciosa) calls in New York's Inspector Ochoa
(Gardenia) for assistance. Gardenia soon suspects Bronson is at
work. He tracks him to a secluded area one night where the architect has gone to ambush one of the wrongdoers, and in a shootout
Gardenia saves Bronson's life but is himself mortally wounded. When
the last thug is let go by the courts and sent to a mental hospital,
Bronson takes measures to break into the facility and, posing as a
doctor, he confronts the criminal. During a fight in which he is
injured, the patient is electrocuted by shock treatment equipment.
Bronson escapes only to return home to find that Ireland has found
out the truth about his activities and has left him.

DEATH WISH II is a superbly executed sequel; one which continues the story smoothly. Like the initial entry, it resulted in solid box office and proved very popular, especially in mid-America. The film's finale is a real knockout, with Bronson's shadow silhouetted against a tenement building as he continues his "hunt."

When plans were announced for DEATH WISH III in 1984, star Charles Bronson vetoed the script and for a spell the producers considered using Chuck Norris in the main role, but script revisions made the production palatable and superstar Bronson again took on the mantle of Paul Kersey for this London-filmed outing.

This time architect Bronson has returned to the East and is living quietly just outside New York City. When an old neighborhood pal (Martin Balsam) living in East New York is attacked by muggers and nearly killed, Bronson returns home and finds that the street scum control the area. The police, however, take him into custody and a district attorney (Deborah Raffin) warns him not to renew his vigilante activities. He agrees but later the woman, while visiting the neighborhood, is brutally attacked by criminals. Bronson unites the decent citizens of the war zone into a vigilante group and they start cleaning up the territory. At the finale, the District Attorney agrees with Bronson that a gun is the only kind of rehabilitation a hardened hoodlum understands. By this time, as the Hollywood Reporter noted, "the body count at times seems to rival the gross national product." The largest flaw of this entry is that the motivation for Bronson's killing rampage is far less personal or real than in the two prior editions.

The success of the DEATH WISH trio stems from two ingredients: the strong sense of fighting back at criminals and wanton crime the movies instill in the average viewer, and the magnetism of macho star Bronson. Regarding the latter, Bruce Williamson best summed it up in Playboy magazine when he reviewed the initial episode: "By touching an exposed nerve in fearful contemporary America, director [Michael] Winner has handed granite-faced Bronson the role most likely to show moviegoers at home what European audiences saw in him ages ago--a rough-cut superstar and folk-hero par excellence!"

DESERT FURY (Paramount, 1947) C 94 mins.

Producer, Hal B. Wallis; director, Lewis Allen; based on the novel by Ramona Stewart; screenplay, Robert Rossen; music, Miklos Rozsa; assistant director, Dick McWhorter; art director, Perry Ferguson; set decorators, Sam Comer, Syd Moore; sound, Harry Lindgren; camera, Charles Lang, Edward Cronjager; editor, Warren Low.

John Hodiak (Eddie Bendix); Lizabeth Scott (Paula Haller); Burt Lancaster (Tom Hanson); Wendell Corey (Johnny Ryan); Mary Astor (Fritzie Haller); Kristine Miller (Claire Lindquist); William Harrigan (Judge Berle Lindquist); James Flavin (Pat Johnson); Jane Novak (Mrs. Lindquist); Ana Camargo (Rose).

Wendell Corey, John Hodiak, Lizabeth Scott, and Ray Teal in
DESERT FURY (1947).

DESERT FURY is an offbeat gangster melodrama with a convoluted plot and a hectic background. Producer Hal B. Wallis first
planned the production in 1946, but after intended supporting player
Burt Lancaster made such an impression in THE KILLERS (see:
B/V), Wallis had Lancaster's role expanded in the new film.   He
further garnered publicity by casting his "favorite" Lizabeth Scott
as the co-star, and before filming started, had them team as guest
performers in the all-star Paramount revue, VARIETY GIRL (1947).
Wendell Corey made his film debut in this production.   When DES-
ERT FURY was finally released it was something of an enigma, a
brooding film noir-type melodrama with flashy performances, Techni-
color, and a turgid plot.   And for all the rewriting and expanding,
Lancaster's part was still the least viable of the picture's five leads.
        In Nevada, one-time madame Fritzie Haller (Mary Astor), now
the owner of a gambling casino, is at odds with her nineteen-year-
old rebellious daughter Paula (Scott).   A gangster, Eddie Bendix
(John Hodiak), on the lam with his bodyguard (Wendell Corey),
takes refuge in a nearby cabin and renews his acquaintance with
old flame Astor; but now he is more attracted to Scott, who is also
courted by local lawman Tom Hanson (Lancaster).   Friction develops
not only between Astor and her daughter over the latter's relationship with the mobster, but also between Scott and Lancaster and
the gangster and his "protective" gunman.   Scott is eventually reunited with Lancaster following the shooting death of Hodiak.

Beautiful desert locales and well etched character delineations are the main assets of this flashy melodrama. Mary Astor easily steals the show as the glamorous but earthy Fritzie, while Wendell Corey made his screen debut as the brooding gunman whose relationship with his boss appears to be multi-faceted.

DETROIT 9000 (General Film, 1983) C 108 mins.

Executive producers, Donald Gottlieb, William Siberkleit, Junius Griffin; producerk Charles Stroud; director, Arthur Marks; screenplay, Orville Hampton; music, Luchi de Jesus and Holland; camera, Harry May.

Alex Rocco (Lieutenant Danny Basset); Hari Rhodes (Sergeant Jesse Williams); Vonetta McGee (Roby Hrris); Ella Edwards (Helen Duebin); Scatman Crothers (Reverend Markham); John Nichols, Martha Jean (Themselves).

One of the motifs of the gangster film genre has been to set the stories of police versus mobsters in various U.S. urban locales, although in Hollywood's heyday these cities were backlot affairs with perhaps on-location shots for added realism. Since the demise of the studio system, most such features have been lensed on location, such as MODERN DAY HOUDINI (q.v.) in Indianapolis and this outing done in Detroit. The digits following the city's name in the title refer to the code for a police officer in trouble.

Although termed a black exploitation feature, DETROIT 9000 is actually a well integrated feature with white actor Alex Rocco sharing star billing with black thespian Hari Rhodes, both playing Detroit cops on the trail of jewel thieves. The gangsters employ an Indian fence from Canada to help them carry out a big jewel heist, but the man is then murdered and the two cops, Lieutenant Danny Basset (Rocco) and Sergeant Jesse Williams (Rhodes), get after the gang, with Rocco eventually getting the money from the robbery before being gunned down.

Full of typical genre action and loaded with requisite blood and gore, DETROIT 9000 contains a subplot about the first black candidate for governor of Michigan, whose fundraiser is victimized by the hoodlums, and various Detroit personalities, such as TV interviewer Martha Jean and then police commissioner John Nichols, who was a candidate for Motor City mayor.

DEVIL'S HARBOR (Twentieth Century-Fox, 1954) 70 mins.

Producer, Charles Deane; director, Montgomery Tully; screenplay, Charles Deane; camera, Geoffrey Faithful; editor, Peter Seabourne.

Richard Arlen (John); Greta Gynt (Peggy); Donald Houston (Mallard); Mary Germaine (Margaret); Elspeth Gray (Mrs. Mallord);

Mary Germaine and Richard Arlen in DEVIL'S HARBOR (1954).

Vincent Ball (Williams); Howard Lang (Marne); Anthony Vicars (Inspector Hunt); Edwin Richfield (Daller); Michael Balfour (Bennett); Arnold Adrian (Mark); Sidney Bromley (Enson); Stuart Saunders (Ryan); Patricia Salonika (Pat); Doreen Holliday (Susie); Peter Bernard (Sam).

John (Richard Arlen), an American running a freight boat on London's Thames River, accidentally receives a package containing stolen cortisone. The gangsters who purloined the valuable medicine are out to retrieve it and Arlen meets a pretty lady (Greta Gynt) who aids him when the hoodlums discover his whereabouts. Eventually the boatman teams with the police and the leader (Vincent Ball) of the mobsters is exposed. While fighting with Arlen on top of an empty warehouse, Ball tumbles to his death in the Thames.

Released in Great Britain by Monarch in 1954 as DEVIL'S POINT, this Richard Arlen starrer received major distribution in the U.S. the same year by Twentieth Century-Fox as DEVIL'S HARBOR. Overall the film is nothing more than a run-of-the-mill production bolstered by charismatic Arlen as the innocent man caught between lawbreakers and the law. This picture was the first of two starring vehicles the actor made in England; the other was STOLEN TIME (1955), which was released here by Allied Artists in 1958 as BLONDE BLACKMAILER and had Arlen as a dupe released from jail after serving seven years for a crime he did not commit and his attempt to clear his name. He meets pretty black-mailer (Susan Shaw) and soon becomes entangled with hoodlums and murder.

THE DEVIL'S PARTY (Universal, 1938) 62 mins.

Producer, Edmund Grainger; director, Ray McCarey; based on the novel Hell's Kitchen Has a Party by Borden Chase; screenplay, Roy Chanslor; musical director, Charles Previn; song, Jimmy McHugh and Harold Adamson; camera, Milton Krasner; editor, Philip Cahn.

Victor McLaglen (Marty Malone); William Gargan (Mike O'Mara); Paul Kelly (Jerry Donovan); Beatrice Roberts (Helen McCoy); Frank Jenks (Sam); John Gallaudet (Joe O'Mara); Samuel S. Hinds (Justice Harrison); Joseph Downing (Frank Diamond); Arthur Hoyt (Webster).

Four street youths become fast pals and agree to meet annually as the years pass to renew their friendship. One of them, Marty Malone, however, is arrested on an arson charge and sent to reform school and he grows up (as played by Victor McLaglen) to be a cardsharp and the owner of a nightclub. The others, Mike O'Mara (William Gargan), Joe O'Mara (John Gallaudet), and Jerry Donovan (Paul Kelly), mature into useful members of society with the first two becoming policemen and the third a priest. When McLaglen sends two of his henchmen to collect a gambling debt, murder results and the two policemen investigate the case, with Gallaudet being killed. With the assistance of the priest, McLaglen sees the error of his ways and sacrifices himself in the name of justice.

It was a popular theme of 1930s films to trace a group of friends from childhood to adulthood (and, for some of them, to death). And because the naturalistic theory that environment shapes personalities was such a strong part of Depression-era thinking, films such as this were created in the name of morality (and of course hopefully resulted in profitable entertainments).

DICK TRACY RETURNS (Republic, 1938) fifteen chapters

Associate producer, Robert Beche; directors, William Witney, John English; based on the cartoon by Chester Gould; screenplay, Barry Shipman, Franklyn Adreon, Ronald Davidson, Rex Taylor, Sol Shor; music, Alberto Colombo; camera, William Nobles; editors, Helene Turner, Edward Todd.

Ralph Byrd (Dick Tracy); Lynn Roberts (Gwen); Charles Middleton (Pa Stark); Jerry Tucker (Junior); David Sharpe (Ron Merton); Lee Ford (Mike McGurk); Michael Kent (Steve); John Merton (Champ); Raphael Bennett (Trigger); Jack Roberts (Dude); Ned Glass (The Kid); Edward Foster (Joe Hanner); Alan Gregg (Snub); Reed Howes

(Rance); Robert Terry (Reynolds); Tom Seidel (Hunt); Jack Ingram (Slasher).

Chapters: 1) The Sky Wreckers; 2) The Runway of Death; 3) Handcuffed to Doom; 4) Four Seconds to Live; 5) Death in the Air; 6) Stolen Secrets; 7) Tower of Death; 8) Cargo of Destruction; 9) The Clock of Doom; 10) High Voltage; 11) The Kidnapped Witness; 12) The Runaway Torpedo; 13) Passengers to Doom; 14) In the Hands of the Enemy; 15) G-Men's Dragnet.

Following the success of Republic's 1937 cliffhanger DICK TRACY, based on Chester Gould's comic strip, the studio devised DICK TRACY RETURNS in which Ralph Byrd repeated his outstanding work in the title role. As a result, "DICK TRACY RETURNS was a more polished serial than its predecessor, because it was made a crucial year after DICK TRACY, and primarily due to the directing team of William Witney and John English. It provided much action that could be later reused in the further serial adventures of DICK TRACY. Its main drawback was in the use of economy chapters." (Jim Harmon, Donald F. Glut, The Great Movie Serials, 1972).
 The story has G-Man Dick Tracy (Byrd) and recruit Ron Merton (David Sharpe) sent to the West Coast to combat the terrorism caused by the notoroius Stark family gang, headed by the murderous Pa Stark (Charles Middleton). The Starks murder the recruit, but Byrd captures the youngest family member (Ned Glass) and one by one eliminates the other brothers until only Middleton and Champ (John Merton) remain alive. The G-men trap the duo in their hideout, an abandoned rock crushing plant, and Merton is killed but Middleton, threatening to blow up everyone with nitroglycerin, forces Byrd into a plane. At a high altitude, the G-man barrel rolls the plane over and parachutes to safety, while Middleton is killed in the plane crash.
 Based on the real-life exploits of Ma Barker and her killer brood, with the main villain changed to a man, DICK TRACY RETURNS was a straight-out gangster serial. Unlike most of the "Dick Tracy" cliffhangers and features, it did not resort to science fiction plot ploys to carry the storyline.
 Following this adventure, Dick Tracy remained with the FBI for his next serial, DICK TRACY'S G-MEN (see: B/V).

DR. MABUSE, THE GAMBLER see: DR. MABUSE, DER SPIELER

DR. MABUSE, DER SPIELER (Ufa, 1922) 122 mins.

Director, Fritz Lang; based on the novel by Norbert Jacques; screenplay, Lang, Thea Von Harbou; art directors, Carl Starl-Urach, Otto Hunte, Erich Kettelhut, Karl Vollbrecht; costumes, Vally Reinecke; camera, Carl Hoffmann.

Gertrude Welcker, Rudolf Klein-Rogge, Alfred Abel in DR. MABUSE, DER SPIELER (1922).

Rudolph Klein-Rogge (Dr. Mabuse); Gertrude Weicker (Contess Stolst); Aud Egede Nissen (Cara); Alfred Abel (Count Told); Bernhard Goetzke (Wenk); Paul Richter (Edgar Hull).

Part 1: Der Grosse Spieler--ein Bild der Zeit; Part 2: Inferno--ein Spiel von Menschen unserer Zeit

Fritz Lang's two-part silent feature DR. MABUSE is considered one of the classic crime melodramas of the post-World War I German cinema. With its contemporary setting and lack of reliance on expressionistic sets which were popular in German movies of that era, this movie is a wonderful recreation of the chaotic world of Germany following its defeat in World War I. Based on Norbert Jacques' 1921 novel, Dr. Mabuse, der Spieler (Dr. Mabuse, the Gambler), the movie ran in excess of two hours each when originally issued in two separate parts. While the British and French versions of the motion picture were close to the German original, the U.S. version was badly mutilated and condensed into one 90-minute feature when issued here in 1927. Later this version was re-released as THE FATAL PASSIONS.

The idea of a master criminal, a man of many disguises, was nothing new to literature or the cinema: Sir Arthur Conan Doyle's Professor Moriarity predated Dr. Mabuse by several decades. Still,

the larger-than-life Mabuse struck a cord with European cinema
goers and most likely the character was seen as a sign of the
decadence so prevalent in postwar Europe, especially Germany.
While appearing a bit vapid when viewed today, DR. MABUSE made
a tremendous impression at the time of its release and is still one
of the best recalled European gangster movies of the Twenties.

The evil Dr. Mabuse (Rudolph Klein-Rogge) has the power to
hypnotize his victims. He controls a vast secret organization made
up of thieves, murderers, and counterfeiters, and he has acquired
a vast fortune through illegal means and by his manipulation of
others. The public prosecutor (Bernhard Goetzke) is investigating
the area's gambling dens and suspects that the two men who cheated
a young man (Paul Ritcher), actually hypnotized by Klein-Rogge,
are really the same person.

In disguise, the prosecutor goes to a gambling club where
Klein-Rogge nearly hypnotizes him and there he meets Countess
Told (Gertrude Welcker) for whom he develops an affection although
she is married to a man (Alfred Abel) who is a gambling victim of
the arch criminal. Klein-Rogge attempts to murder the prosecutor,
but fails. When the police raid his gambling den, Klein-Rogge later
kidnaps the countess to take the place of his favorite dancer (Aud
Egede Nissen) who is murdered. Part I ends here.

The second section opens with the bombing of the prosecutor's
office and the suicide of the Count. The prosecutor talks with the
deceased's psychiatrist, actually Dr. Mabuse, who suggests he witness a performance by a hypnotist (also Mabuse). During the show
Klein-Rogge hypnotizes the prosecutor into committing suicide in his
speeding car, but the police save him and they return to raid Mabuse's hideout. The latter escapes through the sewers to the work-
room of his counterfeiters. There he goes mad and imagines he is
surrounded by all the people whom he has cheated and murdered.
The deranged fiend is taken off to a mental institution.

In An Illustrated History of the Horror Film (1967), Carlos
Clarens wrote that DR. MABUSE "... has an aura of timeless evil
and total corruption that has lost none of its power today. Mabuse,
the arch-criminal, rules the decadent, bankrupt city from behind
multifarious disguises: we see him as a banker, psychiatrist, gambler and drunken sailor. Although he plots to plunge the nation
into chaos by putting counterfeit money into circulation, Mabuse's
first aim in life seems to be the total control of the people who come
into contact with him." In many ways, this continental mastermind
is the precursor of the Chicago gang lords so popular in Thirties'
cinema of Hollywood.

DOG DAY (UGC, 1984) C 104 mins.

Producer, Norbert Saada; director, Yves Boisset; based on the
novel by Jean Herman [Jean Vautrin]; screenplay, Boisset, Michel
Audiard, Dominique Roulet, Serge Korber, Herman; art director,
Jacques Dugied; music, Francis Lai; costumes, Rosine Lan; makeup,

Joel Lavau; sound, Jean-Louis Ducarme; camera, Jean Boffety; editor, Albert Jurgenson.

Lee Marvin (Jimmy Cobb); Miou-Miou (Jessica); Victor Lanaux (Horace); Jean Carmet (Socrate); David Bennet (Chim); Tina Louise (Noemie Blue); Bernadette Lafont (Segolene); Jean-Pierre Kalfon (Torontopoulos); Grace de Capitani (Lily); Henry Guybet (Marceau); Pierre Clementi (Snake); Jean-Calude Breyfus (Le Barrec).

Old-time American gangster Jimmy Cobb (Lee Marvin) is the head of a gang of French crooks stealing loot from a delivery truck at a small-town French bank. Deliberately leading the gang into a police ambush, Marvin escapes with the money and is chased through rural France by the police using helicopters and dogs. He finds refuge with a pig farm family which includes a lecherous father (Victor Lanoux), his passive wife (Miou-Miou), his nymphomaniacal crippled sister (Bernadette Lafont), his brother (Jean Carmet), and the family's young son (David Bennet), who is immersed in the gangster tradition. The two brothers, however, take Marvin as their prisoner and he murders the sister when she tries to seduce him. The wife attempts to help him escape, but she does so in the hope he will kill her husband. With the police closing in and with no hope of escape, Marvin commits suicide and the youth takes the credit for his demise.

The primary interest of this French production (originally released as CANILOUE) is Lee Marvin's interpretation of the lead role. His performance is reminiscent of his screen work in the genre in the 1950s and the 1960s.

DOG DAY AFTERNOON (Warner Bros., 1975) C 130 mins.

Producers, Martin Bregman, Martin Elfand; director, Sidney Lumet; based on the article by P. F. Kluge; screenplay, Frank Pierson; production designer, Charles Bailey; art director, Doug Higgins; set decorator, Robert Drumheller; assistant director, Burtt Harris; sound, Richard Vorisek, James Sabat; camera, Victor J. Kemper; editor, Dede Allen.

Al Pacino (Sonny); John Cazale (Sal); Sully Boyar (Bank Manager Mulvaney); Penny Allen (Chief Cashier Sylvia); Charles Durning (New York Detective Moretti); James Broderick (FBI Agent Sheldon); Chris Sarandon (Leon); Susan Peretz (Angie); Judith Malina (Vi); Gary Springer (Robber).

DOG DAY AFTERNOON is a peculiar entity based on an actual robbery in Brooklyn in August 1972 in which the heist money allegedly was intended for a sex-change operation for the male lover of the gang leader. While this remains the crux of the movie version, the film interpolates a great deal of comedy and tragedy, often confusing the viewer.

Sonny (Al Pacino) and his pal (John Cazale) and another
young man (Gary Springer) hold up a New York City neighborhood
bank branch, taking hostage the manager (Sully Boyar) and the
female clerks. Called to the scene are the police, led by Detective
Moretti (Charles Durning) who is quietly aided by a FBI agent
(James Broderick). Also flocking to the scene are spectators and
the grasping news media, as well as a gay liberation group. Eventually, plans are made to concede to the robbers' wish to fly to Al-
geria, but in a finale double-cross Cazale is shot by the police and
Pacino is captured.

Overlong at 130 minutes, DOG DAY AFTERNOON is best for
its performances, especially Al Pacino as Sonny, John Cazale as
the strangely mixed up Sal, and Chris Sarandon as Leon, the piti-
ful young man who wants a sex change operation.

In addition to these trimmings, DOG DAY AFTERNOON has
its moral: the bad guys are really the good guys, and the real
villains are the business people (in this case, bankers) who get
rich from the masses.

DOG EAT DOG (Ajay Films, 1966) 84 mins.

Executive producer, Arthur Cohn; producer, Carl Szokol; directors,
Ray Nazarro, Albert Zugsmith; based on the novel When Strangers
Meet by Robert Bloomfield; screenplay, Robert Hill, Michael Elkins;
art director, Wolf Witziemann; music, Carlo Savina; camera, Riccardo
Pallotiini; editor, Gene Ruggiero.

Cameron Mitchell (Lylle Corbett); Jayne Mansfield (Darlene); Elisa-
beth Flickenschildt (Xenia); Isa Miranda (Sandra); and: Dody
Heath, Pinkas Braun, Werner Peters, Ivor Salter, Ines Taddio,
Aldo Camarda.

This United States-Italian-West German coproduction was filmed
in 1963 in Rome and Yugoslavia and issued the next year in West
Germany as EINER FRISST DEN ANDEREN and in Italy as LA MORTE
VESTITA DI DOLLARI. Basically a rudimentary gangster melodrama,
the movie did have Cameron Mitchell and Jayne Mansfield for audience interest when the film was issued in the States in 1966 in a
dubbed version.

Gangsters Lylle Corbett (Mitchell) and his confederates rob a
bank of $1,000,000 and head to a small Adriatic Sea island accompa-
nied by Darlene (Mansfield), a moll attracted by the loot. Once
there Mitchell is almost killed by his pal, and he pursues him and
Mansfield to a neighboring isle. In the meantime, a hotel manager
and his sister (Isa Miranda) discover the loot which the gansters
have hidden in a house inhabited by a mad woman (Elisabeth Flickenschildt). Several murders later, Miranda steals the booty and tries
to kill Mitchell, but in a struggle they tumble into the ocean and
drown, as does Mansfield. After all their deaths, the mad woman
watches the money float out on the ocean.

DON'T STEAL MY BABY see: BLACK MARKET BABY

DOPE ADDICT see: REEFER MADNESS

DOPED YOUTH see: REEFER MADNESS

DOUBLE CROSS (Producers Releasing Corp., 1941) 64 mins.

Producer, John G. Bachmann; director, Albert Kelly; story, John A. Albert; screenplay, Milton Ralson, Ron Ferguson; camera, Arthur Martinelli.

Kane Richmond (Jim); Pauline Moore (Ellen); Wynne Gibson (Fay); John Miljan (Nick); Richard Beach (Steve); Mary Gordon (Mrs. Murray); Robert Homans (Captain Murray); William Halligan (Mayor); Frank C. Moran (Cookie); Heinie Conklin (Miggs); Daisy Ford (Nurse); Edward Keane (Police Commissioner); Walter Shumway (Sergeant Tucker); Ted Wray (Sergeant Rand); Jimmie Fox (Camerashop Proprietor); Harry Harvey (Protective Agency Manager).

Following the murder of his policeman pal, law enforcer Jim (Kane Richmond) plots to bring the gangster kingpin murderer to justice. The latter (John Miljan), however, tries to kill the cop's police captain father (Robert Homans) and take control of the city. Richmond teams with the mobster's gang, pretending to be a hoodlum, but he is found out and is forced to drive the gang's truck to an ambush of the police (among whom is his father). At the last minute Richmond knocks out his guard and radios his father and the police surprise the hoodlum in a bloody shootout.

Although it contains a good action finale, DOUBLE CROSS is one of PRC's lesser efforts. The film wastes its respectable cast; especially fetching Pauline Moore who quit the screen after this assignment.

DOUBLE DYNAMITE (RKO, 1951) 80 mins.

Producer-director, Irving Cummings, Jr.; based on characters created by Mannie Manheim; story, Leo Rosten; screenplay, Melville Shavelson; additional dialogue, Harry Crane; music, Leigh Harline; songs, Julie Styne and Sammy Cahn; art directors; Albert S. D'Agostiono, Field Gray; set decorators, Darrell Silvera, Harley Miller; assistant director, James Lane; makeup, Gordon Bau; sound, Phil Brigandi, Clem Portman; camera, Robert de Grasse; editor, Harry Marker.

Jane Russell (Mildred Goodhue); Groucho Marx (Emil J. Keck); Frank Sinatra (Johnny Dalton); Don McGuire (Bob Pulsifer);

Howard Freeman (R. B. Pulsifer, Sr.); Nestor Paiva (Man with
Sun Glasses); Frank Orth (Mr. Kofer); Harry Hayden (McKissack);
William Edmunds (Bengaanicci); Russ Thorson (Tailman); Joe Devlin
(Frankie Boy); Lou Nova (Max); Benny Burt (Waiter); Bill Snyder
(Wire Service Man); Bill Erwin, Charles Regan, Dick Gordon, Mike
Lally, Jack Jahries, Gil Perkins, Jack Gargan (Men); Claire Du
Brey (Hatchet-Faced Lady); Charles Coleman (Santa Claus); Ida
Moore (Little Old Lady); Jean De Briac (Maitre D'); George Chand-
ler (Messenger); William Bailey (Bank Guard); Lillian West (Hotel
Maid); Harold Goodwin (Lieutenant); Charles Sullivan (Sergeant).

Bank clerks Mildred Goodhue (Jane Russell) and Johnny Dalton (Frank Sinatra) are in love but are too impoverished to wed.
One day Sinatra accidentally saves the life of a bookie gangster
(Nestor Paiva) and the latter, out of gratitude, makes it possible
for him to win $60,000 at the race track. Sinatra, however, can-
not disclose his good fortune since a similar amount turns up missing at the bank. For advice he goes to Emil (Groucho Marx), a
waiter at a cafe where the couple often meet, and ends up in trouble with his girl, gangsters, and the law, but eventually resolves
the matter.
While the teaming of busty Jane Russell, wisecracking Groucho
Marx, and crooning Frank Sinatra appears to be a "dynamite" trio,
the result is a tired comedy which employs the gangster theme as a
weak springboard for its plot. The film sat on the shelf for three
years awaiting studio mogul Howard Hughes' decision to release it.

DUE MAFIOSA CONTRO AL CAPONE [Two Mafia Man Against Al
   Capone] (FIDA/Atlantida, 1966) C 103 mins.

Director, Giorgio Simonelli; screenplay, Sollazzo, Ciorciolini; music,
Piero Umiliani; camera, Francisco Sanchez.

Franco Franchi (Franco); Ciccio Ingrassia (Ciccio); Moria Orfei
(Rosalia); Marc Lawrence (Joe Minasi); Jose Calvo (Al Capone);
Jesus Puente (Tony Agnello); Luigi Pavese (New York City Police
Chief); and: Angela Luce Savino, Michele Malaspina, Gino Buz-
zanca, Frank Brana, Solvi Stubing, Laura Brown, Enzo Andronico,
Fred Coplan, Oreste Palella, Ignazio Leone.

In New York City, the police chief (Luigi Pavese) is berating
two of his most incompetent agents, Franco (Franco Franchi) and
Ciccio (Ciccio Ingrassia), for their stupidest mistake to date, arresting his wife and daughter. To get even with them, he sends
them on a suicide mission to Chicago to clean up the Windy City,
which is rampant with lawlessness. By accident they are introduced to Al Capone (Jose Calvo) who assigns them to murder two
of his enemies, and with the help of another agent, they are able
to get the rival mobsters out of the way and ingratiate themselves
with Scarface. As a result, the inept duo are made the gang lord's

assistants and placed in charge of all illegal activities in the city. All goes well until a gangster is released from prison and recognizes the two and tells Calvo, who plans to kill them. However, the police intervene and Franchi and Ingrassia become instant national heroes.

During the 1960s the Italian "comedy" team of Franco Franchi and Ciccio Ingrassia made scores of feature films which spoofed every conceivable movie genre. This outing lambasted the gangster prototype in the team's typical looney way. While it was popular in its homeland, the film played here only on TV and met with tepid reaction.

DUKE OF THE NAVY (Producers Releasing Corp., 1942) 63 mins.

Producer, John T. Coyle; director, William Beaudine; story-screenplay, Gerald D. Adams, Beaudine; music director, Clarence Wheeler; camera, Mark Stengler; editor, Guy V. Thayer, Jr.

Ralph Byrd (Breezy Duke); Veda Ann Borg (Maureen); Stubby Kruger (Cookie); Herbert Corthell (General Courtney); Margaret Armstrong (Mrs. John T. Duke); Val Stanton (Sniffy); Paul Bryar (Bunco Bisbee); Sammy Cohen (Murphy); Red Knight (Tex); Lester Towne (Peewee); William Beaudine, Jr. (Bingo); Zack Williams (Congo).

Sailors Breezy Duke (Ralph Byrd) and Cookie (Stubby Kruger) are on shore leave and the former is mistaken for the son of a candybar king and takes up residence at the hotel suite belonging to the man's mother (Margaret Armstrong). A con man, General Courtney (Herbert Corthell), sells the two sailors a bogus treasure map. When the duo actually discover buried jewels, the mobster and his cohorts get on their trail, but the crooks are soon captured.

This "compact programmer, considerably above the average for this company (PRC)" (Variety) is a fast paced, humorous affair which takes nice digs at hoodlums, shown here being led by a slick con artist. At no time does this entry take itself seriously and it moves quickly under William Beaudine's steady direction. Ralph Byrd, best known as the screen's "Dick Tracy," here does deft low-key comedy, and he is well complemented by swimming champion Stubby Kruger as his cohort. Beda Ann Borg adds allure and laughs as the crook's pretend daughter.

EAST END CHANT see: LIMEHOUSE BLUES

EINER FRISST DEN ANDEREN see: DOG EAT DOG

EMANUELLE REPORTS FROM A WOMAN'S PRISON see: CAGED
WOMEN

THE ENFORCER (Warner Bros., 1976) C 96 mins.

Producer, Robert Daley; director, James Fargo; based on charac-
ters created by Harry Julian Fink, R. M. Fink; story, Gail Morgan
Hickman, S. W. Schurr; screenplay, Stirling Silliphant, Dean
Reisner; music, Jerry Fielding; art director, Allen E. Smith; set
decorator, Ira Bates; costumes-wardrobe, Glenn Wright; assistant
directors, Joe Cavalier, Joe Florence, Billy Ray Smith; makeup,
Joe McKinney; stunt coordinator, Wayne Van Horn; sound, Bert
Hallberg; sound effects editor, Keith Stafford; special effects, Joe
Unsinn; camera, Charles W. Short; editors, Ferris Webster, Joel
Cox.

Clint Eastwood (Detective Harry Callahan); Harry Guardino (Lieu-
tenant Bressler); Bradford Dillman (Captain McKay); John Mitchum
(DiGeorgio); DeVeren Bookwalter (Bobby Maxwell); John Crawford
(Mayor); Tyne Daly (Kate Moore), Tom O'Neill.

    Following his box-office blockbusters DIRTY HARRY (1971)
(see: B/V) and MAGNUM FORCE (1973) (q.v.), Clint Eastwood insisted he would not return to the screen in the role of vigilante
cop Dirty Harry Callahan. During a popularity lull in the mid-1970s,

Tom O'Neill and Clint Eastwood in THE ENFORCER (1976).

however, Eastwood did play the part again in THE ENFORCER, the rationale given that the script was too good to refuse. In reality, this film is much weaker than its predecessors and contains the usual extreme violence formula plus a needless battle-of-the-sexes subplot for "comedy" relief. Further, Eastwood's teaming with actress Tyne Daly has minimal screen chemistry and the overall movie is a disappointment. As a result, it would be another half-dozen years before the superstar returned to playing Dirty Harry in the not-much-better SUDDEN IMPACT (q.v.). (THE ENFORCER grossed $24,000,000 at the box office.)

Filmed in San Francisco and the site of Alcatraz, the plot finds maverick cop Dirty Harry (Eastwood) combating murderous terrorists who have been plaguing the city. Much to his chagrin, chauvanistic Harry is assigned a plucky female rookie, Kate Moore (Daly), as his partner and Eastwood has to simultaneously fight the hoodlums and train his unwanted sidekick. Eventually, the two develop an admiration for one another, but Daly is killed battling the culprits before Eastwood and his much used .44 magnum brings them to a just end.

Once again, the undercurrent theme reflects that law and order (herein the police hierarchy) is not necessarily geared to the public welfare, and that often it is the outsider (i.e. Dirty Harry) who can efficiently and successfully step in to override the criminal element.

The critics, ever anxious to find fault with Eastwood's bonanza box office series, were quick to carp about this production. "Every single character in this lackluster script," complained Jean Hoelscher (Hollywood Reporter), "exists as a stereotype or a parody.... Actually, it's not the violence that is objectionable. Rather it's the lack of artistic meaning behind the violence that makes the whole thing so pointless." "The action is reasonably fast and competently photographed," acknowledged Richard Eder (The New York Times), "But it is maggoty with nonideas. These nonideas come in the form of a whole gallery of corrupt or foolish liberal types who interfere with Harry's mission."

ENTER THE DRAGON (Warner Bros., 1973) C 98 mins.

Producers, Fred Weintraub, Paul Heller, in association with Raymond Chow; director, Robert Clouse; screenplay, Michael Allin; art director, James Wong Sun; music, Lalo Schifrin; sound, Robert Lin; camera, Gilbert Hubbs; editors, Kurt Hirshler, George Watters.

Bruce Lee (Lee); John Saxon (Roper); Jim Kelly (Williams); Shih Kien (Han); Bob Wall (Oharra); Ahna Capri (Tania); Angelo Mao Ying (Su-Lin); Betty Chung (Mei Ling); Geoffrey Weeks (Braithwaite); Yang Sze (Bolo); Peter Archer (Parsons).

Hong Kong martial arts expert Lee (Bruce Lee) is hired by the British government to gain evidence to convict Han (Shih Kien)

Shih Kien and Bruce Lee in ENTER THE DRAGON (1973).

of drug smuggling and white slavery. Under the guise of taking
part in a tournament on Kien's island, Lee is to infiltrate the for-
tress and obtain the data. Lee also has a vendetta to settle since
Kien's henchman (Bob Wall) caused the death of his sister (Angela
Mao). Lee comes to the island with two other fighters from America
(Jim Kelly and John Saxon), both on the run from the police and
mobsters. With the aid of island guard Mai Ling (Betty Chung),
Lee gains the proof he needs against Kien.

ENTER THE DRAGON was the first American-Hong Kong produced martial arts movie and it was the last completed film to star
genre favorite Bruce Lee, who died soon thereafter. It proved a
financial success (grossing $8,400,000) and was packed with action
(Lee himself directed the combat scenes) from start to finish. Its
plot nicely combines the gangster (here in the guise of the island
strongman making and selling drugs and abducting young girls for
prostitution) and kung fu genres into one actionful outing.

ESCAPE FROM ALCATRAZ (Paramount, 1979) C 112 mins.

Executive producer, Robert Daley; producer-director, Donald Siegel;

Advertisement for ESCAPE FROM ALCATRAZ (1979).

based on the book by J. Campbell Bruce; screenplay, Richard
Tuggle; production designer, Allen Smith; set decorator, Edward J.
McDonald; assistant director, Luigi Alfano; sound, Bert Hallberg,
camera, Bruce Surtees; editor, Ferris Webster.

Clint Eastwood (Frank Morris); Patrick McGoohan (Warden); Roberts
Blossom (Doc); Jack Thibeau (Clarence Anglin); Fred Ward (John
Anglin); Paul Benjamin (English); Larry Hankin (Charley Butts);
Bruce M. Fischer (Wolf); Frank Ronzio (Litmus).

ESCAPE FROM ALCATRAZ marked the fifth screen teaming of
star Clint Eastwood and director Don Siegel, the latter just having
made the classic Western, THE SHOOTIST. The duo, of course, is
best known for 1971's DIRTY HARRY (see: B/V), and their return
to the genre held much promise. Despite the fact that Variety
weighed it "one of the finest prison films ever made" and Vincent
Canby (The New York Times) lauded it as "a first-rate action movie
that is about the need and the decision to take action, as well as
the action itself," the movie is disappointing. Full of stock characters and dragged out situations, the climax is hardly startling
since it is based on the June 1962 Alcatraz escape from the "Big
Rock" which resulted in the facility being closed the following year.
    Prison lifer Frank Morris (Eastwood) is sent to Alcatraz,
which is ruled by a charming yet ruthless warden (Patrick McGoohan). There he meets assorted prisoner types, including a huge
thug (Bruce M. Fischer) who lusts for him, an intellectual (Frank
Ronzio), an artist (Roberts Blossom), and the leader (Paul Benjamin) of the blacks, with whom he ingratiates himself. Eventually,
Eastwood conceives a way to escape and enlists the aid of two others. They make good their break and are never heard from again.
    Filmed on location at the now-abandoned Alcatraz, the film
has a good feel for prison life, but its plot is not interesting and
the movie runs too long.
    The same escape was also detailed the next year in the tele-
film, ALCATRAZ: THE WHOLE STORY (q.v.).

ESCAPE FROM SAN QUENTIN (Columbia, 1957) 81 mins.

Producer, Sam Katzman; director, Fred F. Sears; screenplay, Raymond T. Marcus; music, Laerindo Almedda; song, Almedda and
Johnny Desmond; camera, Benjamin H. Kline; editor, Saul H. Goodkind.

Johnny Desmond (Mike Gilbert); Merry Anders (Robbie); Richard
Devon (Roy Gruber); Roy Engel (Hap Graham); William Bryant
(Richie); Ken Christy (Curly Gruber); Larry Blake (Mack); Don
Devlin (Piggy); Victor Millan (Mendez); John Merrick (Sampson);
Norma Frederic (Jerry); Barry Brooks (Georgie); Lennie Smith
(Bud).

Merry Anders and Johnny Desmond in ESCAPE FROM SAN QUENTIN (1957).

Sadistic convict Roy Gruber (Richard Devon) plans a prison break and taken along fellow inmates Mike Gilbert (Johnny Desmond) and Hap Graham (Roy Engel), although he savagely berates the latter following their break. Desmond pilots a plane which takes him and Devon to freedom, while Engel is able to make his getaway on foot. Reaching home, Desmond meets Robbie (Merry Anders) his soon to be ex-wife's (Peggy Maley) younger sister, and the two fall in love. Devon, however, tries to use the girl in his attempt to meet his father (Ken Christy) who has loot stashed for his son's final dash to freedom. Eventually, Desmond turns on Devon and aids the police in capturing him.

Sam Katzman toplined popular singer Johnny Desmond as box-office "bait." In the feature he sings one song, "Lonely Lament," which he also wrote. However, it is Richard Devon who steals the acting honors as the evil Gruber.

THE EVIL THAT MEN DO (ITC Film Distributors/Tri-Star Pictures, 1984) C 89 mins.

Executive producer, Lace Hool; producer, Pancho Khoner; associate producers, David Pringle, Jill Ireland; director, J. Lee Thompson; based on the novel by R. Lance Hill; screenplay, David Lee Henry,

John Crowther; music, Ken Thorne; assistant director, Gordon A. Webb; second unit director, Ernie Orsatti; camera, Javier Ruvalcaba Cruz; editor, Peter Lee Thompson.

Charles Bronson (Holland); Theresa Saldana (Rhiana); Joseph Maher (Moloch); Jose Ferrer (Lomelin); Rene Enriquez (Max); John Glover (Briggs); Raymond St. Jacques (Randolph); Antoinette Bower (Moloch's Sister).

Here is a gangster motion picture which reverses the usual genre plot ploy. The hero is a former mob hit man turned good guy who is on the trail of a sadistic mobster doctor who sells his services to the military regimes of various Central American nations.
Retired hit man Holland (Bronson), living in peace on a remote island, is visited by Lomelin (Jose Ferrer), a Mexico City professor. The latter tells him of the barbarism being indulged in by Dr. Moloch (Joseph Maher), a scientist who develops various tortures which he sells to the dictators of Central American regimes. He is now in Guatemala for the next two weeks and Bronson is persuaded to terminate him for no fee. Using a friend's widow (Theresa Saldana) and small daughter as cover, Bronson stalks the terrorist, killing his bodyguards one by one and kidnapping the man's lesbian sister (Antoinette Bower). The latter is accidentally killed by agents working for a corrupt U.S. ambassador, and Bronson is forced to kill him and another hit man. Soon there is the showdown between Maher and Bronson, and the former is killed. Bronson returns to his island retreat with Saldana and her daughter.
This Mexican location thriller is a very violent film and grossed well at the box-office. Once again it depicted the "new age" criminal; the terrorist leaders who foment trouble all in the name of a cause, but usually in the way of self aggrandizement.

THE EXECUTIONER: PART II (21st Century Distribution, 1984) C 85 mins.

Producer, Renee Harmon; director, James Bryant; screenplay, Renee Harmon.

Christopher Mitchum (Lieutenant Roger O'Malley); Aldo Ray (Police Commissioner); Antoine John Mottet (Mike); Renee Harmon (Celia Amherst), Dan Bradley, Jim Draftfield.

Those optimistic critics and film historians who insist that films are technically better than ever should be chained to a viewing room chair and made to endure at least two showings of THE EXECUTIONER: PART II. This mindless effort harkens back to the poverty row and exploitation days of the 1930s, 1940s, and 1950s; in fact, hardly any film from that period is as technically incompetent as this one. Made in the early 1980s, this picture was lensed without sound in Los Angeles with a handheld camera and dubbed postproduction. Filled with grainy stock footage, the film is often out of focus and the dubbing does not often match the ratio of the footage.

Police Lieutenant Roger O'Malley (Christopher Mitchum) is ordered by his boss (Aldo Ray) to locate the street vigilante who has been blowing up muggers and other vermin with hand grenades. In reality, the wanted man is Mike (Antoine John Mottet), who saved Mitchum's life when the two were stationed in Vietnam. Mottet is out to get vengeance on the gangster kingpin Tatoo Man (Antonio Casals), who kidnapped Mitchum's daughter, and the two men unite to save the girl and rub out the gangster before Mitchum lets Mottet escape.

With its plot similarity to DEATH WISH (q.v.) and its sequels, this trite offering attempts to gain mileage by its title, which is in no way a sequel or followup to the 1970 spy thriller, THE EXECUTIONER.

AN EYE FOR AN EYE (Avco Embassy, 1981) C 106 mins.

Executive producer, Robert Rehme; producer, Frank Capra, Jr.; associate producers, James Bruner, Milan Mrdjenovich; director, Steve Carver; story, James Bruner; screenplay, William Gray, Bruner; production designer, Sandy Veneziano; art director, Vance Lorenzini; assistant directors, Yoram Ben-Ami, Louis S. Muscate, Donald P. Borchers; music, William Goldstein; camera, Roger Shearman; editor, Anthony Redman.

Chuck Norris (Sean Kane); Christopher Lee (Morgan Canfield); Richard Roundtree (Captain Stevens); Matt Clark (Tom); Mako (Chan); Maggie Cooper (Heather); Rosalind Chao (Linda); Toru Tanaka (Giant); Stuart Pankin (Nicky); Terry Kiser (Davie); Mel Novak (Montoya); Richard Prieto (Stark); Sam Hiona (Ambler); Dorothy Dells (Cab Driver); Dov Gottesfeld (Doctor); J. E. Freeman (Tow Truck Dude); Joe Bellan (Truck Driver); Daniel Forest (VW Driver); Joseph DeNicola (Parlor Manager); Jeff Bannister (Man on Walkie-Talkie); Robert Behling (Coroner); Edsel Fung (Proprietor); Harry Wong (Shop Owner); Nancy Fish, Gary T. New, Joe Lerer, Michael Christy (Reporters); Earl Nichols (Officer Ed); Don Pike (Watcher); Tim Culbertson (Policeman).

Martial arts expert Sean Kane (Chuck Norris), a former San Francisco policeman, becomes involved with a pretty girl (Maggie Cooper) after his partner and the latter's girlfriend are murdered by a drug smuggling gang. Plagued by nightmares and guilt over the killings, Norris enlists the aid of his ex-boss (Richard Roundtree) and sets out to take revenge on the mob, led by Morgan Canfield (Christopher Lee) and his menacing henchman giant (Toru Tanaka). Helped by old-time martial arts master Chan (Makol), Norris corners the villains in their lair.

Although basically an excuse for violence and martial arts

exhibitions, AN EYE FOR AN EYE is a solidly made actioner with good work by Chuck Norris and Christopher Lee. Although its basic revenge plotline has been overworked, the film has such good pacing that the thin storyline is hardly noticeable in the midst of the karate chops, kicks, and killings. Especially impressive is the mammoth villain Giant, memorably etched by Toru Tanaka. He proves to be one of the most formidable foes faced by Norris in his epics to date, and the contrasting wry humor of aged James Chan (Mako) is a nice balance.

EYES OF THE UNDERWORLD (Universal, 1942) 61 mins.

Associate producer, Ben Pivar; director, Roy William Neill; story, Maxwell Shane; screenplay, Michael L. Simmons, Arthur Stawn; camera, George Robinson; editor, Frank Gross.

Richard Dix (Police Chief Richard Bryant); Wendy Barrie (Betty Standing); Lon Chaney (Benny); Lloyd Corrigan (J. C. Thomas); Don Porter (Edward Jason); Billy Lee (Mickey Bryan); Marc Lawrence (Gordon Finch); Edward Pawley (Lance Merlin); Joseph Crehan (Kirby); Wade Boteler (Sergeant Clancy); Steve [Gaylord] Pendleton (Hub Geisey); Mike Raffetto (District Attorney).

A plague of tire and car thefts strikes the United States when it's announced that the production of these items has been halted for the duration of World War II. In Lawnsdale, police chief Richard Bryant (Richard Dix) orders Lieutenant Kirby (Joseph Crehan) to be in charge of halting the local thefts. Crehan, however, is actually in league with gang leader Lance Merlin (Edward Pawley), the head of the operation, and he also is enlisted by a government undercover agent (Don Porter) to investigate Dix's criminal past. Finding this out, Pawley hires another gangster (Marc Lawrence) to frame Dix with an edited recording attempting to blackmail the law officer. This is used to eliminate Dix from his job, with Crehan replacing him. Dix's secretary (Wendy Barrie), who has been caring for his young son (Billy Lee), believes him innocent, as does his chauffeur-assistant (Lon Chaney). They eventually learn of the secret garage headquarters where the gang operates, and Chaney forces a confession from Pawley's driver (Gaylord [Steve] Pendleton). The criminals are incarcerated.

"A modest little item turned out with the customary quota of gun battles" (New York Journal-American), EYES OF THE UNDERWORLD was a well made dual bill item which benefitted from its topical plotline. Here gangsters were using the war effort and the need for rationing to benefit their own illegal activities. The typically stalwart Universal cast added a great deal of zest to the proceedings, and the finale is particularly well staged. Realart reissued the film in 1951, retitled as CRIMINALS OF THE UNDERWORLD.

F MAN (Paramount, 1936) 65 mins.

Producer, Val Paul; director, Edward F. Cline; story, Richard Connell; screenplay, Eddie Welch, Henry Johnson, Paul Gerard Smith; art directors; Hans Dreier, Earl Hedrick; camera, Leo Tovar; editor, Paul Weatherwax.

Jack Haley (Johnny Dime); William Frawley (Hogan); Grace Bradley (Evelyn); Adrienne Marden (Molly Carter); Onslow Stevens (Mr. Shaw); Franklin Parker (Carig); Norman Willis (Jerry); Edward McWade (Mr. Whitney); Robert Middlemass (Cartwright); Walter Johnson (Dougherty); Spencer Charters (Sheriff).

During the 1930s, there were few really good spoofs of the gangster film genre; A SLIGHT CASE OF MURDER (1938) (see: B/V) being one of the best. F MAN predates that classic and is a "good, zippy comedy, judiciously salted with burlesque" (Variety) but due to its short running time (65 minutes) it was relegated to double bill programs.

Jack Haley stars as small town soda fountain clerk Johnny Dime, longing to be a G-man. He bothers the FBI so much they finally make him a "F-man," a nonexistent position. Haley, though, takes the job seriously and ferrets out a gang of racketeers and becomes embroiled with their moll (Grace Bradley), much to the chagrin of his girlfriend (Adrienne Marden). He also causes a real federal agent (William Frawley) to be captured by the hoodlums, but Haley rescues him and with the aid of a squirt gun corrals the culprits.

Much of F MAN's success belongs to the bumbling comedy antics of Jack Haley, whose Johnny Dime uses Sherlock Holmes-Craig Kennedy modern scientific detection methods to bring in criminals but usually just confounds the situation.

FACE BEHIND THE MASK (Columbia, 1941) 69 mins.

Producer, Wallace McDonald; director, Robert Florey; based on the radio play by Thomas Edward O'Connell; screenplay, Allen Vincent, Paul Jarrico; music director, Morris W. Stoloff; camera, Franz A. Planer; editor, Charles Nelson.

Peter Lorre (Janos Szaby); Evelyn Keyes (Helen Williams); Don Beddoe (Jim O'Hara); George E. Stone (Dinky); John Tyrrell (Watts); Stanley Brown (Harry); Al Seymour (Benson); James Seay (Jeff); Warren Ashe (Johnson); Charles Wilson (Chief O'Brien); George McKay (Terry Finnegan).

A Hungarian watchmaker, Janos Szaby (Peter Lorre) is forced to immigrate to the United States and is horribly burned in a tenement fire. When plastic surgery fails to restore his face, a kindly doctor (George E. Stone) makes him a lifelike mask. Due to his

Peter Lorre and Evelyn Keyes in THE FACE BEHIND THE MASK (1941).

handicap, Lorre is unable to find work and drifts into crime and soon becomes the gang leader. Despite his occupation, he falls in love with a blind girl (Evelyn Keyes) who uses her natural instincts to perceive Lorre's goodness. When the gang thinks she has betrayed them to the police, they kill her and Lorre takes revenge by killing them one by one, eventually dying himself.

Considered just another "B" programmer at the time of release, THE FACE BEHIND THE MASK has taken on cult status in recent years. Its tragic story, combined with sensitive performances by Peter Lorre and Evelyn Keyes, plus the steady direction of Robert Florey and low-keyed photography by Franz Planer, make the movie very different from the average quickie of the period.

In promoting the feature, Columbia Pictures actually played down its gangster elements and billed it as a horror film, and Variety noted that Peter Lorre's screen makeup was "... likely to cause intestinal flipflops among the more squeamish trade."

FAKE-OUT (M. Riklis, 1982) C 96 mins.

Executive producer, Tino Barzie; producer-director, Matt Cimber; screenplay, Cimber, John Goff; music, Arthur B. Rubinstein; stunt coordinator, Remy Julienne; camera, Eddy Van Der Enden; editor, B. A. Schoenfeld.

Pia Zadora (Bobbie Warren); Telly Savalas (Lieutenant Thurston); Desi Arnaz, Jr. (Detective Clint Morgan); and: Larry Storch.

Following their work on the lust-filled adaptation of James M. Cain's BUTTERFLY (1981), star Pia Zadora and producer-director-scripter Matt Cimber reteamed for this gangster film which attempts to balance drama and comedy and fails in each arena. Shot in Las Vegas with activities focused at the Riviera Hotel (owned by Zadora's husband Meshulan Riklis, who financed this film), the movie is an excuse for the public to oogle the body and charms of the sex-kitten star.

Las Vegas nightclub star Bobbie Warren (Zadora) is arrested by a police lieutenant (Telly Savalas) and tossed into prison until she will testify against her gangster lover. Behind bars, she is gang-raped by the female inmates. As a result she is set free, and upon returning to Las Vegas two mob hoodlums try to shoot her and she is given a police bodyguard (Desi Arnaz, Jr.) with whom she tumbles in love.

THE FAKERS (Independent-International, 1969) C 92 mins.

Executive producers, Rex Carlton, Fred Gebhardt; producer, Al Adamson; associate producers, Bob Kinoshita, Jerry Evans; director, Adamson; screenplay, Evans; music, Don McGinnis; music themes, Nelson Riddle; song, Riddle and John Gabriel, McGinnis and David McKechnie; assistant director, Mike Haggerty; sound, Bob Dietz; camera, Laszlo Kovacs, Frank Ruttencutter, Gary Graver; editor, John Winfield.

Broderick Crawford (Brand); Scott Brady (FBI Agent); Kent Taylor (Count Von Delberg); Keith Andes (Bremonte); John Carradine (Shop Owner); John Gabriel (Mark Adams); Robert Dix (Cunk); rin O'Donnell (Von Delberg's Daughter); Vicki Volante (Carol Bechtol); Anne Randall (Amanda); Jack Starrett (Rocky); Emily Banks (FBI Agent); Dan Kemp (Henchman); William Bonner, Jerry Mills (Bloody Devils); Bambi Allen, Jill Woelfel (Pickup Girls); California's Hessians (Bike Riders); and: Carol Brewster, Gene Shane, Rhae Andrace, Jane Wald, Greydon Clark, John Cardos, Kent Osborne, Philip Difermian, Colonal Harlan Sanders.

A wild motorcycle gang is in the pay of neo-Nazi Count von Delberg (Kent Taylor) and his lovely associate (Anne Randall). After killing two men who are enemies of the organization, they agree to create havoc wherever possible. In Las Vegas, Mark Adams (John Gabriel), an FBI agent who has infiltrated the Mafia, is assigned by his underworld boss to arrange a deal with the Count for the syndicate to distribute counterfeit money made from World War II German plates. The FBI chief (Broderick Crawford) realizes his undercover agent is against three very dangerous elements: gangsters, neo-Nazis, and murderous bikers. The bikers, however, are killed by

Advertisement for THE FAKERS [a.k.a. HELL'S BLOODY DEVILS] (1969).

Randall after they try to gang rape her. Later she is caught spying on Taylor and he slashes her to death. Leading other FBI agents, Gabriel wipes out most of the syndicate gang in a gun battle. Taylor dies in a plane explosion as he tries to escape.

With such enticing advertising as "Madmen on Motorcycles," "Blasting Open Crime's Most Sadistic Secret Society!" and "See-- Barbaric Brutality! Female Love Slaves!" this independent film release openly panders to the blood-and-guts trade. Packed with sex and maximum sadism and violence, the movie wasted a veteran cast in its inept melodramatics. Only Laszlo Kovacs' cinematography of the Utah terrain provides visual satisfaction.

Made under the title OPERATION M in 1968, the film is also known as HELL'S BLOODY DEVILS. On television, the violent biker sequences are eliminated.

THE FALL GUY (RKO, 1930) 70 mins.

Producer, William Le Baron; associate producer, William Sistrom; director, A. Leslie Pearce; based on the play by George Abbott, James Gleason; screenplay, Tim Whelan; art director; Max Rec; sound, George Ellis; camera, Leo Tover; editor, Archie Marshek.

Jack Mulhall (Johnny Quinlan); Mae Clarke (Bertha Quinlan); Ned Sparks (Dan Walsh); Pat O'Malley (Charles Newton); Thomas Jackson (Nifty Herman); Wynne Gibson (Lottie Quinlan); Ann Brody

Jack Mulhall and Pat O'Malley in THE FALL GUY (1930).

(Mrs. Bercowich); Elmer Ballard (Hutch); Alan Roscoe (Detective Keefe).

When soda jerk Johnny Quinlan (Jack Mulhall) loses his job he reluctantly goes to work for racketeer Nifty Herman (Thomas Jackson) whom Mulhall thinks is a bootlegger. Jackson gives him a suitcase for safe keeping and he takes it home and hides it, but his wife (Wynne Gibson) shows it to her sister's boyfriend (Pat O'Malley), a government agent, who recognizes it as belonging to a narcotics ring he has been trailing. Mulhall is arrested but later tricks Jackson into revealing that he, Mulhall, did not know the valise's contents. As a reward, Mulhall becomes O'Malley's new assistant.

This "simple little story" (Photoplay magazine) was taken from George Abbott's and James Gleason's 1928 play and was one of the early talkie attempts at poking fun at the gangster genre. Stars Jack Mulhall and Mae Clarke definitely contributed more to the gangster movie category than evidenced by this fluff. Mulhall, in the previous year, successfully played the first dual roles in a sound gangster film in DARK STREETS (q.v.); one year later Clarke was the recipient of a grapefruit in the face in the classic genre melodrama, THE PUBLIC ENEMY (see: B/V).

THE FAMILY (International Coproductions/EDP Films, 1974) C
100 mins.

Producers, Giorgio Papi, Arrigo Colombo; director, Sergio Sollima; screenplay, Sauroi Scavolini, Gianfranco Calligarich, Lina Wertmuller, Sollima; art director, Francesco Bronzi; music, Ennio Morricone; camera, Aldo Tonti; editor, Nino Baragli.

Charles Bronson (Jeff); Jill Ireland (Vanessa); Umberto Orsini (Steve); Telly Savalas (Weber); Michael Constantin (Killain); Ray Sanders (Prisoner); Benjamin Lev (Young Prisoner); George Savalas (Shapiro); Peter Dane (TV M.C.).

New Orleans hit man Jeff (Charles Bronson) ends in prison due to the machinations of his lady love Vanessa (Jill Ireland). Upon his release, he is determined to get even, but she convinces him she had nothing to do with his imprisonment. He then plans to kill Weber (Telly Savalas), the corrupt gangster kingpin Ireland names as the true culprit. He carries out his mission only to find that another hoodlum (Michael Constantin) is trying to blackmail him back behind bars. Bronson finally figures out that Ireland is behind the operation and he kills her, only to be shot himself by the police.

Full of sex, nudity, and violence, this was one of those Charles Bronson features which was tremendously popular everywhere but in the United States. Filmed in 1970 in Italy (as CITTA VIOLENTA [Violent City]), with location shooting in New Orleans,

the movie proved to be a turgid melodrama which gave Bronson another in his long line of strong, silent, revengeful protagonists.
Jill Ireland, usually a weak acting link in her husband's features,
is particularly effective as the scheming, two-timing gal.

Originally 109 minutes when released abroad, it was chopped
down for U.S. distribution in 1974 on a double bill with BIG BAD
MAMA. For U.S. television it was further edited to eliminate the
nudity and some violence, making the continuity all the more convoluted.

FAREWELL, MY LOVELY (Avco Embassy, 1975) C 97 mins.

Executive producers, Elliott Kastner, Jerry Bick; producers,
George Pappas, Jerry Bruckheimer; director, Dick Richards; based
on the novel by Raymond Chandler; production designer, Dean
Tavoularis; art director, Angelo Graham; set decorator, Bob Nelson; music, David Shire; sound, Tom Overton; camera, John Alonzo; editors, Walter Thompson, Joel Cox.

Robert Mitchum (Phillip Marlowe); Charlotte Rampling (Mrs. Grayle);
John Ireland (Nulty); Sylvia Miles (Mrs. Florian); Jack O'Halloran
(Moose Malloy); Anthony Zerbe (Brunette); Harry Dean Stanton
(Billy Rolfe); Jim Thompson (Mr. Grayle); John O'Leary (Marriott);
Kate Murtagh (Amthor); Walter McGinn (Tommy Ray); Jimmy Archer

Harry Dean Stanton, John Ireland, and Robert Mitchum in FARE-
WELL, MY LOVELY (1975).

(Georgie); Joe Spinell (Nick); Sylvester Stallone (Kelly/Konnie);
Burt Gilliam (Cowboy).

This is the third screen edition of Raymond Chandler's well-
regarded novel; the first two being: THE FALCON TAKES OVER
(1942) and its remake, MURDER, MY SWEET (q.v.) in 1945. Both
features emphasized the fiction's main theme of detective Phillip
Marlowe being embroiled with two beautiful women and the theft of
a jade necklace, resulting in several homicides. That theme was
again employed in this outing, but here the underlying corruption
of the law by gangsters demands equal time in the proceedings.
Also, this version greatly tampers with the original story, often to
the plot's disadvantage. This picturization, nonetheless, beautifully recaptures the feel of 1941 Los Angeles and is a fitting tribute
to the film noir vogue so prevalent in that decade.

World-weary and aging private detective Phillip Marlowe (Robert Mitchum) is following a case in a predominately black section of
Los Angeles and confronts strong man Moose Malloy (Jack O'Halloran)
who hires him to find Velma, his lost lady love who disappeared
while O'Halloran was in the penitentiary. Mitchum seeks the missing woman, but needing funds, he accompanies slippery Lindsay
Marriott (John O'Leary) as he tries to buy back a stolen necklace
which belongs to a wealthy friend. At the meet, Mitchum is knocked
out and O'Leary murdered. The police lieutenant (John Ireland)
pins the crime on Mitchum. Meanwhile, Velma's trail leads Mitchum
to drunken Jesse Florian (Sylvia Miles), a widow whose spouse
owned the bar where Velma performed. Mitchum also learns that
the stolen necklace was owned by Mrs. Grayle (Charlotte Rampling)
and, upon visiting her, he discovers she is the young, sexy wife of
an old, yet still powerful retired judge (Jim Thompson). The case
then leads Mitchum to lesbian brothel owner Frances Amthor (Kate
Murtagh) and there he is beaten and drugged, but manages to escape. Finally the detective concludes that the city's gangster chief,
Laird Brunette (Anthony Zerbe), holds the key to both the stolen
necklace and the whereabouts of Velma. Aboard Zerbe's gambling
ship, Mitchum pieces together that Rampling and Velma are the
same woman. When O'Halloran shows up, Rampling kills him and
Mitchum is forced to shoot her as the police arrive on the scene.

Robert Mitchum's interpretation of Phillip Marlowe highlights
this entrancing feature. Although he is 20 years too senior for the
lead part, he nonetheless embodies the qualities which Chandler
gave to his fictional creation. Reading the Marlowe books and stories, one visualizes a Robert Mitchum in the key assignment. While
the screen star's Marlowe is aging and tired, he is also resourceful
and quick with a wisecrack--all traits drawn from the literary original.

FAST-WALKING (Pickman, 1982) C 115 mins.

Executive producer, Joseph Harris; producer, James B. Harris;

associate producer, Richard McWhorter; director, James B. Harris; based on the novel The Rap by Ernest Brawley; screenplay, James B. Harris; art director, Richard Haman; music, Lalo Schifrin; camera, King Baggot; editor, Douglas Stewart.

James Woods (Fast-Walking Miniver); Tim McIntire (Wasco); Kay Lenz (Moke); Robert Hooks (William Galliot); M. Emmet Walsh (Sergeant Sanger); Timothy Agoglia Carey (Bullet); Susan Tyrrell (Evie); Charles Weldon (Jackson); John Friedrich (Squeeze); Sandy Ward (Warden); Lance LeGault (Lieutenant Barnes); Deborah White (Elaine); Helen Page Camp (Lady in Visitor's Room); Sydney Lassick (Ted).

Fast-Walking Miniver (James Woods) is a discontented prison guard who smokes marijuana on the job and earns extra money by aiding his wheeler-dealer cousin-prisoner Wasco (Tim McIntire) in various nefarious activities behind bars. In addition he is helping a local brothel owner (Susan Tyrrell) with her business. When black militant William Galliot (Robert Hooks) is brought to the prison, two counterplots quickly develop: one to assassinate the man and the other to help him escape. McIntire, who is a part of the former plan, brings in his light-headed girlfriend (Kay Lenz) to seduce Woods into aiding his cause; the guard is also promised $50,000 by black leaders who want their man sprung. As the situation worsens, Woods is caught in the midst of something he cannot handle, while McIntire eventually becomes the victim of his own greed.

With filming accomplished at the closed-down Montana State Prison, FAST-WALKING nicely captures the oppressive atmosphere of life behind bars, but the lack of compelling protagonists hurts the story. Only the black leader is sympathetic, since the film claims he was railroaded into prison. Woods' character has absolutely nothing to recommend him, hardly the kind of person necessary to be the heroic crux of a prison melodrama. Tim McIntire's portrayal of the seedy, wily Wasco is attention-grabbing in its quirky way, especially when he reiterates how much he loves life behind the bars.

THE FAT MAN (Universal, 1951) 77 mins.

Producer, Aubrey Schenck; director, William Castle; based on the radio series derived from the work of Dashiell Hammett; story, Leonard Lee; screenplay, Harry Essex, Lee; music, Bernard Green; music director, Joseph Gershenson; art directors, Bernard Herzbrun, Edward Ilou; set decorators, Russell A. Gausman, Ruby R. Levitt; assistant director, Joe Kenny; makeup, Bud Westmore; sound, Leslie I. Carey, Robert Prichard; camera, Irving Glassberg; editor, Edward Curtiss.

J. Scott Smart (Brad Runyan); Julie London (Pat Boyd); Rock

Jayne Meadows and Emmett Kelly in THE FAT MAN (1951).

Hudson (Roy Clark); Clinton Sundberg (Bill Norton); Jayne Meadows (Jane Adams); John Russell (Gene Gordon); Jerome Cowan (Lieutenant Stark); Emmett Kelly (Ed Deets); Lucille Barkley (Lola Gordon); Robert Osterloh (Fletcher); Harry Lewis (Happy Stevens); Teddy Hart (Shifty); Marvin Kaplan (Pinkie); Ken Niles (Dr. Bromley); Mary Young (Saleswoman); Tristram Coffin (Missing Persons Officer); Tom Keene (Mac); Harry Tyler (Landlord); George Wallace (Carl); Cheerio Meredith (Scrubwoman); Art Lind, Everett Hart, Abe Goldstein (Clowns); Eric Alden (Guard); Jack Chefe (Chef); Bob Roark (Tony).

Based on the character created by Dashiell Hammett in The Maltese Falcon, the Fat Man was changed to the side of the law when the ABC radio program "The Fat Man" debuted in 1945 with J. Scott "Jack" Smart in the title role. The mystery program quickly developed into one of the more popular whodunits on the air and spawned this feature film with Smart recreating the title role for the big screen. "It's a loosely contrived, talky mystery melodrama with enough suspense moments to see it through the more general situation." (Variety)

While attending a convention in Manhattan, a California dentist is murdered and although the death is initially ruled a suicide, the man's widow (Jayne Meadows) hires detective Brad Runyan (Smart) to investigate. Back in California, the private eye traces the trail to murdered gangster Roy Clark (Rock Hudson), who was involved with several other hoodlums in splitting money from a robbery caper. Following another killing, the Fat Man corners the culprit, a circus clown (Emmett Kelly), whose ambition is to finance his own sideshow.

J. Scott Smart's screen portrayal no doubt paved the way for William Conrad to star in a similar role in TV's popular "Cannon" series two decades later. The movie is additionally highlighted by good work by future stars Rock Hudson and Julie London, the latter as Hudson's screen wife, and John Russell as one of the more determined gangsters.

THE FATAL PASSIONS see: DR. MABUSE, DER SPIELER

FBI GIRL (Lippert, 1951) 74 mins.

Producer-director, William Berke; story, Rupert Hughes; screenplay, Richard Landau, Dwight Babcock; art director, F. Paul Sylos; set decorator, Charence Steensen; assistant director, T. O. Collings; makeup, Del Armstrong; wardrobe, Al Berke; sound, John Carter; music, Darrell Calker; camera, Jack Greenhalgh; editor, Phil Cahn.

Cesar Romero (Glen Stedman); George Brent (Jeff Donley); Audrey Totter (Shirely Wayne); Tom Drake (Carl Chercourt); Raymond Burr (Blake); Raymond Greenleaf (Governor Grisby); Tommy Noonan,

Pete Marshall (Television Act); Margia Dean (Natalie Craig); Alexander Pope (George Denton); Richard Monohan (Donald); Don Garner (Paul Craig); Jan Kayne (Davis), Walter Coy (Priest), Byron Foulger (Morgue Attendant); Joel Marston (Hotel Clerk); Marie Blake (Landlady); Joi Lansing (Susan Matthew); and: O. Z. Whitehead.

A Senate investigating committee is weighing allegations against Governor Grisby (Raymond Greenleaf), wanted on a murder charge from years before under his real name of John Williams. The governor proves to be the tool of a corrupt mobster (Raymond Burr), who has established a plan to steal Grisby-Williams' prints from the FBI file.

When the scheme goes awry and the FBI employee (Margia Dean) who was to get the prints is killed, two agents (Cesar Romero and George Brent) handle the case. They talk to Shirley Wayne (Audrey Totter), another FBI clerk, who was the dead girl's roommate, and come to believe her boyfriend Carl (Tom Drake), a lobbyist, is somehow implicated in the caper.

When Totter tells this to Drake, he checks into the matter and is ordered by Burr to have Totter steal the prints. Totter is given decoy prints, which leads to the final showdown and to Burr's death while trying to escape in a helicopter from the police, et al.

Despite its limited budget, FBI GIRL is pleasant fare and Raymond Burr particularly effective as the slimy gangster ruler. "FBI GIRL ... is a curious combination of factual and fanciful action. On the factual side are the multiple facets of the fingerprint department of the Federal Bureau of Investigation, plus the bureau's workaday use of walkie-talkie radios, helicopters and such. These scenes hold definite interest.... Strictly on the fanciful side is the plot.... I imagine many a real-life FBI agent will squirm somewhat on seeing it, and you may share their reaction." (Kay Proctor, Los Angeles Examiner)

FEDERAL AGENT AT LARGE (Republic, 1950) 60 mins.

Producer, Stephen Auer; director, George Blair; screenplay, Albert DeMond; music, Stanley Wilson; songs, Jack Elliott; Ned Washington and Gabriel Ruiz; music director, Jerry Roberts; assistant director, Lee Lukather; art director, Frank Arrigo; set decorators, John McCarthy, Jr., Charles Thompson; special effects, Howard Lydecker, Theodore Lydecker; camera, John MacBurnie; editor, Arthur Roberts.

Dorothy Patrick (Solitaire); Robert Rockwell (Dr. Ross Carrington); Kent Taylor (Matt Ready/Lopita); Thurston Hall (Big Bill Dixon); Frank Puglia (Angelo "Angel" Badille); Roy Barcroft (Nels Berger); Denver Pyle (Jumpy Jordan); Jonathan Hale (Goodwin); Robert Kent (Monahan); Kenneth MacDonald (Captain); Sonia Darrin (Mildred); Frank McFarland (Duke Warren); John McGuire (Customs Officer).

Gold is being smuggled into the United States from Mexico and the Treasury Department orders agent Matt Ready (Kent Taylor) to investigate. He determines that pretty but deadly Solitaire (Dorothy Patrick) is the head of the operation and he joins the gang in the guise of Lopita, a big city gangster. He goes along with the group on a trip to Mexico, where he discovers that a local man (Frank Puglia) is working with the mobsters to send his daughter to college. He also finds that archaeologist Ross Carrington (Robert Rockwell) is an innocent blind for the gang and is being romanced by Patrick. The criminals are using Rockwell's archaeological dig as a front since they are secreting the gold in Aztec pottery which passes through customs without inspection. Taylor documents this with a wire recorder, but before he can complete his mission he is killed. The recording reaches its destination, and the gang is trapped.

FEDERAL AGENTS VS. UNDERWORLD, INC. (Republic, 1949)
    twelve chapters

Associate producer, Franklyn Adreon; director, Fred Brannon; screenplay, Basil Dickey, Sol Shor, Royal Cole, William Lively; music, Stanley Wilson; special effects, Howard Lydecker, Theodore Lydecker; camera, John MacBurnie; editors, Cliff Bell, Sam Starr.

Kirk Alyn (Dave Worth); Rosemary La Planche (Laura); Roy Barcroft (Gordon); Carol Forman (Nila); James Dale (Steve Evans); Bruce Edwards (Professor Williams); James Craven (Professor Clayton); Tristram Coffin (Chambers); Tom Steele (Mort); Dale Van Sickel (Professor Graves); Jack O'Shea (Ali); Marshall Reed (O'Hara); Bob Wilke (Zod); Robert St. Angelo (Native); George Douglas (Courier); Dave Anderson (Porter).

    Chapters: 1) The Golden Hands; 2) The Floating Coffin; 3) Death in the Skies; 4) Fatal Evidence; 5) The Trapped Conspirator; 6) Wheels of Disaster; 7) The Hidden Key; 8) The Enemy's Mouthpiece; 9) The Stolen Hand; 10) Unmasked; 11) Tombs of the Ancients; 12) The Curse of Kurigal.

    Serial fans no doubt believed they were to witness a rip roaring cliffhanger with blazing tommy guns, slick gangsters, and all kinds of illegal big city activities when they paid admissions to watch the initial chapter of FEDERAL AGENTS VS. UNDERWORLD, INC. Instead, and despite the serial's intriguing title, they were feted to an exotic, international crime plot more in line with items such as LOST CITY OF THE JUNGLE. Once the surprise was over, fans could settle down to a solidly paced Republic cliffhanger.
    Federal agent Dave Worth (Kirk Alyn) is hunting the kidnapped Professor Clayton (James Craven), who has discovered the Golden Hands of Kurigal, a treasure which provides the location of a hidden treasure. It seems that an organization of international

gangsters called Underworld, Inc. has nabbed the professor and the group is led by Nila (Carol Forman), an international thief. She latches onto one of the Golden Hands and must find the other. Meanwhile, Alyn suspects her of being behind the kidnapping but is nearly killed by her henchman (Roy Barcroft) when he tries to gain information on her at the Immigration Bureau. Agent Steve Evans (James Dale) rescues Alyn from a warehouse where he had been imprisoned by the gangsters, and they head to the local museum where the other Golden Hand is stored. Forman, in the guise of a cleaning woman, bribes Craven's assistant (Bruce Edwards) for the Golden Hand, but G-men arrive to prevent the sale. Forman is cornered and Underworld, Inc. is no more.

A 110-minute feature version of the serial was released in 1966 as GOLDEN HANDS OF KURIGAL.

FEDERAL MAN (Eagle Lion, 1950) 67 mins.

Producer, Jack Schwarz; director, Robert Tansey; screenplay, Sam Neuman, Nat Tanchuck; music director, Darrel Calker; art director, Fred Preble; set decorator, Harry Reif; assistant director, Arthur Hammond; sound, Glen Glenn; camera, Clark Ramsey; editor, Reg Browne.

William Henry (Sherrin); Pamela Blake (Mrs. Palmer); Robert Shayne (Stuart); Lyle Talbot (Johnson); George Eldredge (Brandon); Movita Castanena (Lolita); John Laurenz (Rodriguez); William Edwards (Mr. Palmer); Lori Irving (Betty Herbert); Ben Moselle (Mack) Dennis Moore (Harry); Noel Cravat (Rocky); Paul Hoffman (George); Joseph Turkel (Sneeze).

Narcotics runners are an established facet of the gangster motion picture, and this programmer examines federal narcotics bureau agents following a gang working between the United States and Mexico. Although a studio-bound production, the film manages to provide a "feel" for its supposed Mexican locales, and its semi-documentary approach, utilizing much of the apparatus agents require to reel in drug smugglers, is most effective. Another appealing aspect of this movie is that it avoids cliched romance in favor of action and plot development.

Brandon (George Eldredge) operates a dope smuggling network which ranges from the United States into Mexico. When a narcotics agent is murdered by the gangsters, the Agency unleashes a full force to bring them to justice with agent Sherrin (William Henry) rounding up the dope ring.

FEDERAL MANHUNT (Republic, 1939) 54 mins.

Producer, Armand Schaefer; director, Nick Grinde; story, Sam Fuller, William Lively; screenplay, Maxwell Shane; camera, Ernest Miller; editor, Murray Seldeen.

Robert Livingston (Bill); June Travis (Anne); John Gallaudet
(Rennick); Ben Welden (Goldie); Horace MacMahon (Soapy); Charles
Halton (Lauber); Gene Morgan (Hawlings); Matt McHugh (Kilgore);
Sybil Harris (Mrs. Banning); Jerry Tucker (Scoop); Margaret Mann
(Mrs. Ganter); Frank Conklin (Beeber).

Hardened criminal Rennick (John Gallaudet) arranges to wed
his fiancee at the chapel in Alcatraz but uses the event to cover
his prison break, leaving the bride-to-be (June Travis) behind.
Once outside prison, he meets with other gangsters who use the
criminals' underground railroad in an attempt to smuggle him out of
the States. Gallaudet thus eludes several G-men, but federal agent
Bill (Robert Livingston) joins the case and eventually Travis becomes disenchanted with the criminal and betrays him to Livingston.
While The New York Times called this Republic programmer
"melodramatic mischief," Variety noted, "Writer and director have
combined to lift this one out of the usual class of prison-break and
manhunt yarns, contributing some refreshing new angles."

THE FEMALE BUNCH (Burbank International, 1969) C 88 mins.

Executive producer, Mardi Rustam; producer, Raphael Nussbaum;
directors, Al Adamson, John Carlos; story, Nussbaum; screenplay,
Jale Lockwood, Brent Nimrod; music, Jaime Mendoza; theme song,
John Gay and Berry Nighbert; camera, Scott Lloyd Davies; editors,
George Goncharoff, Brent Nimrod.

Lon Chaney (Monty); Jenifer Bishop (Grace); Russ Tamblyn (Russ);
Nesa Renet (Sandy); Geoffrey Land (Jim); Regina Carrol (Waitress);
Don Epperson (Singer); John Cardos (Mexican Farmer); Albert Cole
(Barkeeper); A'Lesha Lee, Jackie Taylor, Lesley MacRae (Gang
Members); and: William Bonner, Bobby Clark.

On an old ranch near the Mexican border, a group of hell-
raising young women led by Grace (Jenifer Bishop) make their living by smuggling narcotics with the aid of drunken former Hollywood stuntman named Monty (Lon Chaney, Jr.). Although no man
except Chaney is allowed on the ranch, the girls often visit small
Mexican border towns to trade in heroin and engage in orgies of
alcohol and sex. At one of these parties, Denise (Jackie Taylor)
falls for drifter Russ (Russ Tamblyn), but when Bishop catches
them in the hay, she burns a brand into Tamblyn's forehead. Later
the women burn a Mexican farmer's (John Cardos) house and hang
him with barbed wire. This so repulses new member Sandy (Nesa
Renet) that she runs away. Later Tamblyn returns to have a showdown, and finally only he and Bishop are left. It is Chaney, done
"dirt" by Grace, who plays the last ironic twist.
With tag lines such as "They Dare To Do What Other Women
Only Dream About" and "Women Who Live by Their Own Rules ...
Men Who Die for Them!" THE FEMALE BUNCH is a violent, sex-

filled exploitation melodrama which focuses on the distaff gangster operation, one connected with the mob through their illegal drug activities. Made by director Al Adamson in 1969 under the title A TIME TO RUN, additional sexual scenes were spliced into the proceedings by director John Cardos. Allegedly, some sequences were lensed at the notorious Spahn Ranch in Chatsworth, California, shortly before it was destroyed by fire in 1970. The ranch had been the home of the infamous Manson Family. For the record, THE FEMALE BUNCH was the final film appearance by horror film great Lon Chaney.

FIGHTING BACK (Paramount, 1982) C 98 mins.

Presenter, Dino DeLaurentiis; executive producers, David Permut, Mark Travis; producer, D. Constantine Conte; co-producers, David Lowe, Alex DeBenedetti; associate producer, Tom Hedley; director, Lewis Teague; screenplay, Hedley, David Z. Goodman; art director, Robert Gundlach; costumes, John Boxer; music, Piero Piccioni; assistant directors, Jose Loipez Rodero, Ellen Rauch; camera, Franco DiGiacomo; editors, John J. Fitzstephens, Nicholas Smith.

Tom Skerritt (John); Patti LuPone (Lisa); Michael Sarrazin (Vince); Yaphet Kotto (Ivanhoe); David Rasche (Michael); Donna DeVarona (Sara); Gina DeAngelis (Vera); Jonathan Adam Sherman (Danny); Pat Cooper (Harry); Jim Lovelett (Tom); Joe Ragno (Mike); Sal Richards (Bill); Frank Sivero (Frank); Lewis Van Bergen (Laz); Jim Moody (Lester); Peter Brocco (Donato); Patch MacKenzie (Lilly); Pete Richardson (Eldorado); Jean Erlich (Snowflake); Bob Ryan (Neighbor); George Manos (Carlo); Joseph R. Sicari (Salesman); Maurice Golchin (Mario); Maria Ferrer (Delfina); Robert Hitt (Centner); Sandrino Giglio (Mr. Moresco); Antoinette Iannelli (Mrs. Moresco); Earle Hyman (Police Chief); and: Mandel Kramer, Ted Ross, Josh Mostel, Dean Bennett, Ralph Monaco, Tony Munafo, Lenny Del Genio, Peter Dryden, Verone Scruggs, Andrew Edwards.

South Philadelphia delicatessen owner John D'Angelo (Tom Skerritt) becomes enraged with the gangs roaming his neighborhood after one group causes his wife (Patti LuPone) to miscarry while another cuts off his mother's (Gina DeAngelis) finger. Rather than run, he vows to fight back. He organizes the locals into a strong vigilante group to combat the street hoodlums. One of the group's members is police officer Vince Morelli (Michael Sarrazin) and at first the law aids the group, but after a time friction begins to develop when the vigilantes take the law into their own hands. Skerritt's wife begins to worry that he may be changing due to his celebrity status as the leader of the underdogs, while the corrupt local politicians dislike the change in the balance of power and fear the surging popularity of the vigilante organization.
"The film is quite effective in posing the question of just how far a citizen can go in taking the law into his own hands.... But

each new plot development is so predictable that it becomes difficult to get involved in this particular story." (Variety)

The basic problem with FIGHTING BACK is that it leaves too many grey areas. The film should either be stating that everyone, including crime victims, must follow the law, or it must go all out in the other direction and be like the DEATH WISH (q.v.) features which preach that a person not only has a right to defend home and hearth, but also has the right to rid the earth of human vermin.

FIGHTING FOOLS (Monogram, 1949) 69 mins.

Producer, Jan Grippo; director, Reginald LeBorg; screenplay, Edmond Seward, Gerald Schnitzer, Bert Lawrence; art director, David Milton; set decorator, Raymond Boltz, Jr.; assistant directors, Mel Shyer, Ed Morey, Jr.; makeup, Charles Huber; sound, Earl Sitar; camera, William Sickner; editor, William Austin.

Leo Gorcey (Terrence Aloysius "Slip" Mahoney); Huntz Hall (Horace Debussy "Sach" Jones); Billy Benedict (Whitey); David Gorcey (Chuck); Bennie Bartlett (Butch); Gabriel Dell (Gabe Moreno the Reporter); Frankie Darro (Johnny Higgins); Lyle Talbot (Blinky Harris); Bernard Gorcey (Louie Dumbrowski); Teddy Infuhr (Boomer Higgins); Dorothy Vaughan (Mrs. Higgins); Evelynne Eaton (Bunny Talbot); Frank Moran (Goon); Bill Cartledge (Joey Prince); Anthony

Leo Gorcey, Huntz Hall, David Gorcey, Bennie Bartlett, and Billy Benedict in FIGHTING FOOLS (1949).

Warde (Marty); Ralph Peters (Beef); Tom Kennedy (Rosemeyer the Arena Guard); Ben Welden (Lefty Conlin); Eddie Gribbon (Highball); Marty Mason (Noodles); Paul Maxey (Editor); Robert Walcott (Jimmy Higgins); Meyer Grace (Lug); Frank Hagney (Tough Customer); Bert Hanlon (Dave Dorgan); Bert Conway (Dynamite Carson); Bud Gorman (Call Boy); Roland Dupree (Young Man in Sweetshop); Stanley Andrews (Boxing Commissioner); Johnny Duncan (Fighter in Gym); Sam Hayes (Sam Radar the Announcer); Mike Pat Donovan (Pete the Bartender); Jack Mower (Fight Announcer); Joe Greb (Ad Lib); Eddie Rio (Handler); Carl Sklover (Knockdown Timekeeper); Joe Gray, Larery Anzalone, Johnny Kern, Al Bayne (Fighters).

"The Bowery Boys" series at Monogram often delved into the established gangster genre for its plotlines and this outing combined the boys' typical ghetto humor with prize fighting and hoodlums to develop a "moderately entertaining programmer" (Variety). Well directed by Reginald LeBorg, this feature boasted a fine cast of competent character players, highlighted by Lyle Talbot's performance as corrupt fight manager Blinky Harris. Of course, Leo Gorcey as Slip contributed his usual assaults on the English language while Huntz Hall as Sach provided his standard buffoonery.

When a young boxer--a pal of the Bowery Boys--dies after a boxing match set up by gangsters through a crooked manager (Talbot), Gorcey, Hall, Gabe (Gabriel Dell), and the rest of the boys bring the culprits to justice. The dead boy's brother (Frankie Darro) quits the ring after his sibling's death, but the Bowery contingent persuade him to put his gloves back on and fight for the title. He wins the championship.

FIGHTING ROOKIE (Mayfair, 1934) 67 mins.

Producer, Larry Darmour; director, Spencer Gordon Bennet; story, Homer King Gordon; screenplay, George Morgan; art director, Paul Palmentola; assistant director, Harry Knight; sound, Tom Lambert; camera, James S. Brown, Jr.; editor, Fred Bain.

Jack LaRue (Jim Trent); Ada Ince (Molly Malone); DeWitt Jennings (Police Commissioner); Matthew Betz (Lonie Cantor); Arthur Belasco (Turner Bates); Thomas Brower (Tom Malone); Max Wagner (Jake the Henchman); Ferris Taylor (Police Captain); Bob Reeves (Cop); Wally Wales (Gambler); Frank Meredith (Cop on Raid); Otto Hans (Hans the Houseboy).

A young policeman (Jack LaRue) is told to get the goods on a hoodlum (Matthew Betz) and his confederates. But during a warehouse robbery, the gangsters make it appear LaRue was intoxicated while on duty. When the police commissioner later acknowledges he was framed, the rookie cop agrees to pretend he is thrown off the force. He then joins with the gangsters and in doing so loses the confidence of his girl (Ada Ince), his former co-workers, and his best buddy. LaRue does obtain the needed records to convict the hoodlum and his pals.

THE FIGHTING ROOKIE was one of several gangster and action pictures producer Larry Darmour made for the independent Mayfair Pictures. Star Jack LaRue had scored a sensation in 1933 as the oily, sensuous gangster in Paramount's prestige production of THE STORY OF TEMPLE DRAKE (see: B/V) and although he never rivaled James Cagney, Edward G. Robinson, or George Raft, LaRue did star in a large number of gangster movies and was one of the screen's better purveyors of the slick, crooked, well-dressed hoodlum who appeals to the ladies. In this outing, however, he had a rare hero's role and he carried it off nicely. As Film Daily noted, "An unusually original plot treatment lifts this out of the ruck of underworld plays."

The film proved commercial enough that producer Darmour reunited LaRue and director Spencer Gordon Bennet the next year for CALLING ALL CARS with LaRue again in a heroic part.

FINAL CHAPTER--WALKING TALL (American International, 1977) C
    112 mins.

Producer, Charles A. Pratt, director, Jack Starrett; story, Howard Kreitsek; screenplay, Kreitsek, Samuel A. Peeples; music, Walter Scharf; art director, Joe Altadonna; costumes/wardrobe, Michael W. Hoffman, Chris Zamara; assistant director, Carl Olsen; stunt coordinator, Paul Nuckles; sound, John K. Wilkinson, Robert Miller; camera, Robert B. Hauser; editor, Housely Stevenson.

Bo Svenson (Buford Pusser); Margaret Blye (Luan); Forrest Tucker, Lurene Tuttle (Pusser's Parents); Morgan Woodward (The Boss); Libby Boone (Pusser's Secretary); Leif Garrett, Dawn Lyn (Pusser's Children); Bruce Glover (Pusser's Deputy); Taylor Lacher (Martin French); Sandy McPeak (Lloyd Tatum); Logan Ramsey (John Witter); Robert Phillips (Johnny); Clay Tanner (O. Q. Teal); David Adams (Robbie Teal); Vance Davis (Aaron); H. B. Haggerty (Bulo); John Malloy (Producer).

See: WALKING TALL

FINGER PRINTS (Universal, 1931) ten chapters

Director, Ray Taylor; story, Arthur B. Reeve; screenplay, George Morgan, George H. Plympton, Basil Dickey.

Kenneth Harlan (Gary Gordon); Edna Murphy (Lola Mackey); Gayne Whitman (Kent Martin); Gertrude Astor (Jane Madden); William Worthington (John Mackey); William Thorne (Joe Burke); Monte Montague (Officer Rooney).

Chapters: 1) The Dance of Death; 2) A Fugitive of Fear;
3) Toll of the Sea; 4) The Sinister Shadow; 5) The Plunge of
Peril; 6) The Finger of Fate, 7) The Depths of Doom, 0) The
Thundering Terror; 9) Flames of Fury; 10) The Final Reckoning.

FINGER PRINTS was the first sound serial to use the gangster format for its plotline; the hoodlums here are a band of smugglers called the River Gang. Running only ten episodes, this outing benefitted from a substantial script and quick pacing.

Secret Service Agent Gary Gordon (Kenneth Harlan) must
capture a smuggling gang, and he finds that his girlfriend's (Edna
Murphy) father (Willing Worthington) is a member. When the latter's
partner (William Thorne) is murdered, cohort Kent Martin (Gayne
Whitman) claims he has enough evidence to convict Worthington of
the crime and blackmails him for the hand of Murphy in marriage,
despite the fact that Whitman is loved by loyal Jane (Gertrude Astor). When the blackmail gambit fails, Whitman kidnaps Murphy
and absconds with her to a cave hideout. But Harlan rescues her
and Whitman finally confesses to homicide, thus clearing the father
of the crime.

FINGERMAN (Allied Artists, 1955) 81 mins.

Producer, Lindsley Parsons; director, Harold Schuster; story, Morris Lipsius, John Lardner; screenplay, Warren Douglas; music, Paul
Dunlap; camera, William Sickner; editor, Maurice Wright.

Frank Lovejoy (Casey Martin); Forrest Tucker (Dutch Becker);
Peggie Castle (Gladys Baker); Timothy Carey (Lou Terpe); John
Cliff (Cooper); William Leicester (Rogers); Glen Gordon (Carlos
Armor); John Close (Walters); Hugh Sanders (Mr. Burns); Eve-
lynne Eaton (Lucille); Charles Maxwell (Amory); Lewis Charles
(Lefty Stern); Henry Kulky (Louie); Joi Lansing (Girl at Bar).

Four-time loser Casey Martin (Frank Lovejoy) participates in
a truck hijacking and is hauled in by Treasury agents who offer
him a deal. He can have his freedom if he will work with them to
gain evidence against mobster Dutch Becker (Forrest Tucker).
Eventually, he agrees to be the fingerman in the operation.
Through a former hooker (Peggie Castle), Lovejoy is able to connect with Tucker, and in the process falls in love with Castle.
She is later murdered for being disloyal and Lovejoy is all the more
determined to bring Tucker to task. He succeeds.

Supposedly a true story with the names changed, this taut
programmer was made in a semi-documentary style so popular with
crime melodramas thanks to the success of TV's "Dragnet." Forrest Tucker as the mobster grabs the limelight as the cold, ruthless murderer who hides behind a business-like facade.

FIVE GOLDEN DRAGONS (Warner-Pathe/Anglo Amalgamated, 1968) C 70 mins.

Producer, Harry Alan Towers; director, Jeremy Summers; screenplay, Peter Welbeck; assistant director, Anthony Waye; art director, Scott MacGregor; music, Malcolm Lockyer; songs, Lockyer and Hal Shapers; Lockyer and Sid Colin; sound, Brian Marshall; camera, John von Kotze; editor, Donald J. Cohen.

Bob Cummings (Bob Mitchell); Rupert Davies (Commissioner Sanders); Margaret Lee (Magda); Maria Perschy (Margret); Klaus Kinski (Gert); Maria Rohm (Ingrid); Sieghardt Rupp (Peterson); Brian Donlevy, Dan Duryea, Christopher Lee, Goerge Raft (The Golden Dragons).

Filmed in Hong Kong, this British-West German coproduction was another in a series of cheaply made but exotic melodramas from producer Harry Alan Towers, who was responsible for the "Fu Manchu" series produced about the same time. English and West German versions were shot simultaneously, but with different directors, and the movie received scattered U.S. release in 1968, although its main visibility has been via television.
Set in Hong Kong, expatriate American playboy Bob Mitchell (Bob Cummings) arrives and is soon involved with two sexy women (Maria Perschy, Margaret Lee) and is soon in the midst of several murders and as well as being hunted by a hitman (Klaus Kinski) who works for a secret organization called The Golden Dragons. Cummings finally deduces that the Dragons' leaders want to sell out their interests to the Mafia, and his untimely arrival threatens the deal.

THE FLYING SQUAD (British Lion, 1932) 81 mins.

Producer, S. W. Smith; director, F. W. Kraemer; based on the novel by Edgar Wallace; screenplay, Bryan Edgar Wallace.

Harold Huth (Mark McGill); Carol Goodner (Ann Perryman); Edward Chapman (Sedeman); Campbell Gullan (Tiser); Harry Wilcoxon (Inspector Bradley); Abraham Sofaer (Li Yoseph); Joseph Cunningham (Simmonds).

THE FLYING SQUAD (Associated British, 1940) 64 mins.

Producer, Walter C. Mycroft; director, Herbert Brenon; based on the novel by Edgar Wallace; screenplay, Doreen Montgomery; camera, Claude Friese-Greene, W. Harvey.

Sebastian Shaw (Inspector Bradley); Phyllis Brooks (Ann Perryman); Jack Hawkins (Mark McGill); Basil Radford (Sederman); Ludwig Stossel (Li Yoseph); Manning Whiley (Ronnie Perryman);

Kathleen Harrison (Mrs. Schifan); Cyril Smith (Tiser); Henry Oscar (Commissioner); Kynaston Reeves (Magistrate).

Edgar Wallace's 1928 novel was the basis for two British productions, with both features pretty much following the identical plotline of murder and smuggling. The 1940 version utilized Hollywood star(let) Phyllis Brooks, whose comely looks and talent had decorated many a stateside gangster film.

Edgar Wallace died in 1932, the year British Lion produced the initial version of THE FLYING SQUAD. The famous thriller writer had been chairman of the board of the company and had written and even directed features for British Lion based upon his works. This time his son, Byran Edgar Wallace, adapted his father's book to the screen and it was produced by S. W. Smith, the producer who had worked with the senior Wallace on his previous studio efforts. The story tells of the chief (Harold Huth) of a smuggling net who murders a man. When the victim's pretty sister (Carol Goodner) arrives from Paris, Huth convinces her the crime was really committed by Flying Squad member Bradley (Henry Wilcoxon), but the latter tricks a confession out of the gangster which leads to the arrest of the dope smugglers.

In 1940 Associated British Film Distributors remade the property with Miss Brooks pursuing her brother's killer. Working with a Scotland Yard detective (Sebastian Shaw), she joins a smuggling band and gains sufficient evidence to prove its leader is the murderer.

FOLLOW THE LEADER (Monogram, 1944) 65 mins.

Producers, Sam Katzman, Jack Dietz; associate producer, Barney A. Sarecky; director, William Beaudine; story, Ande Lamb; screenplay, William X. Crowley, Beryl Sachs; set decorator, Ernest Hickerson; music director, Edward Kay; assistant director, Arthur Hammond; sound, Glen Glenn; camera, Marcel Le Picard; editor, Carl Pierson.

Leo Gorcey (Muggs McGinnis); Huntz Hall (Glimpy Freedhoff); Dave Durand (Danny); Bud Gorman (James Aloysius "Skinny" Bogerty); Bobby Stone (Speed); Jimmy Strand (Dave); Gabriel Dell (W. W. "Fingers" Belmont); Jack LaRue (Larry); Joan Marsh (Millie McGinnis); Billy Benedict (Spider O'Brien); Mary Gordon (Mrs. McGinnis); Bernard Gorcey (Ginsberg); J. Farrell MacDonald (Clancy); Bryant Washburn (Colonel); Gene Austin, Sherrill Sisters (Entertainers); Sunshine Sammy Morrison (Scruno in Dream).

This outing thrust the East Side kids into combat against crooks robbing government warehouses and then reselling the merchandise which was vital for the war effort.

Muggs (Gorcey) is discharged from the Army because of poor eyesight and returns home only to find that one of his club members (Jimmy Strand) has been arrested and accused of stealing from

a government warehouse where he works. The real culprit, however, is new club member Spider (Benedict). When Benedict is
later killed by his boss for too much casual talk, Gorcey convinces
the police and Army to let him take Benedict's place at the warehouse and learn more about the gang. Meanwhile, Gorcey's pretty
sister (Joan Marsh) is a cigarette girl at a club run by the man
(Jack LaRue) who is behind the stealing. Before long, Gorcey has
solved the caper and returns to the Army as a sergeant.

FOLLOW THE LEADER opens slowly with strained comedy between Leo Gorcey and Huntz Hall in the company barracks and gets
even worse with the use of poor back screen projection when they
are supposedly outside with other soldiers. The supporting players give this entry added substance, especially Mary Gordon as
Gorcey's loving mother, Joan Marsh as his loyal sister, J. Farrell
MacDonald as the neighborhood cop, Bryant Washburn as a colonel,
and Bernard Gorcey as Ginsberg the delicatessen owner. An added
treat in the nightclub scene is Gene Austin singing "Now and Then"
accompanied by the Sherrill Sisters; later Doris Sherrill (then Mrs.
Gene Austin) vocalizes "I Want to be the Leader" while Austin accompanies her on the piano.

FOR THE DEFENSE (Paramount, 1930) 62 mins.

Producer, David O. Selznick; director, John Cromwell; story,
Charles Furthman; screenplay, Oliver H. P. Garrett; sound, Harold
M. McNiff; camera, Charles Lang; editor, George Nichols, Jr.

William Powell (William Foster); Kay Francis (Irene Manners); Scott
Kolk (Defoe); William B. Davidson (District Attorney Stone); John
Elliott (McGann); Thomas Jackson (Daly); Harry Walker (Miller);
James Finlayson (Parrott); Charles West (Joe); Charles Sullivan
(Charlie); Ernest Adams (Eddie Withers); Bertram Marburgh (Judge
Evans); Edward Le Saint (Judge).

A detective (Thomas Jackson) is reviewing the practices of
successful criminal defense lawyer William Foster (William Powell),
who is adored by successful actress Irene Manners (Kay Francis).
Powell refuses to wed her and, to make him jealous, she pretends
to love lazy playboy Defoe (Scott Kolk). Returning one evening
from a roadhouse, with Francis driving, their car hits and kills a
pedestrian and Kolk takes the blame. When he goes to trial, Powell
defends him. As the evidence mounts, Powell learns it was actually Francis driving the car and he attempts, under the influence of
alcohol, to bribe a juror to get a hung jury. Jackson, though,
convinces the juror to confess to the would-be bribe and Powell is
arrested and pleads guilty. He is sent to prison for five years,
with Francis promising to wait for him.
Photoplay magazine termed this slick melodrama "good." It
was a top-notch production highlighted by Oliver H. P. Garrett's
realistic scenario and dialogue. Allegedly based on real life Gotham

attorney William J. Fallon, the film provides suave William Powell with a meaty assignment, while co-star Kay Francis is her alluring self as the selfish stage actress. (The real life Fallon would also be the subject of Warner Bros.' 1932 film THE MOUTHPIECE, starring Warren William.)

FOR THE DEFENSE is noteworthy as a gangster movie which does not rely on the usual gritty underworld of hoodlums for its plot. Instead it concentrates on the mouthpieces who defend such characters. William Foster's character exemplifies the type of well-educated and intelligent lawyer who makes a practice of handling underworld cases and becoming rich and notorious in the process. Too rarely has Hollywood focussed on the legal profession's involvement with mobsters, usually providing only brief cameo portrayals of stereotyped fast-talking legal men. While this film is hardly an expose of such individuals, it does provide another angle of the gangster motif.

FORBIDDEN (Universal, 1953) 84 mins.

Producer, Ted Richmond; director, Rudolph Mate; story, William Sackheim; screenplay, Sackheim, Gil Doud; art directors, Bernard Herzbrun, Richard Riedel; music, Frank Skinner; camera, William Daniels; editor, Edward Curtiss.

Tony Curtis (Eddie Darrow); Joanne Dru (Christine); Lyle Bettger (Justin Keit); Marvin Miller (Chalmer); Victor Sen Yung (Allan); Peter J. Mamakos (Sam); Mae Tai Sing (Soo Lee); Howard Chuman (Hon-Fai); Weaver Levy (Tang); Harold Fong (Wong); David Sharpe (Leon); Aen Ling Chow, Leemoi Chu (Girl Dealers); Alan Dexter (Barney); Barry Bernard (Black); Harry Lauter (Holly); Reginald Sheffield (Englishman); Alphonse Martell (Guest); Al Ferguson (Harbor Master); Jimmy Gray (Guard); Spencer Chan (Chin).

Mobster lord Justin Keit (Lyle Bettger) discovers his moll Christine (Joanne Dru) has left the country, taking evidence with her that could convict him. He hires gangster Eddie Darrow (Tony Curtis) to follow the girl to Macao where she has a new husband. Curtis' mission is to kill her before she gets Bettger arrested. It develops that Dru is the girl Curtis once loved and in Macao the two rekindle their affair only to find themselves menaced by the gangster and the woman's husband and native pals. A timely explosion removes the bad guys, leaving the two lovers to a life of happiness.

This "carbon little 'B' melodrama" (The New York Times) was a flimsy outing full of double-crossings which even failed to deliver real exotic locales--the Macao of the film was all accomplished on the Universal backlot.

FORCE OF EVIL (Metro-Goldwyn-Mayer, 1948) 78 mins.

Producer, Bob Roberts; director, Abraham Polonsky; based on the
novel Tucker's People by Ira Wolfert; screenplay, Polonsky, Wolfert;
music, David Raksin; music director, Rudolph Polk; art director,
Richard Day; set decorator, Edward G. Boyle; assistant director,
Robert Aldrich; makeup, Gus Norin; sound, Frank Webster; camera,
George Barnes; editor, Art Seld.

John Garfield (Joe Morse); Beatrice Pearson (Doris Lowry); Thomas
Gomez (Leo Morse); Roy Roberts (Ben Tucker); Marie Windsor (Ed-
na Tucker); Howland Chamberlin (Fred Bauer); Paul McVey (Hobe
Wheelock); Jack Overman (Juice); Tim Ryan (Johnson); Barbara
Woodell (Mary); Raymond Largay (Bunty); Stanley Prager (Wally);
Beau Bridges (Frankie); Allan Mathews (Badley); Barry Kelley
(Egan); Sheldon Leonard (Ficco); Jan Dennis (Mrs. Bauer); Geor-
gia Backus (Mrs. Morse); Sid Tomack (Two and Two).

Brothers Joe Morse (John Garfield) and Leo Morse (Thomas
Gomez) work for big-time racketeers in the numbers game. Through
the love of Doris Lowry (Beatrice Pearson), Garfield, an attorney
who abandoned his high level ideals for the easy racketeering life,
wants to break away from the mob. Eventually, he assists in the
dismantling of the numbers operation.
Taken from Ira Wolfert's (who co-scripted the screenplay with
director Abraham Polonsky) 1943 novel Tucker's People, FORCE OF
EVIL is one of John Garfield's lesser forays into the gangster film
genre. Variety notes the film "... fails to develop the excitement
hinted at in the title.... A poetic almost allegorical, interpretation
keeps intruding on the tougher elements of the plot...."
While John Garfield maximizes his role of Joe Morse, it is the
on-site shooting in New York City and the supporting work of
Thomas Gomez as his brother and Roy Roberts as the chief mobster
which provide the sombre film with its zest.

FORCED VENGEANCE (Metro-Goldwyn-Mayer/United Artists, 1982)
C 90 mins.

Producer, John B. Bennett; director, James Fargo; screenplay,
Franklin Thompson; production designer, George B. Chan; music,
William Goldstein; assistant directors, Stan Zabka, Patty Chan; cam-
era, Rexford Metz; editor, Irving C. Rosenblum.

Chuck Norris (Josh); Mary Louise Weller (Claire); Camila Griggs
(Joy); Michael Cavanaugh (Stan); David Opatoshu (Sam); Seiji
Sakaguchi (Cam); Frank Michael Liu (David); Bob Minor (Leroy);
Lloyd Kino (Inspector); Leigh Hamilton (Sally); Howard Caine (Milt);
Robert Emhardt (Carl); Roger Behrstock (Ron); Jimmy Shaw (In-
spector).

Chuck Norris' martial arts features are hardly created for the critics or for upper-crust film enthusiasts, but for the masses who thrive on his swift style of meting out justice. FORCED VENGEANCE is the kind of feature which has all the components necessary to make it a box office success. From its opening slow motion kung fu battle sequences through its Hong Kong-based story, FORCED VENGEANCE never runs dry of violence or the throbbing action so craved by the star's followers.

Norris is Josh Randall, the strong arm man for honest Hong Kong gambling tycoon Sam Paschal (David Opatoshu). After collecting a gambling debt for his boss in California, Norris returns to the Orient, where mobsters are attempting to "buy out" his boss. When the latter refuses to accede, he and his son are killed and his daughter (Camila Griggs) is threatened. Norris, who loves Griggs, sets out to even the score, especially against the gangster king (Michael Cavanaugh) responsible.

FORT APACHE, THE BRONX (Twentieth Century-Fox/Time-Life Films, 1981) C 120 mins.

Executive producer, David Susskind; producers, Martin Richards, Tom Fiorello; co-producers, Mary Lea Johnson, Gill Champion; director, Daniel Petrie; suggested by the experiences of Thomas Mulhearn, Pete Tessitore; production designer, Ben Edwards; art director, Christopher Nowak; music, Jonathan Tunick; assistant

Paul Newman and Edward Asner in FORT APACHE, THE BRONX (1981).

directors, Alex Hapsas, Joe Ray; costumes, John Boxer; camera, John Alcott; editor, Rita Roland.

Paul Newman (Murphy); Edward Asner (Connolly); Ken Wahl (Corelli); Danny Aiello (Morgan); Rachel Ticotin (Isabella); Pam Grier (Charlotte); Kathleen Beller (Theresa); Tito Goya (Jumper/Detective); Miguel Pinero (Hernando); Jaime Tirelli (Jose); Lance William Guercia (Track Star); Ronnie Clanton (Pimp); Clifford David (Dacey); Sully Boyar (Dugan); Michael Higgins (Heffernan); Rik Colitti (Pantuzzi); Irving Metzman (Applebaum); Frank Adu (Clendennon); John Aquiono (Finley); Norman Matlock (Lincoln); John Ring (Donahue); Tony Di Benedetto (Moran); Terence Brady, Randy Jurgenson, Marvin Cohen (Cops at Bar); Paul Gleason, Beinaldo Medina (Detectives); Darryl Edwards, Donald Petrie (Rookies); Thomas A. Carlin (Man with Flat Tire); Frederick Allen (Corelli's Brother); Dominic Chianese (Corelli's Father); Mike Cichette (Wild-Eyed Man); Apu Gueciao (Stabbed Boy); Kim Delgado, Reyno, Dadi Pinero, Cleavant Derricks (Suspects); Dolores Hernandez (Pregnant Girl); Santos Morales (Girl's Father); Ruth Last (Girl's Mother); Jose Rabelo (Girl's Uncle); Gilbert Lewis (Mob Leader); Eric Mourino, Jessica Costello (Boy and Girl on Roof); Gloria Irizarry (Drug Dealer); Manuel Santiago (Intern); Joaquin LaHabana (Transvestite); Fred Strothers (Hospital Buyer); Sylvia "Kuumba" Williams (Bartender); Patricia Dratel (Hostage); Thomas Fiorello (Fence).

"Driving relentlessly to make points that are almost pointless, FORT APACHE, THE BRONX is a very patchy picture, strong on dialog and acting and exceedingly weak on story." (Variety)

At a deteriorated uptown Bronx police station which deals with the riffraff and criminal elements of the depressed area, the police attempt to enforce the law under the near dictatorship of Connolly (Edward Asner) a strict law-and-order commander. Two of his men, Murphy (Paul Newman) and Corelli (Ken Wahl), agree with his viewpoint but know the law must bend on occasions. When they find one of their cohorts (Danny Aiello) has killed a youth, they are torn between loyalty to a pal and their duty of the law. Two other policemen are murdered by a drug-crazed cop hater (Pam Grier) and Newman and Wahl set out to trap the murderer.

Basically a series of vignettes concerning the myriad of criminal elements in the combat zone of the Bronx, this movie is dedicated to the "law abiding citizens" of that realm--who protested the making of the film, figuring correctly it would depict only the sleazy side of their impoverished community. In its gritty, low-life way, FORT APACHE, THE BRONX is not without interest pictorially, but its many subplots do little to sustain viewer interest.

Paul Newman, too old for his part, keeps the picture together via his stout performance. The supporting cast is gripping, but most of the roles are only fleeting bits.

40 POUNDS OF TROUBLE see: LITTLE MISS MARKER

FRAMED (RKO, 1930) 62 mins.

Producer, William Le Baron; associate producer, Henry Hobart; director, George Archainbaud; screenplay, Paul Schofield; dialog, Wallace Smith; sound, Clem Portman; camera, Leo Tover; editor, Jack Kitchen.

Evelyn Brent (Rose Manning); Regis Tomey (Jimmy McArthur [Carter]); Ralf Harolde (Chuck Gaines); Maurice Black (Bing Murdock); William Holden (Inspector McArthur); Robert Emmett O'Connor (Sergeant Schultze); Eddie Kane (Headwaiter).

When a police inspector (William Holden) murders her father, pretty Rose Manning (Evelyn Brent) swears revenge. Five years pass and she is now a nightclub hostess where a bootlegger (Ralf Harolde) courts her. She has her sights on Jimmy Carter (Regis Toomey) whom she learns is the police inspector's son. Jealous Harolde orders his henchman (Maurice Black) to kill Toomey, but before this can happen, Holden, hoping to end the boy's romance with Brent, raids the night spot. When Brent tries to warn Toomey, Harolde attacks her and Toomey comes to the rescue by killing the mobster. To save the young man, Brent then accuses Black of the crime, and Holden, now assured she really loves his son, agrees they can wed.

Evelyn Brent had been one of the silent screen favorites who had easily made the transition to sound films, but she left her home base studio, Paramount, in 1930, and FRAMED, for RKO, was her first freelance assignment. The film was also issued in a silent version.

FRENCH CONNECTION II (Twentieth Century-Fox, 1975) C 119 mins.

Producer, Robert L. Rosen; director, John Frankenheimer; story, Robert and Laurie Dillon; screenplay, the Dillons, Alexander Jacobs; production designer, Jacques Saulnier; art directors, Gerard Viard, Georges Glon; music, Don Ellis; assistant director, Bernard Stora; sound, Ted Soderberg, Bernard Bats; camera, Claude Renoir; editor, Tom Rolf.

Gene Hackman (Popeye Doyle); Fernando Rey (Alain Charnier); Bernard Fresson (Inspector Barthelemy); Jean Pierre Castaldi, Charles Millot (Barthelemy Aides); Cathleen Nesbitt (Mrs. Charnier); Pierre Collet, Alexandre Fabre (Doyle's Tail); Philippe Leotard (Charnier's Bag Man); Ed Lauter (U.S. Colonel); Jacques Dynam (Immigration Officer); Raoul Delfosse (Dutch Captain).

THE FRENCH CONNECTION (1971) (see: B/V) was an amazingly successful Academy Award winning film which helped revive interest in gangster yarns. That vogue was solidified the following year with the release of THE GODFATHER (see: B/V). As a result, THE FRENCH CONNECTION II was released in 1975 with Gene

Gene Hackman in FRENCH CONNECTION II (1975).

Hackman recreating his Academy Award winning characterization as New York City cop Popeye Doyle, a character based on real life law enforcer Eddie Egan. In this episode, compulsive Hackman continues his search for French drug dealer Alain Charnier (Fernando Rey) who eluded the cop at the finale of Part I. His quest takes him to Rey's headquarters in Marseilles, but there the self-assured Hackman finds the local authorities uncooperative. When he is seen on a local beach by Rey, the gangster has Hackman kidnapped and taken to a brothel where he is forcefully addicted to drugs and after several weeks is left for dead on the steps of the police headquarters. Hackman does not die, however, and undertakes a strenuous drug withdrawal program, aided by French policeman Barthelemy (Bernard Fresson). Cured of his addiction, Hackman sets out yet again to corner Rey and following a complex pursuit, he gets his man.

Thanks to Claude Renoir's photography and the Marseilles locales, THE FRENCH CONNECTION II holds visual interest, but its plot is overlong and uninteresting. Too much screen time is relinquished to Hackman and his character's personal quirks. For the most part, THE FRENCH CONNECTION II is an unworthy sequel.

GAMBLING DAUGHTERS (Producers Releasing Corp., 1941) 65 mins.

Producer, T. H. Richmond; director, Max Nosseck; story, Sidney Sheldon, Ben Roberts; screenplay, Joel Kay; camera, Mack Stengler.

Cecilia Parker (Diana Cameron); Roger Pryor (Chance London); Robert Baldwin (Jimmy Parker); Gale Storm (Lilliam); Sig Arno (Professor Bedoin); Janet Shaw (Katherine); Charles Miller (Walter Cameron); Eddie Foster (Nick); Alfred Hall (Dean); Judy Kilgore (Gloria); Gertrude Messinger (Jane); Marvelle Andre (Dorothy); Roberta Smith (Mary).

Wealthy socialites Diana Cameron (Cecilia Parker) and Lillian (Gale Storm) are attracted to the wild side of life and soon are caught in the net of corrupt gangster Chance London (Roger Pryor). When Parker creates a huge debt, Pryor forces her to steal to pay it back and then blackmails her. An insurance investigator, Jimmy Parker (Robert Baldwin), is on the case and uncovers London's racket and comes to Parker's rescue.

Combining exploitation, murder, and gambling, this PRC production was a "fairly amusing whodunit" (Variety) highlighted by responsive acting by Cecilia Parker as the beautiful but hapless heroine and Roger Pryor as the slick gangster. Gale Storm, at the beginning of her career, impressed as the heroine's friend while leading man Robert Baldwin (wed to Parker in real life) was mediocre as the film's serio-comic hero.

GAMBLING SHIP (Paramount, 1933) 70 mins.

Producers, Max Marcin, Louis Gasnier; director, Marcin; based on stories by Peter Ruric; adaptor, Claude Binyon; screenplay, Marcin, Seton I. Miller; camera, Charles Lang.

Cary Grant (Ace Corbin); Benita Hume (Eleanor La Velle); Roscoe Karns (Blooey); Glenda Farrell (Jeanne Sands); Jack LaRue (Pete Manning); Arthur Vinton (Joe Burke); Charles Williams (Baby Face); Edwin Maxwell (District Attorney).

While traveling on a transcontinental train, Ace Corbin (Cary Grant) a gambler avoiding the headlines of a murder trial, pretends to be a tycoon and meets pretty Eleanor La Velle (Benita Hume), a gangster's moll on the make for a sugar daddy, who claims she is a part of the society set. She is the girlfriend of heavily-in-debt gambling ship owner Joe Burke (Arthur Vinton), who wants Grant to purchase the floating casino. Grant becomes interested when he realizes his old rival Pete Manning (Jack LaRue) owns a competing gambling boat. Taking over Vinton's business, Grant lures the gambling trade away from LaRue and the latter bombs Grant's ship and then his gang boards the craft, killing Vinton. In the meanwhile LaRue is washed overboard and drowns. Grant and Hume, now in love, reach shore safely.

This sad potboiler is typical of the inane gangster movies issued by major studios during the 1930s. Its preposterous plot defeats its fine cast and the whole production sinks under the ponderous direction of Louis Gasnier. Carole Lombard was scheduled originally for the female lead but rejected the role and British newcomer Benita Hume took over. Cary Grant, in his first top-billed casting, plays Ace Corbin adequately. Roscoe Karns and Glenda Farrell as wisecrackers are delightful, as is villainous Jack LaRue.

GAMBLING SHIP (Universal, 1939) 62 mins.

Producer, Irving Starr; director, Aubrey H. Scotto; based on the story "Lady Luck" by G. Carleton Brown, Emanuel Manheim; adaptor, Alex Gottlieb; camera, George Meehan; editor, Ed Curtis.

Robert Wilcox (Larry Mitchell); Helen Mack (Mollie Riley); Ed Brophy (Innocent); Joseph Sawyer (Tony Garzone); Irving Pichel (Professor); Selmer Jackson (Steve Riley); Sam McDaniels (Speedy); Dorothy Vaughn (Matron); Al Hill (Fingers); John Harmon (Cramer); Rudolph Chavers (Snowflake); Tim Davis (Nick).

Although not a remake of the 1933 Paramount film, supra, this Universal programmer does have plot similarities to that earlier production. Both deal with rival gamblers and their seaboard operations and both contain the usual modicum of romance. Also, neither production is particularly believable.

A crooked gambling tycoon named Professor (Irving Pichel) operates a gambling ship and uses dishonest methods to put a rival (Selmer Jackson) out of business. Although an onboard explosion kills Jackson, his daughter (Helen Mack) assumes control and the ship begins to thrive. Pichel plans to finish her as well, but a special investigator, Larry Mitchell (Robert Wilcox), is assigned to the case and becomes part of the mobster's henchmen. In the midst of evidence gathering, he becomes enamored of Mack.

An interesting note is that star Robert Wilcox, many years after alcoholism ended his career, had a run-in with an actual gangster, even knocking him out in a fight after the man romanced Wilcox's wife, actress Diana Barrymore, who related the incident in her tell-all autobiography, Too Much Too Soon (1957).

LE GANG DES OTAGES [The Hostage Gang] (Gaumont, 1973) C 80 mins.

Director, Edouard Molinaro; screenplay, Alphonse Bodard, Molinaro; camera, Raoul Coutard; editor, Robert Ishardon.

Daniel Cauchy (Leader); Bulle Ogler (Liliane); Gilles Segal (Serge).

A substrata of gangsterdom, the hoodlums who take advantage of those involved in organized crime as well as innocent citizens, is covered in this French movie which rates a B+. Based on an actual case, the film was topical when released, but its lack of internationally known performers hurt its commercial appeal.

A small time gang leader (Daniel Gauchy) with his cohort (Gilles Segal) is arrested and brought to trial for a series of crimes. With the aid of his sexually free girlfriend (Bulle Ogler), who smuggles arms to her lover and his buddy in a magistrate's office, the two escape from the courthouse where they are being tried and they take hostages with them. They then attempt to use organized crime figures as go-betweens for their eventual escape but are finally foiled.

GANGS, INC. (Producers Releasing Corp., 1941) 69 mins.

Producer, Maurice [King] Kozinsky; director, Phil Rosen; screenplay, Martin Mooney; music, Johnny Lange, Lew Porter; camera, Arthur Martinelli; editor, Martin G. Cohn.

With: Joan Woodbury, John Archer, Linda Ware, Jack LaRue, Vince Barnett, Gavin Gordon, Philip Trent, William Halligan, Alan Ladd, George Pembroke, Selmer Jackson, Kenneth Harlan, Bryant Washburn, Alden Chase, Robert Strange, Alex Callam.

When her family is harmed by the machinations of a corrupt gangster (Jack LaRue), a young woman (Joan Woodbury) infiltrates

the racketeer's operation to get the goods on him. When she learns
that two undercover investigators (John Archer, Alan Ladd) are
working on the case, she helps them obtain needed information.
For her illegal part in gaining the data, she is sentenced to prison,
but goes there satisfied she has ruined the mobster.

Produced on a $20,000 budget and churned out in a few days
by director Phil Rosen, this efficient gangster film was the first
production effort of Maurice and Frank Kozinsky, better known as
the King Brothers. The duo would make many other low budget
films, including DILLINGER (1945) (see: B/V) which is considered
a classic. This debut production was first released as PAPER BUL-
LETS but was changed to CRIME, INC for more box office allure.
The film proved to be a big moneymaker the second time around
when PRC reissued it in 1943 as GANGS, INC, with supporting
player Alan Ladd given star billing, having caused a sensation the
year before in THIS GUN FOR HIRE (see: B/V).

GANGS OF NEW YORK (Republic, 1938) 67 mins.

Director, James Cruze; suggested by the book by Herbert Asbury;
story, Sam Fuller; screenplay, Wellyn Totman, Fuller, Charles
Francis Royal; additional dialog, Jack Townley; music director,
Alberto Colombo; camera, Ernest Miller; editor, William Morgan.

Robert Gleckler (seated), Charles Bickford, George Magrill, Harold
Huber, Pat McKee, Maxie Rosenbloom, Fred Kohler (seated), and
John Wray (seated) in GANGS OF NEW YORK (1938).

Charles Bickford (Rocky Thorpe/John Franklin); Ann Dvorak (Connie); Alan Baxter (Dancer); Wynne Gibson (Orchid); Harold Huber (Panatella); Willard Robertson (Sullivan); Maxie Rosenbloom (Tombstone); Charles Trowbridge (Attorney Lucas); John Wray (Maddock); Jonathan Hale (Warden); Fred Kohler (Kruger); Howard Phillips (Al Benson); Robert Gleckler (Nolan); Elliot Sullivan (Hopkins); Maurice Cass (Phillips).

Notorious gangster Rocky Thorpe (Charles Bickford) is about to be released from jail and, to penetrate his gang, the mobster's law enforcer lookalike, John Franklin (Charles Bickford), takes his place as the gang leader. As a result, Franklin rounds up the requisite evidence to keep Thorpe behind bars. Along the way his ruse is almost destroyed by moll Wynne Gibson, while Franklin romances pretty Connie (Ann Dvorak).

Taken from Herbert Asbury's book (1928), this Republic programmer was "a first-rate gangster melodrama" per Variety and the trade paper added, "James Cruze's direction is A-1 throughout, the dialog is punchy and Ernest Miller has done a bangup contribution in photography." It should be noted the movie also contained an outstanding cast with Charles Bickford strong in his dual assignment, Alan Baxter, Maxie Rosenbloom, John Wray, and Harold Huber as hoods, and Wynne Gibson effective as the gilded gun moll.

The movie was a substantial moneymaker for fledgling Republic Pictures and engendered a sequel two years later, GANGS OF CHICAGO (see: B/V).

THE GANGSTER CHRONICLES (NBC-TV, 2/12/81 to 5/8/81) C 480 mins.

Executive producers, Jack Laird, Jack McAdams, Matthew Rapf; supervising producer, James McAdams; producers, Stuart Cohen, Mark Rodgers, John G. Stephens; directors, Richard Sarafian, Leo Penn, Nicholas Sgarro, Vincent McEveety; teleplay, Richard McKoker [Richard Alan Simmons]; music, Billy Goldenberg, John Cacavas; theme music, Goldenberg.

Michael Nouri (Charlie Luciano); Joe Penny (Benny Siegel); Brian Benben (Michael Lasker); Madeline Stowe (Ruth Lasker); Chad Redding (Joy Osler); Kathleen Lloyd (Stella Siegel); Markie Post (Chris Brennan); Richard Castellano (Joe Masseria); Louis Giambalvo (Al Capone); Jonathan Banks (Dutch Schultz); Allan Arbus (Mrs. Goodman); Joseph Mascolo (Salvatore Maranzano); Robert Davi (Vito Genovese); Robert Burke (Albert Anastasia); Jon Polito (Tommy Lucchese); David Wilson (Vincent "Mad Dog" Coll); Kenneth Tigar (Thomas Dewey); Frank Cherry (Peter Coll); Robert F. Lyons (Legs Diamond); Paul Lieber (Davey Levine); Theresa Saldana (Gina Genovese); Louis Welch (Tony Roscini); Dominic Barto (Morello); Jay Varella (Batista); Tony Raymond (Charlie Luciano as a Boy); Paul Regina (Charlie Luciano as a Teenager); Tony Lattore (Michael

Lasker as a Boy); John Friedrich (Michael Lasker as a Teenager); Cyril O'Reilly (Benny Siegel as a Boy); Mitchell Schorr (Benny Siegel as a Teenager); E.G. Marshall (Narrator, Episodes #1-#7); Danny Dark (Narrator, Episodes #8-#10).

Richard Alan Simmons created and wrote (as Richard McKoker) this well done chronology of the Prohibition era which was shown on NBC-TV in a padded three-hour time period. Nonetheless, the tele-film flavorfully captures the era of lawlessness and delves into the psychology of the creation of gangsters, most of them here of Italian origins. Due to this touchy ethnic situation, the program not only required parental discretion but also contained a disclaimer that it did not intentionally bring adverse reflection to any ethnic group through stereotyping.

THE GANGSTER CHRONICLES details the career of Charles "Lucky" Luciano (Michael Nouri), from his days as the son of Italian immigrants in New York City where he suffered the Lower East Side's poverty and prejudice, to his rise as a gangland leader and association with Michael Lasker (Biran Benben), the Jewish brains behind the operation. The initial segment concludes with the expansion of Luciano's gangster domain and his story is fol-lowed in later segments, culminating in his being deported as an undesirable alien in 1946.

Relying less on violence and more on characterization, this video outing is satisfying, highlighted by Michael Nouri's well-shaded interpretation of the title character, who was also the sub-ject of the theatrical feature, LUCKY LUCIANO (see: B/V) in 1974.

GANGSTERS OF THE SEA see: OUT OF SINGAPORE

THE GAUNT STRANGER see: THE RINGER

GET CARTER (Metro-Goldwyn-Mayer, 1971) C 111 mins.

Producer, Michael Klinger; director, Mike Hodges; based on the novel Jack's Return Home by Ted Lewis; screenplay, Hodges; mu-sic, Roy Budd; song, Budd and Jack Fishman; production design-er, Asheton Gorton; art director, Roger King; costumes, Vangie Harrison; assistant director, Keith Evans; sound, Chris Wangler; special effects, Jack Wallis; camera, Wolfgang Suschitzky; editor, John Trumper.

Michael Caine (Jack Carter); Ian Hendry (Eric); Britt Eklund (Anna); John Osborne (Kinnear); Tony Beckley (Peter); George Sewell (Con); Geraldine Moffatt (Glenda); Dorothy White (Margaret); Rosemaria Dunham (Edna); Petra Markham (Doreen); Alum Armstrong (Keith); Bryan Mosley (Brumby); Glynn Edwards (Albert); Bernard Hepton (Thorpe); Terence Rigby (Gerald Fletcher); John Bindon (Sid Fletcher); Godfrey Quigley (Eddie).

Bryan Mosky and Michael Caine in GET CARTER (1971).

"GET CARTER is a gangster movie set in the contemporary north of England. And like the best gangster movies out of the American 30s and 40s, it has the cold, hard gleam of newly polished chromium.... It is, as they say, a movie-movie, full of surprising images and bizarre confrontations, fast, though, action and cryptic exposition which forces the watcher to stay on his toes and do a lot of his own putting-together" (Charles Champlin, Los Angeles Times). "GET CARTER is a doggedly nasty piece of business made in blatant but inept imitation of POINT BLANK [see: B/V]. While the violence in POINT BLANK defines some surreal and chilling points about the savagery of contemporary urban life, the mayhem in GET CARTER is a gruesome and almost pornographic visual obsession" (Time magazine).

Taken from Ted Lewis' 1970 novel, this Certificate X British melodrama detailed the story of London hired killer Jack Carter (Michael Caine) returning home to Newcastle for his younger brother's funeral. The dead man, an honest businessman, had been murdered by the mob. Caine methodically finds out who was responsible for the murder and kills each of them, his trek taking him through the city's underworld.

In Film Review 1971-72 (1971), F. Maurice Speed declared, "As tough incisive and coldly brutal as any American effort in the same category.... The film had the advantage of a smooth, convincing portrayal of a casual assassin from Michael Caine."

One year later, Metro-Goldwyn-Mayer remade the feature,

this time as a black exploitation entry set in Los Angeles, and called HIT MAN (q.v.). It starred Bernie Casey as the revenge-bent gunman.

GET CHRISTIE LOVE! (Wolper Productions/ABC-TV, 1/22/74) C 78 mins.

Executive producer, Lawrence Turman; producer, Peter Nelson; associate producer, Eddie Seta; director, William A. Graham; based on the novel The Ledger by Dorothy Uhnak; teleplay, George Kirgo; music, Allyn Ferguson, Jack Elliott; camera, Meredith Nicholson; editor, Jim Benson.

Teresa Graves (Christie Love); Harry Guardino (Captain Casey Reardon); Louise Sorel (Helena Varga); Paul Stevens (Enzo Cortino); Andy Romano (Sergeant Seymour Greenberg); Debbie Dozier (Amy); Tracy Roberts (Gwen Fenley); Lee Paul (Max Loomis); Lynne Holmes (Celia Jackson); Bill Henderson (Sergeant Stoner Martin); Totis Vandis (Spiliolis); Davis Roberts (Myron Jones); Richard Hurst (Sergeant Tom Farrell); Byron Chung (Ykari).

Dorothy Uhnak's novel Law and Order was originally filmed as a TV pilot called THE BAIT (1973) and then reworked into this vehicle for lovely black actress Teresa Graves, who has since abandoned show business for religious work. "Tough cop ... soft lady ... out to rip the heart out of the mob. NO wonder the mob's qut to GET CHRISTIE LOVE!" read the ads for this telefilm. The feature generated the series, "Get Christie Love" which ran on ABC-TV from 1974-75 starring Graves.
Here police detective Christie Love (Graves) is ordered by her superior (Harry Guardino) to work undercover to get the goods on those behind a big drug operation. When she finds the drug pushers have connections with the underworld, she is targeted for extinction by the mob.

THE GET-AWAY (Metro-Goldwyn-Mayer, 1941) 88 mins.

Producer, J. Walter Ruben; director, Edward Buzzell; story, Ruben, Wells Root; screenplay, Root, W. R. Burnett; camera, Sidney Wagner; editor, James E. Newcom.

Robert Sterling (Jeff Crane); Charles Winninger (Dr. Josiah Glaze); Donna Reed (Maria Theresa O'Reilly); Henry O'Neill (Warden Alcott); Dan Dailey, Jr. (Sonny Black); Don Douglas (Jiff Duff); Ernest Whitman (Moose); Grant Withers (Parker); Chester Gan (Sam); Charles Wagenheim (Hutch); Guy Kingsford (George); Matty Fain (Bryan).

This is a remake of PUBLIC HERO NO. 1 (see: B/V) produced

by Metro-Goldwyn-Mayer a half-dozen years earlier. Unlike most revampings, this one was "a fast moving melodrama that carries plenty of sock for the action addicts" (Variety). The same reviewer noted, "[Director] Edward Buzzell injects plenty of suspense and excitement in the fast-moving tale of the G-Men vs. crime." Although this programmer uses stock footage from the original feature, it was done with care and didn't spoil the overall effect.

Robert Sterling starred as Jeff Crane, an FBI undercover man who is sent to prison to get in good with gangster Sonny Black (Dan Dailey, Jr.) and learn about his illegal operations. To do so, he sets up a prison break and he and Dailey escape. Complications arise when Sterling falls in love with the hood's pretty sister (Donna Reed). To hide his identity, Sterling takes part in several of the gang's heists. As a result Sterling is denounced by his law enforcement superiors. Finally, he corners the gang and brings them to justice.

THE GIRL FROM CHICAGO (Warner Bros., 1927) 61 mins.

Director, Ray Enright; based on the book Business Is Best by Arthur Somers Roche; screenplay, Graham Baker; assistant director, Frank Shaw; camera, Hal Mohr.

Rockcliffe Fellowes and Myrna Loy in THE GIRL FROM CHICAGO (1927).

Conrad Nagel (Handsome Joe); Myrna Loy (Mary Carlton); William Russell (Big Steve Drummond); Carrol Nye (Bob Carlton); Paul Panzer (Dopey); Erville Alderson (Colonel Carlton).

Southern belle Mary Carlton (Myrna Loy) lives with her invalid planter father (Erville Alderson) on their plantation and she receives a letter from her brother (Carroll Nye) stating that he is in prison in New York City for a murder he did not commit and that he is facing the electric chair. She goes to Gotham to save him and learns he has been involved with gangster Handsome Joe (Conrad Nagel) and the gang he frequents. Pretending to be a gun moll, Loy becomes friendly with Nagel and his pal (William Russell), with the latter liking her so much he gives her a speakeasy party. When she spurns Russell, he admits to the crime for which her brother went to jail and she also finds out that Nagel is really an undercover policeman. Together they overcome the crooks.
This fairly entertaining picture, with its soap opera plot, remains of interest due to its cast, especially Conrad Nagel and Myrna Loy who later made easy transitions to sound, although it required several years for Myrna Loy to obtain her proper niche in features.

THE GIRL IN 313 (Twentieth Century-Fox, 1940) 54 mins.

Producer, Sol M. Wurtzel; director, Ricardo Cortez; story, Hilda Stone; screenplay, Barry Trivers, Clay Adams; music, Emil Newman; camera, Edward Cronjager; editor, Louis Loeffler.

Florence Rice (Joan Matthews); Kent Taylor (Gregg Dunn); Lionel Atwill (Russell Woodruff); Katharine Aldridge (Sarah Sorrell); Mary Treen (Jenny); Jack Carson (Pat O'Farrell); Elyse Knox (Judith Wilson); Joan Valerie (Francine Edwards); Dorothy Dearing (Emmy Lou Bentley); Dorothy Moore (Happy); Jacqueline Wells (Lorna); Charles C. Wilson (Brady); William Davidson (Grayson).

Joan Matthews (Florence Rice), a pretty young detective, is hired to look into the operations of a jewel stealing gang. She enlists the aid of Gregg Dunn (Kent Taylor), an undercover man working for an indemnity insurance company which must pay claim for gems stolen by the hoodlums. The two work with one of the victims of the thefts, a jeweler (Lionel Atwill), and trace the crooks' headquarters to a swank hotel. Eventually Rice understands that Atwill is the leader of the gang and that Taylor is in cahoots with them. Taylor is later killed by a police detective.
GIRL IN 313 was one of two 1940 sequels to the previous year's success, ELSA MAXWELL'S HOTEL FOR WOMEN, which had introduced Linda Darnell to screengoers. This outing was well directed by veteran matinee idol Ricardo Cortez.
It is interesting to note that this production had a downbeat ending with the shooting of "hero" Kent Taylor. Veteran villain Lionel Atwill took the film's acting honors as the suave, crooked gangster leader.

THE GIRL WHO CAME BACK (First Division, 1935) 65 mins.

Producer, George R. Batcheller; director, Charles Lamont; screen-play, Ewart Adamson; assistant director, Melville Shyer; camera, M. A. Anderson.

Sidney Blackmer (Rhodes); Shirley Grey (Gilda); Noel Madison (Brewster); Mathew Betz (Smoky); Torben Meyer (Zarabella); May Beatty (Aunty); Frank LaRue (Burke); Robert Adair (Mathews); Ida Darling (Mrs. Rhodes); Edward Martindel (Madison); John Dilson (Wadsworth); Lou Davis (Sims); Don Brodie (Jason).

Gangster's moll Gilda (Shirley Grey) vows to give up the rackets and goes to California where she becomes involved in an extortion game and meets mobster Brewster (Noel Madison), who is planning a jewel robbery. She also falls in love with honest businessman Rhodes (Sidney Blakmer) and to protect him, she goes straight and double-crosses her "pals," leading to their downfall.

This low-grade melodrama is highlighted by good performances by Shirley Grey in the title role, Sidney Blackmer as her man, and Noel Madison and Matthew Betz as slick mobsters.

GIRLS OF THE BIG HOUSE (Republic, 1945) 68 mins.

Associate producer, Rudolph E. Abel; director, George Archainbaud; screenplay, Houston Branch; music, Joseph Dubin; music director, Morton Scott; songs, Jack Elliott; Sanford Green; and June Carroll; art director, Gano Chittenden; set decorator, Earl B. Wooden; sound, Victor Appel; special effects, Howard Lydecker, Theodore Lydecker; camera, John Alton; editor, Arthur Roberts.

Lynne Roberts (Jeanne Crail); Virginia Christine (Bernice); Marian Martin (Dixie); Adela Mara (Harriet); Richard Powers [Tom Keene] (Barton Sturgis); Geraldine Wall (Head Matron); Tala Birell (Alma Vlasek); Norma Varden (Mrs. Thelma Holt); Stephen Barclay (Smiley); Mary Newton (Dr. Gale Warren); Erskine Sanford (Professor O'Neill); Sarah Edwards (Dormitory Matron); Ida Moore (Mother Fielding); William Forrest (District Attorney); Verna Felton (Agnes).

Jeanne Crail (Lynne Roberts), the daughter of a small town college president, is framed on a trumped up charge by big city hoodlums to cover up their crimes and is sentenced to women's prison although her lawyer boyfriend (Richard Powers) vows to obtain her freedom. Once behind bars, she is resented by the veteran inmates and is treated badly by them with a murder taking place because three of them have been romanced by the same man (Stephen Barclay). Eventually Powers proves Roberts' innocence and she is released.

With its well staged behind bars sequences, GIRLS OF THE BIG HOUSE is more than adequate, enchanced by fine performances by Adele Mara, Virginia Christine, Tala Birlell, and Marian Martin

as prisoners and former cowboy star Tom Keene, billed here as
Richard Powers, as the boyfriend.

It is worthwhile to compare this competent 1940s' programmer
with films made more than three decades later covering virtually
the same territory. Had this feature been produced in the mid-
1970s it would have, by necessity, had to include such by now
obligatory items as sadism, nudity, and lesbianism. Such has been
the "coming of age" of the gangster film genre since World War II.

THE GLASS ALIBI (Republic, 1946) 68 mins.

Producer-director, W. Lee Wilder; screenplay, Mindret Lord; set
designer, Frank Welch; assistant director, Bart Carre; music director, Alexander Laszlo; sound, Feral Redd; camera, Henry Sharp;
editors, Asa Clark, John F. Link.

Paul Kelly (Max Anderson); Douglas Fowley (Joe Eykner); Anne
Gwynne (Belle Marlin); Maris Wrixon (Linda Vale); Jack Conrad
(Benny Brandini); Selmer Jackson (Dr. Lawson); Cyril Thurston
(Riggs); Cy Kendall (Red Hogan); Walter Soderling (Coroner); Vic
Potel (Gas Attendant); George Chandler (Bartender); Phyllis Adair
(Nurse); Ted Stanhope (Drug Clerk); Dick Scott (Frank); Eula
Guy (Connie); Forrest Taylor (Charlie).

THE GLASS ALIBI is one of the more underrated melodramas
of the 1940s and it is probably producer-director W. Lee Wilder's
(Billy's brother) best feature. After this outing, Wilder was unable to duplicate the success he had attained and his career continued through a series of mediocre efforts, including another
gangster film, CAXAMBU (q.v.). With its taut script by Mindret
Lord and fast-paced plot, in addition to a downbeat ending, THE
GLASS ALIBI is certainly a film worth reappraising.

Nationally hunted gangster Red Hogan (Cy Kendall) eludes
the police and takes refuge in the Malibu Beach home of socialite
Linda Vale (Maris Wrixon). He phones his moll Belle Marlin (Anne
Gwynne) to meet him and they will head to Mexico, but Gwynne is
in the arms of her lover, newspaper reporter Joe Eichner (Douglas
Fowley) who calls the law and leads his old pal Inspector Max Anderson (Paul Kelly) to Kendall and the hoodlum is arrested. After
phoning in his big scoop, Fowley finds himself enchanted by the
beautiful Wrixon. After being told she has only six months to live,
he begins romancing her, planning to wed her and gain her fortune.
He entices Gwynne to go along with the scheme and to put up the
front money needed to show Wrixon he wants her and not her fortune.

Fowley and Wrixon wed, but eight months pass and she does
not die. Desperate for money, Fowley comes up with a scheme to
eliminate Wrixon and have the perfect alibi. Working it out with
Gwynne, he shoots Wrixon and makes it look like a suicide. He
leaves and then returns again a few hours later only to find Kelly

there with the policeman accusing him of murdering his wife, insisting that his Palm Springs story is just a "glass alibi" that can be easily broken. But it proves that Wrixon actually died of a heart attack, not the bullet wound. Then just as Fowley is about to get off the hook, it is learned that Gwynne has been killed and that Fowley's fingerprints are all over the scene of the crime. When confronted, Fowley insists that Kendall, who has escaped from prison, is the culprit, with revenge his motive. However, Kendall has been killed by the police, so the newspaperman stands trial and is given the death sentence for Gwynne's murder.

A neat twist ending, although an unhappy one, adds zest to THE GLASS ALIBI and makes it a precursor to THE JAGGED EDGE (1985). As the fast-talking, calculating, but ultimately corrupt newspaperman, Douglas Fowley does the best work of his screen career. He is matched by Anne Gwynne as the slinky, conniving, bitchy moll and by the sadly underrated Maris Wrixon as the striking but naive victim.

GLORIA (Columbia, 1980) C 123 mins.

Executive producer, Sam Shaw; producer, John Cassavetes; associate producer, Stephen Kesten; director-screenplay, Cassavetes; production designer, Rene D'Auriac; costumes, Peggy Farrell; assistant director, Mike Haley, Tom Fritz; camera, Fred Schuler; editor, Jack McSweeney.

Gena Rowlands (Gloria Swenson); Juan Adames (Philip Dawn); Buck Henry (Jack Dawn); Julie Carmen (Jeri Dawn); Lupe Garnica (Margarita Vargas); Jessica Castillo (Joan Dawn); Basilio Franchina (gang boss); Tony Kensich, Tom Noonan, Ronnie Maccone (Gangsters); Ralph Dolman, Israel Castro, Carlos Castro (Kids); Philomena Spagnole (Old Lady); Gregory Gleghorne (Kid in Elevator); Kyle-Scott Jackson, Gary Klarr (Policemen); Ramon Rodriguez (Escape Cab Driver); George Yudzevich (Heavyset Man); Asa Quawee (Cab Driver #2).

Actor-director John Cassavetes has developed a strong cult following due to the features he has helmed, including FACES (1968), HUSBANDS (1970), MINNIE AND MOSKOWITZ (1971), A WOMAN UNDER THE INFLUENCE (1974), and THE KILLING OF A CHINESE BOOKIE (1976) (q.v.). Most of these arty features have starred his talented wife Gena Rowlands, who also headlines this powerful foray by Cassavetes into the traditional gangster genre.

Gloria (Rowlands) is an aging gangster's moll who finds herself in the midst of an unsavory situation and whose better instincts lead her to break with the past. Her one-time gang boss lover (Basilio Franchina) orders the killing of a bookkeeper (Buck Henry) and his wife (Julia Carmen) because the man has tried to doublecross him financially. Rowlands witnesses the slaughter and rescues the couple's young son Phil (Juan Adames). The two flee the

mobster's goons since they are marked for murder for having observed the shooting. Rowlands rushes the boy from one low-life
New York City hiding place to another in hopes of escaping from
the hoodlums. In Pittsburgh, they find sanctuary.

Vincent Canby, in The New York Times, stated GLORIA "...
is a very peculiar, lumpy mixture. It's Hollywood-style hookum ...
It has its charms but not for a minute is it believable, and it's
certainly never embarrassingly moving in the schmaltzy way of such
Hollywood kidflicks as PAPER MOON or even THE CHAMP." It
should be noted that Gena Rowlands' dynamic performance as the
title character is multi-dimensional and so riveting that it gives
focus to this off-center study.

THE GLOVE (Pro International, 1980) C 90 mins.

Executive producer, William B. Silberkleit; producer, Julian Roff-
man; director, Ross Hagen; screenplay, Hubert Smith Hoffman;
music, Robert O. Ragland; camera, Gary Graver; editor, Bob
Fitzgerald.

John Saxon (Sam Kellough); Roosevelt Grier (Victor Hale); Joanna
Cassidy (Sheila Michaels); Joan Blondell (Mrs. Fitzgerald); Jack
Carter (Walter Stratton); Keenan Wynn (Bill Schwartz); Aldo Ray
(Prison Guard); Michael Pataki (Harry Iverson); Misty Bruce (Lisa);
Howard Honig (Lieutenant Kruger).

The title of this film (also known as BLOOD MAD) refers to
the riot glove, a weapon developed in the late 1960s to aid in stopping student riots and later outlawed after its (ab)use in prisons.
Made of metal and cloth, the Glove is a vile weapon and the one
item the makers of this exploitation feature chose to showcase.

Sam Kellough (John Saxon), a former policeman and baseball
player who is down on his luck, makes his living now by chasing
down people who have jumped bail. He is offered $20,000 by a
prison guards association to track down and capture Victor Hale
(Roosevelt Grier), who has brutally attacked a prison guard (Aldo
Ray) to get even for the use of the Glove on him while he was behind bars. Saxon's quest leads him to meet a variety of character
types along the way. Eventually there is the deadly showdown.

Variety best summed up this low calibre production: "Social
consciousness in the violent finale is very poorly-conceived as the
film-makers contrive to whip up audience support for mob violence
and then cop out with a 'There has to be another way' line of dialog."

THE GODFATHER SAGA (1977)

For credits: see: B/V.

Advertisement for THE GODFATHER SAGA (1977).

Telecast November 12-15, 1977, on NBC-TV as MARIO PUZO's "THE GODFATHER": THE COMPLETE NOVEL FOR TELEVISION, this nine-hour feature was a creative re-editing of the two GODFATHER features with additional footage (not seen in the theatrical releases) interwoven. The result is an overlong but entrancing look into the workings of organized crime as seen through the activities of a fictional Mafia family and how their business reflects on their personal lives.

The chronicle opens in 1918 Italy where young Vito Corleone (Robert DeNiro) sees his family murdered by an evil landowner and he migrates to Manhattan where he marries and works in a shop until he loses his job because a gangster who runs an extortion racket threatens his boss. Needing money, DeNiro joins two hoodlums in a life of petty crime. He rises in the ranks, takes over an olive oil importing firm, and becomes a respected community member.

More than three decades later, a much older Vito Corleone (Marlon Brando) is the head of one of the most powerful Mafia families in America. At the wedding of his daughter (Talia Shire), he grants requests and one of them is from his godson singer Johnny Fontane (Al Martino) who wants a movie role denied him by a studio head (John Marley); a favor Brando carries out. Refusing to join rival families in dope operations, Brando is shot, but he survives in poor health. His son Michael (Al Pacino), aided by adopted lawyer-brother Tom Hagen (Robert Duvall), takes over the family interests. Pacino avenges the attempt on his father's life by killing a corrupt policeman, but he is forced to flee to Sicily as a mob war takes place between the families; one of the victims is another Corleone brother, Sonny (James Caan).

In Sicily, Pacino marries the beautiful merchant's daughter Apollonia (Simonetta Stefanelli), but she is the victim of a car bomb intended for him. After Caan's death, Brando calls a halt to the family wars and Pacino returns home and marries his long-time girlfriend Kay (Diane Keaton) and moves the family business operations to Las Vegas to get in on the gambling trade.

As more years pass, Brando dies and Pacino rules the organization with an iron hand. When he refuses to pay extortion money to a corrupt Senator (G. B. Spradlin), Pacino is targeted for assassination but the attempt fails and he eventually gets the goods on the politician. In Havana he meets with Jewish mobster kingpin Hyman Roth (Lee Strasberg) to set up gambling operations in Havana with the government's backing. However, the Castro revolution ends their plans. Back in Las Vegas, Pacino discovers his wife is leaving him and that he is the focus of a government group surveilling organized crime.

For anyone who has appreciated the two theatrical features, THE GODFATHER is an imaginative new presentation of old material. Much of the overt violence and sex were greatly toned down for this TV outing. Nevertheless the total impact of crime and violence on the lives of both the protagonists and the innocent remain strong statements. Even in this diluted, re-edited accounting, the basic material is a powerful indictment against (organized) crime.

Since practically all of the characters depicted in this epic
are of Sicilian origin, the following advisory was given both before
and during the presentation: "THE GODFATHER is a fictional ac
count of the activities of a small group of ruthless criminals. The
characters do not represent any ethnic group and it would be er-
roneous and unfair to suggest that they do."

A planned new sequel, GODFATHER III, Starring anyone from
John Travolta to Sylvester Stallone, has yet to become a reality.

THE GOLD RACKET (Grand National, 1937) 66 mins.

Producer, George A. Hirilman; associate producer, Ben Pivar;
director, Louis J. Gasnier; story, Howard Higgin; screenplay,
David Levy; music, Robert Jahns; camera, Mack Stengler; editor,
Joseph H. Lewis.

Conrad Nagel (Alan O'Connor); Eleanor Hunt (Bobbie Reynolds);
Fuzzy Knight (Scotty); Frank Milan (Steve); Charles Delaney (Joe);
Karl Hackett (Lefty); Warner Richmond (Doc); Albert J. Smith
(Fraser); Edward Le Saint (Dixon); W. L. Thorne (McKenzie);
Paul Weigel (Assayer); Fred Malatesia (Ricardo).

Federal Bureau of Investigation agents Alan O'Connor (Conrad Nagel) and pretty Bobbie Reynolds (Eleanor Hunt) must determine who is smuggling gold into the United States from Mexico.
They base themselves in a small border town where Hunt becomes
a cabaret singer to gain evidence on gang leader Steve (Frank
Milan). Obtaining the required information, Nagel and Hunt put an
end to the outlaws' airplane operation smuggling the gold ore.

THE GOLD RACKET was one of a quartet of modest "B" films
starring Conrad Nagel and Eleanor Hunt as government operatives.
They also fought gangsters in BANK ALARM and YELLOW CARGO
(qq.v.) while they challenged espionage workers in NAVY SPY
(1937). Variety notes this entry "romps haphazardously through
considerable gunplay, a bit of comedy, mediocre music and not
much romance." Overall, though, the film is a solid double-bill
movie with charming interplay between the two leads.

THE GOLDEN EYE (Monogram, 1948) 69 mins.

Producer, James S. Burkett; director, William Beaudine; based on
characters created by Earl Derr Biggers; screenplay, W. Scott
Darling; music, Edward J. Kay; camera, William Sickner; editors,
Otho Lovering, Ace Herman.

Roland Winters (Charlie Chan); Mantan Moreland (Birmingham);
Victor Sen Young (Tommy Chan); Tim Ryan (Lieutenant Ruark);
Bruce Kellogg (Bartlett); Wanda McKay (Evelyn); Ralph Dunn
(Driscoll); Forrest Taylor (Manning); Evelyn Brent (Sister Teresa);

Lois Austin (Mrs. Driscoll); Lee "Lasses" White (Pete); Edmund Cobb, John Merton (Miners).

Sometimes called THE MYSTERY OF THE GOLDEN EYE, this "Charlie Chan" entry came late in the series and proved to be the best of the half-dozen features with Roland Winters starring as the Chinese detective. Similar in locale to Earl Derr Biggers early Chan novel The Chinese Parrot (1926), the feature is a flavorful combination of the detective, gangster, and Western genres, amplified by Scott Darling's intriguing whodunit scenario.

Charlie Chan (Winters) is summoned to an Arizona dude ranch by an old friend (Forrest Taylor) who has been badly injured falling down a mine shaft. Number two son Tommy (Victor Sen Yung) and chauffeur Birmingham Brown (Mantan Moreland) also accompany Winters on the trek. At the ranch the detective finds his old pal, Lieutenant Ruark (Tim Ryan), is on hand disguised as a tipsy guest. After substantial investigation, Winters ferrets out that the Golden Eye mine is really worthless but is being used by smugglers bringing in gold ore from Mexico and passing it off as a domestic find. Winters also learns that a nun (Evelyn Brent) is a member of the criminal outfit and that the mine owner is really dead, with someone, havily bandaged, taking his place.

GOLDEN HANDS OF KURIGAL see: FEDERAL AGENTS VERSUS UNDERWORLD, INC.

GOVERNMENT AGENT VS. PHANTOM LEGION (Republic, 1951) twelve chapters

Associate producer, Franklin Adreon; director, Fred C. Brannon; screenplay, Ronald Davidson; assistant director, Fred A. Ritter; music, Stanley Wilson; special effects, Howard Lydecker, Theodore Lydecker; camera, John L. Russell, Jr.

Walter Reed (Hal); Mary Ellen Kay (Kay); Dick Curtis (Regan); John Pickard (Sam); Fred Coby (Cady); Pierce Lyden (Armstrong); George Meeker (Willard); John Phillips (Patterson); Mauritz Hugo (Thompson); Edmund Cobb (Turner); Eddie Dew (Barnett); George Lloyd (Coroner); Dale Van Sickel (Brice); Tom Steele (Brandt); Arthur Space (Crandall); Norval Mitchell (District Attorney); Frank Meredith (Motorcycle Officer).

Chapters: 1) River of Fire; 2) The Stolen Corpse; 3) The Death Drop; 4) Doorway to Doom; 5) Deadline for Disaster; 6) Mechancial Homicide; 7) The Flaming Highway; 8) Sea Saboteurs; 9) Peril Underground; 10) Execution by Accident; 11) Perilous Plunge; 12) Blazing Retribution.

Members of the Truck Owners' Association have been having

their rigs hijacked and the government dispatches agent Hal Duncan
(Walter Reed) to investigate the matter. He works with four owners, Armstrong (Pierce Lydon), Crandall (Arthur Space), Thompson (Mauritz Hugo), and Willard (George Meeker), and their pretty
secretary Kay (Mary Ellen Kay). To get the hijackers, the agent
drives one of Lyden's trucks and is captured by the gangster and
finds they are lead by a mysterious man known only as "The
Voice." He also learns the gang is selling the truck's cargo to a
foreign nation. He manages to escape and continues to pursue the
gang and unmasks the culprit, one of the four Association leaders.
The chief villain dies in a fight with Reed.
        Serials were going downhill fast when this cliffhanger came
along, but in its dozen chapters there were such actionful sequences as a trapdoor escape, an explosion caused by a bullet
setting off hand grenades and a gasoline drum, and the dispatch-
ing of the villain by having him impaled on jagged glass. There
were endless chases and fights and a fair mystery plot, although
cliffhanger veterans could spot immediately that one of the business
quartet was the bad guy.
        It should be noted that gangsters vanished from the serial
scene after this outing as cliffhangers unsuccessfully tried to cling
to screen life with plots revolving around science fiction, spies,
and the durable Wild West.

GRAND JURY (RKO, 1936) 60 mins.

Producer, Lee Marcus; director, Albert Rogell; story, James Grant,
Thomas Lennon, screenplay, Joseph A. Fields, Philip Epstein; mu-
sic director, Alberto Colombo; camera, Joseph August; editor, Jack
Hively.

Fred Stone (Commodore); Louise Latimer (Edith); Owen Davis, Jr.
(Steve); Moroni Olson (Bodyguard); Frank M. Thomas (Taylor);
Guinn Williams (Britt); Harry Beresford (Evans); Russell Hicks
(Hanity); Harry Jans (Sullivan); Robert Emmet Keane (Walters);
Robert Middlemass (Chief); Margaret Armstrong (Martha); Charles
Wilson (Editor).

        When gangsters commit a brutal murder, a former crusading
Commodore (Fred Stone), his pretty granddaughter (Louise Latimer), and a fledgling newspaper reporter (Owen Davis, Jr.) jump
on their trail and uncover a respected businessman (Frank M.
Thomas) as the power behind the gang.
        The only solid aspect of this anemic gangster outing is Fred
Stone's wily performance as the Commodore, although those who
recall his superb screen work in ALICE ADAMS (1935) and TRAIL
OF THE LONESOME PINE (1936) will be disappointed at the paucity
of his part.

Edward G. Robinson and Janet Leigh in GRAND SLAM (1968).

GRAND SLAM (Paramount, 1968) C 121 mins.

Producers, Harry Colombo, George Papi; director, Giuliano Montaldo; screenplay, Mino Roli, Marcello Fondato, Antonio De La Loma, Caminito; music, Ennio Morricone; music conductor, Bruno Nicolai; art directors, Alberto Boccianti, Juan Alberto Soler; assistant directors, Mauro Sacripanti, Carlos Luiz Corito, Federico Canudas; sound, Umberto Picistrelli; camera, Antonio Macasoli; editor, Nino Baragli.

Janet Leigh (Mary Ann); Robert Hoffman (Juan-Paul Audry); Edward G. Robinson (Professor James Anders); Adolfo Celi (Mark Muilford); Klaus Kinski (Erich Weiss); Georges Riguad); Riccardo Cucciolla (Agostini Rossi); Jussara (Setuaka); Miguel Del Castillo (Manager).

Retiring after thirty years as a professor, mild-mannered James Anders (Edward G. Robinson) returns to New York City from Rio de Janeiro and visits an old friend, powerful mobster Mark Muilford (Adolfo Celi). He suggests a big heist to the gangster. The plan is to rob a company safe in Rio which contains $10,000,000 in diamonds. Since Robinson intimately knows the ins and outs of the operation, Celi agrees to his plan for the job and it's agreed

they will divide the loot. Four specialists are hired to complete the
robbery and they work under the cover of the city's festive carnival. The crime is carried out, but two of the thieves are killed by
the police while a third man is shot by his comrade who does not
want to share the loot. Taking the cache back to the gangster,
this man too is murdered, but Celi finds the case is empty. In
Rome, Robinson meets Mary Ann (Janet Leigh), the company's secretary, and she gives him the diamonds; the whole devious plot
having been devised by the elderly man. All goes awry, though,
when a young boy on a scooter grabs the travel bag with the diamonds and makes a successful getaway.

Paramount released this Italian-made heist drama in 1968 and
thanks so the drawing power of Janet Leigh and Edward G. Robinson it did fairly well at the box office. The film had been issued
the previous year in its homeland as AD OGNI COSTO [At Any
Cost]. It was one of three gangster movies starring Robinson in
Italy in the 1960s, and it was the only one which took the genre
seriously, although the results were still unmemorable.

THE GREAT HOSPITAL MYSTERY (Twentieth Century-Fox, 1937)
    59 mins.

Director, James Tinling; based on a story by Mignon Eberhart;
screenplay, William Conselman, Rose Meredith, Jerry Cady; music
director, Samuel Kaylin; camera, Harry Jackson; editor, Nick
DeMaggio.

Jane Darwell (Miss Keats); Sig Rumann (Dr. Triggert); Sally Blane
(Ann Smith); Thomas Beck (Dr. David McKerry); Joan Davis (Flos-
sie Duff); William Demarest (Mr. Beatty); George Walcott (Allen
Tracy); Wade Boteler (Madoon); Howard Phillips (Tom Kirby); Ruth
Peterson (Desk Nurse); Carl Faulkner, Frank C. Fanning (Police-
men); Margaret Brayton (Chart Room Nurse); Lona Andrews (Miss
White); Tom Mahoney (Bank Guard).

When racketeers realize a young man has seen them commit
two murders, they shoot him and he is taken to a hospital where
they seek to finish him off before he can talk. The police set a
trap, hiding the fact that the witness has already died. The hospital's head nurse, Miss Keats (Jane Darwell), is aware that something is amiss but she cannot fathom what it is, while a young doctor (Thomas Beck) and his lady love (Sally Blane) are also involved,
as is a light-headed nurse (Joan Davis). Eventually the gunman
(William Demarest) is arrested.

More of a murder mystery hanging the crux of its plot on
gangsters, THE GREAT HOSPITAL MYSTERY is one of those
entries that seemed commonplace in its day but in retrospect is
pleasingly entertaining. It was offbeat to cast comic William
Demarest as the heavy.

Fozzie Bear, Miss Piggy, and Kermit the Frog in THE GREAT MUPPET CAPER (1981).

THE GREAT MUPPET CAPER (Universal/Associated Film Distribution, 1981) C 95 mins.

Executive producer, Martin Starger; producers, David Lazer, Frank Oz; associate producer, Bruce Sharman; director, Jim Henson; screenplay, Tom Patchett, Jay Tarses, Jerry Juhl, Jack Rose; production designer, Harry Lange; art directors, Charles Bishop, Terry Ackland-Snow, Leigh Malone; choreography, Anita Mann; music and lyrics, Joe Raposo; costumes, Julie Harris; assistant director, Dusty Symonds; Muppet costumes, Calista Hendrickson, Mary Strieff, Joanne Green, Carol Spier, Danielle Obinger; camera, Oswald Morris; editor, Ralph Kemplen.

Jim Henson: Kermit, Rowlf, Dr. Teeth, Waldorf, Swedish Chef; Frank Oz: Miss Piggy, Fozzie Bear, Animal, Sam the Eagle; Dave Goelz: The Great Gonzo, Beauregard, Zoot, Dr. Bunsen Honeydew; Jerry Nelson: Floyd, Pops, Lew Zealand; Richard Hunt: Scooter, Stalter, Sweetums, Janice, Beaker; Charles Grodin (Nicky Holiday); Diana Rigg (Lady Holiday); John Cleese, Robert Morley, Peter Ustinov, Jack Warden (Guest Stars); Steve Whitmore: Rizzo the Rat, Lips; Carroll Spinney: Oscar the Grouch; Erica Creer (Marla); Kate Howard (Carla); Della Finch (Darla); Michael Robbins (Guard); Joan Sanderson (Dorcas); Peter Mughes (Maitre D'); Peggy

Aitchinson (Prison Guard); Tommy Godfrey (Bus Conductor); Katia Borg, Valili Kemp, Michele Ivan-Zadeh, Chai Lee (Models).

After a lengthy television run in the 1970s and their successful film debut in THE MUPPET MOVIE (1979), Jim Henson's Muppets invaded the world of gangsters in this family-oriented motion picture which retains all the special charm associated with the well-loved puppet characters, which creator-director Henson here deftly interpolates with real actors. Not only is the script a strong one in the amusement department, but the production also boasts well staged musical outings featuring Miss Piggy, one being a beautifully executed water ballet.

Kermit the Frog, Fozzie Bear, and The Great Gonzo are newspapermen in London out to solve a jewelry robbery at Lady Holiday's (Diana Rigg) fashion salon. Kermit thinks Miss Piggy is Lady Holiday and he falls for her, much to the plump pig's joy. Trouble ensues, however, when Rigg's brother (Charles Grodin) also makes a play for Miss Piggy and attempts to set her up as the culprit of the caper.

In reviewing the charm of this feature, Variety analyzed, "As before, much of the dialog neatly walks the line between true wit and silly (and sometimes inside) jokes. Seeing these cute creatures interact in full-figure with live actors may not represent the novelty now that it did the first time...."

THE GREAT SKYCOPTER RESCUE (Star Cinema, 1981) C 90 mins.

Executive producer, George Foldes; producer-director, Lawrence D. Foldes; associate producer, Stanley Isaacs; screenplay, Foldes, Henry Edwards, Tony Creschales; music, Steve Myland; camera, Nicholas von Sternberg; editors, Ted Nicholaou, Dan Perry.

Aldo Ray (Sheriff); William Marshall (Jason); Terry Michos (Jimmy); Terri Taylor (Terri); Paul Tanashian (Will); Russell Johnson (Benson); and: Alex Mann, Richard C. Adams, Maria Redman, Linda Redman, Kim Manners, Liza Ferrell, John Carter, Stanley Isaacs, Ron Schmeck.

Two young men (Terry Michos, Paul Tanashian), satiated with their lives, become friends and the latter interests the former in becoming a sky copter flier. In a small California town they romance two locals (Terri Taylor, Maria Redman) and learn the area is coveted by a gangster leader (William Marshall) intending to build a large condominium project which will upset the area's ecology. To push through his scheme, the crook pays off the boorish local sheriff (Aldo Ray) and hire biker thugs to harass the townspeople into complacency. However, the sky copter fliers team with their fellow aviators to thwart the gangsters.

Similar to the much better thriller SKYRAIDERS (1976), a political kidnapping caper starring James Coburn, this low budgeter

was hampered by mediocre performances (especially by William
Marshall as the hammy mobster). Only Nicholas von Sternberg's
photography gave imagination to the proceedings.

GREEN ICE (ITC Films International, 1981) C 115 mins.

Producer, Jack Wiener; associate producer, Colin M. Brewer; di-
rector, Ernest Day; based on the book by Gerald Browne; screen-
play, Edward Anhalt, Ray Hassett, Anthony Simmons, Robert de
Laurentis; music, Bill Wyman; art directors, Alan Tomkins, Leslie
Tomkins, Pamela Carlton; special effects, Martin Gutteridge; camera,
Gilbert Taylor, editor, John Jympson.

Ryan O'Neal (Wiley); Anne Archer (Holbrook); Omar Sharif (Ar-
genti); Domingo Ambriz (Miguel); John Larroquotta (Claude); Philip
Stone (Kellerman); Michael Sheard (Jasp); and: Manuel Ojeda, Tara
Feliner, Sandra Kerns, Raul Martinez, Enrique Novi, Miguel Angel
Fuentes, Deloy White.

    In Mexico, electronics engineer Wiley (Ryan O'Neal) meets
pert socialite Holbrook (Anne Archer) and the duo is befriended by
Argenti (Omar Sharif) who takes them to his home in Colombia.
There O'Neal encounters an old pal (John Larroquotte) who is
friendly witha left-wing terrorist (Domingo Ambriz) who claims
Sharif is the leader of a Bogota emerald empire with the gems being stashed in the top floor of a high rise business building. The
trio decide to steal the emeralds, and, using three large balloons,
they land atop the building, break into its vault, and steal the
gems. The terrorist, however, is killed during the crime, but the
other two with Archer head to Key West where they are pursued
by Sharif and his murderous minions.
    GREEN ICE has little to recommend it beyond exotic Mexican
locale and a spirited performance by Omar Sharif as the international
gangster.

THE GUN RUNNERS see: THE BREAKING POINT

GUNS DON'T ARGUE (Visual Drama, 1957) 92 mins.

Producer, William J. Faris; associate producer, Terry Turner;
directors, Bill Karn and Richard C. Kahn; screenplay, Phillips H.
Lord. Faris.

Myron Healey (John Dillinger); Jim Davis (Bill Baxter); Lyle Talbot
(Dr. Guellfe); Jean Harvey (Ma Barker); Paul Dubov (Alvin Kar-
pis); Sam Edwards (Fred Barker); Richard Crane (Homer Van
Meter); Tamar Cooper (Bonnie Parker); Baynes Baron (Clyde
Barrow); Doug Wison (Pretty Boy Floyd); Regina Gleason, Jeanne

Carmen (Gun Molls); and: Lash LaRue, Sydney Mason, Ralph
Moody, Ann Morriss, Aline Towne, Jeanne Bates, Hellen Van Tuyl,
Knobby Schaeffer, Russell Whitney, Coulter Irwin, Robert Kondoll,
Gam Flint, Bill Baldwin.

Touted as "The Factual Story of the Short But Vicious Lives
of America's Public Enemies" and "How the Nation's Mad-Dog Killers
Traded Slugs for a Slab with the G-Men," this theatrical release
was composed of footage from the 1952 NBC-TV program, "Gang-
busters." Two years before Visual Drama released GANG BUSTERS
(see: B/V), also made up of segments from the TV program, but
that feature dealt with only one criminal, John Omar Pinson (Myron
Healey), while this production hosted almost the entire array of
Depression-era desperadoes.

The telefilm recounts the adventures of G-man Bill Baxter
(Jim Davis) and his confreres in battling such infamous under-
world figures as Bonnie Parker (Tamar Cooper) and Clyde Barrow
(Baynes Baron), John Dillinger (Myron Healey), Homer Van Meter
(Richard Crane), Alvin Karpis (Paul Dubov), and Dr. Guellfre
(Lyle Talbot), the medical man who tries to change Karpis' face
and fingerprints. In addition, there were: Ma Barker (Jean Har-
vey) and her killer brood, and Pretty Boy Floyd (Doug Wilson).

The Motion Picture Exhibitor reviewed, "This decidedly different type of film fare unfolds in documentary fashion so well....
Although overly-long, and at times repetitious due to the nature of
subject matter, this is paced with machine gun battles, gore, murders, hold-ups, kidnapping, etc...."

HAIL! MAFIA (Goldstone Film Enterprises, 1966) C 90 mins.

Producer-director, Raoul J. Levy; story, Pierre-Vial Lesou; screenplay, Levy; dialog, Jean Cau; art director, Jean Andre; music,
Hubert Rostaing; Pierre Goumy; assistant director, Jacques Bar-
zaghi; camera, Raoul Coutard; editor, Victoria Mercanton.

Henry Silva (Schaft); Jack Klugman (Phil); Eddie Constantine
(Rudy Hamburg); Elsa Martinelli (Sylvia); Micheline Presle (Daisy);
Michel Lonsdale (Secretary); Carl Studer (Ruidosa); Rick Cooper
(Ben); Tener Riggs Eckelberry (Hyman); Daniel O'Brian (Karl);
and: Marcel Pagliero, Danielle Couprayen, Jean-Marc Allegre.

Since the 1950s, American actor-singer Eddie Constantine has
built a strong following in Eruope for his screen roles in cheap imitation gangster yarns, but that popularity has never spread to his
homeland. Finally in 1966 one of his features, HAIL! MAFIA, received considerable distribution in the United States. However the
effort was a minor one and Constantine, in the tertiary role, was
outbilled by better known character actors Henry Silva and Jack
Klugman. Moreover, the picture got lost in the era's spy film
craze, which was outdistancing gangster stories at the box office.

The corrupt officials running a large construction company hire gangster Schaft (Henry Silva) to murder American Rudy Hamburg (Constantine) living in France. The aim is to prevent him from testifying before a Senate investigating committee. Joining Silva in Paris is another mobster, Phil (Jack Klugman), who also wants Constantine dead. The duo set out to destroy the expatriate American, but Silva receives orders to cease the hunt since the construction company has been cleared of charges against it. Klugman continues to pursue Constantine and the trio are finished in a shootout.

This film was first issued in France in 1965 as JE VOUS SALUE, MAFIA and was seen the next year in Italy as DA NEW YORK: MAFIA UCCIDE!

HAMMER (United Artists, 1972) C 92 mins.

Executive producer, Phillip Hazelton; producer, Al Adamson; director, Bruce Clark; screenplay, Charles Johnson; art director, Skip Troutman; stunt coordinator, Eric Cord; wardrobe, Harold Crawford; assistant director, Byron Roberts; music, Solomon Burke, camera, Bob Steadman; editor, George Folsey, Jr.

Fred Williamson (B. J. Hammer); Bernie Hamilton (Davis); Vonetta McGee (Lois); Charles Lampkin (Big Sid); Elizabeth Harding (Rhoda); Mel Stewart (Professor); D'Urville Martin (Sonny); Stack Pierce (Roughhouse); Jamal Moore (Henry Jones); Nawana Davis (Mary); John Quade (Riley); Johnny Silver (Tiny); John De Carlos (Bruiser); Perrie Loft (Nagi); Leon Isaac (Bobby Williams); Philip Jackson (Landlord); Al Richardson (Black Militant); Tracy Ann King (Black Magic Woman); George Wilber (Irish Joe Brady); Gene Le Bell (Referee); Jimmy Lennon (Ring Announcer).

New York City dock laborer B. J. Hammer (Fred Williamson) is good with his fists both in and out of the ring and comes to the attention of local crime boss Big Sid (Charles Lampkin) who sponsors his boxing career. Quickly rising in the fight game, Williamson doesn't suspect that gangsters are behind his success until he is told to throw a big fight or his girlfriend (Vonetta McGee), Lampkin's secretary, will be murdered. Then Williamson finds he is owned by white syndicate boss Brenner (William Smith) and he plots to eliminate the big man.

"HAMMER is a straightforward entry in the black action film genre, with emphasis placed on violence and kindred particulars" (Variety). "The filmmakers seem to be more interested in capitalizing on racial emotions than in indicating a sense of responsibility" (New York Daily News). A typical example of the good guy black versus bad man whitey exploitation cinema, HAMMER offers former footabll star Fred Williamson in one of his first genre features. It was followed by such box-office successes as BLACK CAESAR (1973) and its sequel HELL UP IN HARLEM (1974) (see both: B/V).

Jeff Morrow, Kent Taylor, and Miriam Colon in HARBOR LIGHTS (1963).

HARBOR LIGHTS (Twentieth Century-Fox, 1963) 68 mins.

Producer, Maury Dexter; associate producer, Frank Marrero; director, Dexter; story-screenplay, Henry Cross; music, Paul Sawtell, Bert Shefter; assistant director, Frank Parmenter; makeup, Bob Mark; sound, Jack Solomon, Harry M. Leonard; camera, John Nickolaus, Jr.; editor, Jodie Copelan.

Kent Taylor (Dan Crown); Jeff Morrow (Cardinal); Miriam Colon (Gina Rosario); Antonio Torres Martino (Captain Acosta); Art Bedard (Captain Aristarchus); Braulio Castillo (Manolo); Jose de San Anton (Father Riva); Luis Antonio Martinez (Vallejo); Jose Manuel Caicoya (Mortician); Robert Rivera Negron (Storekeeper); Allan Sague (Hotel Clerk); Victor Mojica, Alfredo Perez, Tino Garcia (Cardinal's Men); Ralph Rodriguez (Alex Crown).

Gambler Dan Crown (Kent Taylor) comes to San Juan, Puerto Rico, to visit his borther Alex, but is informed by the local police chief (Antonio Torres Martino) that he has been found murdered. Taylor tells the police he has no knowledge of his brother's activities but later he finds pretty Gina Rosario (Miriam Colon) searching his hotel room and the two team to seek the murderer. A rich importer (Jeff Morrow) sends for Taylor and he advises him he is looking for something which his brother had in his possession. A priest (Jose de San Anton) informs Taylor that the brother was in church the day before he died and a clue leads to the church statue of St. Francis. In it they discover a valuable uncut diamond the deceased had smuggled into the country. Taylor is attacked by Morrow's hit men, but the police arrive.

Shot in Puerto Rico, the mystery of this substandard entry is the rationale for its title, since no part of its "action" occurs on the waterfront (despite the film's advertising to the contrary).

HARBOR OF MISSING MEN (Republic, 1950) 60 mins.

Producer, Sidney Picker; director, R. G. Springsteen; screenplay, John K. Butler; art director, Frank Arrigo; set decorator, Charles Thompson; assistant director, Lee Lukather; music-music director, Stanley Wilson; makeup, Howard South; sound, Dick Tyler; camera, John MacBurnie; editor, Arthur Roberts.

Richard Denning (Brooklyn); Barbara Fuller (Mae Leggett); Steven Geray (Captain Corcoris); Aline Towne (Angelike); Percy Helton (Rummy Davis); George Zucco (H. G. Danziger); Paul Marion (Philip Corcoris); Ray Teal (Frank); Robert Osterloh (Johnny); Fernanda Eliscu (Mama Corcoris); Gregory Gay (Captain Koretsky); Jimmie Kelly (Carl); Barbara Stanley (Leodora); Neyle Morrow (Christopher); Charles LaTorre (John).

Smuggling and hijackers are two solid elements of the gangster film lore and both are exploited in this Republic quickie which is "a neatly paced actioner" (Variety). With its ocean and ship locales and a full blown performance by George Zucco as the smuggling racket mobster, HARBOR OF MISSING MEN is a satisfying if low budget melodrama.

Richard Denning stars as Brooklyn, the owner of a fishing boat, who makes extra money by engaging in smuggling for Danziger (Zucco), the chief of the illegal operations. Returning home with money for Zucco from one of his jobs, Denning is hijacked by two cohorts and when he fails to appear with the money, the gangster has him marked as a traitor and calls in thugs to put him on the spot. Escaping his captors, Dennings takes refuge with a fisherman (Paul Marion) and becomes enamored of his lovely daughter (Aline Towne) who persuades him to abandon crime. Going to Zucco, Denning convinces him he didn't steal the money and the mobster directs his goons to the duo who did. As a result Zucco and one of the hijackers are killed while the other goes to prison. Denning, knowing Towne will wait for him, turns himself over to the law.

HARD BOILED MAHONEY (Monogram, 1947) 63 mins.

Producer, Jan Grippo; director, William Beaudine; screenplay, Cyril

Endfield; additional dialog, Edmond Seward, Tim Ryan; music director, Edward J. Kay; art director, David Milton; set decorator, George Milo; assistant director, Frank Fox; sound, Eldon Ruberg; special effects, Augie Lohman; camera, James Brown; editor, William Austin.

Leo Gorcey (Terence "Slip" Mahoney/Robert Westerfield); Huntz Hall (Sach/AK 9); Bobby Jordan (Bobby); Billy Benedict (Whitey/ AK 7); Gabriel Dell (Gabe); David Gorcey (Chuck); Teala Loring (Eleanor Williams); Dan Seymour (Dr. Armand); Bernard Gorcey (Louie Dumbrowski); Patti Brill (Alice/AK 13); Betty Compson (Selena Webster); Danny Beck (Lennie the Meatball); Pierre Watkin (Dr. Rolfe Carter); Noble Johnson (Hasson); Carmen D'Antonio (Dr. Armand's Secretary); Byron Foulger (Professor Quizard); Teddy Pavelec (Thug); Pat O'Malley (Police Lieutenant); Jack Cheatham (Police Sergeant); William Ruhl, Tom Faust (Bits).

An early entry in Monogram Pictures' "The Bowery Boys" series, which itself was an offshoot of the studio's earlier "East Side Kids" (mis)adventures, HARD BOILED MAHONEY is definitely one of the more interesting capers of the Lower East Side comic youths. In fact, the movie incorporates several elements rarely utilized in the series; chiefly the film-noir mystique of having gang leader Slip Mahoney (Leo Gorcey) as a loner hero thrust into situations which are totally alien to him. The use of the mystic racket is straight out of MURDER, MY SWEET (q.v.), one of the more popular film noir features of the 1940s. Not to fear, the Bowery Boys retain their slapstick comedy here, but in many respects the feature is a step above most of the series' entries.

Slip Mahoney (Gorcey) and Sach (Huntz Hall) are working for a detective and go to his office to collect their money. There a woman, Selena Webster (Betty Compson), thinks they are really gumshoes and hires Gorcey to find another woman (Teala Loring). When he traces her Gorcey learns Loring does not know his employer (Compson), but she does talk about a man named Armand (Dan Seymour) who turns out to be a fortune teller. After being knocked out by Seymour's henchman (Noble Johnson), Gorcey is revived by Compson who advises him that Seymour uses his fake racket for blackmail and that Loring has letters she needs to rid herself of the bogus mystic. When Seymour comes to Louie Dumbrowski's (Bernard Gorcey) sweet shop to meet with Loring, the Boys capture the culprit.

HARD CONTRACT (Twentieth Century-Fox, 1969) C 106 mins.

Producer, Marvin Schwartz; director/story/screenplay, S. Lee Pogostin; art director, Ed Graves; set decorators, James W. Payne, Fernando Gonzalez; music, Alex North; assistant directors, Julio Sempere, Kip Gowans; wardrobe, Gladys de Segonzac; makeup, Giuliiano Laurenti; special camera effects, L. B. Abbott, Art Cruickshank; camera, Jack Hilyard; editor, Harry Gersdtad.

James Coburn (John Cunningham); Lee Remick (Sheila); Lilli Palmer
(Adrianne); Burgess Meredith (Ramsey); Patrick Magee (Alexi);
Sterling Hayden (Michael Carlson); Claude Dauphin (Maurice); Helen
Cherry (Evelyn Carlson); Karen Black (Ellen); Sabine Sun (Belgian
Prostitute).

Filmed on location in Spain's Torremolinos and Madrid and
Tangiers and Brussels, this high-handed melodrama attempts to
delve into the psyche of a hired assassin, a type usually presented
in gangster movies as a cold fish who murders for money and pleasure. This presentation digs deeper into such a gangster character,
but the overall result is tedious.

Hired killer John Cunningham (James Coburn) is contracted
by businessman Ramsey Williams (Burgess Meredith) to eliminate
three men in Europe. In Spain he meets Sheila (Lee Remick) and
her jet-set friends and when she learns he sleeps only with hookers
she pretends to be one and they initiate an affair. There he carries out the first third of his contract and then goes with Remick
to Tangiers and on to Brussels to kill the second man, but by now
he is emotionally involved with the woman and barely carries out
his assignment. He finds out the next victim is to be the retired
hitman Michael Carlson (Sterling Hayden), living peaceably with his
family in Madrid. Coburn now has tremendous doubts about his
work and he meets Hayden and is befriended by the man. Meanwhile, Meredith arrives to ensure that the last of the contract is
completed and Hayden invites Coburn, Remick, and Meredith to be
guests at his ranch. There Coburn plots to kill everyone by driving off a cliff, but at the final moment he and Sheila run away together.

HARD GUY (Producers Releasing Corp., 1941) 67 mins.

Producers, George Merrick, Arthur Alexander; director, Elmer
Clifton; story-screenplay, Oliver Drake; camera, Eddie Linden;
editor, Charles Henkel.

Jack LaRue (Vic); Mary Healy (Julie); Kane Richmond (Steve);
Iris Adrian (Goldie); Gayle Mellott (Doris); Jack Mulhall (Cassidy);
Howard Banks (Anthony); Ben Taggart (Sherwood); Montague Shaw
(Tremaine, Sr.); Ina Gest (Mona); Arthur Gardner (Dick); Eddie
Durant and His Rhumba Band (Themselves).

Nightclub proprietor Vic (Jack LaRue) is a gangster steeped
in all kinds of illegal activities, chief of which is his shakedown
racket. He forces the pretty girls who work for him to marry rich
men and then takes money from their unhappy fathers for quick
annulments. When one of the girls, rhumba dancer Doris (Gayle
Mellott) refuses to go through with such a ruse, LaRue coldly
murders her. The girl's younger sister (Mary Healy) takes a job
as a club cigarette girl to get the goods on the killer. She is aided

by Steve (Kane Richmond), the gun-toting son of a former Oklahoma governor. After LaRue is brought to justice, Healy and Richmond marry.

The main attraction here is Jack LaRue as the slick, murderous wrongdoer. LaRue had a lengthy screen career in such roles and although he never attained the level of James Cagney, Edward G. Robinson, or George Raft, he was one of the screen's top purveyors of tough guys.

HARD TIMES (Columbia, 1975) C 92 mins.

Executive producer, Paul Maslansky; producer, Lawrence Gordon; director, Walter Hill; story, Bryan Gindorff, Bruce Henstell; screenplay, Hill, Gindorff, Henstell; music, Barry De Vorzon; art director, Trevor Williams; set decorator, Dennis Peeples; assistant director, Michael Daves; sound, Arthur Piantadosi, Donald Johnson; camera, Philip Lathrop; editor, Roger Spottiswoode.

Charles Bronson (Chaney); James Coburn (Speed); Jil Ireland (Lucy); Strother Martin (Poe); Maggie Blye (Gayleen); Michael McGuire (Gandil); Robert Tessier (Jim Henry); Nick Dimitri (Street); Felice Orlandi (Le Beau); Bruce Gover (Doty); Edward Walsh (Pettibon); Frank McRae (Hammerman); Maurice Kowalewski (Cesare); Naomi Stevens (Madam); Robert Castleberry (Counterman); Beck Allen (Poe's Date); Joan Kleven (Carol); Anne Welsch (Secretary); Lyla

Charles Bronson and Jill Ireland in HARD TIMES (1975).

Hay Owen (Diner Waitress); Jim Nickerson (Barge Fighter); John Greamer (Apartment Manager); Fred Herner (Cesare's Hitter); Chuck Hicks (Speed's Hitter); Walter Scott, Max Kleven (Pool Players); Valerian Smith (Handler); Bob Minor (Zack); Charles W. Schaeffer, Jr., Leslie Boano (Card Players); Ronnie Philips (Cajun Fighter); The Greater Liberty Baptist Church Choir & Congregation (Themselves).

Chaney (Charles Bronson) arrives in 1936 New Orleans and enters an illegal bare-knuckle prizefight and wins, capturing the attention of Speed (James Coburn), whose fighter he has beaten. Conman Coburn offers to manage Bronson and the next night he winds another match and moves into a cheap hotel where he meets attractive but lonely Lucy (Jill Ireland). Bronson continues to win a series of street fights and he acquires the services of cut man Poe (Strother Martin). After a big moneymaking victory, Bronson decides to call it quits and settle down with Ireland, but Coburn loses all his money in a crap game and is threatened with death by gangster Le Beau (Felice Orlandi), to whom he owes the money. Although it means losing Ireland, who wants someone more dependable, Bronson agrees to one last fight to save Coburn and he takes on the giant Street (Nick Dimitri) whom he defeats after a brutal bout. With Coburn's debt paid, Bronson leaves New Orleans.

Filmed on location in New Orleans, and sometimes titled THE STREET FIGHTER, HARD TIMES is a gritty, realistic melodrama which beautifully captures the feel of the Depression era. While the film's gangster aspects are downplayed to focus on a major loner, the production is full of lowlife underworld types and even one of the protagonists (Coburn) is hardly part of the law's long arm. The illegal sport of street fighting is finely detailed here and the film--which grossed over $25,000,000 domestically--is an entertaining outing.

As Time magazine decided, "HARD TIMES is unassuming, tough, and spare, a tidy little parable about strength and honor."

HARD TO HOLD see: PAID TO DANCE

HE LAUGHED LAST (Columbia, 1956) 76 mins.

Producer, Jonie Taps; director, Blake Edwards; story, Richard Quine, Edwards; screenplay, Edwards; music, Arthur Morton; music supervisor, Fred Karger; camera, Henry Freulich; editor, Jack W. Ogilvie.

Frankie Laine (Gino Lupo); Lucy Marlow (Rosemary Lebeau); Anthony Dexter (Dominic); Dick Long (Jimmy Murphy); Alan Reed (Big Dan Hennessy); Jesse White (Max Lassiter); Florenz Ames (George Eagle); Henry Slate (Ziggy); Paul Dubov (Buly Boy Barnes); Peter Brocco (Al Fusary); Joe Forte (Dave Hoffman); Robin Morse (Two Gun

Tommy); Dale Van Sickel (Harry); Mara McAfee (Nurse Rafferty); David Tomack, John Truex, John Cason, Richard Benedict (Hoods).

Believing he will take over the underworld operations of mobster Big Dan Hennessy (Alan Reed), second-in-command Max Lassiter (Jesse White) has his boss ambushed but gets a real surprise when the mobster expires, leaving his fortunes to club dancer Rosemary Le Beau (Lucy Marlow), much to the chagrin of her policeman fiancee Jimmy Murphy (Richard Long). Marlow comes to love the high life, including owning a nightclub run by singer Gino Lupo (Frankie Laine) and dancing tango with hoofer Dominic (Anthony Dexter). Lassiter, however, gets even by moving in on the girl, but the old mob stops him and Marlow and Long are reconciled.

HE LAUGHED LAST is a delightful gangster spoof, complete with tough hoodlums, a dumb blonde heroine, a clean-cut hero, and all the trappings of the glittering Roaring '20s.

HEADLINE HUNTERS (Republic, 1955) 70 mins.

Associate producer, William J. O'Sullivan; director, William Witney; screenplay, Frederic Louis Fox, John K. Butler; assistant director, Roy Wade; music, R. Dale Butts; costumes, Adele Palmer; sound, Melvin M. Metcalfe, Jr.; camera, John Russell, Jr.; editor, Arthur E. Roberts.

John Daheim, Ben Cooper, and Rod Cameron in HEADLINE HUNTERS (1955).

Rod Cameron (Hugh "Woody" Woodruff); Julie Bishop (Laura Stewart); Ben Cooper (David Flynn); Raymond Greenleaf (Paul Strout); Chubby Johnson (Ned Towers); John Warburton (District Attorney Keys); Nacho Galindo (Ramon); Joe Besser (Coroner); and: Virginia Carroll, Howard Wright, Stuart Randall, Edward Colmans, Joe Besser.

Just out of college, a cub reporter (Ben Cooper) joins a big city newspaper only to find that the journalist (Rod Cameron) he has idolized is now jaded about his profession. The writer's girlfriend (Julie Bishop) tries to help the young man's morale and when he is sent to cover a minor story, he becomes involved in a killing engineered by racketeers. Cooper is convinced that the city's corrupt district attorney is behind the crime ring. Breaking the older reporter out of his apathy, the young man joins forces with the newsman to bring out the facts in the case and smash the local corruption.

Another in a long series of movies about news reporters getting evidence on gangsters, HEADLINE HUNTERS is thin going except for its good cast.

This film's title is sometimes used on TV as an alternate tag for a much more exciting movie, HEADLINE SHOOTER, a 1933 RKO release about newspaper photographers and their quest for news photos.

THE HELEN MORGAN STORY (Warner Bros., 1957) 117 mins.

Producer, Martin Rackin; director, Michael Curtiz; screenplay, Oscar Saul, Dean Riesner, Stephen Longstreet, Nelson Gidding; art director, John Beckman; choreography, LeRoy Prinz; camera, Ted McCord; editor, Frank Bracht.

Ann Blyth (Helen Morgan); Paul Newman (Larry); Richard Carlson (Wade); Gene Evans (Whitey Krause); Alan King (Ben); Cara Williams (Dolly); Virginia Vincent (Sue); Walter Woolf King (Florenz Ziegfeld); Dorothy Green (Mrs. Wade); Ed Platt (Haggerty); Warren Douglas (Mark Hellinger); Sammy White (Sammy); Peggy De Castro, Cheri De Castro, Babette De Castro (Singers); Jimmy McHugh, Rudy Vallee, Walter Winchell (Themselves); Gogi Grant (The Singing Voice of Helen Morgan).

Comely singer Helen Morgan (Ann Blyth) loves punk hoodlum Larry Maddox (Paul Newman) in the Roaring Twenties era, but after seducing her, he departs. Scarred by the desertion, she continues her career and due to her fine singing voice climbs the ladder of success and becomes a top star in clubs and on Broadway, but then has the misfortune to love a lawyer (Richard Carlson) who is already married. Newman returns to her life, but he is now a full-fledged gangster and he slips in and out of her sphere, driving Blyth to drink. Despite further success, the star becomes an alcoholic and ruins her career. She ends up in a hospital detoxification ward with Newman coming to comfort her before he is led off to prison after being convicted of a hijacking charge.

THE HELEN MORGAN STORY followed such show business exposes as I'LL CRY TOMORROW (1955) and LOVE ME OR LEAVE ME (see: B/V), but it was the least popular of the trio as it proved to be nothing more than a glossy melodrama uplifted by Ann Blyth's good performance. Robert Milton Miller wrote in Star Myths: Show-Business Biographies on Film (1983), the movie "... unlike most show-business bio-films, makes extensive use of the compositional and lighting codes which are generally associated with the critical term film noir. The criminal activities of her romantic nemesis become all the more familiarly appropriate to those framing devices, but the ultimate innovational act comes in the authenticity-tinged narration by the actual voice of newsman Walter Winchell, who appears on camera as himself, emceeing the story's apocryphal, all-star-attended comeback celebration, paying tribute to a recovered Helen Morgan at the reopening of her own, long-shuttered New York nightclub."

For the record, the feature's chief asset is its soundtrack of vintage songs. Ironically, Ann Blyth (whose actual singing voice was much like that of Helen Morgan) was dubbed by full-voiced Gogi Grant. On television, Polly Bergen had earlier appeared as the famed songstress on "Playhouse 90" (4/16/57, CBS-TV) and received far more acclaim for her star interpretation than would Blyth.

HELLINGER'S LAW (Universal/CBS-TV, 3/10/81) C 110 mins.

Executive producers, Jack Laird, James McAdams; producer, Charles Floyd Johnson; director, Leo Penn; story, Lawrence Vail, Ted Leighton; teleplay, Laird, Vail; music, John Cacavas; art director, Howard E. Johnson; costumes, Burton Miller; camera, Charles Correll; editors, Bill Parker, John J. Dumas, Leon Ortiz-Gil.

Telly Savalas (Nick Hellinger); Morgan Stevens (Andy Clay); Ja'net DuBois (Dottie Singer); Roy Poole (Judge Carroll); Rod Taylor (Clint Tolliver); Melinda Dillon (Anne Gronouski); James Sutorius (Lon Braden); Tom McFadden (Detective Roy Donovan); Lisa Blake Richards (Cara Braden); Kyle Richards (Julie Braden); Arlen Dean Snyder (District Attorney Fred Whedon); Tom Christopher (Bill Rossetti); M. Emmet Walsh (Mr. Graebner); Robert Phalen (Dave Fredericks); Jack Ramage (Douglas Langley); Patsy Rahn (Laura Weire); Don Hamner (District Attorney Stevenson); Frank McCarthy (Paul Savage); Cindy Fisher (Jill Gronouski); Bill Cross (Leo); Paul Larson (Philadelphia Judge); Paul Picerni (TV Director); John Christy Ewing (Assistant Director); Marcy Pullman (Mrs. Carlson).

Top-notch Philadelphia criminal lawyer Nick Hellinger (Telly

Savalas) is hired to defend an accountant (James Sutorius) who is working for a business which, in reality, is controlled by the mob. The problem is that the man is actually a government undercover agent out to get the goods on a syndicate boss (Rod Taylor) and he must be proved innocent at any cost. During the investigation, Savalas unearths the fact that the syndicate chief is involved personally with another government agent (Tom Christopher), a prosecuting attorney (Melinda Dillon), and a policeman (Tom McFadden).

Following his long run in the popular "Kojak" series (CBS-TV, 1973-78), Telly Savalas returned to the small screen in this pilot which co-starred Morgan Stevens as his younger law partner. The "pilot was superior to the series content of shows currently on the air." (Variety) and gave Savalas ample opportunity to expound on his flashy-type characterizations so associated with him via the role of Theo Kojak. As a crime thriller, the telefilm was more than passable, aided by its Houston, Texas, locales.

HELL'S BLOODY DEVILS see: THE FAKERS

HELL'S HOUSE (Capitol Films Exchange, 1932) 72 mins.

Producer, Benjamin F. Zeidman; director-story, Howard Higgin; screenplay, Paul Gangelin, B. Harrison Orkow; camera, Allen S. Siegel; editor, Edward Schroeder.

Pat O'Brien, Bette Davis, and Junior Durkin in HELL'S HOUSE (1932)

Junior Durkin (Jimmy Mason); Pat O'Brien (Matt Kelly); Bette Davis (Peggy Gardner); Junior Coghlan (Shorty); Charley Grapewin (Uncle Henry); Emma Dunn (Aunt Emma); Morgan Wallace (Frank Gebhardt); Hooper Atchley (Captain of the Guards); Wallis Clark (Judge Robinson); James Marcus (Superintendent Thompson); Mary Alden (Mrs. Mason).

Gangster Matt Kelly (Pat O'Brien) runs a bootlegging operation and he gives teenager Jimmy Mason (Junior Durkin) a job. When the police raid the joint and find Durkin there, he is arrested but he refuses to tell the law who owns the place and a judge (Wallis Clark) sentences him to three years in reform school. There he is beaten by a sadistic guard (Hooper Atchley) and the place is run by a crooked superintendent (Mames Marcus). Durkin befriends Shorty (Junior Coughlan), who has a heart ailment, and when the latter dies, a newsman (Morgan Wallace) attempts an expose of the place, but the staff is alerted before a state inspection occurs. Durkin escapes and heads to O'Brien's apartment where he finds the latter's girlfriend (Bette Davis) who explains she is trying to help O'Brien to get Durkin out of the state school. When the police arrive, O'Brien vindicates his young pal.

Filmed as JUVENILE COURT, this poverty row indictment of the reform school system is of interest today because it gave fledgling screen performer Bette Davis an early leading role. With the coming of the video cassette craze, HELL'S HOUSE has surfaced again via several companies who deal in public domain features.

DER HEXER see: THE RINGER

THE HEXER see: THE RINGER

HIDEOUT (Republic, 1949) 61 mins.

Associate producer, Sidney Picker; director, Philip Ford; based on the novel by William Porter; screenplay, John K. Butler; music, Stanley Wilson; art director, Frank Hotaling; set decorators, John McCarthy, Jr., George Milo; assistant director, Roy Wade; makeup, Bob Mark; sound, Dick Tyler; camera, John Macburnie; editor, Richard L. Van Enger.

Adrian Booth (Hannah Kelly); Lloyd Bridges (George Browning); Ray Collins (Philip J. Fogarty); Sheila Ryan (Edie Hansen); Alan Carney (Evans); Jeff Corey (Beecham); Fletcher Chandler (Joe Bottomley); Don Beddoe (Dr. Hamilton Gibbs); Charles Halton (Gabriel Wotter); Emory Parnell (Arnie Anderson); Nana Bryant (Sybil Elwood Kaymeer); Paul E. Burns (Janitor); Douglas Evans (Radio Announcer); Smoki Whitfield (Pullman Porter).

Lloyd Bridges in HIDEOUT (1949).

Aging con man Arthur Burdett (Ray Collins) takes on the
guise of a deceased named Philip J. Fogerty. After masterminding
a diamond robbery and doublecrossing his cohorts (Alan Carney,
Jeff Corey), he moves to Hilltop, Iowa, where the real Fogerty once
attended college. Pretending to be a retired businessman, Collins
has another assistant (Adrian Booth) placed as secretary to the city
attorney (Lloyd Bridges), who is running for mayor. Due to a
residency requirement, however, Booth loses the job and is replaced
by Edie (Sheila Ryan). A diamond cutter (Charles Halton) arrives
in town but is murdered and Bridges sets out to solve the case, believing Booth can help him since she is Fogerty's new secretary.
The con man, however, decides to have Booth help him and he plans
to have her murdered, but she and Bridges are captured by Carney
and Corey and taken to a remote area where Booth shoots both men.
Bridges realizes Booth has been part of the gang but lets her go,
and he and the police chief (Emory Parnell) arrest "Fogerty" just
as he is receiving an honorary doctorate from the local college.
    HIDEOUT is a fast paced yarn highlighted by Ray Collins'
performance as the slick but corrupt gangster and Adrian Booth as
the femme fatale. Director Philip Ford used the then popular film
noir motif for this programmer, which has most of its action set at
night. Lloyd Bridges was only adequate in the part of the city's
attorney.

HIJACK! (ABC-TV, 9/26/73) C 78 mins.

Producers, Aaron Spelling, Leonard Goldberg; associate producer,
Peter Dunne, director, Leonard J. Horn; story, Michael Kelly; tele-
play, James D. Buchanan, Michael Kelly, Ronald Austin; music,
Allyn Ferguson, Jack Elliott; art director, Paul Sylos; camera,
Arch R. Dalzell; editor, Leon Carrere.

David Janssen (Jake Wilinson); Keenan Wynn (Donny McDonald);
Lee Purcell (Eileen Noonan); Jeanette Nolan (Mrs. Briscoe); Wil-
liam Schallert (Frank Kleiner); Tom Tully (Mr. Noonan); Ron Fein-
berg (Bearded Man); John A. Zee (Man with Glasses); William Mims
(Highway Patrolman); James Gavin (Helicopter Pilot); Dallas Mitchell
(Houston Dispatcher); Morris Buchanan (Los Angeles Dispatcher);
James Burke, Walter Wyatt (Cowboys); Robert Golden (Weigh Sta-
tion Officer).

Truckers Jake (David Janssen) and Donny (Keenan Wynn),
who have had a run of extreme bad luck, agree to trek a secret
cargo from Los Angeles to Houston. En route, they discover the
merchandise they are hauling is actually top-secret government ma-
terials and that a gang is planning to hijack their truck. The two
drivers must play a cat-and-mouse game with the criminals as they
attempt to reach their destination safely.
Filmed in California's Antelope Valley, HIJACK was a "typical
tailored-for-TV melodramatic hijink" (TV Guide) which offered solid
performances by David Janssen and Keenan Wynn in the leads.

HI-JACKED (Lippert, 1950) 66 mins.

Executive producer, Murray Lerner; associate executive producer,
Jack Leewood; producer, Sigmund Neufield; director, Sam Newfield;
story, Ray Schrock, Fred Myton; screenplay, Myton, Orville Hampton; art director, F. Paul Sylos; set decorator, Harry Reif; music,
Paul Dunlap; assistant director, Eddie Davis; sound, Frank Webster;
camera, Phil Tannura; editor, Edward Mann.

Jim Davis (Joe Harper); Marsha Jones (Jean); Sid Melton (Killer);
David Bruce (Matt); Paul Cavanagh (Hagen); Ralph Sanford (Clark);
Iris Adrian (Agnes); George Eldredge (Digbey).

Former convict Joe Harper (Jim Davis) wins a job driving a
freight truck and after he is hijacked, the company begins to suspect he might be implicated with the criminals. After a second hijacking, Davis is fired but receives support from his wife (Marsha
Jones) and fellow rig driver (Sid Melton). Davis intends to prove
his innocence and eventually discovers that the trucking company's
dispatcher (David Bruce) is behind the operations. He learns when
the next hijacking is scheduled to occur and tips off the police.

HI-JACKED is a fast paced, tough programmer. Jim Davis is particularly credible as the trucker falsely accused of working with the thieves.

HIT MAN (Metro-Goldwyn-Mayer, 1972) C 90 mins.

Producer, Gene Corman; director, George Armitage; based on the novel Jack's Return Home by Ted Lewis; screenplay, Armitage; music, H. B. Barnum; art director, Lynn Griffin; assistant director, George Van; sound, Alex Vanderkar; camera, Andrew Davis; editor, Morton Tubor.

Bernie Casey (Tyrone Tackett); Pamela Grier (Gozelda); Lisa Moore (Laurel); Betty Waldron (Irvelle); Sam Laws (Sherwood); Candy All (Rochelle Tackett); Don Diamond (Theotis); Edmund Cambride (Zito); Bob Harris (Shag); Rudy Challenger (Julius); Tracy Ann King (Nite); Christopher Joy (Leon); Roger E. Mosley (Baby Huey).

Hooked up with the West Coast pornography racket and its control by the underworld, Tyrone Tackett (Bernie Casey) leaves his Oakland home base to come to Los Angeles for the funeral of his murdered brother. He finds that the killing was instigated by rivals in the porno trade and he decides to even the score. His only helper is friend Laurel (Lisa Moore). Among those involved in the revenge are: gangster kingpin Zito (Edmund Cambride), hit man Shag (Bob Harris), porno stars Julius (Rudy Challenger) and Gozelda (Pam Grier), and prostitute Irvelle (Betty Waldron). By the finale, Casey has settled his grudge with all concerned.
    HIT MAN was yet another in the violent black exploitation cycle which flooded theaters in the early 1970s. It was loud, brutal, and erotic, with its subtheme of the porno film industry.
    By this period, the hero of such epics was often on the wrong side of the law and usually was out to eliminate rivals rather than living up to the letter of the law. This feature, however, does have the hoodlum hero out to avenge his brother's murder as well as the on-camera rape of his niece (Candy All), all of which leads to her father's death. The film has its lighter moments; especially the sequence where a slick used car dealer (Sam Laws) wants to film a TV commercial but cannot get a perfect take due to his street language.
    This film is a Hollywood remake of the British entry, GET CARTER (1971) (q.v.).

HIT THE ICE (Universal, 1943) 82 mins.

Producer, Alex Gottlieb; director, Charles Lamont; story, True Boardman; screenplay, Robert Lees, Frederic Rinaldo, John Grant; songs, Harry Revel and Paul Francis Webster; assistant director, Howard Christie; art directors, John B. Goodman, Harold MacArthur;

set decorators, Russell A. Gausman, A. J. Greene; music director, Charles Previn; choreography, Sammy Lede; ice skating numbers, Harry Losee; sound, Robert Prichard; camera, Charles Van Enger; editor, Frank Cross.

Bud Abbott (Flash); Lou Costello (Weejie); Ginny Simms (Marcia); Patric Knowles (Dr. Elliott); Elyse Knox (Peggy Osborne); Sheldon Leonard (Silky Fellowsby); Marc Lawrence (Phil); Joe Sawyer (Buster); Johnny Long and His Orchestra (Themselves); Joseph Crehan, Wade Boteler (Train Conductors); Edward Gargan, Eddie Dunn (Cops); Pat Flaherty (Police Lieutenant); Dorothy Vaughn (Nurse); Minerva Urecal (Wife); Mantan Moreland (Redcap); Bobby Barber (Train Porter); Ken Christy (Fire Chief); Billy Wayne (Man in Bed); Rebel Randall (Woman in Bed); Cordelia Campbell (Skater); Eddie Parker (Ambulance Driver).

Two bumbling photographers, Flash (Bud Abbott) and Weejie (Lou Costello), go on a call with a childhood doctor friend (Patric Knowles). They end up at a burning building and Costello is slightly injured and taken to a hospital where three gangsters (Sheldon Leonard, Marc Lawrence, Joseph Sawyer) are staying with the leader pretending to be ill in order to map out a heist of the bank across the street. The hoodlums believe the photographers are actually gangsters from Detroit sent to aid them by covering their escape. The crooks rob the bank and the two hapless picture takers are left taking the blame. They chase the hoodlums to Sun Valley where their leader has gone with Knowles and a nurse (Elyse Knox). At the resort, the duo are hired as waiters and Costello falls in love with a pretty band singer (Ginny Simms). After much ado, they clear their names.

Originally this well-balanced feature was to have been entitled OH DOCTOR and the plot called for Lou Costello to play a hypochondriac, but after several script changes the end product was this comedy. Besides the pratfalls and sight gaps of the comedy team, there was the pleasant music of Johnny Long and His Orchestra and songstress Ginny Simms.

HOLD YOUR MAN (Metro-Goldwyn-Mayer, 1933) 80 mins.

Director, Sam Wood; story, Anita Loos; adaptors, Loos, Howard Emmett Rogers; song, Nacio Herb Brown and Arthur Freed; art directors, Cedric Gibbons, Merrill Pye; set decorator, Edwin B. Willis; gowns, Adrian; sound, Douglas Shearer; camera, Harold Rosson; editor, Frank Sullivan.

Jean Harlow (Ruby Adams); Clark Gable (Eddie Huntington Hall); Stuart Erwin (Al Simpson); Dorothy Burgess (Gypsy); Muriel Kirkland (Bertha); Garry Owen (Slim); Barbara Barondess (Saide); Paul Hurst (Aubrey Mitchell); Elizabeth Patterson (Miss Tuttle); Theresa Harris (Lily Mae Crippen); Blanche Friderici (Mrs. Wagner); George

Reed (Reverend Crippen); Louise Beavers (Maid); Jack Cheatham, Frank Hagney (Cops); Jack Randall (Dance Extra); G. Pat Collins (Phil Dunn); Harry Semels (Neighbor); Nora Cecil (Miss Campbell the Sewing Instructress); Eva McKenzie (Cooking Teacher).

Petty crook Eddie Hall (Clark Gable) is on the lam from the law for defrauding a man of $40 and ends up hiding in the apartment of hooker Ruby Adams (Jean Harlow), who shelters him when he tells the cops he is her husband. The two begin an affair with Harlow dropping her boyfriend (Stuart Erwin) for Gable, who only wants to use her. He sets up a scheme to extort money out of laundry owner Aubrey Mitchell (Paul Hurst), who is attracted to Harlow. Harlow agrees to entertain Hurst in her apartment, but when Gable arrives he becomes angered and accidentally kills the man. He runs away and Harlow is charged with the crime and sentenced to three years in prison. Once incarcerated, she finds she is pregnant and that her cellmate is Gypsy (Dorothy Burgess), Gable's ex-love. Eventually, Gable and Harlow are secretly wed in her prison and then Gable, redeemed, takes responsibility for the manslaughter. After serving his term, he finds Harlow and their young son waiting for him.

HOLD YOUR MAN has all the necessary basic ingredients to be a sizzling cinema melodrama. Unfortunately, the Hays Office had, by this time, put the stops on overt sexual actitivity in feature films and the performers had to rely totally on characterization to bring out the sensual aspect of their relationship. Thus this drama of petty crooks wasn't strong enough in plotting and soon became maudlin soap opera. Of the screen team's half-dozen cinema pairings between 1932 and 1937, this was the weakest.

HOLT OF THE SECRET SERVICE (Columbia, 1941) fifteen chapters

Producer, Larry Darmour; director, James W. Horne; screenplay, Basil Dickey, George Plympton; Wyndham Gittens; assistant director, Carl Hiecke; music, Lee Zahler; camera, James S. Brown; editors, Dwight Caldwell, Earl Turner.

Jack Holt (Jack Holt/Nick Farrell); Evelyn Brent (Kay Drew); Montague Shaw (Mulvey); Tristam Coffin (Valden); John Ward (Arnold); Ted Adams (Quist); Joe McGuinn (Crimp); Edward Hearn (Jim); Ray Parsons (Severn); Jack Cheatham (Frank).

Chapters: 1) Chaotic Creek; 2) Ramparts of Revenge; 3) Illicit Wealth; 4) Menaced by Fate; 5) Exits to Terror; 6) Deadly Doom; 7) Out of the Past; 8) Escape to Peril; 9) Sealed in Silence; 10) Named to Die; 11) Ominous Warnings; 12) The Stolen Signal; 13) Prisoner of Jeopardy; 14) Afire Afloat; 15) Yielded Hostage.

The country is being flooded with counterfeit money and the Secret Service assigns agent Jack Holt (himself) to investigate,

Jack Holt (with gun) and Tristram Coffin in HOLT OF THE SECRET
SERVICE (1941).

aided by another operative, Kay Drew (Evelyn Brent). They locate the gang responsible for the bogus currency and in order to
infiltrate the operation, Jack pretends to be notorious criminal Nick
Farrell with Brent as his wife. He makes friends with gang member
Crimp (Joe McGuinn) and they head to the gangster's hideout in
the north woods, where after several narrow escapes, they emerge
victorious.

This cliffhanger marked Jack Holt's final film in his Columbia
contract, having been with Harry Cohn's studio since 1928 and having starred in over 50 bread-and-butter features for that company.
By 1941 the opinionated studio head and his first big star were bitter enemies, but Holt's name was used in the serial's title because
Cohn recognized the box-office draw of Jack Holt. Teaming Holt
with one-time sex symbol Evelyn Brent makes this chapterplay a
nostalgic outing.

The serial was later re-edited into six chapters and televised
as part of the PBS-TV series, "Action-Packed Cliffhangers."

HOMICIDE BUREAU (Columbia, 1939) 56 mins.

Producer, Jack Fier; director, C. C. Coleman, Jr.; screenplay,
Earle Snell; music director, Morris Stoloff; camera, Benjamin Kline;
editor, James Sweeney.

Gene Morgan, Bruce Cabot, Marc Lawrence, and Moroni Olsen in
HOMICIDE BUREAU (1939).

Bruce Cabot (Jim Logan); Rita Hayworth (J. G. Bliss); Marc Law-
rence (Chuck Brown); Richard Fiske (Hank); Moroni Olsen (Captain
Haines); Norman Willis (Briggs); Gene Morgan (Blake); Robert
Paige (Thurston); Lee Prather (Jaimison); Eddie Featherston
(Specks); Stanley Andrews (Police Commissioner); John Tyrell
(Poolroom Employee); Charles Trowbridge (Henly); George Lloyd
(Boat Captain); Ann Doran (Nurse); Joseph De Stefani (Miller);
Beatrice Curtis (Stewardess); Beatrice Blinn (Woman); Dick Curtis
(Radio Broadcaster); Stanley Brown (Police Photographer); George
De Normand (Trigger); Harry Bernard (Joe); Nell Craig, Georgia
Cooper (Committee Women); Kit Guard (Mug); Gene Stone (Man);
Ky Robinson (Casey); Dick Rush (Cop); Lee Shumway (Police
Switchboard Operator); Wedgwood Nowell (Committee Man); Lester
Dorr (Gangster).

After several murders occur, a detective (Bruce Cabot) believes that gangsters running an operation which steals and then
resells scrap iron is responsible, and he is assisted in his detection by a crusading newspaper reporter (Robert Paige). With data
garnered by pretty police laboratory expert J. G. Bliss (Rita Hayworth), the two men are able to crack the underworld operation.
    Made by the Irving Briskin unit at Columbia Pictures, HOMI-
CIDE BUREAU is a bottom-drawer production. Films of the 1930s

placed gangsters in all types of rackets for novelty's sake, and
this entry had them stealing scrap iron, hardly a subject geared
to attract viewers, Rita Hayworth's role here is relatively small
and there are no romantic interludes between her and the leading
men.

THE HOODLUM (United Artists, 1951) 61 mins.

Executive producer, Jack Schwartz; producer, Maurice Kosloff;
associate producers, Sam Neuman, Nat Tanchuck; director, Max
Nosseck; story-screenplay, Neuman, Tanchuck; art director, Fred
Preble; set decorator, Harry Reif; makeup, Harry Thomas; music,
Darrell Calker; wardrobe, Oscar Rodriguez; assistant director,
Arthur Hammond; sound, Earl Snyder; camera, Clark Ramsey;
editor, Jack Killifer.

Lawrence Tierney (Vincent Lubeck); Allene Roberts (Rosa); Edward
Tierney [Scott Brady] (Johnny Lubeck); Lisa Golm (Mrs. Lubeck);
Marjorie Riordan (Eileen); and: Stuart Randall, Ann Zika, John De-
Simone, Tom Hubbard, Eddie Foster, O. Z. Whitehead, Richard Bar-
ron, Rudy Rama, Gene Roth.

Lawrence Tierney and Gene Roth in THE HOODLUM (1951).

Ever since he played DILLINGER (see: B/V), Lawrence Tierney was typecast in tough guy roles; mainly as hoodlums. This Jack Schwartz production continued that tradition with the actor offering a strong performance as a no-good crook who doublecrosses everyone, including his mother, brother, and mistress, the latter committing suicide as a result. Termed "a satisfactory programmer" by Variety, the movie is purely a vehicle for Tierney. To be noted is Tierney's real life brother Edward in the role of the screen tough's brother. Edward would later change his screen name to Scott Brady.

Lawrence Tierney is a convict who has been in prison for five years but is released on the mercy pleas of his mother. His brother gives him a job in his service station to satisfy parole requirements and while working there, the ex-convict notices an armored truck at the bank across the street. He plans to rob the vehicle and enlists the teamwork of several of his former underworld cronies. Using a funeral as a blind for their robbery, the gangsters commit the caper, but several of them are killed and later Lawrence Tierney is gunned down by the law. Once again, the motto is clearly: crime does not pay!

THE HOSTAGE GANG see: LE GANG DES OTAGES

HUMAN CARGO (Twentieth Century-Fox, 1936) 65 mins.

Producer, Sol M. Wurtzel; director, Allan Dwan; based on the novel I Will Be Faithful by Kathleen Shepard; adaptors, Jefferson Parker, Doris Malloy; art director, Duncan Cramer; costumes, William Lambert; camera, Daniel B. Clark; editor, Louis Loeffler.

Claire Trevor (Bonnie Brewster); Brian Donlevy (Packy Campbell); Alan Dinehart (Lionel Crocker); Ralph Morgan (District Attorney Carey); Helen Troy (Susie); Rita Cansino [Hayworth] (Carmen Zoro); Morgan Wallace (Gilbert Fender); Herman Bing (Fritz Schultz); John McGuire (Spike Davis); Ralf Harolde (Tony Sculla); Wade Boteler (Bob McSweeney); Harry Wood (Ira Conklin); Stanley Blystone, Ivan "Dusty" Miller, Pat Hartiga, Tom O'Grady (Detectives); Herman Bing (Schultz); Paul McVey (Ship's Officer); Tom Rickett (Reporter); Harry Semels (Baretto); Wilfred Lucas (Detective Lieutenant); Edward Cooper (Butler); Frederick Vogeding (Captain); John Rogers (Foreigners' Agent); Arno Frey (German Husband); Rosalie Hegedus (German Mother); Hans Fuerberg, Milla Davenport (German Characters); Otto H. Fries (German Cook); Alphonse Martell (Frenchman); Hector V. Sarno (Italian); Eddie Buzard (Copy Boy); Claudia Coleman (Sob Sister).

Gangsters are smuggling aliens into the United States, murdering those who dare to disclose their activites. The Immigration Service has no success in tracking down the traffickers in human lives although the local district attorney (Ralph Morgan) wants to prosecute those involved. A newspaper reporter (Brian Donlevy) pursuing the case finds he has a rival (Claire Trevor) from another paper. She is a socialite who, bored with life, has taken a news-writing job. Although opponents, they work together to gain evidence against the racketeers and they find an illegal alien (Rita [Hayworth] Cansino) who agrees to testify against the gang. Their research a success, the two reporters plan to wed.

With its topical plot, good cast, and fine direction by Allan Dwan, HUMAN CARGO has "movement, suspense and punch to maintain unflagging interest" (Motion Pictures Herald). It was a forthright expose of the smuggling of aliens. Brian Donlevy, in his first film under his new 20th Century-Fox contract, and the studio's "B" queen, Claire Trevor, made a watchable team in the lead roles while a young Rita Hayworth gained notice as the gal who helped to break up the gangsters' alien-smuggling racket.

THE HUMAN MONSTER (Monogram, 1940) 76 mins.

Producer, John Argyle; director, Walter Summers; based on the novel The Dark Eyes of London by Edgar Wallace; screenplay, Patrick Kirwin, Walter Summers, Argyle; music, Guy Jones; camera, Ronald Anscombe; editor, E. G. Richards.

Bela Lugosi (John Dearborn/Dr. Orloff); Hugh Williams (Inspector Holt); Greta Gynt (Diana Stuart); Edmond Ryan (Lieutenant O'Reilly); Wilfred Walter (Jake the Monster); Alexander Field (Grogan); Arthur E. Owen (Dumb Lew); Julie Suedo (Secretary); Gerald Pring (Henry Stuart); Bryan Herbert (Walsh); Mayt Hallatt (Policewoman); Charles Denrose (The Drunk).

Edgar Wallace's 1924 thriller novel was the basis of this British production starring Bela Lugosi in dual roles as the seemingly honest (but really murderous) head of an insurance company, while also masquerading as a blind proprietor of a mission for the sightless. In the latter part, the actor's voice was dubbed by O. B. Clarence. The movie is a top-notch thriller, combining the usual Wallace ingredients of mystery, suspense, and horror into a veritable field day for Bela Lugosi fans. When Monogram released the feature in the U.S. in 1940, Variety noted its "asset is the presence of Bela Lugosi in a more villainous characterization than he's been in for some time." (The original British release title was DARK EYES OF LONDON.)

Insurance company head John Dearborn (Lugosi) sells clients insurance and then murders them after they pay large premiums. He carries out the murders in the guise of Dr. Orloff, the head of a mission for the blind who pretends to be blind and uses hulking Blind Jake (Wilfred Walter) to carry out the actual murders. A Scotland Yard man (Hugh Williams) and an American police detective (Edmond Ryan) are ordered to solve the case. They enlist the aid

of a young woman (Greta Gynt) who is investigating the death of
her father, one of the insurance company's clients. It is deduced
that Dearborn and Orloff are the same man. The crook is killed by
Walter after his friend is done in by Lugosi as Orloff.

Plot elements from this film would be used in the later Lugosi
starrer, BOWERY AT MIDNIGHT (q.v.), while the Edgar Wallace
novel was refilmed in West Germany in 1961 as DIE TOTEN AUGEN
VON LONDON and issued in the States as DEAD EYES OF LONDON
(q.v.).

HUNTED MEN (Paramount, 1938) 63 mins.

Producer, Stuart Walker; director, Louis King; based on the play
by Albert Duffy, Marian Grant; screenplay, Horace McCoy, William
R. Lipman; music director, Boris Morros; assistant director, Lef-
fert; camera, Victor Milner; editor, Ann Bauchans.

Lloyd Nolan (Joe Albany); Mary Carlisle (Jane Harris); Lynne Over-
man (Peter Harris); J. Carrol Naish (Morton Rice); Anthony Quinn
(Mac); Larry "Buster" Crabbe (James Flowers); Johnny Downs
(Frank Martin); Dorothy Peterson (Mrs. Mary Harris); Delmer
Watson (Robert Harris); Regis Toomey (Donovan); Louis Miller
(virgie); George Davis (Waiter); Hooper Atchley (Headwaiter).

HUNTED MEN offered Lloyd Nolan one of his best screen
roles, that of a gangster on the lam who is humanized by the en-
virons of a typically American middle class family before engaging
in a fatal shootout with the law. According to Variety, "... had
this picture been released five years ago during the gangster cycle
it would have cleaned up."

Nolan is Joe Albany, a gangster who has bumped off a cohort (Larry "Buster" Crabbe) and is hiding from the law. He
hitches a ride with tipsy Peter Harris (Lynne Overman) whom Nolan
needs as a front. Once at Overman's house, Crabbe is attracted
to the pretty daughter (Mary Carlisle) and he also takes a shine to
her younger brother Robert (Delmer Watson) who wants to be a G-
Man. This amuses Nolan, who buys the lad some toys, including a
camera. When the film is developed at the drugstore, the police
discover Nolan, who refuses to surrender and is killed.

Writing in B Movies (1973), Don Miller says of HUNTED MEN,
"Among the many points in the film's favor, foremost was the refusal to compromise with a happy ending by scenarists William R.
Lipman and Horace McCoy, even though Nolan's portrayal is sympathetic. His performance and the writing of his role, delved considerably more deeply than most routine hoodlum characterizations."

I AM THE CHEESE (Almi, 1983) C 100 mins.

Executive producers, Jack Schwartzman, Albert Schwartz, Michael

S. Landes; producer, David Lange; director, Robert Jiras; based
on the novel by Robert Cormier; screenplay, Lange, Jiras; music,
Jonathan Tunick; camera, David Quaid; editor, Nicholas Smith.

Robert Macnaughton (Adam); Hope Lange (Betty); Don Murray
(David); Robert Wagner (Dr. Brint); Cynthia Nixon (Amy); Frank
McGurran (Young Adam); Russell Goslant (Gardener); Robert
Cormier (Hertz); Dorothea Macnaughton (Produce Lady); Milford
Keene (Harvester); Lee Richardson (Grey); Joey Jerome (Whipper);
Ronnie Bradbury (Corn); Robert Dutil (Jed); Jeff Rumney (Counter-
man); David Lange (Montgomery); Christopher Murray (Eric); Sudie
Bond (Edna); John Fiedler (Arnold); John Bernek (Store Owner);
Paul Romero (Coke).

Too seldom have motion pictures taken an in-depth look at
the psychological effect the underworld has on innocent bystanders,
particularly children. This low-budget feature, running at a very
leisurely pace, delves into this theme but the use of three different
time levels in the story's context confuses the viewer. The film is
more than half over before the plot gimmick comes to light.

Filmed in Vermont, the picture details the daily activities of
Adam Farmer (Robert Macnaughton), a fifteen-year-old boy who is
institutionalized and undergoing treatment by psychiatrist Dr. Brint
(Robert Wagner). Much of the boy's past is lost to him and the
physician attempts to draw this out during their sessions. At other
times the youth is allowed to ride his bicycle around the guarded
grounds, and during these interludes he pretends he is free or
back at home with a girl (Cynthia Nixon) he knew as a younger
boy. Believing that the people around him are his enemies, Macnaughton escapes from the retreat on his bike and begins to relive
his past.

He recalls living with his father (Don Murray) and mother
(Hope Lange) in a small town and the strange visitors who came to
see his father. He remembers discovering his dad was a newspaperman who had testified against gangsters and had taken on a new
identity in a small town to protect himself and his family. Finally
the boy recalls seeing his parents murdered in a fake car accident
and that the people who are treating him are actually those responsible for the homicides.

I COVER THE UNDERWORLD (Republic, 1955) 70 mins.

Producer, William J. O'Sullivan; director, R. G. Springsteen;
screenplay, John K. Butler; music, R. Dale Butts; camera, Reggie
Lanning; editor Tony Martinelli.

Sean McClory (Gunner O'Hara/John O'Hara); Joanne Jordan (Joan
Marlowe); Ray Middleton (Police Chief); Jaclynne Greene (Gilda);
Lee Van Cleef (Flash Logan); James Griffith (Smiley Di Angelo);
Hugh Sanders (Tim Donovan); Roy Roberts (District Attorney);

208 / I COVER THE UNDERWORLD

Lee Van Cleef, Harry Tyler, Jaclynne Greene, Sean McClory in I
COVER THE UNDERWORLD (1955).

Peter Mamakos (Charlie Green); Robert Crosson (Danny Marlowe);
Frank Gerstle (Dum-Dum Wilson); Willis Bouchey (Warden Lewis L.
Johnson); Philip Van Zandt (Jake Freeman).

　　When his gangster brother Gunner O'Hara (Sean McClory) is
scheduled for parole, divinity student John O'Hara (Sean McClory)
convinces the city's police chief (Ray Middleton) to hold off the
parole so he can infiltrate his brother's gang and bring them to
justice.　Taking on the guise of his corrupt sibling, the young man
gains the evidence needed to clear up the waterfront operations,
mainly with the aid of his brother's gal (Jaclynne Greene).　Along
the way he romances attractive club performer Joan Marlowe (Joanne
Jordan).　Just as he is about to bring in the gang, his brother escapes from jail but is mistakenly shot by one of his own men and in
a shootout with the law, the gang is finally dispersed.
　　While the film's title suggests an expose of the underworld,
it only provides stock ingredients.

I COVER THE WATERFRONT (United Artists, 1933) 72 mins.

Director, James Cruze; based on the book by Max Miller, adaptor, Wells Root; additional dialogue, Jack Jerne; song, Edward Heyman and Johnny Green; camera, Ray June; editor, Grant Whytock.

Claudette Colbert (Julie Kirk); Ben Lyon (Joseph Miller); Ernest Torrence (Eli Kirk); Hobart Cavanaugh (McCoy); Maurice Black (Ortegus); Harry Beresford (Old Chris); Purnell Pratt (John Phelps; George Humbert (Silva); Rosita Marstina (Mrs. Silva); Claudia Coleman (Mother Morgan); Wilfred Lucas (Randall); Lee Phelps (Reporter); Al Hill (Sailor).

Producer Edward Small turned out this medium-budget programmer which became a popular item due to its headlining Claudette Colbert, a big Paramount Pictures star. Ben Lyon, still a popular player even after peaking in HELL'S ANGELS (1930), was her co-star and the picture was directed by James Cruze who had made his reputation in the silent era, especially with THE COVERED WAGON (1923).

Newspaper reporter Joseph Miller (Lyon) is on the trail of gangsters smuggling aliens into the country. The chief culprit is Eli Kirk (Ernest Torrence), a tuna fisherman, who has been using his boats to bring in the illegal aliens. When the authorities have gotten too close on occasion, Torrence has unhesitatingly thrown his human cargo overboard, drowning the hapless victims. Lyon gets wind that Torrence is the culprit and when he finds that the man has an attractive daughter (Colbert) he romances her to get close to her father. Her disgust at learning Lyon's true mission is assuaged when she realizes her dad's actual profession.

The atmospheric I COVER THE WATERFRONT is highlighted by Ernest Torrence's sharp performance as the outwardly kind but inwardly cruel fisherman.

This feature was remade in 1961 as SECRET OF DEEP HARBOR (q.v.).

I STAND ACCUSED (Republic, 1938) 63 mins.

Associate producer-director, John A. Auer; screenplay, Gordon Kahn; additional dialogue, Alex Gottlieb; music director, Cy Feuer; camera, Jack Marta; editor, Murray Seldeen.

Robert Cummings (Fred); Helen Mack (Alison); Lyle Talbot (Eastman); Thomas Beck (Paul); Gordon Jones (Blackie); Robert Paige (Joe Gilman); Leona Roberts (Mrs. Davis); Robert Middlemass (Mitchell); Thomas E. Jackson (Gilroy); John Hamilton (Brewer); Howard Hickman (Gilbert); Harry Stubbs (Mr. Moss); Robert Strange (Ryan).

Two young attorneys, Fred (Robert Cummings) and Eastman

(Lyle Talbot), open an office together and nearly starve before Cummings starts representing a murderer who works for a gangster running a slot machine extortion racket. Cummings, having the proper "influences," begins winning a number of cases and becomes very successful but this causes friction with his wife (Helen Mack), mother (Leona Robert), and partner. Meanwhile, Talbot becomes an assistant district attorney and works to clean up the rackets but often finds himself losing cases to his ex-partner. Finally Cummings realizes the error of his ways and turns state's evidence for his friend, bringing the mob to justice.

I STAND ACCUSED is one of those gangster yarns which eclipsed the genre's popularity in the late 1930s. It lacked what such films required the most--realism.

I TAKE THIS OATH (Producers Releasing Corp., 1940) 61 mins.

Producer, Sigmund Neufeld, director, Sherman Scott [Sam Newfield]; story, William A. Gillman, Jr.; screenplay, George Bricker; music director, David Chudnow; camera, Jack Greenhalgh; editor, Holbrook Todd.

Gordon Jones (Hannigan); Joyce Compton (Betty Casey); Craig Reynolds (Joe Kelly); J. Farrell MacDonald (Inspector Ryan); Robert Homans (Police Inspector Mike Hannigan); Guy Usher (Captain Casey); Mary Gordon (Mrs. Hannigan); Sam Flint (Uncle Jim Kelly); Brooks Benedict (Burly); Veda Ann Borg (Flo); Ed Piel Sr. (Riley); Budd Buster (Jones).

I TAKE THIS OATH deserves a place in film history as the first feature to carry the release emblem of Producers Releasing Corporation (PRC), a poverty row company which issued many gangster tales throughout the 1940s.

Police Inspector Mike Hannigan (Robert Homans) uncovers the evidence needed to put gangsters in prison, but he is murdered before he can carry out his mission. His son Steve (Gordon Jones), a police trainee, joins the force and sets out to avenge his dad's death and bring in the culprits. In doing so, he causes a lot of problems and almost loses his gal (Joyce Compton).

I TAKE THIS OATH has an interesting plot twist in that the young rookie cop finally learns that his best friend's (Craig Reynolds) uncle (Sam Flint) is the leader of the gang and his father's murderer and it is Jones' friend who dies from a bullet intended for the policeman.

I WAS A CONVICT (Republic, 1939) 62 mins.

Producer, Herman Schlom; director, Aubrey Scotto; story, Robert D. Andrews; screenplay, Ben Markson, Andrews; musical director, Cy Feuer; camera, Edward Snyder; editor, Murray Seldeen.

Barton MacLane (Ace King); Beverly Roberts (Judy); J. B. Harrison (Clarence Kolb); Janet Beecher (Mrs. Harrison); Horace Mac-Mahon (Missouri Smith); Ben Welden (Rocks); Leon Ames (Jackson); Clara Blandick (Aunt Sarah); Russell Hicks (District Attorney); John Harmon (Matty); Chester Clute (Evans).

 Rich businessman J. B. Harrison (Clarence Kolb) is sent to prison for income tax evasion and while there becomes friends with fellow convicts Ace King (Barton MacLane) and Missouri Smith (Horace MacMahon). Upon release, he gives them jobs in his manufacturing firm and MacLane romances Kolb's pretty daughter Judy (Beverly Roberts). MacLane, however, plans to steal what he can from Kolb and make a getaway, but his love for Boerts prevails and he goes straight, eventually heading the firm.
 I WAS A CONVICT gives Barton MacLane something other than his usual hardened, murderous convict role and he handles the comedy dialogue deftly.

ILLEGAL TRAFFIC (Paramount, 1938)

Associate producer, director, Louis King; story-screenplay, Robert Yost, Lewis Foster, Stuart Anthony; camera, Henry Sharpe.

J. Carrol Naish (Lewis Zomar); Mary Carlisle (Carol Butler);

Larry "Buster" Crabbe, Judith Barrett, and J. Carrol Naish in ILLEGAL TRAFFIC (1938).

Robert Preston (Bent Martin); Pierre Watkin (Jigger); Larry "Buster" Crabbe (Steve); George McKay (Old Man Butler); Richard Denning (Silk Patterson); Philip Warren (Dittmar); Sheila Darcy (Mathilde); Dolores Casey (Mamie); Richard Stanley (Cagey Miller); John Hart (Davis); Regis Toomey (Windy); William H. Davidson (Dalton); Joseph Crehan (Chief Daley); Monte Blue (Captain Moran); Archie Twitchell (Duke); Morgan Conway (State's Attorney Ryan).

Businessman Lewis Zomar (J. Carrol Naish) and Jigger (Pierre Watkin) supposedly helm a legal transportation firm, but in actuality their trucks transport gangsters away from the scenes of their crimes. Several G-men attempt to penetrate the racket but are killed. Finally Captain Moran (Monte Blue) assigns ambitious agent Bent Martin (Robert Preston) to the case. The G-man thoroughly studies the operation and learns that Naish is the grou's mastermind. In a final confrontation, Naish is killed.

Well directed by Louis King and containing an excellent cast, ILLEGAL TRAFFIC is a top-notch "B" feature, especially benefitting from strong performances by J. Carrol Naish as the hoodlum and Robert Preston as the law enforcer.

INCIDENT ON A DARK STREET (Twentieth Century-Fox/NBC-TV, 1/13/73) C 100 mins.

Executive producer, David Gerber; producer, E. Jack Neumann; director, Buzz Kulik; teleplay, Neumann; music, Elmer Bernstein; camera, Charles F. Wheeler; editor, Rita Roland.

James Olson (Joseph Dubbs); David Canary (Pete Gallagher); Robert Pine (Paul Hamilton); Richard Castellano (Frank Romeo); William Shatner (Deaver Wallace); Murray Hamilton (Edmund); Gilbert Roland (Dominic Leopold); John Kerr (Attorney Gallagher); Kathleen Lloyd (Louise Trenier); Wesley Lau (John Pine); Donald Barry (Miles Henderson); David Doyle (Luke Burgess); Gordon Pinsent (Mayor); James Davidson (Arthur Trenier); and: Jerome Thor; Mark Jenkins; Marienne Clark; Susan Stafford, Marian Collier, Earl Ebi, Michelle Nichols, Michael W. Siokey, Jed Allen, Robyn Millian.

When a man is murdered leaving a nightclub, the U.S. Attorney's office finds the syndicate is involved. As a result, U.S. Attorney Joseph Dubbs (James Olson) uncovers not only organized crime in the building contract business as well as a dope smuggling racket, but also pinpoints corrupt city hall officials in league with the mobsters.

In TV Guide, Judith Crist called this telefeature, "A top-notch tailored-for-television flick ... an above-average crime drama." What makes this TV movie so interesting is not its rehash of the day-to-day workings of a crime fighting government agency, but its trio of villains played slickly by William Shatner (as a crooked businessman), Gilbert Roland (as the syndicate boss), and Richard Castellano (as an Italian gangster).

INCOGNITO (Gaumont, 1958) 100 mins.

Director, Patrice Dally; screenplay, Albert Siminon, Bon Barsman, Yvan Audouard, Dally; camera, Michel Kelber; editor, Claude Nicole.

Eddie Constantine (Stanley); Danick Patersson (Barbara); Tilda Thamar (Blonde); Gaby Andre (Redhead); Dario Moreno (Fernando).

American actor-singer Eddie Constantine carved out a successful career for himself in 1950s Europe as a cabaret performer and actor, eventually headlining more than fifty feature films. Although largely unknown in the United States, Constantine was extremely popular in Europe, especially in the decade from the mid-1950s onward. He became identified with his portrayals of the tough, tongue-in-cheek detectives and secret agents combatting global villains. His cheaply made features were largely takeoffs of American gangster films and were loaded with amusing sight gags, vapid plots, and lots of shapely females.

Here he is Stanley, a U.S. secret service agent pretending to be an American vice-consul to find incriminating evidence on a counterfeiting operation in Nice run by a woman who uses the guise of the outfit being led by Latin gangsters.

INSIDE DETROIT (Columbia, 1955) 80 mins.

Producer, Sam Katzman, director, Fred F. Sears; screenplay, Robert R. Kent, James H. Gordon; music conductor, Mischa Bakaleinikoff; camera, Henry Freulich; editor, Gene Havlick.

Dennis O'Keefe (Blair Vickers); Pat O'Brien (Gus Linden); Tina Carver (Joni Calvin); Margaret Field (Barbara Linden); Mark Damon (Gregg Linden); Larry Blake (Max Harkness); Ken Christy (Ben Macauley); Joseph Turkel (Pete Kink); Paul Bryar (Sam Foran); Robert E. Griffin (Hoagy Mitchell); Guy Kingsford (Jenkins); Dick Rich (Toby Gordon); Norman Leavitt (Preacher); Katherine Warren (Ethel Linden), and Herman Boden.

After serving five years in prison for racketeering, one-time union boss Gus Linden (Pat O'Brien) is about to be released and he plans to move in and take over his old job which is now held by honest Blair Vickers (Dennis O'Keefe). When an attempt is made on O'Keefe's life, it is believed that O'Brien is behind the union headquarter's bombing, and policeman Max Harkness (Larry Blake) is assigned to protect O'Keefe. Meanwhile, O'Brien is released from jail and he and his mistress (Tina Carver) open a modeling agency which is a front for their prostitution racket. O'Brien continues his efforts to get rid of O'Keefe, but this only results in injury to his daughter (Margaret Field) who loves O'Keefe and the death of his disillusioned son (Mark Damon) before O'Brien is again arrested for his assorted crimes.

Dennis O'Keefe, Mark Damon, Ken Christy, Herman Boden, and
Larry Blake in INSIDE DETROIT (1955).

Apparently based on an actual incident involving the attempted
murder of the Reuther brothers in the early 1950s, this downbeat
melodrama is a "familiar good-versus-racketeer type of actioner, using the housecleaning by the United Auto Workers local in Detroit
to springboard a documentary-styled treatment" (Variety). Dennis
O'Keefe and Pat O'Brien are solid in the lead roles, lending credibility to the overall production.

INSIDE INFORMATION (Univeral, 1939) 61 mins.

Producer, Irving Starr; director, Charles Lamont; story, Martin
Mooney, Burnet Hershey; screenplay, Alex Gottlieb; camera, Arthur
Martinelli; editor, Harry Keller.

June Lang (Kathleen Burke); Dick Foran (Danny Blake); Harry
Carey (Captain Dugan); Mary Carlisle (Crystal); Addison Richards
(Banford); Joseph Sawyer (Grazzi); Grant Richards (Bixby); Paul
McVey (Crawford); Selmer Jackson (Huxley); Frederick Burton
(Commissioner); John Harmon (Frenchy).

The old chestnut of new scientific methods versus tried and
true police activities in cornering criminals is the crux of this

melodrama. Variety labeled it, "A pleasing dish, all in all, being neither obnoxious through exaggeration nor outstanding as serious screen entertainment." The film benefitted from Harry Carey as the police captain bent on keeping traditional methods while Dick Foran compliments him as the young rookie sold on scientific crime detection.

A large number of unsolved jewel robberies have taken place in Captain Dugan's (Carey) precinct and he is baffled by them. He is also under pressure from local businessman Banford (Addison Richards) to get the robberies solved and in addition he is forced to break in several new recruits, including Danny Blake (Foran). The latter is not only espousing new crime detection methodology, but is romancing Carey's niece (June Lang). Finding a heel print at the scene of one of the robberies, Foran traces it to one of the gang members and gets promoted to plainsclothes cop. But when one of his later theories proves false, he is suspended. He then works on his own and locates the crooks' headquarters, but later complications end him in jail. At last he succeeds in proving that Richards is masterminding the crime wave.

INSIDE THE WALLS OF FOLSOM PRISON (Warner Bros., 1951)
    87 mins.

Producer, Bryan Foy; director-screenplay, Carne Wilbur; music, William Lava; orchestrator, Charles Maxwell; art director, Douglas Bacon; set decorator, William Kuehl; makeup, Gordon Bau, assistant director, Jean McMahon; sound, Stanley Jones; camera, Edwin Du-Par; editor, Owen Marks.

Steven Cochran (Chuck Daniels); David Brian (Mark Benson); Philip Carey (Red Pardue); Ted de Corsia (Warden Rickey); Scott Forbes (Frazier); Lawrence Tolan (Daly); Dick Wesson (Tinker); Paul Picerni (Jeff Riordan); William Campbell (Ferretti).

Prison reform pictures were, and are, a dime a dozen, but INSIDE THE WALLS OF FOLSOM PRISON is one of the better efforts in this vein, due to a meaty plot and actual filming at the correctional facility. Four years later, writer-director Crane Wilbur (a one-time silent screen movie idol) wrote another prison reform outing, WOMEN'S PRISON (q.v.).

Set in the 1920s, Folsom Prison is a harsh institution run by a cruel warden (Ted de Corsia) and his evil guards. Due to the severity, the prisoners, led by Chuck Daniels (Steve Cochran), are hardly cooperative and plan a break. This is thwarted by the appointment of Mark Benson (David Brian) as the captain of the guards and he sets about making reforms which transform the prison into a more humane place. In the meantime, Brian has earned the rancor of the warden, who has the reformer fired. Thereafter, Cochran leads the prisoners in a bloody revolt in which many inmates die. The ensuing investigation leads to permanent reforms.

INTRIGUE (United Artists, 1947) 90 mins.

Producer, Sam Bischoff; director, Edwin L. Marin; story, George Slavin; screenplay, Barry Trivers, Slavin; music, Louis Forbes; song, Harry Akst and Samuel Lerner; art director, Arthur Lonergan; set decorator, Robert Priestly; assistant director, Joseph Depew; sound, William H. Lynch, Joseph I. Kane; camera, Lucien Andriot; editor, George Arthur.

George Raft (Brad Dunham); June Havoc (Tamara Baranoff); Helena Carter (Linda Parker); Tom Tully (Mark Andrews); Marvin Miller (Ramon); Dan Seymour (Karidian); Philip Ahn (Lui Chen); Jay C. Flippen (Mike); Marc Krah (Nicco); Charles Lane (Hotel Clerk); Edna Holland (Miss Carr); Michael Visaroff (Captain Masters); Peter Chong (Newspaper Editor); Maria San Marco (Ling); Michael Ansara (Radio Operator); Victor Sen Yung (Cable Clerk); Paul Fierra (Warehouseman); Stan Ross (Assistant Warehouseman); Rod Red Wing (Manuscript Thief); Leon Lontoc (Mechanic); Hassan Ezzat, Robert Gilbert, Alex Montoya, Hassan Khayyan, Al Rhein (Karidian's Henchmen); Nancy Hsuieh (Little Chinese Girl).

Former flyer Brad Dunham (George Raft) has been expelled from the Army after being accused of smuggling. To prove his innocence he comes to war-torn Shanghai to infiltrate the gangster mob which framed him. There he meets pert Linda Arnold (Helena Carter) who is trying to help the city's starving waifs. Raft and Carter are attracted to one another, but Raft won't permit romance to get in the way of his mission. He works for exotic black market operator Tamara Baranoff (June Havoc) and at the same time works in league with foreign correspondent Marc Andrews (Tom Tully), who is piecing together the story on who is behind the area's black market operations. The mob's gunman Ramon (Marvin Miller) kills the reporter just as he is about to break the story. Raft thereafter gets the goods on Havoc and her boss (Semour), bringing them to justice.

Although it did not fare well at the box-office, INTRIGUE is enhanced by Raft's stoic performance as the hero. One of the more creative aspects of the film was its promotional copy:

> "A Raft of lightning action.
> A Raft of racy romance.
> A Raft of heart-stopping thrills!"

IRISH LUCK (Monogram, 1939) 55 mins.

Producer, Grant Withers; director, Howard Bretherton; story, Charles M. Brown; screenplay, Mary C. McCarthy; camera, Harry Neumann; editor, Russell Schoengarth.

Frankie Darro (Buzzy O'Brien); Dick Purcell (Lanahan); Lillian

Elliott (Mrs. O'Brien); Sheila Darcy (Kitty Monahan); James Flavin (Finger); Dennis Moore (Jim); Mantan Moreland (Jefferson); Howard Mitchell (Hotel Manager).

Gangsters are selling government bonds they have stolen and are using a hotel as their headquarters. Bellhop Buzzy O'Brien (Frankie Darro) fancies himself a detective because his dad was once a plainsclothes cop. When a murder takes place at the hotel, attractive Kitty Monahan (Sheila Darcy) is the chief suspect of the policeman (Dick Purcell) handling the case and the house detective (James Flavin). Darro, however, looks into the matter and finds that mobsters are behind the killing and clears Darcy.

The initial feature produced by actor Grant Withers, who later did MUTINY IN THE BIG HOUSE (q.v.), this Frankie Darro vehicle "turns out as forthright entertainment" (Variety). While the gangsters take a back seat to Frankie Darro's sleuthing chores, the mystery-comedy is a pleasant outing. Mantan Moreland, who would later become Darro's co-star in this Monogram series, has some good moments as the hotel porter.

ISLAND MONSTER see: IL MOSTRO DELL'ISOLA

ISLAND OF DOOMED MEN (Columbia, 1940) 68 mins.

Producer, Wallace MacDonald; director, Charles Barton; screenplay, Robert D. Andrews; music director, Morris W. Stoloff; camera, Benjamin Kline; editor, James Sweeney.

Peter Lorre (Steve Dane); Rochelle Hudson (Lorraine); Robert Wilcox (Mark Sheldon); Don Beddoe (Brand); George E. Stone (Siggy); Kenneth McDonald (Doctor); Charles Middleton (Cort); Stanley Brown (Eddie); Earl Gunn (Mitchell).

Sadistic prison pictures had been in vogue for some time when Columbia issued this pot boiler. As the critic for the New York Daily Mirror assessed, "Addicts will eat it up." The main emphasis here is on Peter Lorre's quirky performance as the prison's sinister warden, with the actor doing his best to be the most sadistic as possible.

An island prison camp is supervised by evil Stephen Dane (Peter Lorre) whose inhumane treatment of prisoners has made the place a living hell, although it is supposed to be a place for the rehabilitation of convicts. Living behind an electrified stockade with his unhappy wife (Rochelle Hudson) whom he mentally torments, the vile warden uses the men for slave labor, controlling them with whip-carrying guard Cort (Charles Middleton), gunman Brand (Don Beddoe), and a drunken doctor (Kenneth MacDonald). The government sends undercover agent Mark Sheldon (Robert Wilcox) to the isle in the guise of a prisoner, and he is able to bring about the end of the warden's corrupt reign and to romance Hudson.

ISLAND OF LOST MEN (Paramount, 1939) 63 mins.

Producer, Adolph Zukor; associate producer, Eugene Zukor; director, Kurt Neumann; based on the play Hangman's Whip by Norman Reilly Raine, Frank Butler; screenplay, William R. Lipman, Horace McCoy; art directors; Hans Dreier, Franz Bachelin; camera, Karl Sturss; editor, Ellsworth Hoagland.

Anna May Wong (Kim Ling); J. Carrol Naish (Gregory Prin); Eric Blore (Herbert); Ernest Truex (Frobenius); Anthony Quinn (Chang Tai); William Haade (Hambly); Broderick Crawford (Tex Ballister); Rudolf Forster (Professor Sen); Richard Loo (General Ahn Ling); Philip Ahn (Sam Ring); Torben Meyer (Cafe Manager); Lal Chand Mehra (Hindu); George Kirby (Waiter); Vivien Oakland (Blonde); Jack Perry (Blonde's Escort); Ruth Rickaby, Ethyl May Halls (Tourists); Bruce Mitchell (Ship's Officer).

It is hard to believe that a more preposterous story ever came from Paramount Pictures' scripters during the 1930s. This sad offering, which is laughable, is one of those potboilers which give "B" movies a tarnished name. Added to this, the script wastes its talented cast badly.

Gangster Gregory Prin (J. Carrol Naish) rules a small Asiatic island with an iron fist assisted by Tex Ballister (Broderick Crawford). The duo kidnap and rob a Chinese general (Richard Loo) and in Shanghai his daughter Ling (Anna May Wong) meets Naish and accompanies him to his island to find her dad. The man is nowhere to be found but both Naish and his follower (Anthony Quinn) fall in love with the woman and the latter plans to leave the isle with her. Naish and Crawford set a trap for them by giving them a boat with little petrol, but Naish's servant (Eric Blore), angry at his master for killing his pet chimp, provides the needed gasoline and the two escape to the island where the general has taken sanctuary. Meanwhile the natives on the island revolt. Crawford kills himself and Naish is left to the wrath of the natives.

IT'S YOUR MOVE (Kinesis/Minmer/Tecisa, 1968) C 89 mins.

Producer, Franco Porro; director, Robert Riz; screenplay, Riz, Massimilliano Capriccoli, Ennio De Concini, Jose G. Maesso, Leonardo Martin, Juan Cesarabea; music, Manuel Asins Arbo; set decorator, Rafael Ferri; camera, Antonio Macasoli; editor, Mario Morra.

Edward G. Robinson (MacDowell); Terry-Thomas (Jerome); Maria Grazi Buccella (Monique); and: Adolpfo Celi, Manuel Zarzo, Jorge Riguard, Jose Bodalo, Louis Bazzochchi, Rossella Como.

In the late 1960s, Edward G. Robinson journeyed to Italy where he performed in a quartet of gangster features, three of which LA BLONDE DE PEKIN [The Blonde from Peking] (see. D/V), AD OGNI COSTO, and OPERATION ST. PETER'S (qq.v.)--were issued in the United States in 1968 by Paramount. The fourth feature, UNO SCACCO TUTTO MATTO, was shown in England as MAD CHECKMATE but its only U.S. release came via TV as IT'S YOUR MOVE.

Retired Englishman MacDowell (Robinson), now living in Italy, plots a bank heist by bringing in gang members who look like bank workers. Thus he manages to pull off the robbery, but in the escape one of the robbers is mistaken for his lookalike by the man's wife and his cohorts think he is trying to run out with the loot and give chase. The money changes hands several times while the police accuse Robinson of having four people prisoner in the cellar of his villa. The four, however, are secretly returned to the bank and when the police arrive to corroborate that, the manager claims the people were at work. An investigation shows that the money is in the safe and that no robbery was committed. Robinson's cohorts then appear, claiming they were locked inside the bank's heating system while repairing it. All are released and at the fadeout the indomitable Robinson, undefeated by the experience, is planning still another robbery caper.

IZZY & MOE (CBS-TV, 9/23/85) C 100 mins.

Producer, Robert Halmi, Sr.; associate producer, Steven Felder; director, Jackie Cooper; teleplay, Robert Boris; music, Jackie Gleason; production designer, Tony Corbett; art director, Mike Moran; stunt coordinator, Victor Magnotta; second unit director, Skott Snider; camera, Peter Stein; editor, Eric Albertson.

Jackie Gleason (Izzy); Art Carney (Moe); Cynthia Harris (Dallas); Zohra Lampert (Esther); Dick Latessa (Murphy); Thelma Lee (Mrs. Perlman); Drew Snyder (McCoy); Jesse Doran (Dutch); Roy Brocksmith (Sheriff Bledsoe); Robyn Finn (Sarah); William Hickey (Hotel Desk Clerk); Peter Jason (Bartender); Andrea Lin (Ellen); Steve McNaughton (Doctor); Tracy Sallows (Paula); Mary Tanner (Lilly); Rick Washburn (Jake); Tom Wiggin (Harris).

"Together Again" is how CBS-TV promoted this telefeature which reunited Jackie Gleason and Art Carney of TV's "The Honeymooners" fame; it was the first time they had worked together professionally in eight years and the first time in three decades they had not portrayed Ralph Kramden and Ed Norton in tandem. Reviewing the results in TV Guide, Judith Crist determined, "It's lushly period, laid back and charming, with the charisma of the two stars irresistible."

At the start of the Prohibition era, third-rate vaudevillians Izzy (Gleason) and Moe (Carney) are down on their luck. Gleason

220 / JAIL BAIT

is out of work, and the new Federal Prohibition Act has closed
Carney's bar. Gleason answers an advertisement for agents to enforce the new "dry" law and due to the dearth of applicants, he is
hired and persuades a reluctant Carney to become his partner.
Their boss (Dick Latessa) and fellow agent McCoy (Drew Snyder)
are dubious that the two aging men can cope with the regime of
murderous gangster Dutch (Jesse Doran) who runs the booze racket.
However, Gleason and Carney utilize their stage background in a
variety of disguises and schemes which make them the most successful of Prohibition agents, able even to break up the private bar of
the city's district attorney. The more publicity they gain from
their successes, the more Doran vows revenge against them and
their boss.

The main appeal of this gangster comedy is its stars as well
as the fantasy look at the Roaring Twenties. The feature is low on
outright violence. Even the murder of Doran's rival is carried out
beyond camera range.

JAIL BAIT (Howco, 1954) 70 mins.

Producer-director, Edward D. Wood, Jr.; screenplay, Wood, Alex
Gordon; music, Hoyt Curtin; camera, Bill Thompson; editors,
Charles Clemont, Igor Kantor.

Lyle Talbot (Inspector Johns); Dolores Fuller (Marilyn Gregor);
Steve Reeves (Lieutenant Bob Lawrence); Herbert Rawlinson (Dr.
Boris Gregor); Theodora Thurman (Loretta); Clancey Malone (Don
Gregor); Timothy Farrell (Vic Brady); John Robert Martin (Detec-
tive McCall); Cotton Watts & Chick (Novelty Act); Bud Osborne
(Night Watchman); Mona McKinnon (Miss Willis); Don Nagel (De-
tective Davis); LaVada Simmons (Miss Lytell); Regina Claire (News-
paper Woman); John Avery (Police Doctor).

With the surge of interest in the film career of Edward D.
Wood, Jr., the man who produced such "classics" as PLAN 9 FROM
OUTER SPACE (1958) and the unissued NIGHT OF THE GHOULS
(1959), it is no wonder that perverse movie buffs searched out this
title, Wood's second directed feature. The movie has been around
for years, appearing on TV as THE HIDDEN FACE. Produced for
slightly over $20,000 and containing not one nubile nymphet (as
promised by its theatrical title), JAIL BAIT is a straight-out gangster film which "leaves much to be desired" (Variety).

A young man, Don Gregor (Clancey Malone), gets in trouble
with the law and teams with hardened criminal Vic Brady (Timothy
Farrell). During the robbery of a theater, he accidentally kills a
night watchman (Bud Osborne). Horrified at what he has done,
the young man goes to his father, a famous plastic surgeon (Herbert Rawlinson), to confess. Before the youth can reach the police, Farrell kills him. Later Farrell demands that Rawlinson alter
his face. The doctor complies, but having learned the truth of his

son's murder, he gives the culprit the face of his deceased boy. In a gun battle with the police, Farrell is killed.

For the record, Herbert Rawlinson died one day after filming was completed. The picture, shot in and around the Monterey Theatre in Monterey Park, California, takes its music soundtrack from MESA OF LOST WOMEN (1952) and its one production number (with Cotton Watts and Chick) is lifted from the 1951 Lippert feature, YES SIR, MR. BONES. Producer-director-scripter Wood made yet another gangster cheapie, THE SINISTER URGE (q.v.), in 1961.

JAILBREAK (Warner Bros., 1936) 60 mins.

Director, Nick Grinde; story, Jonathan Finn; screenplay, Robert Andrews, Joseph Hoffman; camera, Arthur Todd.

June Travis (Jane Rogers); Craig Reynolds (Ken Williams); Barton MacLane (Detective Captain Rourke); Richard [Dick] Purcell (Ed Slayden); Addison Richards (Dan Varner); George E. Stone (Weeper); Eddie Acuff (Sig Patton); Joseph King (Big Mike Eagan); Joseph Crehan (Warden); Mary Treen (Gladys Joy); Henry Hall (Pop Anderson); Charles Middleton (Dan Stone); Robert Emmett Keane (City Editor).

While in prison, Ed Slayden (Richard [Dick] Purcell) and Ed Varner (Addison Richards) develop a deep hatred for one another. The two escape during a prison break and after a multiple murder takes place on a Long Island estate, a police detective (Barton MacLane) learns the two are behind the revenge killings.

Perhaps the film's least realistic aspects are its make-believe presentation of life behind bars, while its sudden change in ambiance to murder mystery also confuses matters.

JE VOUS SALUE, MAFIA see: HAIL! MAFIA

JIMMY THE KID (New World, 1982) C 85 mins.

Producer, Ronald Jacobs; director, Gary Nelson; based on the novel by Donald E. Westlake; screenplay, Sam Bobrick; assistant director, Donald Roberts; music, John Cameron; camera, Dennis Dalzell; editor, Richard C. Meyer.

Gary Coleman (Jimmy); Paul LeMat (John); Dee Wallace (May); Don Adams (Harry); Walter Olkewicz (Andrew); Ruth Gordon (Bernice); Cleavon Little (Herb); Fay Hauser (Nina); Avery Schreiber (Dr. Stevens); Pat Morita (Maurice).

Just out of prison, two dimwitted criminals (Paul LeMatt, Walter Olkewicz) kidnap a rich child and hold him for ransom. The idea came to them from a cheap paperback story one of them read while in the clinker. Abetting them in the caper is the mother (Ruth Gordon) of one of the crooks and the scatterbrained moll (Dee Wallace) of the other. They select Jimmy Lovejoy (Gary Coleman) as their victim. He turns out to be the unhappy son of recording stars (Cleavon Little, Fay Hauser) who have a combination country-soul act. The duo kidnap the youth and demand the ransom. The parents hire a "crack" detective (Don Adams) to rescue their offspring.

Produced as a theatrical vehicle for televison comedy star Gary "Different Strokes" Coleman, this batty gangster yarn has its appeal to the younger trade, although most of the plot and dialogue are geared to adults. Unfortunately, Coleman's wise cracking youth is not strong enough to carry a feature and Don Adams' big screen rehash of his TV "Get Smart" role does little to enhance the proceedings. Avery Schreiber, it should be noted, is especially good in a brief assignment as the boy's shifty and conniving shrink.

JINX MONEY (Monogram, 1948) 68 mins.

Producer, Jan Grippo; director, William Beaudine; suggested by the story by Jerome T. Golard; screenplay, Edmond Seward, Tim Ryan, Gerald Schnitzer; art director, David Milton; set decorator, Raymond Boltz, Jr.; assistant director, Wesley Barry; music director, Edward J. Kay; costumes, Richard Bachler; sound, Tom Lambert; camera, Marcel Le Picard; editor, William Austin.

Leo Gorcey (Terence Aloysius "Slip" Mahoney); Huntz Hall (Horace Debussy "Sach" Jones); Billy Benedict (Whitey); David Gorcey (Chuck); Bennie Bartlett (Butch); Sheldon Leonard (Lippy Harris); Gabriel Dell (Gabe); Donald MacBride (Captain James Q. Broderik); Betty Caldwell (Candy McGill); John Eldredge (Lullaby Kane); Ben Weldon (Benny the Meatball); Lucien Littlefield (Tipper); Bernard Gorcey (Louie Dumbrowski); Benny Baker (Augie Pollack); Ralph Dunn (Jack "Cold Deck" Shapiro); Wanda McKay (Virginia); Tom Kennedy (Officer Rooney); William Ruhl (Sergeant Ryan); Stanley Andrews (Bank President); George Eldredge (Tax Man); William H. Vedder (Meek Man); Mike Pat Donovan (Bank President).

After winning $50,000 in cards from gangsters, a gambler is murdered and the hoodlums try to retrieve the money which is found in the gutter by Slip Mahoney (Leo Gorcey) and Sach Jones (Huntz Hall). A police captain (Donald MacBride) is on the case, but when the boys try to hide the money, a gunman demands the loot--but he too is killed. Meanwhile, beautiful Candy (Betty Caldwell) tricks Gorcey into meeting gangster Lippy Harris (Sheldon Leonard) who forces him to call Hall and order him to bring along the loot. Eventually the law catches up with the wrongdoers and all is saved.

"JINX MONEY scriptwriters obviously started with a fully

developed gangster story before the boys were written into it. This makes the film more subtle than its counterparts, and the boys don't carry the burden of the story. They are seen only in scenes for which adolescents are appropriate.... JINX MONEY has a split personality: it shows the boys engaging in teen-agers' activities, but it also has a plot too intricate for children to understand." (The Films of the Bowery Boys, by David Hayes and Brent Walker, 1985).

JOHNNY DANGEROUSLY (Twentieth Century-Fox, 1984) C 90 mins.

Executive producers, Bud Austin, Harry Colomby; producer, Michael Hertzberg; associate producer, Neil A. Machlis; director, Amy Heckerling; screenplay, Norman Steinberg, Bernie Kukoff, Colomby, Jeff Harris; production designer, Joseph R. Jennings; costumes, Patricia Norris; music, John Morris; assistant director, Bill Beasley; sound, Jerry Jost; camera, David M. Walsh; editor, Perm Herring.

Michael Keaton (Johnny Dangerously); Joe Piscopo (Vermin); Marilu Henner (Lil); Maureen Stapleton (Mom); Peter Boyle (Dundee); Griffin Dunne (Tommy); Richard Dimitri (Maroni); Glynnis O'Connor (Sally); Byron Thames (Young Johnny); Danny DeVito (Burr); Dom DeLuise (The Pope); Ray Walston (Vendor); Sudi Bond (Cleaning Lady).

In the 1930s, a young boy (Byron Thames) is forced into a life of crime to pay his mother's (Maureen Stapleton) hospital bills. As a result, he becomes mixed up in the big city rackets and grows up to become Johnny Dangerously (Michael Keaton), a crime boss. He is pals with a kindly mobster (Peter Boyle) and at odds with a rival (Joe Piscopo) and his honest district attorney brother (Griffin Dunne). Eventually Keaton's underworld activities lead him to prison.

Although the gangster milieu has often made good comedy grist in small doses, few films which have kidded the genre have been successful. For every funny satire like A SLIGHT CASE OF MURDER (see: B/V) there have been dozens of misfires like JOHNNY DANGEROUSLY. Full of foul language and crude jokes, the film quickly becomes tiresome due to Michael Keaton's too broad impersonation of James Cagney, and a variety of cameos (Dom De Luise, Ray Walston, Danny DeVito, Glynnis O'Connor) do little to salvage the sinking morass.

Issued as a Christmas comedy, the movie proved to be a bomb which Variety slammed as "this season's low-brow selection." The trade paper also noted the feature was directed by a woman (Amy Heckerling), one of the few gangster movies to date by a member of her sex. The paper went on to add, "Too much shouldn't be made of that now.... After all, it took four men to write it." As Kevin Thomas concluded in the Los Angeles Times, "JOHNNY DANGEROUSLY foolishly defies a truth that should be painfully self-

evident by now. If you insist on trying to send up the old gangster
movies still one more time ... you'd better be pretty funny. Occasionally, the scattershot humor actually hits the mark, mainly in a
flurry of amusing anachronisms--e.g., 'You tell me another gang
that's got a dental plan.' ... Sloppy as a period piece and unac-
countably grainy and bleached-out in appearance, JOHNNY DAN-
GEROUSLY is as hard on the eyes as it is on the ears."

JUVENILE COURT see: HELL'S HOUSE

JUVENILE COURT (Columbia, 1938) 60 mins.

Producer, Ralph Cohn; director, D. Ross Lederman; story-
screenplay, Michael L. Simmons, Robert E. Kent, Henry Taylor;
music director, Morris Stoloff; assistant director, Wilbur McCaugh;
sound, Lodge Cunningham; camera, Benjamin Kline; editor, Byron
Robinson.

Paul Kelly (Gary Franklin); Rita Hayworth (Marcia Adams); Frankie
Darro (Stubby Adams); Hally Chester (LeRoy); Don Latorre (Mickey);
David Gorcey (Pighead); Dick Ellis (Ears); Allan Ramsey (Davy);
Charles Hart (Squarehead); Howard Hickman (Governor Stanley);
Joseph DeStefani (Judge); John Tyrrell (Dutch Adams); Dick Curtis

Rita Hayworth, Eddie Brian, and Paul Kelly in JUVENILE COURT
(1938).

(Detective); Kane Richmond (Bradley); James Blaine, Lee Shumway,
Edmund Cobb, Tom London, George Chesebro, Eddie Hearn (Cops);
Edward LeSaint (Mr. Lambort); Leo Prather (Mr. Allen), Gloria
Blondell (Gary's Secretary); Stanley Andrews (Mayor); Harry
Bailey, Steve Clark, Stanley Mack, Dan Wolheim (Men); Cleo Ridg-
ley, Dorothy Vernon, Eva McKenzie (women); Bud Osborne (Driver);
Lester Dorr (Druggist); Vernon Dent (Schultz); George Billings
(Kid); Helen Dixon (Matron); Nick Copeland (Drunk); Reginald
Simpson, Sam Ash, Don Reed (Reporters).

Made as a tribute to the programs of the Police Athletic
League in fighting juvenile delinquency, JUVENILE COURT was
tattered going, ground out by producer Irving Briskin's low-budget
unit at Columbia. With Rita Hayworth as its leading lady, the programmer does hold interest and in its conception it is somewhat
similar to the 1932 feature HELL'S HOUSE (original title: JUVENILE
COURT).

Young Stubby Adams (Frankie Darro) becomes involved with
his peers in lawless activities and comes under the influence of
gangsters. This worries his pretty sister Marcia (Hayworth) and
she urges a public defender (Paul Kelly) to woo her brother away
from the street gang. Through the activities of the Police Athletic
League, this is accomplished. She and Kelly fall in love.

KANSAS CITY CONFIDENTIAL (United Artists, 1952) 98 mins.

Producer, Edward Small; director, Phil Karlson; story, Harold R.
Greene, Rowland Brown; screenplay, George Bruce, Harry Essex;
camera, George Diskant; editor, Buddy Small.

John Payne (Joe Rolfe); Coleen Gray (Helen Foster); Preston Fos-
ter (Timothy Foster); Lee Van Cleef (Tony Romans); Neville Brand
(Boyd Kane); Jack Elam (Pete Harris); Howard Negley (Andrews);
Marta Siletti (Tomaso); Dona Drake (Teresa); Helen Kleeb (Mrs.
Crane); Vivi Janis (Mrs. Rogers); Ted Ryan (Olson); George Wal-
lace (Moreill); Don Orlando (Dias).

Former Kansas City police captain Timothy Foster (Preston
Foster) devises an intricate bank robbery plan. Wearing a mask to
conceal his identity, he enlists the aid of three hoodlums (Lee Van
Cleef, Neville Brand, Jack Elam) who also wear masks and who are
unknown to one another. The heist is carried off successfully and
the police arrest former convict Joe Rolfe (John Payne) for the
crime. He clears himself and vows to find the real culprits. The
chase leads to Guatemala where he romances Foster's pretty daughter (Coleen Gray) and discovers her father has masterminded the
robbery and now is scheming to doublecross his confederates to
collect the insurance money. In a shootout, Foster dies and Payne
wins both the girl and the reward money.

Outside of its initial scenes, most of this melodrama does not
take place in Kansas City. "It's a fast-moving, suspenseful entry

for the action market," declared <u>Variety</u> and that reviewer noted the similarities between the film's plotline and the actual Brink's robbery in Boston and the exploits of gangster-"actor" Willie Sutton.
   Although overlong, KANSAS CITY CONFIDENTIAL is a hard-hitting underworld melodrama benefiting from several well-staged action sequences (i.e. the split second timing of the holdup and the final gun battle).

THE KANSAS CITY MASSACRE (ABC-TV, 9/19/75) C 100 mins.

Producer, Dan Curtis; associate producer, Robert Singer; director, Curtis; story, Bronson Howitzer; teleplay, Howitzer, William F. Nolan; music, Robert Cobert; art director, Trevor Williams; camera, Paul Lohmann; editors, Dennis Virkler, Richard A. Harris.

Dale Robertson (Melvin Purvis); Bo Hopkins (Charles Arthur "Pretty Boy" Floyd); Robert Walden (Adam Richetti); Mills Watson (Frank Nash); Scott Brady (Hubert Tucker McElway); Matt Clark (Verne Miller); John Karlen (Sam Cowley); Lyn Loring (Vi Morland); El-liott Street (Lester Gillis "Baby Face" Nelson); Harris Yulin (Johnny Lazia); Philip Bruns (Captain Jackson); Sally Kirkland (Wilma Floyd); William Jordan (John Dillinger); Morgan Paull (Alvin Karpis); James Storm (Larry Devol); Lester Maddox (Governor Garfield Burns).

   Following the capture of notorious criminal Machine Gun Kelly (as told in the telefilm MELVIN PURVIS G-MAN [see: B/V]), the Federal Bureau of Investigation orders Midwest Bureau Chief Melvin Purvis (Dale Robertson) to transport another gangster by train to Kansas City utilizing the services of state and local law enforcement officers. From there, the hoodlum is to be taken by car to Leaven-worth Prison but unknown to the G-Man, the transfer is a signal for rival gangsters to kidnap the prisoner. The scheme includes such wanted notorious mobsters as Pretty Boy Bloyd (Bo Hopkins), Baby Face Nelson (Elliott Street), Alvin Karpis (Morgan Paull), and crime king Johnny Lazia (Harris Yulin). The shootout between the police and the gangsters became known as the infamous Kansas City Massacre.
   This flavorful telefeature was Dale Robertson's second TV starrer as real-life G-Man Melvin Purvis and it successfully recre-ated the Depression era and its ambiance of lawlessness. The gun battle climax was especially well choreographed as was the sequence where lawmen surround the farm house where a bevy of gangsters are holding up, resulting in a gory shootout. The movie is also etched with a number of finely shaded characterizations, including Robertson as the cigar-smoking dandy Purvis, Bo Hopkins as the murderous Pretty Boy Floyd, and a well done cameo by former Georgia governor Lester Maddox as Oklahoma Governor Garfield Burns, who masterminds the assignment which leads to the show-down.
   A TV series was planned around the exploits of Melvin Purvis

with Dale Robertson to continue in the title role. Unfortunately the ratings weren't up to those of its predecessor and the project was dropped.

KILL (Cocinor, 1971) C 102 mins.

Producers, Alexander and Ilya Salkind; director-screenplay, Romain Gary; camera, Edmond Richard; editor, Robert Dwyre.

Jean Seberg (Emily); James Mason (Alan); Stephen Boyd (Killian); Curt Jurgens (Chief); Daniel Emilfork (Inspector); Henri Garcin (Lawyer).

　　Weary American Interpol agent Alan (James Mason) flies to Italy to study the activities of gangsters involved in the international smuggling of heroin. Longing for romantic adventure, his repressed wife (Jean Seberg) travels there also and meets Killian (Stephen Boyd), another disillusioned agent who believes the only way to eradicate hard core criminals is to execute them. Seberg falls in love with Boyd and the gangsters, who know the agents are after them, plant several corpses in her car. As a result, Mason abandons his plans to capture the mobsters legally and teams with Boyd and Seberg to kill the drug pushers.
　　This Spanish-Italian co-production was a very brutal outing. None of its participants, unfortunately, gave very convincing performances. The Hollywood Reporter thought it "visually harsh and endlessly brutal" while the International Herald Tribune labeled it "an exceptionally violent and lurid melodrama."
　　The film had limited United States release under the alternate title KILL! KILL! KILL!

KILL ME IF YOU CAN (Columbia/NBC-TV, 9/25/77) C 100 mins.

Producer, Peter Katz; director, Buzz Kulik; teleplay, John Gay; music, Bill Conti; art directors, Carl Brauner, Ross Bellah; camera, Gerald Perry Finnerman; editor, Les Green.

Alan Alda (Caryl W. Chessman); Talia Shire (Rosalie Asher); John Hillerman (George Davis); Barnard Hughes (Judge Fricke); Virginia Kiser (Virginia Gibbons); Edward Mallory (Warden Teets); Walter McGinn (J. Miller Leavy); Ben Piazza (Bill Edmunds); John Randolph (Judge Lewis Goodman); Herb Vigran (Hart--Jury Foreman); Maxine Stewart (Mrs. Asher); Rose Mortillo (Sara Loper).

　　Caryl Chessman, the famous "red light bandit," was the subject of the theatrical release CELL 2455, DEATH ROW (see: B/V) issued five years before his execution in San Quentin in 1960. While that feature, based on Chessman's own book, favored capital punishment, this TV movie took Chessman's story and utilized it as

Alan Alda in KILL ME IF YOU CAN (1977).

a springboard to oppose the death penalty. Since this movie's original telecast, more and more states have returned to the use of
capital punishment.

Captured in 1948 and tried and convicted of murder, Caryl
Chessman (Alan Alda) is shown waging a legal battle on death row
to keep from being executed. A highly intelligent man who uses
his high IQ to fight the system, Alda is aided by his attorney (Talia
Shire), and together they win eight stays of execution while Alda
writes books defending his case. However, in 1960 the final appeals
are fruitless and he is sent to the gas chamber.

Movies on TV (1985) called the TV film a "powerful and all
too rare polemic against capital punishment." Alan Alda received
an Emmy nomination for his in-depth performance.

THE KILLING OF A CHINESE BOOKIE (Faces Distribution Corp.,
   1976) C 135 mins.

Producer, Al Ruban; associate producer, Phil Burton; director-
screenplay, John Cassavetes; production designer, Sam Shaw; sound,
Bo Harwood; camera, Fred Elmes; editor, Tom Cornwell.

Ben Gazzara (Cosmo Vitelli); Timothy Agoglia Carey (Flo); Azizi
Johari (Rachel); Meade Roberts (Mr. Sophistication); Seymour Cas-
sel (Mort Weil); Alice Friedland (Sherry); Donna Gordon (Margo);
Robert Phillps (Phil); Morgan Woodward (John); Virginia Carring-
ton (Betty); John Red Kullers (Eddie); Al Rubana (Marty Reitz);
Soto Joe Hugh (Chinese Bookie).

Cosmo Vitelli (Ben Gazzara) is the owner of a run-down burlesque joint on Hollywood's Sunset Strip and he is into the mob for
a $23,000 gambling debt. In order to pay off the bill, the racke-
teers force him to murder a bookie, something Gazzara is opposed
to.

Director-actor John Cassavetes utilized this flimsy plot to
string out a 135-minute feature which might appeal to his followers,
but certainly not to anyone else. With an overdose of background
material on the strip club, its denizens, and the Hollywood underworld, and despite good performances by Gazzara and Woodward
(as the syndicate boss), the movie is still a snail's paced bore.

Vincent Canby (The New York Times) best summed up the
picture: "Watching this film is like listening to someone use a lot
of impressive words, the meaning of which are just wrong enough
to keep you in a state of confusion, but occasionally right enough
to hold your attention."

Four years after this fiasco, Cassavetes again invaded the
gangster movie turf, this time with GLORIA (q.v.), which was not
much of an improvement.

Elvis Presley, Walter Matthau, and Carolyn Jones in KING CREOLE
(1958).

KING CREOLE (Paramount, 1958) C 116 mins.

Producer, Hal B. Wallis; director, Michael Curtiz, based on the novel A Stone for Danny Fisher by Harold Robbins; screenplay, Michael V. Gazzo, Herbert Baker; music arranger, Walter Scharf; choreography, Charles O'Curran; camera, Russell Harlan; editor, Warren Low.

Elvis Presley (Danny Fisher); Carolyn Jones (Ronnie); Walter Matthau (Maxie Fields); Dolores Hart (Nellie); Dean Jagger (Mr. Fisher); Liliane Montevecchi (Nina); Vic Morrow (Shark); Paul Stewart (Charlie Le Grand); Jan Shepard (Mimi Fisher); Brain Hutton (Sal); Jack Grinnage (Dummy); Dick Winslow (Eddie Burton); Raymond Bailey (Mr. Evans).

Elvis Presley, the king of rock 'n roll, was given a two-month deferment from his celebrated Army induction to make this Paramount release. Following its completion, he went into the armed service and was stationed in West Germany. For the next two years no new Elvis movies or recordings were made, thus giving KING CREOLE added popularity with his fans, both as a movie and for its RCA Victor soundtrack. This production was his finest feature, and under veteran director Michael Curtiz the star provided his best cinema performance.

Taken from Harold Robbins' explosive novel, A Stone for Danny Fisher (1951), but diluted for the big screen, the movie details struggling New Orelans musician Danny Fisher (Presley) who starts out working as a busboy at a Bourbon Street nightclub. His singing talents come to the fore and he is headlining at the club and becomes a local sensation. He falls in love with pretty Nellie (Dolores Hart) but he is also romanced by sexy Bonnie (Carolyn Jones) who is the moll of gangster kingpin Maxie Fields (Walter Matthau). When a young punk (Vic Morrow) holds up the drugstore where Presley's father (Dean Jagger) works, it is Presley who gets the blame and it almost ruins his career. However, with the help of Hart he is able to prove his innocence.

Not only did KING CREOLE provide Elvis with his best motion picture, but it also gave him two of his most memorable songs: "Hard Headed Woman" and "Trouble."

KING OF CHINATOWN (Paramount, 1938) 54 mins.

Associate producer, Stuart Walker; director, Nick Grinde; story, Herbert Biberman; screenplay, Lillie Hayward, Irving Reis; music director, Boris Morros; art directors, Hans Dreier, Robert Odell; camera, Leo Tover; editor, Eda Warren.

Anna May Wong (Dr. Mary Ling); Akim Tamiroff (Frank Baturin); J. Carrol Naish (The Professor); Sidney Toler (Dr. Chang Ling); Philip Ahn (Robert "Bob" Li); Anthony Quinn (Mike Gordon);

Barnadene Hayes (Dolly Warren); Roscoe Karns (Rep Harrigan);
Ray Mayer (Potatoes); Richard Denning, Archie Twitchell (Interns);
Elward Marr (Bert); George Anderson (Detective); Charles H. Wood,
George Marrill (Gangsters); Charles Trowbridge (Dr. Jones); Lily
King (Chinese Woman); Wong Chong (Chinese Man); Chester Gan
(Mr. Foo); Pat West (Announcer); Guy Usher (Investigator).

This Stuart Walker production was one of a number of "B"
double-bills which Paramount churned out in the late 1930s and
early 1940s in the established gangster genre. Like its contempo-
raries, the film is a short-running, tightly constructed affair with
solid entertainment value and a superb cast. Variety noted the
movie "carries sufficient action and underworld intrigue to satisfy
as support ... and hit the fancy of the family trade." Akim Tamiroff is especially impressive as the philanthropic gangster, as is
J. Carrol Naish as his doublecrossing partner. This entry provides
the exotic Anna May Wong with one of her better sound film roles.
Frank Baturin (Tamiroff) operates all the illegal rackets in
Chinatown, especially gambling. He is also trying to strongarm the
local merchants into paying him protection money, but his aggres-
sive partner (Naish) takes over the organization by gunning him
down in front of Dr. Ling's (Sidney Toler) office. Toler's daughter (Wong), also a physician, witnesses the shooting and immediately operates on Tamiroff, saving his life. While he is convalescing,
Naish and the gangsters terrorize the area and the law moves in to
round them up. When Tamiroff is well enough to meet Naish in the
showdown, both are killed. Before he dies, Tamiroff insures that
Wong has sufficient funds for an ambulance unit in the area.

LADY KILLER (Warner Bros., 1933) 67 mins.

Director, Roy Del Ruth; based on the story "The Finger Man" by
Rosalind Keating Shaffer; adaptors, Ben Markson, Lillie Hayward;
screenplay, Markson; assistant director, Chuck Hansen; art direc-
tor, Robert Haas; costumes, Orry-Kelly; music director, Leo F.
Forbstein; makeup, Perc Westmore; camera, Tony Gaudio; editor,
George Amy.

James Cagney (Dan); Mae Clarke (Myra); Leslie Fenton (Duke);
Margaret Lindsay (Lois); Henry O'Neill (Ramick); Willard Robertson
(Conroy); Douglas Cosgrove (Jones); Raymond Hatton (Pete); Rus-
sell Hopton (Smiley); William Davidson (Williams); Marjorie Gateson
(Mrs. Marley); Robert Elliott (Brannigan); John Marston (Kendell);
Douglass Dumbrille (Spade); George Chandler (Thompson); George
Blackwood (The Escort); Jack Don Wong (Oriental); Frank Sheridan
(Los Angeles Police Chief); Edwin Maxwell (Jeffries the Theatre
Manager); Phil Tead (Usher Sargeant Seymour); Dewey Robinson
(The Movie Fan); H. C. Bradley (Man With Purse); Harry Holman
(J. B. Roland); Harry Beresford (Dr. Crane); Olaf Hytten (But-
ler); Harry Strang (Ambulance Attendant); Al Hill (Casino Cashier);

Dennis O'Keefe (Man in Casino); James Burke (Handout); Robert
Homans (Jailer); Sam McDaniel (Porter); Herman Bing (Western
Director); Spencer Charters (Los Angeles Cop); Luis Alberni (Di-
rector); Sam Ash (Hood); Ray Cooke (Property Man); Harold
Waldridge (Letter Handler).

Termed "An all-time high in roughneck character work, even
for this rough-and-tumble star" by Variety, this Warner Bros. release is a delicious tongue-in-cheek look at the gangster genre,
showcasing the studio's then top star, James Cagney. This fun
film reunited Cagney with Mae Clarke and Leslie Fenton, who had
previously supported him in the austere THE PUBLIC ENEMY (1931)
(see: B/V), the feature which brought him screen stardom. Here
Cagney has a field day as a pugnacious hoodlum turned movie lum-
inary and the movie even tries to top the grapefruit-in-the-face
scene with Mae Clark from their first teaming: the valiant actress
is dragged around the set by her hair and thrown down a hallway
by battling Cagney.

Fast-talking Dan Quigley (Cagney) is a movie theater usher
who loves films. To survive, however, he is forced into crime and
becomes a top mobster in the big city. When the police close in, he
hightails it westward to Hollywood and by accident gains a small
role as a movie Indian and is a hit. He develops into a top movie
star and is the toast of the town. Things begin to sour for him.
His old mob appears on the scene, complete with his moll (Clarke)
who interrupts his romance with Hollywoodite Lois Underwood (Margaret Lindsay). The gangsters suggest Cagney help them fleece
movie stars' homes, but he refuses and finds that Clarke also has
reformed. Once the gang is captured and Cagney is cleared of any
implication in their shenanigans, he and Clarke wed.

LAS VEGAS SHAKEDOWN (Allied Artists, 1955) 76 mins.

Producer, William F. Broidy; director, Sidney Salkow; screenplay,
Steve Fisher; music, Edward J. Kay; camera, John Martin; editor,
Chandler House.

Dennis O'Keefe (Joe Barnes); Coleen Gray (Julia Rae); Charles
Winninger (Mr. Raff); Thomas Gomez (Sirago); Dorothy Patrick
(Dorothy Reid); Mary Beth Hughes (Mabel); Elizabeth Patterson
(Mrs. Raff); James Millican (Wheeler Reid); Robert Armstrong
(Doc); Joseph Downing (Matty); Lewis Martin (Collins); Mara
McAfee (Angela); Charles Fredericks (Sheriff Woods); Regina Glea-
son (Maxine Miller); Murray Alper (House Manager); James Alexan-
der (Sam Costar); Frank Hantey (Martin); Allen Mathews (Rick).

Gangster Sirago (Thomas Gomez) wants to own Joe Barnes'
(Dennis O'Keefe) Las Vegas gambling casino and offers to purchase
it, but O'Keefe refuses. Thereafter the hoodlum plans to kill him,
using his two thugs (Robert Armstrong, Joseph Downing) to carry

Dennis O'Keefe and Coleen Gray in LAS VEGAS SHAKEDOWN (1955).

out the hit mission. Meanwhile O'Keefe has become enamored with Julie Rae (Coleen Gray), a school teacher who plans to write a book on the impossibilities of coming out ahead by gambling. The two fall in love and become engaged, but must dodge Gomez's hit men. Gomez himself goes mad and kills several people before he is eliminated.

Containing "some formula melodramatics of the GRAND HOTEL style" (Variety), the film uses its Las Vegas backdrops to good advantage. Even more interesting is its depiction of the denizens of the gambling capitol, including a compulsive gambler (Mary Beth Hughes), a married couple (James Millican, Dorothy Patrick) there for a divorce, and a banker (Charles Winninger) from a small town who has come to glitter city with his wife (Elizabeth Patterson) on their first gambling spree.

THE LAST CROOKED MILE (Republic, 1946) 67 mins.

Associate producer, Rudolph E. Abel; director, Philip Ford; based on the radio play by Robert L. Richards; screenplay, Jerry Sackhelm; art director, Frank Hotaling; set decorators, John McCarthy, Jr., George Milo; music director, Richard Cherurn; special effects, Howard Lydecker, Theodore Lydecker; camera, Alfred Keller; editor, William P. Thompson.

Donald Barry (Tom Dwyer); Ann Savage (Sheila Kennedy); Adele
Mara (Bonnie); Tom Powers (Floyd Sorelson); Sheldon Leonard (Ed
MacGuire); Nestor Paiva (Farrar); Harry Shannon (Lieutenant
Blake); Ben Welden (Haynes); John Miljan (Lieutenant Mayrin);
Charles D. Brown (Detrich); John Dehner (Jarvis); Anthony Caruso
(Charlie); George Chandler (Roller Coaster Attendant); Earle Hod-
gins (Carnival Pitch Man).

Gangster Jarvis (John Dehner) and three henchmen rob a
bank of a $300,000 payroll. One of the bandits is killed at the
scene and the rest die in a car crash while eluding the law. The
money, however, is not recovered and Floyd Sorelson (Tom Powers),
the representative for the insurance company for the bank, hires
private detective Tom Dwyre (Donald Barry) to investigate. Barry
heads to Ocean City where the getaway car is part of a carnival ex-
hibit owned by Farrar (Nestor Paiva) and there he meets an ex-
flame (Adele Mara). Together they discover the corpse of the murdered mechanic who serviced the getaway vehicle. The path leads
to another gangster associate (Sheldon Leonard) of Paiva, and the
suspects include Powers and Ann Savage, John Dehner's moll.

Although primarily a director of "B" Westerns and programmers, Philip Ford turned out this top-drawer feature early in his
career. The film fits into the then voguish film noir category with
its many night scenes, tawdry locales, and low-life characters. The
movie is influenced by the Philip Marlowe novels of Raymond Chandler, with this picture's gumshoe hero being a flippant ladies' man.

THE LAST WILL OF DR. MABUSE see: THE TESTAMENT OF DR.
MABUSE

THE LAUGHING POLICEMAN (Twentieth Century-Fox, 1973) C
111 mins.

Producer-director, Stuart Rosenberg; based on the novel by Per
Wahloo, Maj Sjowall; screenplay, Thomas Rickman; music, Charles
Fox; assistant director, Mike Moder; set decorator, Doug Von Koss;
sound, Theodore Soderberg, Jerry Jost; camera, David Walsh; editor, Robert Wyman.

Walter Matthau (Jake Martin); Bruce Dern (Leo Larsen); Lou Gos-
sett (Larrimore); Albert Paulsen (Camerero); Anthony Zerbe (Lieu-
tenant Styner); Anthony Costello (Dave Evans); Cathy Lee Crosby
(Kay Butler); Shirley Ballard (Martin's Wife); David Belrose, Dawn
Frame (Martin's Children); Louis Guss (Niles); Mario Gallo (Bobby
Mow); Paul Koslo (Dealer).

This tale of a San Francisco policeman pursuing hardened
criminals is based on a book from the Swedish writing team of Per
Wahloo and Maj Sjowall, with the locale switched from Stockholm to

the Bay City. What is captivating about this film is its middle-of-the-road stance between ultra-liberal views on individual rights and law-and-order followers, resulting in a picture which shows the plight of the law enforcer doing his duty and bringing criminals to justice while often fighting the system as much as the underworld.

While shadowing criminal Niles (Louis Guss) onto a downtown bus, policeman Dave Evans (Anthony Costello) becomes one of the victims when all the passengers are murdered by a rider with a shotgun. Assigned to the case is the dead man's partner, Jake Martin (Walter Matthau) and fellow cops Leo Larsen (Bruce Dern) and Larrimore (Lou Gossett), all under severe pressure from their harassed chief (Anthony Zerbe) to solve the murders. After a time Matthau abandons the rulebook and delves far enough to come up with supposedly honest businessman Camerero (Albert Paulsen), who was once accused of murdering his girlfriend. It proves he is the crux of this baffling case.

With lensing in San Francisco and its penetrating look into the daily life of policeman Matthau and the effects of his job on his domestic life, THE LAUGHING POLICEMAN is a satisfying police thriller which eschews the more typical aspects of the gangster genre in deference to the workaday routines of law enforcers. Unfortunately, in choosing this path, the filmmakers failed to win commercial approval at the box office.

LAW AND ORDER (Paramount Television/NBC-TV, 5/6/76) C 144 mins.

Producer, E. Jack Neumann; associate producer, Richard Rosetti; director, Marvin J. Chomsky; based on the novel by Dorothy Uhnak; teleplay, Neumann; art director, Robert E. Smith; music, Richard Hazard; camera, Jacques R. Marquette; editors, Donald R. Rode, Gerald J. Wilson.

Darren McGavin (Deputy Chief Brian O'Malley); Keir Dullea (Johnny Morrison); Robert Reed (Aaron Levine); James Olson (Inspector Ed Shea); Suzanne Pleshette (Karen Day); Teri Garr (Rita Wusinski); Biff McGuire (Lieutenant Lenihan); Jeanette Nolan (Margaret O'Malley); Scott Brady (Sergeant Brian O'Malley, Sr.); Will Geer (Pat Crowley); Art Hindle (Patrick O'Malley); Allan Arbus (Arthur Pollack); Whitney Blake (Mary-Ellen Corlwey); Tom Clancy (Hennessey); James Whitmore, Jr. (Pete Caputo); Lurene Tuttle (Mrs. Brian O'Malley, Sr.); James Flavin (Captain Toomey); Paul Jenkins (Lieutenant Kevin O'Malley); Robert Hegyes (Angelo); Beverly Hope Atkinson (Lola); Brad Dexter (Patrolman Tierney); Redmond Gleeson (Reverend Martin O'Malley); Jack Knight (Lieutenant Fitzgerald); Patrick O'Moore (Father Damian); Frank Ramirez (Rodriguez); Marian Collier (Sister Providencia); Fredd Wayune (Sergeant Haran); Paul Lichtman (Rabbi Schulman); and: Dan Priest, Harry Basch.

The lengthy telefeature, based on Dorothy Uhnak's novel,

Scott Brady and Darren McGavin in LAW AND ORDER (1976).

tells the story of three generations of New York City policemen against the backdrop of corruption in the modern day force.

Contemporary Manhattan cop Brian O'Malley (Darren McGavin), a deputy chief of public affairs, is having problems both on the job and at home. The latter involves his son, a patrolman (Art Hindle) who while on the job is caught in the midst of a controversy concerning charges of corrpution on the force. In flashbacks, McGavin recalls his own difficult relations with his police sergeant father (Scott Brady) and his own painful discoveries about misconduct by fellow officers while still a rookie. The combination of these memories and his son's idealistic persistence in wanting the truth known leads McGavin to making an intense investigation into the department which has been his whole life.

LAW OF THE UNDERWORLD (RKO, 1938) 58 mins.

Producer, Robert Sisk; director, Lew Landers; based on the play by John B. Hymer, Samuel Shipman; adaptors, Bert Granet, Edmund L. Hartmann; camera, Nicholas Musuraca; editor, Ted Chusman.

Chester Morris (Gene Fillmore); Anne Shirley (Annabelle); Eduardo Ciannelli (Rocky); Walter Abel (Rogers); Richard Bond (Tommy); Lee Patrick (Dorothy); Paul Guilfoyle (Batsy); Frank M. Thomas (Captain Gargan); Eddie Acuff (Bill); Jack Arnold (Eddie); Jack Carson (Johnny); Paul Stanton (Barton); George Shelley (Frank); Anthony Ward (Larry).

Businessman Gene Fillmore (Chester Morris) is the head of an underworld operation, and two young people in love (Anne Shirley, Richard Bond) become accidentally involved with the gang. Against Morris' orders, underling Rocky (Eduardo Ciannelli) kills a clerk in a jewelry store holdup. The cops are tipped off that the youngsters committed the crime and they are arrested. When he finds that Ciannelli used the two young people as decoys and they will go to prison because they have no alibis, Morris confesses all to the law.

"Everything runs to extreme simplicity and easy recognition, the narrative, the direction and the acting" (Variety).

This film is a remake of the 1930 feature, THE PAYOFF (q.v.), which starred Lowell Sherman as the gangster and Marion Nixon and William Janney as the lovers.

LEPKE (Warner Bros., 1975) C 109 mins.

Executive producer, Yoram Globus; producer-director, Menachem Golan; story, Wesley Lau; screenplay, Lau, Tamar Hoffs; production designer, Jack Degovia; assistant director, Fred Miller; sound, Bob Casey; camera, Andrew Davis; editors, Dov Hoenig, Aaron Stell.

Tony Curtis (Louis "Lepke" Buchalter); Anjanette Comer (Bernice Buchalter); Michael Callan (Robert Kane); Warren Berlinger (Gurrah Shapiro); Gianni Russo (Albert Anastasia); Vic Tayback (Lucky Luciano); Milton Berle (Mr. Meyer); and: Mary Wilcox, Jack Ackerman, Louis Guss, Vaughn Meader, Lillian Adams, Albert Cole, Zitto Kazann, Johnny Silver, J. S. Johnson.

With the resurgence of interest in the gangster picture caused by THE GODFATHER (1972) (see: B/V), a rash of underworld figures were paraded on screen in the 1970s, including some obscure individuals like Louis "Lepke" Buchalter, a Jewish mobster of the Depression era. The result was a gory, but run-of-the mill, melodrama which was "a stale rehash of stock gangster pic situations, without originality of theme or treatment" (Variety).
The movie chronicles the rise of Lepke (Tony Curtis) from his days as a punk hoodlum on the streets of New York to his rise as a major 1930s mobster, doing battle with the likes of fellow hoodlums Albert Anastasia (Gianni Russo) and Lucky Luciano (Vic Taybeck), as well as the law. Curtis keeps his family life separate from his lawless activities and finds support from his innocent wife (Anjanette Comer) and her father (Milton Berle). Eventually Curtis' long time pal (Michael Callan) and lawyer turns him over to the Justice Department.
Films In Review's Hugh James noted, "Menahem Golan's direction is pedestrian with some strange time lapses.... Tony Curtis gives a good performance as the New York-Jewish narrator."

LIMEHOUSE BLUES (Paramount, 1934) 66 mins.

Director, Alexander Hall; story, Arthur Phillips; screenplay, Phillips, Cyril Hume, Grover Jones; song, Sam Coslow; camera, Harry Fischbeck.

George Raft (Harry Young); Jean Parker (Toni); Anna May Wong (Tu Tuan); Kent Taylor (Eric Benton); Montagu Love (Pug Talbot); Billy Bevan (Herb); John Rogers (Smokey); Robert Lorraine (Inspector Sheridan); E. Alyn Warren (Ching Lee); Wyndham Standing (Assistant Commissioner Kenyong); Louis Vincenot (Rhama); Eily Malyon (Woman Who Finds Pug); Forrester Harvey (McDonald); Robert "Bob" A-Dair (Policeman in Pug's House); Elsie Prescott (Woman Employment Agent); James May (Taxi Driver); Colin Kenny (Davis); Eric Blore (Man Slummer); Colin Tapley (Man Fighting with Wife); Rita Carlyle (His Wife); Desmond Roberts (Constable); Tempe Pigott (Maggie); Otto Yamaoka (Chinese Waiter on Boat); Dora Mayfield (Flower Woman); Ann Sheridan (Girl with Couples).

Half-caste Chinese Harry Young (George Raft) abandons New York for London where he rises quickly in the gangster world and becomes the owner of a waterfront cafe as well as the kingpin in the smuggling racket. All goes well until he meets Toni (Jean

Parker), a Cockney down on her luck and drawn to prostitution. Raft loves her, much to the dismay of his mistress (Anna May Wong). Actually, Parker loves Eric (Kent Taylor), the proprietor of a small pet store in the Limehouse district. When the area's main fence (Montagu Love) betrays him, Raft has him murdered and he also plans to eliminate Taylor so he can have Parker. However, Wong goes to the police and tells them about Raft's mobster activities and then commits suicide. Trapped by the law, Raft stops the intended murder of Taylor before being killed by Scotland Yard men.

A romantic potboiler relying on its exotic ethnics to create audience interest, this film is a very unrealistic gangster exercise. Although he contributed fine performances in several major films, Raft was out of his element in this film, the part being more suitable to a less dashing figure like Charles Laughton.

For its television showings, the film was retitled EAST END CHANT.

THE LINEUP (Columbia, 1958) 85 mins.

Producer, Jaime Del Valle; director, Don Siegel; based on the teleseries created by Lawrence L. Klee; screenplay, Stirling Silliphant; music, Mischa Bakleinikoff; camera, Hal Mohr; editor, Al Clark.

Eli Wallach (Dancer); Robert Keith (Julian); Warner Anderson (Lieutenant Guthrie); Richard Jaeckel (Sandy McLain); Mary La Roche (Dorothy Bradshaw); William Leslie (Larry Warner); Emile Meyer (Inspector Al Quine); Marshall Reed (Inspector Fred Asher); Raymond Bailey (Philip Dressler); Vaughn Taylor (The Man); Cheryl Callaway (Cindy); Bert Holland (Porter); George Eldredge (Dr. Turkel); Robert Bailey (Staples).

This taut melodrama is based on the highly successful police drama series "The Lineup," which ran on CBS-TV from 1954 to 1960 and starred Warner Anderson, Tom Tully, and Marshall Reed. Only Anderson and Reed repeated their roles in the theatrical version, as co-star Tom Tully felt his part would be too minor. For the picturization, Anderson was provided a new sidekick named Al Quine, well played by Emile Meyer. This feature was helmed by Don Siegel, who also directed the teleseries pilot.

Two San Francisco detectives (Anderson, Meyer) investigate the murder of a cab driver involved with a drug smuggling operation. They also discover a railroad porter murdered, the man having previously put a bag in the hack of the murdered cabbie. At the same time, two syndicate hit men (Eli Wallach, Robert Keith) arrive in the city, sent to recover the narcotics smuggled in from Hong Kong. With a hoodlum (Richard Jaeckel) as their driver, the two killers track the packages and eliminate all those holding the narcotics. After several murders, the detectives connect the various killings as the hit men find the last two holders (Mary LaRoche,

Cheryl Callaway). They take the woman and her daughter hostage
and at an amusement part meet The Man (Vaughan Taylor), the
boss of the operation, whom Wallach kills. With the police after
them, the hit men are cornered on an elevated freeway, with Wallach shooting his partner and then falling to his death.

Discussing this production in Don Siegel, Director (1974),
Stuart Kaminsky writes, "... THE LINEUP is surely one of Don
Siegel's best films ... Sterling Silliphant's screenplay may well be
better than IN THE HEAT OF THE NIGHT, for which he won an
Academy Award, and the film may well be better than some of
Siegel's more admired works [including several Clint Eastwood
features]."

LITTLE CIGARS (American International, 1973) C 92 mins.

Producer, Albert Band; director, Chris Christenberry; screenplay,
Louis Garfinkle, Frank Ray Perilli; music, Harry Betts; assistant
director, Foster H. Phinney; art director, Alfeo Bocchicchio; camera, John M. Stephens; editor, Ed Newman.

Angel Tompkins (Cleo); Billy Curtis (Slick Bender); Jerry Maren
(Cadillac); Frank Delfino (Monty); Felix Silla (Frankie); Emory
Souza (Hugo); Joe De Santis (Travers).

On the lam from her sadistic gangster boyfriend (Joe De Santis) and his two murderous hitmen, dizzy blonde moll Cleo (Angel
Tompkins) stumbles onto a quintet of midgets (Billy Curtis, Jerry
Maren, Frank Delfino, Felix Silla, Emory Souza) who present a
medicine show while two of them simulatenously fleece their audience's cars. Slick Bender (Curtis) is the gang leader and Tompkins joins them to bring in the male trade. Finally she convinces
the men to carry out a series of robberies as they head across the
country, and she and Curtis become lovers. After a big heist,
Tompkins persuades Curtis to dump his friends and make a getaway with the loot. The remaining four gang members trail the
cheats to San Francisco and plot their revenge.

The novelty of midgets as gangsters does not wear thin as
does the use of the "wee people" in the spy spoof UNDER THE
RAINBOW (1981). The movie is to be commended for the fact that
"... the five midgets cast for probably the first time on screen
play themselves as the little people and not in the offbeat character parts they usually are called upon to portray" (Variety). Angel
Tompkins as the looker and Billy Curtis as the crafty gang leader
are particularly effective.

LITTLE MISS MARKER (Universal, 1980) C 112 mins.

Executive producer, Walter Matthau; producer, Jennings Lang;
director, Walter Bernstein; based on the story by Damon Runyon;

Screenplay, Bernstein; production designer, Edward C. Carfagno; music, Henry Mancini; assistant directors, Ronald J. Martinez, Judith Vogelsang; camera, Philip Lathrop; editor, Eve Newman.

Walter Matthau (Sorrowful Jones); Julie Andrews (Amanda); Tony Curtis (Blackie); Bob Newhart (Regret); Lee Grant (The Judge); Sara Stimson (The Kid); Brian Dennehy (Herbie); Kenneth McMillan (Brannigan); Andrew Rubin (Carter); Joshua Shelley (Benny); Randy Herman, Jessica Rains, John P. Finnegan (Clerks); Nedra Volz (Mrs. Clancy); Jacquelyn Hyde (Lola); Tom Pedi (Vittorio); Jessica Rains (Clerk); Henry Slate (Teller); Alvin Hammer (Morris); Dom Bexley (Sam); Jack DeLeon (Manager); and: Ralph Manza, Jack Mullaney, Mark Anger, Colin Gilbert, Ed Ness, William Ackridge, Charles A. Venegas, Robert E. Ball, Jorge B. Cruz.

Between -10- (1979), in which she wore a see-through blouse, and S.O.B. (1981), in which she bared her breasts in shedding her MARY POPPINS (1964) image, Julie Andrews appeared in this fourth rendition of the fairytale Damon Runyon story. Having been filmed previously in 1934 (see: B/V) with Shirley Temple and Adolphe Menjou, followed by mediocre versions with Bob Hope in SORROWFUL JONES (1949) (see: B/V) and 40 POUNDS OF TROUBLE (1962) with Tony Curtis, the property aged considerably and one wonders just why it was remade yet again. Janet Maslin (The New York Times) pondered, "If LITTLE MISS MARKER were a lot more witty and a bit less overdecorated, it might recall the good-time-Charlie spirit of THE STING."

Like its predecessors, the tale revolves around a little girl (Sara Stimson) being left with gambling house owner Sorrowful Jones (Walter Matthau) to cover a gambling debt with the little tyke eventually softening the hard guy's heart. She also ingratiates herself with lovely widow Amanda (Andrews), who ends up in a romance with Matthau, at odds with gangster Blackie (Curtis) over both Andrews and the rackets.

Matthau contributes another of his slobby but good-hearted roles, while Andrews is the clothes-conscious heroine, Curtis the black-hearted villain, Brian Dennehy his thug associate, and Bob Newhart as Matthau's loyal associate. Little Sara Stimson steals the show as "The Kid."

As in most Damon Runyon stories, everything is geared to be cute and charming rather than real and vivid.

THE LITTLE RED SCHOOLHOUSE (Chesterfield, 1936) 59 mins.

Producer, George R. Batcheller; director, Charles Lamont; story-screenplay, Paul Perez; camera, M. A. Anderson.

Frank Coghlan, Jr. (Frank Burke); Dickie Moore (Dickie Burke); Ann Doran (Mary Burke); Lloyd Hughes (Roger Owen); Corky (Himself); Richard Carle (The Professor); Ralf Harolde (Pete

Scardoni); Frank Sheridan (Warden Gail); Matthew Betz (Bill);
Kenneth Howell (Schuyler Tree); Sidney Miller (Sidney Levy);
Gloria Browne (Shirley); Don Brodie (Ed); Lou Davis (Mac).

Disillusioned and unhappy with his life, a young orphan
(Junior Coghlan) leaves behind his pal (Dickie Moore) and runs
away with dog Corky. He arrives in the big city but cannot adjust
to life there and soom comes under the control of gangsters who
frame him for a criminal act he did not commit. He is sentenced
to the boys' penitentiary but his ex-school teacher (Lloyd Hughes),
who loves the boy's sister (Ann Doran), comes to his rescue by
finding the evidence to exonerate him of the crime. Coghlan goes
back to school, once again content with his simplistic life.

This delightful poverty row quickie was first issued by
Chesterfield Pictures, but when that company failed, its distribution was picked up by the newly formed Grand National Pictures.
Frank Coghlan, Jr. (billed here as Junior Coghlan) does admirably
as the boy who abandons his studies only to get mixed up with
mobsters. Veteran stage star Richard Carle is the elderly, shifty
city slicker gang leader.

LOAN SHARK (Lippert, 1952) 79 mins.

Producer, Bernard Luber; director, Seymour Friedman; story, Martin Rackin; screenplay, Rackin, Eugene Ling; camera, Joseph Biroc;
editor, A. Joseph.

George Raft (Joe Gargen); Dorothy Hart (Ann Nelson); Paul Stewart
(Donnelli); John Hoyt (Phillips); Henry Slate (Paul Nelson); William
Phipps (Ed Haines); Russell Jackson (Thompson); Benny Baker
(Tubby); Larry Dobkin (Walter Karr); Charles Meredith (Pennick);
Harlan Warde (Lieutenant White); Spring Mitchell (Nancy); Margie
Dean (Ivy); Ross Elliott (Norm); Robert Bice (Steve Casmer);
Robert Williams (Scully); Michael Ragan (Maxie); Virginia Caroll
(Netta); Helen Westcott (Martha Haines); William "Bill" Phillips
(Baski); George Eldredge (George); William Tannen (Rourke); Jack
Daley (Borrower).

LOAN SHARK is George Raft's most satisfying starring vehicle of the 1950s. Not only is it well constructed--a taut expose
of the loan shark rackets--the movie also provides the star with an
interesting characterization that he handles well. Although he is
too old for the role, Raft's strong, silent, tough image suits the
part. Moreover, he and striking Dorothy Hart have the proper romantic chemistry while Paul Stewart and John Hoyt project slick
villainy and Benny Baker etches an amusing character study of
Raft's lazy buddy.

Released from prison, Joe Gargen (Raft) lives with his
widowed sister (Helen Westcott) whose husband had been murdered by loan shark racketeers. In reality, Raft is helping the

police smash the loan shark racket and through Westcott's pretty friend (Hart), a secretary at the Acme Tire Company, Raft wins a job at the plant where the loan sharkers are active. At the plant, he is befriended by easygoing worker Tubby (Baker), who introduces him to the loan shark operators and Raft obtains a loan from them. Working for the scam, Raft quickly rises to the top as a collector, impressing boss Donelli (Stewart). Eventually he meets the refined Phillips (Hoyt), who is supposed to be the operation's head man, but Raft realizes there's a still bigger boss. After the loan sharkers discover he is an undercover agent he forces a shootout with the big boss (Larry Dobkin) in a deserted theatre, with Hoyt and the boss being killed and the loan shark racket destroyed.

LONE WOLF McQUADE (Orion, 1983) C 107 mins.

Producers, Yoram Ben-Ami, Steve Carver; director, Carver; story, H. Kaye Dyal, B. J. Nelson; screenplay, Nelson; music, Francesco DeMasi; camera, Rober Shearman; editor, Anthony Redman.

Chuck Norris (J. J. McQuade); David Carradine (Rawley Wilkes); Barbara Carrera (Lola); Leon Issac Kennedy (Jackson); Robert Beltran (Kayo); L. Q. Jones (Dakota); Dana Kimmell (Sally); R. G. Armstrong (Tyler); Jorge Cervera, Jr. (Jefe); Sharon Farrell (Molly); Daniel Frishman (Falcon); William Sanderson (Snow); John Anderson (Burnside).

Weapons belonging to the United States Army are being hijacked, and they eventually end up in the hands of Central American terrorist groups. Texas Ranger J. J. McQuade (Chuck Norris) is assigned to ferret out the individuals behind the thefts and he and his partner (Robert Beltran) hunt the thieves. They learn that the gang is led by Rawley Wilkes (David Carradine), who is allied with the Mexican mafia. With the help of FBI Agent Jackson (Leon Isaac Kennedy), Norris and Beltran locate Carradine's secluded airport where the hijacked shipments are flown south. They attack the well guarded sanctuary and after a showdown between Norris and Carradine, the gang is routed.

Basically a modern-day Western with gangster trappings, LONE WOLF McQUADE is an actionful Chuck Norris vehicle in which he receives excellent box-office support from David Carradine of TV's "Kung Fu" fame and Leon Isaac Kennedy who starred in the two PENITENTIARY features and the remake of BODY AND SOUL (qq.v.). As to be expected from a Norris-Carradine feature, there is a good deal of martial arts. However, the main reliance for excitement is an almost endless array of weaponry, including tanks, machine guns, bazookas, and hand grenades. Guns are a-blazin' from start to finish and the body count mounts as the picture progresses to its airstrip shoot-out finale.

"Director Steve Carver lifts motifs from all sorts of earlier pics and doesn't manage to maintain the [Sergio] Leone-esque

intensity of the opening scene, but achieves the bottom line of getting lots of rough stuff up there on the screen" (Variety).
Produced on a modest $5,000,000 budget, the feature to date
has grossed over $50,000,000 worldwide.

THE LONG GOOD FRIDAY (Black Lion Films, 1980) C 105 mins.

Producer, Barry Hanson; director, John Mackenzie; screenplay,
Barrie Keeffe; music, Francis Monkman; art director, Vic Symonds;
assistant director, Simon Hunkly; sound, David John; camera, Phil
Meheux; editor, Mike Taylor.

Bob Hoskins (Harold); Helen Mirren (Victoria); Dave King (Parky);
Brian Hall (Alan); Eddie Constantine (Charlie); Stephen Davies
(Tony); Derek Thompson (Jeff); Bryan Marshall (Harris); P. H.
Moriarty (Razors); Paul Freeman (Colin); Charles Cork (Eric);
Paul Barber (Erroll); Patrti Love (Carol).

At his country estate for a long holiday weekend, London
mobster boss (Bob Koskins) negotiates with a backer (Eddie Constantine) to set up a large building project for the 1988 London
Olympics. Things go awry, however, when multiple explosions
occur and several of his henchmen are murdered. The mobster
learns that the Irish Republic Army is behind the incidents since
government money (targeted to insure that the largely Irish construction work force does not strike) is stolen and the gangster is
blamed. Hoskins rallies his minions to do battle with the IRA, but
he ends up the loser.
   A "classy item" (Variety), this low-keyed very British production is surprisingly anti-government and also anti-IRA, the latter
depicted to have a well oiled assassination machine. One of the few
gangster movies to be overtly political, the feature is a well-acted
melodrama with a taut plotline.

LOVE AND BULLETS (ITC Film Distributors, 1979) C 95 mins.

Presenter, Sir Lew Grade; producer, Pancho Kohner; director,
Stuart Rosenberg; screenplay, Wendell Mayes, John Melson; music,
Lalo Schifrin; production designer, John De Cuir; costumes, Dorothy
Jeakins; assistant director, Jack Aldworth; sound, Gene Garvin,
John Bramall; camera, Fred Koenekamp, Anthony Richmond; editor,
Michael Anderson.

Charles Bronson (Charlie Congers); Rod Steiger (Joe Bomposa);
Jill Ireland (Jackie Pruit); Strother Martin (Louis Monk); Bradford
Dillman (Brickman); Henry Silva (Vittorio Farroni); Paul Koslo
(Huntz); Sam Chew (Cook); Michael Gazzo (Lobo); Val Avery
(Caruso); Bill Gray (Mike Durant); Andy Romano (FBI Agent
Marty); Robin Clarke (FBI Agent George); Cliff Pellow (Police
Captain); Lorraine Chase (Vittorio's Girlfriend).

Following the car bomb murder of police informant Mike Durant (Bill Gray), Arizona police are anxious to gain information on alleged Mafia don Joe Bomposa (Rod Steiger). They send undercover policeman Charles Congers (Charles Bronson) to Switzerland to get Jackie Pruit (Jill Ireland), the don's mistress, hoping she will provide them with information on the gangster. Complications arise when Italian kidnappers abduct the woman and Bronson must rescue her. In Switzerland he wisks Ireland away from the gang and the two fall in love, although they are always running from the kidnappers. Eventually Bronson dispatches the gang, but Ireland is killed in the process. Before she dies, she gives the cop needed information to convict Steiger.

Although Charles Bronson fans were enthusiastic about the production, the more objective Monthly Film Bulletin branded it a "slackly organized sequence of chases and betrayals."

LOVE MADNESS see: REEFER MADNESS

LOVE THAT BRUTE (Twentieth Century-Fox, 1950) 85 mins.

Producer, Fred Kohlmar; director, Alexander Hall; screenplay, Karl Tunberg, Darrell Ware, John Le Mahin; music, Cyril Mockridge; music director, Lionel Newman; art directors, Lyle Wheeler, Richard Irvine; set decorators, Thomas Little; Stuart Reiss; assistant director, Arthur Jacobson; makeup, Ben Nye; costumes, Rene Hubert; choreography, Billy Daniels; sound, Arthur Kirback, Harry M. Leonard; camera, Lloyd Ahern; editor, Nick De Maggio.

Paul Douglas (Big Ed Hanley); Jean Peters (Ruth Manning); Cesar Romero (Pretty Willie); Keenan Wynn (Bugs); Joan Davis (Mamie); Arthur Treacher (Quentin); Peter Price (Harry); Jay C. Flippen (Biff); Harry Kelley (Burly Detective); Leon Belasco (Durray); Edwin Max (Puggy); Sid Tomack (Louie); Phil Tully (Detective Lieutenant); Clara Blandick (Landlady); Jimmie Hawkins (Freddie Van Zandt); Judith Ann Vroom (Gwendolyn).

LOVE THAT BRUTE is a pleasant comedy which kids the gangster film genre. "A farce with plenty of sparkle and speed" (Variety). The movie, a remake of the studio's TALL, DARK AND HANDSOME (1941) which starred Cesar Romero and Virginia Gilmore, is a splendid vehicle for Paul Douglas and it provides Jean Peters with one of her better screen parts. In addition, there's Cesar Romero, Joan Davis, and Keenan Wynn in top-notch supporting roles. The feature's only drawback is its lack of proper detail in recreating the Roaring Twenties era.

Douglas headlines as burly, tough Chicago gangster Big Ed Hanley who loves country girl Ruth Manning (Peters) and offers her a job as governess in his home. He doesn't mention that he does not have a family. Douglas pretends to be a widower with

Jean Peters in LOVE THAT BRUTE (1950).

two children and enlists a younger member (Peter Price) of his
gang to be his son. While carrying out a duel of wits with gangster rival Pretty Willie (Romero), Douglas' charade is found out by
Peters who thinks he is a murderer. Through a mistake by his
associate (Wynn) all the rival hoodlums Douglas is supposed to have
killed (but who are actually kept imprisoned in his basement) escape
and the wild chase is on. Eventually, Douglas and Peters bid good-
bye to the underworld milieu and head for a life of happiness in a
small town.

MAD CHECKMATE see: IT'S YOUR MOVE

MAFIA PRINCESS (Group W/NBC-TV, 1/19/86) C 100 mins.

Executive producer, Jack Farren; producer, Lew Gallo; director,
Robert Collins; based on the book by Antoinette Giancana; teleplay,
Robert W. Lenski; music, Lee Holdridge; art director, Claude Bon-
niere; assistant director, Don Buchsbaum; camera, Alexander
Gruszynski; editor, John Marc Vasseur.

Susan Lucci (Antoinette Giancana); Tony Curtis (Salvatore "Sam"
Giancana); Kathleen Widdoes (Angelina Giancana); David McIlwraith
(Dr. Raymond Spiros); Louie di Bianco (Jimmy Lucca); Tony DeSan-
tis (Joey Leone); Chuck Shamata (Fat Louie); Jonathan Welsh (Dr.
Towers); Ken Pogue (Committee Member); Dennis Strong (Richard
Smith); Antoinette Giancana (Communion Guest); and: Bill Lake,
John MacKenzie, Ann-Marie MacDonald, Jacquie Presly, Richard
Comar, Bruce Pirrie, Allan Aarons, Marilyn Smith, Tom MacCarone,
Virginia Reh, Marvin Goldhar, Shawn Lawrence, Chas Lawther, Dan
Hennessey.

   Opening in Chicago in the early 1950s, this telefeature, via
flashbacks, delves into the complicated love-hate relationship between Mafia kingpin Salvatore "Sam" Giancana (Tony Curtis) and
his daughter (Susan Lucci). Relayed in quick jumping segments,
the production lacks the necessary cohesion and for the most part
is lacking in sufficient character development. Many important aspects of the film (i.e. Mafia activities, inter-Family relationships,
involvement of the Mafia in politics) remain nebulous. Actually
there is ample storyline for a good mini-series, but chopped to a
100-minute telefilm, the result is unrewarding. The film's prime
assets are its three lead players, with Susan Lucci and Kathleen
Widdoes excelling in their daughter and mother roles and Tony Curtis outstanding in his etching of one of the most powerful underworld figures of this century.
   The narrative opens with Lucci asking her father to give up
the Mafia and Curtis replying, "The only way you quit is feet
first." He then recalls how he was sent to prison thirty years
before for bootlegging but still continued to run his underworld

Advertisement for MAFIA PRINCESS (1986).

empire from behind bars. When he gets out he muscles in on the
city's black numbers racket. Although devoted to his wife (Widdoes) and small daughter, Curtis is too involved in the Mafia and
his rise to power to be a good family man and his child is sent to
a convent for rearing. As an adult she gets into Hollywood films
through her father's influence and changes her name to Toni Jordan. She loses her Navy man fiancee and finds out about her dad's
mistress. Her mother dies and Curtis rejects Lucci. After attempting suicide, she is sent to an institution where she is given shock
treatments. A year later she falls in love with a physician (David
McIlwraith) and becomes pregnant but has an abortion and Curtis
has the man badly beaten. To spite her father, the girl marries a
divorced bartender (Tony De Santis) but the marriage founders due
to her drinking and sexual escapades. When her father is jailed
for refusing to testify before a grand jury, Lucci has a breakdown.
After therapy, she tells her father she is getting divorced and he
rejects her. Ten years later she tries to smooth over their differ-
ences but he is assassinated. At his funeral, Lucci realizes that
Curtis really loved her and wanted to protect her by keeping her
out of his tumultuous life.

    While the production received much press, it was a diversion
quickly forgotten. As Daily Variety opined, "The soaps go Italian,
... but the wine's been watered.... [It] trails unconvincingly
after its self-serving fictional heroine with all the snap of over-
cooked pasta."

MAGNUM FORCE (Warner Bros., 1973) C 122 mins.

Producer, Robert Daley; director, Ted Post; based on a story by
John Milius and original material by Harry Julian Fink, R. M. Fink;
screenplay, Milius, Michael Cimino; music, Lalo Schifrin; art direc-
tor, Jack Collis; set decorator, John Lampbear; assistant director,
Wes McAfee; second unit director, Buddy Van Horn; sound, James
Alexander; camera, Frank Stanley; editor, Ferris Webster.

Clint Eastwood (Detective Harry Callahan); Hal Holbrook (Lieutenant
Briggs); Felton Perry (Early Smith); Mitchell Ryan (Charlie McCoy);
David Soul (Davis); Tim Matheson (Sweet); Robert Urich (Grimes);
Kip Niven (Astrachan); Christine White (Carol McCoy); Adele
Yoshioka (Sunny).

    Clint Eastwood returned in his popular role of vigilante cop
Dirty Harry Callahan in MAGNUM FORCE, issued two years after
his sensational DIRTY HARRY (see: B/V) release. While this sequel (nor its own two follow ups to date) is as good as the original,
it did better at the box office, with a gross of $20.1 million com-
pared to $17.9 million for the initial outing.

    A series of murders are gripping San Francisco, the targets
being syndicate leaders. Investigating the case with his partner
Early Smith (Felton Perry), detective Callahan (Eastwood) believes

Clint Eastwood in MAGNUM FORCE (1973).

that four young rookies (David Soul, Tim Matheson, Kip Niven, Robert Urich) are taking the law into their own hands to rid the community of crime leaders set free by an overly liberal judicial system. When an older member (Mitchell Ryan) of the force is killed, Eastwood suspects his old foe and boss Lieutenant Briggs (Hal Holbrook) is behind the vigilante force. When it is learned that Eastwood is on their trail, the rogue cops mark him for elimination, but Eastwood corners them in an old aircraft carrier docked in a junkyard and there he eliminates the avengers. His partner is killed in the shootout.

Variety reported, "The interesting twist in MAGNUM FORCE is that Eastwood stumbles on a group of bandit cop avengers, all of whom have that advertising agency and Hitler Youth look characteristic of most witnesses before the Ervin Watergate committee. The plot thus forces Eastwood to render judgment in favor of the present system." Gene Siskel (Chicago Tribune) offered, "Those familiar with DIRTY HARRY will recognize the story premise of MAGNUM FORCE as the liberal flip side of the earlier reactionary film.... The problem with MAGNUM FORCE is that this new side of Harry-- his antivigilantism--is never made believable in the context of his continuing tendency to brandish his .45 Magnum revolver as if it were his phallus. The new, 'Clean Harry' doesn't quite cut it."

Since this entry grossed over $20,000,000, at least two more "Dirty Harry" films were sure to follow: THE ENFORCER (1977) and SUDDEN IMPACT (1983) (qq.v.).

A year after its release, the TV film DEATH SQUAD (q.v.) appeared, its plotline closely paralleling MAGNUM FORCE's execution squad plot gimmick.

THE MAN WHO DIED TWICE (Republic, 1958) 70 mins.

Producer, Rudy Ralston; director, Joe Kane; screenplay, Richard C. Sarafian; art director, Ralph Oberg; set decorator, John McCarthy, Jr.; songs, Jerry Gladstone and Al DeLory; assistant director, Leonard Kunody; makeup, Bob Mark; sound, Edwin B. Levinson; camera, Jack Marta; editor, Fred Knudtson.

Rod Cameron (Bill Brennon); Vera Ralston (Lynn Brennon); Mike Mazurki (Rak); Gerald Milton (Hart); Richard Karlan (Santoni); Louis Jean Heydt (Hampton); Don Megowan (T. J. Brennon); John Maxwell (Chief Hampton); Bob Anderson (Sergeant Williams); Paul Picerni (George); Don Haggerty (Frank); Luana Anders (Young Girl Addict); Jesslyn Fax (Sally Hemphill).

Republic Pictures was at the end of its trail when this gangster melodrama was produced. The final film of Vera Ralston, the wife of studio chief Herbert J. Yates, the movie was produced by Vera's brother Rudy. Only an average crime picture, the movie is slow but its story has redeeming qualities--several nice plot twists and winning performances by Rod Cameron as the man searching for his brother's killer and Mike Mazurki as a homicidal gang member. When the film was released theatrically, it was co-featured with MGM's ANDY HARDY COMES HOME, while on TV--mainly due to its title--it was categorized as a horror entry.
Businessman T. J. Brennon (Don Megowan) is murdered in a car explosion and not long after his widow (Ralston), a nightclub singer, suffers a nervous breakdown after seeing two undercover agents murdered. Her brother-in-law (Cameron) arrives, intent on finding out who murdered his sibling. He discovers that his brother was involved in a narcotics racket and that the two dead cops were investigating the operation. When an attempt is made on Ralston's life, Cameron understands that the culprit is his brother, who is not dead at all and who wants his wife out of the way because she witnessed the killings he instigated. In a shootout, Megowan is shot down on a rooftop, leaving Ralston and Cameron to find happiness together.

THE MAN WHO WOULD NOT DIE (Centaur Releasing, 1975) C 83 mins.

Executive producer, Rick Lede; producers, Lawrence M. Dick, Robert Arkless; director, Arkless; based on the novel The Sailcloth Shroud by Charles Williams; screenplay, George Chesbro, Stephen Taylor, Arkless; music, Art Harris; song, Harris and Cahn; camera, Lowell McFarland; editor, Arline Garson.

Dorothy Malone (Paula Stafford); Keenan Wynn (Victor Slidell);
Aldo Ray (Frank Keefer); Alex Sheafer (Skipper Mark Rogers);
Joyce Ingalls (Patricia Regan); Fred Scollay (Lieutenant Willotts);
James Monks (Reagan); Jesse Osuna (Agent Shearer); Dennis
McMullen (Harry); Hal Lasky (Reporter); Kathy Triffon (Jackie);
Valerie Shorr (Girlfriend); Rick Lede (Detective Ramirez); Barry
Simco (C. P. P. Murthy); John Peters (Yardman); and: James
Cook.

The skipper (Alex Shaefer) of a Caribbean boat and his first
mate (Aldo Ray) pick up a mysterious passenger who took the
identity of a rich man, and after the boat sets sails he dies of a
heart attack. Later the skipper realizes the dead man was not who
he claimed to be and suddenly finds that he is the target of the
local police, the FBI, and mobsters. Eventually he learns the deceased had stolen bonds from Las Vegas gangsters and the mob
leader (Keenan Wynn) tries to retrieve them, killing the mate before dying himself.
Filmed in the Caribbean, this outing received scant theatrical
release although it is an absorbing melodrama with its visuals superior to its plot. Despite top billing, poorly photographed Dorothy
Malone has only a small role as a woman who knew the dead man.

THE MAN WITH BOGART'S FACE (Twentieth Century-Fox, 1980) C
106 mins.

Executive producer, Melvin Simon; producer, Andrew J. Fenady;
director; Robert Day; based on the novel by Fenady; screenplay,
Fenady; music, George Dunning; production designer, Richard
McKenzie; costumes, Oscar Rodriguez, Jack Splangler, Voulee
Giokaris; assistant director, David McGiffert; sound, James J.
Klinger; camera, Richard C. Glouner; editor, Eddie Saeta.

Robert Sacchi (Sam Marlow); Franco Nero (Hakim); Michelle Phillips
(Gena); Olivia Hussey (Elsa); Misty Rowe (Duchess); Victor Buono
(Commodore Anastas); Herbert Lom (Mr. Zebra); Dick Bakalyan
(Lieutenant Bumbera); Sybil Danning (Cynthia); Gregg Palmer
(Sergeant Hacksaw); Jay Robinson (Wolf Zinderneuf); George Raft
(Petey Cane); Yvonne De Carlo (Teresa Anastas); Mike Mazurki
(Himself); Henry Wilcoxon (Mr. Chevalier); Victor Sen Yung (Mr.
Wing); Joe Theismann (Jock); Alshia Brevard (Mother); Buck
Kartalian (Nicky).

Film farces aren't always successful, especially those which
are offshoots of gangster-detective film classics, such as THE BLACK
BIRD (1975) (q.v.). THE MAN WITH BOGART'S FACE, however,
is a delightful exception to that rule: it is a picture which both
retains the flavor and zest of the film noir detective thrillers of the
1940s yet lightly kids the genre so as not to take itself too seriously. The main gimmick here is the use of Humphrey Bogart's dra-

matic lookalike Robert Sacchi in the role of sleuth Sam Marlow, and the result is a movie that is a lot of fun.

After undergoing plastic surgery to look like Humphrey Bogart, Sam Marlow (Sacchi) sets up a detective agency with dumb blonde Duchess (Misty Rowe) as his secretary. He is hired by Elsa Borsht (Olivia Hussey) to investigate the murder of her father, a German refugee somehow involved in the disappearance of matching blue sapphires supposedly used for the eyes of a bust of Alexander the Great. He finds that others are also after the precious gems: Greek shipper Anastas (Victor Buono), Turkish rogue Hakim (Franco Nero), gangster Mr. Zebra (Herbert Lom), and Nazi war criminal Zinderneuf (Jay Robinson). Sacchi soon finds himself at odds with the local police detective (Richard Bakalyan) but allied with beautiful Gena (Michelle Phillips) in finding the gems and the murderer, who also kills Hussey before Sacchi finally solves the caper aboard Buono's yacht.

Full of inside jokes and delightful cameos (George Raft, Yvonne De Carlo, Mike Mazurki, Henry Wilcoxon), the movie is an amusing farce which shamefully died in its theatrical release.

The feature received some distribution as SAM MARLOW, PRIVATE EYE.

MANDALAY (Warner Bros., 1934) 65 mins.

Director, Michael Curtiz; story, Paul Hervery Fox; adaptors, Austin Parker, Charles Kenyon; costumes, Orry-Kelly; art director, Anton Grot; song, Irving Kahal and Sammy Fain; camera, Tony Gaudio; editor, Thomas Pratt.

Kay Francis (Tanya); Lyle Talbot (Dr. Gregory Burton); Ricardo Cortez (Tony Evans); Warner Oland (Nick); Lucien Littlefield (Mr. Peters); Ruth Donnelly (Mrs. Peters); Reginald Owen (Police Captain); Raphaela Ottiano (Countess); Etienne Girardot (Mr. Abernathie); Halliwell Hobbs (Colonel Dawson Ames); Herman Bing (Mr. Kleinschmidt); Henry C. Bradley (Mr. Warren); Torbin Meyer (Van Brinker); David Torrance (Captain); Bodil Rosing (Mrs. Kleinschmidt); Shirley Temple (Betty); James B. Leong (Ram Singh); Lillian Harmer (Louisa); Otto Frisco (Fakir); George Huerrera (Steward); Desmond Roberts (Sergeant).

In the Far East exotic Tanya (Kay Francis), a young woman with an extremely soiled past, is the mistress of racketeer and gun runner Tony Evans (Ricardo Cortez) who supposedly commits suicide in order to avoid the law. Cast adrift romantically when she believes her lover is dead, Francis is asked by Nick (Warner Oland) to perform in his club as well as be his mistress. Instead, she romances a drunken doctor (Lyle Talbot) and attempts to rehabilitate him. Cortez, however, reappears and seeks to persuade Francis to help him open a cafe as a front for his ongoing illegal activities, but she instead departs with her physician beau.

Lyle Talbot and Kay Francis in MANDALAY (1934).

Set in Rangoon, this posh melodrama exploited the sultry
dramatics of Kay Francis, in vogue with Depression-weary audiences.
Besides the chic Miss Francis, the film offers good work by Lyle Talbot (one of her frequent co-stars) as the doctor, Ricardo Cortez as
the gangster, and Warner Oland as the shady cafe proprietor, plus
a brief glimpse of little Shirley Temple as a ship passenger. This
atmospheric production reflected director Michael Curtiz's great
ability to make a modest tale seem far more entertaining and lavish.

MANHANDLED (Paramount, 1949) 98 mins.

Producers, William H. Pine, William C. Thomas; director, Lewis R.
Foster; based on the novel The Man Who Stole a Dream by L. S.
Goldsmith; screenplay, Foster, Whitman Chambers; assistant direc-
tor, Howard Pine; costumes, Edith Head, Odette Myrtel; art direc-
tor, Lewis H. Creber; set decorator, Alfred Keggeris; music, Darryl
Claker; music director, David Chudnow; sound, William Fox; camera,
Ernest Laszlo; editor, Howard Smith.

Dorothy Lamour (Merl Kramer); Sterling Hayden (Joe Cooper); Dan Duryea (Karl Benson); Irene Hervey (Mrs. Alton Bennet); Philip Reed (Guy Bayard); Harold Vermilyea (Dr. Redman); Alan Napier (Mr. Alton Bennett); Art Smith (Detective Lieutenant Dawson); Irving Bacon (Sergeant Fayle); Philip Reed (Guy Bayard); Benny Baker (Mr. Boyd); Keye Luke (Chinese Laundryman).

Gangster Karl Benson (Dan Duryea) romances lonely Merl Kramer (Dorothy Lamour) while using her as a patsy for his various crooked schemes, including robbery and blackmail. Insurance investigator Joe Cooper (Sterling Hayden) is tracing jewels stolen by Duryea and he encounters Lamour who has been accused of killing a woman (Irene Hervey) whom Duryea was blackmailing. Lamour, however, has no alibi and she and Hayden must locate a man (Benny Baker) whom she saw in the hotel lobby the night the woman was murdered, since the man can identify Duryea as having been at the scene. When Lamour is cleared she and Hayden face life together.

This low-budget Pine-Thomas was a good drama with a few comedy touches lightening the proceedings. Its offbeat casting of ex-sarong star Dorothy Lamour in a serious drama was not appreciated by moviegoers.

MANHATTAN NIGHT OF MURDER (Allianz-Film/Constantin-Film, 1966) 87 mins.

Director, Harald Phillip; screenplay, Alex Berg; music, Peter Thomas; camera, Walter Tuch.

George Nader (Jerry Cotton); Richard Munch (Phil); and: Heinz Weiss, Monika Grimm.

New York City business people are being terrorized by an extortion gang which agrees to protect them against criminal activities but at a high price. Those who refuse the deal are quickly dispatched. The Federal Bureau of Investigation sends its ace G-man Jerry Cotton (George Nader) to investigate the happenings and he succeeds in placing his sidekick Phil (Richard Munch) in the gang, but he cannot stop them until he finds the true identity of the mobster controlling the extortion game.

Never released theatrically in the United States, this West German production (released in its homeland as MORDNACHT IN MANHATTAN) appears in a dubbed version on U.S. television. It is one of a popular film series which American star George Nader made as agent Jerry Cotton in Europe during the 1960s. Most of these entries are naive but fast paced gangster yarns held together by Nader's likable performance.

Isabel Jewell, Lyle Clement, Warren Hull, and Wolf the dog in
MARKED MEN (1940).

MARKED MEN (Producers Releasing Corp., 1940) 63 mins.

Producer, Sigmund Neufeld; director, Sherman Scott; story, Harold
Greene; screenplay, George Bricker; camera, Jack Greenhalgh;
editor, Holbrook N. Todd.

Warren Hull (Bill Carver); Isabel Jewell (Linda Harkness); John
Dilson (Dr. Harkness); Paul Bryar (Joe Mallon); Charles Williams
(Charlie Sloane); Lyle Clement (Marshall Tait); Budd L. Buster
(Marvin); Al St. John (Gimpy); Eddie Featherstone (Marty); Ted
Erwin (Mike); Art Miles (Blimp); Wolf the Dog (Gray Shadow).

  Sent to prison for a crime he didn't commit, Bill Carver (Warren Hull) is pulled into a prison break by gangster Joe Mallon (Paul
Bryar) and while the escape is successful, a man is killed in the
attempt. Hull finds refuge in a small town where he romances the
local doctor's (John Dilson) daugher (Isabel Jewell). All the time
he realizes he will always be a hunted man until he proves his innocence. He therefore locates the five convicts who escaped with
him, and using the ruse of escaping from a sheriff and his posse,
takes the wanted men into the desert and forces a confession from
Bryar.
  Variety judged this PRC economy entry, "passably exciting,

melodramatic story herewith is bungled by quickie production methods, inept acting and poor direction." Actually, Warren Hull handles the lead rather well, especially in the Arizona desert finale,
and veteran comedian Al St. John appears as one of the lesser
gangsters, while the hero received some aid from Gray Shadow, a
wolf dog.

MEAN STREETS (Warner Bros., 1973) C 110 mins.

Executive producer, E. Lee Perry; producer, Jonathan T. Taplin;
director, Martin Scorsese; screenplay, Scorsese, Mardik Martin;
assistant director, Russell Vreeland; camera, Kent Wakeford; editor, Sid Levin.

Robert DeNiro (Johnny Boy); Harvey Keitel (Charlie); David
Proval (Tony); Amy Robinson (Teresa); Richard Romanus (Michael);
Cesare Danova (Giovanni); Victor Argo (Mario); George Memmoli
(Joey); Martin Scorsese (Man in Car).

Following his initial foray into the gangster film genre with
BOXCAR BERTHA (see: B/V) in 1972, director Martin Scorsese
received critical acclaim for MEAN STREETS, an "often brilliant,
generally unsatisfying little Italy meller" (Variety) which he shot
mostly in New York City in four weeks on a $500,000 budget. In
addition to bringing Scorsese into the cinema limelight, this feature
also made a star of Robert DeNiro, who was seen to advantage in
THE GODFATHER II (see: B/V) at the same time.
    MEAN STREETS revolves around the lives of three second-
generation Italian-American buddies, all slightly rebellious and ado-
lescent-oriented, despite being in their mid-twenties. Johnny Boy
(DeNiro), Charlie (Harvey Keitel), and Tony (David Proval) stay
close to the streets of their bleak Italian ghetto, chasing broads
and making a living involving such scams as loan sharking and the
numbers rackets. Proval works also as a bartender, while Keitel,
who is romancing DeNiro's cousin (Amy Robinson), is about to take
over a restaurant owned by his Mafia-member uncle (Cesare Danova).
DeNiro later gets into debt with slick but murderous loan shark
Michael (Richard Romanus) and almost loses his life before paying
off his debts.
    The film's main focus is on its triad of leading men, and in
this regard, Variety opined, "... most viewers will remain very
much outside the drama, spectators to a veristic documentary that
is seldom moving despite a great deal of hysteria and violence."
    In analyzing this feature, Leslie Taubman wrote in Magill's
Survey of Cinema (1981), "The film is violent, but it is also an
intimate drama. There are many scenes using the natural, low-
level lighting which is characteristic of the bars and poolhalls
where the film was shot. The realism of the scenes shot with a
handheld camera seem to bring the story into the same perspective
as the characterizations.... The characterizations are ... given
in a matter-of-fact, gradual unfolding."

Robert DeNiro in MEAN STREETS (1973).

MEET DANNY WILSON (Universal, 1952) 86 mins.

Producer, Leonard Goldstein; director, Joseph Pevney; story-screenplay, Don McGuire; musical director, Joseph Gershenson; camera, Maury Gertsman; editor, Virgil Vogel.

Frank Sinatra (Danny Wilson); Shelley Winters (Joy Carroll); Alex Nichol (Mike Ryan); Raymond Burr (Nick Driscoll); Tommy Farrell (Tommy Wells); Vaughan Taylor (T. W. Hatcher).

Barroom singers Danny Wilson (Frank Sinatra) and Mike Ryan (Alex Nicol) are having a tough time making a living until they are spotted by entertainer Joy Carroll (Shelley Winters) who gets them a job in a club run by mobster Nick Driscoll (Raymond Burr). The latter takes a liking to Sinatra and offers to promote his career for half the profits, and the young man agrees. Meanwhile, both Sinatra and Nicol chase Winters, but she is attracted to Nicol. Sinatra's career blossoms and he quickly rises to the top and even makes a movie before having a falling out with Nicol over Winters. Burr then appears on the Hollywood scene demanding his percentage of Sinatra's earnings. In a shootout, Burr wounds Nicol. Sinatra hunts the mobster and finds him back in Chicago--at Wrigley Field he shoots the gangster.

This tale parallels the career of crooner Frank Sinatra from his rise from the streets to stardom and to his alleged gangster associations. The movie is paced efficiently and Sinatra performs a number of standard tunes (including: "How Deep Is the Ocean," "That Old Black Magic"). Although he is basically portraying himself, his interpretation of Danny Wilson is professionally done. Raymond Burr provides another of his standard but effective overbearing gangster portraits.

MEN OF AMERICA (RKO, 1933) 55 mins.

Associate producer, Pandro S. Berman; director, Ralph Ince; story, Humphrey Pearson, Henry McCarty; adaptor, Samuel Ornitz, Jack Jungmeyer; camera, J. Roy Hunt; editor, Edward Schroeder.

Bill Boyd (Jim Parker); Charles "Chic" Sales (Smokey Joe); Dorothy Wilson (Annabelle); Ralph Ince (Cicero); Henry Armetta (Tony Garboni); Inez Palange (Mrs. Garboni); Theresa Conover (Postmistress); Alphonse Ethier (Oley Jensen); Ling (Chinese Joe).

This RKO programmer is an ingratiating minor offering, thanks to the performance of Charles "Chic" Sales as old-time Indian fighter Smokey Joe, a store owner in a tiny Western town invaded by gangsters. The scenes in the early portion of the story which focus on the area's veteran citizens--those men of several nationalities who tamed and settled the area--are charming and present a vivid picture of bygone America.

In the small Western town of Paradise Valley, life is leisurely, mostly centered around Jalco' general store where the oldsters congregate and spin tales. When Jim Parker (Bill Boyd) moves there, the old men are suspicious of him, especially when a crime wave hits the community. Actually it is led by on-the-lam gangster Cicero (Ralph Ince) and his gang of rowdies. After a local farmer (Henry Armetta) is killed by the hoodlums, the seniors team with Boyd to combat the city foe and the gangsters surrender after a lengthy gun battle.

MEN OF SAN QUENTIN (Producers Releasing Corp., 1942) 77 mins

Producers-directors, Martin Mooney, Max M. Kiong; story, Mooney; screenplay, Ernest Booth; camera, Clark Ramsey; editor, Dan Miller.

J. Anthony Hughes (Jack Holden); Eleanor Stewart (Anne Holden); Dick Curtis (Butch Mason); Charles Middleton (Sanderson); Jeffrey Sayre (Jimmy); George Breakstone (Louis); Art Mills (Big Al); Michael Mark (Convict in Ravine); John Ince (Board Chairman); Joe Whitehead (Joe Williams); Skins Miller (Himself); Jack Shay (Phone Guard); Jack Cheatham (Court Gate Guard); Dave Demarest (Guard Gaines); Nancy Evans (Mrs. Doakes).

Wickedly sadistic deputy prison warden Sanderson (Charles Middleton) is at odds with progressive new guard Jack Holden (J. Anthony Hughes) who demands reforms. When a prison break and murder occurs, Middleton thrusts the blame on Hughes but the former is killed during a riot and Hughes is promoted to warden. With the support of his wife (Eleanor Stewart), he institutes reforms, but his program almost backfires when another riot takes place. He quells it and proves his humanitarian theories correct.
The only bonus item of this poorly directed feature is its authentic look--it was lensed entirely in an actual prison and the film's music was provided by the prison's band. Charles Middleton is especially strong as the evil deputy warden and good support comes from Western badman Dick Curtis as a rebellious convict.

MEN WITHOUT NAMES (Paramount, 1935) 67 mins.

Producer, Albert Lewis; director, Ralph Murphy; story, Dale Van Every; screenplay, Marguerite Roberts, Kubec Glasmon; camera, Ben Reynolds; editor, Stuart Heisler.

Fred MacMurray (Richard Hood); Madge Evans (Helen Sherwood); Lynne Overman (Gabby Lambert); David Holt (David Sherwood); John Wray (Sam "Red" Hammond); J. C. Nugent (Major Newcomb); Leslie Fenton (Monk); Herbert Rawlinson (Crawford); Dean Jagger (Jones); Grant Mitchell (Andrew Webster); Clyde Dilson (Butch);

Arthur Aylesworth (Drew); Helen Shipman (Becky); Harry Tyler (Steve).

Following his success as an amiable leading man to Claudette Colbert in THE GILDED LILY (1935), Paramount put Fred MacMurray into starring roles in two police melodramas. In CAR 99 (1935) he was a Michigan State Police officer trailing a bank robbery gang. Next came MEN WITHOUT NAMES, which found him as an undercover G-man chasing hoodlums. The entry was strongly directed by Ralph Murphy, and the new star had very fine support from Lynne Overman as his partner and by Madge Evans as the love interest. Regarding this compact programmer, Don Miller wrote in B Movies (1973), "... it came at the beginning of the G-Man cycle in vogue, and its brief running time ... compared favorably, minute for minute, with more elaborate, and noisier, crime-doesn't-pay treatises."

G-man Richard Hood (MacMurray) assumes the identity of gangster Dick Grant and reaches a small Kansas community where mobsters have established their headquarters and are terrorizing the area. He infiltrates the gang and is aided by his agency cohort Gabby Lambert (Overman) and a news reporter Helen Sherwood (Evans) with whom he falls in love. In cornering the gangsters, Overman is killed.

MIAMI EXPOSE (Columbia, 1956) 73 mins.

Producer, Sam Katzman; director, Fred F. Sears; story-screenplay, James B. Gordon; music, Mischa Bakaleinkioff; camera, Benjamin H. Kline; editor, Al Clark.

Lee J. Cobb (Bart Scott); Patricia Medina (Ella Hodges); Edward Arnold (Oliver Tubbs); Michael Granger (Louis Ascot); Eleanore Tanin (Anne Easton); Alan Napier (Raymond Sheridan); Barry Lauter (Tim Grogan); Chris Alcaide (Morrie Pell); Hugh Sanders (Chief Charlie Landon); Barry L. Connors (Stevie).

Mobster Raymond Sheridan (Alan Napier) gets the help of corrupt lobbyist Oliver Tubbs (Edward Arnold) in making gambling legal in Florida so he can control all gaming interests. He is opposed by rival crook Louis Ascot (Michael Granger), who fears losing his hold on the now illegal operations. When a policeman is murdered after investigating a killing instigated by the rival mobs, lawman Bart Scott (Lee J. Cobb) attempts to get the goods on both rivals by using testimony from moll Lila Hodges (Patricia Medina), who wants to escape her past. Cobb hides her in an Everglades retreat until she can testify, in the meantime coping with killers out to eliminate her.

MIAMI EXPOSE was the final film of veteran actor Edward Arnold--an old hand at the gangster genre--who died during the film's production.

THE MIDNIGHT CLUB (Paramount, 1933) 65 mins.

Directors, Alexander Hall, George Somnes, based on the novel by
E. Phillips Oppenheim; screenplay, Seton I. Miller, Leslie Charteris;
camera, Theodor Sparkuhl; editor, Eda Warren.

Clive Brook (Colin Grant); George Raft (Nick Mason); Helen Vinson
(Iris Whitney); Alison Skipworth (Lady Barrett-Smythe); Sir Guy
Standing (Commissioner Hope); Alan Mowbray (Arthur Bradley);
Ferdinand Gotschalk (George Rubens); Ethel Griffies (The Duchess);
Forrester Harvey (Thomas Roberts); Billy Bevan, Charles McNaugh-
ton (Detectives); Paul Perry (Grant's Double); Celeste Ford (Iris'
Double); Pat Somerset (Bradley's Double); Rita Carlyle (Nick's
Landlady); Jean de Briac (Headwaiter); Leo White (Waiter).

American policeman Nick Mason (George Raft) is ordered to
London to assist a Scotland Yard commissioner (Sir Guy Standing)
in bringing in a gang of jewel thieves. He finds that nobleman
Colin Grant (Clive Brook) is the head of the operation, aided by
Iris Whitney (Helen Vinson), his lady love, and by Lady Barrett-
Smythe (Alison Skipworth). Once enmeshed in the caper, Raft becomes attracted to Vinson and doesn't want to surrender her to the
law. At the climax, Brook ignores his airtight alibi and turns himself in on condition that Vinson goes free.

THE MIDNIGHT CLUB is a pleasant mixture of British gangster-
ism, mystery, and humor which "... is a lively and entertaining
comedy of the sort of London underworld that exists in the novels
of E. Phillips Oppenheim" (New York Herald-Tribune). In fact, the
film was derived from one of Oppenheim's novels and was co-adapted
to the screen by Leslie Charteris, soon to become famous for his detective character Simon Templar, "The Saint." Although Clive Brook
is topbilled as the crime chief, it is policeman George Raft who domi-
nates this feature, especially with his brand of stateside gangster
slang and his humorous encounters with gang member Vinson and
her Cockney use of the King's English.

THE MIDNIGHT MAN (Universal, 1974) C 117 mins.

Producers-directors, Roland Kibbee, Burt Lancaster; based on the
novel The Midnight Lady and the Morning Man by David Anthony;
screenplay, Kibbee, Lancaster; music, Dave Grusin; song, Grusin
and Morgan Ames; production designer, James D. Vance; set decorator, Joe Stone; assistant directors, Brad Aronson, Warren Smith;
sound, Melvin M. Metcalfe; camera, Jack Priestley; editor, Frank
Morriss.

Burt Lancaster (Jim Slade); Susan Clark (Linda); Cameron Mitchell
(Quartz); Morgan Woodward (Clayborne); Harris Yulin (Sheriff
Casey); Joan Lorring (Quartz's Wife); Richard Winterstein (Deputy

Burt Lancaster in THE MIDNIGHT MAN (1974).

Sheriff); William Splawn (Bar Owner); Catherine Bach (Natalie Clay-
borne); Ed Lauter, Mills Watson, Bill Hicks (Robbery Gang); William
Lancaster (Natalie's Boyfriend); Robert Quarry (Psychologist);
Charles Tyner (Janitor); Lawrence Dobkin (Professor Mason);
Quinn Redeker (Clayborne's Aide); Peter Dane (Artist); Eleanor
Ross (Robbers' Friend).

One-time policeman Jim Slade (Burt Lancaster) has spent
several years in prison for the murder of his wife's lover and upon
release he comes to a small South Carolina college town to rebuild
his life. Through the aid of a policeman friend (Cameron Mitchell)
and his wife (Joan Lorring), Lancaster gets a job on campus security. He is also helped in his readjustment by parole officer Linda
(Susan Clark). When Mitchell tries to stop the robbery of a cafe
by a masked gang, he is badly injured. Not long after, a co-ed
(Catherine Bach) is found murdered and her boyfriend (William
Lancaster) is a suspect. The murdered girl is the daughter of a
senator (Morgan Woodward), and unsatisfied with the official investigation of her homicide, Burt Lancaster delves into the matter
and finds he is in the midst of a criminal ring run by his pal,
whom he is forced to capture.

Star Burt Lancaster and Roland Kibbee produced, directed, and wrote the script for this overlong and flabby mystery thriller which has an interesting plot (when not mired down in focusing on the ex-con's adjustment to civilian life). The subplot based on gangster activities is well hidden until near the finale and the intervening time is spent with Lancaster delving into Bach's murder and learning of other killings, brutal beatings, blackmail, and incest. This film marked Joan Lorring's screen return and benefitted from Robert Quarry's cameo as a lecherous professor.

MIDNIGHT ROSE (Universal, 1928) 5,689'

Presenter, Carl Laemmle; director, James Young; story-continuity, J. Grubb Alexander; titles, Tom Reed; camera, Joseph Brotherton; editor, Byron Robinson.

Lya De Putti (Midnight Rose); Kenneth Harlan (Tim Regan); Henry Kolker (Corbin); Lorimer Johnston (English Edwards); George Larkin (Joe the Wop); Gunboat Smith (Casey); Wendell Phillips Franklin (Sonny); Frank Brownlee (Grogan).

Cabaret dancer Midnight Rose (Lya De Putti) loves gangster Tim Regan (Kenneth Harlan) and he goes straight, despite warnings from his gang. When one of his associates dies, Harlan adopts the deceased's four-year-old boy (Wendell Phillips Franklin) and asks De Putti to marry him to give the youngster a mother. Soon De Putti grows weary of domestic life and returns to the cabaret run by her ex-lover (Henry Kolker). Upset by the turn of events, Harlan returns to his gang but is sent to jail when Kolker squeals on his activities. When Harlan is released (after Kolker confesses) he is reunited with De Putti and Franklin, along with De Putti's baby (by Harlan).
This soggy melodrama was one of seven Hollywood films made by German actress Lya De Putti who had caused such a sensation in the German-made VARIETY (1925). She would leave California in 1928 at the advent of sound and return to Germany, where she died in 1935. The cast included Gunboat Smith, the one-time "White Hope" heavyweight boxing champion.

MIDNIGHT TAXI (Twentieth Century-Fox, 1937) 69 mins.

Producer, Milton H. Feld; director, Eugene Forde; story, Borden Chase; adaptors, Lou Breslow, John Patrick; camera, Barney McGill; editor, Al De Gaetato.

Brian Donlevy (Chick Gardner); Frances Drake (Gilda Lee); Alan Dinehart (Philip Strickland); Sig Rumann (John Rudd); Gilbert Roland (Flash Dillon); Harold Huber (Lucky Todd); Paul Stanton (J. W. McNeary); Lon Chaney, Jr. (Erickson); Russell Hicks (Barney Flagg); Regis Toomey (Hilton).

Frances Drake, Alan Dinehart, Harold Huber and Gilbert Roland in
MIDNIGHT TAXI (1937).

The Federal Bureau of Investigation has agent Chick Gardner
(Brian Donlevy) look into counterfeiting activities and he uncovers
a gang which includes Flash Dillon (Gilbert Roland), Strickland
(Alan Dinehart), and Lucky Todd (Harold Huber), plus moll Gilda
Lee (Frances Drake). Donlevy worms his way into the operation
and along the way falls in love with Drake. The mobsters deduce
his true identity and plan to eliminate him, but Drake rescues him.

Coming late in the mid-1930s gangster film cycle, MIDNIGHT
TAXI made a scant impression, although it was competent entertainment. The picture is a good example of the rollercoaster effect the
film industry had on entertainers' careers. The supporting cast included one-time stars Regis Toomey, Creighton Hale, and Agnes
Ayres, while future star Lon Chaney, Jr. was given his first role
in his two-year Twentieth Century-Fox stock contract.

MILLION DOLLAR MANHUNT (Anglo Amalgamated Film Distributors,
    1962) 67 mins.

Producer, William G. Chalmers; director, Maclean Rogers; based on
the novel Requiem for a Redhead by Al Bocca; screenplay, Rogers;
art director, John Stoll; music, Wilfred Burns; camera, Ernest
Palmer; editor, Peter Mayhew.

Richard Denning (Keen); Carole Mathews (Hedy); Ronald Adam (Scammel/Dumetrius); Danny Green (Yottie); Brian Worth (Ridgeway); Jan Holden (Sally); Hugh Moxey (Sergeant Coutts); Elwyn Brook-Jones (Mitchell); Peter Swanwick (Bonnet).

Twelve million dollars in counterfeit money is sought by international gangsters who want the currency which the Germans expertly printed in Berlin before the collapse of the Third Reich. The money was taken from Berlin before the arrival of the Allies and smuggled into London and intelligence agent Keen (Richard Denning) is assigned to the case. He becomes attracted to one of the suspects, German nightclub singer Hedy (Carole Mathews), who is a member of the criminal gang. The leader of the gangsters, Dumetrius (Ronald Adam) has taken on the identity of a recently killed British staff officer and when he tries to get the currency by committing a murder, Mathews deserts the operation and agrees to aid Denning. Using photographs taken of the gang leader in Berlin, where he murdered the officer, Denning plans to trap Adam but the latter kills Mathews and then meets his own death by falling from a high ledge during a fight with the agent.

This 1956 British production was initially entitled ASSIGNMENT REDHEAD. Although its plot is passable, the casting of Richard Denning as a British secret agent and Carole Mathews as a German cabaret chirp is hard to accept.

MISSING DAUGHTERS (Columbia, 1939) 63 mins.

Director, C. C. Coleman, Jr.; screenplay, Michael L. Simmons, George Bricker; music, Morris W. Stoloff; camera, Henry Freulich; editor, Gene Havlick.

Richard Arlen (Wally King); Rochelle Hudson (Kay Roberts); Marian Marsh (Josie Lamonte); Isabel Jewell (Peggy); Edward Raquello (Lucky Rogers); Dick Wessel (Brick McGirk); Eddie Kane (Nick); Wade Boteler (Captain McGraw); Don Beddoe (Al Farrow); Claire Rochelle (Doris).

Gangsters operating a dance hall racket and obtaining young girls as dancers and then using them for other nefarious activities was documented two years earlier in PAID TO DANCE (q.v.), and this outing was no better than that programmer.

Gangster Lucky Rogers (Edward Raquello) is involved in the dance hall racket and he uses a phony talent scout Al Farrow (Don Beddoe) to procure innocent girls as dancers-hostesses; those who refuse to provide the hoodlum with additional kinds of income are eliminated. When her sister is found floating in the river, a victim of the racket, Kay Roberts (Rochelle Hudson) teams with Wally King (Richard Arlen), a newspaper-radio columnist investigating the dance hall game. With the aid of the local police chief (Wade Boteler), they bring about the mobster's downfall.

MR. MAJESTYK (United Artists, 1974) C 104 mins.

Producer, Walter Mirisch; director, Richard Fleischer; screenplay, Elmore Leonard; music, Charles Bernstein; assistant director, Buck Hall; sound, Harold M. Etherington; camera, Richard H. Kline; editor, Ralph E. Winters.

Charles Bronson (Vince Majestyk); Al Lettieri (Frank Renda); Linda Cristal (Nancy Chavez); Lee Purcell (Wiley); Paul Koslo (Bobby Kopas); Taylor Lacher (Gene Lundy); Frank Maxwell (Detective Lieutenant McAllen); Alejandro Rey (Larry Mendoza); Gordon Rhodes (Deputy Harold Ritchie).

Colorado melon farmer Vince Majestyk (Charles Bronson) evokes the wrath of a crooked labor racketeer by using migrant workers to pick his crop instead of the man's hirelings. As a result a trumped up assault charge is levied against him and he is jailed, handcuffed to recently arrested syndicate kingpin Frank Renda (Al Lettieri). An ambush by the mobster's gang sets both men free and Lettieri offers Bronson money to drive him to Mexico but the latter refuses and notifies the police of the hoodlum's whereabouts. The law, however, fails to capture the wanted man and the latter vows to get even with Bronson. By now most of the migrant workers have vanished due to harassment by the racketeer, who joins forces with Lettieri to trap Bronson. Bronson is aided now only by two of the migrants: Nancy Chavez (Linda Cristal), with whom he has a romance, and Larry Mendoza (Alejandro Rey). Realizing that the law is of no use to him against the gangsters, Bronson lures the adversaries into the mountains he knows so well and begins stalking them, eventually shooting Lettieri and capturing the racketeer.

MR. MAJESTYK is a typically actionful and violent Charles Bronson thriller, well produced and acted. The movie provides the star's fans with all the expected ingredients in his features, but it received the ire of many liberal film critics because it centered on Bronson's attempts to save his life against the gangsters instead of being a treatise on the plight of today's migrant workers. With its Colorado locales and efficient plot, plus good performances by Linda Cristal and Al Lettieri, the movie is solid entertainment.

MR. REEDER IN ROOM 13 see: ROOM 13

MODELS, INC. (Mutual, 1952) 72 mins.

Producer, Hal E. Chester; associate producer, Bernard W. Burton; director, Reginald Le Borg; story-adaptor, Alyce Canfield, screenplay, Harry Essex, Paul Yawitz; music, Herschel Burke Gilbert; camera, Stanley Cortez; editor, Burton.

John Howard, Howard Duff, and Benny Baker in MODELS, INC. (1952).

Howard Duff (Lennie Stone); Coleen Gray (Rusty Faraday); John Howard (John Stafford); Marjorie Reynolds (Peggy Howard); Louis Jean Heydt (Cronin); Ed Max (Looie); Benny Baker (Freddy); James Seay (Detective Sergeant Mooney); Charles Cane (Big Jim); Sue Carlton (Ann); Lou Lubin (Max); Mary Hill (Millie); Frank Ferguson (Banker Reynolds).

Gold-digging Rusty Faraday (Coleen Gray) sets her sights on the honest owner of a modeling agency-school, John Stafford (John Howard). The latter becomes enamoured with her and all goes well until the woman's ex-lover, gangster Lennie Stone (Howard Duff) is released from jail and comes back into her life. He plans to use the agency and its models in a shakedown operation by which the girls will pose for lewd photos and various oddballs will pay to photograph them and then be blackmailed. Gray, however, tries to get rid of Duff and marries Howard, but the ex-convict is tracked to her home by the police who want him for parole viola-tion. In a gun battle Duff kills Gray before being shot himself. Howard reopens his business and finds love with his loyal secre-tary (Marjorie Reynolds).

MODERN DAY HOUDINI (Mid America Promotions, 1983) C 90 mins.

Executive producer, Bill Shirk; producers, Ron Hostetler, Eddie Beverly, Jr.; director, Beverly; screenplay, Steven Meyers; music, Jeffrey Boze; camera, Steve Posey; editor, Hostetler.

Bill Shirk (Shirk); Milbourne Christopher (Weiss); Peter Lupus (Sharky); Dick the Bruiser [Dick Afflis] (The Bruiser); Gary Todd (Doug); Terry Mann (Polly); Cynthia Johns (Stormy); Elizabeth Bechtel (Sylvia); Sam Graves (Mike); Robert James Poorman, Jr. (Hardin); Dave Dugan (Butch); Larry Battson (Bubba).

The owner (Bill Shirk) of an Indianapolis radio station finds out a gang of crooks, fronted by a businessmen's organization headed mostly by blacks, is attempting to take over his operation. The man is determined to stop this power play and enlists the aid of several influential citizens as well as engaging in a series of magic stunts to raise the money to thwart the tycoon's plot.

Filmed in Indianapolis and allegedly Indiana's first locally produced "major" feature, MODERN DAY HOUDINI is a sad affair. Listless direction, poor editing, a saggy script, and a mostly no-name cast do nothing for the proceedings and star Bill Shirk, the owner of Indianapolis radio station WXLW known for his wild pub-licity stunts, is unable to carry the feature. The only cast not-ables are Indiana natives Peter Lupus (of TV's "Mission: Impos-sible" fame) and long time professional heavyweight wrestling cham-pion Dick the Bruiser (Dick Afflis).

MONEY MADNESS (Film Classics, 1948) 73 mins.

Producer, Sigmund Neufeld; director, Peter Stewart [Sam Newfield]; screenplay, Al Martin; music director, Leo Erdody; art director, Elias H. Reif; set decorator, Eugene C. Stone; makeup, Harry Ross; assis-tant director, Stanley Neufield; sound, Ben Winkler; camera, Jack Greehalgh; editor, Holbrook N. Todd.

Hugh Beaumont (Fred Howard/Steve Clark); Frances Rafferty (Julie); Harlan Warde (Donald); Cecil Weston (Cora); Ida Moore (Mrs. Fer-guson); Danny Morton (Rogers); Joel Friedkin (Dr. Wagner); Lane Chandler (Policeman); Molly Lamont (Martha); Dick Elliott (Custo-mer).

Bank robber Fred Howard (Hugh Beaumont) buses to a small California town and hides the $200,000 he stole in a Denver bank heist in a local safety deposit box. As Steve Clark he becomes a taxi driver and romances Julie Saunders (Frances Rafferty), who lives with her widowed aunt (Cecil Watson). Beaumont schemes to murder Watson, marry Rafferty, stash the money in her attic, and then claim it belonged to the late aunt. When Rafferty finds that he has poisoned her aunt, she is forced to go along with Beaumont. However, her attentive attorney (Harlan Warde) learns the truth and in a police confrontation with a cop (Lane Chandler) Beaumont is gunned down.

MONEY MADNESS loses some of its punch by beginning its narrative with the character of Julie Saunders being sentenced to ten years in prison and then relating the intricacies of how she fell into such a predicament. On the other hand, the film is well executed and nicely paced by director Peter Stewart (Sam Newfield). Hugh Beaumont, later famous as the oh-so-understanding father in the teleseries "Leave It to Beaver," is particularly effective as the underworld heel who switches from being a good humored, easygoing guy to a cold, calculated, psychotic murderer.

MONSTER OF THE ISLAND see: IL MOSTRO DELL'ISOLA

LA MORTE VESTITA DI DOLLARI see: DOG EAT DOG

IL MOSTRO DELL'ISOLA [MONSTER OF THE ISLAND] (Roman Films, 1953) 87 mins.

Director, Roberto Montero; story, Alberto Vecchietti; screenplay, Montero, Vecchietti; music, Carlo Innocenzi; camera, Augusto Tiezzi; editor, Iolanda Benvenuti.

Boris Karloff (Don Gaetano); Franco Marzi (Andreani); Renata Vicario (Gloria); Patrizia Remiddi (Mirella Andreani); Germana Paolieri (Senora Andreani); and: Iole Fiero, Carlo Duse, Giuseppe Chinnici, Giulio Battiferri, Domenico De Ninno, Clara Gaberini, Salvatore Sciebetta.

With its title and famous monster movie star, this 1953 movie would appear to be a horror film, but in reality it is an Italian-made gangster tale. It did not play in the United States until 1957 and then only in Italian language theaters, although a dubbed version does appear on U.S. TV as ISLAND MONSTER.

Drug trafficking is on the increase on the island of Ischia and the Italian government sends an undercover agent (Franco Marzi) to learn who is masterminding the smuggling operation. He arrives with his young daughter (Patrizia Remiddi) and meets attractive singer Gloria (Renata Vicario) who knows some of the gang members. He is aided in his investigation by Don Gaetano (Boris Karloff), a wealthy local businessman. Later the gangsters kidnap Marzi's daughter and threaten to murder her unless he stops his activities. However, Vicaro helps Marzi find the gang's hideout, where he is not only captured but finds that Karloff is the ringleader of the operation. With the police closing in, Karloff uses the little girl as a means of escape but is thwarted and the gang is captured.

MOTOR PATROL (Lippert, 1950) 68 mins.

Producer, Barney Sarecky; director, Sam Newfield; story, Maurice Tombragel; screenplay, Tombragel, Orville Hampton; art director; Frank P. Sylos; set decorator, Harry Reif; music director, Ozzie Caswell; makeup, Harry Ross; assistant director, Stanley Neufield; sound, Glen Glenn; special effects, Ray Mercer; camera, Ernest W. Miller; editor, Stanley Frazen.

Don Castle (Ken); Jane Nigh (Connie); Reed Hadley (Flynn); Bill Henry (Larry); Gwen O'Connor (Jean); Sid Melton (Omar); Dick Travis (Bill); Frank Jenks (Mac); Louis Fuller (Tom Morgan); Charles Victor (Russ); Onslow Stevens (Lieutenant Dearborn); Charles Wagenheim (Bud Haynes); Frank Jacquet (Miller).

To milk every conceivable aspect possible from the gangster motif and the lawmen who fight the hoodlums, Hollywood films have depicted the police in practically every avenue of their daily work: from G-men to border patrolmen. Here the hero is a member of the motor patrol out to halt an auto theft operation.
When traffic patrolman Larry (Bill Henry) learns too much about their illegal activities, he is murdered by gangsters running a stolen car ring. His buddy, patrolman Ken (Don Castle), who is engaged to the dead man's sister (Gwen O'Connor), demands revenge. His department superior (Reed Hadley) gives him permission to solve the case. He pretends to be a gangster from Chicago and wins his way into the gang's good graces. The ruse works well and he determines the operation is run by Connie (Jane Nigh). In the final shootout, the gang is overwhelmed by the police.

MOTORCYCLE GANG (American-International, 1957) 78 mins.

Producer, Alex Gordon; director, Edward L. Cahn; story-screenplay, Lou Rusoff; art director, Don Ament; music, Albert Glasser; sound, Ben Winkler; camera, Frederick E. West; editor, Richard C. Meyer.

Anne Neyland (Terry); Steve Terrell (Randy); John Ashley (Nick); Carl Switzer (Speed); Raymond Hatton (Uncle Ed); Russ Bender (Joe); Jean Moorehead (Marilyn); Scott Peters (Hank); Eddie Kafafian (Jack); Shirley Falls (Darlene); Aki Aleong (Cyrus Wong);

Wayne Taylor (Phil); Hal Bogart (Walt); Phyllis Cole (Mary);
Suzanne Sydney (Birdie); Edmund Cobb (Bill); Paul Blaisdell
(Don); Zon Murray (Hal); Felice Richmond (Hal's Wife).

The financial success of Columbia's THE WILD ONE (see:
B/V) in 1954 resulted in a raft of juvenile delinquency pictures
centering around motorcycle bikers and their cohorts. Since many
of these depict riders as young thugs/hoodlums, they qualify as a
sub-genre of the gangster movie. While these lawbreakers may not
necessarily have direct connections with organized crime, they are
criminals nonetheless, carrying on an anarchical lifestyle destined to
put them at odds with law enforcers.

Biker Nick (John Ashley) gets out of jail after serving fifteen
months for a hit-and-run incident and he wants revenge on fellow
cyclist Randy (Steve Terrell) who was only put on probation. He
wants to engage his rival in an illegal race, but Terrell has joined
a police-sponsored club and now wants to abide by the rules in order to race in a regional event. Female biker Terry (Anne Neyland)
flirts with both youths, hoping to get them to fight. Goaded into
the race, Terrell is injured and hospitalized, but his club still wants
him in the regional meet. During that event, Terrell drops out
when he finds that Ashley and his gang are terrorizing the people
of a nearby town. With the aid of the police the thugs are put
back in prison and he returns to Neyland.

"MOTORCYCLE GANG kicks up a cloud of dust as soon as it
hits the screen, and the haze becomes a persistent one, never let-
ting enough story break through" (Variety). The one nice element
of this below par programmer is producer Alex Gordon's penchant
for utilizing Hollywood veterans, and the movie showcases such
screen stalwarts as Raymond Hatton, Carl "Alfalfa" Switzer, and
Edmund Cobb. It should be noted that villain John Ashley later
became the producer of the popular action NBC-TV series, "The
A-Team."

MURDER AT THE BASKERVILLES (Astor, 1941) 70 mins.

Producer, Julius Hagen; director, Thomas Bentley; based on the
story by Sir Arthur Conan Doyle; screenplay, Arthur Macrae, H.
Fowler Mear; camera, Sydney Blythe; editor, Alan Smith.

Arthur Wontner (Sherlock Holmes); Lyn Harding (Professor Mori-
arty); Judy Gunn (Diana Baskerville); Ian Fleming (Dr. Watson);
Lawrence Grossmith (Sir Henry Baskerville); Arthur Macrae (Jack
Trevor); Eve Gray (Mrs. Straker); Martin Walker (John Straker);
John Turnbill (Inspector Lestrade); Robert Horton (Colonel Ross);
Arthur Goullet (Colonel Sebastian Moran); Minnie Rayner (Mrs.
Hudson); D. J. Williams (Silas Brown); Ralph Truman (Bert
Prince); Gilbert Davis (Miles Stamford).

This is an expanded screen version of Sir Arthur Conan

Doyle's 1894 short story, and was the fifth and final feature film to star Arthur Wontner as Sherlock Holmes. Many Holmes purists consider Wontner one of the best screen purveyors of the character, but this entry is probably the weakest of his quintet of movies about the famous detective. By the time this feature was produced, the actor was 62 years old, far too advanced in years to play the energetic Sherlock. In addition, the film took place in modern times, lacking the ingratiating flavor of the gaslight era. In The Films of Sherlock Holmes (187), Chris Steinbrunner and Norman Michaels determined, "Like most last entries in screen series, ... [this] is not top drawer. But it is still a workmanlike adaptation of the classic Conan Doyle horse-kidnapping story, with many fine touches. It faces, however, the recurring problem of fitting a spare short story into a feature-film format, and therefore embellishes with zeal."

Set two decades after the famous events at Baskerville Hall, Holmes (Wontner) and Dr. Watson (Ian Fleming) are again called to the locale by Henry Baskerville (Lawrence Grossmith), this time to celebrate the twentieth anniversary of Wontner having solved the noted crime. There, however, he finds that Grossmith's race horse, Silver Blaze, has been stolen just prior to a big race, with his groom (Robert Horton) murdered and Grossmith's daughter's (Judy Gunn) fiance (Arthur Macree) suspected of the crime. Wontner deduces that the infamous gangster Professor Moriarty (Lyn Harding) and his henchman Colonel Moran (Arthur Goullet) are behind the problem and despite an attempt on his life and the kidnapping of Fleming, Wontner solves the case.

Originally released in England as SILVER BLAZE it was four years before Astor Pictures released the property in the U.S., giving it a more pungent marquee title.

MURDER, MY SWEET (RKO, 1945) 93 mins.

Executive producer, Sid Rogell; producer, Adrian Scott; based on the novel Farewell, My Lovely by Raymond Chandler; screenplay, John Paxton; art directors, Albert S. D'Agostino, Carroll Clark; music, Roy Webb; music director, C. Bakaleinikoff; special effects, Vernon L. Walker; camera, Harry J. Wild; editor, Joseph Noriega.

Dick Powell (Philip Marlowe); Claire Trevor (Mrs. Grayle); Anne Shirley (Anne Riordan); Otto Kruger (Jules Amthor); Mike Mazurki (Moose Malloy); Miles Mander (Mr. Grayle); Douglas Walton (Lindsay Marriott); Don Douglas (Lieutenant Randall); Ralf Harolde (Dr. Sonderborg); Esther Howard (Mrs. Jesse Florian); John Indrisano (Chauffeur); Jack Carr (Short Guy); Shimen Ruskin (Elevator Operator); Ernie Adams (Bartender); Dewey Robinson (The Boss); Larry Wheat (Butler); Sammy Finn (Headwaiter); Bernice Ahi (Dancer); Don Kerr (Cab Driver); Paul Phillips (Detective Nulty); Ralph Dunn, George Anderson (Detectives); Paul Hilton (Boy).

Raymond Chandler's novel Farewell, My Lovely (1940) originally was to deal with the relationship between gangsters and the law in a corrupt California community. But by the time it was completed, this storyline aspect became a subplot with a murder mystery angle wrapped around it. In this form it was filmed in 1942 by RKO as THE FALCON TAKES OVER, with the lead character of shamus Philip Marlowe converted to fit the "Falcon" series lead, debonair sleuth Gay Falcon (George Sanders), a character created by Michael Arlen. In 1945, RKO remade the Chandler property, bringing back the character of Philip Marlowe and breathing new life into the film career of crooner Dick Powell, who played hard-boiled Marlowe to perfection.

Los Angeles-based detective Philip Marlowe (Powell) is in a black district working on a case when he is strongarmed by giant Moose Malloy (Mike Mazurki) who hires him to find his former flame Velma who vanished while he was in prison. The case takes Powell to Jesse Florian (Esther Howard), a lush whose late husband owned the bar where Velma once sang. Meanwhile dapper Lindsay Marriott (Douglas Walton) hires Powell to accompany him in buying back a jade necklace which hoodlums had stolen from a friend, and at the scene Powell is blackjacked and Walton murdered. Pretty Anne Riordan (Anne Shirley) finds the body and later informs Powell that Mrs. Grayle (Claire Trevor), the young wife of a rich, elderly politician, once owned the necklace. The trail leads to mystic Jules Amthor (Otto Kruger), whom Powell suspects of being the head of the jewel robbery gang. Trevor later tells Powell that Walton used his psychic racket for blackmail. On the way to see Kruger, Powell is drugged and taken to the establishment of drug runner Dr. Sonderborg (Ralf Harolde), from which he escapes. With the aid of policeman Randall (Don Douglas), one of the few men on the local force not allied with gangsters, he finds that Mazurki has murdered Howard. Powell forces one of the tainted cops to reveal where Mazurki is. The trail leads to a gambling ship owned by an underworld kingpin and the events soon push to a rapid conclusion. It proves that Trevor is Velma and it was she who murdered Walton. Trevor shoots Mazurki, but when later cornered, she kills herself.

MURDER, MY SWEET was one of the more popular detective movies of the 1940s and its box-office success paved the way for the filming of most of Raymond Chandler's novels dealing with iconoclastic Philip Marlowe. This movie is a tightly organized rendition of the Chandler work, highlighted by Dick Powell's flippant yet very likable interpretation of Marlowe, and wrestler Mike Mazurki's superb performance as the super strong hoodlum looking for his lost love. The casting of Claire Trevor as the woman with a past and Anne Shirley (in her final film role) as the sugar sweet girl adds interest to the proceedings, as does the film's look at the then-popular psychic racket.

In 1975, this Chandler novel would be filmed for a third time, reverting to the book's original title, FAREWELL, MY LOVELY (q.v.).

MURDER ON LENOX AVENUE (Colonnade Pictures, 1941) 65 mins.

Producer-director, Arthur Dreifuss; story, Frank Wilson; screenplay, Vincent Valentini, Bryna Ivens; music, Donald Heywood; art
director, William Salter; assistant director, Charles Wasseman; camera, George Webber; editor, Robert Crandall.

Alberta Perkins (Mercedes); Sidney Easton (Speed Simmons); Alec
Lovejoy (Flirver Johnson); Dene Larry (Ola Wilkins); J. Augustus
"Gus" Smith (Pa Wilkins); Ernie Ransom (Jim Braxton); Earl Sydnor
(Gregory); Norman Astwood (Marshall); Herman Green (Loman);
George Williams (Monstante); Mamie Smith (Hattie); Cristola Williams
(Rosaline); Emily Santos (Emily), Flo Lee (Flo); Wahneta San
(Wahneta).

 This feature was filmed in New York City and geared for the
Negro theater circuit. Its story has a basis in fact since in the
1930s Harlem business people formed the Colored Merchants Association to rid their community of racketeers. This crudely made feature
examines this event against the background of fictional characters
and their actions. Like most movies of its ilk, the film contains
such genre subplots as a rent party, a nightclub, and plenty of
jazz music. It should be noted that the film was created mostly by
blacks, although its final script was by a white writer (Vincent
Valentini) and it was directed by Arthur Dreifuss, who had a long
Hollywood career.
 The plot centers around honest Pa Wilkins (Gus Smith) who
wants his daughter Ola (Dene Larry) to wed Jim Braxton (Ernie
Ransom), the son of his deceased war buddy. Dene, however,
loves educator Greg (Earl Syndor) who wants her to go South with
him to teach. Ransom, who has impregnated pretty Mercedes (Alberta Perkin), works for gangster Speed Simmons (Sidney Easton)
and his deformed hit man. Easton has set up a local business group
but the members throw him out because he has been taking rake-
offs and they now get Smith to run the league. In revenge,
Easton wants Ransom to murder Smith and he agrees after Larry
rejects him in favor of Sydnor. At a meeting at the Progress Hall,
Ransom plans to carry out the murder, but Larry and Synder arrive
with the news that Perkin has killed himself. When Smith confronts
Ransom, the hit man attempts to shoot him, but Ransom gets in the
way and is killed. Smith tells his people they must unite to rid
their community of the gangsters.
 The acting by this movie's large cast is uneven, but one of
its supporting players is Mamie Smith, who gives a well defined
performance as the pregnant girl's mother. (To be noted is that
Mamie Smith made history in 1921 when her recording of "Crazy
Blues" started the blues music craze, paving the way for famous
blues artists like Bessie Smith and Victoria Spivey. In this movie,
Miss Smith offers a fine vocal rendition of "I'll Get You For This.")

Barton MacLane, Charles Bickford, and I. Stanford Jolly (hidden to right) in MUTINY IN THE BIG HOUSE (1939).

MUTINY IN THE BIG HOUSE (Monogram, 1939) 55 mins.

Producer, Grant Withers; director, William Nigh; story, Martin Mooney; screenplay, Robert Andrews; camera, Harry Neumann; editor, R. F. Schoengarth.

Charles Bickford (Father Joe); Barton MacLane (Red); Pat Moriarity (Warden); Dennis Moore (Johnny); William Royle (Cap); Charles Foy (Ritsy); George Cleveland (Dad); Nigel DeBrulier (Mike); Ed Foster (Duke); Richard Austin (Jim); Russell Hopton (Frankie), I. Stanford Jolly (Bit).

 Martin Mooney based his original story for this film on an incident that had occurred a decade before at a Canon City, Colorado, prison where a prison priest, Father Patrick O'Neil, stopped a riot in which several guards and inmates were killed. As a result, he was awarded the Carnegie medal for bravery.
 Here Charles Bickford stars as Father Joe, a prison chaplain who tries to help a young convict (Dennis Moore) who has been sent to the big house for a $10 forgery. At odds with the priest is hardened criminal Red (Barton MacLane) who tries to make a real hoodlum out of the young man and for a time succeeds until Moore realizes the error of his ways and goes over to the priest's

278 / MY SON IS GUILTY

side. MacLane, however, instigates a bloody prison riot which Bickford manages to quell, thus ending MacLane's evil hold over his fellow inmates.

In B Movies (1973), author Don Miller terms this Monogram production "... in many ways one of their best ... [a] commendable work...." The film contains what is probably Barton MacLane's most stereotyped role as the loud-mouthed, cold-blooded, incorrigible gangster, a characterization for which he was famous. It should be noted that the film was produced by actor Grant Withers, who had a brief, but decent, career as a producer at Monogram before going on to become one of the screen's most dastardly villains, especially in Westerns.

MY SON IS GUILTY (Columbia, 1940) 63 mins.

Producer, Jack Fier; director, Charles Barton; story, Karl Brown; screenplay, Harry Shumate, Joseph Carole; camera, Benjamin Kline; editor, William Lyon.

Bruce Cabot (Ritzy Kerry); Jacqueline Wells (Julia Allen); Harry Carey (Tim Kerry); Glenn Ford (Barney); Wynne Gibson (Claire Moreill); Don Beddoe (Duke Mason); John Tyrrell (Whitey Morris); Bruce Bennett (Lefty); Dick Curtis (Monk); Edgar Buchanan (Dan).

Tim Kerry (Harry Carey), an old-line beat policeman in New York's Hell's Kitchen, tries to reform his hoodlum son Ritzy (Bruce Cabot) after the young man is released. Cabot, however, becomes involved with his old gang members after his girl (Jacqueline Wells) rejects him for another man (Glenn Ford) and Cabot joins with the gang now run by a woman mobster (Wynne Gibson). As a result of his criminal activities, the young man tries to murder his father but instead kills another officer, and in a showdown Carey is forced to shoot his wayward offspring.

Sporting a fine cast and steady direction by Charles Barton, MY SON IS GUILTY is a substantial gangster "B" outing. Its downbeat plot holds one's attention and its recreation of Manhattan's tough Hell's Kitchen neighborhood is well executed. Of particular interest is the psychological diversity between father and son: the scripters suggest that environment and not blood ties are more important in the determination of whether a person goes right or wrong.

THE MYSTERIOUS MAGICIAN see: THE RINGER

MYSTERY SHIP (Columbia, 1941) 65 mins.

Producer, Jack Fier; director, Lew Landers; story, Alex Gottlieb; screenplay, David Silverstein, Houston Branch; camera, L. W. O'Connell; editor, James Sweeney.

Paul Kelly (Allan Harper); Lola Lane (Patricia Marshall); Larry
Parks (Tommy Baker); Trevor Bardette (Ernst Madok); Cy Kendall
(Condor); Roger Imhof (Captain Randall); Eddie Laughton (Turillo);
John Tyrrell (Sam); Byron Foulger (Wasserman); Dick Curtis (Van
Brock); Dwight Frye (Rader); Kenneth MacDonald (Gorman).

Gangsters, murderers, and fifth columnists are taken out of
prison and placed aboard a ship to be taken to an unnamed country
to which they are being deported.   Infiltrating the gang of criminals
to make sure they do not take over the vessel is G-man Tommy
Baker (Larry Parks) while his partner (Paul Kelly) is in charge of
the voyage.   The latter's lady love, reporter Patricia Marshall (Lola
Lane), stows away to get a big scoop.   Along the way the criminals
try to take over but are thwarted by the G-men.

While an actionful entry from the Columbia "B" unit, MYSTERY
SHIP has scant cinema realism.   Only the presence of perennial
screen bad guys Cy Kendall, Trevor Bardette, Eddie Laughton,
Dick Curtis, Dwight Frye, and Kenneth MacDonald add life to the
mundane proceedings.

THE NAKED STREET (United Artists, 1955) 84 mins.

Producer, Edward Small; director, Maxwell Shane; story, Leo
Katcher; screenplay, Shane, Katcher; art director, Ted Haworth;
music, Emil Newman; sound, Fred Lau; camera, Floyd Crosby, editor, Grant Whytock.

Peter Graves and Anne Bancroft in THE NAKED STREET (1955).

Farley Granger (Nicky Bradna); Anthony Quinn (Phil Regal); Anne
Bancroft (Rosalie Regalzyk); Peter Graves (Joe McFarland); Else
Neft (Mrs. Regalzyk); Jerry Paris (Latzi Franks); Frank Sully
(Nutsy); John Dennis (Big Eddie); Angela Stevens (Janet); Joy
Terry (Margie); G. Pat Collins (Mr. Hough); Mario Siletti (Antonio
Cardini); Whit Bissell (Attorney Blaker); Jeanne Cooper (Evelyn
Shriner); Sara Berner (Millie); James Flavin (Attorney Flanders);
Harry Harvey (Judge Roder); Alex Campbell (Judge Stanley);
Jackie Loughery (Francie); Frank Kreit (Ollie); Joe Turkel (Shim-
my); Harry O. Tyler (Barricks); Sammie Weiss (Lennie).

"There's not too much to discuss about this little gangster
picture. The original story, if briefly told, might have made a
mildly satisfying vignette in a man's pulp magazine.... There's
nothing unusually bad about all this, except it's hard to think of
anyone who'll want to see it. Direction, script and action aren't
bad, but there's not enough solid conflict in the yarn to make a
good man's picture and not enough sympathetic human interest to
make it appealing to women" (Jack Moffitt, Hollywood Reporter).

Gangster Phil Regal (Anthony Quinn) maneuvers the release
of fellow hoodlum Nicky Bradna (Farley Granger) from prison on a
murder charge so he will marry the man's pregnant sister Rosalie
(Anne Bancroft). The baby dies, however, and Granger proves
to be a sadistic husband so Quinn sets him up on a fake murder
charge and he returns to prison to die in the electric chair. To
get revenge, Granger tells all he knows about the man's racketeering operations to newspaper reporter Joe McFarland (Peter Graves)
who falls in love with Bancroft and also brings about Quinn's downfall.

Director-scripter Maxwell Shane, an old hand at crime melodramas, does a workmanlike job, especially aided by Anthony Quinn
and Farley Granger as the hoods and Peter Graves as the crusading
newsman.

THE NARROW MARGIN (RKO, 1952) 71 mins.

Producer, Stanley Rubin; director, Richard Fleischer; story, Martin
Goldsmith, Jack Leonard; screenplay, Earl Felton; art directors, Al-
bert S. D'Agostino, Jack Okey; set decorators, Darrell Silvera,
William Stevens; sound, Francis Sarver, Glen Portman; camera,
George E. Diskant; editor, Robert Swink.

Charles McGraw (Walter Brown); Marie Windsor (Mrs. Neil); Jac-
queline White (Ann Sinclair); Gordon Gebert (Tommy Sinclair);
Queenie Leonard (Mrs. Troil); David Clarke (Kemp); Peter Virgo
(Densel); Don Beddoe (Gus Forbes); Paul Maxey (Jennings); Harry
Harvey (Train Conductor).

A gangster's moll (Marie Windsor) is scheduled to testify
against mobsters in a Los Angeles court and two police detectives

(Charles McGraw, Don Beddoe) are sent to Chicago to extradite her.
On board the westbound train to Los Angeles, one of the detectives
(McGraw) becomes involved with a young widow (Jacqueline White)
with a small son while the other (Beddoe) is murdered. The surviving policeman realizes that the mobsters have sent hit men to
stop them from returning and he must protect the evil-tempered
witness. Windsor, however, is killed before the cop dispatches
the two hoodlums and McGraw only then learns she was a decoy
policewoman while the real witness is the widow.

 THE NARROW MARGIN is a compact thriller done in the film
noir style. It was regarded as a sleeper in its day and a "B"
movie classic by today's film followers. At release Time magazine
stated the film had "... a lean scenario, pungent performances and
inventive direction...." Made in two weeks on a $200,000 budget,
the movie was highly regarded by Howard Hughes, then head of
RKO, and, in the nearly two years he tinkered with it, he thought
of adding sequences to make it an "A" movie but finally decided the
product could not be improved. By then he had lost interest in
the production and threw it into release with scarcely any promo-
tion.

 While Charles McGraw is particularly effective as the stern
detective, it is Marie Windsor as the undercover cop who excels as
she masquerades as the hardened moll. Discussing her performance
in Dames (1969), Ian and Elisabeth Cameron detailed, "So closely
does she fit our and McGraw's preconception of what sort of woman
would marry a gangster that it never occurs to him or to us until
he searches her belongings after her death that she might not be
all she seems. One of Richard Fleicher's purposes throughout is to
undermine audience security which he does by attacking our assump-
tions...."

NEUES VOM HEXER see: THE RINGER

NEW ORLEANS AFTER DARK (Allied Artists, 1959) 69 mins.

Producer, Eric Sayers; director, John Sledge; screenplay, Frank
Phares; assistant director, Clint Bolton; sound, Edward Dutreil;
camera, Willis Winford; editor, John Hemel.

Stacy Harris (Detective Vic Beaujac); Louis Sirgo (Detective John
Conroy); Ellen Moore (Kean Conroy); Tommy Pelle (Pat Conroy);
Wilson Bourg (Nick Liverno); Harry Wood (Carl); Johnny Aladdin
(Fighter); Jeanine Thomas (Sandra); Leo Zinser (Caprini); Kathryn
Copponex (Mary Sherman); Bob Samuels (Pete); Steve Lord (Black-
ie); Louis Gurvich (Omega); Frank Fiasconaro (Solitaire); Allan
Binkley (Bartender); Claude Evans (Frank); Dottie Lee (Stripper);
La Vergne Smith (Herself).

 New Orleans police detectives Vic Beaujac (Stacy Harris) and

Stacy Harris in NEW ORLEANS AFTER DARK (1959).

John Conroy (Louis Sirgo) are on the trail of the perpetrators of a number of murders and the clues lead them to a drug smuggling operation.   Posing as a seaman, Harris is able to infiltrate the gang and eventually expose its leader and arrest the murderer.
    Filmed in New Orleans, "this film takes the viewer on a sometimes intriguing pictorial survey" (Motion Picture Herald) of that city.   Based on actual records from the New Orleans Police Department, the feature was executed in the semi-documentary and intricate investigating style associated with the "Dragnet" TV series, on which star Stacy Harris often appeared in character roles as well as having appeared in Warner Brothers' theatrical version in 1953.   Of interest to music fans was the appearance of popular bistro entertainer La Vergne Smith.
    In 1962, director John Sledge reunited co-stars Stacy Harris and Louis Sirgo in the mystery melodrama FOUR FOR THE MORGUE, issued by MPA Feature Films.

NEW ORLEANS UNCENSORED (Columbia, 1955) 76 mins.

Producer, Sam Katzman; director, William Castle; story, Orville H.

Hampton; screenplay, Hampton, Lewis Meltzer; music conductor, Mischa Bakaleinikoff; camera, Henry Freulich; editors, Gene Havlick, Al Clark.

Arthur Franz (Dan Corbett); Beverly Garland (Marie Reilly); Helene Stanton (Alma Mae); Michael Ansara (Zero Saxon); Stacy Harris (Scrappy Durant); Mike Mazurki (Mike); William Henry (Joe Reilly); Michael Granger (Jack Petty); Frankie Ray (Deuce); Edwin Stafford Nelson (Charlie); Ralph Dupas (Himself); Pete Herman (Pete Heerman); Judge Walter B. Hamlin (Wayne Brandon); Al Chittenden (Himself).

Shot in New Orleans, and using many locals for atmosphere, NEW ORLEANS UNCENSORED is best when regarded as a peep into that city in the mid-1950s. As a gangster melodrama, it is inadequate.

After several crimes are commited and two of his pals are murdered, New Orleans dock worker Dan Corbett (Arthur Franz) suspects gangsters are behind the events and he goes to the local crime commission which appoints him a special agent to study the matter. He learns that gangster Zero Saxon (Michael Ansara) and his henchman Mike (Mike Mazurki) are behind the lawlessness, and with the blonde Marie (Beverly Garland) he stops the hoodlum's activities.

The New York Times labeled the film a "banal story of pilfering and dockside skulduggery" and added, "All the effort applied to NEW ORLEANS UNCENSORED to make it look like a documentary has made it appear patently unreal. The use of non-professionals is fine, when they can act, but in this film the civic leaders who were recruited can't act. This is not crime, but it does show."

NEWS HOUNDS (Monogram, 1947) 68 mins.

Producer, Jan Grippo; director, William Beaudine; story, Tim Ryan, Edmond Seward, George Cappy; screenplay, Seward, Ryan; art director, David Milton; set decorator, Raymond Boltz, Jr.; assistant director, William Calihan; music director, Edward J. Kay; sound, Tom Lambert; camera, Marcel Le Picard; editor, William Austin.

Leo Gorcey (Terrence J. Montgomery "Slip" Mahoney); Huntz Hall (Horace Debussy "Sach" Jones); Bobby Jordan (Bobby); Billy Benedict (Whitey); David Gorcey (Chuck); Gabriel Dell (Gabe); Bernard Gorcey (Louie Dumbrowski); Tim Ryan (John Burke); Anthony Caruso (Dapper Dan Greco); Christine McIntyre (Jane Ann Connelly); Bill Kennedy (Mark Morgan); Robert Emmett Keane (Attorney Mack Snide); Ralph Dunn (Dutch Miller); John H. Elliott (Judge); John Hamilton (Timothy X. Donlin); Leo Kaye (Red Kane); Emmett Vogan (Defense Attorney); Nita Bieber (Mame); Bud Gorman (Copy Boy); Emmett Vogan, Jr. (Johnny Gale); Meyer Grace (Sparring Partner); Gene Stutenroth [Roth] (Dutch's Henchman); Terry Goodman, Russ Whiteman (Bits).

"NEWS HOUNDS adds up to one of the best of Monogram's Bowery Boys series ... Jan Grippo's production has given the boys a plot to work over and that accounts for more substance than usually found in B. B. entries" (Variety).

Slip Mahoney (Leo Gorcey) decides to become a newspaper reporter and he is encouraged by his pals, including Sach (Huntz Hall). He uncovers a gangster-operated sports fixing operation run by "Clothes" Greco (Anthony Caruso) and Dutch Miller (Ralph Dunn). The paper prints his story but Gorcey cannot prove what he has written and the journal is sued for libel. To get the goods on the mobsters and prove Gorcey correct, the boys find stolen photographs which substantiate the sports fixing racket and Gorcey and the paper are cleared--the underworld characters go to prison.

Under William Beaudine's fast-clip direction, NEWS HOUNDS is a pleasant time killer.

THE NICKEL RIDE (Twentieth Century-Fox, 1974) C 106 mins.

Executive producers, David Foster, Lawrence Turman; producer-director, Robert Mulligan; screenplay, Eric Roth; music, Dave Grusin; art director, Larry Paull; set decorator, Jack Stevens, assistant director, Daniel J. McCauley; sound, Don Bassman, Gene Cantamessa; camera, Jordan Croneweth; editor, Nick Brown.

Jason Miller (Cooper); Linda Haynes (Sarah); Victor French (Paddie); John Hillerman (Carl); Bo Hopkins (Turner); Richard Evans (Bobby); Brendan Burns (Larry); Lou Frizzell (Paulie); Jeanne Lange (Jeannie); Bart Burns (Elias); Harvey Gold (Chester); Mark Gordon (Tonozzi).

The decline and fall of a small-time racketeer is the theme of this gangster exercise, competently made by director Robert Mulligan and nicely acted by an excellent cast. Overall, though, the feature is mundane.

Jason Miller stars as Cooper, the minor kingpin of the rackets in a blighted urban area. He works for Carl (John Hillerman) who is actually a liaison between Miller and the big bosses who are in legitimate businesses. Working with Miller is a corrupt policeman (Bart Burns), his friend bar owner Paddie (Victor French), and his girlfriend (Linda Haynes). Miller begins to realize that the big bosses want him out and when a mobster (Bo Hopkins) is brought in from out of town, he starts a fight to retain his tenuous position.

While genre outings like THE GODFATHER (see: B/V) looked at the cream of the crop of criminal kingpins, THE NICKEL RIDE reveals the flip side of the coin. The movie deftly studies the changes in the rackets from the past, focusing on the new breed of racketeer who uses the facade of honesty to cover his nefarious activities, while old-line hoodlums like Miller are anachronisms who must be destroyed.

Gene Hackman in NIGHT MOVES (1975).

NIGHT MOVES (Warner Bros., 1975) C 99 mins.

Producer, Robert M. Sherman; director, Arthur Penn; screenplay, Alan Sharp; music, Michael Small; production designer, George Jenkins; set decorator, Ned Parsons; assistant director, Jack Roe; camera, Bruce Surtees; underwater camera, Jordan Klein; editors, Dede Allen, Stephen A. Rotter.

Gene Hackman (Harry Moseby); Jennifer Warren (Paula); Edward Binns (Ziegler); Harris Yulin (Marty Heller); Susan Clark (Ellen Moseby); Kenneth Mars (Nick); Janet Ward (Arlene Iverson); James Woods (Quentin); Anthony Costello (Marv Ellman); John Crawford (Tom Iverson); Melanie Griffith (Delly).

Private detective Harry Moseby (Gene Hackman), a one-time football star, is hired by former movie star Arlene Iverson (Janet Ward) to locate her runaway teenage daughter Delly (Melanie Griffith), who has a history of promiscuity and drugs. Since Hackman's wife (Susan Clark) is involved with another man (Harris Yulin) and he has too much free time to brood, he accepts the bothersome case. He finds the subject has gone off with a movie stuntman (Anthony Costello), who fought with Griffith's stuntman boyfriend (James Woods) for her sexual favors. Woods informs Hackman that the teenager may be in Florida with her stepfather (John Crawford), and later a movie production man (Edward Binns) tells him where Crawford lives. On Crawford's Florida island, Hackman meets the man's girlfriend (Jennifer Warren) and during a night swim the two find a crashed plane and the body of its pilot. When Hackman tells her of his assignment, Warren agrees to help. After the detective returns to California, Warren phones Hackman and tells him Griffith has been killed in a movie stunt with Binns, although he survived. Hackman learns from Ward that her daughter is actually back home. This leads him back to Florida and the news that Woods is dead and that he and Crawford had been in the smuggling racket and were after a $500,000 statue. In a fight with Hackman, Crawford dies and the former plans to help Warren recover the statue. The rest of Crawford's gang appear and, in a skirmish, only Hackman survives.

    Director Arthur Penn and writer Alan Sharp tried very hard to resurrect the gangster-detective film noir vogue of the 1940s with this heavy melodrama full of hefty violence and steamy sex. The result, nevertheless, was only a mildly entertaining adventure which had too many loose ends. A major problem was that Hackman wasn't right for this Philip Marlowe-type role. Then too, NIGHT MOVES creeped too slowly for audiences to develop enthusiasm.

NIGHT RIDE (Universal, 1930) 58 mins.

Presenter, Carl Laemmle; director, John S. Robertson; based on the story by Henry La Cossitt; adaptor, Edward T. Lowe; dialogue, Tom Reed, Lowe; titles, Charles Logue; sound, C. Roy Hunter; camera, Alvin Wyckoff; editor, Milton Carruth.

Joseph Schildkraut (Joe Rooker); Barbara Kent (Ruth Kearns); Edward G. Robinson (Tony Garotta); Harry Stubbs (Bob O'Leary); De Witt Jennings (Police Captain); Ralph Welles (Blondie); Hal Price (Mac); George Ovey (Ed).

    When two murders and a payroll robbery happen, news reporter Joe Rooker (Joseph Schildkraut) believes they were committed by gangster Tony Carotta (Edward G. Robinson) because he found one of Robinson's special cigarettes at the scene of the crimes. Later, in the reporters' room at the police precinct, Robinson threatens Schildkraut and tells the newsman he will take out his vengeance on the latter's wife (Barbara Kent). When the gangster escapes from police custody and Schildkraut's house is bombed, the reporter hunts down Robinson with the aid of a friend (Harry Stubbs). In the showdown, Schildkraut brings his wife to safety.

    Although he played a crook in his sound film debut, THE HOLE IN THE WALL (1929), NIGHT RIDE provided Edward G. Robinson with his first real screen portrayal of a menacing gangster, a part he would perfect as Cesare "Little Rico" Bandello in LITTLE CAESAR (see: B/V) later that year. His portrayal of Tony Garotta in this "yarn about a hard-boiled gangster and a hard-boiled reporter" (Photoplay) is substantial, presenting the mobster as a thoroughly wicked and grasping individual.

99 AND 44/100% DEAD (Twentieth Century-Fox, 1974) C 97 mins.

Producer, Joe Wizan; director, John Frankenheimer; screenplay, Robert Dillon; music, Henry Mancini; songs, Mancini and Alan and Marilyn Bergman; art director, Herman Blumenthal; assistant director, Kurt Neumann; sound, Glenn Anderson, Theodore Soderberg; camera, Ralph Woolsey; editor, Harold F. Kress.

Richard Harris (Harry Crown); Edmond O'Brien (Uncle Frank); Bradford Dillman (Big Eddie); Ann Turkel (Buffy); Constance Ford (Dolly); David Hall (Tony); Kathrine Baumann (Baby); Janice Heiden (Clara); Chuck Connors (Marvin "Claw" Zuckerman).

As newsman Paul Harvey would say, "Here is a strange!": a gangster film set in the future with comic-book-type characters, a claw-handed villain, a river full of corpses with cement shoes, and huge albino alligators infesting sewers. Further, this is not some shoestring production, but a major Hollywood release with a top-notch director (John Frankenheimer) and cast (Richard Harris, Edmond O'Brien, Chuck Connors, Bradford Dillman, Constance Ford) and music by Henry Mancini.
    Hit man Harry Crown (Richard Harris) is put on the payroll by mobster Uncle Frank (Edmond O'Brien) who is at war with rival Big Eddie (Bradford Dillman). Harris finds he is caught between the two feuding underworld leaders and he must do battle with Dillman's hired assassin (Connors) whose chief weapon is his metal claw hand which uses various detachable instruments of death.
    Writing in The Films of the Seventies (1984), Marc Sigoloff judged the movie an "offbeat and original gangster saga that resembles a live-action comic book ... a strange spoof of the genre, and it works quite well." More on target was Michael Weldon in The Psychotronic Encyclopedia of Film (1983), who wrote that director "Frankenheimer attempted to make a futuristic, comic-book-style gangster satire. The few who've seen it seem to agree he failed." In its day 99 AND 44/100% DEAD had scant release and received pans from the critic majority.

NOWHERE TO HIDE (Viacom Enterprises/CBS-TV, 6/5/77) C 78 mins.

Executive producer, Mark Carliner; producers, Edward Anhalt, Rift Fournier; associate producer, Roberta Maynes; director, Jack Starrett; story, Anhalt, Fournier; teleplay, Anhalt; music, Ray Ellis; art director, Peter M. Wooley; camera, Jacques R. Marquette; editor, John C. Horger.

Lee Van Cleef (Ike Scanlon); Tony Musante (Joey Faber); Charles Knox Robinson (Deputy Ted Willoughby); Lelia Goldoni (Linda Faber); Noel Fournier (Frankie Faber); Russell Johnson (Charles Montague); Edward Anhalt (Alberto Amarici); John Randolph (Narrator); David Proval (Rick); Clay Tanner (Lee); John McLaughlin (Stan); Robert Hevelone (Giff); Richard Narita (Lou); Stafford Morgan (Ken);

Blackie Dammett (John); Bud Davis (Rudy); Vince Di Paolo (Frederico); John Alderman (Vittorio); John Stefano (Pilot); Bill Yeager (Co-Pilot); Jack Starrett (Gus); Brian Cutler (Gaynes); Isaac Ruiz (Herandez); Ric Dano (Torn); Gene Massey (Coxswain); Araceli Rey (Mrs. Amarrei); Huguette Pateraude (Deputy Rowan).

After more than a decade as the star of Westerns, gangster, and action movies in Europe and other points abroad, one-time Hollywood character actor Lee Van Cleef returned home to headline this made-for-TV movie, the pilot for a series which didn't sell. Writing in TV Guide, Judith Crist called it "a pseudocumentary crime drama.... Its only novelty is that Lee Van Cleef, a Western heavy from HIGH NOON on, is the middle-aged hero and does very well." TV MOVIES (1985) judged it "the stuff B movies did so well." To be noted is that writer-producer Edward Anhalt is cast as the syndicate chief.

When former mob hit man Joey Faber (Tony Musante) agrees to testify against his one-time mobster boss (Edward Anhalt), the government assigns U.S. Marshall Scanlon (Lee Van Cleef) to protect him until the gangster's trial. Van Cleef takes Musante, his wife (Leila Goldoni), and child (Noel Fornier) to a deserted island but the mob finds the place and the two men must unite to defeat the crooks.

NUMBERED MEN (First National, 1930) 65 mins.

Director, Mervyn LeRoy; based on the play Jailbreak by Dwight Taylor; screenplay, Al Cohn, Henry McCarthy; sound, Earl Sitar; camera, Sol Polito; editor, Terrell Morse.

Conrad Nagel (Bertie Gray); Bernice Claire (Mary Dane); Raymond Hackett (Bud Leonard); Ralph Ince (King Callahan); Tully Marshall (Lemuel Barnes); Maurice Black (Lou Rinaldo); William Holden (Warden Lansing); George Cooper (Happy Howard); Blanche Frederici (Mrs. Miller); Ivan Linow (Pollack); Frederick Howard (Jimmy Martin).

Taken from Dwight Taylor's play Jailbreak, this "fair entertainment" (Photoplay) was an early sound entry which was boosted by a good cast and steady direction by Mervyn LeRoy. (Some of the scenes were shot on location at San Quentin prison.) Released prior to the big gangster film craze caused by LITTLE CAESAR and PUBLIC ENEMY (see: B/V for both), NUMBERED MEN is an interesting example of the genre in the days prior to the flood of celluloid big city hoodlums. This outing focuses on the day-to-day activities of minor criminals.

Sent to prison for a decade for counterfeiting, Bud Leonard (Raymond Hackett) is happy knowing Mary (Bernice Claire) will wait for him, and he confides this to fellow inmate Bertie Gray (Conrad Nagel). Meanwhile, the man (Maurice Black) who framed

Hackett tries to seduce Claire, but she rejects him. When Claire learns Hackett will work on the prison road gang she gets a job at a farmhouse where the prisoners are fed in hopes of seeing him, but Black sets up an escape attempt and hopes both Hackett and another inmate (Ralph Ince) will be killed. When the escape does occur, Claire stops Hackett, and Ince, who has a grudge against Black, shoots the gangster. Nagel, facing extra prison time anyway, tells the authorities Hackett was innocent in the escape attempt, and Hackett is returned home to Claire.

ODDS AGAINST TOMORROW (United Artists, 1959) 96 mins.

Producer, Robert Wise; associate producer, Phil Stein; director, Wise; based on the novel by William P. McGivern; screenplay, John O. Killens; music, John Lewis; camera, Joseph Brun; editor, DeDe Allen.

Harry Belafonte (Ingram); Robert Ryan (Slater); Shelley Winters (Lorry); Ed Begley (Burke); Gloria Grahame (Helen); Will Kuluva

Gloria Grahame and Robert Ryan in ODDS AGAINST TOMORROW (1959).

(Bacco); Richard Bright (Coco); Lou Gallo (Moriarity); Fred J. Scollay (Cannoy); Carmen DeLavalade (Kitty); Mae Barnes (Annie); Kim Hamilton (Ruth); Lois Thorne (Eadie); Wayne Rogers (Soldier); Zohra Lampert (Girl); William Zuckert (Bartender); Burt Harris (George); Clint Young (Policeman); Ed Preble (Hotel Clerk); Mil Stewart (Operator); Ronnie Stewart (Fan with Dog); Marc May (Ambulance Attendant); Paul Hoffman (Garry); Cicely Tyson (Fra); William Adams (Bank Guard); Floyd Ennis (Solly); Fred Herrick (Bank Manager); Mary Boylan (Bank Secretary); John Garden (Clerk); Allen Nourse (Police Chief).

Johnny Ingram (Harry Belafonte), a black man, is in debt some $75,000 to a bookie and his life is threatened if he does not pay off. He comes across what he thinks will be an easy bank robbery but he needs help to pull it off. He becomes involved with former convict Dave Burke (Ed Begley) and his cohort, Southern drifter Earle Slater (Robert Ryan), and immediately racial hatred develops between Ryan and Belafonte. Still, they make plans to carry off the heist despite opposition from Belafonte's wife (Kim Hamilton). Meanwhile, Ryan has become involved with a vulgar slut (Shelley Winters) and a nymphomaniac (Gloria Grahame) who lives next door to the men. Eventually the easy heist is thwarted due to Ryan's hatred of Belafonte and the trio are captured.
Filmed in New York City and upstate New York, this "sharp, hard and suspenseful melodrama" (The New York Times) is a clever, gritty, and entertaining film etched with fine performances. Unfortunately the movie flopped in distribution due to its downbeat themes.

O'HARA, UNITED STATES TREASURY: OPERATION COBRA (Mark VII Ltd/Universal/CBS-TV, 4/2/71) C 100 mins.

Executive producers, Jack Webb, James B. Moser; producer, Leonard B. Kaufman; associate producer, William Stark; director, Webb; teleplay, Moser; music, Ray Heindorf, William Lava; song, Heindorf; art director, William D. DeCinces; aerial camera, James Gavin; camera, Alric Edens; editor, Warren H. Adams.

David Janssen (James O'Hara); Lana Wood (Fran Harper); Jerome Thor (Marty Baron); Gary Crosby (Harry Fish); Charles McGraw (Agent Joe Flagg); Jack Ging (Agent Garrick); Stacy Harris (Agent Ben Hazzard); William Conrad (Keegan); Jim B. Smith (Phil Phillips); Michael Road (Russ Novack); John David Chandler (Al Garver-- Henchman); Burt Mustin (Len Clancy); Timothy Brown (Tim Shelley); John McCook (Captain Shafer); Jack Webb (Narrator of Foreword); and: Ed Peck, Joe E. Tata, James McEachin.

James O'Hara (David Janssen), the one-time sheriff of a small town, becomes an agent for the Treasury Department and among his assignments is bringing to justice a gang of hashish smugglers.

Lana Wood and David Janssen in O'HARA, UNITED STATES TREAS-
URY: OPERATION COBRA (1971).

The chase takes him around the country as he works with various
cohorts such as Fran Harper (Lana Wood), Joe Flagg (Charles
McGraw), Garrick (Jack Ging), and Ben Hazzard (Stacy Harris) in
bringing to justice the head of the multi-million-dollar-per-year
narcotics operation.

This contrived vehicle served as the pilot for the "O'Hara,
U.S. Treasury" CBS-TV series which starred David Janssen and
ran during the 1971-72 video season. MOVIES ON TV (1985) noted,
"The agents talk in code, using that efficient, manly, clipped, no-
smiling technique which has become Webb's TV trademark; but in
this pilot film, Treasury jargon is constant and fans need a few
subtitles."

A.k.a.: OPERATION COBRA

ONCE UPON A TIME IN AMERICA (Warner Bros., 1984) C 135 mins.

Executive producer, Claudio Mancini; producer, Arnon Milchan;
production executive, Fred Caruso; director Sergio Leone; based
on the novel The Hoods by Harry Grey; screenplay, Leonardo Benvenuti, Piero De Bernardo, Enrico Medioli, Franco Arcalli, Franco
Ferrini, Leone; art director, Carlo Simi; assistant directors, Fabrizio
Sergenti Castellani, Dennis Benatar, Amy Wells; music, Ennio

Morricone; costumes, Richard Bruno, Gabriella Pescucci; camera, Tonino Delli Colli; editor, Nino Baragli.

Robert DeNiro (Noodles); James Woods (Max); Elizabeth McGovern (Deborah); Treat Williams (Jimmy O'Donnell); Tuesday Weld (Carol); Burt Young (Joe); Joe Pesci (Frankie); William Forsythe (Cockeye); James Hayden (Patsy); Darlanne Fleugel (Eve); Larry Rapp (Fat Moe); Dutch Miller (Van Linden); Robert Harper (Sharkey); Richard Bright (Chicken Joe); Gerard Murphy (Crowning); Amy Ryder (Peggy); Olga Karlatos (Woman in Puppet Theatre); Mario Brega (Mandy); Ray Dittrich (Trigger); Frank Gio (Beefy); Angelo Florio (Willie the Ape; Scott Tiler (Young Noodles); Rusty Jacobs (Young Max/David); Brian Bloom (Young Patsy); Adrian Curran (Young Cockeye); Mike Monetti (Young Fat Moe); Noah Moazezi (Dominic); James Russo (Bugsy); Frankie Caserta, Joey Marzella (Bugsy's Gang); Joey Faye (Adorable Old Man).

Italian director Sergio Leone is one of those lionized European directors who has a cult following in Europe and a place in the hearts of highbrow critics in the United States. Actually the filmmaker's reputation rests on a quartet of spaghetti Westerns he made at home in the mid-1960s: PER UN PUGNO DI DOLLARI [A Fistful of Dollars] (1964), PER QUALCHE DOLLARI IN PIU [For a Few Dollars More] (1965), IL BUONO, IL BRUTTO, IL CATTIVO [The Good, the Bad and the Ugly] (1966), and C'ERA UNA VOLTA IL WEST [Once Upon a Time in the West] (1968). Since then, Leone has only helmed the none-too-popular GIU LA TESTA [Duck You Sucker] in 1970 and produced and initiated the story for IL MIO NOME NESSUNO [My Name Is Nobody] four years later. ONCE UPON A TIME IN AMERICA marked his long-heralded return to the big screen, but this "... sprawling saga of Jewish gangsters over the decades is surprisingly deficient in clarity and purpose, as well as excitement and narrative involvement" (Variety). On the other hand, there were many critics who championed the box-office disaster: "The uncut ONCE UPON A TIME IN AMERICA is ... a magnificent fairy tale of crime and history, of melancholy, bloodshed, ribaldry, money and violence, failed love and crazy grandeur. However suspicious you may be, you owe it to yourself to test the accolade" (LA Weekly).

The storyline crisscrosses the lives of several people in a juxtaposition of time frames from the 1920s through the 1960s. The narrative is centered around small-time hoodlum David "Noodles" Aaronson (Robert DeNiro) and his clique of friends, their exploits, betrayals, and love affairs. Due to its excessive length and jumping from time period to time period, the story is hard to follow, wallowing in long periods without dialogue, using brooding pantomime to carry across its alleged message. The main flaw is that the basic story is not very appealing and its prime character is hardly ingratiating. DeNiro's Noodles is a hard rock of a person, hardly ever likable and brutal both in his gangster dealings and in his love life, as witnessed by his rape of two of the women in his life.

The film opens in 1933 with rival gangsters out to get DeNiro by murdering several of his pals and his girlfriend. The narrative then jumps thirty five years with DeNiro returning to Manhattan to meet his old boyhood friend (Larry Rapp) and picking up a great deal of money for some future venture. The tale then reverts to the 1920s and shows how DeNiro and his pals grew up in the city's Lower East Side and became a part of the area's gangland populace. The boys develop into a well-oiled gang carrying out a big diamond robbery and becoming notorious hoods as a result. Later they get the goods on a police chief and fight with others gangsters for control of labor rackets, but this leads to DeNiro and his best pal (James Woods) disagreeing over the robbery of a federal bank. The film then moves forward to 1968 and the final confrontation between DeNiro and Woods.

Reportedly costing over $32,000,000 to complete, this elaborately inflated feature ran 227+ minutes when reviewed at the Cannes Film Festival in 1984, but the 150-minute version issued in the U.S. by Warner Brothers was chopped to 139 minutes for television. Leone, however, reportedly only recognized the full-length version as his.

As with any Leone film, it is not without special interest. The film's sets, especially the recreation of New York City during Prohibition, are authentic and the photography of Tonino Delli Colli provides an aura of professionalism not always substantiated by the plot. While Ennio Morricone's score is hardly one of his best, it does have its passages of pleasurable listening.

It should be noted that a six-hour rendition of the movie was prepared for Italian television. In that version Louise Fletcher plays the role of the Riverdale Directress, a part which does not appear in the 227-minute edition.

ONE DOWN TWO TO GO (Almi, 1982) C 84 mins.

Executive producer, Robert Atwell; producer, Fred Williamson; associate producers, Randy Jurgensen, Stan Wakerfield, David Moon; director, Williamson; screenplay, Jeff Williamson; camera, James Lemmo; editor, Daniel Loewenthal.

Fred Williamson (Cal); Jim Brown (J); Jim Kelly (Chuck); Richard Roundtree (Ralph); Paula Sills (Teri); Laura Loftus (Sally); Tom Signorelli (Mario); Joe Spinell (Joe); Louis Neglia (Armando); Peter Dane (Rossi); Victoria Hale (Maria); Richard Noyce (Hank); John Guitz (Bob); Warrington Winters (Sheriff); Arthur Haggerty (Mojo); Irwin Litvack (Banker); Addison Greene (Pete); Dennis Singletary (Roy); John Dorish (Deputy); Robert Pastner (Slim); Patty O'Brien (Nurse).

The days of black exploitation features such as BLACK CAESAR and HELL UP IN HARLEM (see: B/V for both), both starring Fred Williamson, were dim memories when the star helmed this low-budget project which reunited him with Jim Brown and

Jim Kelly from 1974's THREE THE HARD WAY. This production also added Richard "Shaft" Roundtree for box-office take, while perennial bad guy Joe Spinell provided flair to a mundane actioner.

The pauper's plot has Ralph (Roundtree), a promoter-publicity man, setting up a martial arts tournament only to have gangsters grab the proceeds. To gain revenge, he allies himself with slick Cal (Williamson), tough guy J (Brown), and martial arts expert Chuck (Kelly). Eventually the quartet overwhelm the mobsters.

Of the four male black stars, only Richard Roundtree gives a performance. Technically, the film is below par.

THE 1000 EYES OF DR. MABUSE (Ajay Films, 1966) 103 mins.

Executive producer, Arthur Brauner; producer-director, Fritz Lang; idea, Jan Fethke; screenplay, Lang, Heinz Oskar Wuttig; art directors; Erich Kettelhut, Johanness Ott; music, Bert Grund; costumes, Ina Stein; makeup, Heinz Stamm; sound, Eduard Kessel; camera, Karl-Heinz Linke, Ernst Zahrt; editor, Walter Wischniewsky.

Dawn Addams (Marion Menil); Peter Van Eyck (Henry B. Travers); Gert Frobe (Commissioner Krauss); Wolfgang Preiss (Jordan); Werner Peters (Heironymous P. Mistelzweig); Andrea Checchi (Inspector Berg); Reinhard Holldehoff (Klumpfuss); Howard Vernon (#12); Jean-Jacques Delbo (Servant); Lupo Prezzo (Cornelius); Christiane Maybach (Pretty Blonde); David Camerone (Travers' Secretary); Nico Pepe (Hotel Manager); Werner Buttler (#11); Linda Sini (Corinna); Rolf Mobius (Police Officer); Bruno W. Pantel (Reporter); and: Marie-Luise Nagel, Albert Bessler.

After returning to his homeland of West Germany in the late 1950s to make the two-part feature DAS INDISCHE GRABMAL (1958), director Fritz Lang was offered several motion picture projects, including a remake of his 1933 thriller DAS TESTAMENT DES MR. MABUSE (q.v.), but he turned it down and it was done in 1962 (q.v.) by director Werner Klingler. Instead Lang agreed to do an entirely new Dr. Mabuse movie, for which he co-authored the scenario. The movie was his final directorial effort. Regarding the result, Paul M. Jensen appraises in The Cinema of Fritz Lang (1969), "... the film is weak; it is not boring, but it is ordinary and dated. Old-fashioned technical flaws include very wobbly process shots, schmaltzy music ... and even some slowing-down of the camera's speed to hype the action. The final chase, with machine guns firing from car to car with little apparent effects, belongs in a Thirties gangster movie. Though there is a lot of plot, several threads remain tangled and the scripts contain much talk, but little tension. There are really no characters here at all, just personalities, eccentrics, and types--nothing human."

DIE 1000 AUGEN DES MR. MABUSE is in many ways a pseudo-Dr. Mabuse movie. The character of the madman hypnotist criminal does not actually appear in the film but instead it deals with a master criminal, Dr. Jordan (Wolfgang Preiss), who steals the police file on Mabuse and uses the madman's methods in his plans to amass a great fortune through criminal activities, including the use of gangsters. In the guise of the mild mannered head of a mental clinic, Preiss is responsible for fifteen unsolved crimes connected with a luxurious hotel. Police superintendent Krass (Frobe) investigates the case and notices the similarities between the crimes and those committed by Mabuse years before. Meanwhile, Preiss uses a beautiful patient (Dawn Addans) to ensnarl wealthy American Henry Travers (Peter Van Eyck) whom he plans to murder after the girl has married him so Preiss can take control of the man's fortunes and industries. The plot fails when Addams falls in love with Van Eyck and through them the police are able to gain evidence against Preiss, who dies in a shootout.

Although only mediocre, DIE 1000 AUGEN DES DR. MABUSE was responsible for a rash of West German programmers based on the characters created by Norbert Jacques in his series of novels about Dr. Mabuse, including the aforementioned remake of DAS TESTATMENT, the INVISIBLE DR. MABUSE (1962), DR. MABUSE VS. SCOTLAND YARD (1963), THE SECRET OF DR. MABUSE (1964), and DR. MABUSE (1971), the last being a Spanish-West German co-production.

OPERATION COBRA see: O'HARA, UNITED STATES TREASURY: OPERATION COBRA

OPERATION M: see: THE FAKERS

OPERATION ST. PETER'S (Paramount, 1968) C 88 mins.

Producer, Turi Vasile; director, Lucio Fulci; screenplay, Ennio De Concini, Adriano Baracco, Robert Gianviti, Fulci; assistant director, Francesco Massaro; art director, Giorgio Giovannini; camera, Erico Menczer.

Lando Buzzanca (Napoleon); Edward G. Robinson (Joe); Heinz Ruhmann (Cardinal Braun); Jean-Claude Brialy (Cajella); Pinuccio Ardia (The Baron); Dante Maggio (The Captain); Ugo Fancareggi (Agonia); Marie-Christine Barclay (Marisa); Uta Levka (Samanth); Antonella Delle Porti (Cesira).

Filmed in Italy and issued there in 1967 as OPERAZIONE SAN PIETRO [Operation St. Peter's], this tongue-in-cheek effort was one of a trio of genre outings for veteran Edward G. Robinson, none of which helped his fading screen career.

A gang of bumbling thieves try to rob a bank and end up tunneling into the security cell of the police station and then into a funeral home. Finally their leader (Lando Buzzanca) decides they will steal Michelangelo's statue "La Pieta" from Rome's Vatican Basilica. Surprisingly the heist is accomplished and the gang then enlists the aid of mobsters led by Joe (Robinson) and Samantha (Uta Levka) in disposing of the statue. The gangsters plan to take it outside Italian territorial waters and ransom it back to the Vatican, but when they kill two of the thieves, Buzzanca's girlfriend (Marie-Christine Barclay) convinces him to confess the theft to a priest. This act puts the Cardinal (Heinz Ruhmann) on the trail of the gangsters and he gains the assistance of religious people in finding the statue. At the end, the hoodlums are defeated and the statue is returned in time for Easter services.

OPERAZIONE SAN PIETRO see: OPERATION ST. PETER'S

OUT OF SINGAPORE (Goldsmith, 1932) 61 mins.

Producer, Ken Goldsmith; director, Charles Hutchison; story, Fred Chapin; screenplay, John S. Nattleford; assistant director, Melville De Lay; sound, Freeman Lang; camera, Edward S. Kull; editor, S. Roy Luby.

Noah Beery (Woolf Barstow); Dorothy Burgess (Concha); Miriam Seegar (Mary Carroll); Montague Love (Scar Murray); George Walsh (Steve Trent); Jimmie Aubrey (Bloater); William Moran (Captain Carroll); Olin Francis (Bill); Ethan Laidlaw (Second Mate Miller); Leon Wong (Wong); Horace B. Carpenter (Captain Smith); Fred "Snowflake" Toones (Snowball); Ernest Butterworth (Sailor).

Woolf Barstow (Noah Beery), who has lost the three previous ships he commanded, is signed on as first mate of a cargo ship along with associate Scar Murray (Montagu Love). Beery, coveting the captain's pretty daughter (Miriam Seegar), slowly poisons the skipper and when they reach Singapore he culminates a deal with a corrupt Chinese merchant (Leon Wong) to take on a bogus cargo and then sink the ship for insurance money. While there he rejects his ex-love (Dorothy Burgess) and she gets even by stowing away on the ship. Beery hires a drunk (George Walsh) to work on the ship along with the latter's friend (Jimmie Aubrey) as the cook. Back at sea, the captain (William Moran) makes one last effort to stop Beery but the latter kills him. Burgess convinces Seegar of Beery's evil intentions and enlists the aid of Walsh, who changes his way. Seegar, Walsh, and Aubrey escape and the rest aboard are blown up.
A true poverty row film, the picture is nonetheless fun thanks to Noah Beery and Montagu Love as the shipboard gangsters.
When reissued by Astor Pictures in the 1940s, the film was retitled GANGSTERS OF THE SEA.

OUT OF THE PAST see: AGAINST ALL ODDS

OUTSIDE THE THREE MILE LIMIT (Columbia, 1940) 64 mins.

Director, Lewis D. Collins; story, Albert DeMond, Eric Taylor; screenplay, DeMond; music, Lee Zahler; camera, James S. Brown, Jr.; editor, Dwight Caldwell.

Jack Holt (Conway); Harry Carey (Captain Bailey); Sig Rumann (Van Cleve); Eduardo Ciannelli (Reeves); Donald Briggs (Rothacker); Irene Ware (Dorothy); Dick Purcell (Pierce); Ben Welden (Shores); Paul Fix (Swanson); George Lewis (Morrow).

The penultimate feature entry in Jack Holt's long running action series for Columbia Pictures, OUTSIDE THE THREE MILE LIMIT is an intriguing gangster opus which relies more on plot flow and dialogue than on the usual fist fights and chases.
Holt is Secret Service operative Conway, who works on a gambling boat off the California coast where the owner, gangster Reeves (Eduardo Ciannelli), is suspected of planting bogus money on the customers. Also aboard are two reporters (Irene Ware, Donald Briggs) looking for a big story, and the vessel's honest captain (Harry Carey). When fellow government man Pierce (Dick Purcell) disobeys orders and tries to arrest Ciannelli, he is thrown overboard, and the gangster takes the ship beyond the three-mile limit. The crew, however, in the pay of rival hoodlum Van Cleve (Sig Rumann), a dealer in fake coins, wants $50,000 in real money which Ciannelli has in his possession. The ship ends up in Central America before Holt can bring the crooks to justice.
In The Fabulous Holts (1976), Buck Rainey termed this feature "... a good, solid though inexpensive mystery meller. The acting was subtle, yet active enough to please the patrons at whom the picture is aimed. And, with the exception of a few miniature shots, the film is above par for a picture in this budget bracket, definitely deserving the seal of class."

THE PACE THAT KILLS see: THE COCAINE FIENDS

PAID TO DANCE (Columbia, 1937) 55 mins.

Director, C. C. Coleman, Jr.; story, Leslie T. White; screenplay, Robert E. Kent; music director, Morris Stoloff; camera, George Meehan; editor, Byrd Robinson.

Don Terry (William Dennis); Jacqueline Wells [Julie Bishop] (Joan Bradley); Rita Hayworth (Betty Morgan); Arthur Loft (Jack Miranda); Paul Stanton (Charles Kennely); Paul Fix (Nifty); Louise Stanley (Phyllis Parker); Ralph Byrd (Nickels Brown); Beatrice Curtis (Frances Mitchell); Bess Flowers (Suzy); Beatrice Blinn (Lois); Jane Hamilton (Evelyn); Dick Curtis (Mike Givens); Al Herman (Joe Krause); Thurston Hall (Governor); John Gallaudet

Paul Fix, Jacqueline Wells [Julie Bishop], and Beatrice Curtis in
PAID TO DANCE (1937).

(Barney Wilson); Horace McMahon (LaRue); George Lloyd (Sanders);
Ruth Hilliard (Ruth Gregory); Ann Doran (Rose Trevor); Bud
Jamison (Lieutenant); Bill Irving (Salesman); Eddie Fetherston
(Skipper); Edward Le Saint (Magistrate); Ernest Wood (Francine);
Lee Prather (McDonald); Jay Eaton, Stanley Mack, Ethan Laidlaw,
Arthur Stuart Hull (Men); Georgie Cooper (Mrs. Daniels); Edward
Hearn (Butler); Bill Lally, Dan Wolheim, Dick Rush, Bruce Mitchell
(Cops); George Lollier (Sailor); Jack Cheatham (Radio Cop); Bud
McTaggart (Newsboy); Edward Peil, Sr. (Conductor); Walter Law-
rence (News Vendor); Nell Craig (Woman); Harry Strang (Attendant).

     In a large metropolis, racketeers control the dance hall "busi-
ness" and the police send undercover agent William Dennis (Don
Terry) and Joan Bradley (Jacqueline Wells) to investigate. The
former takes on the guise of a hoodlum and works for mobster Jack
Miranda (Arthur Loft), the boss of the dance hall operation, while
Wells becomes a dancer at the clip joint and acquires the needed
evidence to convict Loft through unhappy hostess Betty Morgan
(Rita Hayworth). Both agents, however, are nearly killed by gangsters before they can shut down the racket.
     Obviously made to cash in on the popularity of Warner Bros.'
MARKED WOMAN (see: B/V), PAID TO DANCE "has all the ear-
marks of being churned out with a minimum of expense and effort"

(Variety). Running under one hour, the film moves quickly but makes little sense as events push by so rapidly they almost defy viewer credulity. Of particular interest is the opportunity to view Rita Hayworth in her salad days.
TV title: HARD TO HOLD

PAROLE FIXER (Paramount, 1940) 57 mins.

Producer, Edward T. Lowe; director, Robert Florey; based on the book Persons in Hiding by J. Edgar Hoover; screenplay, William Lipman, Horace McCoy; music, Boris Morros; art directors, Hans Dreier, John Goodman; camera, George Barnes; editor, Harvey Johnston.

William Henry (Scott Britton); Virginia Dale (Enid Casserly); Robert Paige (Steve Eddson); Gertrude Michael (Collette Menthe); Richard Denning (Bruce Eaton); Faye Helm (Rita Mattison); Anthony Quinn (Francis "Big Boy" Bradmore); Harvey Stephens (Bartley Hanford); Marjorie Gateson (Mrs. Thornton Casserly); Charlotte Wynters (Nellie); Lyle Talbot (Ross Waring); Louise Beavers (Aunt Lindy); Wilfred Roberts (Frank Preston); Jack Carson (George Mattison); John Gallaudet (Edward Bradshaw); Eddie Marr (Edward "Slim" Racky); Morgan Wallace (Ben); Sonny Bupp (Bobby Mattison); Billy Lee (Jimmy Mattison); Harry Shannon (Randall Porter); Russell Hicks (Judge); Edwin Maxwell (Edward Murkil); Mary Hart (Mrs. Tilden); Olaf Hytten (Carter); Ed Mortimer (Mr. Tilden); Byron Foulger (Florist); Doodles Weaver (Edward the Florist's Helper); Paul McGrath (Tyler Craden).

The third of four "B" features Paramount milked from J. Edgar Hoover's book Persons in Hiding (1938), this was the "weakest structurally of the four Hoover films, it was saved largely by its cast, another Paramount example of loading the screen with familiar faces" (Don Miller, B Movies, 1973). Reviewing the feature at the time of its distribution, Variety reported, "Its story structure is typically cops-and-robbers, with several opportunities to display routines and workings of the FBI along scientific lines."
A corrupt lawyer (Paul McGrath) controls a local parole board and uses his mob connections to have hoodlums released from prison. Once out they continue their lives of crime with the mouthpiece obtaining a percentage of their ill-gotten gains. When McGrath masterminds the kidnapping of a wealthy young woman, the FBI brings about the gang's downfall.
As noted above, this entry is bursting with seasoned personalities, most of them members of the studio's stock company: Robert Paige, Gertrude Michael, Richard Denning, Anthony Quinn, Marjorie Gateson, Charlotte Wynters, Lyle Talbot, Louise Beavers, Jack Carson.

Michael O'Shea, Michael Whalen, and James Cardwell in PAROLE, INC. (1948).

PAROLE, INC. (Eagle Lion, 1948) 71 mins.

Producer, Constantin J. David; director, Alfred Zeisler; story, Sherman L. Lowe, Royal K. Cole; screenplay, Lowe; music, Alexander Lasda; camera, Gilbert Warrenton; editor, John D. Faure.

Michael O'Shea (Richard Hendricks); Turhan Bey (Barney Rodescu); Evelyn Ankers (Jojo Dumont); Virginia Lee (Glenda Palmer); Charles Bradstreet (Harry Palmer); Lyle Talbot (Police Commissioner); Michael Whalen (Kid Redmond); Charles Williams (Titus Jones); James Cardwell (Duke Vigill); Paul Bryar (Charles Newton); Noel Cravat (Blackie Olson); Charles Jordan (Monty Cooper).

Government man Richard Hendricks (Michael O'Shea) is after a parole fixing gang which bribes parole boards to spring criminals out of the penitentiary so they can rejoin their mob for more criminal activities. (If this sounds familiar, note the plot premise of PAROLE FIXER, 1937, supra.) To discover the mastermind of the gambit, O'Shea becomes part of the gang, but one of his cohorts is killed and another nearly dies before he can put the finger on corrupt Barney Rodescu (Turhan Bey) who is controlling the parole fixing activities.

Here the emphasis is on the G-man who brings the crooks to justice as well as the actual bagman behind the operation.

PAROLED FROM THE BIG HOUSE (J. D. Kendis, 1938) 57 mins.

Producer, J. D. Kendis; director, Elmer Clifton; screenplay, George
Plympton; camera, Eddie Linden.

Jean Carmen (Pat Mallory); Richard Adams (Slicker Nixon); George
Eldredge (Red Herron); Gwen Lee (Binnie Bell); Milbourne [Milburn]
Stone (District Attorney Downey); Walter Anthony (Joe "Killer"
Britt); Ole Olesen (Torchy); Earl Douglass (Hoke Curtis--alias
"The Duke"); Eddie Kaye (Gunner Carson); Joe Devlin (Jed Cross);
Eleanor De Van (Rita).

Big city District Attorney Downey (Milburn Stone) is fighting
the prison parole board because the latter is releasing hardened
criminals to commit more crimes. One such mobster is Slicker Nixon
(Richard Adams), who forms a protection racket which extorts
money from honest businessmen, including one who is murdered
when he refuses to cooperate. His pretty daughter Pat Mallory
(Jean Carmen) vows revenge and pretends to be a gun moll to become part of the group. She realizes later that gang member Red
Herron (George Eldredge) is a policeman who has joined the "boys"
to get the goods on Adams for the murder of his partner. At the
final shootout, the policeman kills the gangster leader.
Made at the bottom depths of poverty row by the same producer, director, and star who turned out the bad movie classic
WOLVES OF THE SEA (1938), this entry is listless entertainment.
The movie does present a very diverse group of gangsters, with
the gang including a wide array of murderers and thieves as well
as a firebug called Torchy (Ole Olesen) and a marijuana addict
(Gwen Lee). On a positive note, Jean Carmen is fetching as the
heroine and Milburn Stone is impressive in his Thomas E. Dewey-
like performance as the crusading district attorney.

PARTNERS IN CRIME (Paramount, 1937) 66 mins.

Director, Ralph Murphy; based on the novel by Kurt Stell; screenplay, Garnett Weston; camera, Henry Sharp.

Lynne Overman (Hank Hyer); Roscoe Karns (Slim Perkins); Muriel
Hutchison (Odette La Vin); Anthony Quinn (Nicholas Massaney);
Inez Courtney (Lillian Tate); Lucien Littlefield (Mr. Twitchell);
Charles Halton (Silas Wagon); Charles Wilson (Inspector Simpson);
June Brewster (Mabel); Esther Howard (Mrs. Wagon); Nora Cecil
(Housekeeper); Russell Kicks (Mayor Callaghan); Don Brodie (Re-
porter); Archie Twitchell (Photographer).

Hank Hyer was the character in a series of well written and
entertaining detective novels by Kurt Stell, and the character of
Hyer and his newspaperman pal Slim Perkins first came to the screen
in 1937 in MURDER GOES TO COLLEGE with Lynne Overman as the
gumshoe and Roscoe Karns as the newsman. The picture was

Lynne Overman, Inez Courtney, and Roscoe Karns in PARTNERS IN CRIME (1937).

successful enough to spawn a series, but the next outing, PARTNERS IN CRIME, bordered on the lackluster and the proposed series was halted.

A town is controlled by a crooked mayor (Russell Hicks) and racketeers run rampant. Private eye Hank Hyer (Overman) discovers a plot to discredit the mayor's reform opponent, so he sets out to stop this by romancing a gangster's moll (Muriel Hutchison) and by putting his newspaper buddy Slim Perkins (Karns) as a candidate on the independent ticket. The actions bring about the mayor's and the gang's defeat, but for his troubles, well-meaning Overman is escorted out of town.

PARTY GIRL (Tiffany, 1930) 73 mins.

Director, Victor Halperin; based on the novel <u>Dangerous Business</u> by Edwin Balmer; screenplay, Monte Katterjohn, George Draney, Halperin; songs; Harry Stoddard and Marcy Klauber; sound, R. S. Clayton, William R. Fox, Alfred M. Granich, Ben Harper; camera, Henry Cronjager, Robert Newhard; editor, Russell Schoengarth.

Douglas Fairbanks, Jr. (Jay Roundtree); Jeanette Loff (Ellen Powell); Judith Barrie (Leeda Cather); Marie Prevot (Diana Hoster);

John St. Polis (John Roundtree); Sammy Blum (Sam Metten); Harry Northrup (Bert Lowry); Almeda Fowler (Maude Lindsay); Hal Price (Lew Evans); Charles Giblyn (Lawrence Doyle); Sidney D'Albrook (Investigator); Lucien Prival (Paul Newcast); Florence Dudley (Miss Manning); Earl Burtnett's Biltmore Orchestra and Trio (Themselves).

College man Jay Roundtree (Douglas Fairbanks, Jr.) is engaged to marry his father's (John St. Polis) secretary (Jeanette Loff), a one-time party girl. As a lark, he and fraternity brothers crash a business party at a hotel which employs party girls and there he meets Leeda (Judith Barrie), who is secretly pregnant. Taking a liking to Fairbanks, she gets him drunk and when he wakes up the next day in her apartment, she claims he seduced her and they get married. This drives Loff back to the party girl racket but later the police raid a party and find Barrie there. While interrogating her she attempts to escape and is killed falling from a window. Fairbanks and Loff are later reconciled.

PARTY GIRL is an exploitation film which examines the party girl racket, a thinly veiled term for prostitution. The movie also pokes fun at decadent upper class morality as in the scene where the fraternity boys drive their flivver up an elevator and right into the middle of the business party. The film encompasses quite a bit of questionable activity which would NOT have been tolerated after the institution of the 1933 film industry morality code. One such scene has plump party girl Diana (Marie Prevost) being carried into an adjoining room by a gang of rowdies with her yelling for them to quit tickling her as several others watch through the door and laugh at the "goings-on."

Originally reviewed as DANGEROUS BUSINESS and based on Edwin Balmer's 1927 novel of that title, the movie was directed by Victor Halperin who would turn out the low-budget horror film classic WHITE ZOMBIE two years later.

PARTY GIRL (Metro-Goldwyn-Mayer, 1958) 99 mins.

Producer, Joe Pasternak; director, Nicholas Ray; story, Leo Katcher; screenplay, George Wells; music, Jeff Alexander; camera, Robert Bronner; editor, John McSweeney.

Robert Taylor (Thomas Farrell); Cyd Charisse (Vicki Gaye); Lee J. Cobb (Rico Angelo); John Ireland (Louis Canette); Kent Smith (Jeffrey Stewart); Claire Kelly (Genevieve); Corey Allen (Cookie); Lewis Charles (Danny Rimett); David Opatoshu (Lou Forbes); Dem Dibbs (Joey Vulner); Patrick McVey (O'Malley); Barbara Lang (Tall Blonde); Mryna Hansen (Joy Hampton); Betty Utey (Showgirl).

This "new" PARTY GIRL has no relationship to the 1930 release detailed supra. Still it was similar in that it told of the use of party girls, this time by gangsters. Set in 1930s Chicago, the movie unfolds the tale of a corrupt gangster chief (Lee J. Cobb)

Robert Taylor and Cyd Charisse (left center) in PARTY GIRL
(1958).

who employs the services of a crippled attorney (Robert Taylor).
The lawyer, however, falls in love with a pretty dancer (Cyd
Charisse) in the pay of the hoodlum and when he believes her life
is threatened he goes to a prosecutor and tells all he knows about
the gangland activities, setting both himself and his lady love up
for execution. The law comes to the rescue and the couple is
saved.

With its superior recreation of the Prohibition era, amiable
performances by Robert Taylor and Lee J. Cobb as the somewhat
likable mobster, and well-executed dances by Cyd Charisse, PARTY
GIRL is a colorful melodrama displaying the virtues of the big studio
(Metro-Goldwyn-Mayer) even in its swan song days. The film's title tune is sung by Tony Martin, the husband of Cyd Charisse.

THE PAY OFF (RKO, 1930) 65 mins.

Director, Lowell Sherman; story, Samuel Shipman; screenplay, Jane
Murfin; art director, Max Ree; sound, Bailey Sesler; camera, J.
Roy Hunt; editor, Rose Smith.

Lowell Sherman (Gene Fenmore); Marion Nixon (Annabelle); Hugh
Trevor (Rocky); William Janney (Tommy); Helen Millard (Dot);

George F. Marion (Mouse); Walter McGrail (Emory); Robert McWade (Frank); Alan Roscoe (District Attorney); Lita Chevret (Margy); Bert Moorhouse (Spat).

Termed "a pip" by Photoplay magazine, this gangster melo-drama was directed by star Lowell Sherman who portrays a sophis-ticated, well dressed hoodlum with slick manners and underworld cunning. Soon such screen mobsters would be replaced oncamera with more earthy counterparts like those depicted in LITTLE CAE-SAR, THE PUBLIC ENEMY, and SCARFACE (see: B/V for all).
Suave Gene Fenmore (Sherman) is the head of a theft opera-tion. The gang holds up a young engaged couple (Marion Nixon, William Janney). Janney recognizes one of the gang members (Hugh Trevor) and he and his fiancee set out to regain their possessions but are captured by the gang and taken to Sherman, who offers them jobs. Against his orders, Trevor later has them join in a holdup and he kills a man and the youngsters are arrested for the homicide. Sherman, not wanting the innocent couple to be tried, confesses to planning the robbery and turns in Trevor. As a re-sult, his gang kills him.

PENITENTIARY (Jerry Gross Organization, 1979) C 99 mins.

Producer-director-screenplay, Jamaa Fanaka; music, Frankie Gaye; art director, Adel Mazen; camera, Marty Olistein; editor, Betsy Blankett.

Leon Isaac Kennedy (Too Sweet Gordon); Tommy Pollard (Eugene); Hazel Spears (Linda); Badja Djola (Wilson); Gloria Delaney (Inmate); Chuck Mitchell (Lieutenant Arnsworth); Wilbur "Hi-Fi" White (Sweat Pea).

Sent to prison on circumstantial evidence for a crime he didn't commit, Too Sweet Gordon (Leon Isaac Kennedy) quickly learns that might makes right behind bars and he pulverizes his bigger cellmate after the latter tries to rape him. To survive sane, Kennedy de-velops his boxing skills and takes part in prison competition and tournaments and wins sexual visitations with his girlfriend (Hazel Spears) as well as early parole.
This was the third feature film for producer-director-writer Jamaa Fanaka and it was far more interesting than the run-of-the-mill black exploitation pictures, particularly in its sordid but real-istic look at prison environment. According to Variety, "Fanaka's greatest success comes in his delineation of the brutal realities of prison life ... incarceration is shown to be a supreme test of char-acter strength, with some men growing, others going crazy, and a few simply going under."

PENITENTIARY II (Metro-Goldwyn-Mayer/United Artists, 1982) C
103 mins.

Producer, Jamaa Fanaka; associate producers, Albert Shepard,
Ayanne Dulaney; director-screenplay, Fanaka; music, Jack W.
Wheaton; assistant director, Eric Jewett; sound, Russel Williams;
camera, Steve Posey; editor, James E. Nownes.

Leon Isaac Kennedy (Too Sweet Gordon); Glynn Turman (Charles);
Ernie Hudson (Half Dead); Mr. T (Himself); Peggy Blow (Ellen);
Sephton Moody (Charles, Jr.); Donovan Womack (Jesse); Malik
Carter (Seldom); Stan Kamber (Sam); Cepheus Jaxon (Do Dirty);
Marvin Jones(Simp); Ebony Wright (Sugar); Eugenita Wright
(Clarisse); Renn Woods (Nikki); Marci Thomas (Evelyn); Dennis
Libscomb, Gerald Bersn (Announcers); Joe Anthony Cox (Midget).

 Following the successful PENITENTIARY, supra, an independent release from the Jerry Gross Organization, producer-writer-
scripter Jamaa Fanaka reteamed with star Leon Isaac Kennedy for
this followup which won major distribution from Metro-Goldwyn-
Mayer/United Artists. Unfortunately this sequel proved to be a
"cheap, exploitative, preposterously dumb mess" (Variety).
 Too Sweet Gordon (Leon Isaac Kennedy) gets out of prison
through his ring career and retires to the good life. His enemy,
Half Dead (Ernie Hudson), however, wants him killed and he and
his henchman Do Dirty (Cepheus Jaxon) and Simp (Marvin Jones)
trail Kennedy to the house of a girlfriend, whom Hudson knifes to
death, causing the fighter to return to the ring on a path of revenge and regeneration. To clinch the fight with the champ (Donovan Womack), the hoodlums kidnap the boxer's family and hold them
hostage so he will be forced to throw the match. As Kennedy is
taking a terrible beating in the ring, his brother-in-law (Glynn
Turman) captures the gangsters and sets the family free. Word
gets back to the fighter who then scores a knockout.
 Almost as puerile as it sounds, PENITENTIARY II has few
redeeming qualities. The characters of Half Dead, Do Dirty, and
Simp are amusing in a perverse way, and Mr. T even shows up as
himself.

PENTHOUSE (Metro-Goldwyn-Mayer, 1933) 90 mins.

Associate producer, Hunt Stromberg; director, W. S. Van Dyke;
based on the novel by Arthur Somers Roche; screenplay, Frances
Goodrich, Albert Hackett; music, William Axt; camera, Lucien Andriot, Harold Rosson; editor, Robert J. Kern.

Warner Baxter (Jackson Durant); Myrna Loy (Gertie Waxted);
Charles Butterworth (Layton); Mae Clarke (Mimi Montagne); Phil-
lips Holmes (Tom Siddell); C. Henry Gordon (Jim Crelliman); Martha
Sleeper (Sue Leonard); Nat Pendleton (Tony Gazotti); George E.

Stone (Murtoch); Robert Emmett O'Connor (Stevens); Raymond Hatton, Arthur Belasco (Bodyguards).

Wealthy criminal lawyer Jackson Durant (Warner Baxter), who defends underworld clients, finds himself caught in a frame with both the mobsters and the police against him. Since he helped save her society friend from being framed by a mobster, socialite Gertie Waxted (Myrna Loy) decides to help the lawyer by romancing a hoodlum (C. Henry Gordon) and getting the evidence needed to clear Baxter. Baxter, however, manages to gain the data by questioning one of the gang members. Meanwhile the mobster realizes Loy's scheme and plans to kill her, but she is aided by a rival gangster (Nat Pendleton) whom Baxter once saved from the electric chair. In a shootout, both mobsters are eliminated, and now Loy and Baxter continue their romance.

Variety called this melodrama, "First class entertainment for everybody embodied in a brightly written story, played in the best manner and framed in a production of the best modern grade." Warner Baxter and Myrna Loy were especially appealing in tandem as the lawyer and the socialite, while Mae Clarke was a delight as gangster's moll Mimi Montague.

PERSONS IN HIDING (Paramount, 1938) 69 mins.

Producer, Edward T. Lowe; director, Louis King; based on the book by J. Edgar Hoover; screenplay, William R. Lipman, Horace McCoy; assistant director, William Faralla; camera, Harry Fischbeck; editor, Hugh Bennett.

Lynne Overman (Pete Griswold); Patricia Morison (Dorothy Bronson); J. Carrol Naish (Freddie "Gunner" Martin); William Henry (Dan Waldron); Helen Twelvetrees (Helen Griswold); William Frawley (Alec Ingilis); Judith Barrett (Blase Blonde); William Collier, Sr. (Burt Nast); May Boley (Mme. Thompson); Richard Stanley (Flagler); Dorothy Howe (Flo); John Hartley (Joe Butler); Janet Waldo (Ruth Devoe); Richard Denning (Powder); Leona Roberts (Ma Bronson); Phillip Warren (Curly); John Eldredge (Gordon Kingsley); Richard Carle (Zeke Bronson); Roy Gordon (John Nast); John Hart (Stenographer); Lillian Yarbo (Maid).

Federal Bureau of Investigation Director J. Edgar Hoover's best-selling book, Persons in Hiding, was brought to the screen as a "B" programmer and proved so popular that three other features were culled from its pages. The quartet, which also included UNDERCOVER DOCTOR, PAROLE FIXER (qq.v.), and QUEEN OF THE MOB (see: B/V), are good action melodramas which also take a quasi-documentary look at the workings of the Bureau and its agents. This initial outing was based on several FBI cases, most specifically the exploits of Clyde Barrow and Bonnie Parker.

Small-time hoodlum Freddie "Gunner" Martin (J. Carrol Naish) starts out robbing a gas station and continues as a petty crook until he meets young, attractive, and calculating Dorothy Bronson (Patricia Morison) who eggs him on to bigger criminal activities, including robberies, kidnapping, and murder. FBI chief Pete Griswold (Lynne Overman) is assigned to bring in the pair and with the help of fellow agents, local police, and the victims of the duo's crime spree, he closes the case.

"Presentation of the subject is a relief from the generally overtheatric G-man pictures that have gone before.... Inside operation of FBI ... are presented most effectively during story unfolding" (Variety).

Special mention must be made of Patricia Morison's (in her screen debut) performance as the Bonnie Parker-type gun moll who brought about her own and her lover's destruction through a life of crime.

THE PHANTOM STRIKES see: THE RINGER

UNE PIERRE DAN LA BOUCHE [A Stone in the Mouth] (A.A.A. Soporfilm, 1983) C 106 mins.

Director, Marie-Annick Jarlegand; screenplay, Jean-Louis Leconte, Gerard Brach; sets, Jean-Pierre Bazerolle, Colombe Anovilh; music, Egisto Macchi; sound, Philippe Lioret; camera, Henri Alekan; editor, Genevieve Letellier.

Harvey Keitel (The Fugitive); Michel Robin (Victor); Richard Anconina (Marc); Catherine Frot (Jackie); Jeffrey Kime (The Killer); Bruno Balp (Daniel); Genevieve Mnich (Suzanne); Jacques Boudet (Gas Pump Attendant); Greta Rubens (The Woman in the Blockhouse); Gerard Uzes (The Man in the Blockhouse); Hugues Quester (The Driver).

The title of this French drama refers to a gangland gimmick of placing a stone in the mouth of a murdered cohort to demonstrate that he was an informer.

A fleeing gangster (Harvey Keitel) takes refuge in the country estate of an aged, blind actor (Michel Robin), who comes to find some amusement in the plight of his crude intruder. Also on the scene is the actor's no-good nephew (Richard Anconina) and his new girlfriend (Catherine Frot) who sets out to seduce the wounded hoodlum. This angers Anconina and when the rival gangsters arrive to trap their prey, he informs on the man, causing the fugitive to be gunned down and the telltale stone placed in his mouth.

While Michel Robin is a delight as the blind actor, Harvey Keitel provides his usual obscure characterization as the fugitive. His actions give little insight into the character of a gangster on the run, especially one hunted by his peers.

PRISON FARM (Paramount, 1938) 60 mins.

Producer, Stuart Walker, director, Louis King; screen idea, Edwin V. Westrate; screenplay, Eddie Welch; camera, Harry Fischbeck; editor, Edward Dmytryk.

Shirley Ross (Joan Forest); Lloyd Nolan (Larry Harrison); John Howard (Dr. Roy Conrad); J. Carrol Naish (Noel Haskins); Porter Hall (Chiston Bradby); Anna Q. Nilsson (Matron Ames); Esther Dale (Cora Waxley); Morjorie Main (Matron Brand); John Hart (Texas Jack); Diane Wood (Dolly); Howard Mitchell (Guard); Mae Busch (Trixie); Ruth Warren (Josie); Robert Buster (Joe Easy); Phil Warren (Injured Prisoner); Virginia Dabney (Maisie).

In the late 1930s Paramount's "B" unit developed a strong series of dual-bill programmers in the gangster film vein. The movies were tightly scripted, well directed, and boasted large supporting casts with familiar screen names. In many instances the "B" features were stronger than the "A" movies they supported. The series would run into the early 1940s and resulted in a number of fine productions, one of which was PRISON FARM.

Lloyd Nolan, who headlined several of these studio presentations, played a lowlife criminal who agrees to a six-month sentence at a coed prison farm in order to avoid a much larger rap for a serious crime he committed. He forces his girlfriend, innocent Joan Forest (Shirley Ross), to go with him as his accomplice and she too goes to the farm. There a prison doctor (John Howard) tries to help the two but his efforts are thwarted by sadistic guards (J. Carrol Naish, Marjorie Main) and a crooked warden (Porter Hall). Finally the inmates revolt with Nolan being killed and Ross and Howard finding happiness together.

In discussing this production in his book B Movies (1973), Don Miller determined, "It was the usual prison story--in fact, it was all the prison stories ever seen on the screen rolled into one, and done in 60 minutes. And done so well, it became a wonderment that similar yarns weren't as satisfactory, including the more expensive productions.... And it worked beautifully, thanks to [Director Louis] King, the cast, and some exceptionally realistic photography by Harry Fischbeck."

PRIVATE HELL 36 (Filmmakers, 1954) 81 mins.

Producer, Collier Young; associate producer, Robert Eggenweiler; director, Don Siegel; screenplay, Young, Ida Lupino; art director, Walter Keller; set decorator, Edward Boyle; music, Leith Stevens; assistant directors, James Anderson, Leonard Kunody; makeup, David Newell; sound, Thomas Carmen, Howard Wilson; camera, Burnett Guffey; editor, Stanford Tischler.

Ida Lupino (Lilli Marlowe); Steve Cochran (Detective Sergeant

THEY LIVE BY NIGHT . . .

. . . a right kind of guy . . . a wrong kind of woman . . . both making their own

PRIVATE HELL 36

starring **IDA LUPINO**

STEVE COCHRAN   **HOWARD DUFF**

DEAN JAGGER   **DOROTHY MALONE**

Written for the screen by COLLIER YOUNG and IDA LUPINO · Produced by COLLIER YOUNG · Directed by DON SIEGEL
Distributed by Filmakers Releasing Organization

Advertisement for PRIVATE HELL 36 (1954).

Calvin Brimer); Howard Duff (Jack Farnham); Dean Jagger (Captain
Michaels); Dorothy Malone (Francye Farnham); Bridgett Duff (Farnham's Child); Jerry Hausner (Nightclub Boss); Dabbs Greer (Bartender); Chris O'Brien (Coroner); Kenneth Patterson (Superior Officer); George Dockstader (Fugitive); Jimmy Hawkins (Delivery
Boy); King Donovan (Burglar).

"They lived by night ... on the edge of evil and violence ...
that ended in their own Private Hell 36." So read the promotional
tag lines for this feature.

Police detectives Cal Bruner (Steve Cochran) and Jack Farnham (Howard Duff) are tracking $320,000 missing from a murder-
holdup. They come across nightclub singer Lilli Marlowe (Ida Lupino) who can identify the suspect in the case, and she points him
out at a race track but during a high speed chase the culprit is
killed. The detectives find the missing money in the man's car
and Cochran takes part of it ($80,000) and they hide it in unit 36
at a trailer park. When some of the money is missing, the police
captain (Dean Jagger) is suspicious but by now Cochran is deeply
in love with Lupino and wants the money for her. Duff, however,
feels guilty about the theft and drinks too much and frightens his
wife (Dorothy Malone) and tells Cochran they must return the
money. Cochran agrees, but at the trailer he tries to murder
Duff. Instead he is killed by Jagger who has trailed them to the
site.

PRIVATE HELL 36 is a compelling psychological melodrama in
which the law enforcers become the hoodlums, filled with greed and
lust. While not a financially or critically successful movie when released, the film plays rather well today, thanks mainly to Don Siegel's
steady direction, the moody camerawork of Burnett Guffey, and top-
notch performances by the leads.

In 1958 the film was reissued as BABY FACE KILLERS.

PRIZZI'S HONOR (Twentieth Century-Fox, 1985) C 129 mins.

Producer, John Foreman; director, John Huston; based on the novel
by Richard Condon; screenplay, Condon, Janet Roach; assistant
director, Benjy Rosenberg; production designer, Dennis Washington;
art directors, Michael Helmy, Tracy Bousman; set designer, Elizabeth Bousman; set decorators, Bruce Weintraub, Charles Truhan;
music, Alex North; costumes, Donfeld, stunt coordinator, Harry
Madsen; special effects Connie Brink; camera, Andrzej Bartkowiak;
editors, Rudi Fehr, Kaja Fehr.

Jack Nicholson (Charley Partanna); Kathleen Turner (Irene Walker);
Robert Loggia (Eduardo Prizzi); John Randolph (Angelo "Pop" Par-
tanna); William Hickey (Don Corrado Prizzi); Lee Richardson (Domi-
nic Prizzi); Michael Lombard (Filargi "Finlay"); Anjelica Huston
(Maerose Prizzi); George Santopietro (Plumber); Lawrence Tierney
(Lieutenant Hanley); C. C. H. Pounder (Peaches Altamont); Ann

Selepegno (Amalia Prizzi); Vic Polizos (Phil Vittimizzare); Dick
O'Neill (Bluestone); Sully Boyar (Casco Vascone); Antonia Vasquez
(Theresa Prizzi); Tomasino Baratta (Opera Singer); John Calvani
(Don's Bodyguard); Murray Staff (Gallagher); Joseph Ruskin
(Marxie Heller); Ray Serrra (Bocca); Seth Allen (Gomsky); Domi-
nic Barfto (Presto Ciglione); Teddi Siddall (Beulah); Tom Signo-
relli, Raymond Iannicelli (Photographers); Stanley Tucci (Soldier);
Themi Sapountzakis (Policeman); Debra Kelly (Bride at Mexican
Chapel); Scott Campbell (Groom at Mexican Chapel); Beth Raines
(Airport Clark); Michael Sabin (Charley at Age 17); Michael Tuck
(Anchorman "Fred"); Michael Fischetti (Kiely); Kenneth Cervi
(Bodyguard); Marlene Williams (Mrs. Calhane); Joe Kopmar, Eramus
"Charlie" Alfano, Peter D'Arcy, Thomas Lomonaco, Bill Brecht
(Cigar Smokers); Henry Fehren (Bishop); John Codiglia (Cop);
Skip O'Brien (Bartender); Alexandra Ivanoff (Soprano Soloist in
Church); Enzo Citarelli, Theodore Theoharous (Priests).

The Prizzi clan is a powerful Sicilian-American Mafia family
which is controlled by Don Corrado (William Hickey), whose godson
Charley Partanna (Jack Nicholson) is one of their hit men. At the
wedding of Hickey's son's (Lee Richardson) youngest daughter,
Nicholson is attracted to pretty tax consultant Irene Walker (Kathleen Turner) and the two fall in love and plan to wed. Richardson's older daughter (Anjelica Huston) has disgraced the family by
a brief affair with another man when she had been promised to
Nicholson and she looks forward to the marriage which will make
her again acceptable to the family. Nicholson is told to kill a man
(Joseph Ruskin) who has embezzled a large amount of money from
one of the family's Las Vegas casinos, but when the job is done he
finds he has only half the money and it turns out Turner is the
murdered man's widow. She claims she knows nothing about his
activities and that he was dying anyway and that she did not love
him. From his father (John Randolph), Nicholson finds out that
Turner is also a hired killer retained by the family but he tells
Nicholson to marry the woman. The two are wed and Richardson
finds out that Huston has recently slept with Nicholson and that
his father plans to make Nicholson his second-in-command since
Richardson is in ill health. The family then assigns Nicholson to
kidnap the manager (Michael Lombard) of one of their banks since
the man has been embezzling funds, and they plan to ransom him
back and deduct the cost from taxes. Nicholson kidnaps the man
but Turner is forced to kill a woman witness who turns out to be
the police chief's (Lawrence Tierney) wife. The lawman, usually
in the pay of the Prizzi family, vows revenge. Huston wants
Nicholson back and she tells Hickey about Turner being the widow
of the murdered man and urges him to have her killed. Instead
Hickey directs Turner to return the stolen money and pay a penalty.
Meanwhile Turner tells Nicholson that Richardson has hired her to
kill him and urges him to run away with her. Randolph, however,
orders them to stay with the kidnapping so they can dictate terms

to the family, but when he does, Hickey explains to Nicholson that
his loyalty is to the family and that he must kill Turner. Turner
grows suspicious and departs for Hong Kong, but Nicholson stops
her and she tries to shoot him. He stabs her with a stiletto.

An involved and minute look at a Mafia family's operations,
PRIZZI'S HONOR is remindful of THE GODFATHER (see: B/V) although it has none of the expanse or excitement of that film. While
THE GODFATHER delved into the actions of a wide variety of characters, this outing looks mainly at just a few people, those orbiting
around the none-too-bright Charley Partanna, who is obviously being hoodwinked romantically by fellow assassin Irene Walker. Nicholson's performance is one of his quirky best, while Kathleen Turner
is more than satisfying as the beautiful and deadly Irene.

From the start, the critics raved about this feature, lionizing
78-year-old director John Huston, now in the twilight of his lengthy
writing-directing-acting career. Richard Schickel in Time magazine
enthused, "... this wickedly complex movie is not to be taken literally. It is not an inside look at organized crime anymore than it
is a study of the joys and dangers of sexual obsession. It is a
parable of generational conflict.... Its basic irony derives from
the fact that the Prizzi hoods ... represent, despite their line of
work, traditional values.... To preserve it, they are willing to
sacrifice short-term advantage.... [PRIZZI'S HONOR is] a shrewd
and entertaining fable told out of the corner of cynical mouths."
Sheila Benson (Los Angeles Times) was equally laudatory: "It's a
rich, dense character comedy in which Huston ... cocks a playful
but unblinking eye at love, family loyalty and the togetherness of
a happy marriage Sicilian-style." Across the Atlantic, Tom Milne
wrote in the British Monthly Film Bulletin, "Featuring a whole string
of superlative performances, ... PRIZZI'S HONOR is made with the
lazily rigorous economy Huston first evolved in FAT CITY [1972].
Its tortuously complex plot manipulated with insolent ease."

The winner of several New York Film Critics Awards (and
many others from various industry competitions), PRIZZI'S HONOR
claimed several Academy Awards, including Best Supporting Actress
(Anjelica Huston).

PUBLIC ENEMY'S WIFE (Warner Bros., 1936) 65 mins.

Director, Nick Grinde; story, P. J. Wolfson; screenplay, Aben
Finkel, Harold Buckly; art director, Hugh Reticker; camera, Ernest
Haller, editor, Thomas Pratt.

Pat O'Brien (Lee Laird); Margaret Lindsay (Judith Maroc [Roberts]);
Robert Armstrong (Gene Ferguson); Cesar Romero (Maroc); Dick
Foran (Thomas Duncan McKay); Joseph King (Wilcox); Dick Purcell
(Louie); Addison Richards (Warden William); Paul Graetz (Mr.
Schultz); Selmer Jackson (Duffield); Hal K. Dawson (Daugherty);

Alan Bridge (Swartzman); Mary Green, Isabel Withers (Perators);
Kathrin Clare Ward (Matron); Bernice Pilot (Miranda the Black Maid);
Don Downen (Bellhop); Ted Oliver, Jack Mower, Ed Hart, Emmett
Vogan (G-Men); Ralph Dunn (Cap); Harry Harvey, William Wayne,
Bert Kennedy (Mail Clerks); Harry Hayden (Justice of the Peace);
Stuart Holmes (Telephone Repair Chief); Milton Kibbee (Charlie
the Repair Man).

Convicted jewel thief Gene Maroc (Cesar Romero) says he will
kill any man who attempts to marry his wife (Margaret Lindsay),
who is being released from prison after serving three years for a
crime she did not commit. Upon her release, the young woman
promptly divorces Romero and announces her engagement to wealthy
playboy Tom McKay (Dick Foran). Romero then tells authorities he
will testify against hoodlum Corelli (William Frawley) and while he is
being transported to the trial via mail train an elderly lady brings
in a package which turns out to be filled with gas which knocks
out everyone on the train, including Romero and his G-men escorts.
The gangster's henchmen escape with him. Later, when Foran is
injured in a polo accident, G-man Lee Laird (Pat O'Brien) pretends
to be the heavily bandaged playboy and takes part in a bogus marriage ceremony in hopes of bringing Romero out into the open.
When this doesn't work, O'Brien and Lindsay embark on a fake
honeymoon and the gangster kidnaps his ex-wife away from O'Brien
and his associate (Robert Armstrong). The FBI then tracks the
gangster and his captive to a small fishing village and the two G-
men pretend to be fishermen. Romero gets the drop on them but
is killed when fellow agents come to the rescue. O'Brien and Judith
decide to remain married.

Taken from P. J. Wolfson's story, PUBLIC ENEMY'S WIFE is
a sappy affair which promises more than it delivers in entertainment
value. Pat O'Brien's usual flippant self is overbearing in the G-man
role, Robert Armstrong is too dense as his associate, and Margaret
Lindsay offers a too icy heroine. Fortunately Cesar Romero is top
notch as the deadly and revenge-oriented gangster.

In 1940 Warner Bros. remade the Wolfson story as BULLETS
FOR O'HARA in a 50-minute version, finely directed by veteran
William K. Howard. Here the hero is rabbit-foot carying lawman
Mike O'Hara (Roger Pryor) while the gangster is called Tony Van
Dyne (Anthony Quinn) and the heroine is his wife Patricia (Joan
Perry).

PUBLIC HERO NO. 1 see: THE GET-AWAY

THE PURSUIT OF D. B. COOPER (Universal, 1981) C 100 mins.

Executive producers, William Tennant, Donald Kranze; producers,
Daniel Wigutow, Michael Taylor; associate producer, Ron Shelton;

director, Roger Spottiswoode; based on the book Free Fall by J. D.
Reed; screenplay, Jeffrey Alan Fiskin; music, James Horner; song,
Waylon Jennings; production designer, Preston Amos; assistant di-
rectors, Richard Learman, Dan Attias, Louis Muscate, R. Anthony
Brown; camera, Harry Stradling; editors, Robbe Roberts, Allan
Jacobs.

Robert Duvall (Gruen); Treat Williams (Meade); Kathryn Harrold
(Hannah); Ed Flanders (Brigadier); Paul Gleason (Remson); R. G.
Armstrong (Dempsey); Dorothy Fielding (Denise); Nicolas Coster
(Avery); Cooper Huckabee (Homer); Howard K. Smith (Himself);
Christopher Curry (Hippie); Ramon Chavez (El Capitan); Stacy
Newton (Cowboy); Pat Ast (Horse Lady); and: Jack Dunlap, Brad
Sergi, Michael Potter, James Wiers, David Adams, Stephen Blood,
Tom May, Mearl Ross, Gregory Suke, John Herold, Glenda Young,
Christine Dolny, Conrad Marshall, Michael Goodsite, Mearl Ross.

Former Green Beret Meade (Treat Williams) boards a jet plane
with a bogus bomb and in mid-flight steals $200,000 in cash and
parachutes to freedom. Gruen (Robert Duvall), the airline insurance agent, suspects Williams because he was Williams' instructor
when they were both Green Berets, and he sets out to find the
thief as does another former cohort (Paul Gleason). Meanwhile
Williams returns home to get his wife (Kathryn Harrold) and the
two are soon being chased by Duvall and Gleason.
    While this movie has fragments of truth about the actual
event involving the mysterious D. B. Cooper, the name given to
the individual who actually accomplished the mid-air heist, the rest
of this tame drama is pure pap. Just as convoluted as its story is
the film's production history. Originally, director John Frankenheimer initiated this picture, but he was replaced by Buzz Kulik,
who in turn was replaced by Roger Spottiswoode, who received
sole directorial credit on the final product. The result was worthy
of no one, as this series of chases and personal reflections does
little to bring insight into one of the most famous unsolved crimes
in recent years. While the lead players do their best with their
laborious roles, the viewer is the real victim of this pseudo-historical
affair.

QUICKSAND (United Artists, 1950) 79 mins.

Executive producer, Samuel H. Stiefel; producer, Mort Brisken;
director, Irving Pichel; screenplay, Robert Smith; assistant director, Maurie Suess; art director, Emil Newman; set decorator, Pro-
bert Priestley; music, Louis Gruenberg; sound, William Lynch;
camera, Lionel Lindon; editor, Walter Thompson.

Mickey Rooney (Dan); Jeanne Cagney (Vera); Barbara Bates (Helen);
Peter Lorre (Nick); Taylor Holmes (Harvey); Art Smith (Mackey);
Wally Cassel (Chuck); John Galludet (Moriarity); Minerva Urecal
(Landlady); Patsy O'Connor (Millie).

Jeanne Cagney, Mickey Rooney, and Minerva Urecal in QUICKSAND
(1950).

        On a southern coastal highway Dan (Mickey Rooney) and his
girl Helen (Barbara Bates) force a driver to stop and take them to
Mexico, since Rooney is on the run from the law.   The driver is a
lawyer (Taylor Holmes) and he persuades the young man to relate
how he got into this predicament.   A few days earlier ex-sailor
Rooney, now a garage mechanic, broke with Bates and was attracted
to diner cashier Vera (Jeanne Cagney) and in order to take her out
he steals money from his boss.   To pay it back, he buys a watch
for a down payment and then hocks it, but a private detective
working for the jeweler demands the watch or the money, so Rooney
robs a drunk, using the cash to pay off the debts as well as one
owed by Cagney to Nick Dmitrov (Peter Lorre), the shady owner of
a local nightclub and Cagney's former lover.   Realizing how Rooney
got the money, Lorre demands he steal a car from his boss, which
Rooney does.   Then the car's owner (Art Smith) demands Rooney
give him more than the vehicle is worth.   This leads to Rooney and
Cagney robbing Lorre, with Rooney paying off the garage owner
who then calls the law.   Rooney knocks him out, and thinking he
has killed him, runs, but is later deserted by Cagney.   Going to
get his own car, he finds Bates who refuses to leave him, and they
head for Mexico, but the car breaks down and they stop the lawyer.

After completing his account, Rooney decides to reach Mexico by boat and they go to a nearby pier where the lawyer and Bates hear over the radio that the car owner is not dead. The police, however, see Rooney and shoot him as he tries to escape, but his injuries are not serious and the lawyer agrees to defend him.

It is difficult to believe by viewing this low-grade, sleazy melodrama that merely a few years earlier Mickey Rooney was a top Metro-Goldwyn-Mayer star. Nevertheless, QUICKSAND remains one of Rooney's better 1950s outings, although here he takes second place to fetching co-stars Jeanne Cagney and Barbara Bates. And in fairness, the plotline is offbeat in its presentation of how a decent person can go astray into a life of crime, pushed further into the morass by vicious circumstances.

RADAR SECRET SERVICE (Lippert, 1950) 59 mins.

Producer, Barney Sarecky; director, Sam Newfield; screenplay, Beryl Sachs; assistant director, James Parsley; art director, Fred Preble; set decorator, Harry Reif; music, Russell Garcia, Dick Hazard; sound, Earl Snyder, Harry Eddes; camera, Ernest Miller; editor, Carl Pierson.

John Howard (Bill); Adele Jergens (Lila); Tom Neal (Moran); Myrna Dell (Marge); Sid Melton (Pill Box); Ralph Byrd (Static); Pierre Watkin (Hamilton); Robert Kent (Benson); Tristram Coffin (Michael); Riley Hill (Blacky); Bob Carson (Tom); Marshall Reed, John McKee (Bruisers); Holly Bane (Truck Operator); Bob Woodward, Boyd Stockman (Henchmen); Bill Crespinel (Helicopter Operator); Kenne Duncan, Bill Hammond (Michael;s Henchmen); Jane Kayne (Maid).

Two secret service agents (John Howard, Ralph Byrd) must stop a gang of crooks who have stolen uranium ore intended for government use. The gang leaders (Tom Neal, Tristram Coffin) plan to sell the valuable mineral to the highest bidder and take it to their hideout, but the government agents use radar to track down the wrongdoers.

With "fast action and short footage" (Variety), RADAR SECRET SERVICE was a dependable dual bill item employing the topical use of radar to bring in the bad guys. Adequately directed by Sam Newfield and with a strong cast of "B" players, the movie was a pleasant diversion. As the story unfolds, the gangsters, per usual, prove to be far more engaging than their honest counterparts. Of particular interests are Adele Jergens and Myrna Dell as the gang's molls and Sid Melton as its buffoon.

RADIO PATROL (Universal, 1937) twelve chapters

Producers, Barney Sarecky, Ben Koenig; directors, Ford Beebe, Cliff Smith; based on the cartoon strip by Eddie Sullivan, Charlie

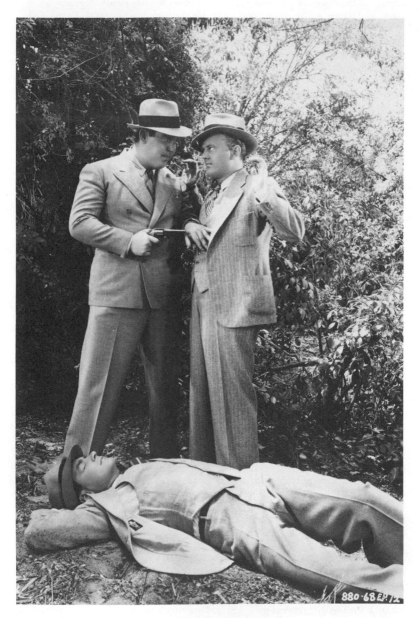

Ray Teal (on ground) in RADIO PATROL (1937).

Schmidt; screenplay, Wyndham Gittens, Norman S. Hall, Ray
Trampe; camera, Jerome Ash.

Grant Withers (Pat O'Hara); Catherine Hughes (Molly); Mickey
Rentschler (Pinky Adams); Adrian Morris (Sam); Max Hoffman, Jr.
(Selkirk); Frank Lackteen (Thata); Leonard Lord (Franklin); Monte
Montague (Pollard); Dick Botiller (Zutta); Silver Wolf (Irish); and:
Jack Mulhall, Earle Dwire, Leonard Lord, Louis Vokali, Wheeler
Oakman, Harry Davenport.

Chapters: 1) A Million Dollar Murder; 2) The Hypnotic Eye;
3) Flaming Death; 4) The Human Clue; 5) The Flash of Doom;
6) The House of Terror; 7) Claws of Steel; 8) The Perfect Crime;
9) Plaything of Disaster; 10) A Bargain with Death; 11) The Hidden Menace; 12) They Get Their Man.

A scientist who has invented a formula for a flexible, bullet-
proof steel is murdered and international gangsters want the secret.
They adopt the man's orphaned son (Mickey Rentschler) in hopes
of getting the formula from him. Their plans are thwarted, however, by radio policeman Pat O'Hara (Grant Withers) and pretty
Molly (Catherine Hughes), the duo being aided by Silver Wolf, a
German Shepherd dog. After several showdowns with the crooks,
the policeman hero ferrets out their leader.
RADIO PATROL was a typically actionful Universal serial,
kept moving at a good pace by veteran genre ace directors Ford
Beebe and Cliff Smith. Grant Withers, who would develop into one
of the screen's most heinous villains, handles the lead role of the
policeman in good form, being equally deft at both the rough stuff
and romantics.

REEFER MADNESS (Motion Pictures Ventures, 1936) 67 mins.

Producer, George A. Hirliman, Sam Diech; director, Louis Gasnier;
story, Lawrence Meade; screenplay, Arthur Hoerl; additional dialogue, Paul Franklin; music director, Abe Meyer; sound, Hans
Weeren; camera, Jack Greenhalgh; editor, Carl Pierson.

Dorothy Short (Mary Lane); Kenneth Craig (Bill Harper); Dave
O'Brien (Ralph Wiley); Lillian Miles (Blanche); Thelma White (Mae
Coleman); Carleton Young (Jack Perry); Warren McCullom (Jimmy
Lane); Pat Toyale (Agnes); Josef Forte (Dr. Alfred Carroll).

Without doubt, REEFER MADNESS is the best known exploitation movie of the 1930s, although its fame did not begin until its
re-release to theaters in the late 1960s and its use by the National
Organization for the Repeal of Marijuana Laws in the early 1970s.
Made as a warning to parents about the dangers of marijuana use
by school-age youths, the movie was cheap, overripe sensationalism
when it was created and its deficiencies have only amplified with

time. Today it is watched chiefly for derision, especially with the widespread use of marijuana since the 1960s, although medical evidence tends to support the movie's basic preachments.

The narrative opens with a high school principal telling parents at a PTA meeting of the dangers of marijuana to their children and then showing a film about the subject. The story then switches to Mae Coleman (Thelma White) and Jack Perry (Carleton Young), two adults who have an apartment near the town's high school and who bring in teenagers and get them hooked on marijuana during wild parties. Already addicted is Ralph Wiley (Dave O'Brien) who has a yen for Mary Lane (Dorothy Short), the clean-cut sister of Jimmy (Warren McCullom) who has been frequenting the parties. Short's boyfriend, Bill Harper (Kenneth Craig), also begins coming to the parties and neglecting his school work and later McCullom loses control of White's car and kills a pedestrian. O'Brien invites Short to one of the parties, gets her high on the drug, and tries to rape her. Craig arrives and fights with O'Brien, and when Young tries to hit O'Brien with a gun, the weapon goes off and a bullet strikes and kills Short. White, however, convinces Carig that he murdered his girl and he goes on trial, but in the courtroom, O'Brien, now addicted to marijuana, begins to feel guilty and the edgy Young gets permission from his gangster boss to kill O'Brien. In a fight between the two, it is Young who dies and the police raid White's apartment and when Craig is convicted of killing Short, White and another denizen (Lillian Miles) of the drug nest tell the judge the truth and the decision is reversed. Short and the drug dealers she informed on are sent to prison; Miles commits suicide, and O'Brien is sent to a mental institution.

Perhaps the most striking thing about viewing REEFER MADNESS is the squeaky clean look of the movie despite its sleazy topic and characters. Everyone in the production, to the lowest of weed addicts, is well groomed, lives in upper middle class surroundings, and appears clean cut. Although the basic theme of the production is anti-marijuana, it also strikes a blow against premarital sex.

REEFER MADNESS was directed by Louis Gasnier, whose credits date back to THE PERILS OF PAULINE (1914) and includes such gangster entries as GAMBLING SHIP and BANK ALARM (qq.v.), and it boasts solid technical work by such fine craftsmen as cinematographer Jack Greenhalgh and editor Carl L. Pierson.

Like most exploitation fare, the movie has been reissued under sundry titles, including: THE BURNING QUESTION, DOPE ADDICT, DOPED YOUTH, LOVE MADNESS, and TELL YOUR CHILDREN.

REPORT TO THE COMMISSIONER (United Artists, 1975) C 112 mins.

Producer, Mike J. Frankovich; director, Milton Katselas; based on the novel by James Mills; screenplay, Abby Mann, Ernest Tidyman; music, Elmer Bernstein; songs, Vernon Burch, Spencer Proffer, Jeffrey Marmelzat; production designer, Robert Clatworthy; set decorator, John Kuri; assistant director, Richard Moder; action

Michael Moriarty and Susan Blakely in REPORT TO THE COMMIS-
SIONER (1975).

coordinator, Paul Baxley; sound, Arthur Piantadosi, Richard Tyler,
Les Fresholtz, Don Cahn, Alfred J. Overton; camera, Mario Tosi;
editor, David Blewitt.

Michael Moriarty (Bo Lockley); Yaphet Kotto (Crunch Blackstone);
Susan Blakely (Patty Butler); Hector Elizondo (Captain D'Angelo);
Tony King (Stick Henderson); Michael McGuire (Lieutenant Han-
son); Edward Grover (Captain Strichter); Dana Elcar (Chief
Perna); Robert Balaban (Joey Egan); William Devane (Assistant
District Attorney); Stephen Elliott (Commissioner); Richard Gere
(Billy); Vic Tayback (Lieutenant Seidensdticker); Noelle North
(Samatha); Bebe Drake Hooks (Dorothy); Albert Seedman (Detec-
tive Schulman); Sonny Grosso, Lee Delano, Vincent Van Lynn, Bob
Golden (Detectives).

New York City police detective Bo Lockley (Michael Moriarty)
is assigned to investigate the disappearance of a young girl (Susan
Blakely). The woman, however, is actually an undercover officer
who has volunteered to share quarters with a black dope dealer
(Tony King). Since the police department has not authorized her

work, Moriarty is not aware of the assignment and, finding the girl, he accidentally shoots her and the department then tries to cover over the situation. After the accident, Moriarty finds King and two end up with guns pointing at each other in an elevator at Saks Fifth Avenue.

Based on James Mills' 1972 best selling novel, which was told in flashback through taped interview transcripts, the film follows its literary source closely. Variety lauded the movie as "a superb suspense drama of the tragic complexities of law enforcement." Filled with admirable performance, the motion picture is another good illustration of later-day gangster cinema stearing away from the machine-gun toting, pin-striped suited ethnic mobster in favor of low-life dope runners, crooked cops, and ambitious politicians.

One astute observer of the film was reviewer Michael Deskey in Films in Review, who noted, "The major cause of this [film's box-office] failure is the casting of and portrayal by Michael Moriarty as the young detective, Bo Lockley. There is a diffuseness about Lockley that puts the picture off kilter: his face is too bland-- weak to the point of effeminacy--to be convincing as somebody who would want to become or be accepted as a cop."

REVOLT IN THE BIG HOUSE (Allied Artists, 1958) 79 mins.

Producer, David Diamond; director, R. G. Springsteen; screenplay, Daniel Hyatt, Eugene Lourie; camera, William Margulies; editor, William Austin.

Gene Evans (Gannon); Robert Blake (Rudy); Timothy Carey (Kyle); John Qualen (Doc); Sam Edwards (Al); John Dennis (Red); Walter Barnes (Starkey); Frank Richards (Jake); Emile Meyer (Warden); Arlene Hunter (Girl).

Until the ending of censorship in the late 1960s, most prison pictures centered on life behind bars but the main plot crux was typically the inevitable prison break. Following the repeal of rigid moral guidelines, the anything-goes atmosphere "permitted" delving into the psychological and sexual aspects of prison life. As a result earlier pictures on the subject appear sterile in their presentations. Still, the older films retain a good amount of entertainment value in their pretend world of prison and one such outing is RE-VOLT IN THE BIG HOUSE, a good dual bill item from the late 1950s.

Long-time criminal Gannon (Gene Evans) has eluded the law for years but is finally sent to prison for a long term. Once there he plans to break out and immediately uses his persuasive powers and ruthless abilities to form a group of loyal supporters including his young Mexican cellmate (Robert Blake). Evans, however, plans to doublecross the men by using them as a diversion at the front of the prison while he makes good his escape via the back wall. Blake finds out his plans and Evans stabs him but the boy warns the other inmates that they will be ambushed by guards. Evans does escape, yet he is later gunned down in a subway.

With lensing at California's Folsom Prison, the movie is atmospheric and R. G. Springsteen's direction keeps the well-defined plot moving consistently. Gene Evans is effective as the self willed hoodlum, and Robert Blake, after a long career as a juvenile performer, came of age as the frightened Rudy.

THE RINGER (British Lion, 1952) 78 mins.

Producer, Hugh Perceval; director, Guy Hamilton; based on the play by Edgar Wallace; screenplay, Val Valentine, Lesley Storm; camera, Ted Scaife.

Herbert Lom (Maurice Meister); Donald Wolfit (Dr. Lombond); Mai Zetterling (Lisa); Greta Gynt (Cora Ann Milton); William Hartnell (Sam Hackett); Norman Wooland (Inspector Bliss); Denholm Elliott (John Lenley); Dora Bryan (Mrs. Hackett); Charles Victor (Inspector Wembley); Walter Fitzgerald (Commissioner); John Stuart (Gardener); John Slater (Bell); and: Campbell Singer.

Maurice Meister (Herbert Lom), a crooked lawyer who handles underworld cases in London, years before cheated a notorious criminal called The Ringer, a man of many disguises, and caused the death of the crook's sister. Now The Ringer has escaped from Australia and has come to England with the intent of killing Lom, and the lawyer takes refuge in his large, burglar-proof home guarded by the police. Also in the house is his pretty young secretary (Mai Zetterling), whose boyfriend the lawyer is defending although he is out to seduce the girl, and a police doctor (Donald Wolfit). Being questioned in the matter is The Ringer's girlfriend (Greta Gynt) and an ex-convict (William Hartnell) who is employed by Lom but who has ties to the criminal. Eventually the master crook fools the police, saves the secretary from Lom, and settles his old score with the unethical attorney.

This handsomely produced and entertaining thriller is actually the fifth screen version of the 1926 Edgar Wallace play, and later novel, which has become a chestnut of the British mystery theater. Full of improbable situations, offbeat characters, shifting plot motifs, and a look at the British gangster underworld, the vehicle set the standard for having a villain who is actually a hero. This edition benefitted from solid production values and fine performances.

The first screen adaption of the Wallace work was done by the mystery master himself and made by British Lion in 1928, a company for which Wallace was chairman of the board of directors. The silent film featured Leslie Faber in the title role. The initial talkie version was also by British Lion and released by Gainsborough in 1931. Gordon Harker enjoyed the title assignment, while John Longden was the police inspector. The movie was issued in the U.S. in 1932 by First Division. Next came a German version entitled DER HEXER made in 1932; Fritz Rasp (who would headline several West German Edgar Wallace films in the 1960s) was The Ringer, and it was directed by Karl Lamac. In 1938 Jon Longden repeated his role as the policeman in a third British version of the property, now called THE GAUNT STRANGER (which was Wallace's original title for the play). Alexander Knox had the lead part with Wilfred Lawson as Meister; work was adapted by Sidney Gilliat. This Associated British release was shown in the U.S. in 1939 by Monogram as THE PHANTOM STRIKES.

Following the 1952 adaptation detailed above, the Germans again revived the story in 1964 as THE HEXER, one of over thirty features made from the author's works by Rialto Films. Joachim Fuchsberger, a veteran of these thrillers, headlined as the police inspector and the movie plays on U.S. TV as THE MYSTERIOUS MAGICIAN. It also inspired a sequel the following year, Rialto's NEUES VOM HEXER, based on Wallace's novel, Again the Ringer. The plot had Scotland Yard teaming with The Ringer to solve murders taking place in wealthy London households.

RIOT (Paramount, 1968) C 98 mins.

Producer, William Castle; director, Buzz Kulik; based on the novel by Frank Elli; screenplay, James Poe; music, Christopher Komeda; songs, Komeda, Robert Wells and Johnnie Lee Willis and Deacon Anderson; production designer, Paul Sylbert; assistant director, Daniel J. McCauley; sound, Walter Gross, John H. Wilkinson, Clem Portman; camera, Robert B. Hauser; editor, Edwin H. Bryant.

Jim Brown (Cully Briston); Gene Hackman (Red Fletcher); Mike Kellin (Bugsy); Gerald S. O'Loughlin (Grossman); Ben Carruthers (Indian Joe Surefoot); Clifford David ("Mary" Sheldon); Bill Walker (Jake); Michael Byron (Murray); Jerry Thompson (Fisk); Ricky Summers, John Neiderhauser (Homosexuals); Warden Frank A. Eyman (Warden).

With filming at the Arizona State Penitentiary and the inclusion of Warden Frank A. Eyman and 600 personnel and inmates of the institution salted in the cast, RIOT beautifully captures the feeling of life behind bars. Variety commended it as a "strong prison drama, handsomely produced...." In fact, the film is one of the best prison pictures of the 1960s and one which is often underrated today, mainly because producer William Castle's previous work, ROSEMARY'S BABY (1968), had been so lionized.

At a state prison, black prisoner Cully Briston (Jim Brown) is taken to isolation for irritating a guard and there he reluctantly takes part in a riot which Red Fletcher (Gene Hackman) starts. The riot is really Hackman's ruse to stall for time because he plans to use a long forgotten tunnel beneath the prison to escape and it must be extended for his plan to work. Several guards are taken hostage during the riot and Hackman works to complete the tunnel. While the news media make the inmates' grievances known, the prisoners enjoy their newfound freedom and even form a kangaroo

court to try informants while Brown stops another psychotic prisoner (Ben Carruthers) from murdering the captive guards. Upon the
warden's (Lyman) return to the prison, he immediately begins to
restore order, but by now Hackman, Brown, and ten others start
their escape through the tunnel and seal the entrance after them.
On the outside, they are ambushed by guards armed with machine
guns and gas bombs. However, Hackman, Brown, and Carruthers
have gas masks and escape through a steam pipe at the bottom of
the guard tower. After killing a guard, Carruthers tries to kill
Brown, but Hackman comes to his defense. Later Carruthers and
Hackman die fighting, while Brown escapes.

ROOM 13 (Constantin, 1964) 90 mins.

Director, Dr. Harald Reinl; based on the novel Zimmer 13 by Edgar
Wallace; screenplay, Quentin Philips; music, Peter Thomas; camera,
Ernst W. Kainke; editor, Jutta Hering.

Joachim Fuchsberger (Jonny Gray); Karin Dor (Denise); Richard
Haeussler (Joe Legge); Kai Fischer (Pia Pasani); Walter Rilla (Sir
Marney); Siegfried Schuerenberg (Sir John); Hans Clarin (Mr.
Igle); Eddie Arent (Dr. Higgins); Benno Hoffmann (Blackstone-
Edwards).

ROOM 13 derives from the 1924 Edgar Wallace novel and it was
the first of five books the prolific mystery author wrote concerning
his continuing character Mr. J. G. Reeder, an inspector for the
Public Prosecutor's Office in London. The property was initially
filmed in 1939 by British National as MR. REEDER IN ROOM 13 and
in it the title character (Gibb McLaughlin) poses as an ex-convict
to unveil a gang involved in thefts, counterfeiting, and blackmail.
When issued in the United States in 1941 by Alliance, it was entitled THE MYSTERY IN ROOM 13.
   This 1964 West German version follows the plot of Wallace's
book, but with one major difference. The character of the enterprising, fussy, and prim Mr. Reeder has been replaced by that of
Detective Jonny Gray (Joachim Fuchsberger). In reviewing ROOM
13, Variety decided, "There is something about Rialto's Edgar Wallace filmizations which deserve praise. They are, unlike most other
similar domestic thrillers, based on properly prepared scripts and
technically well made. This also applies to ROOM 13."
   Room 13 is a Soho dive and the headquarters for gangsters
intent on robbing a train and hiding the loot in the country home
of respected British politician Sir Marney (Walter Rilla) whom they
are blackmailing because of his previous association with their leader (Richard Haeussler). When the robbery occurs, private detective Jonny Gray (Fuchsberger) is called into the caper and eventually solves both that case and the mystery of who has been slit-
ting the throats of several pretty girls.

Dewey Robinson, Ricardo Cortez, Milburn Stone, and Alex Callam in RUBBER RACKETEERS (1942).

RUBBER RACKETEERS (Monogram, 1942) 65 mins.

Producers, Maurice King, Franklin King; director, Harold Young; screenplay, Henry Blankfort; assistant directors, Arthur Gardner, Herman King; camera, L. William O'Connell; editor, Jack Dennis.

Ricardo Cortez (Gilin); Rochelle Hudson (Nikki); Bill Henry (Bill Barry); Barbara Read (Mary Dale); Milburn Stone (Antel); Dewey Robinson (Larkin); John Abbott (Dumbo); Pat Gleason (Curley); Dick Rich (Mule); Alan Hale, Jr. (Red); Sam Edwards (Freddy Dale); Kam Tony (Tom); Dick Hogan (Bert); Marjorie Manners (Lila); Alex Callam (Butch).

    After spending time in prison for income tax evasion, a one-time big bootlegger and racketeer (Ricardo Cortez) establishes an operation stealing tires, which are much in demand due to the war-time rubber shortage. His gang takes worn tires and recaps them with new rubber and puts them on the black market although the "new" tires are dangerous due to the likelihood of blowouts. When his factory buddy is killed because of such a defective tire, defense plant worker Bill Barry (Bill Henry) enlists co-workers to stop the rubber racketeering.
    This King Brothers production is a topical programmer with

gangsters shown as unpatriotic by taking advantage of consumer shortages to make a quick profit at the expense of their country and the lives of others. Veteran Ricardo Cortez is effective as the gang leader.

UNO SACCO TUTTO MATTO see: IT'S YOUR MOVE

THE SAINT IN NEW YORK (RKO, 1938) 72 mins.

Producer, William Sistrom; director, Ben Holmes; based on the novel by Leslie Charteris; adaptors, Charles Kaufman, Mortimer Offner; camera, Joseph August, Frank Redman; editor, Harry Marker.

Louis Hayward (Simon Templar--the Saint); Kay Sutton (Fay Edwards); Sig Rumann (Hutch Rellin); Jonathan Hale (Inspector Fernack); Jack Carson (Red Jenks); Paul Guilfoyle (Hymie Fanro); Frederick Burton (Valcross); Ben Welden (Papinoff); Charles Halton (Vincent Nather); Cliff Bragdonm (Sebastian).

To date Leslie Charteris' famous fictional sleuth Simor Templar, "The Saint," has been the subject of eleven English language theatrical feature films and three telefeatures, in addition to the popular 1960s British teleseries starring Roger Moore and its 1970s counterpart with Ian Ogilvy. The initial "Saint" theatrical film was 1939's THE SAINT IN NEW YORK, based on the novel published four years earlier. Here Britisher Louis Hayward plays the sophisticated crime solver and he would return to the role in 1954 in THE SAINT'S GIRL FRIDAY; the interim installments starring George Sanders or Hugh Sinclair.

THE SAINT IN NEW YORK finds Simon Templar (Hayward) being hired by a Manhattan businessmen's group to eliminate a half-dozen gangsters who are terrorizing the metropolis. In the process, he falls in love with Fay Edwards (Kay Sutton), a moll of one of the mobsters, but she is killed and after he has eliminated the targeted underworld figures, the globe-trotting adventurer departs for South America to join a revolution.

Following this initial series entry, droll George Sanders assumed the role of Simon Templar, and his third appearance in the series, THE SAINT'S DOUBLE TROUBLE, found him portraying both the Saint and his lookalike, gangster Duke Piato, better known as "The Boss." The plot focuses on a Philadelphia-based diamond smuggling ring which Piato heads and their goal of snatching a batch of stolen uncut diamonds which are hidden in a mummy case Templar is sending to his friend, Professor Bitts (Thomas W. Ross). When the treasure-laden artifact arrives in the city, the hoodlums find the Saint is wise to their gambit, causing a confrontation between Templar and his gangster boss double. The movie--not one of the series' best--is notable for wasting Bela Lugosi in a supporting role as a gang member known as The Partner.

After two more series' chapters, Sanders grew bored with the undemanding role and Hugh Sinclair took over for a few features before the series was temporarily halted. In 1954, Louis Hayward returned to the fold in the British-made THE SAINT'S RETURN, which RKO issued here as THE SAINT'S GIRL FRIDAY. Within the story, The Saint investigates the death of a young woman whose murder is connected with a gambling syndicate headquartered in a house near London's Thames River. While bringing the hoodlums to justice, Hayward romances the gambling house seductress (Naomi Chance).

ST. IVES (Warner Bros., 1976) C 93 mins.

Producers, Pancho Kohner, Stanley Canter; director, J. Lee Thompson; based on the novel The Procane Chronicle by Oliver Bleeck; screenplay, Barry Beckerman; music, Lalo Schifrin; production designer, Philip M. Jefferies; set decorator, Robert De Vestel;

Charles Bronson in ST. IVES (1976).

assistant director, Ronald L. Schwary; stunt coordinator, Max
Kleven; sound, Harlan Riggs, Arthur Piantadosi; camera, Lucien
Ballard; editor, Michael F. Anderson.

Charles Bronson (Raymond St. Ives); John Houseman (Abner Pro-
cane); Jacqueline Bisset (Janet Whistler); Maximilian Schell (Dr.
John Constable); Harry Guardino (Detective Deal); Harris Yulin
(Detective Oller); Dana Elcar (Detective Blunt); Michael Lerner
(Lawyer Green); Dick O'Neill (Counterman); Elisha Cook (Room
Clerk); Val Bisolgio (Finley); Burr De Benning (Motorcycle Cop);
Daniel J. Travanti (Parisi).

Superstar Charles Bronson, known for his hard-hitting earthy
roles, once said, "Some day, I would like to have a part where I
can lean my elbow against a mantlepiece and have a cocktail."
About as close as the star ever has come to such a screen situation is ST. IVES, an offbeat crime thriller which provides Bronson
as actionful, yet toned down role, and the sophisticated feature
even permits him to dress well and to mingle with the upper crust,
although the latter are revealed to be crooks.
Bronson is Raymond St. Ives, a former crime reporter and
struggling novelist with few published credits. Wealthy Abner
Procane (John Houseman) hires Bronson to procure five stolen ledgers and in the process Bronson becomes involved with Houseman's
beautiful mistress (Jacqueline Bisset) who has a boyfriend (Maximilian Schell). Before long, Bronson finds himself caught in a maze
of murders, double crosses, and complications which results in his
learning that the real killer is Bisset, who is after her gangster-
keeper's fortunes.
While most critics delighted in the change of pace the movie
provided Bronson, most also felt the movie was essentially dull.
Perhaps the feature's most ingratiating ingredient is Jacqueline
Bisset, who remains long in memory, especially at the finale where
she stands soaking wet and defenseless as Bronson, who has brought
about her downfall, leaves her in the custody of pal policeman Charlie Blunt (Dana Elcar).

SAINT JACK (New World, 1979) C 112 mins.

Executive producers, Hugh M. Hefner, Edward L. Rissien; producer,
Roger Corman; director, Peter Bogdanovich; based on the novel by
Paul Theroux; screenplay, Howard Sackler, Theroux, Bogdanovich;
art director, David Ng; sound, Jean-Pierre Ruh; camera, Robby
Muller; editor, William Carruth.

Ben Gazzara (Jack Flowers); Denholm Elliott (William Leigh); James
Villiers (Frogget); Joss Ackland (Yardley); Rodney Bewes (Smale);
Mark Kingston (Yates); Lisa Lu (Mrs. Yates); Monika Subramanian
(Monika); Judy Lim (Judy); George Lazenby (Senator); Peter Bog-
danovich (Eddie Shuman); Joseph Noel (Gopi); One Kian Bee (Hing);
Tan Yan Meng (Little Hing).

The film career of producer-director-writer-occasional-actor Peter Bogdanovich is an intriguing one, running the gamut from such cinema classics as THE LAST PICTURE SHOW (1971), WHAT'S UP DOC? (1972), and PAPER MOON (1973), to such debacles as DAISY MILLER (1974) and AT LONG LAST LOVE (1975). SAINT JACK, filmed in Singapore in 1978 and issued to fairly decent notices but anemic box office, lies in the middle among the aforementioned features. The film was the first in two years for Bogdanovich following the failure of NICKELODEON (1976).

The story is "about a guy who was about as low as you can get" (Peter Bogdanovich in a speech at the 1983 Denver Film Festival), and it was shot totally in Singapore using residents of that city, some in speaking roles. It tells of American Jack Flowers (Ben Gazzara), a slimy gangster who makes money any way he can, from numbers runnings and drugs to prostitution. Although personally he is vague about America's involvement in Vietnam, he agrees to work for a military intelligence officer (Bogdanovich) who requires him to supply whores for servicemen on leave in the city. Later, however, he is told to get the goods on an antiwar senator (George Lazenby) who is a closet homosexual. Gazzara obtains the needed evidence to smear the man, but has second thoughts and destroys it.

SAINT JACK's chief charm is its exotic locales, with the city reflecting more life than the film. Since the movie's protagonist is basically a bottom-of-the-ladder hoodlum, it is hardly an endearing case study and star Ben Gazzara appears to be ad libbing too frequently. On the other hand, Denholm Elliott is impressive as Gazzara's stalwart British pal, while George "James Bond" Lazenby is fine in his brief walk-on as the senator. Producer-director Bogdanovich is embarrassingly self-indulgent as the military officer.

THE SAINT'S DOUBLE TROUBLE (RKO, 1940) 68 mins.

Producer, Cliff Reid; director, Jack Hively; based on characters created by Leslie Charteris; screenplay, Ben Holmes; music, Roy Webb; special effects, Vernon Walker; camera, J. Roy Hunt; editor, Theron Warth.

George Sanders (Simon Templar--the Saint); Helene Whitney (Anne); Jonathan Hale (Inspector Fernack); Bella Lugosi (Partner); Donald MacBride (Bohlen); John F. Hamilton (Limpy); Thomas W. Ross (Professor Bitts); Elliott Sullivan (Monk).

See: THE SAINT IN NEW YORK

THE SAINT'S GIRL FRIDAY (RKO, 1954) 70 mins.

Producers, Julian Lesser, Anthony Hinds; director, Seymour Friedman; based on characters created by Leslie Charteris; screenplay,

Allan MacKinnon; music, Ivoy Stanley; camera, Walter Harvey; editor, James Needs.

Louis Hayward (Simon Templar--the Saint); Naomi Chance (Carol Denby); Sidney Tafler (Max Lennar); Charles Victor (Chief Inspector Teal); Jane Carr (Katie French); Harold Lan (Jarvis); Russell Enoch (Keith Merton); Diana Dors (Margie); Fred Johnson (Irish Cassidy); Thomas Gallagher (Hoppy Uniatz).

See: THE SAINT IN NEW YORK

SAM MARLOW, PRIVATE EYE see: THE MAN WITH BOGART'S FACE

SAVANNAH SMILES (Gold Coast, 1982) C 107 mins.

Producer, Clark L. Paylow; associate producer, Laurette DeMoro Gafferi; director, Pierre DeMoro; story-screenplay, Mark Miller; music, Ken Sutherland; production designer, Charles Stewart; art director, Allen Terry; assistant director, Dennis White; camera, Stephen W. Gray; editor, Eva Ruggiero.

Mark Miller (Alive); Donovan Scott (Boots); Bridgette Andersen (Savannah Driscoll); Peter Graves (Dobbs); Chris Robinson (Driscoll); Michael Parks (Lieutenant Savage); Barbara Stanger (Joan); Pat Morita (Fr. O'Hara); Philip Abbott (Chief Pruitt); Fran Ryan (Wilma); John Fiedler (Clerk); Ray Anzalone (Greenblatt); Carol Wayne (Coreen).

After making the respectable but obscure Western CHRISTMAS MOUNTAIN (1980) with Slim Pickens, actor-writer Mark Miller and director Pierre DeMoro turned their creative attentions to the gangster film genre with this picturesque, family-oriented, Utah-lensed drama. Having two crooks softened by the charms of a pretty little girl is an old plot ploy and one used to good advantage here by scripter Miller, who has a good cast to bolster the proceedings. SAVANNAH SMILES is a relief from the barrage of foul-mouthed, blood-spattered gangster movies saturating theaters recently.

Young Savannah Driscoll (Bridgette Andersen) runs away from home after being taken for granted by her rich, social climbing parents (Chris Robinson, Barbara Stanger). She meets two small-time criminals (Miller, Donovan Scott) who have unsuccessfully been trying to accomplish robberies in various small towns. Realizing the girl's parents are wealthy, the duo plan to hold her for $100,000 ransom. The parents hire a Texas lawman (Peter Graves) to find their girl. The longer the gangsters remain with the girl, the more ingratiating they find her and finally they fall prey to her charm, even taking her on a picnic and getting her a small dog. Finally, two policemen (Michael Parks, Pat Morita) aid in the return of the girl; the crooks are reformed by her sweetness, and the girl's mother has a change of heart and leaves her spouse because of his child neglect.

SCARFACE (Universal, 1983) C 170 mins.

Executive producer, Louis A. Stroller; producer, Martin Bregman; co-producer, Peter Saphier; director, Brian DePalma; based on the screenplay by Ben Hecht; new screenplay, Oliver Stone; assistant directors, Jerry Ziesmer, Joe Napolitano, Chris Soldo; costumes, Patricia Norris; music, Giorgio Moroder; production designers, Blake Russell, Steve Schwartz, Geoff Hubbard; art director, Ed Richardson; camera, John A. Alonzo; editors, Jerry Greenberg, David Ray.

Al Pacino (Tony Montana); Steven Bauer (Manny Ray); Michelle Pfeiffer (Elvira); Mary Elizabeth Mastrantonio (Gina); Robert Loggia (Frank Lopez); Miriam Colon (Mama Montana); F. Murray Abraham (Omar); Paul Shenar (Alejandro Sosa); Harris Yulin (Bernstein); Angel Salazar (Chi Chi); Arnaldo Santana (Ernie); Pepe Serna (Angel); Michael P. Moran (Nick the Pig); Al Israel (Hector the Toad); Dennis Holohan (Banker); Mark Maregolis (Shadow); Michael Alldredge (Sheffield); Ted Beniades (Seidelbaum); Richard Belzer (M.C. at Babylon Club); Paul Espel (Luis); John Brandon, Tony Perez, Garnett Smith (Immigration Officers); Loren Almaguer (Dr. Munoz); Gil Barreto (Cuban Refugee); Heather Benna (Gutierrez Child); Dawnell Bowers (Miriam); and: Tina Leigh Cameron, Victor Campos, Rene Carrasco, John Carter, Richard Caselnova, Carlos Cestero, Dante D'Andre, Wayne Doba, Ben Frommer, John Gamble, Joe Marmo, Ray Martel, Richard Mendez, Santos Morales.

Tony Montana (Al Pacino) comes to 1980 Florida as one of the thousands of criminals deported by Cuba's Fidel Castro. He becomes involved in a drug deal, emerging with both money and cocaine. His savvy impresses the local gang boss (Robert Loggia) who takes him under his protective wing. Pacino quickly becomes a mover in the organization and develops a close relationship with Alejandro Sosa (Paul Shenar), a Bolivian cocaine connection. Having lusted for this boss' drug-addicted mistress (Michele Pfeiffer), Pacino finally murders Loggia and takes over his territory. Compulsive, greedy Pacino then rules his gangland empire with an iron hand, even killing an old friend whom he suspects has slept with his pretty sister (Mary Elizabeth Mastrantonio) for whom Pacino also yearns. Eventually, excessive drugs and power brings about his downfall.

An updating of the classic, slick, powerful Paul Muni starrer (see: B/V), the new SCARFACE is an overblown, slow moving melodrama which wallows in explicit and excessive violence in deference to a sturdy storyline or strong characterizations. The Miami gangster world represented here is a scum-inhabited realm

where everyone double-crosses everyone else and only money and
drugs are important and the swiftest way to success is violence.
Certainly the spectrum of the gangster movie has changed dramat-
ically since the 1930s when even the worst of hardened criminals
were pictured as being victims of economic circumstances rather
than being innately evil creatures.

In his highly intensive fashion, Al Pacino etches a sharp
portrait of the ambitious, murderous, but weak Tony Montana.
However, the final hour of the feature in which his excesses bring
about his death becomes near ludicrous. Director Brain DePalma
allows the narrative to get out of hand and to become a laughable,
tawdry melodrama.

SCORCHY (American International, 1976) C 99 mins.

Executive producer, Marlene Schmidt; producer-director-screenplay,
Hikmet Avedis; assistant director, Bruce Wilson; music, Igo Kantor;

Connie Stevens as SCORCHY (1976).

sound, Kenneth Hansen; camera, Laszlo Paul; editor, Michael Luciano.

Connie Stevens (Sergeant Jackie Parker--Scorchy); Cesare Danova (Philip Biasnco); William Smith (Carl Henrich); Norman Burton (Chief Frank O'Brien); John David Chandler (Nicky); Joyce Jameson (Mary Davis); Greg Evigan (Alan); Nick Dimitri (Steve); Nate Long (Charlie); Ingrid Cedergren (Suzi); Ellen Thurston (Maria); Ray Sebastian (Counterman); Mike Esky (Dimitri); Gene White (Big Boy); Marlene Schmidt (Claudia Bianco).

Federal undercover agent Jackie Parker, also known as Scorchy (Connie Stevens), is in Seattle to break up the Bianco Brothers' drug operation between that city and Rome. Using an export-import business as a front, the brothers import dope into the country, with one brother (Cesare Danova) and his wife (Marlene Schmidt) operating out of the West Coast city. Stevens infiltrates the gang and gains the trust of the couple, and they assign her to deliver a heroin shipment to the San Juan Islands. There a delay occurs with hijackers murdering the chief's brother-in-law, who was making love to Stevens. She teams with the narcotics' kingpin to get revenge on them. With this accomplished and the missing heroin recovered, Stevens attempts to arrest the gangster, but he escapes in a speedboat with she purusing him in a helicopter to a climactic shootout.

"She's Killed a Man, Been Shot at and Made Love Twice Already This Evening--and the Evening Isn't Over Yet! ... Where There's Scorchy, There's Action!" read the catchlines for this American-International release in which executive producer Marlene Schmidt plays a co-starring role.

Connie Stevens is fairly convincing in the part of the hard-as-nails federal agent in this R-rated violent actioner. Unlike most of its ilk, SCORCHY left no room for a sequel when it killed off the title character at the finale. Boxoffice magazine also complained, "More development of her [Scorchy] background character, and motivation would have been helpful." Still, the trade paper correctly noted, "Nevertheless, the rapid-action film will please its particular audience."

SCOUTS TO THE RESCUE (Universal, 1939) twelve chapters

Directors, Ray Taylor, Alan James; story, J. Irving Crump; screenplay, Wyndham Gittens, George H. Plympton, Basil Dickey, Joseph Poland; music, Charles Previn; camera, Willard Sickner; editor, Saul A. Goodkind.

Jackie Cooper (Bruce Scott); Vondell Darr (Mary Scanlon); Edwin Stanley (Pat Scanlon); William Ruhl (Hal Marvin); Bill Cody, Jr. (Skeets Scanlon); David Durand (Rip Dawson); Ralph Dunn (Pug O'Toole); Jason Robards (Doc); Frank Coghlan, Jr. (Ken); Ivan

Jackie Cooper and David Durand in SCOUTS TO THE RESCUE (1939).

Miller (Turk Mortenson); Victor Adams (Hurst); Sidney Miller (Hermie); Richard Botiller (Leeka).

Chapters: 1) Death Rides the Air; 2) Avalanche of Doom; 3) Trapped by the Indians; 4) River of Doom; 5) Descending Doom; 6) Ghost Town Menace; 7) Destroyed by Dynamite; 8) Thundering Hoofs; 9) The Fire God Strikes; 10) The Battle at Ghost Town; 11) Hurtling Through Space; 12) The Boy Scouts' Triumph.

Following the end of his Metro-Goldwyn-Mayer contract in the late 1930s, erstwhile child star Jackie Cooper, now a less commercial teenager, found the going rough in Hollywood and his screen assignments (when he could obtain them) varied from Monogram programmers to the lead role of Henry Aldrich in Paramount's WHAT A LIFE (1939). Sandwiched between these outings was a twelve-chapter Universal serial, SCOUTS TO THE RESCUE, which slapped Cooper smack in the middle of the gangster genre with the usual fast paced action associated with such chapterplays.

Eagle Scout Bruce Scott (Cooper) takes his Boy Scout troop to Ghost Town, a deserted village. While camping they locate what they believe is a buried treasure. A plane crashes nearby and the scouts rescue a man who turns out to be FBI agent Hal Marvin (William Ruhl). He tells them that the found money is counterfeit and that he is after the gang that is printing the bogus currency. He adds that the gang is led by hoodlum Turk Mortenson (Ivan Miller) and he believes the crook is associated with businessman Pat Scanlon (Edwin Stanley), the father of troop member Skeets (Bill Cody, Jr.). The gangster then takes both father and son prisoner, but Cody escapes only to be menaced by renegade Indians. The scouts fight them off. The G-man then finds evidence which clears Stanley of criminal complicity, and with the aid of the scouts he captures the gangsters.

Not only did ex-child star Jackie Cooper headline this chapterplay, but other former child players appeared in it: Frank Coghlan, Jr., also known as Junior Coghlan, who headlined another gangster picture, THE LITTLE RED SCHOOLHOUSE (q.v.); and Bill Cody, Jr., the son of the Western star, who had a career as the juvenile lead, mainly in "B" Westerns.

SCREAM IN THE NIGHT (Commodore, 1935) 60 mins.

Producer, Ray Kirkwood; director, Fred Newmeyer; screenplay, Norman Springer; technical director, Zarah Tazil; camera, Bert Longenecker.

Lon Chaney, Jr. (Jack Wilson/Butch Curtain); Sheila Terry (Edith Bentley); Richard Cramer (Inspector Green); Zarah Tazil (Mora); Philson [Philip] Ahn (Wu Ting); Manuel Lopez (Johnny Fly); John Ince (Bentley); Merrill McCormick (Arab).

In Singapore Police Inspector Green (Richard Cramer) assigns detectives Jack Wilson (Lon Chaney, Jr.) and Wu Ting (Philson [Philip] Ahn) to capture notorious gangster Johnny Fly (Manuel Lopez), who tries to steal a ruby from a rich man (John Ince) whose daughter (Sheila Terry) is friendly with Chaney. Masquerading as a coolie, Ahn meets Butch Curtain (Chaney), Lopez's henchman, but when Fly tells him the Chinaman is really a detective, Curtain murders him. Meanwhile Curtain is having an affair with Lopez's mistress (Zarah Tazil), who wants to get gems from him, and Lopez kidnaps Terry and holds her prisoner, hoping to use her as ransom for her father's ruby. Wilson and Cramer manage to capture Curtain and through the use of makeup, Wilson pretends to be the hoodlum and locates Lopez, but Tazil sees through the disguise and a fight takes place with Wilson defeating Lopez and Cramer arriving to round up the gang and free Terry.
SCREAM IN THE NIGHT (made as SCREAM IN THE DARK and also called MURDER IN MOROCCO) was the second and last of two gangster thrillers Lon Chaney, Jr. acted in for Commodore Pictures in 1935; the initial entry was THE SHADOW OF SILK LENNOX (q.v.). A tawdry drama, this movie provided Chaney the chance to enact

two roles and his makeup for the grotesque Butch Curtain is similar to that used by his famous father in THE ROAD TO MANDALAY (1926). In its initial distribution, the picture had scant release, but after Chaney became a Universal horror film star in the early 1940s, the picture was re-released in 1943 by Astor Pictures.

THE SEA SPOILERS (Universal, 1936) 62 mins.

Producer, Trem Carr; associate producer, Paul Malvern; director, Frank Strayer; story, Dorrell and Stuart E. McGowan; screenplay, George Waggoner; music director, Herman S. Heller; camera, Archie Stout, John P. Fulton ;editors, H. R. Fritch, Ray Lockhart.

John Wayne (Bob Randall); Nan Grey (Connie Dawson); William Bakewell (Lieutenant Maya); Fuzzy Knight (Hogan); Russell Hicks (Phil Morgan); George Irving (Commander Mays); Lotus Long (Marie); Harry Worth (Nick Austin); Ernest Hilliard (Reggie); George Humbert (Hop Scotch); Ethan Laidlow (Louie); Chester Gan (Oil); Cy Kendall (Detective); Harrison Green (Fats).

In 1936 John Wayne, then mainly associated with "B" Westerns, signed to star in six adventure programmers for producer Trem Carr with release through Universal Pictures. Although low budgeted, these movies were entertaining and varied in their globe-trotting plots: Wayne was a boxer in CONFLICT (1936), a trucker

John Wayne and Fuzzy Knight in THE SEA SPOILERS (1936).

in CALIFORNIA STRAIGHT AHEAD (1937), a newsreel cameraman
in I COVER THE WAR (1937), a hockey player in IDOL OF THE
CROWDS (1937), and a pearl diver in ADVENTURE'S END (1937).
For the initial entry, the lanky star was entangled with gangsters,
this time the kind who are seal poachers and smugglers.

U.S. Coast Guard cutter commander Bob Randall (Wayne)
takes a furlough to visit his actress fiancee, Donnie Dawson (Nan
Grey) aboard a yacht where she is scheduled to be the star entertainer. On board he finds the yacht's owner has been shot and
that a load of stolen sealskins are hidden in the cargo, but Grey
cannot be located. With his pal Hogan (Fuzzy Knight) and the latter's pet seal Mabel, Wayne boards a small fishing boat and begins
searching nearby waters for the girl. He finds her on an expensive yacht, being held prisoner by smugglers using the boat as
their headquarters.

SECRET FILE: HOLLYWOOD (Crown International, 1961) 85 mins.

Producers, Rudolph Cusumano, James Dyer; director, Ralph Cush-
man; story-screenplay, Jack Lewis; art director, Stanley Rusak;
makeup, Bill Condos; assistant director, Gene Pollack; music,
Manuel Francisco; sound, James Fullerton; camera, Gregory Sandor;
editor, James Dyer.

Robert Clarke (Maxwell Carter); Francine York (Nan Torr); Syd
Mason (Hap Grogan); Maralou Gray (Gay Shelton); John Warburton
(James Cameron); Shirley Chandler (Jazz Dancer); Maya De Mar
(Flamenco Dancer); and: Bill White, William Justice, Martha Mason,
Barbara Skyler, Kathy Potter, Eleanor Ames.

Private detective Maxwell Carter (Robert Clarke) loses his
license after being involved in the shooting of a young girl in a
beatnik joint while on a case. About to leave Hollywood, he is
given a job as a reporter on a scandal magazine called "Secret
File Hollywood" by editor Nan Torr (Francine York). York and
Hap Grogan (Syd Mason) run the publication but they work for a
mysterious man who sends them instructions via tape recordings.
York assigns Clarke to get photos of famous film director James
Cameron (John Warburton) in a compromising position with starlet
Gay Shelton (Maralou Gray) and after he does, York uses them to
blackmail Warburton. When the story is published, Warburton's
wife commits suicide and he goes to a newscaster pal (Bill White)
who urges readers to help shut down the scandal rag. After the
suicide, Clarke quits the operation but the police urge him to continue to help them track the real magazine owner. York and Mason
get wise to him after he becomes involved with Gray and they catch
him wiring York's bedroom. Mason takes Clarke for a ride but is
himself killed as Clarke jumps from the car before it careens off a
cliff. The mysterious publisher then murders York but tapes of
his voice sent to Warburton reveal the man's identity. Clarke and

Gray trail Warburton to the television station where the moviemaker confronts the newscaster as the voice on the tape and the killer of his wife. In a scuffle, the newsman is killed with his own gun. Clarke and Gray head to the marriage license bureau.

In the 1950s, the expose magazine racket unfairly indicted some of the biggest names in Hollywood moviemaking. This cheapie production takes advantage of this phenomenon, but it is a stale outing, poorly executed and wretchedly performed by its cast, except for Robert Clarke, Francine York, and John Warburton, who try to make something out of their roles. The film would have been more believable had not the microphone been visible in just about every scene that called for a long shot.

SECRET OF DEEP HARBOR (United Artists, 1961) 70 mins.

Producer, Robert E. Kent; director, Edward L. Cahn; based on the novel I Cover the Waterfront by Max Miller; screenplay, Owen Harris, Wells Root; music, Richard LaSalle; assistant director, Herbert S. Greene; sound, Stanley Cooley; camera, Gilbert Warrenton; editor, Kenneth Crane.

Ron Foster (Skip Hanlon); Barry Kelley (Milo Fowler); Merry Anders (Janey Fowler); Norman Alden (Barney Hanes); James Seay (Travis); Grant Richards (Rick Correll); Ralph Manza (Frank Miner); Billie Bird (Mama Miller); Elaine Walker (Rita); Max Mellinger (Doctor).

Crime reporter Skip Hanlon (Ron Foster) is following gangsters who are being smuggled out of the country by a crime syndicate. He falls in love with pretty Janey Fowler (Merry Anders), the daughter of sea captain Milo Fowler (Barry Kelley), a suspect in the operation. Foster uncovers the fact that the sea captain has been hired by the syndicate to carry out the smuggling operation and he exposes him, thus causing trouble with his lady love. Eventually the reporter and the captain unite to thwart the wrongdoers.

This "ludicrously-plotted, ketchup-spattered, waterfront crime melodrama" (Variety) taken from Max Miller's novel I Cover the Waterfront (1928), was first filmed in 1933 (q.v.) by producer Edward Small. Nowhere matching the original, this edition is a poor second in nearly every department. The gangsters here are a dull lot, their criminal activities hardly in keeping with the fast pace creativity of the atomic age.

SERPICO: THE DEADLY GAME (Paramount/NBC-TV, 4/24/76) C 100 mins.

Producer, Emmet G. Lavery, Jr.; associate producer, Arthur E. McLaird; director, Robert Collins; based on the novel Serpico by Peter Maas; teleplay, Collins; music, Elmer Bernstein; art director, Frank T. Smith; camera, Donald M. Morgan; editor, Patrick Kennedy.

David Birney in SERPICO: THE DEADLY GAME (1976).

David Birney (Frank Serpico); Allen Garfield (The Professor); Burt
Young (Alec Rosen); Tom Atkins (Lieutenant Tom Sullivan); Lane
Bradbury (Carol); Christine Jones (Kim); Will Kuluva (Mr. Ser-
pico); Walter McGinn (David Doyle); Mario Roccuzzo (Angelo Ser-
pico); Sydney Lassick (Goldman); Anthony Charnota (Joe Simone);
Carl Lee (Carothers); Richard C. Adams (Atkins); Madison Arnold
(Polo); Albert Henderson (Sergeant Morgan); Antony Ponziini
(Dominique); Harry Shearer (Hippy); Paulette Brein (Gina); Pat
Angeli (Rosa); Frank Spalar (Choreographer).

New York City policeman Frank Serpico was the subject of a
best-selling book and later a well-received motion picture (see:
B/V) starring Al Pacino. Serpico's dedicated efforts to halt corruption both in and out of the Gotham police department made him
a legendary figure, although not necessarily a popular one on his
home turf. This telefeature continued the adventures of the real-
life cop who, in reality, retired from the police force in 1971 after
a dope peddler shot him in the face.
  SERPICO: THE DEADLY GAME has undercover policeman
Frank Serpico (David Birney), in tandem with Lieutenant Tom Sullivan (Tom Atkins), working to stop corruption within the confines
of the police department and at the same time tracking down and
bringing to justice those involved in a drug smuggling operation
and their connection with a loan shark.
  This adequate telefeature was the pilot for NBC's "Serpico"
series starring David Birney and Tom Atkins which lasted four
months on the air (9/24/76 to 1/28/77).

THE SET-UP (RKO, 1949) 72 mins.

Producer, Richard Goldstone; director, Robert Wise; based on the
poem by Joseph Moncure March; screenplay, Art Cohn; art direc-
tors, Albert S. D'Agostino, Jack Okey; set decorators, Darrell
Silvera, James Altwies; technical adviser, John Indrisano; makeup
Gordon Bau; assistant director, Edward Killy; music director, C.
Bakalienikoff; sound, Phil Brigandi, Clem Portman; camera, Milton
Krasner; editor, Roland Gross.

Robert Ryan (Stoker Thompson); Audrey Totter (Julie Thompson);
George Tobias (Tiny); Alan Baxter (Little Boy); Wallace Ford (Gus);
Percy Helton (Red); Hal Fieberling (Tiger Nelson); Darryl Hickman
(Shanley); Kenny O'Morrison (Moore); James Edwards (Luther Haw-
kins); David Clarke (Gunboat Johnson); Phillip Pine (Souza); Ed-
win Max (Danny); Dave Fresco (Mickey); William E. Greemn (Doc-
tor); Abe Dinovitch (Ring Caller); Jack Chase (Hawkins' Second);
Mike Lally, Arthur Sullivan, William McCarter (Handlers); Herbert
Anderson, Jack Raymonds, Helen Brown, Constance Worth (Married
Couples); Archie Leonard (Blind Man); Ralph Volkie, Tony Merrill,
Lilliam Castle, Frances Mack, Sam Shack, Carl Sklover (Bits); Larry
Anzalone (Mexican Fighter); Paul Dubov, Jess Kirkpatrick (Gamblers);

Audrey Totter and Robert Ryan in THE SET-UP (1949).

Jack Stoney (Nelson's Second); John Butler (Blind Man's Companion); Walter Ridge (Manager); Bernard Gorcey (Tobacco Man); Donald Kerr (Vendor).

With the success of Sylvester Stallone's ROCKY films in the 1970s and 1980s, there has been a resurgence of interest in boxing movies, most of which depict the so-called sport's gangster influences. There has also been a retrospective look at fight films of the past, and one of the most revered is THE SET-UP, a taut, in-depth look at small-time fighters and their mob controllers. In his appraisal of the film, "Knockout in Paradise," in American Classic Screen magazine (July/August, 1978), J. M. Welsh wrote, "It is especially remarkable for its creation of atmosphere in the noir tradition, the murky, soiled world of smalltime boxing arenas, ruined athletes, sadistic fans, corrupt managers, and vengeful gangsters."
The film relates the account of Stoker Thompson (Robert

Ryan), a 35-year-old boxer who is thought to be washed up. He lives in a dive hotel with his wife Julie (Audrey Totter), who wants him to quit the ring, and he fights across the street in a dump of an auditorium called "Paradise City." He is scheduled to fight an up and coming boxer, Tiger Nelson (Hal Baylor), and the local hoodlum, Little Boy (Alan Baxter), who runs the boxing racket, pays Ryan's manager (George Tobias) and trainer (Percy Helton) $50 for him to throw the bout. The two, however, do not think Ryan can win anyway and don't tell him of the special arrangement. For the first few rounds, Ryan takes a terrible beating, but soon the kid wears down and is knocked out in the fourth round. Because he failed to throw the match, Stoker is taken into an alley and badly beaten. His hand is broken so he can never fight again.

Robert Ryan, a former collegiate boxer, had one of his best screen roles as Stoker Thompson, and the supporting cast is equal to his work. Yet the most memorable aspect of the production is its tawdry atmosphere, especially the violence-hungry crowd. To amplify this mood director Robert Wise centered in on several such individuals (a fat man with a new snack for each round; a blind man having the action described to him; a screaming woman who embarrasses her spouse, et al). It all combined to make this film even more realistic.

The entire background of the film is shaded by the influence of gangsters, the main mobster being Little Boy, a cowardly, sadistic, evil man, well played by Alan Baxter. Especially effective is the finale where Ryan lashes out at Baxter when he is cornered and slugs him. The hoodlum then has the boxer's hand crushed in retaliation.

In his book A Reference Guide to the American Film Noir: 1948-1958 (1981), author Robert Ottson analyzes, "Unlike John Garfield in BODY AND SOUL, [Robert] Ryan is not a heroic figure, but a tragic one. His refusal to capitulate to the gamblers takes place in such a shabby milieu, and the size of his triumph is so minuscule, that any heroic notions the viewer might perceive are quickly dashed. In this respect, the film does provide a proper corrective to the unrealities of a film like ROCKY."

SHADOW OF A KILLER see: DEATH RAGE

THE SHADOW OF SILK LENNOX (Commodore, 1935) 60 mins.

Producer-director, Ray Kirkwood; screenplay, Norman Springer; art director, Zarah Tazil; songs, Dean Benton; camera, Robert Cline.

Lon Chaney, Jr. (Silk Lennox); Jack Mulhall (Fingers Farley); Dean Benton (Jimmy Lambert); Marie Burton (Nola); Eddie Gribbon (Lefty); Larry McGrath (Ratsy); Allen Greer (Deacon).

In 1935 Lon Chaney's son, Creighton Chaney, who had been appearing under his own name in films for three years, signed a contract with producer Ray Kirkwood to headline eight films a year, many of them to be Westerns, over a three-year period. After making two gangster yarns, THE SHADOW OF SIL LENNOX and SCREAM IN THE NIGHT (q.v.), the series died along with Kirkwood's Commodore Pictures. It was for this series that Chaney had reluctantly changed his name to Lon Chaney, Jr.

THE SHADOW OF SILK LENNOX tells of a one-time bootlegger (Chaney, Jr.) who operates a night spot which is the headquarters for his many criminal outlets. For some time the police have been unable to get the goods on him, so a police detective (Jack Mulhall) "becomes" criminal Fingers Farley and infiltrates the gang, helping in the planning of a bank robbery. The detective uses club singer Nola (Marie Burton) and her beau (Dean Benton), Chaney's reluctant cohorts, to bring the gangster to justice.

This poverty row entry had Chaney as the villain and as the hero, silent film star Jack Mulhall, who only a few years earlier had played the first dual roles in a talking gangster movie in 1929's DARK STREETS (q.v.).

SHARKEY'S MACHINE (Orion/Warner Bros., 1981) C 119 mins.

Producer, Hank Moonjean; associate producer, Edward Teets; director, Burt Reynolds; based on the novel by William Diehl; screenplay, Gerald Di Pego; production designer, Walter Scott Herndon; costumes, Norman Salling; assistant directors, Benjy Rosenberg, Jim Van Wyck, Don Wilkerson, Paul Moen; choreography, Arthur Ferro; sound, Jack Solomon, Joe Kenworthy; camera, William A. Fraker; editor, William Gordean.

Burt Reynolds (Sharkey); Vittorio Gassman (Victor); Brain Keith (Papa); Charles Durning (Firscoe); Earl Holliman (Hotchkins); Bernie Casey (Arch); Henry Silva (Billy Score); Richard Libertini (Nosh); Darryl Hickman (Smiley); Rachel Ward (Dominoe); Joseph Mascolo (Joe Tipps); Carol Locatell (Mabel); Hari Rhodes (Highball Mary); John Fiedler (Barrett); James O'Connell (Twigs); Val Avery (Man with Siakwan); Suzec Pai (Siakwan); Azarika Wells (Tiffany); Tony King (Kitten); William Diehl (Percy); Dan Inosanto, Weaver Levy (The Two Chins); May Keller Pearce (May); Sheryl Kilby (Lisa); James Lewis, Scott Newell (Police); Glynn Ruben (Pregnant Woman); Bennie Moore (Bus Driver); Brenda Bynum (Aging Hooker); Gus Mann (Flasher); John Arthur (Pusher).

After headlining such mindless box office successes as SMOKEY AND THE BANDIT (1977), SMOKEY AND THE BANDIT II (1980), and THE CANNONBALL RUN (1981), Burt Reynolds attempted to redeem himself within the film community by starring in and directing this tough police melodrama which Variety acclaimed "a seemingly guaranteed winner." In actuality this strung-out, overlong cops-and-gangsters hookum was a poor mixture of DIRTY HARRY (see: B/V) and LAURA (1944) set in Atlanta.

Several veteran cops are suddenly relegated to routine work on the vice squad, a force led by Sharkey (Reynolds). Soon they begin to sniff around to determine why they got there. They discover a connection between a syndicate kingpin (Vittorio Gassman) and a popular gubernatorial candidate (Earl Holliman) in the person of luscious hooker Dominoe (Rachel Ward). When she is mysteriously shot, Reynolds stakes out her apartment and finds himself entranced with the image of the girl, who turns up very much alive. Realizing she is marked for murder, he hides her in an out-of-town retreat where the two fall in love. Later the gangsters remove two of the cop's fingers in an attempt to make him reveal her whereabouts. At the finale the team shoot it out with Gassman's crew, with Reynolds finally downing the syndicate's almost invincible hit man (Henry Silva) in a highrise business complex.

There is little beyond flash to recommend SHARKEY'S MACHINE outside of Vittorio Gassman's well etched portrayal of the sinister gangster and Earl Holliman's convivial but corrupt politico.

SHEBA BABY (American International, 1975) C 90 mins.

Producer, David Sheldon; director-story-screenplay, William Girdler; music, Monk Higgins, Alex Brown; songs, Cleveland and Ranifere; stunt coordinator, Richard Washington; production

Pam Grier in SHEBA BABY (1975).

designer, J. Patrick Kelly III; special effects, Gene Grigg; camera, William Asman; editors, Henry Asman, Jack Davies.

Pam Grier (Sheba); Austin Stoker (Brick); D'Urville Martin (Pilot); Rudy Challenger (Andyh); Dick Merrifield (Shark); Christopher Joy (Walker); Charles Kissinger (Phil); Charles Broaddus (Hammerhead); Maurice Downes (Killer); Ernest Cooley (Whale); Edward Reece, Jr. (Racker); William Foster, Jr. (Waldo); Bobby Cooley (Tank); Paul Grayber (Fin); Sylvia Jacobson (Tail); Leory Clark, Jr. (Customer); Mike Clifford (Policeman); Rose Ann Deel (Policewoman).

Producer-director William Girdler churned out a series of low budget action melodramas prior to his death in 1977. Two of these starred black exploitation queen Pam Grier, with SHEBA BABY firmly in the gangster tradition while ABBY (1974) was a black cast horror film in the mold of THE EXORCIST.

Big city private detective Sheba (Grier) returns to her home town of Louisville, Kentucky, to protect her father who is being harassed by a white mobster and his black goons as they attempt to extort money from him. The underworld figures warn the old man to pay up and tell Grier to get out of town. When she refuses, the father is murdered. Grier then embarks on revenge: rubbing out the henchmen and then harpooning the mobster.

The chief interest in this low grade production is comely. Pam Grier who completed her American-International contract with this feature. The ads label Grier's character "Queen of the Private Eyes," but she seems unable to use her mental acumen to solve the crime; rather relying on her silver .44 to strong arm the heavies.

SHIP OF WANTED MEN (Showmen, 1933) 60 mins.

Director, Lew Collins; screenplay, Ethel Hill; camera, George Meehan; editor, Rose Smith.

Dorothy Sebastian (Irene Reynolds); Fred Kohler (Chuck Young); Leon Waycott [Ames] (Captain John Holden); Gertrude Astor (Vera); Maurice Black (Spinoli); Jason Robards (Craig); James Flavin (Busch).

A group of escaped prisoners steal a boat and head for a Central American island which has no extradition laws. The boat's captain (Leon Waycott), falsely convicted of a crime, has been given command because of his past naval experience, although hardened criminal Chuck Young (Fred Kohler) is really the group's leader. During their voyage, the men rescue a girl (Dorothy Sebastian) who has escaped from a yacht where she has killed a man (Jason Robards) who attempted to rape her. The girl becomes their prisoner, and when they find she has no money the escapees start

to bid for her but the captain comes to her aid and defeats Kohler
in a fight, puts the gang in the ship's hold, and turns them all
over to the Navy.

The Motion Picture Herald said this poverty row outing had a
"vigorous story" that provides "an hour of plentiful action." Despite its sparse settings, the movie is flavorful and holds audience
interest. Obviously some care was taken in executing this feature
as, for example in the use of radio news flashes to introduce the
various criminals, and a highly realistic finale fistfight between the
captain and the gang's leader.

SILVER BLAZE see: MURDER AT THE BASKERVILLES

THE SINISTER URGE (Headliner Productions, 1961) 75 mins.

Producer-director-screenplay, Edward D. Wood, Jr.; camera, William C. Thompson; editor, Wood.

Kenne Duncan (Lieutenant Matt Carson); James "Duke" Moore
(Sergeant Randy Stone); Jean Fontaine (Gloria Henderson); Carl
Anthony (Johnny Ryde); Dino Fantini (Dirk Williams); Jeanne Wil-
lardson (Mary Smith); Harry Keatan (Jaffe); Reed Howes (Police
Inspector); Harvey Dunne (Mr. Romaine); Kenneth Willardson (The-
atrical Agent); Vic McGee (Syndicate Man); Judy Berares (Frances);
Vonnie Starr (Secretary); Oma Soffian (Nurse); Toni Costello, Kathy
Randall, Sylvia Marenco, April Lynn (Models); Fred Mason, Jean
Baree, Clayton Peca (Policemen); Conrad Brooks, Edward D. Wood,
Jr. (Rival Gang Leaders).

Several girls who have posed for pornographic magazines have
been found murdered. Los Angeles police inspector (Reed Howes)
assigns Lieutenant Matt Carson (Kenne Duncan) and Sergeant Randy
Stone (Duke Moore) to bring in the killer(s). When the cops later
raid a pornographic modeling session directed by one-time Hollywood
helmsman Johnny Ryde (Carl Anthony) they begin to connect the
rash of murders with the smut racket. They find the operation is
headed by Gloria Henderson (Jean Fontaine), but it turns out the
killings are being committed by Dirk Williams (Dino Fantini), a young
man who goes haywire with lust after viewing porno product. The
police surround Fontaine's apartment and when he tries to murder
her, Fantini is captured by the law enforcers.

This obscure exploitation melodrama was the final legitimate
theatrical film directed by the "infamous" Edward D. Wood, Jr.,
the creator of such amusingly bad cinema as BRIDE OF THE MON-
STER (1955), and PLAN 9 FROM OUTER SPACE (1958), although
he later helmed a XXX-rated feature, TAKE IT OUT IN TRADE
(1971), which dealt with gangsters preying on the garment industry. THE SINISTER URGE (a.k.a. HELLBORN; THE YOUNG AND
THE IMMORAL), when initially released in 1961, had scant showings,

but in recent years due to the interest in the director's output of "unique" films this property has enjoyed revival theater and video-cassette offerings.

SIZZLE (Aaron Spelling Productions/ABC-TV, 11/29/81) C 100 mins.

Executive producers, Aaron Spelling, Douglas S. Cramer; producers, Cindy Dunne, Lynn Loring; supervising producer, E. Duke Vincent; associate producer, Chip Hayes; director, Don Medford; teleplay, Clyde Ware, Richard Carr; music, Artie Butler; choreography, Carl Jablonski; art directors, Paul Sylos, Tom Trimble; camera, Arch R. Daizell; editors, Michael S. McLean, George W. Brooks.

Loni Anderson (Julie Davis); John Forsythe (Mike Callahan); Roy Thinnes (Wheeler); Richard Lynch (Johnny O'Brien); Leslie Uggams (Vonda); Phyllis Davis (Sally); Judith-Marie Bergan (Louise); Michael V. Gazzo (Tripoli); Michael Goodwin (Danny Clark); Richard Bright (Corky); Martine Bartlett (Freda); Robert Costanzo (Al Capone); Sandy Martin (Freda's Assistant); Paul Larson (Johnson); Charles Picicerni (Hit Man); Yvonne Childress (Mrs. Walters); James O'Connell (Simms); Arnie Moore (Buggs); McKee Anderson (Nurse); Tom Shell (Eddie); Tony Pepper (Bobby); Teal Markland (Guard); Lee Delano (Hood); Mary Armstrong, Susan Serbes (Inmates); Bruce Reed; Walter Edmiston (Electricians).

In the late 1970s gorgeous blonde Loni Anderson caused a sensation as the star of the teleseries WKRP IN CINCINNATI and she followed this project with a surprisingly accomplished portrayal in the title role of the telefeature THE JAYNE MANSFIELD STORY (1980). Next, her TV movie career took her into this Prohibition-era gangster yarn, but the result was more fizzle than SIZZLE. Judith Crist in TV Guide decided the telefilm was in "the pointless-period-piece category" and added, "The sets and costumes are lavish, but what's that delicious cutie from WKRP doing in all that Sturm und Drang? Not very much--or very well."

"They took her innocence, used her beauty, murdered her man. Now she's living for revenge. Heading for the top. Trying to beat them at their own game!" Thus read the advertisement for SIZZLE in which Anderson's character was dubbed "The Hottest Woman in a Red-Hot Town." The chronicle tells of small town night-club chirp Julie Davis (Anderson) who arrives in the big city with boyfriend Danny (Michael Goodwin) who is soon murdered by mobsters for running local moonshine. To even the score, Anderson plays up to big-time hood Mike Callahan (John Forsythe) after the mob forces her into prostitution. The young woman then begins her climb to success as a speakeasy singer, and to gain revenge on those who used her and killed her man, she enlists the aid of Al Capone (Robert Costanzo).

SORROWFUL JONES see: LITTLE MISS MARKER

SPECIAL AGENT (Warner Bros., 1935) 76 mins.

Producer, Martin Mooney; director, William Keighley; idea, Mooney, screenplay, Laird Doyle, Abem Finkel; art director, Esdras Hartley; music director, Leo F. Forbstein; camera, Sid Hickox; editor, Clarence Kolster.

Bette Davis (Julie Carston); George Brent (Bill Bradford); Ricardo Cortez (Nick Carston); Joseph Sawyer (Rich); Joseph Crehan (Police Chief); Henry O'Neill (District Attorney); Irving Pichel (U.S. District Attorney); Jack La Rue (Andrews); Robert Strange (Armitage); Joseph King (Wilson); William B. Davison (Young); J. Carroll Naish (Durrell); Paul Guilfoyle (Secretary to D.A.); Robert Barrat (Head of Internal Revenue Department); Charles Middleton, Thomas Jackson, Jack Mower (Cops); Jack McHugh, Billy Naylor (Newsboys); Garry Owen, John Dilson (Men); Milton Kibbee (Player); Edwin Argue (Looker-On); John Alexander (Manager); Jerry Fletcher (Young Man); Lucille Ward (Matron); Herbert Skinner (Henry); Allan Cavan (Starter); Bob Montgomery, Huey White, Dutch Hendrian (Gangsters); Louis Natheaux (Clark); John Kelly (Copper); Emmett Vogan (Police Announcer); Frank G. Fanning (Driver); Douglas Wood (Judge).

The Internal Revenue Services needs evidence that alleged racketeer Rick Carston (Ricardo Cortez) has been cheating on his tax returns. To gain data for a grand jury indictment, newspaperman Bill Bradford (George Brent) is sent to work as an IRS special agent. Disguised as a reporter, he gets in good both with Cortez and with his bookkeeper (Bette Davis). Later he appeals to Davis' patriotism to help him gain the required information. She agrees to decode and photostat the syndicate's account books. As a result, Cortez is arrested. When he learns that Brent is an undercover agent and that Davis has betrayed him, he has his men kidnap her so she cannot testify. Brent, however, trails the gang to their hideout and with the police, they rescue Davis. Cortez is sentenced to 30 years in prison and Davis and Brent plan to wed.

Based on an idea by producer Martin Mooney, SPECIAL AGENT was "crisp, fast-moving and thoroughly entertaining" (The New York Times). Due to its violence, however, the Hays Office demanded several cuts, weakening to a degree a very strong film.

SQUAD CAR (Twentieth Century-Fox, 1960) 62 mins.

Producer, Ed Leftwich; associate producer, Bill Collins; director, Leftwich; story-screenplay, E. M. Parsons, Scott Flohr; music, Hall Daniels; camera, Henry Cronjager; editor, Edward Dutko.

Vici Raaf (Cameo Kincaid); Paul Bryar (Lieutenant Beck); Don Marlowe (Jay Reinhart); Lyn Moore (Jeanne Haggerty); James Cross (Harry); Jack Harris (Manfred Stahl); Blu Wright (Robert

Don Marlowe and Paul Bryar in SQUAD CAR (1960).

Scalise); Jim Hurley (Bartender); Jimmy Dale (Bank Official); Norman Macdonald (Dell Taylor); Bill Foster (Detective).

Set in Phoenix, Arizona, this tale concerns a nightclub singer (Vici Raaf) who is romancing Treasury agent Manfred Stahl (Jack Harris) who is assigned to destroy old currency but actually keeps it and burns retrieved counterfeit money. Harris is partnered with crop duster pilot Jay Reinhart (Don Marlowe), who is really a smuggler. Marlowe falls in love with a pretty resort swimming instructor (Lyn Moore) who tries to bring him over to the right side of the law. A detective (Paul Bryar) is on the trail of the counterfeiting gang and eventually succeeds.

Filmed in Arizona, the main slant of this minor opus is its depiction of a government agent on the wrong side of the law. At the time of release, the only promotional gimmick the film could offer was that stars Paul Bryar and Don Marlowe were known for their TV action work, the latter as Lieutenant Wilson on the "Dragnet" series.

STAR WITNESS (Warner Bros., 1931) 67 mins.

Director, William Wellman; screenplay, Lucien Hubbard; camera, James Van Trees; editor, Hal McLernon.

Walter Huston (District Attorney Whitlock); Charles "Chic" Sale
(Grandfather Summerville); Frances Starr (Ma Leeds); Grant Mit-
chell (Pa Leeds); Sally Blane (Sue Leeds); Edward Nugent (Jackie
Leeds); Ralph Ince (Maxey Campo); Dickie Moore (Donny Leeds);
George Ernest (Ned Leeds); Tom Dugan (Brown); Robert Elliot
(Williams); Noel Madison (Hogan); Nat Pendleton (Big Jack); Rus-
sell Hopton (Deputy Thorpe); Mike Donlin (Mickey); Fletcher Nor-
ton (Dopey); Guy D'Ennery (Jack Short); Ed Dearing (Sackett);
Allan Lane (Clerk); William A. Wellman (Lineman's Voice).

A middle class family witnesses a street fight in which gangster kingpin Maxey Camp (Ralph Ince) commits murder. When the
gangsters learn the family has witnessed the crime, they intimidate
them by beating up the father (Grant Mitchell) and kidnapping his
young son (Dickie Moore). District Attorney Whitlock (Walter Huston) wants the family members to testify at Ince's trial, but he is
concerned about their ultimate safety. Finally the family's elderly
grandfather (Chic Sale) rescues the boy and then takes the stand
and provides the evidence to send Ince to the electric chair.
Dubbed a "well-knit melodrama" by The New York Times,
STAR WITNESS was a most topical picture when released as urban
street crime involving racketeers was then rampant. Director
William Wellman conveyed his plotline in a fast-paced manner, but
its highlight is Charles "Chic" Sale's performance as the brave,
venerable granddad who thwarts dangers to himself to save his
family and bring the crooks to justice.
Frank Thompson noted in his book William A. Wellman (1983),
"... [the film] is distinguished mainly by Wellman's imaginative
staging of the scenes and the brisk pace he maintains. The gang's
beating of the father is remarkably brutal and the final confrontation with the police is done with Wellman's characteristic just-off-
frame style of staging; the shoot-out is all smoke and feet seen
through banister rails."
In 1939 Warner Bros. remade the feature as THE MAN WHO
DARED (a.k.a. I AM NOT AFRAID) with Charley Grapewin as the
grandfather and Henry O'Neill as the terrorized father. Directed
by Crane Wilbur (who later did INSIDE THE WALLS OF FOLSOM
PRISON, q.v.), Variety observed the remake's "script drags in
numerous spots."

STICK (Universal, 1985) C 109 mins.

Executive producer, Robert Daley; producer, Jennings Lang; associate producer, David Gershenson; director, Burt Reynolds;
based on the novel by Elmore Leonard; screenplay, Leonard,
Joseph C. Stinson; music, Barry De Vorzon, Joseph Conlan; production designer, James Shanahan; art director, Ed Richardson, set
decorator, Philip Abramson; assistant director, Jim Van Wyck;
sound, Charles Darin Knight, Bob Gravenor; camera, Nick McLean;
editor, William Gordean.

Burt Reynolds (Stick); Candice Bergen (Kyle); George Segal (Barry); Charles Durning (Chucky Buck); Jose Parez (Rainy); Richard Lawson (Cornell); Castulo Guerra (Nestor); Dar Robinson (Moke); Alex Rocco (Firestone); Tricia Leigh Fisher (Katie).

"He's a guy who's taken a lot of wrong turns" is how the ads described the title character in STICK, although the catch line could just as well describe star-director Burt Reynolds' own career, especially in conjunction with this underworld melodrama. Taken from Elmore Leonard's (who co-scripted the feature with Joseph C. Stinson) novel (1983), the film took great liberties with the original work and some sources claim that two very different versions of the book were shot by Reynolds, with the released version, which resulted from much reshooting, inferior to the original one. In regards to the finished product, Newsweek magazine complained it was "... lazy, dull and told in imagery as murky as its underlying morality."

Reynolds stars as Stick, a hardened criminal just out of prison who arrives in Fort Lauderdale and accidentally meets big-time drug dealer Chucky Buck (Charles Durning) who takes an immediate dislike to him and orders him murdered. Reynolds takes a chauffeur's job to a wealthy financier (George Segal) and soon falls in love with the man's beautiful financial advisor (Candice Bergen), but he also finds he is being hunted by Durning's hired killers who murder his best friend and threaten his daughter. Needing to protect himself, the girl, and Bergen from the hoods, Reynolds realizes he has something to live for.

STICK has the look of a solid gangster movie but director-star Reynolds appears to have scant empathy for the project or his starring assignment. Janet Maslin noted correctly in The New York Times that "... Mr. Reynolds displays little understanding of the very good reason why audiences usually like him. He is at his most ponderous here, with none of his trademark resiliency or sardonic humor.... STICK has a dull look and the kind of quick pacing that's abrupt rather than staccato."

STILETTO (Avco Embassy, 1969) C 100 mins.

Producer, Norman Rosemont; director, Bernard Kowblski; based on the novel by Harold Robbins; screenplay, A. J. Russell; music, Sid Ramin; art director, Jan Scott; assistant director, Peter Scoppa; sound, Jack C. Jacobsen; camera, Jack Priestley; editor, Frank Mazzola.

Alex Cord (Cesare Cardinali); Britt Eklund (Illeana); Patrick O'Neal (Baker); Joseph Wiseman (Matteo); Barbara McNair (Ahn Dessje); John Dehner (Simpson); Titos Vandis (Tonio); Eduardo Ciannelli (Don Andrea); Roy Scheider (Bennett); Lincoln Kilpatrick (Hannibal Smith); Louis Elias (Mann); Luke Andreas (Macy); Dominic Barto (Franchini); James Tolkan (Edwards).

Successful playboy and foreign auto dealer Cesare Cardinali
(Alex Cord) is secretly a Mafia hit man working for New Yorker
Emilio Matteo (Joseph Wiseman) who saved his life years before in
Italy. After killing a Mafia enemy In a nightclub, Cord is ordered
by Wiseman to eliminate two witnesses who might help the local district attorney (John Dehner) in his fight to indict Wiseman, whom
he successfully has deported back to Italy. After the killings,
Cord visits Wiseman in his homeland and asks to be let out of his
obligations to him, but the gangster refuses, stating that Cord is
too valuable to the organization. Back in the States, Cord finds
the city's Mafia plan to kill him and he makes his girlfriend (Britt
Eklund) go see Wiseman on his behalf, but a lawman (Patrick
O'Neal) who has linked Cord to the killings detains her and forces
her to reveal her mission. Once in Italy, Eklund does convince
Wiseman to meet with Cord in Puerto Rico, where the big Mafia boss
Don Andrea (Eduardo Ciannelli) has ordered Cord killed. Hidden in
a Harlem apartment by a girl (Barbara McNair), Cord is attacked
by the Mafia and escapes, but the girl dies. He goes to Puerto
Rico, followed by the lawman, and meets with Wiseman, but a gun-
ma kills Cord, the lawman shoots Wiseman, and another marksman
murders the lawman.

Taken from Harold Robbins' 1969 best seller, with location
shooting in New York City and Puerto Rico, STILETTO was called
a "confusing but often fast-paced Mafia yarn" by Variety. The
title refers to Alex Cord's role as a stiletto man, or a hired assassin. This violent tale did sport a fine ensemble and it was especially refreshing to see gangster film genre veteran Eduardo Ciannelli well cast as an unrelenting Mafia don.

THE STING II (Universal, 1982) C 103 mins.

Producer, Jennings Lang; director, Jeremy Paul Kagan; screenplay,
David S. Ward; music, Lalo Schifrin; assistant directors, L. Andrew
Stone, Ross Brown, Robert Engelman; boxing choreography, Ron
Stein; choreography, Alton Ruff; songs, Scott Joplin; production
designer, Edward C. Carfagno; camera, Bill Butler; editor, David
Garfield.

Jackie Gleason (Gondorff); Mac Davis (Hooker); Teri Garr (Veronica); Karl Malden (Macalinski); Oliver Reed (Lonnegan); Bert Remsen (Kid Colors); Benny Baker (Gym Manager); Kathalina Veniero
(Blonde with Kid Colors); Jose Perez (Carlos); Larry Bishop (Gal-
laecher); Frank McCarthy, Richard C. Adams (Lonnegan's Thugs);
Harry James (Bandleader); Ron Rifkin (Eddie); Frances Bergen
(Lady Dorsett); Monica Lewis (Band Singer); Daniel-Wade Dalton
(Messenger); Val Avery (O'Malley); Jill Jaress (Gertie); Paul Will-
son (Man in Ticket Line); Sidney Clute (Ticket Clerk); Al Robertson (Redap); Hank Garrett (Cab Driver); Bob O'Connell (Clancy);
John Hancock (Doc Brown); Larry Hankin (Handicap); Jerry Whitney (Page Boy); Michael D. Alldredge (Big Ohio); and: Corey

Eubanks, Tim Rossovich, Sam Theard, Rex Pierson, Angela Robinson, Lise Kristen Gerard, Tony Giorgio, Melodie Bovee, Lesa Weis, Max Wright, Terry Berland.

Motion pictures which use Roman numerals with their titles to indicate sequels to previous blockbusters often obtain the box-office residuals expected of such an advertising measure. THE STING II, however, appears to actually have been hurt by such a move in that audiences were expecting a film in the same vein as the earlier production (see: B/V) with Paul Newman and Robert Redford and were disappointed when they were presented with an entirely different feature which used only the original plot ploy of every character involved in a series of elaborate doublecrosses. This is unfortunate because THE STING II is a slick production which can stand on its own as good entertainment, highlighted by fine performances by Jackie Gleason, Teri Garr, and Mac Davis as the shifty protagonists.

Con man Gondorff (Gleason) is released from prison with pal Hooker (Davis) and plans to fleece a rather dim-witted nightclub owner (Karl Malden) who is allied with an underworld figure (Oliver Reed). Aiding in the scam is sexy Veronica (Garr), who apparently has her own motives to cheat the two hoodlums. As the scam progresses, Davis is called to take part in a big fight in which the two hoodlums will lose their money and at the same time he finds himself falling in love with the girl. The finale has everyone doublecrossed with the gangsters fleeced, Gleason very wealthy, and Davis and Garr matched for life, with Davis discovering that his lady love is really his pal's daughter.

THE STING II has a nice tongue-in-cheek air, making it an effortless, fun diversion. The movie sweetly captures the gloss of the 1930s backgrounds, even to having Harry James and his orchestra providing the film's nightclub entertainment. The supporting cast benefits from Karl Malden as the none-too-bright windbag and Benny Baker as the manager of the sleaziest gym ever revealed on film.

A STONE IN THE MOUTH see: UNE PIERRE DANS LA BOUCHE

THE STONE KILLER (Columbia, 1973) C 95 mins.

Presenter, Dino De Laurentiis; producer-director, Michael Winner; based on the book A Complete State of Death by John Gardner; screenplay, Gerald Wilson; art director, Ward Preston; set decorator, Norman Rockett; assistant director, Joe Ellis; music, Roy Budd; sound, Hugh Strain, Thomas Thompson; camera, Richard Moore; editor, Frederick Wilson.

Charles Bronson (Detective Lou Torrey); Martin Balsam (Vescari); David Sheiner (Detective Lorenz); Norman Fell (Detective Daniels);

Charles Bronson in THE STONE KILLER (1973).

Ralph Waite (Detective Matthews); Eddie Firestone (Junkie); Walter
Burke (J.D.); David Moody (Lipper); Charles Tyner (Psychiatrist);
Paul Koslo (Jazz Musician); Stuart Margolin (Lawrence); John Ritter
(Hart); Byron Mrrow (L.A. Police Chief); Jack Colvin (Jumper);
Frank Campanella (Calabriese); Gene Woodbury (Long); Christina
Raines (Mathews' Daughter); Kelly Miles (Stewardess Dropout).

A series of murders take place in Los Angeles and Police
Detective Lou Torrey (Charles Bronson) is assigned to the case.
He believes the Mafia is involved and through investigation, some
of which is quite brutal, he learns that Mafia don Vescari (Martin
Balsam) is planning a massacre in New York City using trained
Vietnam veterans. Bronson immediately heads to Gotham to thwart
the intended event but arrives too late and is only able to arrest a
few of the mob's men, but not the big mobsters involved in the
slaughter.
Originally called A COMPLETE STATE OF DEATH, THE STONE
KILLER was star Charles Bronson's third feature with both director
Michael Winner and producer Dino De Laurentiis and his first film
done entirely in the United States since his becoming an international
screen favorite. With its lack of romantic interest, the movie was a

straightforward crime thriller with no frills and plenty of violence
to satisfy Bronson's public. The title refers to the underworld
jargon for a man, on either side of the law, who is ruthless and
cold-blooded; here referring to the character played by Bronson
who is part of the law.

While the critics were not enthused with the movie (i.e. the
New York Daily News labeled it a "routine presentation"), the pub-
lic flocked to it. In his book, The Films of Charles Bronson (1980),
Jerry Vermilye analyzes the film's success: "... THE STONE KILL-
ER is a cunning bundle of all the ingredients that [Dino] De
Laurentiis realized the Bronson public wanted and expected of
their superhero.... The inhumanity of Bronson's flint-eyed screen
image had reached its zenith."

STRANGE CARGO (Metro-Goldwyn-Mayer, 1940) 113 mins.

Producer, Joseph L. Mankiewicz; director, Frank Borzage; based
on the novel Not Too Narrow, Not Too Deep by Richard Sale; screenplay, Lawrence Hazard; art director, Cedric Gibbons; music, Frank
Waxman; sound, Douglas Shearer; camera, Robert Planck; editor,
Robert J. Kern.

Clark Gable (Andre Verne); Joan Crawford (Julie); Ian Hunter
(Cambreau); Peter Lorre (Cochon); Paul Lukas (Hessler); Albert
Dekker (Moll); J. Edward Bromberg (Flaubert); Eduardo Ciannelli
(Telz); Victor Varconi (Fisherman); John Arledge (Dufond); Fred-
eric Worlock (Grideau); Paul Fix (Benet); Bernard Nedell (Marfeu);
Francis McDonald (Moussenq); Betty Compson (Suzanne); Charles
Judels (Renard); Jack Mulhall (Dunning); Dewey Robinson (Geor-
ges); Harry Cording, Richard Alexander, Bud Fine, James Pierce,
Hal Wynants, Christian Frank, Mitchell Lewis, Dick Cramer, Ray
Teal, Jack Adair (Guards); Gene Coogan, Eddie Foster, Frank
Lackteen, Harry Semels (Convicts); Art Dupuis (Orderly); Stanley
Andrews (Constable); William Edmunds (Watchman).

A French penal colony in New Guinea is a hellhole and prisoner Andre Verne (Clark Gable) plans to escape but engages in a
fight with the evil Moll (Albert Dekker) and is hospitalized. Dekker then leads fellow prisoners (Ian Hunter, Eduardo Ciannelli,
John Arledge, J. Edward Bromberg, Paul Lukas, and Peter Lorre)
in escaping through the jungle. Gable also later escapes and he
meets entertainer Julie (Joan Crawford), who is out of work because
she has refused the advances of the island's chieftain (Bernard
Nedell). Crawford goes with Gable and to survive they join the
other prisoners. Along the way the escapees begin to die off one
by one, yet each of them is touched by the kindness and humanity
of Hunter and through their hardships they feel he is divine. Most
of them eventually die (including the wicked Dekker, who tries to
kill Gable) except Crawford, Gable, and Hunter. To save himself,
Gable later pushes Hunter off their boat; then he has a sudden

Ian Hunter and Joan Crawford in STRANGE CARGO (1940).

burst of renewed faith and jumps in and saves the man. Back in port, Gable tells Crawford he loves her and asks her to wait for him to complete his sentence.

STRANGE CARGO can probably be best described as a religious gangster yarn, but its emphasis on faith and love of one's fellow men made it a curio even with the top-heavy pairing of stars Clark Gable and Joan Crawford in their seventh and final screen teaming. Actually the movie is endowed with superior performances, especially Albert Dekker as the conniving murderer and Ian Hunter as the benevolent, Christ-like Cambreau.

Without doubt STRANGE CARGO is a bizarre kind of gangster film and one that is difficult to assess in its relationship to other genre entries. While the criminals here are as hardened a lot as ever seen on camera, the redemption aspects of the story soften them, making the feature an oddball entry in the overall gangster movie sweepstakes.

While the film failed to generate much box-office enthusiasm in its day (also hindered by it being heavily censored and/or banned by many morality film boards across the country for its too-Christ-like parable), the picture is constantly revived on TV and gains fresh enthusiasts each generation.

STREET FIGHTER see: HARD TIMES

STREET GANG see: VIGILANTE

STREET OF CHANCE (Paramount, 1930) 75 mins.

Director, John Cromwell; story, Oliver H. P. Garrett; adaptor, Howard Estabrook; dialogue, Lenore J. Coffee; titles, Gerald Geraghty; sound, Harry D. Mills; camera, Charles Lang; editor, Otto Levering.

William Powell (John B. Marsden [Natural Davis]); Jean Arthur (Judith Marsden); Kay Francis (Alma Marsden); Regis Toomey (Babe Marsden); Stanley Fields (Dorgan); Brooks Benedict (Al Mastick); Betty Francisco (Mrs. Mastick); John Risso (Tony); Joan Standing (Miss Abrams); Maurice Black (Nick); Irving Bacon (Harry); John Cromwell (Imbrie).

New York City ace gambler John Marsden, alias Natural Davis (William Powell), gives his younger brother Babe (Regis Toomey) $10,000 as a wedding gift on the condition that he does not use it to gamble. Powell's wife (Kay Francis) is unhappy with his life as a gambler and she informs him she will leave if he doesn't take the money he has won and leave town with her. Powell goes along with his wife's decision but that night his brother wins big and in order to teach him a lesson, Powell cheats and is caught and, true to the gamblers' code, is shot dead.

"Here's a punchful racketeer picture that is going to give
rival producers jaundice until they get a carbon copy in the can.
Bill Powell's finesse and Kay Francis' sincere emoting would be highlights in any picture," is how Photoplay magazine felt about this
underworld melodrama.

Based on the life of famed New York City gambler Arnold
Rothstein, this sophisticated movie was nominated for an Academy
Award for its Howard Estabrook scenario but lost to Frances Marion
for THE BIG HOUSE (see: B/V). William Powell and Kay Francis
caused quite a sensation as the chic husband-wife team, while Regis
Toomey as the younger brother and Jean Arthur as his wife rounded
out the leads with Stanley Fields in for a good supporting role as
gangster Dorgan, the man who catches debonair Powell cheating at
cards.

The feature proved successful enough that Paramount reteamed Powell and Francis in a film based on New York City criminal lawyer William J. Fallon called FOR THE DEFENSE (q.v.). Oliver H. P. Garrett wrote the script (he did the story for STREET
OF CHANCE) and both movies were directed by John Cromwell, who
also played a bit in STREET OF CHANCE.

STREET OF MISSING MEN (Republic, 1939) 64 mins.

Producer, Armand Schaefer; director, Sidney Salkow; idea, Eleanor
Griffen, William Rankin; screenplay, Frank Dolan, Leonard Gee;
music, Cy Feuer; camera, Ernest Miller; editor, Ernest Nims.

Charles Bickford (Cash); Harry Carey (Putnam); Tommy Ryan
(Tommy); Mabel Todd (Dove); Guinn "Big Boy" Williams (T-Bone);
Nana Bryant (Mrs. Putnam); Ralph Graves (Reardon); John Gallau-
det (Kinsella); Regis Toomey (Parker).

Notorious mobster Cash (Charles Bickford) has spent five
years in prison after being sent there by information garnered by
a big city newspaper run by editor Putnam (Harry Carey). Bickford vows revenge and when he is released immediately goes to the
newspaper to kill Carey, but he does not carry out his mission. Instead he becomes the protector of newspaper delivery boy Tommy
(Tommy Ryan) and eventually aids in the delivery of the publication
when rival hoodlums attempt to shut it down, with Bickford dying
for the cause.

Despite its preposterous plot, STREET OF MISSING MEN is
fairly enjoyable, especially for Charles Bickford's performance as
the tough hoodlum who experiences a change of heart and Harry
Carey as the taciturn but just editor. Variety noted the film was
"... paced for the action traffic, and satisfies the needs for average entertainment of the rougher trade."

It should be noted the film was timely, in that Republic Pictures issued it about the same time gangster kingpin Al Capone was
scheduled for parole.

Roger Moore in STREET PEOPLE (1976).

STREET PEOPLE (American International, 1976) C 92 mins.

Producers, Manolo Bolognini, Luigi Borghese; director, Maurizio Lucidi; story, Gianfranco Bucceri, Roberto Leoni; screenplay, Bucceri, Niccola Badalucco, Randall Keiser, Leoni, Laurizio Lucidi; music, Luis Enriquez; art director, Gastone Carsetti; set decorator, Luigi Urbani; assistant directors, Mauro Sacripanti, Franco Fantasia; stunt coordinator, Remo DeAngelis; car scene director, William Garroni; camera, Aiaca Parolin; editor, Renzo Lucidi.

Roger Moore (Ulysses); Stacy Keach (Phil); Ivo Garrani (Salvatore Francesco); Ettore Manni (Bishop Lopetri); Ennio Balbo (Continenza); Fausto Tozzi (Nicoletta); Pietro Martellanz (Pano); Romano Puppo (Fortunate).

Ulysses (Roger Moore) is the lawyer-mouthpiece for his San Francisco Mafia uncle's operation. When a syndicate member hijacks a Mafia dope shipment, Moore and his Grand Prix driver hit man pal (Stacy Keach) are dispatched to find the culprit. They finally discover the heroin has been hidden in a cross the uncle imported from Italy as a church gift.

Merely another in a long string of films spawned in the 1970s by THE GODFATHER (1972) (see: B/V), STREET PEOPLE is most incredulous in its casting of Britisher Roger Moore (best known as "The Saint" on TV and "James Bond" in the movies) in the role of a Mafia member. Writing in Films in Review magazine, Harry Banta noted, "In order to compete with the many competently-made police and crime TV films, the made-for-theatrical release picture must offer something extra. That something extra in STREET PEOPLE is tho now beginning to pall nudity and excessive violence that won the film an 'X' rating."

SUDDEN IMPACT (Warner Bros., 1983) C 117 mins.

Executive producer, Fritz Manes; producer, Clint Eastwood; associate producer, Steve Perry; director, Eastwood; based on characters created by Julian Fink, R. M. Fink; story, Earl E. Smith, Charles B. Pierce; screenplay, Joseph C. Stinson; production designer, Edward Carfagno; music, Lalo Schifrin; assistant director, David Valdes; camera, Bruce Surtees; editor, Joel Cox.

Clint Eastwood (Detective Harry Callahan); Sondra Locke (Jennifer Spencer); Pat Hingle (Chief Jannings); Bradford Dillman (Captain Briggs); Paul Drake (Mick); Audrie J. Neenan (Ray Parkins); Jack Thibeau (Kruger); Michael Currie (Lieutenant Donnelly); Albert Popwell (Horace King); Mark Keyloun (Officer Bennett); Kevyn Major Howard (Hawkins); Bette Ford (Leah); Nancy Parsons (Mrs. Kruger).

Clint Eastwood returned to the successful role of vigilante cop Dirty Harry Callahan for the fourth time in SUDDEN IMPACT, and for the first time in the series he also directed the commercial venture which starred his long-time friend, actress Sondra Locke. The result is a highly violent motion picture, full of endless gunplay and retribution on the villains, geared at pandering to the box office. Unlike the three previous series entries, however, SUDDEN IMPACT has more of a mystery motif to it, with touches of the DEATH WISH (q.v.) trilogy. Not as weak as THE ENFORCER (1976) (q.v.), but not up to the standards of DIRTY HARRY (1971) (see: B/V) or MAGNUM FORCE (1973) (q.v.), the feature was nonetheless popular with Eastwood's huge following, thus paving the way for doubtless more adventures with the one-man demolition machine.

Here Eastwood is shown to be the bane of his San Francisco police superiors due to his ruthless and not always letter-of-the-law tactics in bringing criminals to justice. To get him out of their hair for a spell, he is sent to the coastal town of San Paulo to investigate connections in the town to gangsters on Eastwood's home turf. There the police chief (Pat Hingle) wants no part of Eastwood and fears the worst due to the cop's violent reputation. The town has been plagued by a series of murders and it turns out that a young woman (Sandra Locke) is taking revenge on the men and one lesbian who gang raped her and her sister years before. When Eastwood finds himself in the middle of the case, he is caught between the necessity of bringing the woman to justice yet sympathizing with her motives.

Variety summed up the film's success when it wrote, "Any

moral compuctions one may have about both Eastwood's and Locke's
actions are shoved aside by the fact that all their victims are ir-
redeemable scum, and the Dirty Harry pictures as a group feed in
no small measure on the public's general attitude that the criminal
justice system in the U.S. is far too lenient with certified criminals.
If only there were more Dirty Harrys around." On the other hand,
the more artistically attuned New York Times' Vincent Canby noted,
"The screenplay is ridiculous, and Mr. Eastwood's direction of it
primitive.... Among other things, the movie never gets a firm hold
on its own continuity. Sometimes scenes of simultaneous action
appear to take place weeks or maybe months apart. Not that this
makes much difference."

SUPER FUZZ (Avco Embassy, 1982) C 97 mins.

Director, Sergio Corbucci; screenplay, Corbucci, Sabataino Ciuffini;
production designer, Marco Dentici; assistant director, Amanzio
Todini; camera, Silvano Ippoliti; editor, Eugenio Alabiso.

Terence Hill (Dave Speed); Ernest Borgnine (Willy); Joanne Dru
(Rosy); Marc Lawrence (Torpedo); Julie Gordon (Evelyn); Lee
Sandman (Chief); Herb Goldstein (Silvias); Don Sebastian (Dingo);
Sal Borghese (Paradise Alley); Claudio Ruffini (Tragedy Row);
Sergio Smacchi (Slot Machine).

　　　Miami vice cop Dave Speed (Terence Hill) is dispatched to
India by his chief (Ernest Borgnine) and there a NASA nuclear
rocket explodes, subjecting Hill to mega-rays which bestow him
with super powers. Back in Miami he goes against local mobsters
run by Rosy (Joanne Dru) and Torpedo (Marc Lawrence) and despite their many attempts to dispose of him, Hill survives and puts
and end to the mobsters' activities.
　　　This atrocity was an attempt by popular Italian film star
Terence Hill to switch from spaghetti Westerns to the gangster film
genre, but with minimal success, although the Italian humor no doubt
played well in its homeland. Stateside, however, the picture emerged
a disaster in its clumsy combination of comedy, science fiction, and
gangsters. Little humor or action was engendered by the star's escaping death via the gas chamber, hanging, electrocution, or the
firing squad. Just as limp was Hill's use of his powers to turn
bubble gum into a hot-air balloon, his riding the top of an airplane,
or becoming a human mole and tunneling into China.
　　　Cast-wise, Terence Hill may not be all that well known in the
United States despite exposure in such Italian oaters as MAN OF THE
EAST (1972) or MY NAME IS NOBODY (1973), topbilled over Henry
Fonda in the latter; but those going to see Ernest Borgnine, Joanne
Dru, and Marc Lawrence must have been saddened to see them sad-
dled with this celluloid tripe.

SWEENEY (EMI FILMS, 1977) C 97 mins.

Executive producers, Lloyd Shirley, George Taylor; producer, Ted Childs; director, David Wickes; based on the television series created by Ian Kennedy Martin; screenplay, Ranald Graham; music, Denis King; art director, Bill Alexander; camera, Dusty Miller; editor, Chris Burt.

John Thaw (Regan); Dennis Waterman (Carter); Barry Foster (McQueen); Ian Bannen (Baker); Colin Welland (Chadwick); Diane Keen (Bianca); Michael Coles (Johnson); Joe Melia (Brent); Brian Glover (Mac); Lynda Bellingham (Janice); Morris Perry (Commander); Paul Angelis (S.S. Man); Nick Brimble (Burtonshaw); John Alkin (Daniels); Bernard Kay (Matthews); Anthony Scott (Codaly); Anthony Brown (Superintendent).

During the 1970s, John Thaw and Dennis Waterman starred in the popular British teleseries "Sweeney," created by Ian Kennedy Martin. The two transferred their small-screen parts to the movies with this outing, but the addition of overt sex and violence did little to improve the project's theatrical chances. "Internationally it hasn't enough punch to match U.S. cops and robbers counterparts," reported the ever-vigilant Variety trade newspaper. The chronicle added, "The tv show packed a certain authenticity. This theatrical version, with bodies littered all over London as a result of liberal bursts of machine gun bullets, must put the concept back into the realms of the fairy story class."

The movie's thin plot has policemen Regan (Thaw) and Carter (Waterman) on the trail of gangsters out to gain control of the world oil market and influence Great Britain's economy. They are aided in the case by a drunken government minister (Ian Bannen) and an American newsman (Barry Foster).

SWEET JESUS, PREACHER MAN (Metro-Goldwyn-Mayer, 1972) C 103 mins.

Executive producer, Ronald Goldman; producer, Daniel B. Cady; director, Henning Schellerup; screenplay, John Cerulio, M. Stuart Madden, Abbey Leitch; set decorator, Merolyn Ravety; assistant director, Ernest Williams III; music, Horace Tapscott; special effects, Harry Woolman, Rich Helmen; camera, Paul E. Hipp; second unit camera, Ray Icely; special effects editors, Duane Hartnell, Sharron Miller.

Roger E. Mosley (Holmes/Lee); William Smith (Martelli); Michael Pataki (State Senator Sills); Tom Johnigam (Eddie Stoner); Joe Tornatore (Joey); Damy King (Sweetstick); Marla Gibbs (Beverly Solomon); Sam Laws (Deacon Greene); Phil Hoover (George Orr); Paul Sillman (Roy); Chuck Lyles (Detroit Charlie); Norman Fields (Police Captain); Delia Thomas (Foxey); Amentha Dymally (Mrs.

364 / THE TAKING OF PELHAM 1, 2, 3

Greene); Patricia Edwards (Marion Hicks); Dhuck Douglas, Jr.
(Lenny Solomon); Vincent LaBauve (Bobby Thompson); Chuck
Wells (Eli Stoner); Betty Coleman (Maxine Gibb); Lou Jackson
(Randy Gibbs); Lillian Tarry (Mother Gibbs); T. C. Ellis (Earlo
Saunders); Lee Frost (Policeman); Jo Ann Bruno (Widow Foster);
Reverend K. D. Friend (Funeral Minister); Billy Quinn (Sweet-
stick's Bodyguard).

Black hit man Holmes (Roger E. Mosley) works for syndicate
boss Martelli (William Smith) and goes to Los Angeles and masquerades as a Baptist minister Lee (Mosely) at a ghetto church in order
to observe his boss' underworld holdings. After romance with
three women, a barmaid (Della Thomas), the church secretary (Patricia Edwards), and a widow (Marla Gibbs) whose son (Chuck
Douglas, Jr.) has been shot by a lawman, the bogus preacher decides to take over the area's drug and prostitution trades and make
them his own domain, resulting in a showdown with his former mob
employer.

Variety called this black exploitation item "a mishmash of by
now cliches of the genre delivered with the technical sophistication
of an industrial trailer," and the same reviewer noted, "Muscular
Mosley appears amused by most of the things he's required by plot
to do."

This surprisingly bloodless melodrama was one of the lesser
movies made for the black action trade in the early 1970s.

THE TAKING OF PELHAM 1, 2, 3 (United Artists, 1974) C 104 mins.

Producers, Gabriel Katzka, Edgar J. Scherick; director, Joseph
Sargent; based on the novel by John Godey; screenplay, Peter
Stone; music, David Shire; art director, Gene Rudolf; sound,
Chris Newman; camera, Owen Roizman; editor, Jerry Greenberg.

Walter Matthau (Lieutenant Garber); Robert Shaw (Blue); Martin
Balsam (Green); Hector Elizondo (Grey); Earl Hindman (Brown);
Tony Roberts (Warren LaSalle); James Broderick (Denny Doyle);
Dick O'Neill (Correll); Lee Wallace (The Mayor); Tom Pedi (Caz
Dolowitz); Beatrice Winde (Mrs. Jenkins); Jerry Stiller (Lieutenant
Rico Patrone); Nathan George (Patrolman James); Rudy Bond (Po-
lice Commissioner); Kenneth McMillan (Borough Commander); Doris
Roberts (Mayor's Wife); Julius Harris (Inspector Daniels); Cynthia
Belgrave (The Maid); Anna Berger (The Mother); Gary Bolling (The
Homosexual); Carol Cole (The Secretary); Alex Colon (The Delivery
Boy); Joe Fields (The Salesman); Mari Gorman (The Hooker); Mi-
chael Gorrin (The Old Man); Thomas La Fleur (The Older Son);
Maria Landa (The Spanish Woman); Louise Larabee (The Alcoholic);
George Lee Miles (The Pimp); William Snickowski (The Hippie);
Jerry Holland (Buddy Carmondy); Ruth Attaway (Mayor's Nurse).

An enterprising hijack gang (Robert Shaw, Martin Balsam,

Walter Matthau in THE TAKING OF PELHAM 1, 2, 3 (1974).

Hector Elizondo, Earl Hindman) led by Blue (Shaw) boards a subway under Manhattan and takes control of the car and its passengers, demanding a $1,000,000 ransom. The negotiations are handled
through Lieutenant Garber (Walter Matthau), a Transit Authority
detective who not only has to negotiate via radio with Shaw, but
also must put up with pressure from the city's self-serving mayor
(Lee Washington) to get the hijacking ended and to appease various
cohorts who want to use violent methods to bring in the hoodlums.
Eventually the ransom is paid to the hijackers, but by a ruse they
are captured.

Beyond the vivid characterizations by Walter Matthau and
Robert Shaw, THE TAKING OF PELHAM 1, 2, 3, based on John
Godey's novel of 1973, is a slow, talky feature with extraneous action sequences tossed in to keep the plot from stagnating. Little
attention is paid to the subway's captives and little tension is developed as the film progresses. Except for Shaw's offbeat performance, the lawbreakers are a stereotyped lot and do not appear at
all menacing.

DIE 1000 AUGEN DES MR. MABUSE see: THE 1000 EYES OF DR.
    MABUSE

TELL YOUR CHILDREN see: REEFER MADNESS

DAS TESTAMENT DES DR. MABUSE see: THE TESTAMENT OF DR.
MABUSE (1933)

THE TESTAMENT OF DR. MABUSE (Nero Films, 1933) 115 mins.

Producer, Seymour Nebenzal; director, Fritz Lang; screenplay,
Theo Von Harbou; art directors, Karl Vollbrecht, Emil Hasser;
camera, Fritz Arno Wagner, Karl Vass.

Rudolph Klein-Rogge (Dr. Mabuse); Oskar Beregi (Dr. Baum);
Otto Wernicke (Lohmann); Vera Liessem (Lilli); Gustav Diessel
(Kent); Karl Meixner (Hofmeister); Theodor Loos (Dr. Kramm);
Georg John (Winkler); Theo Lingen (Jeweler); Camila Spira (Anna);
Hadraian M. Netto (Crook in Striped Blazer); P. Oscar Hocker
(Bredow); Rudolf Schundler (Hardy); Paul Henckels (Counter-
feiter); E. A. Licho (Monetary Expert); Heinrich Gotho, Michael
von Newlinski (Crook); Gerhard Bienert (Detective); Karl Platen
(Sanatorium Assistant); and: Klaus Pohl.

See description in next entry.

THE TESTAMENT OF DR. MABUSE (Golden Era, 1965) 88 mins.

Producer, Wolf Brauner; director, Werner Klingler; based on the
screenplay by Thea von Harbou; new screenplay, Ladislas Fodor,
R. A. Stemmle; music, Raimund Rosenberger; assistant director,
Carl von Barany; art director, Helmut Nentwig, Paul Markwitz;
sound, Erwin Schanzle; camera, Albert Benitz; editor, Walter
Wischniewsky.

Gert Frobe (Inspector Lohmann); Helmut Schmid (Johnny Briggs);
Charles Regnier (Mortimer); Senta Berger (Nelly); Wolfgang Preiss
(Dr. Mabuse); Walter Rilla (Professor Polland); Harald Juhnke
(Sergeant Kruger); Leon Askin (Flake); Ann Savo (Wabble-Heidt);
Claus Tinney (Jack); Zeev Berlinski (Gulliver); Albert Bessler
(Paragraph Joe); Arthur Schiliski (Tom).

        After the success of M (1931), director Fritz Lang was of-
fered the opportunity to do another movie about the evil arch-
criminal Dr. Mabuse, based on his successful 1922 (q.v.) two-part
silent thriller. At first he refused, but he saw an opportunity in
such a project to inject anti-Nazi sentiment and so relented and
made the film, which was co-written by his then-wife Thea von
Harbou, a member of the Nazi party. Although the motion picture
was banned in his homeland as soon as it was filmed, a copy of the
French version was smuggled out of the country by Lang for distribution. Lang made LILIOM in France in 1934 and then came to Hollywood where he had a long career before making his last movie in
West Germany in 1960, another Dr. Mabuse thriller, DIE 1000 AUGEN
DES MR. MABUSE (q.v.).

DAS TESTAMENT DES DR. MABUSE takes up where DR. MABUSE left off, with the mad gangster Dr. Mabuse (Rudolf Klein-Rogge) in a mental institution. There he uses his hypnotic powers to take control of the mind of the asylum head, Dr. Baum (Oskar Beregi), and together the two organize a new criminal operation to thrust the world into a state of chaos by various terrorist acts. Following several murders, Berlin Police Inspector Lohman (Otto Wernicke), a character who also appeared in M, investigates and believes that Klein-Rogge's power has been reactivated by some means. Meanwhile a member of Klein-Rogge's gang (Gustav Diessel) has fallen in love with a young woman (Vera Liessem) and wants to go legitimate but is hunted by his ex-cohorts as well as by the law. When Klein-Rogge dies, Beregi continues his underworld activities, but eventually the inspector traces the gang to the asylum and when he confronts the doctor with his crimes, the physician goes insane.

Paul M. Jensen, in The Cinema of Fritz Lang (1969), writes, "The picture is typical of Lang's work in the way it illustrates both the inherent shallowness of his melodramatic stories (despite the possible imitation of Nazi reality) and his great skill at directing set-piece, atmospheric sequences involving incident, not motion. His comment that in the silent days he would often make a list of scenes he wanted to stage, and then have a story written that included these scenes, should be borne in mind while viewing DAS TESTA-MENT which appears to be constructed by this method."

Also known as THE CRIMES OF DR. MABUSE, the movie was first shown in the U.S. in a dubbed version in 1943 as THE LAST WILL OF DR. MABUSE.

In 1962 the movie was remade in West Germany by CCC-Filmkunst in Berlin with direction by Werner Klingler. This stout and entertaining thriller followed the plotline of the original to some degree. It opens like the original with Dr. Mabuse (Wolfgang Preiss) in an insane asylum where he hypnotizes its chief doctor (Helmut Schmid) and the two reorganize his criminal gang. When Preiss dies, the gangsters leave the organization and Inspector Lohmann (Gert Frobe) is able to bring them to justice. As to the quality of this production, the British Monthly Film Bulletin alerted: "Another black mark to the West German industry. One of the worst of the recent batch of Dr. Mabuse fabrications, this one has the temerity to base itself directly on Lang's famous film of 1933.... There is one feeble attempt at 'style,' involving a sub-Wellesian set of mirrors, which is almost a parody of itself; only Wolfgang Preiss as Mabuse, busily scribbling away on hundreds of sheets of paper, brings a whiff of the real atmosphere."

THAT MAN BOLT (Universal, 1973) C 102 mins.

Producer, Bernard Schwartz; directors, Henry Levin, David Lowell Rich; story, Charles Johnson; screenplay, Quentin Werty, Johnson; music, Charles Bernstein; art director, Alexander Golitzen; set decorator, Chester R. Bayhi; assistant director, Phil Bowles;

sound, Melvin M. Metcalfe, Sr.; camera, Gerald Perry Finnerman; editors; Carl Pingitore, Robert F. Shugrue.

Fred Williamson (Jefferson Bolt); Byron Webster (Griffiths); Mike Mayama (Dominique); Teresa Graves (Samantha); Satoshi Nakamura (Kumada); John Orchard (Carter); Jack Ging (Connie); Ken Kamama (Spider); Vassili Lambrinos (DeVargas).

Jefferson Bolt (Fred Williamson), an international courier of syndicate funds, is at odds with global crime kingpin Kumada (Satoshi Nakamura) who wants the loot Williamson is carrying. Williamson also is being followed by two government agents (Byron Webster, John Carter) and after one of his lady loves (Teresa Graves) is killed by a hit man (Vassili Lambrinos), he revenges himself on Nakamura and his minions.

Shot in Las Vegas, Hong Kong, and Los Angeles, this black exploitation-gangster melodrama has a likable hero in Fred Williamson but scant else to recommend it. Full of violence, kung-fu combats, and auto chases, the movie is overlong and substandard.

"THAT ROYALE GIRL" (Paramount, 1925) 114 mins.

Presenters, Adolph Zukor, Jesse L. Lasky; director, D. W. Griffith; based on the novel by Edwin Balmer; screenplay, Paul Schofield; art director, Charles M. Kirk; camera, Harry Fischbeck, Hal Sintzenich; editor, James Smith.

Carol Dempster (Joan Daisy Royle); W. C. Fields (Her Father); James Kirkwood (Deputy District Attorney Calvin Clarke); Harrison Ford (Fred Ketlar--the King of Jazz); Marie Chambers (Adele Ketlar); Paul Everton (George Baretta); George Regas (His Henchman); Florence Auer (Baretta's Girl); Ida Waterman (Mrs. Clarke); Alice Laidley (Clarke's Fiancee); Dorothea Love (Lola Neeson); Dore Davidson (Elman); Frank Allworth (Oliver); Bobby Watson (Hofer).

"THAT ROYALE GIRL" is considered one of D. W. Griffith's lesser silent features, one he was forced to make as a Paramount director and one which did nothing to retain his film career in high gear. Filmed in Chicago, the movie is apparently lost today so fresh evaluation is impossible.

Chicago model Joan Daisy Royle (Carol Dempster) is tinged by her slum origins. She loves jazz band leader Fred Ketlar (Harrison Ford) whose estranged wife (Marie Chambers) has become the mistress of gangster-bootlegger George Baretta (Paul Everton). When Chambers is murdered, her husband is placed on trial and Dempster is called as a witness. The district attorney (James Kirkwood) is attracted to her but he twists her testimony so that Ford is convicted. Convinced the gangster is the real killer, Dempster attends a party at his roadhouse but is discovered and almost abducted when a cyclone destroys the place and all the hoodlums die.

With the information she needs to free Ford, she contacts the governor and he is pardoned. Dempster realizes that she doesn't truly love Ford and starts a romance with the district attorney.

The Chicago locale provides good background for the gangster elements in this melodrama and the well staged storm sequence is based on the actual 1919 Illinois cyclone. W. C. Fields tries to breathe comedy into the film as Dempster's eccentric father, but is not very successful.

THEY RAN FOR THEIR LIVES (Color Vision International, 1968) C 92 mins.

Producer, Samuel Ray Calabrese; associate producer, Stanley R. Caiden; directors, John Payne, (uncredited: Oliver Drake); screenplay, Monroe Manning; music, Raoul Kraushaar; assistant director, Russell Vreeland; stunt coordinator, Boyd Stockman; animal trainer, Gary Gero; sound, Lee Strosnider; camera, Ross Kelsay; editors, Thor Brooks, Sam Aanis.

John Payne (Bob Martin); Luana Patten (Barbara); John Carradine (Laslow); Scott Brady (Joe); Jim Davis (Vince Mallard); Anthony Eisley (Doc Wright); Darwin Lamb (Deputy); Boyd Stockman (Hotel Clerk); Bravo the Dog (Himself).

Filmed in the Valley of Fire near Las Vegas, this low-budget gangster-chase thriller harkened back to the days of simplistic scenarios with its basic tale of a man and his dog saving a young woman from murderous mobsters. Buoyed by scenic locales, an able cast, and decent production values, the film is ingratiating, although a minor effort.

Young Barbara Collins (Luana Patten), the daughter of a murdered oil geologist, is kidnapped by the gangsters who committed the crime. The trio (Jim Davis, Anthony Eisley, and Scott Brady) are after an oil lease document which belonged to the murdered man and they believe the daughter knows its whereabouts. They drug her and take her across the Nevada desert, but she is rescued by a prospector (John Payne) and his dog. The gangsters pursue, but Payne is able to kill Davis in an explosion. Brady is driven mad by the heat and Payne takes him to a nearby sheriff's office where the geologist's crooked partner (John Carradine) overhears him tell the lawman the girl's location. Carradine then hunts the girl, attacks her, and tries to get the document, but the dog forces the culprit off a cliff and he falls to his death. She returns to civilization with Payne and the dog.

THE TIP-OFF GIRLS (Paramount, 1938) 61 mins.

Associate producer, Edward T. Lowe; director, Louis King; screenplay, Maxwell Shane, Robert Yost, Stuart Anthony; art directors,

Larry "Buster" Crabbe, Mary Carlisle, and Gertrude Short in THE TIP-OFF GIRLS (1938).

Hans Dreir, Robert Odell; music, Boris Morros; camera, Theodor Sparkuhl; editor, Ellsworth Hoagland.

Lloyd Nolan (Bob Anders); Mary Carlisle (Marjorie Rogers); J. Carrol Naish (Joseph Valkus); Harvey Stephens (Jason Baardue); Roscoe Karns (Tom Logan); Larry Crabbe (Red Deegan); Evelyn Brent (Rena Terry); Anthony Quinn (Marty); Benny Baker (Scotty); Barlowe Borland (Blacky); Pierre Watkin (George Murkil); John Hart, Harry Templeton, Vic Demourelle, Jr., Jack Pennick, Ethan Laidlaw, Stanley King (Drivers); Stanley Price (Louis); Philip Warren (Steve); Wade Boteler (Pete); John Patterson (Jim); Frank Austin (Gus); Richard E. Allen (Police Lieutenant); Stanley Andrews (Police Sergeant); Oscar "Dutch" Hendrian (Hijacker); Barbara Jackson (Nurse); Joyce Mathews (Tessie); Ruth Rogers, Laurie Lane, Margaret Randall, Cheryl Walker (Waitresses), Gertrude Short (Telephone Operator).

   G-men Bob Anders (Lloyd Nolan) and Tom Logan (Roscoe Karns) are on the track of a hijacking gang and they infiltrate the group by pretending to be gangsters. They learn the gang uses "B" girls, led by Rena Terry (Evelyn Brent), for tips on merchandise shipments as well as acting as fronts for the operation. As a result, the G-men bring the head mobster (J. Carrol Naish) and his gang to justice.

Filmed as HIGHWAY RACKETEERS, this Paramount programmer was one of a series of finely done gangster pictures the studio released in the late 1930s and early 1940s. Bosley Crowther in The New York Times lauded, "Told swiftly, in a clean straight line and convincingly performed ... [it] is a good B-plus action picture."

TO HAVE AND HAVE NOT see: THE BREAKING POINT

TO LIVE AND DIE IN L.A. (Metro-Goldwyn-Mayer/United Artists, 1985) C 116 mins.

Executive producer, Samuel Schulman; producer, co-producer, Bud Smith; Irving H. Levin; director, William Friedkin; based on the novel by Gerald Petievich; screenplay, Friedkin, Petievich; production designer, Lilly Kilvert; art director, Buddy Cone; set decorator, Cricket Rowland; costume designer, Linda Bass; assistant director, Charles Myer; second unit director, Bud Smith; sound, Jean-Louis DuCarme, Rodger Pardee; camera, Robby Muller; editors, Bud Smith, Scott Smith.

William L. Petersen (Richard Chance); Willem Dafoe (Eric Masters); John Pankow (John Vukovich); Debra Feuer (Bianco Torres); John Turturro (Carl Cody); Darlanne Fluegel (Ruth Lanier); Dean Stockwell (Attorney Bob Crimes); Steve James (Jeff Rice); Robert Downey (Thomas Bateman); Michael Greene (Jim Hart); Christopher Allport (Max Waxman); Jack Hoar (Jack); Val DeVargas (Judge Filo Cedillo); Dwier Brown (Doctor); Michael Chong (Thomas Ling); Jackelyn Giroux (Claudia Leith).

Having already explored the gangster movie with the classic THE FRENCH CONNECTION (see: B/V) in 1971 and the much less satisfying THE BRINK'S JOB (q.v.) in 1978, director William Friedkin returned to the genre with this gritty, hard-hitting, but ultimately empty journey into the underbelly of Los Angeles, using the explosive revenge motif to display the unsavory aspects of the city and its denizens. Duane Byrge notes in The Hollywood Reporter that the film "... travels the meanest streets of film noir, and genre buffs will be blown away. Film should also appeal to foreign audiences, especially places like France where romanticized view of the United States syncs up with noir outlook; namely that this country is a corrupt cesspool where everyone's trying to blow everyone else away."

When his partner (John Pankow) is murdered while trailing a highly talented, diabolical counterfeiter (Willem Dafoe), Treasury agent Richard Chance (William L. Petersen) vows revenge, which turns into a psychotic vendetta. His quest takes him through the Los Angeles underworld where Dafoe has connections with crooks in all levels of gangsterdom. Meeting several of the city's low-life inhabitants and even killing one innocent person, Petersen is able to get the gangster after a lengthy auto chase.

According to <u>Variety</u>, the movie "... looks like a rich man's 'Miami Vice.' As hip as can be and as cynical as all getout, William Friedkin's evident attempt to fashion a West Coast equivalent of THE FRENCH CONNECTION is commercially intended, but the intense vulgarity of the characters and the virtuoso stylistic overkill will, like that of YEAR OF THE DRAGON [q.v.], turn off mainstream audiences." More stringent was the <u>LA Weekly</u>'s review: "In his attempt to be 'with it,' metaphysically hip, Friedkin creates psychological and physical landscapes that bear no resemblance to any planet I've ever visited.... Even worse, in its last 15 minutes the film finally discovers its true subject and promptly buries it under intimations of Heavy Meaning." Michael Wilmington (<u>Los Angeles Times</u>) observed, "... the movie's saving grace--beyond its formidable professionalism--may be its avoidance of even disguised sentimentality. There's no <u>ubermensch</u> here to clean up the town, no fairy-tale climax. Here are some mean streets and meaner people, the movie seems to be saying. Look at them a while and see if you flinch."

TODAY'S FBI (ABC-TV, 10/25/81) C 100 mins.

Executive producer, David Gerber; producers, Christopher Morgan, Fred Caruso; director, Virgil W. Vogel; teleplay, Jerry Ludwig; theme music, Elmer Bernstein; music, John Cacavas, Charles R. Cassey; camera, H. John Penner.

Mike Connors (Deputy Assistant Director); Joseph Cali (Agent Nick Frazer); Carol Potter (Agent Maggie Clinton); Richard Hill (Agent Al Gordean); Charles Brown (Agent Dwayne Thompson); Steven Keats (Gene Pauley); Paul Sorvino (Informant); Tony Lo Bianco (Joey D'Amico); Louis Giambalvo (Vinnie Tigner); Joe Silver (Sy Fowler); Patricia Elliott (Sally Kositchek); Raymond Sierra (Harry Colfax); Roberta Maxwell (Phyllis Slater); Tony DiBenedett (Elgort).

FBI agency executive Ben Slater (Mike Connors) puts together a task force of three men and a woman to obtain information to bring a union leader mobster (Joey D'Amico) to justice. The latter is the head of the Stevedores Association of America (SAA), a longshoremen's union. Although D'Amico pretends to be a civic leader who guides his union in refusing to handle imported Soviet goods, he is really a gangster using force and extortion to carry out his activities. Agent Nick Frazier (Joseph Cali) infiltrates the operation as the boss' new chauffeur and develops a liking for the man and almost wavers in his assignment. However, when a businessman (Paul Sorvino) refuses to buckle under the gang's demands and turns informant, the team is able to bring the crook to justice.

This telefeature was the series pilot for a program of the same title (eighteen installments between October 1981 and spring 1982 on ABC-TV), which attempted to revitalize interest in cases from the FBI files. Previously the long-running ABC-TV series, "The F.B.I."

had done the same thing with Efrem Zimbalist, Jr. headlining the 1965-74 program. This video outing had "Mannix" telestar Mike Connors as the FBI chief and was "a notably fast paced and un- usually engrossing specimen of the actioner form" (Variety). His- torically the telefilm was of interest in that the depicted SAA union was very close in reality to the actual International Longshoremen's Association which also refused to handle Russian goods following that nation's rape of Afghanistan.

TOO MANY WINNERS (Producers Releasing Corp., 1947) 60 mins.

Producer, John Sutherland; director, William Beaudine; based on characters and story by Brett Halliday; adaptors, Fred Myton, Scott Darling; screenplay, John Sutherland; set decorator, Tony Thompson; music, Alvin Levin; music supervisor, Dick Carruth; dialogue director, Clifford Hayman; assistant director, Barton Adams; sound, John Carter; camera, Jack Greenhalgh; editor, Harry Rey- nolds.

Hugh Beaumont (Michael Shayne); Trudy Marshall (Phyllis Hamilton); Ralph Dunn (Rafferty); Claire Carleton (Mayme Martin); Charles Mitchell (Tim Rourke); John Hamilton (Police Chief Payson); Gran- don Rhodes (Hardeman); Ben Welden (Madden); Byron Foulger (Edwards); Jean Andren (Mrs. Edwards); George Meader (Clarence); Frank Hagney (Joe); Maurice B. Mozelle (Punk).

Detective Michael Shayne (Hugh Beaumont) and his secretary Phyllis Hamilton (Trudy Marshall) are embarking on a duck hunting expedition when he is called into a case at the Santa Rosita race- track by the local police chief (John Hamilton). Beaumont learns that someone is counterfeiting mutual tickets and hurting the track's profits. He goes undercover to locate the culprits. Along the way he meets a woman (Claire Carleton) who has useful information, but she turns up dead and two thugs try unsuccessfully to eliminate the detective while Marshall, who has followed her boss to the track, aids him in the case. Two more murders occur before Beaumont traps the gangsters. Now he and his helper go off on their delayed vacation.

The last of a quintet of "Michael Shayne" adventures issued by PRC, TOO MANY WINNERS is a decent grade "B" detective ac- tion drama interpolating the gangster theme. Hugh Beaumont car- ries the film quite well with his believable rendition of the literary character, and William Beaudine's brisk direction is a blessing.

TRAPPED (Eagle Lion, 1949) 78 mins.

Producer, Bryan Foy; director, Richard Fleischer; story-screenplay, Earl Felton, George Zuckerman; assistant director, Emmett Emerson; makeup, Ern Westmore; art director, Frank Dunlauf; set decorator,

Barbara Payton and John Hoyt in TRAPPED (1949).

Armor Marlowe; music director, Irving Friedman; music, Sol Kaplan; sound, L. J. Myers; camera, Guy Roe; editor, Alfred DeGaetano.

Lloyd Bridges (Tris Stewart); John Hoyt (Johnny Downey/Johnny Hackett); Barbara Payton (Laurie); James Todd (Sylvester); Russ Conway (Gunby); Bert Conway (Mantz); Robert Karnes (Foreman).

Counterfeit money is flooding the country and the Treasury Department is out to stop the bogus currency. To accomplish this, agency chief Johnny Downey (John Hoyt) enlists one-time counterfeiter Tris Stewart (Lloyd Bridges) whose old plates are being used by the gang. The T-man makes it appear Bridges has escaped from federal prison and he joins the gang run by Sylvester (James Todd). Complications arise in the person of alluring Laurie (Barbara Payton), Todd's girlfriend, who wants Bridges to resume his illegal activities. With Bridges' aid, the T-men stomp out the ring.

TRAPPED is one of those late 1940s and early 1950s melodramas which employed a quasi-documentary background for its narrative format. Here the inner workings of the Treasury Department are depicted. The production, shot on the streets of Los Angeles, "packs in plenty of suspense and strong melodrama," Variety accorded, and it was a most topical entry due to a plethora of counterfeiting operations then flourishing.

The production's most interesting aspect is the presence of

Barbara Payton as the seductive Laurie. In her first major screen
assignment, the blonde beauty stole the film and launched a brief
but impressive career which sadly ended much too soon due to her
overwhelming personal problems.

TRUE CONFESSIONS (United Artists, 1981) C 108 mins.

Producers, Irwin Winkler, Robert Chartoff; associate producer,
James D. Brubaker; director, Ulu Grosbard; based on the novel by
John Gregory Dunne; screenplay, Dunne, Joan Didion; music,
Georges Delerue; assistant directors, Tom Mack, Bill Elvin, Duncan
S. Henderson; production designer, Stephen S. Grimes; art direc-
tor, W. Stewart Campbell; customes, Joe I. Tompkins; choreography,
Alfonse L. Palermo; camera, Owen Roisman; editor, Lynzee Klingman.

Robert DeNiro (Des Spellacy); Robert Duvall (Tom Spellacy);
Charles Durning (Jack Amsterdam); Ed Flanders (Dan T. Campon);
Burgess Meredith (Seamus Fargo); Rose Gregorio (Brenda Samuels);
Cyril Cusack (Cardinal Danaher); Kenneth McMillan (Frank Crotty);
Dan Hedeya (Howard Terkel); Gwen Van Dam (Mrs. Fazenda); Tom
Hill (Mr. Fazenda); Jeanette Nolan (Mrs. Spellacy); Jorge Cervera,
Jr. (Eduardo Duarte); Susan Myers (Bride); Louisa Moritz (Whore);
Darwyn Carson (Lorna Keane); Pat Corley (Sonny McDonough);
Matthew Faison (Reporter); Richard Foronjy (Ambulance Driver);
James Hong (Coroner Wong); Joe Medalis (Deputy Coroner); Ron
Ryan, Louis Basile, Paul Valentine (Detectives); Louise Fitch (Older
Nun); Margery Nelson (Nun); Fredric Cook (Brenda's Trick); Kirk
Brennan (Acolyte); Steve Ariwn (Radio Announcer); Sharon Miller
(Movie Star); Kevin Breslin (Boy); Jeff Howard (Priest); Harry
Duncan (Priest at Banquet); Pierrino Mascarino (Suspect); Michael
Callahan (Sub-Deacon); Luisa Leschin (Tower Girl); Bob Arthur,
Bill Furnell (Newscasters); Sig Frohlich (Waiter).

    With its soap opera title and plot derived from the still un-
solved Black Dahlia murder case of 1940s Hollywood, TRUE CON-
FESSIONS turned out to be a confusing, although well acted, melodrama about two diverse brothers who become enmeshed in the web
of the investigation surrounding the killing. Co-adapted by John
Gregory Dunne from his novel of 1977, the movie is more of an indictment of the politics of the Catholic Church than either a gangster movie or a murder mystery. In fact, the trappings of the political interworkings of the church so overshadow the film's scenario
that the actual mystery proved to be far better handled by the 1975
telefeature WHO IS THE BLACK DAHLIA?
    In a small desert church priest Des Spellacy (Robert DeNiro)
meets with his policeman brother (Robert Duvall) and they relate
the events which took place years before when a priest was found
dead from a heart attack in a brothel and Duvall was assigned to
the case. In the flashback, Duvall questioned his brother about
the matter, which proved to be a delicate one of the church. DeNiro

is very close to the Cardinal (Cyril Cusack), who has selected him as his protege and successor in carrying out church politics such as fundraising and the forced retirement of an elderly priest (Burgess Meredith) no longer useful to the Cardinal. When a young prostitute is found murdered, Duvall is again ordered to investigate and learns that his brother was not only close to the girl but that she was also involved with a gangster businessman (Charles Durning) who has been named the year's Catholic layman due to his heavy church contributions. Both Duvall and DeNiro find themselves caught in the web of the investigation; Duvall does not want to implicate his brother with the murdered prostitute, while DeNiro must keep the money donated to the church by the hateful businessman, who now feels he has been betrayed by the church as Duvall closes in on him for committing the crime. As a result, De-Niro is relegated to an out-of-the-way desert parish where the talk (many years later) occurs.

Two institutions on the "hit" list of Hollywood's new left receive the barbed treatment in TRUE CONFESSIONS: the American businessman and the Catholic Church. The former has long been shown to be the center of corruption, and Charles Durning's broad and despicable Jack Amsterdam is the epitome of the crooked, loud-mouthed entrepreneur who uses every means to grasp all the wealth he can while carrying out every possible indulgence, including the murder of a hooker no longer useful to him.

Since ROSEMARY'S BABY (1968), the Catholic Church has been Hollywood's main religious target. While not openly as anti-Catholic as ALICE SWEET ALICE (1976) (also known as COMMUNION and HOLY TERROR), TRUE CONFESSIONS takes a dim view of the Church's involvement in various secular activities to bring in funds needed to keep its religious mechanisms working.

While TRUE CONFESSIONS is flaw-ridden, it affords the pleasure of reteaming two stars from THE GODFATHER (see: B/V) epics: Robert DeNiro and Robert Duvall. Their emoting as the two brothers is perfect and their performances are a constant viewer joy. Rob Edelman observed in Magill's Survey of the Cinema (1982), "The real star of TRUE CONFESSIONS is the dialogue. John Gregory Dunne and Joan Didion have written a trenchant, gutsy script, based on Dunne's best-selling novel.... The performances are hardly less impressive than the script.... [DeNiro's and Duvall's] performances are toned down, subtle, and affecting. Particularly in the sequences set in 1963, without so much as a sentence uttered between them, they express warmth, affection and, most tellingly, brotherly love."

TWO MAFIA MEN AGAINST AL CAPONE see: DUE MAFIOSA CONTRO
   AL CAPONE

UNDERCOVER DOCTOR (Paramount, 1939) 67 mins.

Producer, Harold Hurley; director, Louis King; based on the story by J. Edgar Hoover; adaptors, Horace McCoy, William R. Lippman; camera, William C. Mellor; editor, Arthur Schmidt.

Lloyd Nolan (Robert Anders); Janice Logan (Margaret Hopkins); J. Carrol Naish (Dr. Bartley Morgan); Heather Angel (Cynthia Weld); Broderick Crawford (Eddie Krator); Robert Wilcox (Tom Logan); Richard Carle (Elmer Porter).

UNDERCOVER DOCTOR is the second of four feature films derived from J. Edgar Hoover's 1938 book Persons in Hiding: it was preceded by PERSONS IN HIDING (q.v.) issued the same year, and PAROLE FIXER (q.v.) and QUEEN OF THE MOB (see: B/V), both issued in 1940. It is the weakest of the celluloid quartet.

Dr. Bartley Morgan (J. Carrol Naish), a successful medical man, finds his main source of income is from public enemy Eddie Krator (Broderick Crawford), his henchman (Robert Wilcox), and gang. FBI agent Robert Anders (Lloyd Nolan) is on the track of the group but does not realize the doctor is involved with them. But with the aid of a society girl (Heather Angey) and the physician's nurse (Janice Logan), he brings in the mobsters to justice.

The character of Dr. Bartley Morgan was based on the real-life Dr. Guellfe, who tries to change the face and fingerprints of gangster Alvin Karpis; the story is told again in GUNS DON'T ARGUE (1957) (q.v.).

UNDERWORLD (Limehouse, 1985) C 100 mins.

Producers, Kevin Attew, Don Hawkins; coproducer, Graham Ford; director, George Pavlou; story, Clive Barker; screenplay, Barker, James Caplin; production designer, Len Huntingford; music, Freur; special effects, Richard Parkis; camera, Sydney Macarthey; editor, Chris Ridsdale.

Denholm Elliott (Dr. Savary); Steven Berkoff (Hugo Moherskille); Larry Lamb (Roy Bain); Miranda Richardson (Oriel); Art Malik (Fluke); Nicola Cowper (Nicole); Ingrid Pitt (Peppardine); Irina Brook (Bianca); Paul Brown (Nygaard); Philip Davies (Lazarus); Gary Olsen (Red Dog); Brian Croucher (Darling); Trevor Thomas (Ricardo); Paul Mari (Dudu).

Unlike many screen genres, the gangster film has not been overly diluted by mixing its plots with other types of movies. Certainly gangsters have roamed the range in several Westerns, and they have come up against kung fu artists, and a few have even sung a song or two in musicals, but mostly they have stayed with their pin-striped suits and tommy guns in the rain-drenched streets of Chicago and the corrupt warmth of Los Angeles. In UNDERWORLD, however, the gangster theme is solidly engrained with the horror and science fiction types to make an "Okay thriller marred by cornball dialog" (Variety).

A scientist (Denholm Elliott), who also traffics in drugs with

the underworld, develops a formula which permits people to live out
their wildest fantasies, but after a time the formula causes a facial
deterioration and only pretty Nicole (Nicola Cowper) has not been
affected. The others contaminated by the drug kidnap the girl,
who was once the girlfriend of a gangster chief (Larry Lamb) who
plans to exterminate his infected cohorts. He hires a detective
(Steven Berkoff) to do the job, but the latter falls in love with
Cowper who is doing her best to help those tainted by the drug
and she convinces the gunman to turn on the gangsters.

VENOM (Paramount, 1982) C 93 mins.

Executive producers, Louis A. Stroller, Richard R. St. Johns;
producer, Martin Bregman; associate producer, Harry Benn; director, Piers Haggard; based on the novel by Alan Scholefield;
screenplay, Robert Carrington; art director, Tony Curtis; assistant directors, Dominic Fulford, Nick Daubeny; camera, Gilbert
Taylor, Denys Coop; editor, Michael Bradsell.

Klaus Kinski (Jacmel); Oliver Reed (Dave); Nicol Williamson (Com-
mander William Bulloch); Sarah Miles (Dr. Marion Stowe); Sterling
Hayden (Howard Anderson); Cornelia Sharpe (Ruth Hopkins); Lance
Holcomb (Philip Hopkins); Susan George (Louise); Mike Gwilyn (De-
tective Constable Dan Spencer); Paul Williamson (Detective Sergeant
Glazer); Michael Gough (David Ball); Hugh Lloyd (Taxi Driver);
Rita Webb (Mrs. Loewenthal); Edward Hardwicke (Lord Dunning);
John Forbes-Robertson (Sergeant Nash); Ian Brimble (Constable
in Police Station); Peter Porteus (Hodges); Maurice Colbourne
(Sampson); Nicholas Donnelly (Police Superintendent); Cyril Con-
way, Sally Lahee (Couple in #17); David Sterne (Driver); Charles
Cork (Driver's Mate); Howard Bell (Constable); Alan Ford (Peters);
Norman Mann (Williams); Tony Meyer (Martin); Michael Watkins
(Rogers); Gerard Ryder (Smith); Moti Makan (Murkerjee); Kath-
erine Wilkinson (Susan Stowe); Eric Richard (Airline Clerk); Arnold Diamond (Head Waiter).

VENOM is a British-made combination of the suspense and
gangster film genres which provides for ninety minutes of good entertainment, as both heroes and villains fight one of the world's
deadliest snakes, a black mamba. While this feature has come under
critical fire in some circles, it is a taut thriller nicely directed by
Piers Haggard, who replaced Tobe ("Texas Chain Saw Massacre")
Hooper in the film's early going.
    In London, young asthmatic Philip Hopkins (Lance Holcomb),
the son of a rich American (Cornelia Sharpe) and the grandson of
a noted writer (Sterling Hayden), is kidnapped by a ruthless German gangster (Klaus Kinski) with the aid of the boy's chauffeur
(Oliver Reed) and maid (Susan George). What the criminals and
the youth do not know is that the latter has purchased a snake
from a local pet store which is really a black mamba intended for

a toxicologist (Sarah Miles). When Reed kills a policeman, the criminals are cornered in the boy's home and the snake escapes and bites George, who dies a horrible death as a result. The reptile takes refuge in the house's heating system and stalks the inhabitants. The police, led by Commander William Bulloch (Nicol Williamson), surround the house as the toxicologist warns them of the situation and a standoff occurs.

Slick production values and a topnotch cast, plus the fascinating behavior of the deadly snake, keep this thriller moving at a healthy clip. Klaus Kinski is effective as the quirky gangster and the London Zoo's actual snake expert, David Ball, appears, the part enacted by Michael Gough.

VIGILANTE (Film Ventures International, 1982) C 90 mins.

Executive producers, John Packard, Jerry Mascacci, Kenneth Pavioa; producers, Andrew Garroni, William Lustig; associate producer, Randy Jurgensen; director, Lustig; screenplay, Richard Vetere; music, Jay Chattaway; camera, James Lemmo; editor, Lorenzo Marinelli.

Robert Forster (Eddie); Fred Williamson (Nick); Richard Bright (Burke); Rutanya Alda (Vickie); Don Blakely (Prago); Joseph Carberry (Ramon), Willie Colon (Rico); Joe Spinell (Eisenberg); Carol Lynley (District Attorney Fletcher); Woody Strode (Rake); Vincent Beck (Judge); Bo Rucker (Horace); Peter Savage (Mr. T).

A New York City neighborhood is plagued by street gangs, pimps, and dope peddlers and a businessman (Fred Williamson) unites with his neighbors into a protection group which sets out to exterminate the scum plaguing their lives. At first Williamson's pal (Robert Forster) does not go along with the vigilante group, but when a street gang kills his baby and knifes his wife (Rutanya Alda), he joins them. The police arrest gang leader Rico (Willie Colon) for the child's murder and the district attorney (Carol Lynley) prosecutes, but a spineless judge (Vincent Beck) sides with the defendant's attorney (Joe Spinell) and the hoodlum is given a two-year suspended sentence. Enraged, Forster attacks the judge and is sent to jail for contempt of court and there two punks try to beat him up, but he is saved by a fellow prisoner (Woody Strode). Getting out of jail, Forster plans to kill the street gang members and the judge. As a result his wife leaves him.

"Even without the ultra-violence, VIGILANTE is simply too grim and nihilistic to justify its existence as entertainment" (Variety). Made in the vein of DEATH WISH (q.v.) and its countless imitators, VIGILANTE is one of those movies which strikes a nerve with law-abiding citizens enraged by the continuing spiraling of urban crimes and the impotence of law enforcement agencies to combat street gangs and the low life preying upon the average person.

A.k.a.: STREET GANG

Jan-Michael Vincent and Andrew Stevens in VIGILANTE FORCE (1976).

VIGILANTE FORCE (United Artists, 1976) C 89 mins.

Producer, Gene Corman; director; screenplay, George Armitage; music, Gerald Fried; art director, Jack Fisk; assistant director, Don Heitzer; stunt coordinator, Joe Buddy Hooker; sound, Darin Knight; camera, William Cronjager; editor, Morton Tubor.

Kris Kirstofferson (Aaron Arnold); Jan-Michael Vincent (Ben Arnold); Victoria Principal (Linda); Bernadette Peters (Dee); Brad Dexter (Mayor); Judson Pratt (Police Chief); David Doyle (Homer Arno); Antony Carbone (Freddie Howe); Andrew Stevens (Paul Sinton); Shelly Novack (Viner); Paul X. Gleason (Michael Loonius); John Steadman (Shakey Malone); Lilyan McBride (Landlady); James Lydon (Tom Cousy).

    A back-country California town has a sudden influx of rowdy oil workers whom the local police cannot handle. Young Ben Arnold (Jan-Michael Vincent) talks the town's mayor (Brad Dexter) into bringing in his Vietnam veteran brother (Kris Kristofferson) to keep the peace. The mayor agrees and Kristofferson is successful in taming the town but soon brings in his wartime buddies who terrorize the citizenry by running the town with an iron fist.
    VIGILANTE FORCE is a formula effort, full of violence, although

it scores with a sincere performance by Kris Kristofferson. Writing in The Films of the Seventies (1984), Marc Sigoloff states, "VIGILANTE FORCE, unlike most low-budget action films, has ideas to justify its violence. The film is a political allegory with the theme that authoritarianism is not the alternative to anarchy. Unfortunately the execution is not up to the idea."

VIOLENT CITY see: THE FAMILY

VOICE OF THE CITY (Metro-Goldwyn-Mayer, 1929) 60 mins.

Director-screenplay, Willard Mack; titles, Joe Farnham; art director, Cedric Gibbons; sound, Douglas Shearer; camera, Maximilian Fabian; editors, William S. Gray, Basil Wrangell.

Robert Ames (Bobby Doyle); Willard Mack (Biff); Sylvia Field (Beebe); James Farley (Wilmot); John Miljan (Wilkes); Clark Marshall (Johnny); Duane Thomspon (Mary); Tom McGuire (Kelly); Alice Moe (Martha); Beatrice Banyard (Betsy).

A young man, Bobby Doyle (Robert Ames) is framed on a murder charge and sent to prison for twenty years. With the help of a drug addict (Clark Marshall) he escapes and hides out at the man's home. The gangster (John Miljan), who framed Ames, wants him back behind bars so he can have the young man's girlfriend (Sylvia Field). Detective Biff Myers (Willard Mack) trails the gangster to Ames' hideout and kills the mobster. A note found on Miljan's body clears Ames of all charges.

This old-fashioned early talkie, also issued in a silent version, was a family affair. Willard Mack not only wrote and directed this creeker, but also played the detective, while his wife, Sylvia Field, was the ingenue.

WALKING TALL (Cinerama Releasing Corp., 1973) C 125 mins.

Executive producer, Charles A. Pratt; producer, Mort Briskin; director, Phil Karlson; screenplay, Briskin; music, Walter Scharf; song, Scharf and Don Black; production designer, Stan Jolley; assistant directors, Ralph Black, David Hall; sound, Andy Gilmore, David Dockendorf; camera, Jack A. Marta; editor, Harry Gerstad.

Joe Don Baker (Buford Pusser); Elizabeth Hartman (Pauline Pusser); Gene Evans (Sheiff Thurman); Noah Beery (Grandpa Pusser); Brenda Benet (Luan); John Brascia (Prentiss); Bruce Glover (Deputy Coker); Arch Johnson (Buel Jaggers); Felton Perry (Deputy Eaker); Richard X. Slattery (Arno Purdy); Rosemary Murphy (Callie Hecker).

Felton Perry and Joe Don Baker (center) in WALKING TALL (1973).

WALKING TALL: PART II (American International, 1975) C 109 mins.

Producer, Charles A. Pratt; director, Earl Bellamy; screenplay, Howard B. Kreitsek; art director, Phil Jefferies; music, Walter Scharf; assistant director, David Hall; stung coordinator, Carey Loftin; sound, John Wilkinson, Andy Gilmore; camera, Keith Smith; editor, Art Seid.

Bo Svenson (Buford Pusser); Luke Askew (Pinky Dobson); Noah Beery (Carl Pusser); John Chandler (Ray Henry); Robert Doqui (Obra Eaker); Bruce Glover (Grady Coker); Richard Jaeckel (Stud Pardee); Brooke Mills (Ruby Ann); Logan Ramsey (John Witter); Angel Tompkins (Marganne Stilson); Lurene Tuttle (Grandma Pusser); Leif Garrett, Dawn Lyn (Pusser Children); William Bryant (FBI Agent).

The exploits of rural Tennessee lawman Buford Pusser in fighting racketeers and corruption became the grist of three theatrical features and a telefeature. Ironically, Pusser himself was set to star in the second of the theatrical outings before being killed in an auto crash in August 1974. While all the Buford Pusser movies took the law-and-order platform in unfolding their narratives, the three theatrical films especially focused on violence. The movies also developed a stock company with Noah Beery playing Pusser's father in the first two films and Forrest Tucker taking over the role for the final theatrical movie and the telefilm, while Lurene Tuttle played the lawman's mother in the trio of big screen outings.

WALKING TALL tells the story of how lawman Buford Pusser (Joe Don Baker) takes on the gambling and prostitution rackets which infest his small town. The racketeers include a madam (Rosemary Murphy), the town's ex-lawman (Gene Evans), and a crooked judge (Douglas Fowley). When Baker begins cleaning up the area, the lawman's family is threatened and his wife (Elizabeth Hartman) is killed. Finally, with the aid of one of the hookers (Brenda Benet), Baker brings the lawless element to justice, although many of them have already been eliminated in the process. Variety noted the movie "... wallows in its own bloody exploitation of episodic carnage while dabbling in do-it-yourself police sociology of dubious merit.... Phil Karlson's slaughter staging is far superior to his dramatic direction."

WALKING TALL proved to be a box-office sleeper and resulted in PART 2--WALKING TALL two years later. With Bo Svenson now in the lead, the hero is up against Witter (Logan Ramsey), the chief of racketeering in the rural area where Svenson is still the law. The gangster hires a race car driver (Richard Jaeckel) to kill the lawman, but both are eventually thwarted. The movie grossed over $9,000,000 theatrically compared to $17,000,000 for the initial outing. The film was successful enough to bring forth a third release: FINAL CHAPTER--WALKING TALL in 1977 with Bo Svenson again enacting the resourceful Pusser. It grossed over $6,000,000 at the box office.

The third episode has Pusser being voted out of office but still fighting corruption, this time in the guise of a racketeer called The Boss (Morgan Woodward). At the finale, however, Pusser is killed in a car wreck, thus ending the theatrical series. Variety complained of this installment that it has "... a clumsy script which lurches from cornball sentimentality to psychotic violence."

The commercial exploits of Buford Pusser were not over, as the late lawman was resurrected for the 1978 telefeature A REAL AMERICAN HERO, which rehashes the events of WALKING TALL. Here Pusser (Brian Dennehy), the sheriff of Selma, Tennessee, takes on a polished bootlegger-moonshiner (Ken Howard). The results were "average" (TV Movies, 1985). Samuel A. Peeples, who co-wrote the third theatrical film, wrote and produced this television outing which was highlighted by Forrest Tucker again portraying the hero's father, Carl Pusser.

WANTED BY THE POLICE (Monogram, 1938) 59 mins.

Executive producer, Scott R. Dunlap; supervisor, Lindsley Parsons; director, Howard Bretherton; story, Donn Mullally, Sally Sandlin; screenplay, Wellyn Totman; camera, Bert Longenecker.

Frankie Darro (Danny); Lillian Elliott (Mrs. Murphy); Robert Kent (Mike); Evalyn Knapp (Kathleen); Matty Fain (Williams); Don Rowans (Owens); Sam Bernard (Stinger); Maurice Hugo (Marty); Thelma White (Lilliam); Wally Costello (Russo); Walter Merrill (Trigger); Ralph Peters (Jess).

Gangsters are using a garage as the headquarters for their auto theft ring and they entice a wayward youth (Frankie Darro) to join their operations by promising him big money. His activities soon come to the attention of his mother (Lillian Elliott) and pretty sister (Evelyn Knapp) and the latter enlists her policeman boyfriend (Robert Kent) to bring Darro around to the right side of the law.
"A prosy little film, as straight-forward and matter-a-fact as its title," is how The New York Times assessed this pleasing programmer. The movie was one of a series of many such features starring perennial juvenile lead Frankie Darro which Monogram produced in the late 1930s and early 1940s.

WHAT'S YOUR RACKET? (Mayfair, 1934) 50 mins.

Director, Fred Guiol; story, George R. Rogan; adaptor, Barry Barringer; camera, James S. Brown, Jr.; editor, Dan Milner.

Regis Toomey (Bert Miller); Noel Francis (Mae Cosgrove); J. Carrol Naish (Dick Graves); Creighton Hale (Jimmie Dean); Fred Malatest (Benton); May Wallace (Mrs. Cosgrove); Lew Kelly (Cameron); David Callia (Jones).

Nightclub entertainer Mae Cosgrove (Noel Francis) robs the home of her racketeer boss (J. Carrol Naish) looking for evidence to convict the man since he was responsible for sending her father, a bank executive, to prison. Following the robbery, Francis falls in love with Bert Miller (Regis Toomey), who is an undercover policeman working to send the mobster to jail. Eventually Toomey and Francis succeed in their mission.
This fast moving poverty row programmer runs a brief fifty minutes and is a worthy addition to the canon of such entries.

WHEN G-MEN STEP IN (Columbia, 1938) 60 mins.

Producer, Wallace MacDonald; director, C. C. Coleman, Jr.; story-adaptors, Arthur T. Horman, Robert C. Bennett; camera, Henry Freulich; editor, Al Clark.

Don Terry (Frederick Garth); Jacqueline Wells [Julie Bishop]
(Marjory Drake); Robert Paige (Bruce Garth); Gene Morgan (Neale);
Paul Fix (Clip Phillips); Stanley Andrews (Preston); Edward Earle
(Morton); Horace MacMahon (Jennings); Huey White (Turk).

Racketeer Frederick Garth (Don Terry) heads a gang involved
in numerous rackets including charity swindles, bookmaking, and
bogus sweepstakes tickets. He claims to be a legitimate businessman but his younger brother (Robert Paige), a G-man, learns he is
a gangster. With the help of his partner (Gene Morgan) and girlfriend (Jacqueline Wells), Paige halts his brother's illegal activities.
    Although Variety termed this Wallace MacDonald production a
"run-of-the-mill G-man meller," the trade paper also admitted, "Without spending a great deal of money, MacDonald has turned out a
'B' that has good backgrounds, moves along at a pretty good pace
and maintains suspense as good as most productions of its kind."
It is worth noting that the head crook portrayed by Don Terry is
offbeat casting, since the actor is usually associated with hero and
second lead roles.

WHEN GANGLAND STRIKES (Republic, 1956) 70 mins.

Associate producer, William J. O'Sullivan; director, R. G. Springsteen; screenplay, John K. Butler, Frederic Louis Fox; music, Van
Alexander; assistant director, Dolph Zimmer; costumes, Adele Palmer; sound, Dick Tyler, Sr.; camera, John L. Russell, Jr.; editor,
Tony Martinelli.

Raymond Greenleaf (Luke Ellis); Marjie Millar (June Ellis); John
Hudson (Bob Keeler); Anthony Caruso (Duke Martella); Marian Carr
(Hazel Worley); Slim Pickens (Slim Pickett); Mary Treen (Emily Par-
sons); Ralph Dumke (Walter Pritchard); Morris Ankrum (Leo Pans-
ler); Robert Emmett Keane (Judge Walters); Addison Richards (Mark
Spurlock); John Galludet (Chip); Paul Birch (Sheriff McBride);
Richard Deacon (Dixon Brackett); Rankin Mansfield (Court Clerk);
Frank Kreig (Chubby Johnson); James Best (Jerry Ames); Fred
Sherman (Arthur Livingston); Nancy Kilgas (Sarah Ames); Dick
Elliott (Foreman); Norman Leavitt (Court Clerk); Peter Mamakos
(Thorndike); Scott Douglas (Reporter); Pauline Drake (Helen Crain);
Jim Hayward (Bert Sample).

Republic Pictures was on its last legs when it issued this
gangster melodrama; a slickly made production with a plot harkening
back to the 1930s. (The film was a remake of 1939's MAIN STREET
LAWYER starring Edward Ellis, Anita Louise, and Margaret Hamilton). While lacking in big names, the picture is not without interest and it is smoothly helmed by veteran action director R. G.
Springsteen, who the same year turned out the studio's last really
good feature, the bucolic classic, COME NEXT SPRING. The Monthly Film Bulletin judged WHEN GANGLAND STRIKES, "A modest and

unsophisticated 'B' melodrama; despite its violent title, the film is pleasant and amiable in a homely sort of way."

Thoughtful small town prosecutor Luke Ellis (Raymond Greenleaf) is forced to throw a case because the man he is prosecuting, racketeer Duke Martell (Anthony Caruso), has uncovered evidence that Ellis' daughter (Marjie Millar) is actually adopted and was born in prison. As a result, Greenleaf is voted out of his job by the locals and is succeeded by Millar's fiance (John Hudson), and later the two learn the truth of her origins. When Millar is arrested on a murder charge, her adopted father defends her and proves the gangster committed the crime.

WHITE LINE FEVER (Columbia, 1975) C 89 mins.

Executive producers, Gerald Schneider, Mort Litwack; producer, John Kemeny; director, Jonathan Kaplan; screenplay, Ken Friedman; music, David Nichtern; art director, Sydney Litwack; set decorator, Sam Jones; assistant director, Don Heitzer; stunt supervisors, Carey Loftin, Nate Long, Joe Hooker; sound, Tex Rudloff, Darren Knight; camera, Fred Koenekamp; editor, O. Nicholas Brown.

Jan-Michael Vincent (Carrol Jo Hummer); Kay Lenz (Jerri Hummer); Slim Pickens (Duane Haller); L. Q. Jones (Buck Wessle); Don Porter (Josh Cutler); Sam Laws (Pops); Johnny Ray McGhee (Carnell); Leigh French (Lucy); R. G. Armstrong (Prosecutor); Martin Kove (Clem); Jamie Anderson (Jamie); Ron Nix (Deputy); Dick Miller (Birdie); Arnold Jeffers (Reporter); Curgie Pratt (Defense Lawyer); John David Garfield (Witness Miller).

Following a stint in the Air Force, Carrol Jo Hummer (Jan-Michael Vincent) returns home to marry his sweetheart Jerri (Kay Lenz) and go into business for himself as an independent trucker. Troubles start, however, when he ignores the request of a trucking company executive (Don Porter) to involve himself in smuggling activities, and his refusal to do so results in other truckers trying to put him out of operation by any means possible (assaults, sabotage, etc.). When his old pal Duane Haller (Slim Pickens) intercedes, he is murdered and Vincent organizes the independent truckers to combat the corrupt element.

While the film proved popular with the moviegoing public (it grossed over $6,000,000 in domestic rentals), Variety noted one of the movie's bigger flaws: "What seems missing ... is more depth and logical transition: Vincent passes too rapidly from a stubborn honest lone wolf to practically a union leader. That sort of telescoping used to work, but today's audiences require more lucidity and logic...."

THE WIDOW FROM CHICAGO (First National, 1930) 64 mins.

Director, Edward Clino; story screenplay, Earl Baldwin; sound, Clifford A. Ruberg; camera, Sol Polito; editor, Edward Schoreder.

Alice White (Polly Henderson); Neil Hamilton (Swifty Dorgan); Edward G. Robinson (Dominic); Frank McHugh (Slug O'Donnell); Lee Shumway (Chris Johnston); Brooks Benedict (Mullins); John Elliott (Detective Lieutenant Finnegan); Dorothy Mathews (Cora); Ann Cornwall (Mazie); E. H. Calvert (Captain Davis); Betty Francisco (Helen); Harold Goodwin (Jimmy Henderson); Mike Donlin (Desk Man); Robert Homans (Patrolman); Al Hill (Johnston's Henchman); Mary Foy (Neighbor Woman); Allan Cavan (Sergeant Dunn).

In his sixth sound film and first for Warner Brothers-First National, Edward G. Robinson was appropriately cast as a gangster, but his reviews were poor and for a brief time his tenure in motion pictures seemed to be short. With his next outing, however, Robinson was to make cinema history as Rico Bandello in LITTLE CAESAR (see: B/V) and his screen future was secure.

New York detectives (John Elliott, Harold Goodwin) are trailing a gangster (Neil Hamilton) on a train en route to Chicago where he is to join Dominic's (Robinson) gang. Hamilton leaps from the train and is presumed dead. Later in the Windy City, Goodwin takes on the guise of the late gangster and joins the hoods, but Robinson learns the truth and kills him. Wanting revenge, the young man's sister (Alice White) pretends to be Hamilton's widow and Robinson hires her for his nightclub. Hamilton then arrives on the scene and after White explains the situation, he agrees to go along with her as he wants to reform. When the gang attempts a holdup, White is forced to shoot a policeman to prove her loyalty to Robinson, but later Hamilton outmatches the hoodlum in a shootout.

WITNESS (Paramount, 1985) C 112 mins.

Producer, Edward S. Feldman; co-producer, David Bombyk; associate producer, Wendy Weir; director, Peter Weir; story, William Kelley, Pamela Wallace, Earl W. Wallace; screenplay, Earl W. Wallace, William Kelley; assistant directors, David McGiffert, Pamela Eilerson; production designer, Stan Jolley; set designer, Craig Edgar; set decorator, John Anderson; music, Maurice Jarre; songs, Sam Cooke, Herb Alpert and Lou Adler, Paul Chiten and Sue Sheridan, Alan Brackett and Scott Shelly; makeup, Michael A. Hancock; police adviser, Captain Eugene Dooley; Amish advisers, John D. King, Nora Dunfee; sound, Barry D. Thomas, Humberto Gatica; camera, Chuck Clifton; editor, Thom Noble.

Harrison Ford (John Book); Kelly McGillis (Rachel Lapp); Josef Sommer (Deputy Commissioner Schaeffer); Lukas Haas (Samuel

Lapp); Jan Rubes (Eli Lapp); Alexander Godunov (Daniel Hoch-
leimer); Danny Glover (McFee); Brent Jennings (Carter); Patti
LuPone (Elaine); Angus MacInnes (Fergie); Frederick Rolf (Stoltz-
fus); Viggo Mortensen (Moses Hochleitner); John Garson (Bishop
Tchantz); Beverly May (Mrs. Yoder); Ed Crowley (Sheriff); Timo-
thy Carhart (Zenovich); Sylvia Kauders (Tourist Lady); Marian
Swan (Mrs. Schaeffer); Maria Bradley (Schaeffer's Daughter);
Rozwill Young (T-Bone); Paul S. Nuss, Emily Mary Haas, Fred
Steinharter, John D. King, Paul Gross, Annemarie Vallerio, Bruce
E. Camburn (Amish); William Francis (Town Man); Tom W. Kennedy
(Ticket Seller); Blossom Terry (Mother in Station); Jennifer Man-
cuso (Little Girl); Michael Levering, Cara Giallanza, Anthony Dean
Rubes (Hoodlums).

Following the death of her Amish farmer husband, Rachel
Lapp (Kelly McGillis) takes her young son (Lukas Haas) to visit
her sister in Baltimore and at a stopover at the Philadelphia train
terminal the boy witnesses the murder of a narcotics officer. After
reporting the incident, the two are placed in the protective custody
of the sister of the investigating officer (Harrison Ford) who is sur-
prised when the boy points out fellow officer McFee (Danny Glover)
as one of the killers. Ford goes to his Deputy Commissioner superior (Josef Sommer) with the theory that Glover was involved in the
theft of drugs from the department a few years prior. When Glover
later shoots him, Ford realizes that Sommer is also involved and he
tells his partner (Brent Jennings) to remove all the case's evidence
from the department files. Ford then takes McGillis and Haas back
to Lancaster County, Pennsylvania, but he is too badly wounded to
return to the city and is cared for by the Amish. In the meanwhile, he and McGillis fall in love. When thugs disturb the peace
of the Amish community, Ford fights them but also learns that Jennings has been killed. In a final confrontation, Ford kills Glover
and his cohorts. Forcing a confession from Sommer, Ford then
leaves McGillis behind and returns to his job. Their cultural backgrounds are too disparate to mesh smoothly.

"In its gently receding quality, there are times when WITNESS
looks rather like a Western, which again may be a deliberate stylistic choice, or simply something that comes with the territory when
the urban thriller goes country," wrote Richard Combs in the British Monthly Film Bulletin. The stark contrast between the harsh
realities and corruption of urban Philadelphia and the serenity of
not-too-far-away Amish country is the highlight of this overlong
and occasionally lethargic thriller. After so many recent films
showing that the police can be as venal as any hardened crook, it
comes as no audience surprise that the culprits of the film are os-
tensibly on the side of the law. Laconic Harrison Ford does his
usual Gary Cooper-ish routine, but it is Kelly McGillis who adds
force to the film. She is a combination of Ingrid Bergman and
Dorothy McGuire, radiating honesty and total conviction.

THE WOMAN RACKET (Metro-Goldwyn-Mayer, 1930) 60 mins.

Directors, Robert Ober, Albert Kelley; based on the play The Night Hostess by Philip Dunning, Frances Dunning; screenplay, Albert Shelby Le Vino; titles, Fred Niblo, Jr.; art director, Cedric Gibbons; wardrobe, David Cox; choreography, Sammy Lee; sound, Russell Franks, Douglas Shearer; camera, Peverell Marley; editors, Basil Wrangell (sound version); Anson Stevenson (Silent version).

Tom Moore (Tom); Blanche Sweet (Julia Barnes); Sally Starr (Buddy); Bobby Agnew (Rags); John Miljan (Chris); Tenen Holtz (Ben); Lew Kelly (Tish); Tom London (Hennessy); Eugene Borden (Lefty); John Byron (Duke); Nita Martan (Rita); Richard Travers (Wardell).

Julia Barnes (Blanche Sweet) is a nightclub hostess in a gambler-run joint. When the police raid the night spot, she meets a policeman (Tom Moore) and they fall in love. After marrying, Sweet tires of the domestic life and longs for the old days. Finally she returns to singing in the club, working for her former mobster partner (John Miljan). When the latter gets her involved in a gang murder it is her husband who comes to her rescue. Sweet is cleared of all charges and gratefully returns to Moore.
Released in silent and sound versions, this early talkie is of interest today because it stars silent screen favorites Blanche Sweet and Tom Moore. This movie was Blanche Sweet's first feature talkie, but she was not happy with the sound medium and after a few more films returned to the Broadway stage where she originated the role later done by Genevieve Tobin in the movie THE PETRIFIED FOREST (see: B/V).

WOMEN'S PRISON (Columbia, 1955) 80 mins.

Producer, Bryan Foy; director, Lewis Seiler; story, Jack DeWitt; screenplay, Crane Wilbur, DeWitt; music, Mischa Bakaleinikoff; camera, Lester H. White; editor, Henry Batista.

Ida Lupino (Amelia Van Zant); Jan Sterling (Brenda Martin); Cleo Moore (Mae); Audrey Totter (Joan Burton); Phyllis Thaxter (Helene Jensen); Howard Duff (Doctor Clark); Warren Stevens (Glen Burton); Barry Kelley (Warden Brock); Gertrude Michael (Sturgess); Vivian Marshall (Dottie); Mae Clarke (Saunders); Ross Elliott (Don Jensen); Adelle August (Grace); Don C. Harvey (Captain Tierney); Juanita Moore (Polyclinic Jones); Edna Holland (Sarah); Lynne Millan (Carol); Mira McKinney (Burke); Mary Newton (Enright); Diane DeLaire (Head Nurse); Frances Morris (Miss Whittier).

At a California co-ed prison, Dr. Clark (Howard Duff), a sincere physician, wants to bring about reform but he is opposed by a stubborn, old-line warden (Barry Kelly) and the superintendent (Ida Lupino), a sexually repressed, sadistic woman who takes

Ida Lupino and Cleo Moore in WOMEN'S PRISON (1955).

particular delight in tormenting the female inmates. When a prisoner (Audrey Totter) dies from the treatment, two inmates (Jan Sterling, Cleo Moore) lead a revolt resulting in manslaughter charges being brought against Lupino. Found guilty, she goes insane and is committed to a mental institution. As a result, one (Phyllis Thaxter) of the women Lupino mistreated is released and prison reforms occur.

Sturdy production values and a fine cast (especially Lupino's vividly theatrical performance) could not save this cliched prison melodrama. The New York Times carped, "You'll be ahead of this rehash in about ten seconds.... Under the direction of Lewis Seiler, the story sputters along toward the standard climactic riot provided by the Crane Wilbur-Jack DeWitt script. The picture does give its subject serious, professional treatment, but it's neither a riot nor a revelation." The real problem with WOMEN'S PRISON is that it was all done before--and so much better--in the gangster-prison film classic CAGED (see: B/V) in 1950.

THE YAKUZA (Warner Bros., 1975) C 112 mins.

Executive producer, Shundo Koji; producer, Sydney Pollack; co-producer, Michael Hamilburg; director, Pollack; screenplay, Paul Schrader; music, Dave Grusin; production designer, Stephen Grimes; art director, Ishida Yoshiyuki; assistant director, D. Michael Moore; second unit director, Grimes; sound, Arthur Piantadosi, Basil Fenton-Smith; camera, Okazaki Kozo, Duke Callaghan; editors, Fredric Steinkamp, Thomas Stanford, Don Guidice.

Robert Mitchum (Harry Kilmer); Takakura Keo (Tanaka Ken); Brian Keith (George Tanner); Herb Edelman (Wheat); Richard Jordan (Dusty); Kishi Keiko (Eiko); Okada Eiji (Tono); James Shigeta (Goro); Christina Kokubo (Hanako); Lee Chirillo (Louise).

Trying to pawn itself off as a "Japanese Godfather," THE YAKUZA (referring to Japan's Mafia) benefits from Robert Mitchum's strong presence in the leading role, but mainly it is an average combination of the gangster and martial arts genres with plenty of violence and bloodletting for the R-rated trade. Variety described the plot rather tongue-in-cheek: "An oversimplified description would be to call the result an uneasy and incohesive combination of an Oriental Mafia story overlaid on a formula of international business swindle, mixed up with a 20-years-later update of SAYONARA. That's crude, but so is the script."

Robert Mitchum is American Harry Kilmer hired by an old friend (Brian Keith) from the post-World War II days of occupied Japan. His task is to locate Keith's young kidnapped daughter (Lee Chirillo) who is being held for ransom by Japanese gangsters because her father supposedly welched on a business deal. In Japan, Mitchum meets his one-time mistress (Kishi Keiko), who now has an adult daughter (Christina Kokubo) and he enlists the aid of Tanaka Ken (Takakura Keo) who owes him a long overdue favor. He

Kishi Keito and Robert Mitchum in THE YAKUZA (1975).

asks the man to infiltrate the gang which the helper accomplishes
through the aid of his older brother (James Shigeta), a higher-up
in Japanese criminal circles. Also supposedly aiding Mitchum is
Dusty (Richard Jordan), who has actually been planted by Keith to
surveil Mitchum's activities. Eventually Mitchum realizes that Keith
is the real hoodlum who has caused several needless murders.
  Alternate TV title: BROTHERHOOD OF THE YAKUZA

YEAR OF THE DRAGON (Metro-Goldwyn-Mayer/United Artists, 1985)
  C 136 mins.

Executive producer, Fred Caruso; producer, Dino De Laurentiis;
director, Michael Cimino; based on the novel by Robert Daley;
screenplay, Oliver Stone, Cimino; production designer, Wolf Kroeger;
art director, Vicki Paul; assistant director, Brian Cook; music, David Mansfield; songs, Lucia Hwong, Frederick Knight, Rod Stewart,
Duane Hitching, and Roland Robinson; costume designer, Marietta
Ciriello; makeup designer, Alberto Favo; technical police consultants,

Stanley White, George Kodisch; stunt coordinators, Bill Burton,
Mike Adams, Buddy Van Horn; sound, David Stephenson, Arthur
Carelli; camera, Alex Thomson; editor, Françoise Bonnot.

Mickey Rourke (Captain Stanley White); John Lone (Go Joey Tai);
Ariane (Tracy Tzu); Leonard Termo (Angelo Rizzo); Ray Barry
(Louis Bukowski); Caroline Kava (Connie White); Eddie Jones (Wil-
liam McKenna); Joey Chin (Ronnie Chang); Victor Wong (Harry Yung);
K. Dock Yip (Milton Bin); Pao Han Lin (Fred Hung); Mark Hammer
(Commissioner Sullivan); Dennis Dun (Herbert Kwong); Jack Kehler
(Alan Perez); Steven Chen (Tony Ho); Paul Scaglione (Teddy Tedes-
co); Joseph Bonaventura (Lagnese); Jilly Rizzo (Schiro); Tony Lip
(Lenny Carranza); Fabia Drake, Tisa Chang (Nuns); Gerald Orange
(Bear Siu); Fan Mui Sang (White Powder Ma); Yuko Yamamoto (Ban
Sung); Doreen Chan (Red Hair); Harry Yip (Old General); Dermot
McNamara (Scappy Peck); Dr. Vallo Benjamin (D. E. A. Man); Myra
Chen (Shanghai Palace Singer); Chin Feng, Yuk Fan Yiu, Richie
Hsiu, Jack Lee, David Lee (Dragon Kings); Irene Jung, Josie Lee,
Jiwon Chang, Kelly Wong, Chi Moy (Dragon Girls); Johnny Shia
(Chia); Aileen Ho. Lisa Lee (Jade Cobra Girls); Paul Lee, Manny
Fung (Jackie Wong's Sons); Bruno Millotti (Italian Waiter); Lucille
D'Agnillo (Mrs. Bukowski); Reverend Julian Szumilo (Roman Catholic
Priest); Quan Eng (Mortician).

　　Chinese New Year in New York's Chinatown is marred by the
murder of Jackie Wong (Ming C. Lee), the unofficial district mayor,
by a street gang. Bigoted police captain Stanley White (Mickey
Rourke) is assigned to the district and promptly orders the local
chieftains to clean up the rampaging street gang problem. Meanwhile, Go Joey Tai (John Lone), wed to the late mayor's daughter,
is trying to oust the dead man's old-fashioned successor (Victor
Wong) in order to upgrade the area's illicit drug traffic and to stop
the relationship with the Italian Mafia. Rourke starts a romance
with Chinese television reporter Tracy Tzu (Ariane). As part of
his clean-up team, Rourke hires an Oriental undercover agent (Dennis Dun), but his bigotry prevents Rourke from maximizing the
young man's help. Later Lone revenges himself on Rourke by having his ex-wife killed. Thereafter Dun is killed after giving Rourke
vital information and then Ariane is raped by Lone's henchmen. At
the finale, Rourke has it out with the hoodlum at the docks and in
a shootout wounds Lone, who then commits suicide.

　　Never having outlived his tremendous box-office fiasco, HEAV-
EN'S GATE (1980), director Michael Cimino struggled to make this
modest story a major event. Damned by the critics and ignored by
filmgoers, the production dropped from distribution rather abruptly,
especially after groups such as the Chinese American Citizens picketed the presentation. Most viewers were not impressed with the
restructuring of the original literary work or by the fact that Mickey
Rourke--with only gray makeup in his hair to age him--was asked
to interpret a character so many light years more mature than he is.

　　"YEAR OF THE DRAGON is RAMBO GOES TO CHINATOWN with

a trickier and more pretentious surface," claimed Andy Klein in the
LA Reader. He further analyzed, "... [the film] presents Stan
[Rourke] as a walking one-man disaster area and still treats him
with absolute validation.... The whole movie seems like a justifica-
tion of arrogance, precisely the kind of arrogance for which the
director was lambasted five years ago." More charitable was Sheila
Benson (Los Angeles Times), who queried, "With its potholes and
its excesses, why does ... [it] linger so long and so hauntingly?
Because it's part 'documentary' part grand opera. Working on lo-
cations in Vancouver, northernmost Thailand, Mott Street and
Brooklyn, but mostly on a sound stage in Wilmington, N.C. Cimino's
technicians have created a Chinatown of mythic proportions.... Its
reality is enhanced by the performances of so many Asian actors....
The intelligent use of partial subtitles lets us hear the sharp inflec-
tions, the anger and the explosions of their speech for ourselves."

YELLOW CARGO (Grand National, 1936) 63 mins.

Producer, George A. Hirliman; director-screenplay, Crane Wilbur;
camera, Mack Stengler; editor, Tony Martinelli.

Conrad Nagel (Alan O'Connor); Eleanor Hunt (Bobbie Reynolds);
Vince Barnett (Bulb Callahan); Jack LaRue (Al Perrelli); Claudia
Dell (Fay Temple); Henry Strange (Joe Beeze); John Ivan (District
Commissioner); Vance Carroll (Burke Darrell).

Lester Dorr, Claudia Dell, and Conrad Nagel in YELLOW CARGO
(1936).

Given brief release by Pacific Pictures, YELLOW CARGO was picked up by the newly formed Grand National and the movie proved popular enough to spawn three follow-ups, all issued the next year. Like YELLOW CARGO, THE GOLD RACKET and BANK ALARM (qq.v.) were gangster movies, while NAVY SPY dealt with espionage. This well made quartet of programmers was highlighted by the ingratiating performances of Conrad Nagel and Eleanor Hunt as government agents.

YELLOW CARGO has F.B.I. agents Alan O'Connor (Nagel) and Bobbie Reynolds (Hunt) trailing alien smugglers. They learn that the gangster leader (Jack LaRue) of the operation is using the guise of a Hollywood producer to smuggle Chinese aliens into the United States by taking extras to Catalina Island and then returning with their yellow cargo. Nagel takes a job as an extra with the company while Hunt pretends to be a newspaper reporter covering the movie's production and she also goes on location with a dumb photographer (Vince Barnett). When they are discovered, the two agents are nearly killed, but they emerge victorious.

ABOUT THE AUTHORS

JAMES ROBERT PARISH, Los Angeles-based vice president of marketing for a national direct marketing firm, was born in Cambridge, Massachusetts. He attended the University of Pennsylvania and graduated Phi Beta Kappa with a degree in English. A graduate of the University of Pennsylvania Law School, he is a member of the New York Bar. As president of Entertainment Copyright Research Co., Inc., he headed a major researching facility for the film and television industries. Later he was a film reviewer-interviewer for Motion Picture Daily and Variety. He is the author of over 65 volumes, including: The Fox Girls, Good Dames, The Slapstick Queens, The RKO Gals, The Tough Guys, The Jeanette MacDonald Story, The Elvis Presley Scrapbook, and The Hollywood Beauties. Among those he has co-written are The MGM Stock Company, The Debonairs, Liza!, Hollywood Character Actors, The Hollywood Reliables, The Funsters, The Best of MGM, and his ongoing series, Actors' Television Credits. With Michael R. Pitts, he has co-written such tomes as The Great Western Pictures, The Great Science Fiction Pictures, Hollywood on Hollywood, Film Directors Guide; The U.S., and The Great Gangster Pictures (base volume and supplement).

MICHAEL R. PITTS has written seven other books with James R. Parish for Scarecrow Press and he has also written Radio Soundtracks (and Volume II), Hollywood on Record, Famous Movie Detectives, and The Bible on Film for the same publisher. In addition, Mr. Pitts has written Horror Film Stars and Hollywood and American History and is working on several other book projects. His magazine articles have been published in the United States and abroad. A graduate of Ball State University in Muncie, Indiana, with a BS degree in history and a Masters of Arts degree in journalism, Mr. Pitts resides in Chesterfield, Indiana, with his wife, Carolyn, and daughter, Angela.